ADVANCE PRAISE FOR
AMERICAN DESTINY
NARRATIVE OF A NATION

"The writing style is exceptionally clear, and I think students would have little problem reading this book."
—Raymond J. Haberski, Jr., Marian College

"This text's strengths are its quality content, writing style, and organization. This text is distinguished by its excellent scholarship and readability."
—David Montgomery, Bakersfield College

"The writing is one of the best features of the book. It is clear, forceful, energetic, and at times colorful. . . . I also like some of the explanations of complex events—they are admirably concise and easy to understand."
—Lawrence F. Kohl, University of Alabama

"The three greatest strengths of this text are its essentially traditional approach, careful and balanced conclusions, and pleasing writing style."
—Vernon L. Volpe, University of Nebraska at Kearney

"The greatest strength is the clear, fast-paced, interesting writing. The writing is neither too difficult nor too simple and, in short, is a great strength of the book."
—David Thomas, Union University

"I especially like the authors' commitment to clarity and conciseness and their emphasis on social history. And their use of narrative style is what I look for in a text. The length of the subtopics is one of the outstanding features of the book. Clearly and concisely written and not too long. The captions in this text are concise and do not repeat information, they are interestingly written and offer highlights that supplement the text material."
—Patricia Ann Owens, Wabash Valley College

TO OUR READERS

When I began work on my doctorate at Columbia in 1976, I was assigned to John A. Garraty's seminar on the historian's craft. At that time, I knew two things quite clearly: that I wanted to join the crusade to promote the new social history and extend its insights into new gender topics; and that Professor Garraty's fame resided

John A. Garraty (left) and Mark C. Carnes (right).

©1999 Joel Gordon

in the far-removed fields of economic and political history. Without attending a single class, I applied to be shifted to a seminar more in keeping with my interests. Whether from bureaucratic inertia or transcendent wisdom, the history department refused my request. I was stuck with Garraty, and in consequence my life was changed. In that seminar, Garraty preached a particular doctrine on historical writing. He insisted that the writer's sole duty was to readers, who might become confused by unclear phrases or tired by excess words. He expounded on the details of a complex process whereby the murky abstractions of the past were distilled into clean, clear narrative. This literary alchemy was all the more wondrous for being so devoid of artifice. Enthralled, I stayed with Garraty—that first year, and all subsequent ones. I became an acolyte who has spent the past two decades learning to apply his craft to social and cultural topics. To collaborate with him in synthesizing all of American history in *American Destiny: Narrative of a Nation* is the fulfillment of a dream.

MARK C. CARNES

Ann Whitney Olin Professor of History
Barnard College, Columbia University

Mark C. Carnes of Barnard College and Columbia University brings to *American Destiny: Narrative of a Nation* his scholarly specialization in cultural and social issues, especially gender, as well as his special interest in postwar America. Those areas of specialization complement mine in politics and the economy. Although this volume is the work of two authors, it is as nearly the product of a single historical sensibility as is possible. Mark studied with me in graduate school. Even before he received his doctorate from Columbia in 1982, I invited him to join me as co-editor of the final supplement of the *Dictionary of American Biography*. Since then, we have co-authored one book (*Mapping America's Past,* 1996), and for over a decade we have served as co-general editors of the 24-volume *American National Biography* (1999). Over the many years of our collaborations, one of our favorite topics of discussion has been the craft of historical writing. We share a commitment to clarity and conciseness. We strive to avoid jargon and verbiage. We believe that while the political history of the nation provides a useful narrative framework, its people are what give the story meaning.

JOHN A. GARRATY
Gouverneur Morris Professor of History, Emeritus
Columbia University

Penguin Academics

AMERICAN DESTINY
NARRATIVE OF A NATION

Volume Two: Since 1865

MARK C. CARNES
Ann Whitney Olin Professor of History
Barnard College, Columbia University

JOHN A. GARRATY
Gouverneur Morris Professor of History, Emeritus
Columbia University

Longman

New York   San Francisco   Boston
London   Toronto   Sydney   Tokyo   Singapore   Madrid
Mexico City   Munich   Paris   Cape Town   Hong Kong   Montreal

To Our Children:
Stephanie
and
Kathy, Jack, and Sarah

Vice President and Publisher:	Priscilla McGeehon
Acquisitions Editor:	Ashley Dodge
Development Manager:	Betty Slack
Development Editor:	Janice Wiggins
Executive Marketing Manager:	Sue Westmoreland
Production Manager:	Ellen MacElree
Project Coordination and Electronic Page Makeup:	Nesbitt Graphics, Inc.
Cover Designer/Manager:	Wendy Ann Fredericks
Cover Photo:	Gateway Arch, St. Louis, Missouri, © Paul Edmondson/Getty Images Stone.
Cartographer:	Maps.com
Photo Researcher:	Photosearch, Inc.
Manufacturing Manager:	Dennis J. Para
Printer and Binder:	R.R. Donnelley & Sons Company
Cover Printer:	Phoenix Color Corps.

Library of Congress Cataloging-in-Publication Data

Carnes, Mark C. (Mark Christopher), 1950–
   American destiny: narrative of a nation / Mark C. Carnes, John A. Garraty.
     p. cm.
   Includes index.
   ISBN 0-321-10568-0 (single v. ed.) — ISBN 0-321-10399-8 (v. 1) — ISBN 0-321-10567-2 (v. 2)
    1. United States—History. I. Garraty, John Arthur, 1920- II. Title.

E178.6 .C33 2003
973—dc21   2002073155

Please visit our website at http://www.ablongman.com

ISBN 0-321-10568-0 (Single Volume Edition)
ISBN 0-321-10399-8 (Volume One)
ISBN 0-321-10567-2 (Volume Two)

1 2 3 4 5 6 7 8 9 10—DOC— 05 04 03 02

BRIEF CONTENTS

DETAILED CONTENTS

CHAPTER 28 | WAR AND PEACE   908

CHAPTER 29 | THE AMERICAN CENTURY   942

CHAPTER 30 | FROM CAMELOT TO WATERGATE   979

CHAPTER 31 | SOCIETY IN FLUX   1018

MAPS, GRAPHS, AND FEATURE ESSAYS

GRAPHS

FEATURE ESSAYS: RE-VIEWING THE PAST

PREFACE

"American Destiny"—these words, so laden with portent, may strike some readers as an unsuitable title for a sober work of history. Such words have been invoked on behalf of countless partisan causes and feverish enthusiasms: in John Louis O'Sullivan's 1845 editorial proclaiming it "our manifest destiny to overspread the continent allotted by Providence for the free development of our yearly multiplying millions"; in Daniel Webster's terse repudiation of the looming sectional crisis: "One country, one constitution, one destiny"; in Walt Whitman's celebration, after that crisis had erupted in civil war, of "one common indivisible destiny for ALL"; and in Franklin D. Roosevelt's speaking during the Great Depression of his generation's "rendezvous with destiny." Modern politicians have found such expressions irresistible; Ronald Reagan, who betrayed an otherwise cheerful ignorance of Puritan theology, told a Republican gathering: "We will achieve our destiny to be a shining city on a hill for all mankind to see."

Even the nation's critics have been obliged to address the popular belief in an American destiny, if only to repudiate it. For instance, in 1853 Henry David Thoreau bristled that the American people might "go their way to their manifest destiny, a filibustering toward heaven by the great western route"; he intended to look in a different direction. In 1862 Frederick Douglass asserted that "the destiny of America" was also the destiny of black Americans. One hundred and one years later, Martin Luther King, Jr., writing from a jail in Birmingham, Alabama, resurrected Douglass's words: Insofar as "the goal of America is freedom," he declared, "our destiny is tied up with America's destiny." Suffragist Elizabeth Cady Stanton similarly feared for the nation unless it allowed each woman to become "arbiter of her own destiny."

But if most Americans have accepted the concept of a national purpose, they have endlessly debated where the nation was headed and the nature of the force impelling it there. Some have discerned the hand of God lifting the nation up— or perhaps hurling it down. Others have claimed that the nation's destiny was dictated by accident of geography or economics, by the "laws" of social evolution or the "spirit" of democratic liberalism, by the "patterns" of demography or "processes" of modernity, and so on. Our book, however, maintains that no single model explains the complexity of American history. Because historians are poor prophets, we make no attempt to peer into the future. For us, the concept of an

American destiny describes a pervasive if inchoate longing that has exerted a powerful hold on the American imagination.

The subtitle—"Narrative of a Nation"—may also strike readers as provocative. Some historians object to the subjectivity and sweep of narrative history; others, to the intellectual concept of an American nation. The latter contend that the diverse peoples of the United States cannot be encompassed within the analytical boundaries of a single nation. They point to the wealth of information historians have gathered in recent decades on particular racial and ethnic groups; on the experiences of women in many different social and cultural contexts; on the lives of children, the elderly, and those confronting various physical and emotional challenges; on gays and lesbians, farmers and factory workers, western miners and eastern capitalists, and many more.

The proliferation of this scholarship has shown that "the American people" is so vast a subject that it is beyond comprehension. Consequently, we do not claim to have written a history of "the American people." Rather, we describe how the voices and actions of its many peoples have produced a particular political structure—the United States, a single nation—and how that nation has in turn influenced the lives of everyone.

Narrative history is subjective. We must decide, quite arbitrarily, which stories to tell and how to tell them. Historical sources are incomplete and biased; our judgments more art than science. We have tried, by digging into the muck of the past, to haul out the bits that make sense to us and to present them so as to tell a coherent story. Though some contend that the past is too murky to yield clear meanings, we persist because no one is satisfied with the mud.

Of course, a plausible story may not be good history. We underscore this point by including feature essays on popular movies which, while "based on" true stories, often include a bewildering assortment of historical facts and fictions. We hope that our essays will provide guidance on which of Hollywood's stories contain some measure of truthfulness, which do not, and how viewers can tell the difference. The essays also serve as reminder that all historical narratives are interpretations, and all contain biases of selection, presentation, voice, and argument. When considering the past, people should be critical of what they see—and read.

Hollywood makes so many movies with historical themes because audiences want to see them. Hollywood has proven to be unusually effective at exploiting this craving, but people have always looked to the past, whether chronicling a hunt for mammoth beasts in a cave painting or recounting the foundation stories of their civilizations in the Bible or the Mahabarata. Our lives have grown out of the rich fabric of the past, many of whose elements cannot be readily analyzed or even discerned. For us, a less elusive element, but surely an important one, is the American nation, itself the product of the myriad actions, ideas, and forces described in the following pages. By considering its past, we better understand ourselves—and perhaps our own destiny.

MARK C. CARNES

JOHN A. GARRATY

16

RECONSTRUCTION
AND THE SOUTH

On April 5, 1865, Abraham Lincoln visited Richmond. The fallen capital lay in ruins, sections blackened by fire, but the president was able to walk the streets unmolested and almost unattended. Everywhere black people crowded around him worshipfully; some fell to their knees as he passed, crying "Glory, Hallelujah," hailing him as a messiah. Even white townspeople seemed to have accepted defeat without resentment.

A few days later, in Washington, Lincoln delivered an important speech on Reconstruction, urging compassion and open-mindedness. On April 14 he held a Cabinet meeting at which postwar readjustment was considered at length. That evening, while Lincoln was watching a performance of the play *Our American Cousin* at Ford's Theater, a half-mad actor, John Wilkes Booth, slipped into his box and shot him in the back of the head with a small pistol. Early the next morning, without having regained consciousness, Lincoln died.

The murder was part of a complicated plot organized by die-hard prosoutherners. Seldom have fanatics displayed so little understanding of their own interests, for with Lincoln perished the South's best hope for a mild peace. After his body had been taken home to Illinois, the national mood hardened; apparently the awesome drama was still unfolding—retribution and a final humbling of the South were inevitable.

PRESIDENTIAL RECONSTRUCTION

Despite its bloodiness, the Civil War had caused less intersectional hatred than might have been expected. Although civilian property was often seized or destroyed, the invading armies treated the southern population with remarkable forbearance, both during the war and after Appomattox. While he was ensconced in Richmond behind Lee's army, Northerners boasted that they would "hang Jeff Davis to a sour apple tree," and when he was captured in Georgia in May 1865, he was at once clapped into irons preparatory to being tried for treason and murder. But feeling against Davis subsided quickly. In 1867 the military turned him over to the civil courts, which released him on bail. He was never brought to trial. A few other Confederate officials spent short periods behind bars, but the only Southerner executed for war crimes was Major Henry Wirz, the commandant of Andersonville military prison.

The legal questions related to bringing the defeated states back into the Union were extremely complex. Since Southerners believed that secession was legal, logic should have compelled them to argue that they were out of the Union and would thus have to be formally readmitted. Northerners should have taken the contrary position, for they had fought to prove that secession was illegal. Yet the people of both sections did just the opposite. Senator Charles Sumner and Congressman Thaddeus Stevens, in 1861 uncompromising expounders of the theory that the Union was indissoluble, now insisted that the Confederate states had "committed suicide" and should be treated like "conquered provinces." Lincoln believed the issue a "pernicious abstraction" and tried to ignore it.

The process of readmission began in 1862, when Lincoln reappointed provisional governors for those parts of the South that had been occupied by federal troops. On December 8, 1863, he issued a proclamation setting forth a general policy. With the exception of high Confederate officials and a few other special groups, all Southerners could reinstate themselves as United States citizens by taking a simple loyalty oath. When, in any state, a number equal to 10 percent of those voting in the 1860 election had taken this oath, they could set up state government. Such governments had to be republican in form, must recognize the "permanent freedom" of the slaves, and must provide for black education. The plan, however, did not require that blacks be given the right to vote.

The "Ten Percent Plan" reflected Lincoln's lack of vindictiveness and his political wisdom. He realized that any government based on such a small minority of the population would be, as he put it, merely "a tangible nucleus which the remainder . . . may rally around as fast as it can," a sort of puppet regime, like the paper government established in those sections of Virginia under federal control. The regimes established under this plan in Tennessee, Louisiana, and Arkansas bore, in the president's mind, the same relation to finally reconstructed states that an egg bears to a chicken. "We shall sooner have the fowl by hatching it than by smashing it," he remarked. He knew that eventually representatives of the southern states would again be sitting in Congress, and he wished to lay the groundwork for a strong Republican party in the section. Yet he realized that Congress had no intention of seating representatives from the "10 percent" states at once.

The Radicals in Congress disliked the 10 percent plan, partly because of its moderation and partly because it enabled Lincoln to determine Union policy toward the recaptured regions. In July 1864 they passed the Wade–Davis bill, which provided for constitutional conventions only after a majority of the others in a southern state had taken a loyalty oath. Confederate officials and anyone who had "voluntarily borne arms against the United States" were barred from voting in the election or serving at the convention. Besides prohibiting slavery, the new state constitutions would have to repudiate Confederate debts. Lincoln disposed of the Wade–Davis bill with a pocket veto and there matters stood when Andrew Johnson became president following the assassination.

Lincoln had picked Johnson for a running mate in 1864 because he was a border-state Unionist Democrat and something of a hero as a result of his courageous service as military governor of Tennessee. From origins even more lowly than Lincoln's, Johnson had risen to be congressman, governor of Tennessee, and United States senator. He was able and ambitious but fundamentally unsure of himself, as could be seen in his boastfulness and stubbornness. His political strength came from the poor whites and yeomen farmers of eastern Tennessee, and he was fond of extolling the common man and attacking "stuck-up aristocrats."

Andrew Johnson, as recorded by Mathew Brady's camera in 1865. Johnson, Charles Dickens reported, radiated purposefulness but no "genial sunlight."

Thaddeus Stevens called Johnson a "rank demagogue" and a "damned scoundrel," and it is true that he was a masterful rabble-rouser. But few men of his generation labored so consistently on behalf of small farmers. Free home-steads, public education, absolute social equality—such were his objectives. The father of communism, Karl Marx, a close observer of American affairs at this time, wrote approvingly of Johnson's "deadly hatred of the oligarchy."

Johnson was a Democrat, but because of his record and his reassuring pen-chant for excoriating southern aristocrats, the Republicans in Congress were ready to cooperate with him. "Johnson, we have faith in you," said Senator Ben Wade, author of the Wade–Davis bill, the day after Lincoln's death. "By the gods, there will be no trouble now in running the government!"

Johnson's reply, "Treason must be made infamous," delighted the Radicals, but the president proved temperamentally unable to work with them. Like Randolph of Roanoke, his antithesis intellectually and socially, opposition was his specialty; he soon alienated every powerful Republican in Washington.

Radical Republicans listened to Johnson's diatribes against secessionists and the great planters and assumed that he was antisouthern. Nothing could have been further from the truth. He had great respect for states' rights and he shared most of his poor white Tennessee constituents' contempt of blacks. "Damn the negroes, I am fighting these traitorous aristocrats, their masters," he told a friend during the war. "I wish to God," he said on another occasion, "every head of a family in the United States had one slave to take the drudgery and menial service off his family."

The new president did not want to injure or humiliate all white Southerners. He issued an amnesty proclamation only slightly more rigorous than Lincoln's. It assumed, correctly enough, that with the war over most southern voters would freely take the loyalty oath; thus it contained no 10 percent clause. More classes of Confederates, including those who owned taxable property in excess of $20,000, were excluded from the general pardon. By the time Congress con-vened in December 1865, all the southern states had organized governments, ratified the Thirteenth Amendment abolishing slavery, and elected senators and representatives. Johnson promptly recommended these new governments to the attention of Congress.

REPUBLICAN RADICALS

Peace found the Republicans in Congress no more united than they had been during the war. A small group of "ultra" Radicals were demanding immediate and absolute civil and political equality for blacks; they should be given, for example, the vote, a plot of land, and access to a decent education. Senator Sumner led this faction. A second group of Radicals, headed by Thaddeus Stevens in the House and Ben Wade in the Senate, agreed with the ultras' objectives but were prepared to accept half a loaf if necessary to win the support of less radical colleagues.

Nearly all Radicals distinguished between the "natural" God-given rights described in the Declaration of Independence, and social equality. "Equality," said Stevens, "does not mean that a negro shall sit in the same seat or eat at the same table with a white man. That is a matter of taste which every man must decide for himself." This did not reflect personal prejudice in Stevens's case.

Mathew Brady's photograph of the stalwart radical Republican Thaddeus Stevens. Stevens served in the House from 1859 until his death in 1868.

When he died, he was buried in a black cemetery. Here is his epitaph, which he wrote himself: "I repose in this quiet and secluded spot, not from any natural preference for solitude, but finding other cemeteries limited as to race, by charter rules, I have chosen this that I might illustrate in my death the principles which I advocated through a long life, equality of man before his Creator."

The moderate Republicans wanted to protect exslaves from exploitation and guarantee their basic rights but were unprepared to push for full political equality. A handful of Republicans sided with the Democrats in support of Johnson's approach, but all the rest insisted at least on the minimal demands of the moderates. Thus Johnsonian Reconstruction was doomed.

Johnson's proposal had no chance in Congress for reasons having little to do with black rights. The Thirteenth Amendment had the effect of increasing the representation of the southern states in Congress because it made the Three-fifths Compromise meaningless. Henceforth those who had been slaves would be counted as whole persons in apportioning seats in the House of Representatives. If Congress seated the Southerners, the balance of power might swing to the Democrats. To expect the Republicans to surrender power in such a fashion was unrealistic. Former Copperheads gushing with extravagant praise for Johnson put them instantly on guard.

Southern voters provoked northern resentment by their choice of congressmen. Georgia elected Alexander H. Stephens, vice president of the Confederacy, to the Senate, although he was still in a federal prison awaiting trial for treason! Several dozen men who had served in the Confederate Congress had been elected to either the House or the Senate, together with four generals and many other high officials. The southern people understandably selected locally re-spected and experienced leaders, but it was equally reasonable that these choices would sit poorly with Northerners.

Finally, the so-called Black Codes enacted by southern governments to con-trol former slaves alarmed the North. These varied in severity from state to state, but all, as one planter admitted, set out to keep the blacks "as near to a state of bondage as possible."

Blacks were allowed to own certain kinds of property; other rights were guaranteed. However, blacks could not bear arms, be employed in occupations other than farming and domestic service, or leave their jobs without forfeiting back pay. The Mississippi code required them to sign labor contracts for the year in January, and, in addition, drunkards, vagrants, beggars, "common night-walk-ers," and even "mischief makers" and persons who "misspend what they earn" and who could not pay the stiff fines assessed for such misbehavior were to be "hired out . . . at public outcry" to the white persons who would take them for the shortest period in return for paying the fines. Such laws, apparently designed to get around the Thirteenth Amendment, outraged Northerners.

For all these reasons the Republicans in Congress rejected Johnsonian Reconstruction. Quickly they created a joint committee on Reconstruction, headed by Senator William P. Fessenden of Maine, a moderate, to study the ques-tion of readmitting the southern states.

The committee held public hearings that produced much evidence of the mistreatment of blacks. Colonel George A. Custer, stationed in Texas, testified: "It is of weekly, if not of daily occurrence that Freedmen are murdered." The nurse Clara Barton told a gruesome tale about a pregnant woman who had been brutally whipped. Others described the intimidation of blacks by poor whites. The hearings strengthened the Radicals, who had been claiming all along that the South was perpetuating slavery under another name.

President Johnson's attitude speeded the swing toward the Radical position. While the hearings were in progress, Congress passed a bill expanding and ex-tending the Freedmen's Bureau, which had been established in March 1865 to care for refugees. The bureau, a branch of the War Department, was already ex-ercising considerable coercive and supervisory power in the South. Now Congress sought to add to its authority in order to protect the black population. Although the bill had wide support, Johnson vetoed it, arguing that it was an un-constitutional extension of military authority in peacetime. Congress then passed a Civil Rights Act that, besides declaring specifically that blacks were citizens of the United States, denied the states the power to restrict their rights to testify in court, to make contracts for their labor, and to hold property. In other words, it put teeth in the Thirteenth Amendment.

Once again the president refused to go along, although his veto was sure to drive more moderates into the arms of the Radicals. On April 9, 1866, Congress repassed the Civil Rights Act by a two-thirds majority, the first time in American history that a major piece of legislation became law over the veto of a president. This event marked a revolution in the history of Reconstruction. Thereafter Congress, not President Johnson, had the upper hand.

In the clash between the president and Congress, Johnson was his own worst enemy. His language was often intemperate, his handling of opponents inept, his analysis of southern conditions incorrect. He had assumed that the small southern farmers who made up the majority in the Confederacy shared his prejudices against the planter class. They did not, as their choices in the postwar elections demonstrated. In fact, Johnson's hatred of the southern aristocracy may have been based more on jealousy than on principle.

The president misread northern opinion. He believed that Congress had no right to pass laws affecting the South before southern representatives had been readmitted to Congress. However, in the light of the refusal of most southern whites to grant any real power or responsibility to the freedmen (an attitude that Johnson did not condemn), the public would not accept this point of view. Johnson placed his own judgment over that of the overwhelming majority of northern voters, and this was a great error, morally and tactically. By encouraging white Southerners to resist efforts to improve the lot of blacks, Johnson played into the hands of the Radicals.

The Radicals were in effect demanding not merely equal rights for freedmen but extra rights; not merely the vote but special protection of that right against the pressure that southern whites would surely apply to undermine it. This idea flew in the face of conventional American beliefs in equality before the law and individual self-reliance. Such protection would involve interference by the federal government in local affairs, a concept at variance with American practice. Events were to show that the Radicals were correct—that what amounted to a political revolution in state–federal relations was essential if blacks were to achieve real equality. But in the climate of that day their proposals encountered bitter resistance, and not only from white Southerners.

Thus, while the Radicals sought partisan advantage in their battle with Johnson and sometimes played on war-bred passions in achieving their ends, they were taking large political risks in defense of genuinely held principles.

Agents of the Freedmen's Bureau helped defend former slaves against white attacks and provided them with food, clothing, and medical care. They also set up schools. However, hostility toward the activities of the Freedmen's Bureau was widespread. In 1866, during a race riot in Memphis, mobs killed 46 blacks and burned this Freedmen's schoolhouse.

THE FOURTEENTH AMENDMENT

In June 1866 Congress submitted to the states a new amendment to the Constitution. The Fourteenth Amendment was, in the context of the times, a truly radical measure. First the amendment supplied a broad definition of American citizenship: "All persons born or naturalized in the United States, and subject to the jurisdiction thereof, are citizens of the United States and of the State wherein they reside." Obviously this included blacks. Then it struck at discriminatory legislation like the Black Codes: "No State shall make or enforce any law which shall abridge the privileges or immunities of citizens of the United States; nor shall any State deprive any person of life, liberty, or property, without due process of law." The next section attempted to force the southern states to permit blacks to vote. If a state denied the vote to any class of its adult male citizens, its representation was to be reduced proportionately. Under another clause, former federal officials who had served the Confederacy were barred from holding either state or federal office unless specifically pardoned by a two-thirds vote of Congress. Finally, the Confederate debt was repudiated.

While the amendment did not specifically outlaw segregation or prevent a state from disenfranchising blacks, the southern states would have none of it. Without them the necessary three-fourths majority of the states could not be obtained.

President Johnson vowed to make the choice between the Fourteenth Amendment and his own policy the main issue of the 1866 congressional elections. He embarked on "a swing around the circle" to rally the public to his cause. He failed dismally. Northern women objected to the implication in the amendment that black men were more fitted to vote than white women, but a large majority of northern voters were determined that African Americans must have at least formal legal equality. The Republicans won better than two-thirds of the seats in both houses, together with control of all the northern state governments. Johnson emerged from the campaign discredited, the Radicals stronger and determined to have their way. The southern states, Congressman James A. Garfield of Ohio said in February 1867, have "flung back into our teeth the magnanimous offer of a generous nation. It is now our turn to act."

THE RECONSTRUCTION ACTS

Had the southern states been willing to accept the Fourteenth Amendment, coercive measures might have been avoided. Their recalcitrance and continuing indications that local authorities were persecuting blacks finally led to the passage, on March 2, 1867, of the First Reconstruction Act. This law divided the former Confederacy—exclusive of Tennessee, which had ratified the Fourteenth Amendment—into five military districts, each controlled by a major general. It gave these officers almost dictatorial power to protect the civil rights of "all persons," maintain order, and supervise the administration of justice. To rid themselves of military rule, the former states were required to adopt new state constitutions guaranteeing blacks the right to vote and disfranchising broad classes of ex-Confederates. If the new constitutions proved satisfactory to Congress, and if the new governments ratified the Fourteenth Amendment, their representatives would be admitted to Congress and military rule ended. Johnson's veto of the act was easily overridden.

Although drastic, the Reconstruction Act was so vague that it proved unworkable. Military control was easily established. But in deference to moderate Republican views, the law had not spelled out the process by which the new constitutions were to be drawn up. Southern whites preferred the status quo, even under army control, to enfranchising blacks and retiring their own respected leaders. They made no effort to follow the steps laid down in the law. Congress

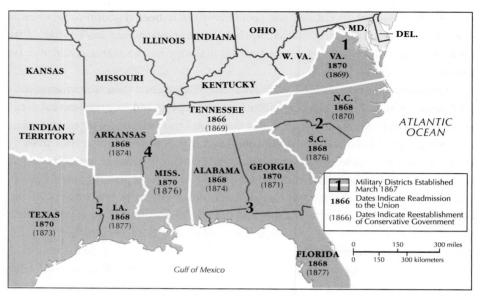

Return to the Union During Reconstruction

therefore passed a second act, requiring the military authorities to register voters and supervise the election of delegates to constitutional conventions. A third act further clarified procedures.

Still white Southerners resisted. The laws required that the constitutions be approved by a majority of the registered voters. Simply by staying away from the polls, whites prevented ratification in state after state. At last, in March 1868, a full year after the First Reconstruction Act, Congress changed the rules again. The constitutions were to be ratified by a majority of the voters. In June 1868 Arkansas, having fulfilled the requirements, was readmitted to the Union, and by July a sufficient number of states had ratified the Fourteenth Amendment to make it part of the Constitution. But it was not until July 1870 that the last southern state, Georgia, qualified to the satisfaction of Congress.

Congress Takes Charge

To carry out this program in the face of determined southern resistance required a degree of single-mindedness over a long period seldom demonstrated by an American legislature. The persistence resulted in part from the suffering and frustrations of the war years. The refusal of the South to accept the spirit of even the mild reconstruction designed by Johnson goaded the North to ever more overbearing efforts to bring the ex-Confederates to heel. President Johnson's stubbornness also influenced the Republicans. They became obsessed with the need to defeat him. The unsettled times and the large Republican majorities, always threatened by the possibility of a Democratic resurgence if "unreconstructed" southern congressmen were readmitted, sustained their determination.

These considerations led Republicans to attempt a kind of grand revision of the federal government, one that almost destroyed the balance between judicial, executive, and legislative power established in 1789. A series of measures passed between 1866 and 1868 increased the authority of Congress over the army, over the process of amending the Constitution, and over Cabinet members and lesser appointive officers. Even the Supreme Court was affected. Its size was reduced and its jurisdiction over civil rights cases limited. Finally, in a showdown caused by emotion more than by practical considerations, the Republicans attempted to remove President Johnson from office.

The chief issue was the Tenure of Office Act of 1867, which prohibited the president from removing officials who had been appointed with the consent of the Senate without first obtaining Senate approval. In February 1868 Johnson "violated" this act by dismissing Secretary of War Edwin M. Stanton, who had been openly in sympathy with the Radicals for some time. The House, acting under the procedure set up in the Constitution for removing the president, promptly impeached him before the bar of the Senate, Chief Justice Salmon P. Chase presiding.

In the trial, Johnson's lawyers easily established that he had removed Stanton only in an effort to prove the Tenure of Office Act unconstitutional. They demonstrated that the act did not protect Stanton to begin with, since it gave Cabinet members tenure "during the term of the President by whom they may have been appointed," and Stanton had been appointed in 1862, during Lincoln's first term!

Nevertheless the Radicals pressed the charges (11 separate articles) relentlessly. To the argument that Johnson had committed no crime, the learned Senator Sumner retorted that the proceedings were "political in character" rather than judicial. Thaddeus Stevens, directing the attack on behalf of the House, warned the senators that although "no corrupt or wicked motive" could be attributed to Johnson, they would "be tortured on the gibbet of everlasting obloquy" if they did not convict him. Tremendous pressure was applied to the handful of Republican senators who were unwilling to disregard the evidence.

Seven of them resisted to the end, and the Senate failed by a single vote to convict Johnson. This was probably fortunate. The trial weakened the presidency, but if Johnson had been forced from office on such flimsy grounds, the independence of the executive might have been permanently undermined. Then the legislative branch would have become supreme.

THE FIFTEENTH AMENDMENT

The failure of the impeachment did not affect the course of Reconstruction. The president was acquitted on May 16, 1868. A few days later, the Republican National Convention nominated General Ulysses S. Grant for the presidency. At the Democratic convention Johnson had considerable support, but the delegates nominated Horatio Seymour, a former governor of New York. In November Grant won an easy victory in the Electoral College, 214 to 80, but the popular vote was close: 3 million to 2.7 million. Although he would probably have carried the Electoral College in any case, Grant's margin in the popular vote was supplied by southern blacks enfranchised under the Reconstruction acts, about 450,000 of whom supported him. A majority of white voters probably preferred Seymour. Since many citizens undoubtedly voted Republican because of personal admiration for General Grant, the election statistics suggest that a substantial white majority opposed the policies of the Radicals.

The Reconstruction acts and the ratification of the Fourteenth Amendment achieved the purpose of enabling black Southerners to vote. The Radicals, however, were not satisfied; despite the unpopularity of the idea in the North, they wished to guarantee the right of blacks to vote in every state. Another amendment seemed the only way to accomplish this objective, but passage of such an amendment appeared impossible. The Republican platform in the 1868 election had smugly distinguished between blacks voting in the South ("demanded by every consideration of public safety, of gratitude, and of justice") and in the North (where the question "properly belongs to the people").

However, after the election had demonstrated how important the black vote could be, Republican strategy shifted. Grant had carried Indiana by less than 10,000 votes and lost New York by a similar number. If blacks in these and other closely divided states had voted, Republican strength would have been greater.

Suddenly Congress blossomed with suffrage amendments. After considerable bickering over details, the Fifteenth Amendment was sent to the states for ratification in February 1869. It forbade all the states to deny the vote to anyone "on account of race, color, or previous condition of servitude." Once again nothing was said about denial of the vote on the basis of sex, which caused feminists, such as Elizabeth Cady Stanton, to be even more outraged than they had been by the Fourteenth Amendment.

Most southern states, still under federal pressure, ratified the amendment swiftly. The same was true in most of New England and in some western states. Bitter battles were waged in Connecticut, New York, Pennsylvania, and the states immediately north of the Ohio River, but by March 1870 most of them had ratified the amendment and it became part of the Constitution.

Fifteenth Amendment went into effect, President Grant called it
What civil change and . . . the most important event that has occurred
"the nation came to life." The American Anti-Slavery Society formally dis-
itself, its work apparently completed. "The Fifteenth Amendment confers
in the African race the care of its own destiny," Radical Congressman James A.
Garfield wrote proudly after the amendment was ratified. "It places their fortunes in their own hands."

"BLACK REPUBLICAN" RECONSTRUCTION: SCALAWAGS AND CARPETBAGGERS

The Radicals had at last succeeded in imposing their will on the South.
Throughout the region former slaves had real political influence; they voted, held
office, and exercised the "privileges" and enjoyed the "immunities" guaranteed
them by the Fourteenth Amendment. Almost to a man they voted Republican.

The spectacle of blacks not five years removed from slavery in positions of
power and responsibility attracted much attention at the time and has since been
examined exhaustively by historians. The subject is controversial, but certain
facts are beyond argument. Black officeholders were neither numerous nor

"Colored Rule in a Reconstructed (?) State," by Thomas Nast, appearing in Harper's Weekly (1874). Though a proponent of black rights, Nast offers a racist depiction of black legislators. The white legislator, at his desk, barely suppresses a smirk.

inordinately influential. None was ever elected governor of a state, re dozen and a half during the entire period served in Congress. Blacks here in a minor offices and were influential in southern legislatures, although (except South Carolina) they never made up the majority. Certainly they did not share the spoils of office in proportion to their numbers.

The real rulers of the "black Republican" governments were white: the "scalawags"—Southerners willing to cooperate with the Republicans because they accepted the results of the war and to advance their own interests—and the "carpetbaggers"—Northerners who went to the South as idealists to help the freed slaves, as employees of the federal government, or more commonly as settlers hoping to improve themselves.

That blacks should fail to dominate southern governments is certainly understandable. They lacked experience in politics and were mostly poor and uneducated. They were nearly everywhere a minority. Those blacks who held office during Reconstruction tended to be better educated and more prosperous than most southern blacks. A disproportionate number had been free before the war. Of those freed by the Thirteenth Amendment, a large percentage had been house servants or artisans, not field hands. Mulatto politicians were also disproportionately numerous and (as a group) more conservative and economically better off than other black leaders.

In South Carolina and elsewhere, blacks proved in the main able and conscientious public servants: able because the best tended to rise to the top in such a fluid situation and conscientious because most of those who achieved importance

During Reconstruction, 14 blacks won election to the House of Representatives and two, Hiram Revels and Blanche K. Bruce, served in the Senate. Revels, at far left, won the Mississippi Senate seat that Jefferson Davis had once held. He later became president of Alcorn University. Congressman R. Brown Elliot, at far right, had been educated at Eton in England.

sought eagerly to demonstrate the capacity of their race for self-government. Even at the local level, where the quality of officials was usually poor, there was little difference in the degree of competence displayed by white and black office-holders. In power, the blacks were not vindictive; by and large they did not seek to restrict the rights of ex-Confederates.

Not all black legislators and administrators were paragons of virtue. In South Carolina, despite their control of the legislature, they broke up into factions re-peatedly and failed to press for laws that would improve the lot of poor black farm workers. In *The Prostrate South* (1874), James S. Pike, a northern newspaper-man, wrote: "The rule of South Carolina should not be dignified with the name of government. It is the installation of a huge system of brigandage." Like many northern commentators, Pike exaggerated the immorality and incompetence of the blacks, but waste and corruption were common during Reconstruction gov-ernments. Half the budget of Louisiana in some years went for salaries and "mileage" for representatives and their staffs. One Arkansas black took $9000 from the state for repairing a bridge that had cost only $500 to build. A South Carolina legislator was voted an additional $1000 in salary after he lost that sum betting on a horse race.

However, the corruption must be seen in perspective. The big thieves were nearly always white; blacks got mostly crumbs. Furthermore, graft and callous disregard of the public interest characterized government in every section and at every level during the decade after Appomattox. Big-city bosses in the North em-bezzled sums that dwarfed the most brazen southern frauds. The New York City Tweed Ring probably made off with more money than all the southern thieves, black and white, combined. While the evidence does not justify the southern cor-ruption, it suggests that the unique features of Reconstruction politics—black suffrage, military supervision, carpetbagger and scalawag influence—do not ex-plain it.

The "black Republican" governments displayed qualities that grew directly from the ignorance and political inexperience of the former slaves. There was a tragicomic aspect to the South Carolina legislature during these years, its many black members—some dressed in old frock coats, others in rude farm clothes—rising to points of order and personal privilege without reason, discoursing pon-derously on subjects they did not understand. But those who complained about the ignorance and irresponsibility of blacks conveniently forgot that the tendency of nineteenth-century American democracy was away from educational, finan-cial, or any other restrictions on the franchise. Thousands of white Southerners were as illiterate and uncultured as the freedmen, yet no one suggested depriving them of the ballot.

The Freedmen's Bureau built 4329 schools, attended by some 250,000 exslaves, in the postwar South. Many of the teachers in these schools were abolitionists or missionaries from New England. The schools drew African Americans of all ages, from children to grandparents, who were eager for the advantages offered by education.

In fact, the Radical southern governments accomplished a great deal. They spent money freely but not entirely wastefully. Tax rates zoomed, but the money financed the repair and expansion of the South's dilapidated railroad network, rebuilt crumbling levees, and expanded social services. Before the Civil War, southern planters possessed a disproportionate share of political as well as economic power, and they spent relatively little public money on education and public services of all kinds.

The former slaves grasped eagerly at the opportunities to learn. Nearly all appreciated the immense importance of knowing how to read and write; the sight of elderly men and women poring laboriously over elementary texts beside their grandchildren was common everywhere. Schools and other institutions were supported chiefly by property taxes, and these, of course, hit well-to-do planters hard. Hence much of the complaining about the "extravagance" of Reconstruction governments concealed traditional selfish objections to paying for public projects. Eventually the benefits of expanded government services to the entire population became clear, and when white supremacy was reestab-

lished, most of the new services remained in force, and the corruption and inefficiency inherited from the carpetbagger governments continued.

THE RAVAGED LAND

The South's grave economic problems complicated the rebuilding of its political
system. The section had never been as prosperous as the North, and wartime destruction left it desperately poor by any standard. In the long run the abolition of
slavery released immeasurable quantities of human energy previously stifled, but
the immediate effect was to create confusion. Freedom to move without a pass,
to "see the world," was one of the exslaves' most cherished benefits of emancipation. Understandably, many at first equated legal freedom with freedom from
having to earn a living, a tendency reinforced for a time by the willingness of the
Freedmen's Bureau to provide rations and other forms of relief in war-devastated

*Photograph of Richmond in ruins, April 1865. Note the two women in hoopskirts. The hoopskirt, on which
as much as 20 yards of cloth were fastened to a steel hoop, became fashionable in the 1850s. Because of
textile shortages during the war, hoopskirts were denounced as an extravagance. But as the war weakened social distinctions, some well-to-do women insisted on wearing hoopskirts to reassert their social position.*

areas. Most, however, soon accepted the fact that they must earn a living; a small plot of land of their own ("40 acres and a mule") would complete their independence.

This objective was forcefully supported by the relentless Congressman Thaddeus Stevens, whose hatred of the planter class was pathological. "The property of the chief rebels should be seized," he stated. If the lands of the richest "70,000 proud, bloated and defiant rebels" were confiscated, the federal government would obtain 394 million acres. Every adult male exslave could easily be supplied with 40 acres. The beauty of his scheme, Stevens insisted, was that "nine-tenths of the [southern] people would remain untouched." Dispossessing the great planters would make the South "a safe republic," its lands cultivated by "the free labor of intelligent citizens." If the plan drove the planters into exile, "all the better."

Although Stevens's figures were faulty, many Radicals agreed with him. "We must see that the freedmen are established on the soil," Senator Sumner declared. "The great plantations, which have been so many nurseries of the rebellion, must be broken up, and the freedmen must have the pieces." Aside from its vindictiveness, the extremists' view was simplistic. Land without tools, seed, and other necessities would have done the freedmen little good. Congress did throw open 46 million acres of poor-quality federal land in the South to blacks under the Homestead Act, but few settled on it. Establishing former slaves on small farms with adequate financial aid would have been of incalculable benefit to them. This would have been practicable, but extremely expensive. It was not done.

The former slaves therefore had either to agree to work for their former owners or strike out on their own. White planters, influenced by the precipitous decline of sugar production in Jamaica and other Caribbean islands that had followed the abolition of slavery there, expected freed blacks to be incapable of self-directed effort. If allowed to become independent farmers, they would either starve to death or descend into barbarism. Of course the blacks did neither. True, the output of cotton and other southern staples declined precipitously after slavery was abolished. Observers soon came to the conclusion that a free black produced much less than a slave had produced. "You can't get only about two-thirds as much out of 'em now as you could when they were slaves," an Arkansas planter complained.

However, the decline in productivity was not caused by the inability of free blacks to work independently. They simply chose no longer to work like slaves. They let their children play instead of forcing them into the fields. Mothers devoted more time to child care and housework, less to farm labor. Elderly blacks worked less.

Noting these changes, white critics spoke scornfully of black laziness and shiftlessness. "You cannot make the negro work without physical compulsion," was the common view. Even General O. O. Howard, head of the Freedmen's Bureau, used the phrase "wholesome compulsion" in describing the policy of forcing blacks to sign exploitive labor contracts. A leading southern magazine complained in 1866 that black women now expected their husbands "to support them in idleness." It would never have made such a comment about white housewives. Moreover, studies show that emancipated blacks earned almost 30 percent more than the value of the subsistence provided by their former masters.

The family life of exslaves was changed in other ways. Male authority increased when husbands became true heads of families. (Under slavery the ultimate responsibility for providing for women and children was the master's.) When blacks became citizens, the men acquired rights and powers denied to all women, such as the right to hold public office and serve on juries. Similarly, black women became more like white women, devoting themselves to separate "spheres" where their lives revolved around housekeeping and child rearing.

SHARECROPPING AND THE CROP-LIEN SYSTEM

Before the passage of the Reconstruction acts, plantation owners tried to farm their land with gang labor, the same system as before, only now paying wages to the former slaves. This method did not work well because it kept blacks under the direction of whites and thus reminded them of slavery. African Americans wanted to be independent, to manage not merely their free time but their entire lives for themselves. "The colored people of this vicinity are so proud," a white Virginian noted, "that they think it is somewhat a second slavery to hire by the month or year." Since the voluntary withdrawal of so much black labor from the workforce had produced a shortage, the blacks had their way. "I had to yield," another white planter admitted, "or lose my labor."

Quite swiftly, a new agricultural system known as sharecropping emerged. Instead of cultivating the land by gang labor as in antebellum times, planters broke up their estates into small units and established on each a black family. The planter provided housing, agricultural implements, draft animals, seed, and other supplies, and the family provided labor. The crop was divided between them, usually on a fifty–fifty basis. If the landlord supplied only land and housing, the laborer got a larger share. This was called share tenancy.

Sharecropping gave blacks the day-to-day control of their lives that they craved and the hope of earning enough to buy a small farm. But this proved extremely

After the Civil War, most blacks worked as sharecroppers on land owned by whites. In this photograph, black sharecroppers pick cotton, a major cash crop of the South. Because the price for cotton remained low, sharecroppers often fell into debt and were tied to the land almost as tightly as under slavery.

difficult. As late as 1880 blacks owned less than 10 percent of the agricultural land in the South, although they made up more than half of the region's farm population. Mississippi actually prohibited the purchase of farmland by blacks.

Many white farmers in the South were also trapped by the sharecropping system and by white efforts to keep blacks in a subordinate position. New fencing laws kept them from grazing livestock on undeveloped land, a practice common before the Civil War. But the main cause of southern rural poverty for whites as well as for blacks was the lack of enough capital to finance the sharecropping system. Like their colonial ancestors, the landowners had to borrow against October's harvest to pay for April's seed. Thus the crop-lien system developed, and to protect their investments, lenders insisted that the grower concentrate on readily marketable cash crops: tobacco, sugar, and especially cotton.

The system injured everyone. Diversified farming would have reduced the farmers' need for cash, preserved the fertility of the soil, and, by placing a premium on imagination and shrewdness, aided the best of them to rise in the world. Under the crop-lien system, both landowner and sharecropper depended on credit supplied by local bankers, merchants, and storekeepers for everything from seed, tools, and fertilizer to overalls, coffee, and salt. Crossroads stores proliferated, and a new class of small merchants appeared. The prices of goods sold on credit were high, adding to the burden borne by the rural population. The small southern merchants were almost equally victimized by the system, for they also lacked capital, bought goods on credit, and had to pay high interest rates.

Seen in broad perspective, the situation is not difficult to understand. The South, drained of every resource by the war, was competing for funds with the North and West, both vigorous and expanding and therefore voracious consumers of capital. Reconstruction, in the literal sense of the word, was accomplished chiefly at the expense of the standard of living of the producing classes. The crop-lien system and the small storekeeper were only agents of an economic process dictated by national, perhaps even worldwide, conditions.

Compared with the rest of the country, progress was slow. Just before the Civil War cotton harvests averaged about 4 million bales. During the conflict, output fell to about half a million, and the former Confederate states did not enjoy a 4-million-bale year again until 1870. In contrast, national wheat production in 1859 was 175 million bushels and in 1878, 449 million. About 7000 miles of railroad were built in the South between 1865 and 1879; in the rest of the nation nearly 45,000 miles of track were laid.

But in the late 1870s cotton production revived. It soon regained, and thereafter long retained, its title as "king" of the southern economy. This was true in large measure because of the crop-lien system.

The South made important gains in manufacturing after the war. The tobacco industry, stimulated by the sudden popularity of the cigarette, expanded rapidly.

Southern Agriculture, 1850–1900

Cotton production recovered to its prewar level by 1880, but tobacco and sugar production lagged. Not until 1900 did tobacco growers have a better year than they had in 1860. The years following 1870 saw a general downward trend in wholesale prices for farm commodities. (Statistics are for the 11 states of the Confederacy.)

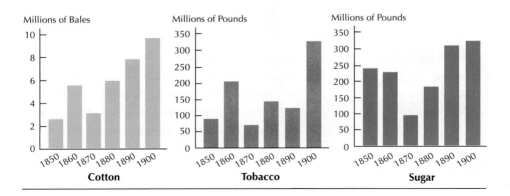

Virginia and North Carolina tobacco towns like Richmond, Lynchburg, and Durham flourished. The exploitation of the coal and iron deposits of northeastern Alabama in the early 1870s made a boomtown of Birmingham. The manufacture of cotton cloth increased, productive capacity nearly doubling between 1865 and 1880. Yet the mills of Massachusetts alone had eight times the capacity of the entire South in 1880. Despite the increases, the South's share of the national output of manufactured goods declined sharply during the Reconstruction era.

THE WHITE BACKLASH

Radical southern governments could sustain themselves only as long as they had the support of a significant proportion of the white population, for except in South Carolina and Louisiana, the blacks were not numerous enough to win elections alone. The key to survival lay in the hands of the wealthy merchants and planters, mostly former Whigs. People of this sort had nothing to fear from black economic competition. Taking a broad view, they could see that improving the lot of the former slaves would benefit all classes.

Southern white Republicans used the Union League of America, a patriotic club founded during the war, to control the black vote. Employing secret rituals, exotic symbols, and other paraphernalia calculated to impress unsophisticated people, they enrolled the freedmen in droves and marched them to the polls en masse.

Powerless to check the League by open methods, dissident Southerners established a number of secret terrorist societies, bearing such names as the Ku Klux Klan, the Knights of the White Camelia, and the Pale Faces. The most notorious of these organizations was the Klan, which originated in Tennessee in 1866. At first it was purely a social club, but by 1868 it had been taken over by vigilante types dedicated to driving blacks out of politics, and it was spreading rapidly across the South. Sheet-clad night riders roamed the countryside, frightening the impressionable and chastising the defiant. Klansmen, using a weird mumbo jumbo and claiming to be the ghosts of Confederate soldiers, spread horrendous rumors

A graphic warning by the Alabama Klan "of the fate in store for" scalawags and carpetbaggers, "those great pests of Southern society," from the Tuscaloosa Independent Monitor, September 1, 1868.

and published broadsides designed to persuade the freedmen that it was unhealthy for them to participate in politics:

Niggers and Leaguers, get out of the way,
We're born of the night and we vanish by day.
No rations have we, but the flesh of man—
And love niggers best—the Ku Klux Klan;
We catch 'em alive and roast 'em whole,
Then hand 'em around with a sharpened pole.
Whole Leagues have been eaten, not leaving a man,
And went away hungry—the Ku Klux Klan. . . .

When intimidation failed, the Klansmen resorted to force. After being
whipped by one group in Tennessee, a recently elected justice of the peace reported: "They said they had nothing particular against me . . . but they did not intend any nigger to hold office." In hundreds of cases the KKK murdered their opponents, often in the most gruesome manner.

Congress struck at the Klan with three Force Acts (1870–1871), which placed
elections under federal jurisdiction and imposed fines and prison sentences on
persons convicted of interfering with any citizen's exercise of the franchise.
Troops were dispatched to areas where the Klan was strong, and by 1872 the federal authorities had arrested enough Klansmen to break up the organization.

Nevertheless the Klan contributed substantially to the destruction of Radical
regimes in the South. Its depredations weakened the will of white Republicans
(few of whom really believed in racial equality), and it intimidated many blacks,
who gave up trying to exercise their rights. The fact that the army had to be
called in to suppress it was a glaring illustration of the weakness of the Reconstruction governments.

Gradually it became respectable to intimidate black voters. Beginning in
Mississippi in 1874, terrorism spread through the South. Instead of hiding behind
masks and operating in the dark, these terrorists donned red shirts, organized
into military companies, and paraded openly. Mississippi redshirts seized militant
blacks and whipped them publicly. Killings were frequent. When blacks dared to
fight back, heavily armed whites easily put them to rout. In other states similar
results followed.

Before long the blacks learned to stay home on election day. One by one,
"Conservative" parties—Democratic in national affairs—took over southern
state governments. Intimidation was only a partial explanation of this development. The increasing solidarity of whites, northern and southern, was equally
significant.

Northerners increasingly doubted that it was still necessary to maintain a large army in the South. In 1869 the occupying forces were down to 11,000 men. After Klan disruption and intimidation had made a farce of the 1874 elections in Mississippi, Governor Ames appealed to Washington for help. President Grant's attorney general, Edwards Pierrepont, refused to act. "The whole public are tired out with these autumnal outbreaks in the South," he told Ames. "Preserve the peace by the forces of your own state."

Nationalism was reasserting itself. Had not Washington and Jefferson been Virginians? Was not Andrew Jackson Carolina-born? Since most Northerners had little real love or respect for blacks, their interest in racial equality flagged once they felt reasonably certain that blacks would not be reenslaved if left to their own devices in the South.

GRANT AS PRESIDENT

Other matters occupied the attention of northern voters. The expansion of industry and the rapid development of the West, stimulated by a new wave of railroad building, loomed more important to many than the fortunes of exslaves. Beginning in 1873, when a stock market panic struck at public confidence, economic difficulties plagued the country for nearly a decade. Heated controversies arose over tariff policy, with western agricultural interests seeking to force reductions from the high levels established during the war, and over the handling of the wartime greenback paper money, with debtor groups and many manufacturers favoring expansion of the dollar supply and conservative merchants and bankers arguing for retiring the greenbacks in order to return to a "sound" currency.

More damaging to the Republicans was the failure of Ulysses S. Grant to live up to expectations as president. Qualities that had made Grant a fine military leader for a democracy—his dislike of political maneuvering and his simple belief that the popular will could best be observed in the actions of Congress—made him a poor chief executive. When Congress failed to act on his suggestion that the quality of the civil service needed improvement, he announced meekly that if Congress did nothing, he would assume the country did not want anything done. Grant was honest, but his honesty was of the naive type that made him the dupe of unscrupulous friends and schemers.

His most serious weakness as president was his failure to deal effectively with economic and social problems, but the one that injured him and the Republicans most was his inability to cope with government corruption. Grant did not cause the corruption, nor did he participate in the remotest way in the rush to "fatten at the public trough," as the reformers of the day might have put it. But he did nothing to prevent the scandals that disgraced his administration. Out of a misplaced belief in the sanctity of friendship, he protected some of the worst culprits and allowed calculating tricksters to use his good name and the prestige of his office to advance their own interests at the country's expense.

The worst of the scandals—such as the Whiskey Ring affair, which implicated Grant's private secretary, Orville E. Babcock, and cost the government millions in tax revenue, and the defalcations of Secretary of War William W. Belknap in the management of Indian affairs—did not become public knowledge during Grant's first term. However, in 1872 Republican reformers, alarmed by rumors of corruption and disappointed by Grant's failure to press for civil service reform, organized the Liberal Republican party and nominated Horace Greeley, the able but eccentric editor of the *New York Tribune,* for president.

The Liberal Republicans were mostly well educated, socially prominent types—editors, college presidents, economists, along with a sprinkling of businessmen and politicians. Their liberalism was of the laissez-faire variety; they were for low tariffs and sound money, and against what they called "class legislation," meaning measures benefiting particular groups, whether labor unions or railroad companies or farm organizations. Nearly all had supported Reconstruction at the start, but by the early 1870s most were including southern blacks

In 1872, Republicans who opposed Grant's renomination bolted the party and nominated Horace Greeley. These Liberal Republicans—some of them former Radicals—sought to conciliate the South. In this cartoon, Thomas Nast, a Grant supporter, condemns the actions of Greeley and Charles Sumner as they push a black man to shake hands with a Klan member and a Copperhead.

among the special interests that ought to be left to their own devices. Their observation of urban corruption and of unrestricted immigration led them to disparage universal suffrage, which, one of them said, "can only mean in plain English the government of ignorance and vice."

The Democrats also nominated Greeley in 1872, although he had devoted his political life to flailing the Democratic party in the *Tribune*. That surrender to expediency, together with Greeley's temperamental unsuitability for the presidency, made the campaign a fiasco for the reformers. Grant triumphed easily, with a popular majority of nearly 800,000.

Nevertheless, the defection of the Liberal Republicans hurt the Republican party in Congress. In the 1874 elections, no longer hampered as in the presidential contest by Greeley's notoriety and Grant's fame, the Democrats carried the House of Representatives. It was clear that the days of military rule in the South were ending. By the end of 1875 only three southern states—South Carolina, Florida, and Louisiana—were still under Republican control.

The Republican party in the South was "dead as a doornail," a reporter noted. He reflected the opinion of thousands when he added: "We ought to have a sound sensible republican . . . for the next President as a measure of safety; but only on the condition of absolute noninterference in Southern local affairs, for which there is no further need or excuse."

THE DISPUTED ELECTION OF 1876

Against this background the presidential election of 1876 took place. Since corruption in government was the most widely discussed issue, the Republicans passed over their most attractive political personality, the dynamic James G. Blaine, Speaker of the House of Representatives, who had been connected with some chicanery involving railroad securities. Instead they nominated Governor Rutherford B. Hayes of Ohio, a former general with an unsmirched reputation. The Democrats picked Governor Samuel J. Tilden of New York, a wealthy lawyer who had attracted national attention for his part in breaking up the Tweed Ring in New York City.

In November early returns indicated that Tilden had carried New York, New Jersey, Connecticut, Indiana, and all the southern states, including Louisiana, South Carolina, and Florida, where Republican regimes were still in control. This seemed to give him 203 electoral votes to Hayes's 165, and a popular plurality in the neighborhood of 250,000 out of more than 8 million votes cast. However, Republican leaders had anticipated the possible loss of Florida, South Carolina, and Louisiana and were prepared to use their control of the election machinery in those states to throw out sufficient Democratic ballots to alter the results if doing so would change the national outcome. Realizing that the electoral votes of those states were exactly enough to elect their man, they telegraphed their henchmen on the scene, ordering them to go into action. The local Republicans then invalidated Democratic ballots in wholesale lots and filed returns showing Hayes the winner. Naturally the local Democrats protested vigorously and filed their own returns.

The Constitution provides (Article II, Section 1) that presidential electors must meet in their respective states to vote and forward the results to "the Seat of the Government." There, it adds, "the President of the Senate shall, in the Presence of the Senate and House of Representatives, open all the Certificates, and the Votes shall then be counted." But who was to do the counting? The House was Democratic, the Senate Republican; neither would agree to allow the other to do the job. On January 29, 1877, scarcely a month before inauguration day, Congress created an electoral commission to decide the disputed cases. The commission consisted of five senators (three Republicans and two Democrats), five representatives (three Democrats and two Republicans), and five justices of the Supreme Court (two Democrats, two Republicans, and one "independent" judge, David Davis). Since it was a foregone conclusion that the others would vote for their party no matter what the evidence, Davis would presumably swing the balance in the interest of fairness.

But before the commission met, the Illinois legislature elected Davis senator! He had to resign from the Court and the commission. Since independents were rare even on the Supreme Court, no neutral was available to replace him. The vacancy went to Associate Justice Joseph P. Bradley of New Jersey, a Republican.

Evidence presented before the commission revealed a disgraceful picture of election shenanigans. On the one hand, in all three disputed states Democrats had clearly cast a majority of the votes; on the other, it was unquestionable that many blacks had been forcibly prevented from voting.

In truth, both sides were shamefully corrupt. The governor of Louisiana was reported willing to sell his state's electoral votes for $200,000. The Florida election board was supposed to have offered itself to Tilden for the same price. "That seems to be the standard figure," Tilden remarked ruefully.

Most modern authorities take the view that in a fair election the Republicans would have carried South Carolina and Louisiana but that Florida would have gone to Tilden, giving him the election, 188 electoral votes to 181. In the last analysis, this opinion has been arrived at simply by counting white and black noses: Blacks were in the majority in South Carolina and Louisiana. Amid the tension and confusion of early 1877, however, even a Solomon would have been hard pressed to judge rightly amid the rumors, lies, and contradictory statements, and the electoral commission was not composed of Solomons. The Democrats had some hopes that Justice Bradley would be sympathetic to their case, for he was known to be opposed to harsh Reconstruction policies. On the eve of the commission's decision in the Florida controversy, he was apparently ready to vote in favor of Tilden. But the Republicans subjected him to tremendous political pressure. When he read his opinion on February 8, it was for Hayes. Thus, by a vote of 8 to 7, the commission awarded Florida's electoral votes to the Republicans.

According to Tilden's campaign manager, angry Democrats in 15 states, chiefly war veterans, were readying themselves to march on Washington to force the inauguration of Tilden. Tempers flared in Congress, where some spoke ominously of a filibuster that would prevent the recording of the electoral vote and leave the country, on March 4, with no president at all.

THE COMPROMISE OF 1877

Forces for compromise had been at work behind the scenes in Washington for some time. Although northern Democrats threatened to fight to the last ditch, many southern Democrats were willing to accept Hayes if he would promise to remove the troops and allow the southern states to manage their internal affairs by themselves. Ex-Whig planters and merchants who had reluctantly abandoned the carpetbag governments and who sympathized with Republican economic

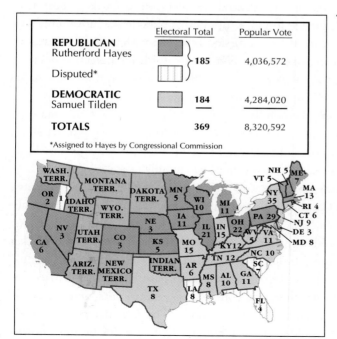

The Compromise of 1877

	Electoral Total	Popular Vote
REPUBLICAN Rutherford Hayes		4,036,572
Disputed*	} 185	
DEMOCRATIC Samuel Tilden	184	4,284,020
TOTALS	369	8,320,592

*Assigned to Hayes by Congressional Commission

policies hoped that by supporting Hayes they might contribute to the restoration of the two-party system that had been destroyed in the South during the 1850s. Ohio Congressman James A. Garfield urged Hayes to find "some discreet way" of showing these Southerners that he favored "internal improvements." Hayes replied: "Your views are so nearly the same as mine that I need not say a word."

With the tacit support of many Democrats, the electoral vote was counted by the president of the Senate on March 2, and Hayes was declared elected, 185 votes to 184.

Like all compromises, this agreement was not entirely satisfactory; like most, it was not honored in every detail. Hayes recalled the last troops from South Carolina and Louisiana in April. He appointed a former Confederate general, David M. Key of Tennessee, postmaster general and delegated to him the congenial task of finding Southerners willing to serve their country as officials of a Republican administration. But the alliance of ex-Whigs and northern Republicans did not flourish; the South remained solidly Democratic. The major significance of the compromise, one of the great intersectional political accommodations of American history, was that it ended Reconstruction and inaugurated a new political order in the South. More than the Constitutional amendments and federal statutes, this new regime would shape the destinies of the four million freedmen.

For most, this future was to be bleak. Forgotten in the North, manipulated and then callously rejected by the South, rebuffed by the Supreme Court, voiceless in national affairs, they and their descendants were condemned in the interests of sectional harmony to lives of poverty, indignity, and little hope. Meanwhile, the rest of the United States continued its golden march toward wealth and power.

MILESTONES

1863	Lincoln announces "Ten Percent Plan" for Reconstruction
1865	Establishment of the Freedmen's Bureau
	General Lee surrenders at Appomattox Court House
	Assassination of Abraham Lincoln; Andrew Johnson becomes President
	Johnson's amnesty plan
	Ratification of Thirteenth Amendment
1865–1866	Enactment of Black Codes by southern states
1866	Civil Rights Act passes over Johnson's veto
	Johnson campaigns for his Reconstruction policy
1867	First Reconstruction Act
	Tenure of Office Act
1868	House of Representatives impeaches Johnson
	Fourth Reconstruction Act
	Senate acquits Johnson
	Ratification of Fourteenth Amendment
	Ulysses S. Grant is elected president
1868–1872	Ku Klux Klan in action
1870	Ratification of Fifteenth Amendment
1870–1871	Force (Ku Klux Klan) Act destroys Klan
1872	Liberal Republican party nominates Horace Greeley for president
	Grant is reelected president
1876	Disputed presidential election
1877	Electoral Commission awards disputed votes to Rutherford B. Hayes
	Hayes agrees to Compromise of 1877

17

IN THE WAKE OF WAR

When Americans turned from fighting and making weapons to more constructive occupations, they transformed their agriculture, trade, manufacturing, mining, and means of communication. Immigration increased rapidly. Cities grew in size and number, exerting on every aspect of life an influence at least as pervasive as that exercised on earlier generations by the frontier. More and more Americans were flocking to the towns and cities, supporting themselves by laboring at machines or by scratching accounts in ledgers. At the same time farm production rose to new heights, invigorated by new marketing methods and the increased use of machinery. Railroad construction stimulated and unified the economy, helping to make possible still larger and more efficient enterprises. The flow of gold and silver from western mines excited people's imaginations and their avarice, while petroleum, the "black gold" discovered in Pennsylvania shortly before the war, gave rise to a new industry soon to become one of the most important in the nation. These developments amounted to more than a mere change of scale; they altered the structure of the economy and the society.

THE TRIUMPH OF SELF-INTEREST

After Appomattox the immense resources of the United States, combined with the high value most Americans assigned to work and achievement, made the people strongly materialistic. From colonial times they had assumed that prosperity was the natural state of things, and they had shown an inordinate respect for wealth. The Civil War further encouraged the glorification of money and the things it could buy. The North's capacity to produce the tools of war had helped preserve the Union; the role of businessmen and manufacturers in winning the struggle was clear to every soldier from General Grant to the lowliest private.

After the failures of Reconstruction, Americans seemed even more enamored of material values. They were tired of sacrifice, eager to act for themselves. They professed to believe strongly in a government policy of noninterference, or laissez-faire. "'Things regulate themselves' . . . means, of course, that God regulates them by his general laws," Professor Francis Bowen of Harvard wrote in his *American Political Economy* (1870).

Impressed by such logic and never especially noted for their sophistication, taste, or interest in preserving the resources of the country, the people now tolerated the grossest kind of waste and seemed to care little about corruption in high places, so long as no one interfered with their personal pursuit of profit. Mark Twain, raised in an earlier era, called this a Gilded Age, dazzling on the surface, base metal below.

Certain intellectual currents encouraged the exploitative drives of the people. Charles Darwin's *The Origin of Species* was published in 1859, and by the 1870s his theory of evolution was beginning to influence opinion in the United States. That nature had ordained a kind of inevitable progress, governed by the natural selection of those individual organisms best adapted to survive in a particular environment, seemed eminently reasonable to most Americans, for it fitted well with their own experiences. "Let the buyer beware; that covers the whole business," the sugar magnate Henry O. Havemeyer explained to an investigating committee. "You cannot wet-nurse people from the time they are born until the time they die. They have to wade and get stuck, and that is the way men are educated."

Yale professor William Graham Sumner sometimes used the survival-of-the-fittest analogy in teaching undergraduates. "Professor," one student asked Sumner, "don't you believe in any government aid to industries?" "No!" Sumner replied, "It's root, hog, or die." The student persisted: "Suppose some professor of political science came along and took your job away from you. Wouldn't you be sore?" "Any other professor is welcome to try," Sumner answered promptly. "If he gets my job, it is my fault. My business is to teach the subject so well that no one can take the job away from me." Sumner's argument described what came to be known as *social Darwinism,* the belief that the activities of people, that is, their business and social relationships, were governed by the Darwinian principle that "the fittest" will always "survive" if allowed to exercise their capacities without restriction.

Few businessmen were directly influenced by Darwin's ideas. Most eagerly accepted any aid they could get from the government, many were active in philanthropy, some felt a deep sense of social responsibility. Nevertheless, most were sincere individualists. They believed in competition, being convinced that the nation would best prosper if all people were free to seek their personal fortunes by their own methods.

CONGRESS ASCENDANT

A succession of weak presidents presided over the White House. Although the impeachment proceedings against Andrew Johnson had failed, Congress dominated the government. Within Congress, the Senate generally overshadowed the House of Representatives. In his novel *Democracy* (1880), the cynical Henry Adams wrote that the United States had a "government of the people, by the people, for the benefit of Senators." Critics called the Senate a "rich man's club," and it did contain many millionaires, among them Leland Stanford, founder of the Central Pacific Railroad; the mining tycoon James G. "Bonanza" Fair of Nevada;

An 1887 cartoon indicting the Senate for closely attending to the Big (read, fat) Trusts rather than to the needs of the public (whose "entrance" to the Senate is "closed"). Drawn by Joseph Keppler, a caricaturist who was born and trained in Germany, this type of grotesque satire greatly influenced late nineteenth-century American comic arts.

Philetus Sawyer, a self-made Wisconsin lumberman; and Nelson Aldrich of Rhode Island, whose wealth derived from banking and a host of corporate connections. However, the true sources of the Senate's influence lay in the long tenure of many of its members (which enabled them to master the craft of politics), in the fact that it was small enough to encourage real debate, and in its long-established reputation for wisdom, intelligence, and statesmanship.

The House of Representatives, on the other hand, was one of the most disorderly and inefficient legislative bodies in the world. "As I make my notes," a reporter wrote in 1882 while sitting in the House gallery,

> *I see a dozen men reading newspapers with their feet on their desks. . . . 'Pig Iron' Kelley of Pennsylvania has dropped his newspaper and is paring his fingernails. . . . The vile odor of . . . tobacco . . . rises from the two-for-five-cents cigars in the mouths of the so-called gentlemen below. . . . They chew, too! Every desk has a spittoon of pink and gold china beside it to catch the filth from the statesman's mouth.*

An infernal din rose from the crowded chamber. Desks slammed; members held private conversations, hailed pages, shuffled from place to place, clamored for the attention of the Speaker—and all the while some poor orator tried to discuss the question of the moment. Speaking in the House, one writer said, was like trying to address the crowd on a passing Broadway bus from the curb in front of the Astor House in New York. On one occasion in 1878 the adjournment of the House was held up for more than 12 hours because most of the members of an important committee were too drunk to prepare a vital appropriations bill for final passage.

The great political parties professed undying enmity to each other, but they seldom took clearly opposing positions on the questions of the day. Democrats were separated from Republicans more by accidents of geography, religious affiliation, ethnic background, and emotion than by economic issues. Questions of state and local importance, unrelated to national politics, often determined the outcome of congressional elections and thus who controlled the federal government.

The fundamental division between Democrats and Republicans was sectional, a result of the Civil War. The South, after the political rights of blacks had been drastically circumscribed, became heavily Democratic. Most of New England was solidly Republican. Elsewhere the two parties stood in fair balance, although the Republicans tended to have the advantage. A preponderance of the well-to-do, cultured Northerners were Republicans. Perhaps in reaction to this concentration, immigrants, Catholics, and—except for blacks—other minority groups tended to vote Democratic. But there were so many exceptions that these generalizations are of little practical importance. German and Scandinavian immigrants usually voted Republican; many powerful business leaders supported the Democrats.

The bulk of the people—farmers, laborers, shopkeepers, white-collar workers—distributed their ballots fairly evenly between the two parties in most elections; the balance of political power after 1876 was almost perfect—"the most spectacular degree of equilibrium in American history." Between 1856 and 1912 the Democrats elected a president only twice (1884 and 1892), but most contests were extremely close. Majorities in both the Senate and the House fluctuated continually. Between 1876 and 1896 the "dominant" Republican party controlled both houses of Congress and the presidency at the same time for only one 2-year period.

THE POLITICAL AFTERMATH OF WAR

Four questions obsessed politicians in these years. One was the "bloody shirt." The term, which became part of the language after a Massachusetts congressman dramatically displayed to his colleagues in the House the blood-stained shirt of an Ohio carpetbagger who had been flogged by terrorists in Mississippi, referred to the tactic of reminding the electorate of the northern states that the men who had taken the South out of the Union and precipitated the Civil War had been Democrats and that they and their descendants were still Democrats. Should their party regain power, former rebels would run the government and undo all the work accomplished at such sacrifice during the war. "Every man that endeavored to tear down the old flag," a Republican orator proclaimed in 1876, "was a Democrat. Every man that tried to destroy this nation was a Democrat. . . . The man that assassinated Abraham Lincoln was a Democrat. . . . Soldiers, every scar you have on your heroic bodies was given you by a Democrat."

Every scoundrel or incompetent who sought office under the Republican banner waved the bloody shirt in order to divert the attention of northern voters from his own shortcomings, and the technique worked so well that many decent candidates could not resist the temptation to employ it in close races. Nothing, of course, so effectively obscured the real issues of the day.

Waving the bloody shirt was related intimately to the issue of the rights of blacks. Throughout this period Republicans vacillated between trying to build up their organization in the South by appealing to black voters—which required them to make sure that blacks in the South could vote—and trying to win conservative white support by stressing economic issues such as the tariff. When the former strategy seemed wise, they waved the bloody shirt with vigor; in the latter case, they piously announced that the blacks' future was "as safe in the hands of one party as it is in the other."

The question of veterans' pensions also bore a close relationship to the bloody shirt. Following the Civil War, Union soldiers founded the Grand Army of the Republic (GAR). By 1890 the organization had a membership of 409,000. The GAR put immense pressure on Congress, first for aid to veterans with service-connected disabilities, then for those with any disability, and eventually for all former Union soldiers. Republican politicians played on the emotions of the exsoldiers by waving the bloody shirt, but the tough-minded leaders of the GAR demanded that they prove their sincerity by treating in open-handed fashion the warriors whose blood had stained the shirt.

The tariff was another perennial issue in post–Civil War politics. Despite considerable loose talk about free trade, almost no one in the United States except for a handful of professional economists, most of them college professors, believed in eliminating duties on imports. Manufacturers desired protective tariffs to keep out competing products, and a majority of their workers were convinced that wage levels would fall if goods produced by cheap foreign labor entered the United States untaxed. Many farmers supported protection, although almost no competing agricultural products were being imported. Congressman William McKinley of Ohio, who reputedly could make reciting a tariff schedule sound like poetry, stated the majority opinion in the clearest terms: high tariffs foster the growth of industry and thus create jobs. "Reduce the tariff and labor is the first to suffer," he said.

A third political question in this period was currency reform. During the Civil War, it will be recalled, the government, faced with obligations it could not meet by taxing or borrowing, suspended specie payments and issued about $450 million in paper money. The greenbacks did not command the full confidence of a people accustomed to money readily convertible into gold or silver. Greenbacks seemed to threaten inflation, for how could one trust the government not to issue them in wholesale lots to avoid passing unpopular tax laws? Thus, when the war ended, strong sentiment developed for withdrawing the greenbacks from circulation and returning to a bullion standard.

In fact, beginning during Reconstruction, prices declined sharply. The deflation increased the real income of bondholders and other creditors but injured debtors. Farmers were particularly hard hit, for many of them had borrowed heavily during the wartime boom to finance expansion.

Here was a question of real significance. Many groups supported some kind of currency inflation. A National Greenback party nominated Peter Cooper, an iron manufacturer, for president in 1876. Cooper received only 81,000 votes, but a new Greenback Labor party polled over a million in 1878, electing 14 congressmen. However, the major parties refused to confront each other over the currency question. While Republicans professed to be the party of sound money, most western Republicans favored expansion of the currency. And while one wing of the Democrats flirted with the Greenbackers, the conservative, or "Bourbon," Democrats favored deflation as much as Republicans did.

The final major political issue of these years was civil service reform. That the federal bureaucracy needed overhauling nearly everyone agreed. As American society grew larger and more complex, the government necessarily took on more functions. The need for professional administration increased. The number of federal employees rose from 53,000 in 1871 to 256,000 at the end of the century. Corruption flourished; waste and inefficiency were the normal state of affairs. The collection of tariff duties offered perhaps the greatest opportunity for venality. The New York Custom House, one observer wrote in 1872, teemed with "corrupting merchants and their clerks and runners, who think that all men can be bought, and . . . corrupt swarms [of clerks], who shamelessly seek their price."

With a succession of relatively ineffective presidents and a Congress that squandered its energies on private bills, pork-barrel projects, and other trivia, the administration of the government was strikingly inefficient.

Every honest observer could see the need for reform, but the politicians refused to surrender the power of dispensing government jobs to their lieutenants without regard for their qualifications. They argued that patronage was the lifeblood of politics, that parties could not function without armies of loyal political workers, and that the workers expected and deserved the rewards of office when their efforts were crowned with victory at the polls. Typical was the attitude of the New York assemblyman who, according to Theodore Roosevelt, had "the same idea about Public Life and the Civil Service that a vulture has of a dead sheep." When reformers suggested establishing the most modest kind of professional, nonpartisan civil service, politicians of both parties subjected them to every kind of insult and ridicule even though both the Democratic and Republican parties regularly wrote civil service reform planks into their platforms.

BLACKS AFTER RECONSTRUCTION

Minorities were treated with callousness and contempt in the postwar decades. That the South would deal harshly with the former slaves once federal control was relaxed probably should have been expected. Men like Governor Wade

Hampton of South Carolina had promised to respect black civil rights. "We . . . will secure to every citizen, the lowest as well as the highest, black as well as white, full and equal protection in the enjoyment of all his rights under the Constitution," Hampton said in 1877. This pledge was not kept.

President Hayes had urged blacks to trust southern whites. A new Era of Good Feelings had dawned, he announced after making a goodwill tour of the South shortly after his inauguration. By December 1877 he had been sadly disillusioned. "By state legislation, by frauds, by intimidation, and by violence of the most atrocious character, colored citizens have been deprived of the right of suffrage," he wrote in his diary. However, he did nothing to remedy the situation. Frederick Douglass called Hayes's policy "sickly conciliation."

Hayes's successors in the 1880s did no better. "Time is the only cure," President Garfield said, thereby confessing that he had no policy at all. President Arthur gave federal patronage to antiblack groups in an effort to split the Democratic South. In President Cleveland's day blacks had scarcely a friend in high places, North or South. In 1887 Cleveland explained to a correspondent why he opposed "mixed schools." Expert opinion, the president said, believed "that separate schools were of much more benefit for the colored people." Hayes, Garfield, and Arthur were Republicans, Cleveland a Democrat; party made little difference. Both parties subscribed to hypocritical statements about equality and constitutional rights, and neither did anything to implement them.

For a time blacks were not totally disfranchised in the South. Rival white factions tried to manipulate them, and corruption flourished as widely as in the machine-dominated wards of the northern cities. In the 1890s, however, the southern states, led by Mississippi, began to deprive blacks of the vote despite the Fifteenth Amendment. Poll taxes raised a formidable economic barrier, one that also disfranchised many poor whites. Literacy tests completed the work; a number of states provided a loophole for illiterate whites by including an "understanding" clause whereby an illiterate person could qualify by demonstrating an ability to explain the meaning of a section of the state constitution when an election official read it to him. Blacks who attempted to take the test were uniformly declared to have failed it.

In Louisiana, 130,000 blacks voted in the election of 1896. Then the law was changed. In 1900 only 5000 votes were cast by blacks. "We take away the Negroes' votes," a Louisiana politician explained, "to protect them just as we would protect a little child and prevent it from injuring itself with sharp-edged tools."

Almost every Supreme Court decision after 1877 that affected blacks somehow nullified or curtailed their rights. The *Civil Rights Cases* (1883) declared the

Civil Rights Act of 1875 unconstitutional. Blacks who were refused equal accommodations or privileges by hotels, theaters, and other privately owned facilities had no recourse at law, the Court announced. The Fourteenth Amendment guaranteed their civil rights against invasion by the states, not by individuals. Finally, in *Plessy* v. *Ferguson* (1896), the Court ruled that even in places of public accommodation, such as railroads and, by implication, schools, segregation was legal as long as facilities of equal quality were provided. "If one race be inferior to the other socially, the Constitution of the United States cannot put them upon the same plane." Now, total segregation was imposed throughout the South. Separate schools, prisons, hospitals, recreational facilities, and even cemeteries were provided for blacks, and these were almost never equal to those available to whites.

Most Northerners supported the government and the Court. Social Darwinist ideas seemed to demonstrate that since there were physiological differences between whites and blacks and since the whites were in control of the country, the whites were "the fittest" by nature. Newspapers presented a stereotyped, derogatory picture of blacks, no matter what the circumstances. Northern magazines, even high-quality publications such as *Harper's, Scribner's,* and *The Century,* repeatedly made blacks the butt of crude jokes. "The Negro's day is over," the tough-minded William Graham Sumner explained. "He is out of fashion."

The southern insistence on segregating public schools, buttressed by the separate but equal decision of the Supreme Court in *Plessy* v. *Ferguson,* imposed a crushing financial burden on poor, sparsely settled communities, and the dominant opinion that blacks were not really educable did not encourage these communities to make special efforts on their behalf.

BOOKER T. WASHINGTON: A "REASONABLE" CHAMPION FOR BLACKS

Since nearly all contemporary biologists, physicians, and other supposed experts on race were convinced that blacks were inferior beings, educated Northerners generally accepted black inferiority as fact. The English observer James Bryce, who had a wide acquaintance among Americans of this type, absorbed their social Darwinist point of view. Negroes, Bryce wrote, were inherently docile, pliable, submissive, lustful, childish, impressionable, emotional, heedless, and "unthrifty." They had "no capacity for abstract thinking, for scientific inquiry, or for any kind of invention." Being "unspeakably inferior," they were "unfit to cope with a superior race."

Like Bryce, most Americans did not especially wish blacks ill; they simply refused to consider them quite human and consigned them complacently to oblivion, along with the Indians, who were also dismissed as racially inferior by Darwinians. A vicious circle was established. By denying blacks decent educational opportunities and good jobs, the dominant race could use the blacks' resultant ignorance and poverty to justify the inferior facilities offered them.

Southern blacks reacted to this deplorable situation in a variety of ways. Some sought redress in racial pride and what would later be called black nationalism. Some became so disaffected that they tried to revive the African colonization movement. "Africa is our home," insisted Bishop Henry M. Turner, a huge, plain-spoken man who had served as an army chaplain during the war and as a member of the Georgia legislature during Reconstruction. "Every man that has the sense of an animal must see there is no future in this country for the Negro." Another militant, T. Thomas Fortune, editor of the New York *Age* and founder of the Afro-American League (1887), called on blacks to demand full civil rights, better schools, and fair wages and to fight against discrimination of every sort. "Let us stand up like men in our own organization," he urged. "If others use . . . violence to combat our peaceful arguments, it is not for us to run away from violence."

For a time, militancy and black separatism won few adherents among southern blacks. For one thing, life was better than it had been under slavery. Segregation actually helped the numbers of southern blacks who became barbers, undertakers, restaurateurs, and shopkeepers because whites were reluctant to supply such services to blacks. Even when whites competed with black businesses, the resentment caused by segregation led blacks to patronize establishments run by people of their own race. According to the most conservative estimates, the living standard of the average southern black more than doubled between 1865 and 1900. But this only made many southern whites more angry and vindictive.

This helps explain the tactics of Booker T. Washington, one of the most extraordinary Americans of that generation. Washington had been born a slave in Virginia in 1856. Laboriously he obtained an education, supporting himself while a student by working as a janitor. In 1881, with the financial help of northern philanthropists, he founded Tuskegee Institute in Alabama. His experiences convinced Washington that blacks must lift themselves up by their own bootstraps but that they must also accommodate themselves to white prejudices. A persuasive speaker and a brilliant fund-raiser, he soon developed a national reputation as a "reasonable" champion of his race. (In 1891 Harvard awarded him an honorary degree.)

In 1895 Washington made a now-famous speech to a mixed audience at the Cotton States International Exposition in Atlanta. To the blacks he said: "Cast

Booker T. Washington's famous Atlanta address in 1895 received mixed reactions in the black community. His most fervent challenge came from W. E. B. Du Bois, a professor at Atlanta University, who rejected Washington's call for patience and accommodation as a means to end racial segregation.

down your bucket where you are," by which he meant stop fighting segregation and second-class citizenship and concentrate on learning useful skills. "Dignify and glorify common labor," he urged. "Agitation of questions of racial equality is the extremest folly." Progress up the social and economic ladder would come not from "artificial forcing" but from self-improvement. "There is as much dignity in tilling a field as in writing a poem."

Washington asked the whites of what he called "our beloved South" to lend the blacks a hand in their efforts to advance themselves. If you will do so, he promised, you will be "surrounded by the most patient, faithful, law-abiding, and unresentful people that the world has seen."

This "Atlanta Compromise" delighted white Southerners and won Washington financial support in every section of the country. He became one of the most powerful men in the United States, consulted by presidents, in close touch with business and philanthropic leaders, and capable of influencing in countless unobtrusive ways the fate of millions of blacks.

Blacks responded to the compromise with mixed feelings. Accepting Washington's approach might relieve them of many burdens and dangers. Being obsequious might, like discretion, be the better part of valor. But Washington was asking them to give up specific rights in return for vague promises of future help. The cost was high in surrendered personal dignity and lost hopes of obtaining real justice.

Washington's career illustrates the terrible dilemma that American blacks have always faced: the choice between confrontation and accommodation. This choice was particularly difficult in the late nineteenth century.

Washington chose accommodation. It is easy to condemn him as a toady but difficult to see how, at that time, a more aggressive policy could have succeeded. Behind the scenes he lobbied against restrictive measures, marshaled large sums of money to fight test cases in the courts, and worked hard in northern states to organize the black vote and make sure that black political leaders got a share of the spoils of office. He may not have been an admirable man, but he was a useful one. His defects point up more the unlovely aspects of the age than those of his own character.

WHITE VIOLENCE AND VENGEANCE

By the time of the Atlanta Compromise, however, Washington's calls for "sagacious silence," as one black militant put it, could scarcely be heard over the anguished cries of the victims of white violence. For decades, some southern whites had tried to replace the legal subjugation of slavery with psychological subjugation through terror. "They had to have a license to kill anything but a nigger," a black Southerner recalled. "We was always in season." From 1890 through 1910 nearly a hundred blacks were lynched each year.

These numbers, which omit those blacks who were executed after biased though nominally legal trials, fail to tell the whole story of the intensification of violence against blacks. An example was the lynching in 1899 of Sam Hose in a town outside Atlanta. Hose, a black laborer, killed his boss in self-defense. He was seized by a white mob and chained to a tree. His ears, fingers, toes, and genitals were cut off and his face was skinned. Then, while still alive, he was doused with kerosene and set on fire. A crowd numbering in the thousands watched, in the words of one newspaper account, "with unfeigning satisfaction." The dead man's body parts were auctioned: small bones went for 25 cents; his liver, "crisply cooked," for 10 cents.

White fears were excited by feverish rumors of black males as rapists and predators. "There is a black vampire hovering over our beloved North Carolina," Rebecca Strowd warned the White Government Leagues in 1898. Violence and violent rhetoric succeeded in disfranchising southern black men and driving them, often literally, out of public spaces. Ironically, this created an opportunity for black women to fill the leadership void, taking increasingly prominent roles as spokespersons in religious and reform associations.

The public activities of black women reformers and of white supremacists such as Rebecca Strowd contradicted ideals of feminine domesticity, but their arguments affirmed middle-class sensibilities. Thus black women insisted that whites uphold Christian brotherhood, while women such as Strowd called upon white men to do their duty in protecting their womenfolk. By advancing middle-class ideology, however, these women distanced themselves from the working classes of both races. Few male sharecroppers or industrial workers could hope to earn enough to enable their wives to devote themselves exclusively to the home or to the cultivation of middle-class proprieties. And many working-class women, having sampled the independence as well as the harshness of paid work, were unpersuaded of the appeal of domesticity.

THE WEST AFTER THE CIVIL WAR

Although the image of the West as the land of great open spaces is accurate enough, the region contained several bustling cities. San Francisco, with a population approaching 250,000 in the late 1870s, had long outgrown its role as a rickety boomtown where the forty-niners bought supplies and squandered whatever wealth they had sifted from the streams of the Sierras. Though still an important warehouse and supply center, it had become the commercial and financial heart of the Pacific Coast and a center of light manufacturing, food processing, and machine shops. Denver, San Antonio, and Salt Lake City were far smaller, but growing rapidly and equally "urban."

There was, in short, no one West, no typical Westerner. If the economy was predominantly agricultural and extractive, it was also commercial and entering the early stages of industrial development. The seeds of such large enterprises as Wells Fargo, Levi Strauss, and half a dozen important department store empires were sown in the immediate postwar decades.

Above all, however, the West epitomized the social Darwinist, "every man for himself" psychology of post-Reconstruction American society. In 1879 several thousand southern blacks suddenly migrated to western Kansas. When asked why they moved, one of their leaders replied: "The white people [in the South] treat our people so bad." The treatment of blacks in Kansas was not much better, certainly not better than the way blacks were treated in the northern states. California had been a free state from the moment of its entry into the Union as part of the Compromise of 1850, but it treated its black citizens poorly, even refusing to ratify the Fifteenth Amendment.

Beginning in the mid-1850s a steady flow of Chinese migrated to the United States, most of them to the west coast. About four or five thousand a year came, until the negotiation of the Burlingame Treaty of 1868, the purpose of which was to provide cheap labor for railroad construction crews. Thereafter the annual influx more than doubled, although before 1882 it exceeded 20,000 only twice. When the railroads were completed and the Chinese began to compete with native workers, a great cry of resentment went up on the west coast. Riots broke out in San Francisco in 1877. Chinese workers were called "groveling worms," "more slavish and brutish than the beasts that roam the fields." The California constitution of 1879 denied the right to vote to any "native of China" along with idiots, the insane, and persons convicted of "any infamous crime."

When Chinese immigration increased in 1882 to nearly 40,000, the protests reached such a peak that Congress passed a law prohibiting all Chinese immigration for ten years. Later legislation extended the ban indefinitely.

THE PLAINS INDIANS

For 250 years the Indians had been driven back steadily, yet on the eve of the Civil War they still inhabited roughly half the United States. By the time of Hayes's inauguration, however, the Indians had been shattered as independent peoples, and in another decade the survivors were penned up on reservations, the government committed to a policy of extinguishing their way of life.

In 1860 the survivors of most of the eastern tribes were living peacefully in Indian Territory, what is now Oklahoma. In California the forty-niners had made short work of the local tribes. Elsewhere in the West—in the deserts of the Great Basin between the Sierras and the Rockies, in the mountains themselves, and on the semiarid, grass-covered plains between the Rockies and the edge of white civilization in eastern Kansas and Nebraska—nearly a quarter of a million Indians dominated the land.

By far the most important lived on the High Plains. From the Blackfeet of southwestern Canada and the Sioux of Minnesota and the Dakotas to the Cheyenne of Colorado and Wyoming and the Comanche of northern Texas, the Plains tribes possessed a generally uniform culture. All lived by hunting the hulking American bison, or buffalo, which ranged over the Plains by the millions. The buffalo provided the Indians with food, clothing, and even shelter, for the famous Indian tepee was covered with hides. On the treeless plains, dried buffalo dung was used for fuel. The buffalo was also an important symbol in Indian religion.

Although they seemed the epitome of freedom, pride, and self-reliance, the Plains Indians had begun to fall under the sway of white power. They eagerly adopted the products of the more technically advanced culture—cloth, metal tools, weapons, cheap decorations. However, the most important thing the whites gave them had nothing to do with technology: It was the horse.

The horse was among the many large mammals that became extinct in the Western Hemisphere around 9000 B.C. Cortés reintroduced the horse to America in the sixteenth century. Multiplying rapidly thereafter, the animals soon roamed wild from Texas to the Argentine. By the eighteenth century the Indians of the Plains had made them a vital part of their culture.

Horses thrived on the Plains and so did their masters. Mounted Indians could run down buffalo instead of stalking them on foot. They could move more easily over the country and fight more effectively too. They could acquire and transport more possessions and increase the size of their tepees, for horses could drag heavy loads heaped on A-shaped frames (called *travois* by the French), whereas earlier Indians had only dogs to depend on as pack animals. The frames of the *travois,* when disassembled, served as poles for tepees. The Indians also adopted modern weapons: the cavalry sword, which they particularly admired, and the rifle. Both added to

An Oglala Sioux named Kills Two painted this portrayal of an Indian horse dance. Horses were vital to survival for the Sioux, as their inclusion in such ceremonies demonstrates.

their effectiveness as hunters and fighters. However, like the whites' liquor and diseases, horses and guns caused problems. The buffalo herds began to diminish, and warfare became bloodier and more frequent.

INDIAN WARS

The government showed little interest in honoring agreements with Indians. A gold rush into Colorado in 1859 sent thousands of greedy prospectors across the Plains to drive the Cheyenne and Arapaho from land guaranteed them in 1851. By 1860 most of Kansas and Nebraska had been cleared. Other trouble developed in the Sioux country. Thus it happened that in 1862, after federal troops had been pulled out of the West for service against the Confederacy, most of the Plains Indians rose up against the whites. For five years intermittent but bloody clashes kept the entire area in a state of alarm.

This was guerrilla warfare, with all its horror and treachery. In 1864 a party of Colorado militia fell on an unsuspecting Cheyenne community at Sand Creek and killed an estimated 450. "Kill and scalp all, big and little," Colonel J. M. Chivington, a minister in private life, told his men. "Nits make lice." A white observer described the scene: "They were scalped, their brains knocked out; the

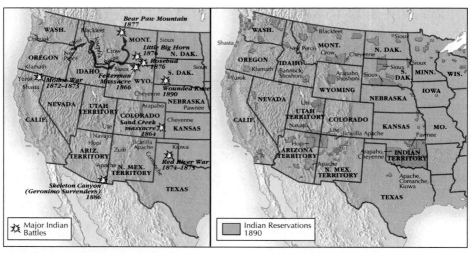

Major Indian Battles and Reservations

men used their knives, ripped open women, clubbed little children, knocked them in the head with their guns, beat their brains out, mutilated their bodies in every sense of the word." General Nelson A. Miles called this "Chivington massacre" the "foulest and most unjustifiable crime in the annals of America," but it was no worse than many incidents in earlier conflicts with Indians.

In turn the Indians slaughtered dozens of isolated white families, ambushed small parties, and fought many successful skirmishes against troops and militia. They achieved their most notable triumph in December 1866, when the Oglala Sioux, under their great chief Red Cloud, wiped out a party of 82 soldiers under Captain W. J. Fetterman. Red Cloud fought ruthlessly, but only when goaded by the construction of the Bozeman Trail, a road through the heart of the Sioux hunting grounds in southern Montana.

In 1867 the government tried a new strategy. The "concentration" policy had evidently not gone far enough. All the Plains Indians would be confined to two small reservations, one in the Black Hills of the Dakota Territory, the other in Oklahoma, and forced to become farmers. At two great conclaves held in 1867 and 1868 at Medicine Lodge Creek and Fort Laramie, the principal chiefs yielded to the government's demands.

Many Indians refused to abide by these agreements. With their whole way of life at stake, they raged across the Plains like a prairie fire—and were almost as destructive.

That a relative handful of "savages," without central leadership, could hold off the cream of the army, battle-hardened in the Civil War, can be explained by the character of the vast, trackless country and the ineptness of many American military commanders. Indian leadership was also poor in that few chiefs were capable of organizing a campaign or following up an advantage. But the Indians made superb guerrillas. Every observer called them the best cavalry soldiers in the world. Armed with stubby, powerful bows capable of driving an arrow clear through a bull buffalo, they were a fair match for troops equipped with carbines and Colt revolvers. Expertly they led pursuers into ambushes, swept down on unsuspecting supply details, stole up on small parties the way a mountain lion stalks a grazing lamb. They could sometimes be rounded up, as when General Philip Sheridan herded the tribes of the Southwest into Indian Territory in 1869. But once the troops withdrew, braves began to melt away into the emptiness of the surrounding grasslands. The distinction between "treaty" Indians, who had agreed to live on the new reservations, and the "nontreaty" variety shifted almost from day to day. Trouble flared here one week, next week somewhere else, perhaps 500 miles away. No less an authority than General William Tecumseh Sherman testified that a mere 50 Indians could often "checkmate" 3000 soldiers.

The government's maladministration of the reservations doomed its Indian policy. After 1849 the Department of the Interior supposedly had charge of tribal affairs. Most of its agents systematically cheated the Indians. Army officers squabbled frequently with Indian agents over policy, and an "Indian Ring" in the Department of the Interior system typically stole funds and supplies intended for the reservation Indians. "No branch of the national government is so spotted with fraud, so tainted with corruption . . . as this Indian Bureau," Congressman Garfield charged in 1869.

At about this time a Yale paleontologist, Othniel C. Marsh, who wished to dig for fossils on the Sioux reservation, asked Red Cloud for permission to enter his domain. The chief agreed on condition that Marsh, whom the Indians called Big Bone Chief, take back with him samples of the moldy flour and beef that government agents were supplying to his people. Appalled by what he saw on the reservation, Professor Marsh took the rotten supplies directly to President Grant and prepared a list of charges against the agents. General Sherman, in overall command of the Indian country, claimed in 1875: "We could settle Indian troubles in an hour, but Congress wants the patronage of the Indian bureau, and the bureau wants the appropriations without any of the trouble of the Indians themselves." General Sheridan was no lover of Indians. "The only good Indians I ever saw," he said in an oft-quoted remark, "were dead." But he understood why they behaved as they did. "We took away their country and their means of support, broke up their mode of living, their habits of life, introduced disease and decay among them, and it was for this and against this that they made war. Could anyone expect less?"

Grant wished to place the reservations under army control, but the Indians opposed this. They fared no better around army camps than on the reservations. In 1869 Congress created a nonpolitical Board of Indian Commissioners to oversee Indian affairs, but the bureaucrats in Washington stymied the commissioners at every turn.

In 1874 gold was discovered in the Black Hills Indian reservation. By the next winter thousands of miners had invaded the reserved area. Already alarmed by the approach of crews building the Northern Pacific Railroad, the Sioux once again went on the warpath. Joining with nontreaty tribes to the west, they concentrated in the region of the Bighorn River, in southern Montana Territory.

The summer of 1876 saw three columns of troops in the field against them. The commander of one column, General Alfred H. Terry, sent ahead a small detachment of the Seventh Cavalry under Colonel George A. Custer with orders to locate the Indians' camp and then block their escape route into the inaccessible Bighorn Mountains. Custer was vain and rash, and vanity and rashness were grave handicaps when fighting Indians. Grossly underestimating the number of the Indians, he decided to attack directly with his tiny force of 264 men. At the Little Bighorn late in June he found himself surrounded by 2500 Sioux under Rain-in-the-Face, Crazy Horse, and Sitting Bull. He and all his men died on the field.

Because it was so one-sided, "Custer's last stand" was not a typical battle, although it may be taken as symbolic of the Indian warfare of the period in the sense that it was characterized by bravery, foolhardiness, and a tragic waste of life. The battle greatly heartened the Indians, but it did not gain them their cause. That autumn, short of rations and hard-pressed by overwhelming numbers of soldiers, they surrendered and returned to the reservation.

Preparing to surrender to General Crook, Geronimo (mounted, left) and Natiche stand with their respective sons and Geronimo's grandson; the sons wear ceremonial paint. This photograph was taken in the Sierra Madre mountains of Mexico in 1886, just before the surrender.

THE DESTRUCTION OF TRIBAL LIFE

Thereafter, the fighting slackened. For this the building of transcontinental railroads and the destruction of the buffalo were chiefly responsible. An estimated 13 to 15 million head had roamed the Plains in the mid-1860s. Then the slaughter began. Thousands were butchered to feed the gangs of laborers engaged in building the Union Pacific Railroad. Thousands more fell before the guns of sportsmen. Buffalo hunting became a fad, and a brisk demand developed for buffalo rugs and mounted buffalo heads. Railroads made the Army a far more efficient force. Troops and supplies could be moved swiftly when trouble with the tribes erupted. The lines also contributed to the decimation of the buffalo by running excursion trains for hunters; even the shameful practice of gunning down the beasts directly from the cars was allowed.

The discovery in 1871 of a way to make commercial use of buffalo hides completed the tragedy. In the next three years about 9 million head were killed; after another decade the animals were almost extinct. No more efficient way could have been found for destroying the Plains Indians. The disappearance of the bison left them starving, homeless, purposeless.

By 1887 the tribes of the mountains and deserts beyond the Plains had also given up the fight. Typical of the heartlessness of the government's treatment of

The Taxidermist's Department of the Kansas Pacific Railway. Victorian Americans brought vanquished or domesticated "Nature" into their lives whenever possible. Stuffed buffalo, however, failed to become popular: Their hulking heads lacked the noble grandeur of the deer, and their large eyes and puny horns rendered them more pitiable than ferocious.

these peoples was that afforded the Nez Percé of Oregon and Idaho, who were led by the remarkable Chief Joseph. After outwitting federal troops in a campaign across more than a thousand miles of rough country, Joseph finally surrendered in October 1877. The Nez Perce were then settled on "the malarial bottoms of the Indian Territory" in far-off Oklahoma.

The last Indians to abandon the unequal battle were the Apaches of the Southwest, who finally yielded on the capture of their leader, Geronimo, in 1886.

By the 1880s, the advance of whites into the Plains had become, in the words of one congressman, as irresistible "as that of Sherman's to the sea." Greed for land lay behind the pressure, but large numbers of disinterested people, including most of those who deplored the way the Indians had been treated in the past, believed that the only practical way to solve the "Indian problem" was to persuade the Indians to abandon their tribal culture and live on family farms. The "wild" Indian must be changed into a "civilized" member of "American" society.

To accomplish this goal Congress passed the Dawes Severalty Act of 1887. Tribal lands were to be split up into individual allotments. To keep speculators from wresting the allotments from the Indians while they were adjusting to their

An encampment of 4000 Sioux on White Clay Creek near the South Dakota–Nebraska border in the early 1890s. Federal policy sought to "civilize" the Indians, though it failed to give the idea much thought. This vast nomadic community, whose homes and possessions could be moved in a few hours (note the horses and wagons), was more populous than most "urban" areas in the nation (the U.S. Census defined urban as any community with more than 2500 people). But the census had no way of conceiving of "cities" as entities whose location would change.

new way of life, the land could not be disposed of for 25 years. Funds were to be appropriated for educating and training the Indians, and those who accepted allotments, took up residence "separate from any tribe," and "adopted the habits of civilized life" were to be granted United States citizenship.

The sponsors of the Severalty Act thought they were effecting a fine humanitarian reform. "We must throw some protection over [the Indian]," Senator Henry L. Dawes declared. "We must hold up his hand." But no one expected all the Indians to accept allotments at once, and for some years little pressure was put on any to do so.

The Dawes Act had disastrous results in the long run. It assumed that Indians could be transformed into small agricultural capitalists by an act of Congress. It shattered what was left of the Indians' culture without enabling them to adapt to white ways. Moreover, unscrupulous white men systematically tricked many Indians into leasing their allotments for a pittance, and local authorities often taxed Indian lands at excessive rates. In 1934, after about 86 million of the 138 million acres assigned under the Dawes Act had passed into white hands, the government returned to a policy of encouraging tribal ownership of Indian lands.

THE LURE OF GOLD AND SILVER IN THE WEST

The natural resources of the nation were exploited in these decades even more ruthlessly and thoughtlessly than were its human resources. Americans had long regarded the West as a limitless treasure to be grasped as rapidly as possible, and after 1865 they engrossed its riches still faster and in a wider variety of ways. From the mid-1850s to the mid-1870s thousands of gold-crazed prospectors fanned out through the Rockies, panning every stream and hacking furiously at every likely outcropping from the Fraser River country of British Columbia to Tucson in southern Arizona, from the eastern slopes of the Sierras to the Great Plains.

Gold and silver were scattered throughout the area, though usually too thinly to make mining profitable. Whenever anyone made a "strike," prospectors, the vast majority utterly without previous experience but driven by what a mining journal of the period called an "unhealthy desire" for sudden wealth, flocked to the site, drawn by rumors of stream beds gleaming with gold-rich gravel and of nuggets the size of men's fists. For a few months the area teemed with activity. Towns of 5000 or more sprang up overnight; improvised roads were crowded with people and supply wagons. Claims were staked out along every stream and gully. Then, usually, expectations faded in the light of reality: high prices, low yields, hardship, violence, and deception. The boom collapsed and the towns died as quickly as they had risen. A few would have found wealth, the rest only backbreaking labor and disappointment—until tales of another strike sent them dashing feverishly across the land on another golden chase.

In the spring of 1858 it was upon the Fraser River in Canada that the horde descended, 30,000 Californians in the vanguard. The following spring, Pikes Peak in Colorado attracted the pack, experienced California prospectors ("yonder siders") mixing with "greenhorns" from every corner of the globe. In June 1859 came the finds in Nevada, where the famous Comstock Lode yielded ores worth nearly $4000 a ton. In 1861, while men in the settled areas were laying down their tools to take up arms, the miners were racing to the Idaho panhandle, hoping to become millionaires overnight. The next year the rush was to the Snake River Valley, then in 1863 and 1864 to Montana. In 1874 to 1876 the Black Hills in the heart of the Sioux lands were inundated.

The sudden prosperity of the mining towns attracted every kind of shady character—according to one forty-niner "rascals from Oregon, pickpockets from New York, accomplished gentlemen from Europe, interlopers from Lima and Chile, Mexican thieves, gamblers from no particular spot, and assassins manufactured in Hell." Gambling dens, dance halls, saloons, and brothels mushroomed wherever precious metal was found.

Law enforcement was a constant problem. Much of the difficulty lay in the anti-social attitudes of the miners themselves. Gold and silver dominated people's thoughts and dreams, and few paid much attention to the means employed in accumulating this wealth. Storekeepers charged outrageous prices; claim holders "salted" worthless properties with nuggets in order to swindle gullible investors. Ostentation characterized the successful, braggadocio those who failed. During the administration of President Grant, Virginia City, Nevada, was at the peak of its vulgar prosperity, producing an average of $12 million a year in ore. Built on the richness of the Comstock Lode ($306 million in gold and silver was extracted from the Comstock in 20 years), it had 25 saloons before it had 4000 people. By the 1870s its mountainside site was disfigured by ugly, ornate mansions where successful mine operators ate from fine china and swilled champagne as though it were water.

In 1873, after the discovery of the Big Bonanza, a seam of rich ore more than 50 feet thick, the future of Virginia City seemed boundless. Other discoveries shortly thereafter indicated to optimists that the mining boom in the West would continue indefinitely. The finds in the Black Hills district in 1875 and 1876, heralding deposits yielding eventually $100 million, led to the mushroom growth of Deadwood, home of Wild Bill Hickok, Deadwood Dick, Calamity Jane, and such lesser-known characters as California Jack and Poker Alice. The West continued to yield much gold and silver, especially silver, but big corporations produced nearly all of it. The mines around Deadwood were soon controlled by one large company, Homestake Mining. Butte, Montana, was similarly dominated by Anaconda Mining.

This is the culminating irony of the history of the mining frontier: Shoestring prospectors, independent and enterprising, made the key discoveries. They established local institutions and supplied the West with much of its color and folklore. But the stockholders of large corporations, many of whom had never seen a mine, made off with the lion's share of the wealth. Those whose worship of gold was direct and incessant, the prospectors who peopled the mining towns and gave the frontier its character, mostly died poor, still seeking a prize as elusive if not as illusory as the pot of gold at the end of the rainbow.

Each new strike and rush, no matter how ephemeral, brought permanent settlers along with the

Nat Love, a cowboy who earned the name "Deadwood Dick" throughout the Dakotas in the 1880s for his prowess with a lariat. His autobiography, published in 1907, attests to the role blacks played in settling the Wild West.

prospectors: farmers, cattlemen, storekeepers, teamsters, lawyers, and ministers. The boomtowns had to import everything from bread, meat, and liquor to building materials and tools of every sort. Without the well-worn trails blazed by earlier hunters and migrants headed for Oregon and California, and of freighting companies equipped to haul heavy loads over long distances, the towns could not have existed. Some of the gold seekers saw from the start that a better living could be made supplying the needs of prospectors than looking for the elusive metal. Others, failing to find mineral wealth, took up whatever occupation they could rather than starve or return home empty-handed. In every mining town—along with the saloons and brothels—schools, churches, and newspaper offices sprang up.

Creede, Colorado, circa 1890, a mining town whose inhospitability to women is suggested by their absence. One reason is indicated in information compiled for another Colorado mining town, Leadville, which, with a population of 20,000, had 250 saloons, 120 gambling establishments, 100 brothels, and only 4 churches.

The mines also speeded the political organization of the West. Colorado and Nevada became territories in 1861, Arizona and Idaho in 1863, Montana in 1864. Although Nevada was admitted before it had 60,000 residents (in 1864, to ratify the Thirteenth Amendment and help reelect Lincoln), most of these territories did not become states for decades. But because of the miners, the framework for future development was early established.

BIG BUSINESS AND THE LAND BONANZA

While the miners were engrossing the mineral wealth of the West, other interests were snapping up the region's choice farmland. Presumably the Homestead Act of 1862 had ended the reign of the speculator and the large landholder. An early amendment to the act even prevented husbands and wives from filing separate claims. The West, land reformers had assumed, would soon be dotted with 160-acre family farms.

They were doomed to disappointment. Most landless Americans were too poor to become farmers even when they could obtain land without cost. The expense of moving a family to the ever-receding frontier exceeded the means of many, and the cost of a plow, hoes and scythes, draft animals, a wagon, a well, fencing, and of building the simplest house, might come to $1000—a formidable barrier. As for the industrial workers for whom the free land was supposed to provide a "safety valve," they had neither the skills nor the inclination to become farmers. Homesteaders usually came from districts not far removed from frontier conditions. And despite the intent of the law, speculators often managed to obtain large tracts. They hired men to stake out claims, falsely swear that they had fulfilled the conditions laid down in the law for obtaining legal title, and then deed the land over to their employers.

Had the land laws been better drafted and more honestly enforced, it is still unlikely that the policy of granting free land to small homesteaders would have succeeded. Aside from the difficulties faced by small-scale agriculturalists in the West, too many people in every section were eager to exploit the nation's land for their own profit. Immediately after the Civil War Congress reserved 47.7 million acres of public land in the South for homesteaders, stopping all cash sales in the region. But in 1876 this policy was reversed and the land thrown open.

However they attained their acres, frontier farmers of the 1870s and 1880s grappled with novel problems as they pushed across the Plains with their families. The soil was rich, but the climate, especially in the semiarid regions beyond 98° longitude, made agriculture frequently difficult and often impossible. Blizzards, floods, grasshopper plagues, and prairie fires caused repeated heartaches, but periodic drought and searing summer heat were the worst hazards, destroying the hopes and fortunes of thousands.

At the same time, the flat immensity of the land, combined with newly available farm machinery and the development of rail connections with the East, encouraged the growth of enormous corporation-controlled "bonanza" farms. One such organization was the railroad-owned empire managed by Oliver Dalrymple in the Dakota Territory, which cultivated 25,000 acres of wheat in 1880. Dalrymple employed 200 pairs of harrows to prepare his soil, 125 seeders to sow his seed, and 155 binders to harvest his crop.

The Plains became the breadbasket of America in the decades following the Civil War. By 1889 Minnesota topped the nation in wheat production, and ten years later four of the five leading wheat states lay west of the Mississippi. The Plains also accounted for heavy percentages of the nation's other cereal crops, together with immense quantities of beef, pork, and mutton.

Like other exploiters of the nation's resources, farmers took whatever they could from the soil with little heed for preserving its fertility and preventing erosion. The consequent national loss was less apparent because it was diffuse and slow to assume drastic proportions, but it was nonetheless real.

Ada McColl on the prairie near Lakin, Kansas, gathering buffalo chips for fuel. Hers was a hard and lonely life, but many women took satisfaction from it. One homesteading woman wrote that "any woman who can stand her own company, can see the beauty of the sunset, loves growing things, and is willing to put in as much time at careful labor as she does over the washtub, will certainly succeed; will have independence, plenty to eat all the time, and a home of her own in the end."

WESTERN RAILROAD BUILDING

Further exploitation of land resources by private interests resulted from the government's policy of subsidizing western railroads. Here was a clear illustration of the conflict between the idea of the West as a national heritage to be disposed of to deserving citizens and the concept of the region as a cornucopia pouring forth riches to be gathered up and carted off by anyone powerful and determined enough to take them. When it came to a choice between giving a particular tract to railroads or to homesteaders, the homesteaders nearly always lost out. On the other hand, the swift development of western railroads was essential if farmers, miners, and cattle ranchers were to prosper.

Unless the government had been willing to build the transcontinental lines itself—and this was unthinkable in an age dominated by belief in individual exploitation—some system of subsidy was essential. Private investors would not hazard the huge sums needed to lay tracks across hundreds of miles of rugged, empty country when traffic over the road could not possibly produce profits for many years. Grants of land seemed a sensible way of financing construction. The method avoided direct outlays of public funds, for the companies could pledge the land as security for bond issues or sell it directly for cash. Moreover, land and railroad values were intimately linked in contemporary thinking.

Federal land grants to railroads began in 1850 with those allotted to the Illinois Central. Over the next two decades about 49 million acres were given to various lines indirectly in the form of grants to the states, but the most lavish gifts of the public domain were those made directly to builders of intersectional trunk lines. These roads received more than 155 million acres, although about 25 million acres reverted to the government because some companies failed to lay the required miles of track. About 75 percent of this land went to aid the construction of four transcontinental railroads: the Union Pacific–Central Pacific line, running from Nebraska to San Francisco, completed in 1869; the Atchison, Topeka and Santa Fe, running from Kansas City to Los Angeles by way of Santa Fe and Albuquerque, completed in 1883; the Southern Pacific, running from San Francisco to New Orleans by way of Yuma and El Paso, completed in 1883; and the Northern Pacific, running from Duluth, Minnesota, to Portland, Oregon, completed in 1883.

The Pacific Railway Act of 1862 established the pattern for these grants. It gave the builders of the Union Pacific and Central Pacific railroads 5 square miles of public land on each side of their right-of-way for each mile of track laid. The land was allotted in alternate sections, forming a pattern like a checkerboard, the squares of one color representing railroad property, the other government property. Presumably this arrangement benefited the entire nation since half the land close to the railroad remained in public hands.

Grants per mile of track ranged from 5 alternate sections on each side of the track to the Union and Central Pacific to 40 sections to the Northern Pacific. In the latter case, when the indemnity zone was included, homesteaders were barred from an area 100 miles wide, all the way from Lake Superior to the Pacific. More than 20 years after receiving its immense grant, the Northern Pacific was still attempting to keep homesteaders from filing in the indemnity zone. President Cleveland finally put a stop to this in 1887, saying that he could find "no evidence" that "this vast tract is necessary for the fulfillment of the grant."

Historians have argued at length about the fairness of the land-grant system. No railroad corporation waxed fat directly from the sale of its lands, which were sold at prices averaging between $2 and $5 an acre. Collectively the roads took in between $400 million and $500 million from this source, but only over the course of a century. Land-grant lines encouraged the growth of the West by advertising their property widely and by providing cheap transportation for prospective settlers and efficient shipping services for farmers. They were required by law to carry troops and handle government business free or at reduced rates, which saved the government millions over the years. At the same time the system imposed no effective restraints on how the railroads used the funds raised with federal aid. Being able to lay track with money obtained from land grants, the operators tended to be extravagant and often downright corrupt.

The construction of the Central Pacific in the 1860s illustrates how the system encouraged extravagance. The Central Pacific and the Union Pacific were

On the contemporary map (above), the Atlantic and Pacific Railroad land grant in Arizona appears as shaded squares on a checkerboard. The grant cut a 100-mile wide swath across the entire territory (right).

given, in addition to their land grants, loans in the form of government bonds—from $16,000 to $48,000 for each mile of track laid, depending on the difficulty of the terrain. The two competed with each other for the subsidies, the Central Pacific building eastward from Sacramento, the Union Pacific westward from Nebraska. They put huge crews to work grading and laying track, bringing up supplies over the already completed road. The Union Pacific employed Civil War veterans and Irish immigrants; the Central, Chinese immigrants.

This plan favored the Union Pacific. While the Central Pacific was inching upward through the gorges and granite of the mighty Sierras, the Union Pacific was racing across the level plains laying 540 miles of track between 1865 and 1867. Once beyond the Sierras, the Central Pacific would have easy going across the Nevada–Utah plateau country, but by then it might be too late to prevent the Union Pacific from making off with most of the government aid.

The Central Pacific wasted huge sums by working through the winter in the High Sierras. Often the men labored in tunnels dug through 40 foot snowdrifts to get at the frozen ground. To speed construction of the Summit Tunnel, one of the managers had a shaft cut down from above so that crews could work out from the middle as well as in from each end. In 1866, over the most difficult terrain, he laid 28 miles of track, at a cost of more than $280,000 a mile. Experts later estimated that 7 percent of this sum could have been saved had speed not been a factor.

Chinese workers building a railroad trestle in the Sierras (1877). "Without them," Leland Stanford, president of the Central Pacific Railroad said, "it would be impossible to complete the western portion of this great national highway." Some Chinese were drawn from the gold fields farther north, and others were imported from China, under five-year contracts with the railroads in which they were paid $10 or $12 a month.

But the mountains were conquered, and then the crews raced across the Great Basin to Salt Lake City and beyond. The meeting of the rails—the occasion of a national celebration—took place at Promontory, north of Ogden, Utah, on May 10, 1869. Leland Stanford drove the final ceremonial golden spike with a silver hammer. The Union Pacific had built 1086 miles of track, the Central 689 miles.

The only transcontinental railroad built without land grants was the Great Northern, running from St. Paul, Minnesota, to the Pacific. Spending private capital, its guiding genius, James J. Hill, was compelled to build economically and to plan carefully. As a result, his was the only transcontinental line to weather the depression of the 1890s without going into bankruptcy.

THE CATTLE KINGDOM

While miners were digging out the mineral wealth of the West and railroaders were taking possession of much of its land, another group was exploiting endless acres of its grass. For 20 years after the Civil War cattlemen and sheep raisers dominated huge areas of the High Plains, making millions of dollars by grazing their herds on lands they did not own.

Columbus brought the first cattle to the New World in 1493, on his second voyage, and later *conquistadores* took them to every corner of Spain's American

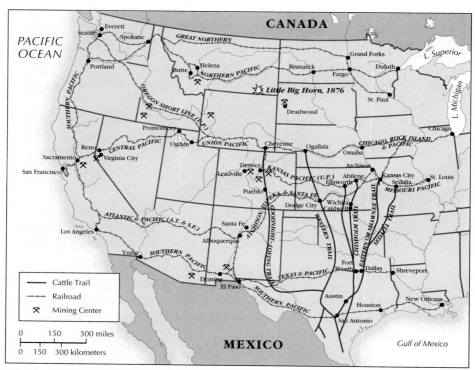

The West: Cattle, Railroads, and Mining, 1850–1893

empire. Mexico proved to be so well suited to cattle raising that many were allowed to roam loose. They multiplied rapidly, and by the late eighteenth century what is now southern Texas harbored enormous herds. The beasts interbred with nondescript "English" cattle, brought into the area by settlers from the United States, to produce the Texas longhorn. Hardy, wiry, ill-tempered, and fleet, with horns often attaining a spread of 6 feet, these animals were far from ideal as beef cattle and almost as hard to capture as wild horses, but they existed in southern Texas by the millions, most of them unowned.

The lack of markets and transportation explains why Texas cattle were lightly regarded. But conditions were changing. Industrial growth in the East was causing an increase in the urban population and a consequent rise in the demand for food. At the same time, the expansion of the railroad network made it possible to move cattle cheaply over long distances. As the iron rails inched across the Plains, astute cattlemen began to do some elementary figuring. Longhorns could be had locally for $3 and $4 a head. In the northern cities they would bring ten times that much, perhaps even more. Why not round them up and herd them northward to the railroads, allowing them to feed along the way on the abundant grasses of the Plains? The land was unoccupied and owned by the federal goverment. Anyone could drive cattle across it without paying a fee or asking anyone's permission. The grass the cattle ate on the way swiftly renewed itself.

In 1866 a number of Texans drove large herds northward toward Sedalia, Missouri, railhead of the Missouri Pacific. This route took the herds through wooded and settled country and across Indian reservations, which provoked many difficulties. At the same time Charles Goodnight and Oliver Loving successfully drove 2000 head in a great arc west to the New Mexico Territory and then north to Colorado.

The next year the drovers, inspired by a clever young Illinois cattle dealer named Joseph G. McCoy and other entrepreneurs, led their herds north by a more westerly route, across unsettled grasslands, to the Kansas Pacific line at Abilene, Kansas, which McCoy described as "a very small, dead place, consisting of about one dozen log huts." They earned excellent profits, and during the next five years about 1.5 million head made the "long drive" over the Chisholm Trail to Abilene, where they were sold to ranchers, feedlot operators, and the agents of eastern meat packers. Other shipping points sprang up as the railroads pushed westward. According to the best estimates 10 million head were driven north before the practice ended in the mid-1880s.

The technique of the long drive, which involved guiding herds of two or three thousand cattle slowly across as much as a thousand miles of country, produced the American cowboy, renowned in song, in story, and on film. Half a dozen of these men could control several thousand steers. Mounted on wiry ponies, they would range alongside the herd, keeping the animals on the move but preventing stampedes, allowing them time to rest yet steadily pressing them toward the yards of Abilene.

The major "cattle towns"—Abilene, Wichita, Ellsworth, Dodge City, and Caldwell—had their full share of saloons, gambling dens, and "dance houses" patronized by cowboys and by other transients bent on having a good time. Most were young, male, and single. Violence punctuated their activities, but tales of individual desperadoes and gangs of outlaws "shooting up" cattle towns and terrorizing honest citizens are fictitious. Police forces were well organized. Indeed, the "respectable" town residents tended to urge leniency for lawbreakers because of the money they and their fellows brought to the towns. Between 1870 and 1885 there were only 45 homicides in these five towns, and some of them had nothing to do with the cattle trade.

OPEN-RANGE RANCHING

Soon cattlemen discovered that the hardy Texas stock could survive the winters of the northern Plains. Attracted by the apparently limitless forage, they began to bring up herds to stock the vast regions where the buffalo had so recently roamed. Introducing pedigreed Hereford bulls, they improved the stock without weakening its resistance to harsh conditions. By 1880 some 4.5 million head had spread across the sea of grass that ran from Kansas to Montana and west to the Rockies.

The prairie grasses offered ranchers a bonanza almost as valuable as the gold mines. Open-range ranching required actual ownership of no more than a few acres along some watercourse. In this semiarid region, control of water enabled a rancher to dominate all the surrounding area back to the divide separating his range from the next stream without investing a cent in the purchase of land. His cattle, wandering freely on the public domain, fattened on grass owned by all the people, to be turned into beefsteak and leather for the profit of the rancher.

Theoretically, anyone could pasture stock on the open range, but without access to water it was impossible to do so. "I have 2 miles of running water," a cattleman said in testifying before the Public Land Commission. "That accounts for my ranch being where it is. The next water from me in one direction is 23 miles; now no man can have a ranch between these two places. I have control of the grass, the same as though I owned it." By having his cowhands take out homestead claims along watercourses in his region, a rancher could greatly expand the area he dominated. In the late 1870s one Colorado cattle baron controlled an area roughly the size of Connecticut and Rhode Island even though he owned only 105 small parcels that totaled about 15,500 acres.

Unlike other exploiters of the West's resources, cattle ranchers did not at first injure or reduce any public resource. Grass eaten by their stock annually renewed itself; the soil was enriched by the droppings of the animals. Furthermore, ranchers poached on the public domain because there was no reasonable way for them to obtain legal possession of the large areas necessary to raise cattle on the Plains. Federal land laws made no allowance for the special conditions of the semiarid West.

BARBED-WIRE WARFARE

Congress refused to change the land laws in any basic way, and this had two harmful effects. First, it encouraged fraud: Those who could not get title to enough land honestly turned to subterfuge. The Desert Land Act (1877) allowed anyone to obtain 640 acres in the arid states for $1.25 an acre provided the owner irrigated part of it within three years. Since the original claimant could transfer the holding, the ranchers set their cowboys and other hands to filing claims, which were then signed over to them. Over 2.6 million acres were taken up under the act, and according to the best estimate, about 95 percent of the claims were fraudulent—no sincere effort was made to irrigate the land.

Second, overcrowding became a problem that led to serious conflicts, even killings, because no one had uncontestable title to the land. The leading ranchers banded together in cattlemen's associations to deal with overcrowding and with such problems as quarantine regulations, water rights, and thievery. In most cases these associations devised effective and sensible rules, but their functions would better have been performed by the government, as such matters usually are.

To keep other ranchers' cattle from those sections of the public domain they considered their own, the associations and many individuals began to fence huge areas. This was possible only because of the invention in 1874 of barbed wire by Joseph F. Glidden, an Illinois farmer. By the 1880s thousands of miles of the new fencing had been strung across the Plains, often across roads and in a few cases around entire communities. "Barbed-wire wars" resulted, fought by rancher against rancher, cattleman against sheepman, herder against farmer. The associations tried to police their fences and to punish anyone who cut their wire. Posted signs gave dire warnings to trespassers. "The Son of a Bitch who opens this fence

In 1885 masked Nebraskans seeking access to water posed for photographer S. D. Butcher, who captioned the picture "Settlers taking the law into their own hands: Cutting 15 miles of the Brighton Ranch fence."

had better look out for his scalp," one such sign announced, another fine statement of the philosophy of the age.

By the 1880s the boom times were ending. Overproduction was driving down the price of beef; expenses were on the rise; many sections of the range were badly overgrazed. The dry summer of 1886 left the stock in such poor condition as winter approached that the *Rocky Mountain Husbandman* urged its readers to sell their cattle despite the prevailing low prices rather than "endanger the whole herd by having the range overstocked."

Some ranchers took this advice; those who did not made a fatal error. Winter that year arrived early and with unparalleled fury. Blizzards raged and temperatures plummeted far below zero. Cattle crowded into low places only to be engulfed in giant snowdrifts; barbed wire took a fearful toll. When spring finally came, the streams were choked with rotting carcasses. Between 80 and 90 percent of all cattle on the range were dead. "We have had a perfect smashup all through the cattle country," Theodore Roosevelt wrote sadly in April 1887 from Elkhorn Ranch.

That cruel winter finished open-range cattle raising. The large companies were bankrupt; many independent operators, Roosevelt among them, became discouraged and sold out. When the industry revived, it was on a smaller, more efficiently organized scale. The fencing movement continued, but now ranchers only enclosed the land they actually owned. It then became possible to bring in pedigreed bulls to improve the breed. Cattle raising, like mining before it, ceased to be an adventure in rollicking individualism and became a business.

By the late 1880s the bonanza days of the West were over. No previous frontier had caught the imagination of Americans so completely as the Great West, with its heroic size, its awesome emptiness, its massive, sculptured beauty. Most of what Professor Webb called the "primary windfalls" of the region—the furs, the precious metals, the forests, the cattle, and the grass—had been snatched up by firstcomers and by individuals already wealthy. Big companies were taking over all the West's resources. Now the frontier was no more.

But the frontier never existed except as an intellectual construction among white settlers and those who wrote about them. To the Indians, the land was simply home. The "conquest of the frontier" was thus an appealing evasion: It transformed the harmful actions and policies of the nation into an expression of human progress, the march westward of "civilization."

"Civilization," though, was changing. The nation was becoming more powerful, richer, and larger, and its economic structure more complex and diversified as the West yielded its treasures. But the East, and especially eastern industrialists and financiers, was increasingly dominating the economy of the entire nation.

MILESTONES

1859	Charles Darwin's *Origin of Species*
	Discovery of the Comstock Lode
1864	Chivington massacre
1869	Union Pacific Railroad completed
	Board of Indian Commissioners established
1873	Timber Culture Act
1875	Civil Rights Act
1876	Battle of the Little Big Horn
1877	Desert Land Act
1878	Timber and Stone Act
1879	Major Powell's *Report on the Lands of the Arid Region*
	Specie payments resumed
1881	Tuskegee Institute founded
1883	*Civil Rights Cases*
1886–1887	Blizzards put an end to open-range ranching
1887	Dawes Severalty Act
1888	James Bryce's *The American Commonwealth*
1890–1900	Blacks deprived of the vote in the South
1895	Booker T. Washington's Atlanta Compromise speech
1896	*Plessy* v. *Ferguson*

18

$$\rightarrow\!\!\!\!\rightarrow \cdot\!\!-\!\!-\!\!-\!\!\cdot \leftarrow\!\!\!\!\leftarrow$$

AN INDUSTRIAL GIANT

When the Civil War began, the country's industrial output, while important and increasing, did not approach that of major European powers. By the end of the century the United States had become far and away the colossus among world manufacturers, dwarfing the production of Great Britain and Germany. The world had never seen such a remarkable example of rapid economic growth. The value of American manufactured products rose from $1.8 billion in 1859 to over $13 billion in 1899. Modern economists estimate that the output of goods and services in the country (the gross national product, or GNP) increased by 44 percent between 1874 and 1883 and continued to expand in succeeding years. This growth was not confined to the Northeast. Wisconsin, for example, underwent a major transformation between 1873 and 1893. An economy based on grain and lumber became a mainly urban-centered industrial economy.

ESSENTIALS OF INDUSTRIAL GROWTH

American manufacturing flourished for many reasons. New natural resources were discovered and exploited steadily, thereby increasing opportunities. These opportunities, in turn, attracted the brightest and most energetic of a vigorous and expanding population. The growth of the country added constantly to the size of the national market, and protective tariffs shielded that market from foreign competition. Foreign capital, however, entered the market freely, in part because tariffs kept out so many foreign goods.

The dominant spirit of the time encouraged businessmen to maximum effort by emphasizing progress, yet it also produced a generation of Robber Barons. The energetic search for wealth led to corrupt business practices such as stock manipulation, bribery, and cut-throat competition and ultimately to "combinations in restraint of trade," a kind of American euphemism for monopoly. European immigrants provided the additional labor needed by expanding industry; 2.5 million arrived in the 1870s, twice that number in the 1880s. These immigrants saw America as a land of opportunity, and for many, probably most, it was that indeed. But for others emigrating to the United States meant a constant struggle for survival; dreary, often unhealthy living conditions; and grinding poverty.

It was a period of rapid advance in basic science, and technicians created a bountiful harvest of new machines, processes, and power sources that increased productivity in many industries and created new industries as well. In agriculture there were what one contemporary expert called "an endless variety of cultivators," better harvesters and binding machines, and combines capable of threshing and bagging 450 pounds of grain a minute. Of course that also meant that many farm families were "displaced" from their homes and livelihoods, and it made farmers dependent on the vagaries of distant markets and powerful economic forces they could not control.

As a result of improvements in the milling of grain, packaged cereals appeared on the American breakfast table. The commercial canning of food, spurred by the "automatic line" canning factory, expanded so rapidly that by 1887 a writer in *Good Housekeeping* could say: "Housekeeping is getting to be ready made, as well as clothing." The Bonsack cigarette-rolling machine created a new industry that changed the habits of millions. George B. Eastman created still another with his development of mass-produced, roll photographic film and the simple but efficient Kodak camera. The perfection of the typewriter by the Remington company in the 1880s revolutionized the way office work was performed. But even some of these inventions were mixed blessings. The harm done by the popularity of cigarettes, for example, needs no explanation.

RAILROADS: THE FIRST BIG BUSINESS

Railroads were important first as an industry in themselves. Fewer than 35,000 miles of track existed when Lee laid down his sword at Appomattox. In 1875 railroad mileage exceeded 74,000 and the skeleton of the network was complete. Over the next two decades the skeleton was fleshed out. In 1890 the mature but

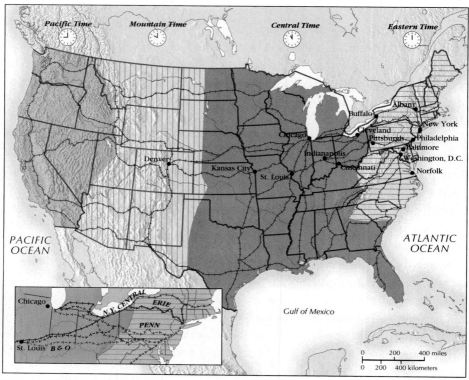

Primary Railroads, 1890

By 1890 trunk lines spanned the country, supplemented by networks of smaller feeder lines. The inset shows the trunk lines of four major companies that dominated rail service in the Northeast and linked up with western lines at Chicago and St. Louis.

still-growing system took in over $1 billion in passenger and freight revenues. (The federal government's income in 1890 was only $403 million.) The value of railroad properties and equipment was more than $8.7 billion. The national railroad debt of $5.1 billion was almost five times the national debt of $1.1 billion! By 1900 the nation had 193,000 miles of track.

The emphasis in railroad construction after 1865 was on organizing integrated systems. The lines had high fixed costs: taxes, interest on their bonds, maintenance of track and rolling stock, and salaries of office personnel. A short train with half-empty cars required almost as many workers and as much fuel to operate as a long one jammed with freight or passengers. To earn profits the railroads had to carry as much traffic as possible. They therefore spread out feeder lines to draw business to their main lines the way the root network of a tree draws water into its trunk.

The Union Railroad Station in Montgomery, Alabama, designed by Henry Hobson Richardson, the nation's foremost architect of the era. Richardson borrowed ideas from the past—the arches evoked the early Middle Ages—but adapted them to contemporary purposes. This building's massiveness and horizontal lines hinted at the power and reach of the railroads.

The lines sought to work out fixed rates for carrying different types of freight, charging more for valuable manufactured goods than for bulky products like coal or wheat, and they agreed to permit rate concessions to shippers when necessary to avoid hauling empty cars. In other words, they charged what the traffic would bear. However, by the 1880s the men who ran the railroads had come to recognize the advantages of cooperating with one another to avoid "senseless" competition. Railroad management was becoming a kind of profession, with certain standard ways of doing things, even with its own professional journals and with regional organizations such as the Eastern Trunk Line Association and the Western Traffic Association.

The railroads stimulated the economy indirectly. Like foreign commerce and the textile industry in earlier times, they were a "multiplier," speeding development. In 1869 they bought $41.6 million worth of cars and locomotives, in 1889 $90.8 million. Their purchases created thousands of jobs and led to countless technological advances.

Because of their voracious appetite for traffic, railroads in sparsely settled regions and in areas with undeveloped resources devoted much money and effort to stimulating local economic growth. The Louisville and Nashville Railroad, for instance, was a prime mover in the expansion of the iron industry in Alabama in the 1880s.

To speed the settlement of new regions, the land-grant railroads sold land cheaply and on easy terms, for sales meant future business as well as current income. They offered reduced rates to travelers interested in buying farms and set up "bureaus of immigration" that distributed brochures describing the wonders of the new country. Their agents greeted immigrants at the eastern ports and tried to steer them to railroad property. They sent agents who were usually themselves immigrants—often ministers—all over Europe to recruit prospective settlers.

Technological advances in railroading accelerated economic development in complex ways. In 1869 George Westinghouse invented the air brake. By enabling an engineer to apply the brakes to all cars simultaneously (formerly each car had to be braked separately by its own conductor or brakeman), this invention made possible revolutionary increases in the size of trains and the speed at which they could safely operate. The sleeping car, invented in 1864 by George Pullman, now came into its own.

To pull the heavier trains, more powerful locomotives were needed. They in turn produced a call for stronger and more durable rails to bear the additional weight. Steel, itself reduced in cost because of technological developments, supplied the answer, for steel rails outlasted iron by many years despite the use of much heavier equipment.

A close tie developed between the railroads and the nation's telegraph network, dominated by the Western Union Company. Commonly the roads allowed Western Union to string wires along their rights-of-way, and they transported telegraphers and their equipment without charge. In return they received free telegraphic service, important for efficiency and safety.

IRON, OIL, AND ELECTRICITY

The transformation of iron manufacturing affected the nation almost as much as railroad development. Output rose from 920,000 tons in 1860 to 10.3 million tons in 1900, but the big change came in the development of ways to mass-produce steel. In its pure form (wrought iron) the metal is tough but relatively soft. Ordinary cast iron, which contains large amounts of carbon and other impurities, is hard but brittle. Steel, which contains 1 or 2 percent carbon, combines the hardness of cast iron with the toughness of wrought iron. For nearly every purpose—structural girders for bridges and buildings, railroad track, machine tools, boiler plate, barbed wire—steel is immensely superior to other kinds of iron.

Iron Ore Shipments, 1870–1900

But steel was so expensive to manufacture that it could not be used for bulky products until the invention in the 1850s of the Bessemer process, perfected independently by Henry Bessemer, an Englishman, and William Kelly of Kentucky. Bessemer and Kelly discovered that a stream of air directed into a mass of molten iron caused the carbon and other impurities to combine with oxygen and burn off. When measured amounts of carbon, silicon, and manganese were then added, the brew became steel. What had been a rare metal could now be produced by the hundreds and thousands of tons. The Bessemer process and the open-hearth method, a slower but more precise technique that enabled producers to sample the molten mass and thus control quality closely, were introduced commercially in the 1860s. In 1870, 77,000 tons of steel were manufactured. Such growth would have been impossible without the huge supplies of iron ore in the United States and the coal necessary to fire the furnaces that refined it. In the 1870s the great iron fields rimming Lake Superior began to yield their treasures. The enormous iron concentrations of the Mesabi region made a compass needle spin like a top. Mesabi ores could be mined with steam shovels, almost like gravel.

Pittsburgh, surrounded by vast coal deposits, became the iron and steel capital of the country, the Minnesota ores reaching it by way of steamers on the Great Lakes and rail lines from Cleveland. Other cities in Pennsylvania and Ohio were important producers, and a separate complex, centering on Birmingham, Alabama, developed to exploit local iron and coal fields.

The petroleum industry expanded even more spectacularly than iron and steel. Edwin L. Drake drilled the first successful well in Pennsylvania in 1859.

This 1895 painting of a steel mill shows steelworkers preparing to pour molten steel, produced by the Bessemer converter, into ingot molds. Later the ingots would be rolled into various shapes. The hard, refined steel produced by the Bessemer process was ideal for railroad track.

During the Civil War, production ranged between 2 million and 3 million barrels a year. By 1890 the figure had leaped to about 50 million barrels.

Technological advances came rapidly. By the early 1870s, refiners had learned how to "crack" petroleum by applying high temperatures to the crude oil in order to rearrange its molecular structure, thereby increasing the percentage of kerosene yielded. By-products such as naphtha, gasoline (used in vaporized form as an illuminating gas), rhigolene (a local anesthetic), cymogene (a coolant for refrigerating machines), and many lubricants and waxes began to appear on the market. At the same time a great increase in the supply of crude oil—especially after the German-born chemist Herman Frasch perfected a method for removing sulfur from low-quality petroleum—drove prices down.

These circumstances put a premium on refining efficiency. Larger plants utilizing expensive machinery and employing skilled technicians became more important. In the mid-1860s only three refineries in the country could process 2000 barrels of crude oil a week; a decade later plants capable of handling 1000 barrels a day were common.

Two other important new industries were the telephone and electric light businesses. Both were typical of the period, being products of technical advances

Alexander Graham Bell making the first telephone call between New York and Chicago. Bell's invention revolutionized communication in America, liberating people from traditional face-to-face exchanges and written correspondence.

and intimately related to the growth of a high-speed, urban civilization that put great stress on communication. The telephone was invented in 1876 by Alexander Graham Bell, who had been led to the study of acoustics through his interest in the education of the deaf. The invention soon proved its value. By 1900 there were almost 800,000 telephones in the country, twice the total for all Europe. The American Telephone and Telegraph Company, a consolidation of over 100 local systems, dominated the business.

When Western Union realized the importance of the telephone, it tried for a time to compete with Bell by developing a machine of its own. The man it commissioned to devise this machine was Thomas A. Edison, but Bell's patents proved unassailable. Edison had already made a number of contributions toward solving what he called the "mysteries of electrical force," including a multiplex telegraph capable of sending four messages over a single wire at the same time. At Menlo Park, New Jersey, he built the prototype of the modern research laboratory, where specific problems could be attacked on a mass scale by a team of trained specialists. During his lifetime he took out more than 1000 patents, dealing with machines as varied as the phonograph, the motion-picture projector, the storage battery, and the mimeograph.

Edison patented the phonograph in 1878, budgeting $18 for its invention. He was photographed in his laboratory on June 16, 1888, at 5:30 A.M., working on a wax cylinder model.

Edison's most significant achievement was the incandescent lamp, or electric lightbulb. Others before him had experimented with the idea of producing light by passing electricity through a filament in a vacuum. Always, however, the filaments quickly burned out. Edison tried hundreds of fibers before producing, in 1879, a carbonized filament that would glow brightly in a vacuum tube for as long as 170 hours without crumbling. At Christmastime he decorated the grounds about his laboratory with a few dozen of the new lights. People flocked by the thousands to see this miracle of the "Wizard of Menlo Park." The inventor boasted that soon he would be able to illuminate entire towns, even great cities like New York.

He was true to his promise. In 1882 his Edison Illuminating Company opened a power station in New York City and began to supply current for lighting to 85 consumers, including the *New York Times* and the banking house of J. P. Morgan and Company. Soon central stations were springing up everywhere until, by 1898, there were about 3000 in the country.

The substitution of electric for steam power in factories was as liberating as that of steam for waterpower before the Civil War. Small, safe electric motors replaced dangerous and cumbersome mazes of belts and wheels. The electric power industry expanded rapidly. By the early years of the twentieth century almost 6 billion kilowatt-hours of electricity were being produced annually. Yet this was only the beginning.

COMPETITION AND MONOPOLY: THE RAILROADS

During the post–Civil War era, expansion in industry went hand in hand with concentration. The principal cause of this trend, aside from the obvious economies resulting from large-scale production and the growing importance of expensive machinery, was the downward trend of prices after 1873. The deflation, which resulted mainly from the failure of the money supply to keep pace with the rapid increase in the volume of goods produced, affected agricultural goods as well as manufactures, and it lasted until 1896 or 1897.

Contemporaries believed that they were living through a "great depression." That label is misleading, for output expanded almost continuously, and at a rapid rate, until 1893, when production slumped and a true depression struck the country. Falling prices, however, kept a steady pressure on profit margins, and this led to increased production and thus to intense competition for markets.

According to the classical economists, competition advanced the public interest by keeping prices low and ensuring the most efficient producer the largest profit. Up to a point it accomplished these purposes in the years after 1865, but it also caused side effects that injured both the economy and society as a whole. Railroad managers, for instance, found it impossible to enforce "official" rate schedules and maintain their regional associations once competitive pressures mounted. In 1865 it had cost from 96 cents to $2.15 per 100 pounds, depending on the class of freight, to ship goods from New York to Chicago. In 1888 rates ranged from 35 cents to 75 cents.

Competition cut deeply into railroad profits, causing the lines to seek desperately to increase volume. They did so chiefly by reducing rates still more, on a selective basis. They gave rebates (secret reductions below the published rates) to large shippers in order to capture their business. Giving discounts to those who shipped in volume made economic sense: It was easier to handle freight in carload lots than in smaller units. So intense was the battle for business, however, that the roads often made concessions to big customers far beyond what the economics of bulk shipment justified. In the 1870s the New York Central regularly reduced the rates charged important shippers by 50 to 80 percent. One large Utica dry-goods merchant received a rate of 9 cents while others paid 33 cents. Two big New York City grain merchants paid so little that they soon controlled the grain business of the entire city.

To make up for losses forced on them by competitive pressures, railroads charged higher rates at way points along their tracks where no competition existed. Frequently it cost more to ship a product a short distance than a longer one. Rochester, New York, was served only by the New York Central. In the 1870s it cost 30 cents to transport a barrel of flour from Rochester to New York City, a distance of 350 miles. At the same time flour could be shipped from Minneapolis to New York, a distance of well over 1000 miles, for only 20 cents a barrel. One Rochester businessman told a state investigating committee that he could save 18 cents a hundredweight by sending goods to St. Louis by way of

New York, where several carriers competed for the traffic, even though, in fact, the goods might come back through Rochester over the same tracks on the way to St. Louis!

Although cheap transportation stimulated the economy, few people benefited from cutthroat competition. Small shippers—and all businessmen in cities and towns with limited rail outlets—suffered; railroad discrimination speeded the concentration of industry in large corporations located in major centers. The instability of rates even troubled interests like the midwestern flour millers who benefited from the competitive situation, for it hampered planning. Nor could manufacturers who received rebates be entirely happy, since few could be sure that some other producer was not getting a larger reduction.

Probably the worst sufferers were the roads themselves. The loss of revenue resulting from rate cutting, combined with inflated debts, put most of them in grave difficulty when faced with a downturn in the business cycle. In 1876 two-fifths of all railroad bonds were in default; three years later 65 lines were bankrupt. Wits called Samuel J. Tilden, the 1876 Democratic presidential candidate, "the Great Forecloser" because of his work reorganizing bankrupt railroads at this time.

Since the public would not countenance bankrupt railroads going out of business, these companies were placed in the hands of court-appointed receivers. The receivers, however, seldom provided efficient management and had no funds at their disposal for new equipment.

During the 1880s the major roads responded to these pressures by building or buying lines in order to create interregional systems. These were the first giant corporations, capitalized in the hundreds of millions of dollars. Their enormous cost led to another wave of bankruptcies when a true depression struck in the 1890s.

The consequent reorganizations brought most of the big systems under the control of financiers, notably J. Pierpont Morgan and such other private bankers as Kuhn, Loeb of New York and Lee, Higginson of Boston.

Critics called the reorganizations "Morganizations." Representatives of the bankers sat on the board of every line they saved and their influence was predominant. They consistently opposed rate wars, rebating, and other competitive practices. In effect, control of the railroad network became centralized, even though the companies maintained their separate existences and operated in a seemingly independent manner. When Morgan died in 1913, "Morgan men" dominated the boards of the New York Central; the Erie; the New York, New Haven and Hartford; the Southern; the Pere Marquette; the Atchison, Topeka and Santa Fe; and many other lines.

COMPETITION AND MONOPOLY: STEEL

The iron and steel industry was also intensely competitive. Despite the trend toward higher production, demand varied erratically from year to year, even from month to month. In good times producers built new facilities, only to suffer heavy losses when demand declined. The forward rush of technology put a tremendous emphasis on efficiency; expensive plants quickly became obsolete. Improved transportation facilities allowed manufacturers in widely separated places to compete with one another.

The kingpin of the industry was Andrew Carnegie. Carnegie was born in Scotland and came to the United States in 1848 at the age of 12. His first job, as a bobbin boy in a cotton mill, brought him $1.20 a week, but his talents perfectly fitted the times and he rose rapidly: to Western Union messenger boy, to telegrapher, to private secretary, to railroad manager. He saved his money, made some shrewd investments, and by 1868 had an income of $50,000 a year.

At about this time he decided to specialize in the iron business. Carnegie possessed great talent as a salesman, boundless faith in the future of the country, an uncanny knack of choosing topflight subordinates, and enough ruthlessness to survive in the iron and steel jungle. Where other steelmen built new plants in good times, he preferred to expand in bad times, when it cost far less to do so. During the 1870s, he later recalled, "many of my friends needed money. . . . I . . . bought out five or six of them. That is what gave me my leading interest in this steel business."

Carnegie grasped the importance of technological improvements. Slightly skeptical of the Bessemer process at first, once he became convinced of its practicality he adopted it enthusiastically. In 1875 he built the J. Edgar Thomson Steel Works, named after a president of the Pennsylvania Railroad, his biggest customer. He employed chemists and other specialists and was soon making steel

Andrew Carnegie in later life. His phenomenal rags-to-riches career was one of the real-life models for Horatio Alger's dime novels on the theme "poor boy makes good."

Worker apartments envelop the Homestead Steel Works. During a strike in 1889, the county sheriff and his men had been chased away by the strikers, who had considerable political power in Homestead. In 1892 Henry Clay Frick took charge of the mills and nearly crushed the unions by bringing in outsiders—strikebreakers as well as the Pennsylvania National Guard.

from iron oxides that other manufacturers had discarded as waste. He was a merciless competitor. When a plant manager announced: "We broke all records for making steel last week," Carnegie replied: "Congratulations! Why not do it every week?" Carnegie sold rails by paying "commissions" to railroad purchasing agents, and he was not above reneging on a contract if he thought it profitable and safe to do so.

By 1890 the Carnegie Steel Company dominated the industry, and its output increased nearly tenfold during the next decade. Profits soared. Alarmed by his increasing control of the industry, the makers of finished steel products such as barbed wire and tubing considered pooling their resources and making steel themselves. Carnegie, his competitive temper aroused, threatened to manufacture wire, pipes and other finished products. A steel war seemed imminent.

However, Carnegie longed to retire in order to devote himself to philanthropic work. He believed that great wealth entailed social responsibilities and that it was a disgrace to die rich. When J. P. Morgan approached him through an intermediary with an offer to buy him out, he assented readily. In 1901 Morgan put together United States Steel, the "world's first billion-dollar corporation." This combination included all the Carnegie properties, the Federal Steel Company (Carnegie's largest competitor), and such important fabricators of finished products as the American Steel and Wire Company, the American Tin Plate

Company, and the National Tube Company. Vast reserves of Minnesota iron ore and a fleet of Great Lakes ore steamers were also included. U.S. Steel was capitalized at $1.4 billion, about twice the value of its component properties but not necessarily an overestimation of its profit-earning capacity. The owners of Carnegie Steel received $492 million, of which $250 million went to Carnegie.

COMPETITION AND MONOPOLY: OIL

The pattern of fierce competition leading to combination and monopoly is well illustrated by the history of the petroleum industry. Irresistible pressures pushed the refiners into a brutal struggle to dominate the business. Production of crude oil, subject to the uncertainties of prospecting and drilling, fluctuated constantly and without regard for need. In general, output surged far ahead of demand.

By the 1870s the chief oil-refining centers were Cleveland, Pittsburgh, Baltimore, and the New York City area. Of these Cleveland was the fastest growing, chiefly because the New York Central and Erie railroads competed fiercely for its oil trade and the Erie Canal offered an alternative route.

The Standard Oil Company of Cleveland, founded in 1870 by a 31-year-old merchant named John D. Rockefeller, emerged as the giant among the refiners. Rockefeller exploited every possible technical advance and employed fair means and foul to persuade competitors either to sell out or to join forces. By 1879 he controlled 90 percent of the nation's oil-refining capacity along with a network of oil pipelines and large reserves of petroleum in the ground.

Standard Oil won the competitive wars because Rockefeller and his associates were the toughest and most imaginative fighters as well as the most efficient refiners in the business. In addition to obtaining from the railroads a 10 percent rebate and drawbacks on its competitors' shipments, Standard Oil cut prices locally to force small independents to sell out or face ruin. Since kerosene was sold in grocery stores, Standard supplied its own outlets with meat, sugar, and other products at artificially low prices to help crush the stores that handled other brands of kerosene. The company employed spies to track down the customers of independents and offer them oil at bargain prices. Bribery was also a Standard practice; the reformer Henry Demarest Lloyd quipped that the company had done everything to the Pennsylvania legislature except refine it.

Although a bold planner and a daring taker of necessary risks, Rockefeller was far too orderly and astute to enjoy the free-swinging battles that plagued his industry. Born in an upstate New York village in 1839, he settled in Cleveland in 1855 and became a produce merchant. During the Civil War he invested in a local refinery and by 1865 was engaged full time in the oil business.

A regally attired John D. Rockefeller, astride a barrel from his Standard Oil refinery, his crown encircled by the railroads he controlled. His actual attire was considerably less conspicuous.

Like Carnegie, Rockefeller was an organizer; he knew little about the technology of petroleum. His forte was meticulous attention to detail: stories are told of his ordering the number of drops of solder used to seal oil cans reduced from 40 to 39 and of his insisting that the manager of one of his refineries account for 750 missing barrel bungs. Not miserliness but a profound grasp of the economies of large-scale production explain this behavior.

Rockefeller competed ruthlessly not primarily to crush other refiners but to persuade them to join with him, to share the business peaceably and rationally so that all could profit. Competition was obsolescent, he argued, though no more effective competitor than he ever lived.

Having achieved his monopoly, Rockefeller stabilized and structured it by creating a new type of business organization, the trust. Standard Oil was an Ohio corporation, prohibited by local law from owning plants in other states or holding stock in out-of-state corporations. As Rockefeller and his associates took over dozens of companies with facilities scattered across the country, serious legal and managerial difficulties arose. How could these many organizations be integrated with Standard Oil of Ohio?

A rotund, genial little Pennsylvania lawyer named Samuel C. T. Dodd came up with an answer to this question in 1879. The stock of Standard of Ohio and of all the other companies that the Rockefeller interests had swallowed up was turned over to nine trustees, who were empowered to "exercise general supervision" over all the properties. In exchange, stockholders received trust certificates, on which dividends were paid. This seemingly simple device brought order to the petroleum business. Competition almost disappeared, prices steadied, profits skyrocketed. By 1892 John D. Rockefeller was worth over $800 million.

The Standard Oil Trust was not a corporation. It had no charter, indeed no legal existence at all. For many years few people outside the organization knew that it existed. The form they chose persuaded Rockefeller and other Standard Oil officials that without violating their consciences, they could deny under oath that Standard Oil of Ohio owned or controlled other corporations "directly or indirectly through its officers or agents." The trustees controlled these organizations—and Standard of Ohio too!

In this 1884 cartoon, "The Monster Monopoly," John D. Rockefeller's Standard Oil Company spreads its tentacles to engulf all manner of businesses, means of transportation, banks, insurance companies, and even the government.

After Standard Oil's duplicity was revealed during a New York investigation in 1888, the word *trust,* formerly signifying a fiduciary arrangement for the protection of the interests of individuals incompetent or unwilling to guard them themselves, became a synonym for monopoly. However, from the company's point of view, monopoly was not the purpose of the trust—that had been achieved before the device was invented. Centralization of the management of diverse and far-flung operations in the interest of efficiency was its chief function. Standard Oil headquarters in New York became the brain of a complex network where information from salaried managers in the field was collected and digested, where top managerial decisions were made, and whence orders went out to armies of drillers, refiners, scientists, and salesmen.

COMPETITION AND MONOPOLY: UTILITIES AND RETAILING

That utilities such as the telephone and electric lighting industries tended to form monopolies is not difficult to explain, for in such fields competition involved costly duplication of equipment and, particularly in the case of the telephone, loss of service efficiency. However, competitive pressures were strong in the early stages of their development. Since these industries depended on patents, Bell and Edison had to fight mighty battles in the courts with rivals seeking to infringe on their rights. When Edison first announced his electric light, capitalists, engineers, and inventors flocked to Menlo Park. He proudly revealed to them the secrets of his marvelous lamp. Many hurried away to turn this information to their own advantage, thinking the "Wizard" a naive fool. When they invaded the field, the law provided Edison with far less protection than he had expected. "My electric light inventions have brought me no profits, only forty years of litigation," Edison later complained. A patent, he said bitterly, was "simply an invitation to a lawsuit."

Competition in the electric lighting business raged for some years among Edison, Westinghouse, and another corporation, the Thomson-Houston Electric Company, which was operating 870 central lighting stations by 1890. In 1892 the Edison and Thomson-Houston companies merged, forming General Electric, a $35 million corporation. Thereafter, General Electric and Westinghouse maintained their dominance in the manufacture of bulbs and electrical equipment as well as in the distribution of electrical power.

The pattern of competition leading to dominance by a few great companies was repeated in many businesses. In life insurance an immense expansion took place after the Civil War, stimulated by the development of a new type of group policy, the "tontine," by Henry B. Hyde of the Equitable Life Company. High-pressure salesmanship prevailed; agents gave rebates to customers by shaving their own commissions; companies stole crack agents from their rivals and raided new territories. They sometimes invested as much as 96 percent of the first year's premiums in obtaining new business. By 1900, after three decades of fierce competition, three giants dominated the industry—Equitable, New York Life, and Mutual Life, each with approximately $1 billion of insurance in force.

In retailing, the period saw the growth of urban department stores. In 1862 Alexander T. Stewart had built an eight-story emporium in New York City that covered an entire block and employed 2000 persons. John Wanamaker in Philadelphia and Marshall Field in Chicago headed similar establishments by the 1880s, and there were others. These department stores advertised heavily, stressing low prices, efficient service, and money-back guarantees. High volume made for large profits. Here is how one of Field's biographers described his methods:

> *His was a one-price store, with the price plainly marked on the merchandise. Goods were not misrepresented, and a reputation for quality merchandise and for fair and honest dealing was built up. . . . Courtesy toward customers was an unfailing rule.*

AMERICAN AMBIVALENCE TO BIG BUSINESS

The growth of huge industrial and financial organizations and the increasing complexity of economic relations frightened people yet made them at the same time greedy for more of the goods and services the new society was turning out. To many, the great new corporations and trusts resembled Frankenstein's monster—marvelous and powerful but a grave threat to society.

To some extent public fear of the industrial giants reflected concern about monopoly. If Standard Oil dominated oil refining, it might raise prices inordinately at vast cost to consumers. Charles Francis Adams, Jr. expressed this feeling in the 1870s: "In the minds of the great majority, and not without reason, the idea of any industrial combination is closely connected with that of monopoly, and monopoly with extortion."

Although in isolated cases monopolists did raise prices unreasonably, generally they did not. On the contrary, prices tended to fall until by the 1890s a veritable "consumer's millennium" had arrived. Far more important in causing resentment was the fear that the monopolists were destroying economic opportunity and threatening democratic institutions. It was not the wealth of tycoons like Carnegie and Rockefeller and Morgan so much as their influence that worried people. In the face of the growing disparity between rich and poor, could republican institutions survive? "The belief is common," wrote Charles Francis Adams's brother Henry as early as 1870, "that the day is at hand when corporations . . . swaying power such as has never in the world's history been trusted in the hands of mere private citizens . . . will ultimately succeed in directing government itself."

Some observers believed either autocracy or a form of revolutionary socialism to be almost inevitable. In 1890 former president Hayes pondered "the wrong and evils of the money-piling tendency of our country, which is changing laws, government, and morals and giving all power to the rich" and decided that he was going to become a "nihilist." Campaigning for the governorship of Texas in 1890, James S. Hogg, a staunch conservative, said: "Within a few years, unless something is done, most of the wealth and talent of our country will be on one side, while arrayed on the other will be the great mass of the people, composing the bone and sinew of this government." John Boyle O'Reilly, a liberal Catholic journalist, wrote in 1886: "There is something worse than Anarchy, bad as that is; and it is irresponsible power in the hands of mere wealth."

As criticism mounted, business leaders rose to their own defense. Rockefeller described in graphic terms the chaotic conditions that plagued the oil industry before the rise of Standard Oil: "It seemed absolutely necessary to extend the market for oil . . . and also greatly improve the process of refining so that oil could be made and sold cheaply, yet with a profit. We proceeded to buy the largest and best refining concerns and centralized the administration of them with a view to securing greater economy and efficiency." Carnegie, in an essay published in 1889, insisted that the concentration of wealth was necessary if humanity was to progress, softening this "Gospel of Wealth" by insisting that the rich must use their money "in the manner which . . . is best calculated to produce the most beneficial results for the community." The rich man was merely a trustee for his "poorer brethren," Carnegie said, "bringing to their service his superior wisdom, experience, and ability to administer." Lesser tycoons echoed these arguments.

The voices of the critics were louder if not necessarily more influential. Many clergymen denounced unrestrained competition, which they considered un-Christian. The new class of professional economists (the American Economic Association was founded in 1885) tended to repudiate laissez-faire. State aid, Richard T. Ely of Johns Hopkins University wrote, "is an indispensable condition of human progress."

REFORMERS: GEORGE, BELLAMY, LLOYD, AND THE MARXISTS

The popularity of a number of radical theorists reflects public feeling in the period. In 1879 Henry George, a California journalist, published *Progress and Poverty*, a forthright attack on the maldistribution of wealth in the United States. George argued that labor was the true and only source of capital. Observing the speculative fever of the West, which enabled landowners to reap profits merely by holding property while population increased, George proposed a property tax that would confiscate this "unearned increment." The value of land depended on society and should belong to society; allowing individuals to keep this wealth was the major cause of the growing disparity between rich and poor, George believed.

George's "single tax," as others called it, would bring in so much money that no other taxes would be necessary, and the government would have plenty of funds to establish new schools, museums, theaters, and other badly needed social and cultural services. While the single tax was never adopted, George's ideas attracted enthusiastic attention. Single tax clubs sprang up throughout the nation, and *Progress and Poverty* became a best-seller.

Even more spectacular was the reception afforded *Looking Backward, 2000–1887,* a utopian novel written in 1888 by Edward Bellamy. This book, which sold over a million copies in its first few years, described a future America that was completely socialized, all economic activity carefully planned. Bellamy compared nineteenth-century society to a lumbering stagecoach upon which the favored few rode in comfort while the mass of the people hauled them along life's route. Occasionally one of the toilers managed to fight his way onto the coach; whenever a rider fell from it, he had to join the multitude dragging it along.

Edward Bellamy, author of the utopian novel, Looking Backward *(1888). Bellamy's socialism, though genteel, unsettled many. The* Household Encyclopaedia *(1892) included this photograph of Bellamy in a section on phrenology, the "science" of ascertaining a person's character and intellectual traits from the shape of his or her cranium. Of Bellamy's, it concluded: "Large perceptive faculties; defective reasoning powers."*

Such, Bellamy wrote, was the working of the vaunted American competitive system. He suggested that the ideal socialist state, in which all citizens shared equally, would arrive without revolution or violence. The trend toward consolidation would continue, he predicted, until one monster trust controlled all economic activity. At this point everyone would realize that nationalization was essential.

A third influential attack on monopoly was that of Henry Demarest Lloyd, whose *Wealth Against Commonwealth* appeared in 1894. Lloyd, a journalist of independent means, devoted years to preparing a denunciation of the Standard Oil Company. Marshaling masses of facts and vivid examples of Standard's evildoing, he assaulted the trust at every point. Although in his zeal Lloyd sometimes distorted and exaggerated the evidence to make his indictment more effective— "Every important man in the oil, coal and many other trusts ought today to be in some one of our penitentiaries," he wrote in a typical overstatement—as a polemic his book was peerless. His forceful but uncomplicated arguments and his copious references to official documents made *Wealth Against Commonwealth* utterly convincing to thousands. The book was more than an attack on Standard Oil. Lloyd denounced the application of Darwin's concept of survival of the fittest to economic and social affairs, and he condemned laissez-faire policies as leading directly to monopoly.

The popularity of these books indicates that the trend toward monopoly in the United States worried many people. But despite the drastic changes suggested in their pages, none of these writers questioned the underlying values of the middle-class majority. They insisted that reform could be accomplished without serious inconvenience to any individual or class. In *Looking Backward* Bellamy pictured the socialists of the future gathered around a radiolike gadget in a well-furnished parlor listening to a minister delivering an inspiring sermon.

Nor did most of their millions of readers seriously consider trying to apply the reformers' ideas. Henry George ran for mayor of New York City in 1886 and lost narrowly to Abram S. Hewitt, a wealthy iron manufacturer, but even if he had won, he would have been powerless to apply the single tax to metropolitan property. The national discontent was apparently not as profound as the popularity of these works might suggest. If John D. Rockefeller became the bogeyman of American industry because of Lloyd's attack, no one prevented him from also becoming the richest man in the United States.

By the 1870s the ideas of Marxian socialists were beginning to penetrate the United States, and in 1877 a Marxist Socialist Labor party was founded. The first serious attempt to explain Marx's ideas to Americans was Laurence Gronlund's *The Cooperative Commonwealth,* which was published in 1884, two years before Marx's *Das Kapital* was translated into English.

Capitalism, Gronlund claimed, contained the seeds of its own destruction. The state ought to own all the means of production. Competition was "Established Anarchy," middlemen were "parasites," speculators "vampires." "Capital and Labor," he wrote in one of the rare humorous lines in his book, "are just as harmonious as roast beef and a hungry stomach." Yet like other harsh critics of that day, Gronlund expected the millennium to arrive in a peaceful, indeed orderly manner. The red flag of socialism, he said, "has no relation to blood." The movement could accommodate "representatives of all classes," even "thoughtful" middleman parasites.

THE GOVERNMENT REACTS TO BIG BUSINESS: RAILROAD REGULATION

Political action related to the growth of big business came first on the state level and dealt chiefly with the regulation of railroads. Even before the Civil War, a number of New England states established railroad commissions to supervise lines within their borders; by the end of the century 28 states had such boards.

Strict regulation was largely the result of agitation by the National Grange of the Patrons of Husbandry. The Grange, founded in 1867 by Oliver H. Kelley, was created to provide social and cultural benefits for isolated rural communities. As it spread and grew in influence—14 states had Granges by 1872 and membership reached 800,000 in 1874—the movement became political too. "Granger" candidates, often not themselves farmers (many local businessmen resented such railroad practices as rebating), won control of a number of state legislatures in the West and South.

Granger-controlled legislatures tried to eliminate unfair or discriminatory railroad rates. The Illinois Granger laws were typical. They established "reasonable" maximum rates and outlawed "unjust" discrimination. The legislature also set up a commission to enforce the laws and punish violators.

The railroads protested, insisting that they were being deprived of property without due process of law. In *Munn* v. *Illinois* (1877), a case that involved a grain elevator whose owner had refused to comply with a state warehouse act, the Supreme Court upheld the constitutionality of this kind of act. Any business that served a public interest, such as a railroad or a grain warehouse, was subject to state control, the justices ruled. Legislatures might fix maximum charges; if the charges seemed unreasonable to the parties concerned, they should direct their complaints to the legislatures or to the voters, not to the courts.

Regulation of the railroad network by the individual states was inefficient, and in 1887 Congress imposed some overarching control by passing the Interstate

Commerce Act. All charges made by railroads "shall be reasonable and just," the act stated. Rebates, drawbacks, the long-and-short-haul evil, and other competitive practices were declared unlawful, and so were their monopolistic counterparts—pools and traffic-sharing agreements. Railroads were required to publish schedules of rates and forbidden to change them without due public notice. Most important, the law established an Interstate Commerce Commission (ICC), the first federal regulatory board, to supervise the affairs of railroads, investigate complaints, and issue cease and desist orders when the roads acted illegally.

The Interstate Commerce Act broke new ground, yet it was neither a radical nor a particularly effective measure. Its terms contradicted one another, some being designed to stimulate, others to penalize, competition. The chairman of the commission soon characterized the law as an "anomaly." It sought, he said, to "enforce competition" at the same time that it outlawed "the acts and inducements by which competition is ordinarily effected."

The new commission had less power than the law seemed to give it. It could not fix rates, only bring the roads to court when it considered rates unreasonably high. Such cases could be extremely complicated; applying the law "was like cutting a path through a jungle." With the truth so hard to determine and the burden of proof on the commission, the courts in nearly every instance decided in favor of the railroads.

State regulatory commissions also fared poorly in the Supreme Court in the last years of the century. Overruling part of their decision in *Munn* v. *Illinois,* the justices declared in *Chicago, Milwaukee and St. Paul Railroad Company* v. *Minnesota* (1890) that the reasonableness of rates was "eminently a question for judicial investigation." Nevertheless, by describing so clearly the right of Congress to regulate private corporations engaged in interstate commerce, the Interstate Commerce Act challenged the philosophy of laissez-faire. Later legislation made the commission more effective. The commission also served as the model for a host of similar federal administrative authorities, such as the Federal Communications Commission (1934).

THE GOVERNMENT REACTS TO BIG BUSINESS: THE SHERMAN ANTITRUST ACT

As with railroad legislation, the first antitrust laws originated in the states, but they were southern and western states with relatively little industry, and most of the statutes were vaguely worded and ill enforced. Federal action came in 1890 with the passage of the Sherman Antitrust Act. Any combination "in the form of trust or otherwise" that was "in restraint of trade or commerce among the several states, or with foreign nations" was declared illegal. Persons forming such combinations were subject to fines of $5000 and a year in jail. Individuals and businesses suffering losses because of actions that violated the law were authorized to sue in the federal courts for triple damages.

Where the Interstate Commerce Act sought to outlaw the excesses of competition, the Sherman Act was supposed to restore competition. If businessmen joined together to "restrain" (monopolize) trade in a particular field, they should be punished and their deeds undone. "The great thing this bill does," Senator George Frisbie Hoar of Massachusetts explained, "is to extend the common-law principle . . . to international and interstate commerce." This was important because the states ran into legal difficulties when they tried to use the common law to restrict corporations engaged in interstate activities.

But the Sherman Act was rather loosely worded, and the Supreme Court emasculated the law. In *United States* v. *E. C. Knight Company* (1895) it held that the American Sugar Refining Company had not violated the law by taking over a number of important competitors. Although the Sugar Trust now controlled about 98 percent of all sugar refining in the United States, it was not restraining trade. "Doubtless the power to control the manufacture of a given thing involves in a certain sense the control of its disposition," the Court said in one of the greatest feats of judicial understatement of all time.

If the creation of the Sugar Trust did not violate the Sherman Act, it seemed unlikely that any other combination of manufacturers could be convicted under the law. However, in several cases in 1898 and 1899 the Supreme Court ruled that agreements to fix prices or divide markets did violate the Sherman Act. These decisions precipitated a wave of outright mergers in which a handful of large companies swallowed up hundreds of smaller ones. Presumably mergers were not illegal. When, some years after his retirement, Andrew Carnegie was asked by a committee of the House of Representatives to explain how he had dared participate in the formation of the U.S. Steel Corporation, he replied: "Nobody ever mentioned the Sherman Act to me, that I remember."

THE LABOR UNION MOVEMENT

At the time of the Civil War only a small percentage of the American workforce was organized, and most union members were cigarmakers, printers, carpenters, and other skilled artisans, not factory hands. Aside from ironworkers, railroad workers, and miners, few industrial laborers belonged to unions. Nevertheless the union was the workers' response to the big corporation: a combination designed to eliminate competition for jobs and to provide efficient organization for labor.

After 1865 the growth of national craft unions, which had been stimulated by labor dissatisfaction during the Civil War, quickened perceptibly. In 1866 a federation of these organizations, the National Labor Union, was founded and by the early 1870s many new trades, notably in railroading, had been unionized.

Most of the leaders of these unions were visionaries out of touch with the practical needs and aspirations of workers. They opposed the wage system, strikes, and anything that increased the laborers' sense of being members of the working class. A major objective was the formation of worker-owned cooperatives.

Far more remarkable was the Knights of Labor, a curious organization founded in 1869 by a group of Philadelphia garment workers headed by Uriah S. Stephens. Like so many labor organizers of the period, Stephens was a reformer of wide interests rather than a man dedicated to the specific problems of indus-

Although the Knights of Labor won some important and highly charged labor disputes, they enshrined middle-class culture. These women delegates to the 1886 convention of the Knights of Labor were probably wage earners themselves, yet they posed for this picture in a Victorian parlor around an infant, whose position at the center of the photograph suggests the primacy of motherhood.

trial workers. He, his successor Terence V. Powderly, and many other leaders of the Knights would have been thoroughly at home in the labor organizations of the Jacksonian era. Like the Jacksonians, they supported political objectives that had no direct connection with working conditions, such as currency reform and the curbing of land speculation. They rejected the idea that workers must resign themselves to remaining wage earners. By pooling their resources, working people could advance up the economic ladder and enter the capitalist class. "There is no good reason," Powderly wrote in his autobiography, *The Path I Trod,* "why labor cannot, through cooperation, own and operate mines, factories, and railroads." Leading Knights saw no contradiction between their denunciation of "soulless" monopolies and "drones" like bankers and lawyers and their talk of "combining all branches of trade in one common brotherhood." Such thinking led the Knights to attack the wage system and to frown on strikes as "acts of private warfare."

If the Knights had one foot in the past, they also had one foot in the future. Rejecting the traditional grouping of workers by crafts, they developed a concept closely resembling modern industrial unionism. They welcomed blacks (though mostly in segregated locals), women, and immigrants, and they accepted unskilled workers as well as artisans. They demanded an eight-hour work day, arguing that increased leisure would give workers time to develop more cultivated tastes and higher aspirations. Higher pay would inevitably follow.

Between 1882 and 1886 successful strikes by local "assemblies" against western railroads, including one against the hated Jay Gould's Missouri Pacific, brought recruits to the Knights of Labor by the thousands. The membership passed 42,000 in 1882, 110,000 in 1885, and in 1886 it soared beyond the 700,000 mark. Alas, sudden prosperity was too much for the Knights. Its national leadership was unable to control local groups. A number of poorly planned strikes failed dismally, and the public was alienated by sporadic acts of violence and intimidation. Disillusioned recruits began to drift away.

Circumstances largely fortuitous caused the collapse of the organization. By 1886 the movement for the eight-hour day had gained wide support among workers, including many who did not belong to unions. Several hundred thousand (estimates vary) were on strike in various parts of the country by May of that year. In Chicago, a center of the eight-hour movement, about 80,000 workers were involved, and a small group of anarchists was trying to take advantage of the excitement to win support.

When a striker was killed in a fracas at the McCormick Harvesting Machine Company, the anarchists called a protest meeting on May 4, at Haymarket Square. Police intervened to break up the meeting, and someone—his identity was never established—hurled a bomb into their ranks. Seven policemen were killed and many others injured.

An anarchist group printed 20,000 of these bilingual handbills on the day of the Haymarket bombing in Chicago in 1886.

THE AMERICAN FEDERATION OF LABOR

Although the anarchists were the immediate victims of the resulting public indignation and hysteria—seven were condemned to death and four eventually executed—organized labor, especially the Knights, suffered heavily. No tie between the Knights and the bombing could be established, but the union had been closely connected with the eight-hour agitation, and the public tended to associate it with violence and radicalism. Its membership declined as suddenly as it had risen, and soon it ceased to exist as a force in the labor movement.

The Knights' place was taken by the American Federation of Labor (AFL), a combination of national craft unions established in 1886. In a sense the AFL was a reactionary organization. Its principal leaders, Adolph Strasser and Samuel Gompers of the Cigarmakers Union, were, like the founders of the Knights of Labor, originally interested in utopian social reforms. They even toyed with the idea of forming a workers' political party. Experience, however, soon led them to concentrate on organizing skilled workers and fighting for "bread-and-butter" issues such as higher wages and shorter hours. "Our organization does not consist of idealists," Strasser explained to a congressional committee. "We do not control the production of the world. That is controlled by the employers. . . . I look first to cigars."

The chief weapon of the federation was the strike, which it used to win concessions from employers and to attract recruits. Gompers, president of the AFL almost continuously from 1886 until his death in 1924, encouraged workers to make "intelligent use of the ballot" in order to advance their interests. The federation worked for such things as eight-hour days, employers' liability, and mine-safety laws, but it avoided direct involvement in politics. "I have my own philosophy and my own dreams," Gompers once told a left-wing French politician, "but first and foremost I want to increase the workingman's welfare year by year. . . . The French workers waste their economic force by their political divisions."

Gompers's approach to labor problems produced solid, if unspectacular, growth for the AFL. Unions with a total of about 150,000 members formed the federation in 1886. By 1892 the membership had reached 250,000, and in 1901 it passed the million mark.

LABOR MILITANCY REBUFFED

The stress of the AFL on the strike weapon reflected rather than caused the increasing militancy of labor. Workers felt themselves threatened from all sides: the growing size and power of their corporate employers; the substitution of machines for human skills; the invasion of foreign workers willing to accept substandard wages. At the same time they had tasted some of the material benefits of industrialization and had learned the advantages of concerted action.

The average employer behaved like a tyrant when dealing with his workers. He discharged them arbitrarily when they tried to organize unions; he hired scabs to replace strikers; he frequently failed to provide the most rudimentary protection against injury on the job. Some employers, Carnegie for example, professed to approve of unions, but almost none would bargain with labor collectively. To do so, they argued, would be to deprive workers of their freedom to contract for their own labor in any way they saw fit.

The industrialists of the period were not all ogres; they were as alarmed by the rapid changes of the times as their workers, and since they had more at stake materially, they were probably more frightened by the uncertainties. Deflation, technological change, and intense competition kept even the most successful under constant pressure.

The thinking of most employers was remarkably confused. They considered workers who joined unions "disloyal," and at the same time they treated labor as a commodity to be purchased as cheaply as possible. "If I wanted boiler iron," Henry B. Stone, a railroad official, explained, "I would go out on the market and buy it where I could get it cheapest, and if I wanted to employ men, I would do the same." Yet Stone was furious when the men he had "bought" joined a union. When labor was scarce, employers resisted demands for higher wages by arguing that the price of labor was controlled by its productivity; when it was plentiful, they justified reducing wages by referring to the law of supply and demand.

Thus capital and labor were often spoiling for a fight, frequently without fully understanding why. When labor troubles developed, they tended to be bitter, even violent. In 1877 a great railroad strike convulsed much of the nation. It began on the Baltimore and Ohio system in response to a wage cut and spread to other eastern lines and then throughout the West until about two-thirds of the railroad mileage of the country had been shut down. Violence broke out, rail yards were put to the torch, dismayed and frightened businessmen formed militia companies to patrol the streets of Chicago and other cities. Eventually President Hayes sent federal troops to the trouble spots to restore order, and the strike collapsed. There had been no real danger of revolution, but the violence and destruction of the strike had been without precedent in America.

The disturbances of 1877 were a response to a business slump, those of the next decade a response to good times. Twice as many strikes occurred in 1886 as in any previous year. Even before the Haymarket bombing centered the country's attention on labor problems, the situation had become so disturbing that President Grover Cleveland, in the first presidential message devoted to labor problems, had urged Congress to create a voluntary arbitration board to aid in settling labor disputes—a remarkable suggestion for a man of Cleveland's conservative, laissez-faire approach to economic issues.

In 1892 a violent strike broke out among silver miners at Coeur d'Alene, Idaho, and a far more important clash shook Andrew Carnegie's Homestead steel plant near Pittsburgh when strikers attacked 300 private guards brought in to protect strikebreakers. Seven guards were killed at Homestead and the rest forced to "surrender" and march off ignominiously. The Homestead affair was part of a struggle between capital and labor in the steel industry. Steel producers insisted that the workers were holding back progress by resisting technological advances, while the workers believed that the company was refusing to share the fruits of more efficient operation fairly. The strike was precipitated by the decision of company officials to crush the union at all costs. The final defeat, after a five-month walkout, of the 24,000-member Amalgamated Association of Iron

Members of the American Railway Union trying to stop trains carrying Pullman cars out of Chicago, as de-picted by an artist. The sheriff, with badge, is at the center of the scene. Both the rioting workers and the company's men carry guns.

and Steel Workers, one of the most important elements in the AFL, destroyed unionism as an effective force in the steel industry and set back the progress of organized labor all over the country.

As in the case of the Haymarket bombing, the activities of radicals on the fringe of the dispute turned the public against the steelworkers. The boss of Homestead was Henry Clay Frick, a tough-minded foe of unions who was deter-mined to "teach our employees a lesson." Frick made the decision to bring in strikebreakers and to employ Pinkerton detectives to protect them. During the course of the strike, Alexander Berkman, an anarchist, burst into Frick's office and attempted to assassinate him. Frick was only slightly wounded, but the attack brought him much sympathy and unjustly discredited the strikers.

The most important strike of the period took place in 1894. It began when the workers at George Pullman's Palace Car factory outside Chicago walked out in protest against wage cuts. (While reducing wages, Pullman insisted on holding the line on rents in the company town of Pullman; when a delegation called on him to remonstrate, he refused to give in and had three of the leaders fired.) Some Pullman workers belonged to the American Railway Union, headed by Eugene V. Debs. After the strike had dragged along for weeks, the union voted to refuse to handle trains with Pullman cars. The union was perfectly willing to han-dle mail trains, but the owners refused to run trains unless they were made up of a full complement of cars.

When Pullman cars were added to mail trains, the workers refused to move them. The resulting railroad strike tied up trunk lines running in and out of Chicago. The railroad owners appealed to President Cleveland to send troops to preserve order. On the pretext that the soldiers were needed to ensure the movement of the mails, Cleveland agreed. When Debs defied a federal injunction to end the walkout, he was jailed for contempt and the strike was broken.

WHITHER AMERICA, WHITHER DEMOCRACY?

Each year more of the nation's wealth and power seemed to fall into fewer hands. As with the railroads, other industries were being influenced, if not completely dominated, by bankers. The firm of J. P. Morgan and Company controlled many railroads; the largest steel, electrical, agricultural machinery, rubber, and shipping companies; two life insurance companies; and a number of banks. By 1913 Morgan and the Rockefeller National City Bank group between them could name 341 directors to 112 corporations worth over $22.2 billion. The "Money Trust," a loose but potent fraternity of financiers, seemed fated to become the ultimate monopoly.

Centralization unquestionably increased efficiency, at least in industries that used a great deal of expensive machinery to turn out goods for the mass market, and in those where close coordination of output, distribution, and sales was important. The public benefited immensely from the productive efficiency of the new empires. Living standards rose.

But the trend toward giantism raised doubts. With ownership falling into fewer hands, what would be the ultimate effect of big business on American democracy? What did it mean for ordinary people when a few tycoons possessed huge fortunes and commanded such influence even on Congress and the courts?

The crushing of the Pullman strike demonstrated the power of the courts to break strikes by issuing injunctions. And the courts seemed only concerned with protecting the interests of the rich and powerful. Particularly ominous for organized labor was the fact that the federal government based its request for the injunction that broke the strike on the Sherman Antitrust Act, arguing that the American Railway Union was a combination in restraint of trade. An indirect result of the Pullman strike was that while serving his sentence for contempt, Eugene Debs was visited by a number of prominent socialists who sought to convert him to their cause. One gave him a copy of Karl Marx's *Capital,* which he found too dull to finish, but he did read *Looking Backward* and *Wealth Against Commonwealth.* In 1897 he became a socialist.

MILESTONES

1859	First oil well drilled in Pennsylvania
1868	Carnegie Steel Company formed
1869	George Westinghouse invents air brake
	Knights of Labor founded
1870	Standard Oil Company formed
1870–1890	Completion of railroad trunk lines
1876	Alexander Graham Bell invents the telephone
1877	Great railroad strike
	Munn v. *Illinois* upholds state regulatory laws
1879	Thomas Edison invents the electric light
	Henry George's *Progress and Poverty*
1884	Laurence Gronlund's *The Cooperative Commonwealth*
1886	Haymarket bombing
	American Federation of Labor founded
	Interstate Commerce Act
1888	Edward Bellamy's *Looking Backward*
1889	Andrew Carnegie's "Gospel of Wealth"
1890	Sherman Antitrust Act
1892	Homestead strike
	General Electric Company formed
1894	Pullman strike
	Henry Demarest Lloyd's *Wealth Against Commonwealth*
1895	*U.S.* v. *E. C. Knight Company* weakens Sherman Act
1901	U.S. Steel Corporation formed

19

AMERICAN SOCIETY
IN THE INDUSTRIAL AGE

The industrialization that followed the Civil War profoundly affected every aspect of American life. New machines, improvements in transportation and communication, the appearance of the great corporation with its uncertain implications for the future—all made deep impressions on the shape and indeed the very character of American society. The growth of cities and the influx of immigrants who knew little about urban life and who neither spoke nor understood English had large effects on the immigrants and the world they inhabited.

MIDDLE-CLASS LIFE

"This middle-class country had got a middle-class president, at last," Ralph Waldo Emerson had noted with satisfaction when Lincoln took office in 1861. Emerson did not endorse an economic class so much as a set of values that were, pointedly, antithetical to those of the antebellum South. Middle-class culture took the best aspects of romanticism—the enshrinement of human potential, the restless striving for personal betterment, the zest for competition and excitement—and tempered them with a passion for self-control and regularity.

But the Civil War sapped middle-class culture of its reforming zeal. The vital energy that had spawned a host of antebellum reform movements became transmuted into greater mass; the fervor of the individual was channeled into institutions. American society and culture underwent a process of "incorporation," as the predominant form of the business world seeped deep into the American consciousness.

The middle-class family similarly lost some of its moral fervor and gained a new substantiality. Historians have long asserted that middle-class family relations were stiff and, in matters pertaining to sexuality, downright prudish. One witless scholar imagined that intercourse occurred "in a dark bedroom into which the husband would creep to create his offspring in silence while the wife endured the connection in a coma." But diaries and letters provide ample proof that many couples experienced emotionally intense and sexually fulfilling relationships. Elaborate and protracted courtship rituals, which doubtless proved frustrating, intensified the expression of love by delaying its gratification. Middle-class mothers at the end of the century had two or three children, four or five fewer than their grandmothers. Their families were smaller mostly because they married later in life and practiced abstinence, though during the last half of the century contraceptive devices were disseminated more readily and abortion was practiced more frequently.

The children in middle-class families, while much treasured, were carefully supervised. Upwardly striving parents were much concerned about the status and prospects of their children's marriage partners, but it was no longer considered proper to interfere with "the course of true love."

While most women remained home to supervise their children, men worked away from home, in shops and offices. Members of the professions and the large and diffuse groups of shopkeepers, small manufacturers, skilled craftsmen, and established farmers that made up the middle class lived in varying degrees of

The glove counter at Rike's Department Store in Dayton, Ohio (1893). Shopping was an excuse for middle-class women to venture from the home into public. Rike's department store was decorated much like the Victorian home: potted ferns, stuffed animals, and carpeted stairways. The salesgirl (far right) was obliged to leave the home to work. She spent much of her income to "keep up appearances" to enable her to mix with middle-class shoppers.

comfort. A family with an annual income of $1000 in the 1880s would have no need to skimp on food, clothing, or shelter. When Professor Woodrow Wilson moved with his family to Wesleyan University in 1888, he was able to rent a large house and employ two full-time servants on his salary of $2500 a year. Indeed, at this time, about a quarter of all urban families employed at least one servant.

Middle-class family life was defined in terms of tangible goods: fashionable clothes and, especially, a large home crowded with furniture, books, lamps and all manner of bibelots. Modern scholars have indicted the morality as well as the aesthetics of this incipient "culture of consumption," criticisms commonly aired by the people themselves. No attack on middle-class culture and its conspicuous consumption exceeds the venom of Thorstein Veblen's *Theory of the Leisure Class* (1899). Fashionable clothing, he observed, induced "aesthetic nausea," prompting women to soon discard them; college athletics was equally wasteful, "since success as an athlete presumes, not only a waste of time, but also a waste of money." (Veblen was never popular on campus and had trouble holding a job.)

SKILLED AND UNSKILLED WORKERS

Wage earners felt the full force of the industrial tide, being affected in countless ways—some beneficial, others unfortunate. As manufacturing and mining became more important, the number of workers in these fields multiplied rapidly: from 885,000 in 1860 to more than 3.2 million in 1890. While workers lacked much sense of solidarity, they exerted a far larger influence on society at the turn of the century than they had in the years before the Civil War.

More efficient methods of production enabled them to increase their output, making possible a rise in their standard of living. The working day still tended to approximate the hours of daylight, but it was shortening perceptibly by the 1880s, at least in many occupations. In 1860 the average had been 11 hours, but by 1880 only one worker in four labored more than 10 hours and radicals were beginning to talk about 8 hours as a fair day's work.

This generalization, however, conceals some important differences. Skilled industrial workers—such types as railroad engineers and conductors, machinists, and iron molders—were quite well off in most cases. But it was still true that unskilled laborers could not earn enough to maintain a family decently by their own efforts alone.

Industrialization created problems for workers beyond the obvious one of earning enough money to support themselves. By and large, skilled workers, always better off than the unskilled, improved their positions relatively, despite the increased use of machinery. Furthermore, when machines took the place of human skills, jobs became monotonous. Mechanization undermined both the artisans' pride and their bargaining power vis-à-vis their employers. As expensive machinery became more important, the worker seemed of necessity less important. Machines more than workers controlled the pace of work and its duration. The time clock regulated the labor force more rigidly than the most exacting foreman. The length of the workday may have declined, but the pace of work and the danger involved in working around heavy, high-speed machinery increased accordingly.

As businesses grew larger, personal contact between employer and hired hand tended to disappear. Relations between them became less human, more businesslike and ruthless. On the other hand, large enterprises usually employed a higher percentage of managerial and clerical workers than smaller companies, thus providing opportunities for more "blue-collar" workers to rise in the industrial hierarchy. But the trend toward bigness made it more difficult for workers to rise from the ranks of labor to become manufacturers themselves, as Andrew Carnegie, for example, had done during the Civil War era.

Another problem for workers was that industrialization tended to accentuate swings of the business cycle. On the upswing something approaching full employment existed, but in periods of depression unemployment became a problem that affected workers without regard for their individual abilities. It is significant that the word *unemployment* (though not, of course, the condition itself) was a late-nineteenth-century invention.

WORKING WOMEN

Women continued to supply a significant part of the industrial working force. But now many more of them were working outside their homes; the factory had almost completely replaced the household as the seat of manufacturing. Textile mills and "the sewing trades" absorbed a large percentage of women, but in all fields women were paid substantially lower wages than men.

Women found many new types of work in these years, a fact commented on by the *New York Times* as early as 1869. They made up the overwhelming majority of salespersons and cashiers in the big new department stores. Partly because of the persistence of the Cult of True Womanhood into the postwar era, managers considered women more polite, easier to control, and more honest than male workers, all qualities especially valuable in the huge emporiums. Over half of the more than 1700 employees in A. T. Stewart's New York store were women.

Educated, middle-class women also dominated the new profession of nursing that developed alongside the expanding medical profession and the establishment of large urban hospitals. To nearly all doctors, to most men, and indeed to many women of that day, nursing seemed the perfect female profession since it required the same characteristics that women were thought to have by nature: self-lessness, cleanliness, kindliness, tact, sensitivity, and submissiveness to male control. Typical was this remark of a contemporary authority: "Since God could not care for all the sick, he made women to nurse." Why it had not occurred to the Lord to make more women physicians, or for that matter members of other prestigious professions like law and the clergy, this man did not explain, probably because it had not occurred to him either.

Middle-class women did replace men as teachers in most of the nation's grade schools, and they also replaced men as clerks and secretaries and operators of the new typewriters in government departments and in business offices. Most men with the knowledge of spelling and grammar that these positions required had better opportunities and were uninterested in office work, so women high school graduates, of whom there was an increasing number, filled the gap.

Both department store clerks and "typewriters" (as they were called) earned more money than unskilled factory workers, and working conditions were more pleasant. According to one advertisement of the period, a "Type-Writer" was an ideal Christmas present for "deserving" young women. "No invention has opened for women so broad and easy an avenue to profitable and suitable employment." Opportunities for promotion for women, however, were rare; managerial posts in these fields remained almost exclusively in the hands of men.

Working Your Way Up

To study mobility in a large industrial country is extraordinarily difficult. Americans in the late nineteenth century believed their society offered great opportunities for individual advancement, and to prove it they pointed to men like Andrew Carnegie and to other poor boys who accumulated large fortunes. How general was the rise from rags to riches is another question.

Americans had been on the move, mostly, of course, in a westward direction, since the colonial period, but studies of census records show that there was considerable geographic mobility in urban areas throughout the last half of the nineteenth century and into the twentieth. Most investigations reveal that only about half the people recorded in one census were still in the same place ten years later. The nation had a vast reservoir of rootless people. For many, the way to move up in the world was to move on.

In most of the cities studied, mobility was accompanied by some economic and social improvement. On the average, about a quarter of the manual laborers traced rose to middle-class status during their lifetimes, and the sons of manual laborers were still more likely to improve their place in society. In New York City about a third of the Italian and Jewish immigrants of the 1890s had risen from unskilled to skilled jobs a decade later. Even in Newburyport, Massachusetts, a town that was something of an economic backwater, most laborers made

An 1890s classroom with 40-plus children, all about the same age, from the same economic and social cir-cumstances, and set to the same assignment by a woman teacher. The urban public school had arrived.

some progress, though far fewer rose to skilled or white-collar positions than in more prosperous cities.

Such progress was primarily the result of the economic growth the nation was experiencing and of the energy and ambition of the people, native-born and immigrant alike, who were pouring into the cities in such numbers. The public education system gave an additional boost to the upwardly mobile.

The history of American education after about 1870 reflects the impact of social and economic change. Although Horace Mann, Henry Barnard, and others had laid the foundations for state-supported school systems, most of these systems became compulsory only after the Civil War, when the growth of cities provided the concentration of population and financial resources necessary for economical mass education. In the 1860s about half the children in the country were getting some formal education, but this did not mean that half the children were attending school at any one time. Sessions were short, especially in rural areas, and many teachers were poorly trained. President Calvin Coolidge noted in his autobiography that the one-room school he attended in rural Vermont in the 1880s was open only in slack seasons when the 20-odd students were not needed in the fields. "Few, if any, of my teachers reached the standard now required," he wrote, adding that his own younger sister had obtained a teaching certificate and actually taught a class when she was only 12.

Thereafter, steady growth and improvement took place. Attendance in the public schools increased from 6.8 million in 1870 to 15.5 million in 1900, a remarkable expansion even when allowance is made for the growth of the population. More remarkable still, during a time when prices were declining steadily, public expenditures for education nearly quadrupled. A typical elementary school graduate, at least in the cities, studied, besides the traditional "Three Rs," history, geography, a bit of science, drawing, and physical training.

Industrialization created many demands for vocational and technical training; both employers and unskilled workers quickly grasped the possibilities. Science courses were taught in some of the new high schools, but secondary education was still assumed to be only for those with special abilities and youths whose families did not require that they immediately become breadwinners. As late as 1890 fewer than 300,000 of the 14.3 million children attending public and private schools had progressed beyond the eighth grade and nearly a third of these were attending private institutions.

Education certainly helped young people to rise in the world, but progress from rags to real riches was far from common. Carnegies were rare. A study of the family backgrounds of 200 late-nineteenth-century business leaders revealed that nearly all of them grew up in well-to-do middle-class families. They were far better educated than the general run, and most were members of one or another Protestant church.

The unrealistic expectations inspired by the rags-to-riches myth more than the absence of real opportunity probably explains why so many workers, even when expressing dissatisfaction with life as it was, continued to subscribe to such middle-class values as hard work and thrift—that is, they continued to hope.

THE "NEW" IMMIGRATION

Industrial expansion increased the need for labor, and this in turn powerfully stimulated immigration. Between 1866 and 1915 about 25 million foreigners entered the United States. Industrial growth alone does not explain the influx. The launching in 1858 of the English liner *Great Eastern,* which was nearly 700 feet from stem to stern and weighed about 19,000 tons, opened a new era in transatlantic travel. Although most immigrants traveled in steerage, which was cramped and almost totally lacking in anything that could be considered an amenity, the Atlantic crossing, once so hazardous, became safe and speedy with the perfection of the steamship. Competition between the great packet lines such as Cunard, North German Lloyd, and Holland-America drove down the cost of the passage, and advertising by the lines further stimulated traffic.

"Push" pressures as well as these "pull" factors had much to do with this "new" immigration. Improvements in transportation produced unexpected and disruptive changes in the economies of many European countries. Cheap wheat from the United States, Russia, and other parts of the world poured into Europe, bringing disaster to farmers throughout Europe. The spreading industrial revolution and the increased use of farm machinery led to the collapse of the peasant economy of central and southern Europe. For rural inhabitants this meant the loss of self-sufficiency, the fragmentation of landholdings, unemployment, and for many the decision to make a new start in the New World.

Political and religious persecutions pushed still others into the migrating stream, but the main reason for immigration remained the desire for economic betterment. "In America," a British immigrant reported, "you get pies and puddings."

While immigrants continued to people the farms of America, industry absorbed an ever-increasing number of the newcomers. In 1870 one industrial worker in three was foreign-born. When congressional investigators examined 21 major industries early in the new century, they discovered that well over half of the labor force had not been born in the United States.

Most of the new millions entered the country by way of New York City. A Serbian immigrant, Michael Pupin, later a distinguished physicist at Columbia University, has left a moving description of what it was like. He arrived in 1874 on the Hamburg-American liner *Westphalia* amid a horde of other newcomers. Disembarking at Hoboken, he was taken by tug to the immigration reception center at Castle Garden on the southern tip of Manhattan Island. He confessed to the authorities that he had only 5 cents to his name and knew no Americans except—by reputation—Franklin, Lincoln, and Harriet Beecher Stowe. But he explained in eloquent phrases why he wanted to live in the land of liberty rather than in the Austro-Hungarian empire.

The officials conferred briefly, then admitted him. After a good breakfast, supplied by the immigration authorities, someone from the Castle Garden Labor Bureau offered him a job as a farmhand in Delaware. Within 24 hours of his arrival he had reached his destination, ready to go to work.

Before 1882, when—in addition to the Chinese—criminals, and persons adjudged mentally defective or liable to become public charges were excluded, entry into the United States was almost unrestricted. Indeed, until 1891 the Atlantic coast states, not the federal government, exercised whatever controls were imposed on newcomers. Even when federally imposed, medical inspection was perfunctory. Public health officials boasted that with "one glance" at each arrival, the inspectors could "take in six details, namely the scalp, face, neck, hands, gait and general condition, both mental and physical." Only those who failed this "test" were examined more closely. On average, only 1 immigrant in 50 was ultimately rejected.

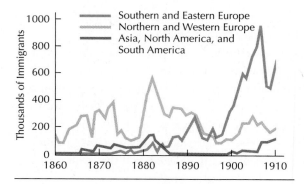

Immigration, 1860–1910

In this graph, Germany is counted as a part of northern and western Europe. Note the tide of new immigration from southern and eastern Europe in the early 1900s.

Private agencies, philanthropic and commercial, served as a link between the new arrivals and employers looking for labor. Until the Foran Act of 1885 outlawed the practice, a few companies brought in skilled workers under contract, advancing them passage money and collecting it in installments from their paychecks, a system somewhat like the indentured servitude of colonial times. Numerous nationality groups assisted (and sometimes exploited) their compatriots by organizing "immigrant banks" that recruited labor in the old country, arranged transportation, and then housed the newcomers in boardinghouses in the United States while finding them jobs. The *padrone* system of the Italians and Greeks was typical. The *padrone,* a sort of contractor who agreed to supply gangs of unskilled workers to companies for a lump sum, usually signed on immigrants unfamiliar with American wage levels at rates that ensured him a healthy profit.

Beginning in the 1880s, the spreading effects of industrialization in Europe caused a shift in the sources of American immigration from northern and western to southern and eastern sections of the Continent. In 1882, 789,000 immigrants entered the United States; more than 350,000 came from Great Britain and Germany, only 32,000 from Italy, and fewer than 17,000 from Russia. In 1907—the all-time peak year, with 1,285,000 immigrants—Great Britain and Germany supplied fewer than half as many as they had 25 years earlier, while Russia and Italy were supplying eleven times as many as then. Up to 1880, only about 200,000 southern and eastern Europeans had migrated to America. Between 1880 and 1910, approximately 8.4 million arrived.

NEW IMMIGRANTS FACE NEW NATIVISM

The "new" immigrants, like the "old" Irish of the 1840s and 1850s, were mostly peasants. They also seemed more than ordinarily clannish; southern Italians typically called all people outside their families *forestieri,* "foreigners." Old-stock Americans thought them harder to assimilate, and in fact many were. Some Italian immigrants, for example, were unmarried men who had come to the United States to earn enough money to buy a farm back home. Such people made hard and willing workers but were not much concerned with being part of an American community.

The "birds of passage" were a substantial minority, but the immigrant who saved in order to bring his wife and children or his younger brothers and sisters to America was more typical. In addition, thousands of immigrants came as family groups and intended to remain. Some, like the eastern European Jewish migrants, were refugees who were almost desperately eager to become Americans, although of course they retained and nurtured much of their traditional culture.

German American and Irish American Catholics had different attitudes that caused them to clash over such matters as the policies of the Catholic University

Contemporary cartoonists reflected the "new nativist" attitude toward unrestricted immigration. Frank Beard's 1885 drawing shows anarchists, socialists, and members of the Mafia (indicated here as the Black Hand) arriving from the sewers of Europe and being resisted by Columbia and her watchdogs "Law" and "Order."

in Washington. Although (or perhaps because) the Haymarket anarchists were German-born, in 1887 one prominent German American denounced the Knights of Labor as a hotbed of radicalism—and was said to have claimed that it was dominated by "Irish ignoramuses." Controversies erupted between Catholic and Protestant German Americans, between Greek American groups supporting various political factions in their homeland, and so on.

Confused by such differences and conflicts, many "older" Americans concluded, wrongly but understandably, that the new immigrants were incapable of becoming good citizens and should be kept out. During the 1880s large numbers of social workers, economists, and church leaders, worried by the problems that arose when so many poor immigrants flocked into cities already bursting at the seams, began to believe that some restriction should be placed on the incoming human tide.

Social Darwinists and people obsessed with pseudoscientific ideas about "racial purity" also found the new immigration alarming. Misunderstanding the findings of the new science of genetics, they attributed the social problems associated with mass immigration to supposed physiological characteristics of the newcomers. Forgetting that earlier Americans had accused pre–Civil War Irish and German immigrants of similar deficiencies, they decided that the peoples of southern and eastern Europe were racially (and therefore permanently) inferior to "Nordic" and "Anglo-Saxon" types and ought to be kept out.

Workers, fearing the competition of people with low living standards and no bargaining power, spoke out against the "enticing of penniless and unapprised immigrants . . . to undermine our wages and social welfare." In 1883 the president of the Amalgamated Iron and Steel Workers told a Senate committee that Hungarian, Polish, Italian, and other immigrants "can live where I think a decent man would die; they can live on . . . food that other men would not touch." A Wisconsin iron worker put it this way: "Immigrants work for almost nothing and seem to be able to live on wind—something I can not do."

Employers were not disturbed by the influx of people with strong backs willing to work hard for low wages. Nevertheless, by the late 1880s many of them were alarmed about the supposed radicalism of the immigrants. The Haymarket bombing focused attention on the handful of foreign-born extremists in the country and loosed a flood of unjustified charges that "anarchists and communists" were dominating the labor movement. Nativism, which had waxed in the 1850s under the Know-Nothing banner and waned during the Civil War, now flared up again, and for similar reasons. Denunciations of "longhaired, wild-eyed, bad-smelling, atheistic, reckless foreign wretches," of "Europe's human and inhuman rubbish," of the "cutthroats of Beelzebub from the Rhine, the Danube, the Vistula and the Elbe" crowded the pages of the nation's press. The Grand Army of the Republic, an organization of Civil War veterans, grumbled about foreign-born radicals.

These nativists, again like the pre–Civil War variety, disliked Catholics and other minority groups more than immigrants as such. The largest nativist organization of the period, the American Protective Association, founded in 1887, existed primarily to resist what its members called "the Catholic menace." The Protestant majority treated "new" immigrants as underlings, tried to keep them out of the best jobs, and discouraged their efforts to climb the social ladder. This prejudice functioned only at the social and economic level. But nowhere in America did prejudice lead to interference with religious freedom in the narrow sense. And neither labor leaders nor important industrialists, despite their misgivings about immigration, took a broadly antiforeign position.

After the Exclusion Act of 1882 and the almost meaningless 1885 ban on importing contract labor, no further restrictions were imposed on immigration until the twentieth century. Strong support for a literacy test for admission developed in the 1890s, pushed by a new organization, the Immigration Restriction League. Since there was much more illiteracy in the southeastern quarter of Europe than in the northwestern, such a test would discriminate without seeming to do so on national or racial grounds. A literacy test bill passed both houses of Congress in 1897, but President Cleveland vetoed it. Such a "radical departure" from the "generous and free-handed policy" of the past, Cleveland said, was unjustified. He added, perhaps with tongue in cheek, that a literacy requirement would not keep out "unruly agitators," who were only too adept at reading and writing.

THE EXPANDING CITY AND ITS PROBLEMS

A steadily increasing proportion of the urban population was made up of immigrants. In 1890 the foreign-born population of Chicago almost equaled the total population of Chicago in 1880; a third of all Bostonians and a quarter of all Philadelphians were immigrants; and four out of five residents of New York City were either foreign-born or the children of immigrants.

After 1890 the immigrant concentration became even more dense. The migrants from eastern and southern Europe lacked the resources to travel to the agriculturally developing regions (to say nothing of the sums necessary to acquire land and farm equipment). As the concentration progressed it fed upon itself, for all the eastern cities developed many ethnic neighborhoods, in each of which immigrants of one nationality congregated. Lonely, confused, often unable to speak English, the Italians, the Greeks, the Polish and Russian Jews, and other

Rural and Urban Population, 1860–1910

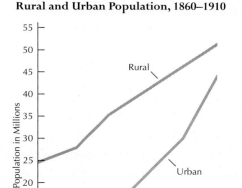

immigrants tended to settle where their predecessors had settled.

Most newcomers intended to become United States citizens, to be absorbed in the famous American "melting pot." But they also wanted to maintain their traditional culture. They supported "national" churches and schools. Newspapers in their native languages flourished, as did social organizations of all sorts. Each great American city became a Europe in microcosm. New York City, the great *entrepôt,* had a Little Italy; Polish, Greek, Jewish, and Bohemian quarters; and even a Chinatown.

Although ethnic neighborhoods were crowded, unhealthy, and crime-ridden, and many of the residents were desperately poor, they were not ghettos in the European sense, for those who lived there were not compelled by law to remain. Thousands "escaped" yearly to better districts. American ghettos were places where hopes and ambitions were fulfilled, where people worked hard and endured hardships in order to improve their own and their children's lot.

Early twentieth-century city life was anything but glamorous for many residential dwellers. Here, cramped slum houses and outhouses are visible from the railroad tracks in Cincinnati, Ohio.

Observing the immigrants' attachment to "foreign" values and institutions, numbers of "natives" accused the newcomers of resisting Americanization and blamed them for urban problems. The immigrants were involved in these problems, but the rapidity of urban expansion explains the troubles associated with city life far more fully than the high percentage of foreigners.

TEEMING TENEMENTS

The cities were suffering from growing pains. Sewer and water facilities frequently could not keep pace with skyrocketing needs. By the 1890s the tremendous growth of Chicago had put such a strain on its sanitation system that the Chicago River had become virtually an open sewer, and the city's drinking water contained such a high concentration of germ-killing chemicals that it tasted like creosote. In the 1880s all the sewers of Baltimore emptied into the sluggish Back Basin, and according to the journalist H. L. Mencken, every summer the city smelled "like a billion polecats." Fire protection became less and less adequate; garbage piled up in the streets faster than it could be carted away; and the streets themselves crumbled beneath the pounding of heavy traffic. Urban growth proceeded with such speed that new streets were laid out more rapidly than they could be paved. Chicago had more than 1400 miles of dirt streets in 1890.

People poured into the great cities faster than housing could be built to accommodate them. The influx into areas already densely packed in the 1840s became unbearable as rising property values and the absence of zoning laws conspired to make builders utilize every possible foot of space, squeezing out light and air ruthlessly in order to wedge in a few additional family units.

Substandard living quarters aggravated other evils such as disease and the disintegration of family life, with its attendant mental anguish, crime, and juvenile delinquency. The bloody New York City riots of 1863, though sparked by dislike of the Civil War draft and of blacks, reflected the bitterness and frustration of thousands jammed together amid filth and threatened by disease. A citizens' committee seeking to discover the causes of the riots expressed its amazement after visiting the slums "that so much misery, disease, and wretchedness can be huddled together and hidden . . . unvisited and unthought of, so near our own abodes."

New York City created a Metropolitan Health Board in 1866, and a state tenement house law the following year made a feeble beginning at regulating city housing. Despite these efforts at reform, in 1890 more than 1.4 million persons were living on Manhattan Island, and in some sections the population density exceeded 900 persons per acre. Jacob Riis, a reporter, captured the horror of the crowded warrens in his classic study of life in the slums, *How the Other Half Lives* (1890):

Impoverished immigrant families, like the one in this 1889 Jacob Riis photograph, often lived in tiny win-dowless rooms in crowded tenement districts.

> *Be a little careful, please! The hall is dark and you might stumble. . . . Here where the hall turns and dives into utter darkness is . . . a flight of stairs. You can feel your way, if you cannot see it. Close? Yes! What would you have? All the fresh air that enters these stairs comes from the hall-door that is forever slamming. . . . The sinks are in the hall-way, that all the tenants may have access—and all be poisoned alike by their summer stenches. . . . Here is a door. Listen! That short, hacking cough, that tiny, helpless wail—what do they mean? . . . The child is dying of measles. With half a chance it might have lived; but it had none. That dark bedroom killed it.*

The unhealthiness of the tenements was notorious. No one knows exactly, but as late as 1900 about three quarters of the residents of New York City's Lower East Side lacked indoor toilets and had to use backyard outhouses to relieve themselves. One noxious corner became known as the "lung block" because of the prevalence of tuberculosis among its inhabitants. In 1900 three out of five babies born in one poor district of Chicago died before their first birthday.

Equally frightening was the impact of overcrowding on the morals of tenement dwellers. The number of prison inmates in the United States increased by 50 percent in the 1880s, and the homicide rate nearly tripled, most of the rise occurring in cities. Driven into the streets by the squalor of their homes, slum youths formed gangs bearing names like Alley Gang, Rock Gang, and Hell's Kitchen Gang. From petty thievery and shoplifting they graduated to housebreaking, bank robbery, and murder. According to Jacob Riis, when the leader of the infamous Whyo Gang, convicted of murder, confessed his sins to a prison chaplain, "his father confessor turned pale . . . though many years of labor as chaplain of the Tombs had hardened him to such rehearsals."

Slums bred criminals—the wonder was that they bred so few. They also drove well-to-do residents into exclusive sections and to the suburbs. From Boston's Beacon Hill and Back Bay to San Francisco's Nob Hill, the rich retired into their cluttered mansions and ignored conditions in the poorer parts of town.

THE CITIES MODERNIZE

As American cities grew larger and more crowded, thereby aggravating a host of social problems, practical forces operated to bring about improvements. Once the relationship between polluted water and disease was fully understood, everyone saw the need for decent water and sewage systems. While some businessmen profited from corrupt dealings with the city machines, more of them wanted efficient and honest government in order to reduce their tax bills. City dwellers of all classes resented dirt, noise, and ugliness, and in many communities public-spirited groups formed societies to plant trees, clean up littered areas, and develop recreational facilities. When one city undertook improvements, others tended to follow suit, spurred on by local pride and the booster spirit.

Gradually the basic facilities of urban living were improved. Streets were paved, first with cobblestones and wood blocks and then with smoother, quieter asphalt. Gaslight, then electric arc lights, and finally Edison's incandescent lamps brightened the cities after dark, making law enforcement easier, stimulating night life, and permitting factories and shops to operate after sunset.

Urban transportation underwent enormous changes. Until the 1880s, horse-drawn cars running on tracks set flush with the street were the main means of urban public transportation. In 1860 New York City's horsecars were carrying about 100,000 passengers a day. But horsecars had serious drawbacks. Enormous numbers of horses were needed, and feeding and stabling the animals was costly. Their droppings (10 pounds per day per horse) became a major source of urban pollution. That is why the invention of the electric trolley car in the 1880s put an end to horsecar transportation. Trolleys were cheaper and less unsightly than horsecars and quieter than steam-powered trains.

A retired naval officer, Frank J. Sprague, installed the first practical electric trolley line in Richmond, Virginia, in 1887–1888. At once other cities seized on

On Sundays in the late nineteenth century, city people crowded into streetcars and thronged to the country-side. Enticed by this taste of bucolic splendor, many chose to live in the suburbs and take the streetcars to work downtown. Soon, the population density of the suburbs resembled that of the cities.

the trolley. Lines soon radiated outward from the city centers, bringing commuters and shoppers from the residential districts to the business district. Without them the big-city department stores could not have flourished as they did. By 1895 some 850 lines were busily hauling city dwellers over 10,000 miles of track, and mileage tripled in the following decade. As with other new enterprises, control of street railways quickly became centralized until a few big operators controlled the trolleys of more than 100 eastern cities and towns.

Streetcars changed the character of big-city life. Before their introduction urban communities were limited by the distances people could conveniently walk to work. The "walking city" could not easily extend more than 2½ miles from its center. Streetcars increased this radius to 6 miles or more, which meant that the area of the city expanded enormously. Dramatic population shifts resulted as the better-off moved away from the center in search of air and space, abandoning the crumbling, jam-packed older neighborhoods to the poor. Thus economic segregation speeded the growth of ghettos. Older peripheral towns that had maintained some of the self-contained qualities of village life were swallowed up, becoming metropolitan centers. The village of Medford, Massachusetts, outside Boston, had 11,000 residents in 1890 when the first trolley line from the city center reached it. By 1905 its population had reached 23,000.

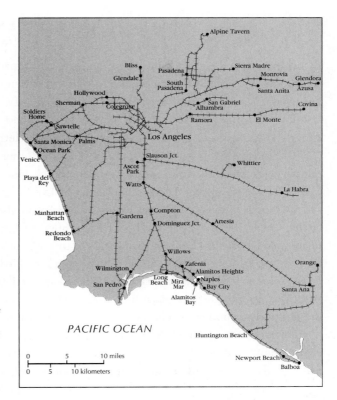

Los Angeles Area Street Railway Network, 1909

By the early 1900s, a street railway network radiated from the settled parts of central Los Angeles for 30 miles and more. Henry Huntington claimed that the Los Angeles and Pacific Electric system "extended into the open country, ahead of, and not behind, the population." (Data from Robert M. Fogelson, The Fragmented Metropolis, *1967.)*

As time passed, each new area, originally peopled by rising economic groups, tended to become crowded and then to deteriorate. By extending their tracks beyond the developed areas, the streetcar companies further speeded suburban growth because they assured developers, bankers, builders, and middle-class home buyers of efficient transport to the center of town. By keeping fares low (5 cents a ride was standard) the lines enabled poor people to "escape" to the countryside on holidays.

But efforts to relieve the congestion in slum districts made little headway. In Brooklyn Alfred T. White established Home Buildings, a 40-family model tenement in 1877; eventually he expanded the experiment to include 267 apartments. Each unit had plenty of light and air and contained its own sink and toilet. Ellen Collins developed a smaller project in Manhattan's Fourth Ward in the 1890s. These model tenements were self-sustaining, but of necessity they yielded only modest returns. The landlords were essentially philanthropists; their work had no significant impact on urban housing in the nineteenth century.

LEISURE ACTIVITIES: MORE FUN AND GAMES

By bringing together large numbers of people, cities made possible many kinds of social activity difficult or impossible to maintain in rural areas. Cities remained unsurpassed as centers of artistic and intellectual life. New York was the outstanding example, as seen in its many theaters and in the founding of the American Museum of Natural History (1870), the Metropolitan Museum of Art (1870), and the Metropolitan Opera (1883), but other cities were equally hospitable to such endeavors. Boston's Museum of Fine Arts, for example, was founded in 1870 and the Boston Symphony in 1881.

Of course less sophisticated forms of recreation also flourished in the urban environment. From 1865 to 1885 the number of breweries in Massachusetts quadrupled. It is only a slight exaggeration to say that in crowded urban centers there was a saloon on every corner; during the last third of the century the number of saloons in the country tripled. Saloons were strictly male working-class institutions, usually decorated with pictures and other mementos of sports heroes, the bar perhaps under the charge of a retired pugilist.

For workingmen the saloon was a kind of club, a place to meet friends, exchange news and gossip, gamble, and eat, as well as to drink beer and whiskey. Saloons also flourished because factory owners and other employers of large numbers of workers tended to forbid the consumption of alcohol on their premises. In addition, the gradual reduction of the workday left men with more free time, which may explain why vaudeville and burlesques, the latter described by one straightlaced critic as a "disgraceful spectacle of padded legs juggling and tight-laced wriggling," also proliferated.

Calvinist-inspired opposition to sports as a frivolous waste of valuable time was steadily evaporating, replaced among the upper and middle classes by the realization that games like golf and tennis were "healthy occupation[s] for mind and body." Bicycling became a fad, both as a means of getting from place to place in the ever-expanding cities and as a form of exercise and recreation.

The postwar era also saw the first important development of spectator sports, again because cities provided the concentrations of population necessary to support them. Curious relationships developed between upper- and working-class interests and between competitive sports as pure enjoyment for players and spectators and sports as something to bet on. Horse racing had strictly upper-class origins, but racetracks attracted huge crowds of ordinary people more intent on picking a winner than on improving the breed.

Professional boxing offers an even better example. It was in a sense a hobby of the rich, who sponsored favorite gladiators, offered prizes, and often wagered large

Luna Park at Coney Island was a vast living theater, in which the strollers were both spectators and actors. At night, a quarter million electric lights turned Luna Park into what its designer, Frederic Thompson, called "a different world—a dream world, perhaps a nightmare world—where all is bizarre and fantastic."

sums on the matches. But the audiences were made up overwhelmingly of young working-class males, from whose ranks most of the fighters emerged. The gambling and also the brutality of the bloody, bare-knuckle character of the fights caused many communities to outlaw boxing, a fact that added to the appeal of the sport for some.

The first widely popular pugilist was the legendary "Boston Strong Boy," John L. Sullivan, who became heavyweight champion in 1882 by disposing of one Paddy Ryan in nine rounds. Sullivan was an immensely powerful man whose idea of fighting, according to his biographer, "was simply to hammer his opponent into unconsciousness," something he did repeatedly during his ten-year reign. Sullivan became an international celebrity and made and lost large sums during this period. He was also the beneficiary of patronage in such forms as a diamond belt worth $10,000 presented to him by some of his admirers. Yet boxing remained a raffish, clandestine occupation. One of Sullivan's important fights took place in France, on the estate of Baron Rothchild, yet when it ended both he and his opponent were arrested.

Three major team games—baseball, football, and basketball—developed in something approaching their modern form during the last quarter of the century. Various forms of what became baseball were played long before that time. Organized teams, in most cases made up of upper-class amateurs, first emerged in the 1840s, but the game only became truly popular during the Civil War, when it was a major form of camp recreation for the troops.

After the war professional teams began to appear (the first, the Cincinnati Red Stockings, paid players between $800 and $1400 for the season), and in 1876 teams in eight cities formed the National League. The American League

Thomas Eakins's Baseball Players Practicing, *painted in 1875, one year before the organization of the National League. The relative similarity of the batter's stance to that favored today suggests the timelessness of this national pastime.*

followed in 1901. After a brief period of rivalry, the two leagues made peace in 1903, the year of the first World Series.

Organized play led to codification of the rules and improvements in technique and strategy, for example, the development of "minor" leagues; impartial umpires calling balls and strikes and ruling on close plays; the use of catcher's masks and padded gloves; the invention of various kinds of curves and other erratic pitches (often enhanced by "doctoring" the ball). As early as the 1870s, baseball was being called "the national game" and losing all upper-class connotations. Important games attracted crowds in the tens of thousands; betting became a problem. Despite its urban origins, its broad green fields and dusty base paths gave the game a rural character that only recently has begun to fade away.

Nobody "invented" baseball, but both football and basketball owe their present form to individuals. James Naismith's invention of basketball is undisputed. In 1891, while a student at a YMCA school, he attached peach baskets to the edge of an elevated running track in the gymnasium and drew up what are still the basic rules of the game. The first basketball was a soccer ball. The game was popular from the start, but because it was played indoors it was not an important spectator sport until much later.

Football was not created by one person in the way that basketball was; it evolved out of English rugby. For many decades it remained almost entirely a college sport (and thus played almost entirely by upper- and middle-class types). Organized collegiate sports dated back to before the Civil War; the first intercollegiate matches were rowing races between Harvard and Yale students. The first intercollege football game occurred when Princeton defeated Rutgers in 1869, and by the 1880s college football had become extremely popular.

Much of the game's modern character, however, was the work of Walter Camp, the athletic director and football coach of Yale. Camp cut the size of teams from 15 to 11, and he invented the scrimmage line, the four-down system, and the key position of quarterback. He publicized the game in a series of books, ranging from *How to Coach a Team* (1886) to *Jack Hall at Yale* (1909). Camp's prestige was such that when he named his first All-American team after the 1889 season, no one challenged his judgment. Well into the twentieth century, the players that Camp selected were *the* All-Americans.

Camp claimed that amateur sports like football taught the value of hard work, cooperation, and fair play. His practice was more questionable. He is known to have recruited players who could not meet Yale's academic standards and to have found means of putting money in his players' pockets. At Yale and elsewhere all the problems that emphasis on athletic achievement poses for modern institutions of higher education existed in microcosm well before 1900.

Spectator sports had little appeal to women at this time and indeed for decades thereafter. And few women participated in organized athletics. Sports were "manly" activities; a woman might ride a bicycle, play croquet and perhaps a little tennis, but to display any concentrated interest in excelling in a sport was considered unfeminine.

CHRISTIANITY'S CONSCIENCE AND THE SOCIAL GOSPEL

The modernization of the great cities was not solving most of the social problems of the slums. As this fact became clear, a number of urban religious leaders began to take a hard look at the situation.

An increasing proportion of the residents of the blighted districts were Catholics, and the Roman church devoted much effort to distributing alms, maintaining homes for orphans and old people, and other forms of social welfare. But church leaders seemed unconcerned with the social causes of the blight; they were deeply committed to the idea that sin and vice were personal, poverty an act of God. They deplored the rising tide of crime, disease, and destitution among their coreligionists, yet they failed to see the connection between these evils and the squalor of the slums. "Intemperance is the great evil we have to overcome," wrote the president of the leading Catholic charitable organization, the Society of St. Vincent de Paul. "It is the source of the misery for at least three-fourths of the families we are called upon to visit and relieve."

Like conservative Protestant clergymen, the Catholic hierarchy tended to be at best neutral toward organized labor. Cardinal James Gibbons spoke favorably of the Knights of Labor in 1886 after the Haymarket bombing, but he took a dim view of strikes. Concrete action by American Catholics, however, was slow in coming, probably because of the conservatism of the clergy and the parochial concerns of lay leaders.

The conservatism of most Protestant and Catholic clergymen did not prevent some earnest preachers from working directly to improve the lot of the city poor. Some followed the path blazed by Dwight L. Moody, a lay evangelist who became famous throughout America and Great Britain in the 1870s. A gargantuan figure weighing nearly 300 pounds, Moody conducted a vigorous campaign to persuade the denizens of the slums to cast aside their sinful ways. He went among them full of enthusiasm and God's love and made an impact no less powerful than that of George Whitefield during the Great Awakening of the eighteenth century or Charles Grandison Finney in the first part of the nineteenth. The evangelists founded mission schools in the slums and tried to provide spiritual and recreational facilities for the unfortunate. They were prominent in the establishment of American branches of the YMCA (1851) and the Salvation Army (1880).

However, the evangelists paid little heed to the causes of urban poverty and vice, believing that faith in God would enable the poor to transcend the material difficulties of life. For a number of Protestant clergymen who had become familiar with the slums, a different approach seemed called for. Slum conditions caused the sins and crimes of the cities; the wretched human beings who committed them could not be blamed, these ministers argued. They began to preach a "Social Gospel" that focused on improving living conditions rather than on saving souls. If people were to lead pure lives, they must have enough to eat, decent homes, and opportunities to develop their talents. Social Gospelers advocated civil service reform, child labor legislation, regulation of big corporations, and heavy taxes on incomes and inheritances.

The most influential preacher of the Social Gospel was probably Washington Gladden. At first, Gladden, who was raised on a Massachusetts farm, had opposed all government interference in social and economic affairs, but his experiences as a minister in Springfield, Massachusetts, and Columbus, Ohio, exposed him to the realities of life in industrial cities, and his views changed. In *Applied Christianity* (1886) and in other works he defended labor's right to organize and strike and denounced the idea that supply and demand should control wage rates. He favored factory inspection laws, strict regulation of public utilities, and other reforms.

Gladden never questioned the basic values of capitalism. But by the 1890s a number of ministers had gone all the way to socialism. The Reverend William D. P. Bliss of Boston, for example, believed in the kind of welfare state envisioned by Edward Bellamy in *Looking Backward*. He founded the Society of Christian Socialists (1889) and edited a radical journal, *The Dawn*. In addition to nationalizing industry, Bliss and other Christian Socialists advocated government unemployment relief programs, public housing and slum clearance projects, and other measures designed to aid the city poor.

THE SETTLEMENT HOUSES

A number of earnest souls began to grapple with slum problems by organizing what were known as settlement houses. These were community centers located in poor districts that provided guidance and services to all who would use them. The settlement workers, most of them idealistic, well-to-do young people, lived in the houses and were active in neighborhood affairs.

The prototype of the settlement house was London's Toynbee Hall, founded in the early 1880s; the first American example was the Neighborhood Guild, opened on the Lower East Side of New York in 1886 by Dr. Stanton Coit. By the turn of the century 100 had been established, the most famous being Jane Addams's Hull House in Chicago (1889), Robert A. Woods's South End House in Boston (1892), and Lillian Wald's Henry Street Settlement in New York (1893).

While some men were active in the movement, the most important settlement house workers were women fresh from college—the first generation of young women to experience the trauma of having developed their capacities only to find that society offered them few opportunities to use them. The settlements provided an outlet for their hopes and energies, and they seized upon the work avidly. An English social reformer who visited Hull House around the turn of the century described the residents as "strong-minded energetic women, bustling about their various enterprises" and "earnest-faced self-subordinating and mild-mannered men who slide from room to room apologetically."

The settlement workers tried to interpret American ways to the new immigrants and to create a community spirit in order to teach, in the words of one of them, "right living through social relations." Unlike most charity workers, who acted out of a sense of upper-class responsibility toward the unfortunate, they expected to benefit morally and intellectually themselves by experiencing a way of life far different from their own and by obtaining "the first-hand knowledge the college classroom cannot give." Lillian Wald, a nurse by training, explained the concept succinctly in *The House on Henry Street* (1915): "We were to live in the neighborhood . . . identify ourselves with it socially, and, in brief, contribute to it our citizenship."

Lillian Wald and other settlement workers soon discovered that practical problems absorbed most of their energies. They agitated for tenement house laws, the regulation of the labor of women and children, and better schools. They employed private resources to establish playgrounds in the slums, along with libraries, classes in everything from child nutrition and home management to literature and arts and crafts, social clubs, and day-care centers. When they observed that many poor families were so occupied with the struggle to survive that they were neglecting or even abandoning their children, they tried to place the children in foster homes in the country.

In Boston Robert A. Woods organized clubs to get the youngsters of the South End off the streets, helped establish a restaurant where a meal could be had for 5 cents, acted as an arbitrator in labor disputes, and lobbied for laws tightening up the franchises of public utility companies. In Chicago Jane Addams developed an outstanding cultural program that included classes in music and art and an excellent "little theater" group. Hull House soon boasted a gymnasium, a day nursery, and several social clubs. Addams also worked tirelessly and effectively for improved public services and for social legislation of all kinds. She even got herself appointed garbage inspector in her ward and hounded local landlords and the garbage contractor until something approaching decent service was established.

This portrait of Jane Addams was completed in 1896 by Alice Kellog Tyler, who worked as an artist at Hull House.

With all their accomplishments, the settlement houses seemed to be fighting a losing battle. "Private beneficence," Jane Addams wrote of Hull House, "is totally inadequate to deal with the vast numbers of the city's disinherited." As a tropical forest grows faster than a handful of men armed with machetes can cut it down, so the slums, fed by an annual influx of hundreds of thousands, blighted new areas more rapidly than the intrepid settlement house workers could clean up old ones. It became increasingly apparent that the wealth and authority of the state must be brought to bear in order to keep abreast of the problem.

CIVILIZATION AND ITS DISCONTENTS

As the nineteenth century died, the majority of the American people, especially those comfortably well-off, the residents of small towns, the shopkeepers, and some farmers and skilled workers, remained confirmed optimists and uncritical admirers of their civilization. However, blacks, immigrants, and others who failed to share equitably in the good things of life, along with a growing number of humanitarian reformers, found little to cheer about and much to lament in their increasingly industrialized society. Giant monopolies flourished despite federal restrictions. The gap between rich and poor appeared to be widening, while the slum spread its poison and the materially successful made a god of their success. Human values seemed in grave danger of being crushed by impersonal forces typified by the great corporations.

In 1871 Walt Whitman, usually so full of extravagant praise for everything American, had called his fellow countrymen the "most materialistic and money-making people ever known":

> *I say we had best look our times and lands searchingly in the face, like a physician diagnosing some deep disease. Never was there, perhaps, more hollowness of heart than at present, and here in the United States.*

By the late 1880s a well-known journalist could write to a friend: "The wheel of progress is to be run over the whole human race and smash us all." Others noted an alarming jump in the national divorce rate and an increasing taste for all kinds of luxury. "People are made slaves by a desperate struggle to keep up appearances," a Massachusetts commentator declared, and the economist David A. Wells expressed concern over statistics showing that heart disease and mental illness were on the rise. These "diseases of civilization," Wells explained, were "one result of the continuous mental and nervous activity which modern high-tension methods of business have necessitated."

Wells was a prominent liberal, but pessimism was no monopoly of liberals. A little later, Senator Henry Cabot Lodge of Massachusetts, himself a millionaire, complained of the "lawlessness" of "the modern and recent plutocrat" and his "disregard of the rights of others." Lodge spoke of "the enormous contrast between the sanguine mental attitude prevalent in my youth and that, perhaps wiser, but certainly darker view, so general today." His one-time Harvard professor, Henry Adams, was still more critical of the way his contemporaries had become money-grubbers. "All one's friends," he complained, along with church and university leaders and other educated people, "had joined the banks to force submission to capitalism."

Of course intellectuals often tend to be critical of the world they live in, whatever its nature; Thoreau denounced materialism and the worship of progress in the 1840s as vigorously as any late-nineteenth-century prophet of gloom. But the voices of the dissatisfied were rising. Despite the many benefits that industrialization had made possible, it was by no means clear around 1900 that the American people were really better off under the new dispensation.

MILESTONES

1858	English liner *Great Eastern* launched
1876	National Baseball League founded
1880	Salvation Army founded
1880s	"New" immigration begins
1882	John L. Sullivan wins heavyweight boxing championship
	Chinese Exclusion Act
1883	Brooklyn Bridge completed
1885	Foran Contract Labor Act
1887	American Protective Association founded
1888	First urban electric streetcar system
1889	Jane Addams founds Hull House
	Walter Camp's first All-American football team
1890	Jacob Riis, *How the Other Half Lives*
	Calvin Woodward opens his Manual Training School

20

INTELLECTUAL
AND CULTURAL TRENDS

Industrialization altered the way Americans thought at the same time that it transformed their ways of making a living. Technological advances revolutionized the communication of ideas more drastically than they did the transportation of goods or the manufacture of steel. The materialism that permeated American attitudes toward business also affected contemporary education and literature, while Charles Darwin's theory of evolution influenced American philosophers, lawyers, and historians profoundly.

New ideas about how children should be educated and what they should be taught emerged along with new methods of communicating information to adults. As society became more complex, the need for specialized training increased, with the result that higher education became more important. Americans began to make significant contributions both in the "hard" sciences, such as chemistry and physics, and in the relatively new "soft" social sciences, such as psychology, political science, and sociology. A new literary flowering comparable to the "renaissance" of the 1840s and 1850s occurred in the 1870s and 1880s. By the end of the century America had finally emerged intellectually from the shadow of Europe.

THE KNOWLEDGE REVOLUTION

Improvements in public education and the needs of an increasingly complex society for every type of intellectual skill caused a veritable revolution in how knowledge was discovered, disseminated, and put to use. Observing the effects of formal education on their children, many older people were eager to experience some of its benefits. Nothing so well illustrates the desire for new information as the rise of the Chautauqua movement, founded by John H. Vincent, a Methodist minister, and Lewis Miller, an Ohio manufacturer of farm machinery. Vincent had charge of Sunday schools for the Methodist church. In 1874 he and Miller organized a two-week summer course for Sunday school teachers on the shores of Lake Chautauqua in New York. Besides instruction, they offered good meals, evening songfests around the campfire, and a relaxing atmosphere—all for $6 for the two weeks.

The 40 young teachers who attended were delighted with the program, and soon the leafy shore of Lake Chautauqua became a city of tents each summer as thousands poured into the region from all over the country. The founders expanded their offerings to include instruction in literature, science, government, and economics. Famous authorities, including, over the years, six presidents of the United States, came to lecture to open-air audiences on every subject imaginable. Eventually Chautauqua supplied speakers to reading circles throughout the country; it even offered correspondence courses leading over a four-year period to a diploma, the program designed, in Vincent's words, to give "the college outlook" to persons who had not had the opportunity to obtain a higher education.

Such success provoked imitation, and by 1900 there were about 200 Chautauqua-type organizations. Intellectual standards in these programs varied greatly; in general they were very low. Entertainment was as important an objective as enlightenment. Musicians (good and bad), homespun humorists, inspirational lecturers, and assorted quacks shared the platform with prominent divines and scholars. Moneymaking undoubtedly motivated many of the entrepreneurs who operated the centers, all of which, including the original Chautauqua, reflected the prevailing tastes of the American people—diverse, enthusiastic, uncritical, and shallow. Nevertheless the movement provided opportunities for thousands seeking stimulation and intellectual improvement.

Still larger numbers profited from the proliferation of public libraries. By the end of the century nearly all the states supported libraries. Private donors, led by the ironmaster Andrew Carnegie, contributed millions to the cause. In 1900 over 1700 libraries in the United States had collections of more than 5000 volumes.

Newspapers were an even more important means of disseminating information and educating the masses. Here new technology supplied the major incentive for change. The development by Richard Hoe and Stephen Tucker of the web press (1871), which printed simultaneously on both sides of paper fed into it from large rolls, and Ottmar Mergenthaler's linotype machine (1886), which cast rows of type as needed directly from molten metal, cut printing costs dramatically. Machines for making paper out of wood pulp reduced the cost of newsprint to a quarter of what it had been in the 1860s. By 1895 machines were printing, cutting, and folding 32-page newspapers at a rate of 24,000 an hour.

The telegraph and transoceanic cables wrought a similar transformation in the gathering of news. Press associations, led by the New York Associated Press, flourished; the syndicated article appeared; and a few publishers—Edward W. Scripps was the first—began to acquire chains of newspapers.

Population growth and better education created an ever-larger demand for printed matter. At the same time, the integration of the economy enabled manufacturers to sell their goods all over the country. Advertising became important, and sellers soon learned that newspapers and magazines were excellent means of placing their products before millions of eyes. Advertising revenues soared just when new machines and general expansion were making publishing an expensive business. The day of the journeyman printer-editor ended. Rich men such as the railroad magnate Jay Gould and the mining tycoon George Hearst invested heavily in newspapers in the postwar decades.

Publishers tended to be conservative, but reaching the masses meant lowering intellectual and cultural standards, appealing to emotions, and adopting popular, sometimes radical, causes. Cheap, mass-circulation papers had first appeared in the 1830s and 1840s, the most successful being the *Sun,* the *Herald,* and the *Tribune* in New York, the *Philadelphia Public Ledger,* and the *Baltimore Sun.* None of them much exceeded a circulation of 50,000 before the Civil War. The first publisher to reach a truly massive audience was Joseph Pulitzer, a Hungarian-born immigrant who made a first-rate paper of the *St. Louis Post-Dispatch.* In 1883 Pulitzer bought the *New York World,* a sheet with a circulation of perhaps 20,000. Within a year he was selling 100,000 copies daily, and by the late 1890s the *World's* circulation regularly exceeded 1 million.

John Singer Sargent's 1905 portrait of Joseph Pulitzer. On his death six years later, Pulitzer's will provided for the endowment of the Columbia School of Journalism and the establishment of Pulitzer Prizes for journalism, letters, and other categories.

Pulitzer achieved this brilliant success by casting a wide net. To the masses he offered bold, black headlines devoted to crime (ANOTHER MURDERER TO HANG), scandal (VICE ADMIRAL'S SON IN JAIL), catastrophe (TWENTY-FOUR MINERS KILLED), society and the theater (LILY LANGTRY'S NEW ADMIRER), together with feature stories, political cartoons, sports pages, comics, and pictures. For the educated and affluent he provided better political and financial coverage than the most respectable New York journals. Pulitzer made the *World* a crusader for civic improvement by attacking political corruption, monopoly, and slum problems. His energetic reporters literally made news, masquerading as criminals and poor workers in order to write graphic accounts of conditions in New York's jails and sweatshops.

"The *World* is the people's newspaper," Pulitzer boasted, and in the sense that it interested men and women of every sort, he was correct. Pulitzer's methods were quickly copied by competitors, especially William Randolph Hearst, who purchased the *New York Journal* in 1895 and soon outdid the *World* in sensationalism. But no other newspaperman of the era approached Pulitzer in originality, boldness, and the knack of reaching the masses without abandoning seriousness of purpose and basic integrity.

Growth and ferment also characterized the magazine world. In 1865 there were about 700 magazines in the country, by the turn of the century more than 5000. Until the mid-1880s, few of the new magazines were in any way unusual. A handful of serious periodicals, such as the *Atlantic Monthly, Harper's,* and *The Century,* dominated the field.

After about 1885 vast changes began to take place. New magazines such as *Forum* (1886) and *Arena* (1889) emphasized hard-hitting articles on controversial subjects by leading experts. The weekly *Literary Digest* (1890) offered summaries of press opinion on current events, and the *Review of Reviews* (1891) provided monthly commentary on the news.

Even more startling changes revolutionized the mass-circulation field. In 1889 Edward W. Bok became editor of the *Ladies' Home Journal.* Besides advice columns ("Ruth Ashmore's Side Talks with Girls"), he offered articles on child care, gardening, and interior decorating, published fine contemporary novelists, and commissioned public figures, such as Presidents Grover Cleveland and Benjamin Harrison, to discuss important questions. He printed colored reproductions of art masterpieces—the invention of cheap photoengraving was of enormous significance in the success of mass-circulation magazines—and crusaded for women's suffrage, conservation, and other reforms.

Bok and his many competitors reached millions of readers. Like Pulitzer in the newspaper field, they found ways of interesting rich and poor, the cultivated and the ignorant. Utilizing the new printing technology to cut costs and drawing heavily on advertising revenues, they sold their magazines for 10 or 15 cents a copy and still made fortunes.

COLLEGES AND UNIVERSITIES

The same forces that were affecting the dissemination of information were also altering higher education and professional training. The number of colleges rose from about 350 to 500 between 1878 and 1898, and the student body roughly tripled. Despite this growth, less than 2 percent of the college-age population attended college, but the aspirations of the nation's youth were rising, and more and more parents had the financial means necessary for fulfilling them.

More significant than the expansion of the colleges were the alterations in their curricula and in the atmosphere permeating the average campus. In 1870 most colleges remained what they had been in the 1830s: small, limited in their offerings, intellectually stagnant. The ill-paid professors were seldom scholars of stature. Thereafter, change came like a flood tide. State universities proliferated; the federal government's land-grant program in support of training in "agriculture and the mechanic arts," established under the Morrill Act of 1862, came into its own; wealthy philanthropists poured fortunes into old institutions and

The earliest colleges were "vocational," their chief purpose being to furnish clergy for the colonists. The colonists, most of whom were farmers, would have been astonished by Cornell University's School of Agriculture, whose purpose was to teach the vocation of farming. At the left of the picture are some of the school's experimental gardens.

founded new ones; educators introduced new courses and adopted new teaching methods; professional schools of law, medicine, education, business, journalism, and other specialties increased in number.

In the forefront of reform was Harvard, the oldest and most prestigious college in the country. In the 1860s it possessed an excellent faculty, but teaching methods were antiquated and the curriculum had remained almost unchanged since the colonial period. In 1869, however, a dynamic president, the chemist Charles W. Eliot, undertook a transformation of the college. Eliot introduced the elective system, gradually eliminating required courses and expanding offerings in such areas as modern languages, economics, and the laboratory sciences. For the first time, students were allowed to borrow books from the library!

Under Eliot's guidance the standards of the medical school were raised. In the law school, Christopher Columbus Langdell introduced the case method of study. In some respects Eliot went too far—the elective system encouraged superficiality and laxness in many students—but on balance he transformed Harvard from a college, "a place to which a young man is sent," to a university, a place "to which he goes."

An even more important development in higher education was the founding of Johns Hopkins in 1876. This university was one of many established in the period by wealthy industrialists; its benefactor, the Baltimore merchant Johns Hopkins, had made his fortune in the Baltimore and Ohio Railroad. Its distinctiveness, however, was due to the vision of Daniel Coit Gilman, its first president.

Gilman modeled Johns Hopkins on the German universities, where meticulous research and freedom of inquiry were the guiding principles. In staffing the institution, he sought scholars of the highest reputation, scouring Europe as well as America in his search for talent and offering outstanding men high salaries for that time—up to $5000 for a professor, roughly ten times the income of a skilled artisan.

The success of Johns Hopkins did not stop the migration of American scholars to Europe; more than 2000 matriculated at German universities during the 1880s. But as Hopkins graduates took up professorships at other institutions and as scholars trained elsewhere adopted the Hopkins methods, true graduate education became possible in most sections of the country.

The example of Johns Hopkins encouraged other wealthy individuals to endow universities offering advanced work. Clark University in Worcester, Massachusetts, founded by Jonas Clark, a merchant and real estate speculator, opened its doors in 1889. Its president, G. Stanley Hall, had been a professor of psychology at Hopkins, and he built the new university in that institution's image. More important was John D. Rockefeller's creation, the University of Chicago (1892). The president of the University of Chicago, William Rainey Harper, was a brilliant biblical scholar—he received his Ph.D. from Yale at the age of 18—and an imaginative administrator. The new university, he told Rockefeller, should be designed "with the example of Johns Hopkins before our eyes."

Like Daniel Coit Gilman, Harper sought topflight scholars for his faculty. He offered such high salaries that he was besieged with over 1000 applications. Armed with Rockefeller dollars, he "raided" the best institutions in the nation. He decimated the faculty of the new Clark University—"an act of wreckage," the indignant President Hall complained, "comparable to anything that the worst trust ever attempted against its competitors." Chicago offered first-class graduate and undergraduate education. During its first year there were 120 instructors for fewer than 600 students, and despite fears that Rockefeller would enforce his social and economic views on the institution, academic freedom was the rule.

State and federal aid to higher education expanded rapidly. The Morrill Act, granting land to each state at a rate of 30,000 acres for each senator and representative, provided the endowments that gave many important modern universities, such as Illinois, Michigan State, and Ohio State, their start. While the federal assistance was earmarked for specific subjects, the land-grant colleges offered a full range of courses, and all received additional state funds. The land-grant universities adopted new ideas quickly. They were coeducational from the start, and most developed professional schools and experimented with extension work and summer programs.

Typical of the better state institutions was the University of Michigan, which reached top rank among the nation's universities during the presidency of James B. Angell (1871–1909). Like Eliot at Harvard, Angell expanded the undergraduate curriculum and strengthened the law and medical schools. He encouraged graduate studies, seeking to make Michigan "part of the great world of scholars," and sought ways in which the university could serve the general community.

Important advances were made in women's higher education. Beginning with Vassar College, which opened its doors to 300 women students in 1865, the opportunity for young women to pursue serious academic work gradually expanded. Wellesley and Smith, both founded in 1875, completed the so-called Big Three women's colleges. Together with the already established Mount Holyoke, and with Bryn Mawr (1885), Barnard (1889), and Radcliffe (1893), they became known as the Seven Sisters.

The only professional careers easily available to women were nursing, teaching, and the new area called social work. Nevertheless, the remarkable women that these institutions trained were conscious of their uniqueness and determined to demonstrate their capabilities. They provided most of the leaders of the early twentieth-century drive for equal rights for women.

Advances in women's higher education opened up new fields of study for women. Here, a group of Smith College students with picks and hammers in hand, set out for a geology field trip in the 1880s.

Not all the changes in higher education were beneficial. The elective system led to superficiality; students gained a smattering of knowledge of many subjects and mastered none. For example, 55 percent of the Harvard class of 1898 took elementary courses and no others during their four years of study. Intensive graduate work often produced narrowness of outlook and research monographs on trivial subjects. Attempts to apply the scientific method in fields such as history and economics often enticed students into making smug (and preposterous) claims to objectivity and definitiveness.

The gifts of rich industrialists sometimes came with strings, and college boards of trustees tended to be dominated by businessmen who sometimes attempted to impose their own social and economic beliefs on faculty members. Although few professors lost their positions because their views offended trustees, at many institutions trustees exerted constant nagging pressures that limited academic freedom and scholarly objectivity. At state colleges, politicians often interfered in academic affairs, even treating professorships as part of the patronage system.

Thorstein Veblen pointed out in his caustic study of *The Higher Learning in America* (1918) that "the intrusion of businesslike ideals, aims and methods" harmed the universities in countless subtle ways. Size alone—the verbose Veblen called it "an executive weakness for spectacular magnitude"—became an end in itself, and the practical values of education were exalted over the humanistic. When universities grew bigger, administration became more complicated and the prestige of administrators rose inordinately. At many institutions professors came to be regarded as mere employees of the governing boards. In 1893 faculty members of Stanford University were officially classified as personal servants of Mrs. Leland Stanford, widow of the founder. This was done in good cause—the Stanford estate was tied up in probate court and the ruling made it possible to pay professors out of Mrs. Stanford's allowance for household expenses—but that such a procedure was even conceivable must have appalled the scholarly world.

As the number of college graduates increased, and as colleges ceased being primarily training institutions for clergymen, the influence of alumni on educational policies began to make itself felt, not always happily. Campus social activities became more important. Fraternities proliferated. Interest in organized sports first appeared as an outgrowth of the expansion of the curriculum, but soon athletic contests were playing a role all out of proportion to their significance. After football evolved as the leading intercollegiate sport (over 50,000 attended the Yale–Princeton game in 1893), it became a source of revenue that many colleges dared not neglect. Since students, alumni, and the public demanded winning teams, college administrators stooped to subsidizing student athletes, in extreme cases employing players who were not students at all. One college president quipped that the B.A. degree was coming to mean Bachelor of Athletics.

Thus higher education reflected American values, with all their strengths and weaknesses. A complex society required a more professional and specialized education for its youth; the coarseness and the rampant materialism and competitiveness of the era inevitably found expression in the colleges and universities.

REVOLUTION IN THE SOCIAL SCIENCES

In the social sciences a close connection existed between the practical issues of the age and the achievements of the leading thinkers. The application of the theory of evolution to every aspect of human relations, the impact of industrialization on society—such topics were of intense concern to American economists, sociologists, and historians. An understanding of Darwin increased the already strong interest in studying the development of institutions and their interactions with one another. Controversies over trusts, slum conditions, and other problems drew scholars out of their towers and into practical affairs.

Among the economists something approaching a revolution took place in the 1880s. The classical school, which maintained that immutable natural laws governed all human behavior and which used the insights of Darwin only to justify unrestrained competition and laissez-faire, was challenged by a group of young economists who argued that as times changed, economic theories and laws must be modified in order to remain relevant. Richard T. Ely, another of the scholars who made Johns Hopkins a font of new ideas in the 1880s, summarized the thinking of this group in 1885. "The state [is] an educational and ethical agency whose positive aid is an indispensable condition of human progress," Ely proclaimed. Laissez-faire was outmoded and dangerous. Economic problems were basically moral problems; their solution required "the united efforts of Church, state and science." The proper way to study these problems was by analyzing actual conditions, not by applying abstract laws or principles.

This approach produced the so-called institutionalist school of economics, whose members made detailed, on-the-spot investigations of labor unions, sweatshops, factories, and mines. The study of institutions would lead both to theoretical insights and to practical social reform, they believed. John R. Commons, one of Ely's students at Johns Hopkins and later professor of economics at the University of Wisconsin, was the outstanding member of this school.

A similar revolution struck sociology in the mid-1880s. Prevailing opinion up to that time rejected the idea of government interference with the organization of society. The influence of the English social Darwinist, Herbert Spencer, who objected even to public schools and the postal system, was immense. Spencer and his American disciples, among them Edward L. Youmans, editor of *Popular Science Monthly,* twisted the ideas of Darwin to mean that society could be changed only by the force of evolution, which moved with cosmic slowness. "You and I can do nothing at all," Youmans told the reformer Henry George. "It's all a matter of evolution. Perhaps in four or five thousand years evolution may have carried men beyond this state of things."

Similar currents of thought influenced other social sciences. In *Systems of Consanguinity* (1871), the pioneer anthropologist Lewis Henry Morgan developed a theory of social evolution and showed how kinship relationships reflected and affected tribal institutions. The new political scientists were also evolutionists and institutionalists. The Founding Fathers, living in a world dominated by Newton's concept of the universe as an immense, orderly machine, had conceived of the political system as an impersonal set of institutions and principles— a government of laws rather than of men. Nineteenth-century thinkers (John C. Calhoun is the best example) concerned themselves with abstractions, such as states' rights, and ignored the extralegal aspects of politics, such as parties and pressure groups. In the 1880s political scientists began to employ a different approach. In his doctoral dissertation at Johns Hopkins, *Congressional Government* (1885), Woodrow Wilson analyzed the American political system. He concluded that the real locus of authority lay in the committees of Congress, which had no constitutional basis at all. Wilson was by no means a radical, but he viewed politics as a dynamic process and offered no theoretical objection to the expansion of state power. "Every means," he wrote in *The State* (1889), "by which society may be perfected through the instrumentality of government . . . ought certainly to be diligently sought."

PROGRESSIVE EDUCATION

Traditionally, American teachers had emphasized the three Rs and relied on strict discipline and rote learning. Typical of the pedagogues of the period was the Chicago teacher, described by a reformer in the 1890s, who told her students firmly: "Don't stop to think, tell me what you know!" Yet new ideas were attracting attention. According to a German educator, Johann Friedrich Herbart, teachers could best arouse the interest of their students by relating new information to what they already knew; good teaching called for professional training, psychological insight, enthusiasm, and imagination, not merely facts and a birch rod. At the same time, evolutionists were pressing for a kind of education that would help children to "survive" by adapting to the demands of their environment.

Forward-looking educators seized on these ideas because dynamic social changes were making the old system increasingly inadequate. Settlement house workers discovered that slum children needed training in handicrafts, good citizenship, and personal hygiene as much as in reading and writing. They were appalled by the local schools, which suffered from the same diseases—filth, overcrowding, rickety construction—that plagued the tenements, and by school systems that were controlled by machine politicians who doled out teaching positions to party hacks and other untrained persons.

The philosopher who summarized and gave direction to these forces was John Dewey, a professor at the University of Chicago. Dewey was concerned with the implications of evolution—indeed, of all science—for education. Essentially his approach was ethical. Was the nation's youth being properly prepared for the tasks it faced in the modern world? The school, Dewey insisted in *The School and Society,* should become an instrument for social reform, "saturating [the child] with the spirit of service" and helping to produce a "society which is worthy, lovely, and harmonious." Education, in other words, ought to build character and teach good citizenship as well as transmit knowledge.

Thomas Eakins's, The Gross Clinic *(1875). To better understand how to depict the body, Eakins resolved to study how it functioned. To that end, in 1873 he enrolled in anatomy classes at the Jefferson Medical College in Philadelphia. This painting is of Samuel Gross, lecturing while removing the dead bone from the thigh of a patient.*

Dewey immediately assumed leadership of what in the next generation was called progressive education. Although the gains made in public education before 1900 were more quantitative than qualitative and the philosophy dominant in most schools was not very different at the end of the century from that prevailing in Horace Mann's day, change was in the air. The best educators of the period were full of optimism, convinced that the future was theirs.

LAW AND HISTORY

Even jurisprudence, by its nature conservative and rooted in tradition, felt the pressure of evolutionary thought and the new emphasis on studying institutions as they actually are. In 1881 Oliver Wendell Holmes, Jr., published *The Common Law.* Holmes argued that "the felt necessities of the time" rather than precedent should determine the rules by which people are governed. "The life of the law has not been logic; it has been experience," he wrote. "It is revolting," he added on another occasion, "to have no better reason for a rule of law than that so it was laid down in the time of Henry IV."

Holmes went on to a long and brilliant judicial career, during which he repeatedly stressed the right of the people, through their elected representatives, to deal with contemporary problems in any reasonable way, unfettered by outmoded conceptions of the proper limits of government authority. Like the societies they regulated, laws should evolve as times and conditions changed, he said.

This way of reasoning caused no sudden reversal of judicial practice. Holmes's most notable opinions as a judge tended to be dissents. But his philosophy reflected the advanced thinking of the late nineteenth century, and his influence grew with every decade of the twentieth.

The new approach to knowledge did not always advance the cause of liberal reform. Historians in the graduate schools became intensely interested in studying the origins and evolution of political institutions. They concluded, after much "scientific" study of old charters and law codes, that the roots of democracy were to be found in the customs of the ancient tribes of northern Europe. This theory of the "Teutonic origins" of democracy, which has since been thoroughly discredited, fit well with the prejudices of people of British stock, and it provided ammunition for those who favored restricting immigration and for those who argued that blacks were inferior beings.

Out of this work, however, came an essentially democratic concept, the frontier thesis of Frederick Jackson Turner, who trained at Johns Hopkins University.

In 1893 Frederick Jackson Turner argued that the boundless expanses of the frontier gave rise to democracy, individualism, and "withal that buoyancy and exuberance which comes with freedom." This photograph of a family in Custer County, Nebraska (1887), shows the individualistic optimism of one frontier family: They have begun to build a house (center); yet their isolation suggests their vulnerability, as does the dugout (upper left) they occupy at present.

In his essay, "The Significance of the Frontier in American History" (1893), Turner argued that the frontier experience, through which every section of the country had passed, had affected people's thinking and the shape of American institutions. The isolation of the frontier and the need during each successive westward advance to create civilization anew, Turner wrote, account for the individualism of Americans and the democratic character of their society.

Turner, and still more his many disciples, made too much of his basic insights. Life on the frontier was not as democratic as Turner believed, and it certainly does not "explain" American development as completely as he said it did. Nevertheless, his work showed how important it was to investigate the evolution of institutions, and it encouraged historians to study social and economic, as well as purely political, subjects. If the claims of the new historians to objectivity and definitiveness were absurdly overstated, their emphasis on thoroughness, exactitude, and impartiality did much to raise standards in the profession. Perhaps the finest product of the new scientific school, a happy combination of meticulous scholarship and literary artistry, was Henry Adams's nine-volume *History of the United States During the Administrations of Jefferson and Madison*.

REALISM IN LITERATURE

When what Mark Twain called the Gilded Age began, American literature was dominated by the romantic mood. Most writers of fiction tended to ignore the eternal conflicts inherent in human nature and the social problems of the age; polite entertainment and pious moralizing appeared to be their only objectives.

The patent unreality, even dishonesty, of contemporary fiction eventually caused a reaction. The most important forces giving rise to the Age of Realism were those that were transforming every other aspect of American life: industrialism, with its associated complexities and social problems; the theory of evolution, which made people more aware of the force of the environment and the basic conflicts of existence; the new science, which taught dispassionate, empirical observation. Novelists undertook the examination of social problems such as slum life, the conflict between capital and labor, and political corruption. They created multidimensional characters, depicted persons of every social class, used dialect and slang to capture the flavor of particular types, and fashioned painstaking descriptions of the surroundings into which they placed their subjects. The romantic novel did not disappear. General Lew Wallace's *Ben Hur* (1880) and Frances Hodgson Burnett's *Little Lord Fauntleroy* (1886) were best-sellers. But by 1880 realism was the point of view of the finest literary talents in the country.

MARK TWAIN

While it was easy to romanticize the West, that region lent itself to the realistic approach. Almost of necessity, novelists writing about the West described coarse characters from the lower levels of society and dealt with crime and violence. It would have been difficult indeed to write a genteel romance about a mining camp. The outstanding figure of western literature, the first great American realist, was Mark Twain.

Twain, whose real name was Samuel L. Clemens, was born in 1835. He grew up in Hannibal, Missouri, on the banks of the Mississippi. After mastering the printer's trade and working as a riverboat pilot, he went west to Nevada in 1861. The wild, rough life of Virginia City fascinated him, but prospecting got him nowhere, and he became a reporter for the *Territorial Enterprise*. Soon he was publishing humorous stories about the local life under the nom de plume Mark Twain. In 1865, while working in California, he wrote "The Celebrated Jumping Frog of Calaveras County," a story that brought him national recognition. A tour

Mark Twain, in a photograph (left) *taken five years before his death in 1910, was both a satirist of American optimism in his writings and its victim in misguided business ventures that brought him to the brink of bankruptcy. He is caricatured* (right) *riding his "Celebrated Jumping Frog of Calaveras County" in this 1872 cartoon by English artist Frederick Waddy.*

of Europe and the Holy Land in 1867 to 1868 led to *The Innocents Abroad* (1869), which made him famous.

Twain's greatness stemmed from his keen reportorial eye and ear, his eagerness to live life to the full, his marvelous sense of humor, and his ability to be at once in society and outside it, to love humanity yet be repelled by human vanity and perversity. He epitomized the zest and adaptability of his age and also its materialism. No contemporary pursued the almighty dollar more assiduously. An inveterate speculator, he made a fortune with his pen and lost it in foolish business ventures. He wrote tirelessly and endlessly about America and Europe, his own times and the feudal past, about tourists, slaves, tycoons, cracker-barrel philosophers—and human destiny. He was equally at home and equally successful on the Great River of his childhood, in the mining camps, and in the eastern bourgeois society of his mature years. But every prize slipped through his fingers. Twain died a dark pessimist, surrounded by adulation yet alone, an alien and a stranger in the land he loved and knew so well.

Twain excelled every contemporary in the portrayal of character. In his biting satire *The Gilded Age* (1873) he created that magnificent mountebank Colonel Beriah Sellers, purveyor of eyewash ("the Infallible Imperial Oriental Optic Liniment") and false hopes, ridiculous, unscrupulous, but lovable. In *Huckleberry Finn* (1884), his masterpiece, his portrait of the slave Jim, loyal, patient, naive, yet withal a man, is unforgettable. When Huck takes advantage of Jim's credulity merely for his own amusement, the slave turns from him coldly and says: "Dat truck dah is trash; en trash is what people is dat puts dirt on de head er dey fren's en makes 'em ashamed." And there is Huck Finn himself, full of deviltry, romantic, amoral—up to a point—and at bottom the complete realist. When Miss Watson tells him he can get anything he wants by praying for it, he makes the effort, is disillusioned, and concludes: "If a body can get anything they pray for, why don't Deacon Winn get back the money he lost on pork? . . . Why can't Miss Watson fat up? No, I says to myself, there ain't nothing in it."

Whether directly, as in *The Innocents Abroad* and in his fascinating account of the world of the river pilot, *Life on the Mississippi* (1883), or when transformed by his imagination in works of fiction such as *Tom Sawyer* (1876) and *A Connecticut Yankee in King Arthur's Court* (1889), Mark Twain always put much of his own experience and feeling into his work. "The truth is," he wrote in 1886, "my books are mainly autobiographies." A story, he told a fellow author, "must be written with the blood out of a man's heart." His innermost confusions, the clash between his recognition of the pretentiousness and meanness of human beings and his wish to be accepted by society, added depths and overtones to his writing that together with his comic genius give it lasting appeal. He could not rise above the sentimentality and prudery of his generation entirely, for these qualities were part of his nature. He never dealt effectively with sexual love, for example, and often—even in *Huckleberry Finn*—contrived to end his tales on optimistic notes that ring false after so many pages portraying life as it is. On balance Twain's achievement was magnificent. Rough and uneven like the man himself, his works catch more of the spirit of the age he named than those of any other writer.

WILLIAM DEAN HOWELLS

Twain's realism was far less self-conscious than that of his longtime friend William Dean Howells. Like Twain, Howells, who was born in Ohio in 1837, had little formal education. He learned the printer's trade from his father and became a reporter for the *Ohio State Journal*. After the Civil War he worked briefly for *The Nation* in New York and then moved to Boston, where he became editor of the *Atlantic Monthly*. In 1886 he returned to New York as editor of *Harper's*.

A long series of novels and much literary criticism poured from Howells's pen over the next 30 years. While he insisted on treating his material honestly, he was not at first a critic of society, being content to write about what he called "the smiling aspects" of life. Realism to Howells meant concern for the complexities of individual personalities and faithful description of the genteel, middle-class world he knew best.

Besides a sharp eye and an open mind, Howells had a real social conscience. Gradually he became aware of the problems that industrialization had created. In 1885, in *The Rise of Silas Lapham,* he dealt with some of the ethical conflicts faced by businessmen in a competitive society. The harsh public reaction to the Haymarket bombing in 1886 stirred him, and he threw himself into a futile campaign to prevent the execution of the anarchist suspects. Thereafter he moved rapidly toward the left; soon he was calling himself a socialist. "After fifty years of optimistic content with 'civilization' . . . I now abhor it, and feel that it is coming out all wrong in the end, unless it bases itself anew on a real equality," he wrote. But he added immediately: "Meanwhile I wear a fur-lined overcoat, and live in all the luxury my money can buy." Howells was more than a reformer, more than an inventor of utopias like Edward Bellamy, though he admired Bellamy and wrote a utopian novel of his own, *A Traveller from Altruria* (1894). In *A Hazard of New Fortunes* (1890), he attempted to portray the whole range of metropolitan life, weaving the destinies of a dozen interesting personalities from diverse sections and social classes. The book represents a triumph of realism in its careful descriptions of various sections of New York and the ways of life of rich and poor, in the intricacy of its characters, and in its rejection of sentimentality and romantic love. "A man knows that he can love and wholly cease to love, not once merely, but several times," the narrator says, "but in regard to women he cherishes the superstition of the romances that love is once for all, and forever."

His own works were widely read, and Howells was also the most influential critic of his time. He helped bring the best contemporary foreign writers, including Tolstoy, Dostoevsky, Ibsen, and Zola, to the attention of readers in the United States, and he encouraged many important young American novelists, among them Stephen Crane, Theodore Dreiser, Frank Norris, and Hamlin Garland.

Some of these writers went far beyond Howells's realism to what they called naturalism. Many, like Twain and Howells, began as newspaper reporters. Working for a big-city daily in the 1890s was sure to teach anyone a great deal about the dark side of life. Naturalist writers believed that the human being was essentially an animal, a helpless creature whose fate was determined by environment. Their world was Darwin's world—mindless, without mercy or justice. They wrote chiefly about the most primitive emotions—lust, hate, greed. In *Maggie, A Girl of the Streets* (1893), Stephen Crane described the seduction, degradation, and eventual suicide of a young woman, all set against the background of a sordid slum; in *The Red Badge of Courage* (1895), he captured the pain and humor of war. In *McTeague* (1899), Frank Norris told the story of a brutal, dull-witted dentist who murdered his greed-crazed wife with his bare fists.

Such stuff was too strong for Howells, yet he recognized its importance and befriended the younger writers in many ways. He found a publisher for *Maggie* after it had been rejected several times, and he wrote appreciative reviews of the work of Garland and Norris. Even Theodore Dreiser, who scorned Howells's writings and considered him hopelessly middle class in point of view, appreciated his aid and praised his influence on American literature. Dreiser's first novel, *Sister Carrie* (1900), treated sex so forthrightly that it was withdrawn after publication.

HENRY JAMES

Henry James was very different in spirit and background from the tempestuous naturalists. Born to wealth, reared in a cosmopolitan atmosphere, twisted in some strange way while still a child and unable to achieve satisfactory relationships with women, James spent most of his mature life in Europe, writing novels, short stories, plays, and volumes of criticism. Although far removed from the world of practical affairs, he was preeminently a realist, determined, as he once said, "to leave a multitude of pictures of my time" for the future to contemplate. He admired the European realists and denounced the "floods of tepid soap and water which under the name of novels are being vomited forth" by the ro-

Henry James (left), *a novelist of exquisite perception, withdrew from America to Europe; his brother, William* (right), *shook off a bout of depression in his twenties, propounded pragmatism, a philosophy that eschewed abstraction, and criticized aesthetes such as his brother: "There is no more contemptible type of human character than that of the nerveless sentimentalist and dreamer, who spends his life in a weltering sea of sensibility and emotion, but who never does a manly concrete deed."*

mancers. "All life belongs to you," he told his fellow novelists. "There is no impression of life, no manner of seeing it and feeling it, to which the plan of the novelist may not offer a place."

Although he preferred living in the cultivated surroundings of London high society, James yearned for the recognition of his fellow Americans almost as avidly as Mark Twain. However, he was incapable of modifying his rarefied, overly subtle manner of writing. Most serious writers of the time admired his books, and he received many honors, but he never achieved widespread popularity. His major theme was the clash of American and European cultures, his primary interest the close-up examination of wealthy, sensitive, yet often corrupt persons in a cultivated but far from polite society.

James dealt with social issues such as feminism and the difficulties faced by artists in the modern world, but he subordinated them to his interest in his subjects as individuals. *The American* (1877) told the story of the love of a wealthy American in Paris for a French noblewoman who rejected him because her family disapproved of his commercial background. *The Portrait of a Lady* (1881) described the disillusionment of an intelligent woman married to a charming but morally bankrupt man and her eventual decision to remain with him nonetheless. *The Bostonians* (1886) was a complicated and psychologically sensitive study of the varieties of female behavior in a seemingly uniform social situation.

James's reputation, greater today than in his lifetime, rests more on his highly refined accounts of the interactions of individuals and their environment and his masterful commentaries on the novel as a literary form than on his ability as a storyteller. Few major writers have been more long-winded, more prone to circumlocution. Yet few have been so dedicated to their art, possessed of such psychological penetration, or so successful in producing a large body of important work.

THE PRAGMATIC APPROACH

It would have been remarkable indeed if the intellectual ferment of the late nineteenth century had not affected contemporary ideas about the meaning of life, the truth of revealed religion, moral values, and similar fundamental problems. In particular the theory of evolution, so important in altering contemporary views of science, history, and social relations, produced significant changes in American thinking about religious and philosophical questions.

Evolution posed an immediate challenge to religion: If Darwin was correct, the biblical account of the creation was obviously untrue and the idea that the human race had been formed in God's image was highly unlikely. A bitter controversy erupted, described by President Andrew D. White of Cornell in *The Warfare of Science with Theology in Christendom* (1896). While millions continued to believe in the literal truth of the Bible, among intellectuals, lay and clerical, victory went to the evolutionists because, in addition to the arguments of the geologists and the biologists, scholars were throwing light on the historical origins of the Bible, showing it to be of human rather than divine inspiration.

The effects of Darwinism on philosophy were less dramatic but in the end more significant. Fixed systems and eternal verities were difficult to justify in a world that was constantly evolving. By the early 1870s a few philosophers had begun to reason that ideas and theories mattered little except when applied to specifics. "Nothing justifies the development of abstract principles but their utility in enlarging our concrete knowledge of nature," wrote Chauncey Wright, secretary of the American

Academy of Arts and Sciences. In "How to Make Our Ideas Clear" (1878), Wright's friend Charles S. Peirce, an amazingly versatile and talented albeit obscure thinker, argued that concepts could be fairly understood only in terms of their practical effects. Once the mind accepted the truth of evolution, Peirce believed, logic required that it accept the impermanence even of scientific laws. There was, he wrote, "an element of indeterminacy, spontaneity, or absolute chance in nature."

This startling philosophy, which Peirce called pragmatism, was presented in more understandable language by William James, brother of the novelist. James was one of the most remarkable persons of his generation. Educated in London, Paris, Bonn, and Geneva—as well as at Harvard—he studied painting, participated in a zoological expedition to South America, earned a medical degree, and was professor at Harvard successively of comparative anatomy, psychology, and finally philosophy. His *Principles of Psychology* (1890) may be said to have established that discipline as a modern science. His *Varieties of Religious Experience* (1902), which treated the subject from both psychological and philosophical points of view, helped thousands of readers to reconcile their religious faith with their increasing knowledge of psychology and the physical universe.

Although he was less rigorous a logician than Peirce, James's wide range and his verve and imagination as a writer made him by far the most influential philosopher of his time. He rejected the deterministic interpretation of Darwinism and all other one-idea explanations of existence. Belief in free will was one of his axioms; environment might influence survival, but so did the *desire* to survive, which existed independent of surrounding circumstances. Even truth was relative; it did not exist in the abstract but *happened* under particular circumstances. What a person thought helped to make thought occur, or come true. The mind, James wrote in a typically vivid phrase, has "a vote" in determining truth. Religion was true, for example, because people were religious.

The pragmatic approach inspired much of the reform spirit of the late nineteenth century and even more of that of the early twentieth. James's hammer blows shattered the laissez-faire extremism of Herbert Spencer. In "Great Men and Their Environment" (1880) he argued that social changes were brought about by the actions of geniuses whom society had selected and raised to positions of power, rather than by the impersonal force of the environment. Such reasoning fitted the preconceptions of rugged individualists yet encouraged those dissatisfied with society to work for change. Educational reformers like John Dewey, the institutionalist school of economists, settlement house workers, and other reformers adopted pragmatism eagerly. James's philosophy did much to revive the buoyant optimism that had characterized the pre–Civil War reform movement.

(text continues on page 682)

Titanic

 James Cameron's *Titanic* was a blockbuster. He made audiences feel what it was like to be on the ship. When the deck tilted to the right, viewers leaned to the left; many gasped as the ship plunged into the icy depths. What sent a shiver down the spine was the knowledge that real people had experienced what was being depicted on the screen.

Cameron well understood the audience's craving to relive a true story. By showing footage of the actual HMS *Titanic* on the floor of the Atlantic, he reminded audiences that what they were seeing had actually happened. He spent scores of millions devising computer-enhanced techniques to ensure that his *Titanic* looked like the one that went down in the North Atlantic on the night of April 14–15, 1912.

But Cameron's *Titanic* was more than a disaster movie. It was also the story of two young people who fall in love. The romance begins when Jack (Leonardo DiCaprio), a struggling artist, spots Rose (Kate Winslet), a wealthy socialite, climbing over the railing and peering despondently into the water below. Obliged to marry a contemptuous (and contemptible) snob, she is miserable. Jack, from a lower deck, scrambles up and persuades her to forego the plunge.

As a reward for saving Rose, Jack is invited to dine with Rose's table. At the dinner, Rose appraises Jack more carefully—and is impressed. He looks good in a tuxedo, displays plenty of moxie, and possesses artistic talent ("Jack, you see things!"). She proposes that she pose for him in the nude. A few hours later they venture belowdecks and, in anticipation of the courtship rituals of future decades, locate an automobile, climb inside, and rip off each other's clothes. Soon the car is bouncing. The windows steam up, and a hand leaves an imprint, fingers outstretched in ecstasy.

Minutes later they are cooled off when the ship has its close encounter of the icy kind. Jack—young, vital, alive—perishes in the frigid waters; but he has imparted to Rose a gift of love, and thus of life. This tale of young lovers, held apart by society, is a nautical "Romeo and Juliet," a brief, pure instant of love, tragically ended by death.

If Cameron's *Titanic* is a love story for the ages, it was also frozen in a particular place and in a particular time. Much as Cameron spent millions to show the ship as it really was, he took similar pains to give a convincing rendering of New York society, especially its clothing, silverware, and social conventions.

Of the latter, the most significant for the story are the elaborate rituals of Victorian courtship. Rose seeks to break free from her impending marriage partly because she despises her fiancé, but also because marriage to him constitutes the final, irreversible step into the gilded cage of a society lady. Jack's presence at the dinner among the "best" of society underscores its shallow materialism and preoccupation with wealth, its disdain for those who lack both, its absurd rules of etiquette, and its repressive attitudes toward sexuality. Viewers of the movie, looking through Rose's eyes, may wonder how such rituals ever came to be.

Some had existed for centuries. The idealization of courtly love and pure womanhood was a commonplace of medieval literature; in the early nineteenth century novelist Jane Austen described the subtle interplay of money and romance in England. But the rituals of New York society in the Gilded Age were characterized by sumptuous and public displays of wealth—glittering balls, and conspicuous "Grand Tours" of Europe.

This new mode of courtship was largely the creation of Mrs. John Jacob Astor, wife of one of New York's wealthiest businessmen, and her friends following the Civil War. Industrialization and urbanization were generating new wealth and destroying the old at a dizzying pace. While prominent businessmen and investment bankers were devising institutions to impose order on this creative industrial chaos, their wives were regularizing its social elite. They decided who should be admitted to New York's "best" families—and who should not. They concluded that it was not enough to be rich; the elite of the nation must also adhere to high standards of etiquette and decorum.

*Leonardo DiCaprio and Kate Winslet
as lovers on the Titanic.*

*A young society couple courting
in New York, about 1914.*

By controlling entrance into society, women such as Mrs. Astor also determined the disposition, through marriage and inheritance, of the nation's largest fortunes. Society women possessed real power.

Although the system was created and supervised by mature women, it demanded the compliance of adolescent girls. The process began when a mother took her daughter on a round of visits to society women, to whom they would present their "calling cards." If mother and daughter were judged suitable, they would be invited in for tea; if the girl behaved with decorum (and if her father's assets proved sound), she would be invited to balls and other formal events. At or near her sixteenth birthday, her parents would hold a ball in her honor, usually at Delmonico's restaurant, marking her "debut" into society. She wore a white gown symbolizing her virginity. A male relative presented her formally to the prominent women. Now she could accept male suitors.

This highly stylized—almost tribal—ritual brought young women to the threshold of womanhood. Marriage awaited beyond the door. Many eagerly anticipated the acquisition of adult status and the social power it entailed. But others regarded this rite with terror. (Novelist Edith Wharton remembered her debut as a "long cold agony of shyness.") In the early twentieth century some young women began to rebel. Elsie Clews, daughter of a Wall Street banker, refused to wear corsets. When her mother wasn't looking, she took off her veil and white gloves. She subse-

quently scandalized Newport by going swimming with a young man without a chaperone (but not without a bathing suit). To her mother's dismay, Clews delayed marriage and went to Barnard College; eventually she became a respected anthropologist (Elsie Clews Parsons).

Kate Winslet's "Rose" was, like Elsie Clews, a prematurely "modern" woman. But Clews tore off only her veil and white gloves, not all her clothes; she dispensed with the rituals of courtship, not its substance. Even in the waning years of the Victorian era, few wealthy young women succumbed to impoverished men, however earnest and appealing.

Victorian courtship was necessarily protracted. Young women did not unburden themselves to strangers; and even to friends, especially of the opposite sex, the process of revealing one's inner feelings unfolded slowly, often after a series of tests and trials. One person's tentative disclosure invited a reciprocal response. Letters and diaries show that, over time, these personal revelations often led to sexual intimacies. Nowadays many people regard Victorian marriages as unfeeling and stiff; but many Victorians maintained that their personal intimacies were the more delicious for having been long delayed.

Cameron's *Titanic looked* like the past; but the heart of the movie is Jack and Rose's romance. While Rose's story addresses some of the anxieties of young society women, it more closely resembles the courtship patterns of Hollywood today than the experiences of young people at the beginning of the last century.

Yet pragmatism brought Americans face to face with somber problems. While relativism made them optimistic, it also bred insecurity, for there could be no certainty, no comforting reliance on any eternal value in the absence of absolute truth. Pragmatism also seemed to suggest that the end justified the means, that what worked was more important than what ought to be. At the time of James's death in 1910, the *Commercial and Financial Chronicle* pointed out that the pragmatic philosophy was helpful to businessmen in making decisions. By emphasizing practice at the expense of theory, the new philosophy encouraged materialism, anti-intellectualism, and other unlovely aspects of the American character. And what place had conventional morality in such a system? Perhaps pragmatism placed too much reliance on the free will of human beings, ignoring their capacity for selfishness and self-delusion.

The people of the new century found pragmatism a heady wine. They would quaff it freely and enthusiastically—down to the bitter dregs.

MILESTONES

1865	Vassar College founded
1869	Charles W. Eliot becomes president of Harvard
1874	Chautauqua movement begins
1876	Johns Hopkins University founded
1881	Oliver Wendell Holmes, Jr., *The Common Law*
1883	Joseph Pulitzer purchases the *New York World*
1886	Ottmar Mergenthaler invents the linotype machine
	William Dean Howells becomes editor of *Harper's*
1889	Edward W. Bok becomes editor of the *Ladies' Home Journal*
1890	William James, *Principles of Psychology*
1893	Frederick Jackson Turner, "Significance of the Frontier in American History"
1899	John Dewey, *The School and Society*

21

POLITICS:
LOCAL, STATE, AND NATIONAL

The major American political parties had nearly always avoided clear-cut stands on controversial questions in order to appeal to as wide a segment of the electorate as possible, but in the last quarter of the nineteenth century, their equivocations assumed abnormal proportions. This was due in part to the precarious balance of power between them. Neither dared declare itself too clearly on any question lest it drive away more voters than it attracted.

POLITICAL STRATEGY AND TACTICS

The rapid pace of social and economic change militated against political decisiveness. No one in or out of politics had as yet devised effective solutions for many current problems. When party leaders tried to deal with the money question, they discovered that the bankers and the professional economists were as confused as the public at large. "We dabble in theories of our own and clutch convulsively at the doctrines of others," a Philadelphia banker confessed. "From the vast tract of mire by which the subject is surrounded, overlaid, and besmeared, it is almost impossible to arrive at anything like a fair estimate of its real nature." How could mere politicians act rationally or consistently in such circumstances?

Reformers could thunder self-righteously against the spoils system, but how could political parties exist without it? Young economists like Richard T. Ely and Henry Carter Adams were insisting that laissez-faire was outmoded, but no one had yet devised the techniques and instruments that would have to be used if the economy was to be measured and managed effectively by a central authority. The embryonic social sciences had not even collected the statistical information necessary for efficient direction of the economy. If the politicians steered clear of the "real" issues, they did so as much out of a healthy respect for their own ignorance as out of any desire to avoid controversy.

CITY BOSSES

City governments were influenced by the religious and ethnic character of the inhabitants and further complicated by the special problems of late nineteenth-century urban life: rapid, helter-skelter growth; the influx of European immigrants; the need to develop costly transportation, sanitation, and other public utility systems; and the crime and corruption that the size, confusion, and anonymity incidental to urban existence fostered.

The difficulties of life in the slums bewildered and often overwhelmed newcomers, both native- and foreign-born. Hopeful, but passive and naive, they could hardly be expected to take a broad view of social problems when so beset by personal ones. This enabled shrewd urban politicians, most of them in this period of Irish origin, the Irish being the firstcomers among the migrants and, according to mobility studies, more likely to stay put, to take command of the city masses and march them in obedient phalanxes to the polls.

Most city machines were loose-knit neighborhood organizations headed by ward bosses, not tightly geared hierarchical bureaucracies ruled by a single leader. "Big Tim" Sullivan of New York's Lower East Side and "Hinky Dink" Kenna of Chicago were typical of the breed. People like Sullivan and Kenna performed many useful services for what they liked to think of as their constituents. They found jobs for new arrivals and distributed food and other help to all in bad times. Anyone in trouble with the law could obtain at least a hearing from the ward boss, and often, if the crime was venial or due to ignorance, the difficulty was quietly "fixed" and the culprit was sent off with a word of caution. Sullivan provided turkey dinners for 5000 or more homeless people each Christmas, distributed new shoes to the poor children of his district on his birthday, and arranged summer boat rides and picnics for young and old alike. At any time of year the victim of some sudden disaster could turn to the local clubhouse for help. Informally, probably without consciously intending to do so, the bosses educated the immigrants in the complexities of American civilization, helping them to leap the gulf between the almost medieval society of their origins and the modern industrial world.

Cartoonist Thomas Nast's indictment of "Boss" Tweed. Nast's caricature was exaggerated but not inaccurate. When Tweed fled to Spain to evade arrest, Spanish authorities, on seeing a Nast cartoon, arrested Tweed and extradited him to the United States. Tweed was convicted and died in prison; Nast was named consul to Ecuador, where he contracted yellow fever and died.

The price of such aid—the bosses were not altruists—was unquestioning political support, which the bosses converted into cash. In New York, Sullivan levied tribute on gambling, had a hand in the liquor business, and controlled the issuance of peddlers' licenses. When he died in 1913, he was reputedly worth $1 million. Yet he and others like him were immensely popular; 25,000 grieving constituents followed Big Tim's coffin on its way to the grave.

Among city bosses, the principal technique for extracting money from the public till was the kickback. To get city contracts, suppliers were made to pad their bills and, when paid for their work with funds from the city treasury, turn over the excess to the politicians. Similarly, operators of streetcar lines, gas and electricity companies, and other public utilities were compelled to pay huge bribes to obtain favorable franchises.

The most notorious of the nineteenth-century city bosses was William Marcy Tweed, whose "Tweed Ring" extracted tens of millions of dollars from New York City during the brief period 1869 to 1871. Tweed was swiftly jailed. More typical was Richard Croker, who ruled New York's Tammany Hall organization from the mid-1880s to the end of the century. Croker held a number of local offices, but his power rested on his position as chairman of the Tammany Hall finance committee. Although more concerned than Tweed with the social and economic services that machines provided, Croker was primarily a corrupt political manipulator; he accumulated a large fortune and owned a $200,000 mansion and a stable of racehorses, one of which was good enough to win the English Derby.

Despite their welfare work and their popularity, most bosses were essentially thieves. Efforts to romanticize them as the Robin Hoods of industrial society grossly distort the facts. However, the system developed and survived because too many middle-class city dwellers were indifferent to the fate of the poor. Except during occasional reform waves, few tried to check the rapaciousness of the politicos.

Many substantial citizens shared at least indirectly in the corruption. The owners of tenements were interested in crowding as many rent payers as possible into their buildings. Utility companies seeking franchises preferred a system that enabled them to buy favors. Honest citizens who had no selfish stake in the system and who were repelled by the sordidness of city government were seldom sufficiently concerned to do anything about it. When young Theodore Roosevelt decided to seek a political career in 1880, his New York socialite friends laughed in his face. They told him, Roosevelt wrote in his autobiography, "that politics were 'low'; that the organizations were not controlled by 'gentlemen'; that I would find them run by saloon-keepers, horse-car conductors, and the like."

Many so-called urban reformers resented the boss system mainly because it gave political power to people who were not "gentlemen" or, as one reformer put it, to a "proletarian mob" of "illiterate peasants, freshly raked from Irish bogs, or Bohemian mines, or Italian robber nests." A British visitor in Chicago struck at the root of the urban problem of the era. "Everybody is fighting to be rich," he said, "and nobody can attend to making the city fit to live in."

PARTY POLITICS:
SIDESTEPPING THE ISSUE

As for national politics, with the Democrats invincible in the South and the Republicans predominant in New England and most of the states beyond the Mississippi, the outcome of presidential elections was usually determined in a handful of populous states: New York (together with its satellites, New Jersey and Connecticut), Ohio, Indiana, and Illinois. The fact that opinion in these states on important questions such as the tariff and monetary policy was divided and that every imaginable religious and ethnic interest was represented in the electorate goes far to explain why the parties hesitated to commit themselves on issues. In every presidential election, Democrats and Republicans concentrated their heaviest guns on these states. Of the 18 Democrats and Republicans nominated for president in the nine elections between 1868 and 1900, only 3 were not from New York, Ohio, Indiana, or Illinois, and all 3 lost.

Partisanship was intense in these states. A story is told of a Democrat from a town in Illinois who was trying to persuade a doctor he knew to settle there. He admitted that the town already had five doctors, more than enough to care for the medical needs of the populace. But all five were Republicans. "If you come here you can commence all the Democratic practice," he assured the doctor. There are, he added sagely, "a set of public men here that will do what they can for you." Campaigns were conducted in a carnival atmosphere, entertainment being substituted for serious debate. Large sums were spent on brass bands, barbecues, uniforms, and banners. Speakers of national reputation were imported to attract crowds, and spellbinders noted for their leather lungs—this was before the day of the loudspeaker—and their ability to rouse popular emotions were brought in to address mass meetings.

With so much depending on so few, the level of political morality was abysmal. Mudslinging, character assassination, and plain lying were standard practice; bribery was routine. Drifters and other dissolute citizens were paid in cash—or more often in free drinks—to vote the party ticket. The names of persons long dead were solemnly inscribed in voting registers, their suffrages exercised by impostors. During the 1880 campaign the Democratic national chairman, hearing that the Republicans were planning to transport Kentuckians into Indiana to vote illegally in that crucial state, urged Indiana Democrats to "check this outrageous fraud." Then, perhaps seeking an easier solution to the problem, he added: "If necessary . . . keep even with them." Since, as this incident demonstrates, both parties indulged in these tactics, their efforts often canceled each other's, yet presidents were sometimes made and unmade in this sordid fashion.

LACKLUSTER LEADERS

The leading statesmen of the period showed as little interest in important contemporary questions as the party hacks who made up the rank and file of their organizations. Consider the presidents.

Rutherford B. Hayes, president from 1877 to 1881, came to office with a distinguished record. He attended Kenyon College and Harvard Law School before settling down to practice in Cincinnati. Although he had a family to support, he volunteered for service within weeks after the first shell fell on Fort Sumter. "A just and necessary war," he called it in his diary. "I would prefer to go into it if I knew I was to die . . . than to live through and after it without taking any part."

Hayes was wounded at South Mountain on the eve of Antietam and later served under Sheridan in the Shenandoah Valley campaign of 1864. Entering the army as a major, he emerged a major general. In 1864 he was elected to Congress; four years later he became governor of Ohio, serving three terms altogether. The Republicans nominated him for president in 1876 because of his reputation for honesty and moderation, and his election, made possible by the Compromise of 1877, seemed to presage an era of sectional harmony and political probity.

*A former officer under General Philip Sheridan,
Rutherford B. Hayes was sympathetic to the plight of
southern blacks, but like many northern politicians of his
generation, took no action to stop the racist oppression.*

Outwardly Hayes had a sunny disposition; inwardly, in his own words, he was sometimes "nervous to the point of disaster." Despite his geniality, he was utterly without political glamor. He played down the tariff issue. On the money question he was conservative. He cheerfully approved the resumption of gold payments in 1879 and vetoed bills to expand the currency. He accounted himself a civil service reformer, being opposed to the collection of political contributions from federal officeholders.

Hayes complained about the South's failure to treat blacks decently after the withdrawal of federal troops, but he took no action. He worked harder for civil service reform, yet failed to achieve the "thorough, rapid, and complete" change he had promised. In most matters, he was content to "let the record show that he had made the requests."

Hayes's successor, James A. Garfield, was cut down by an assassin's bullet four months after his inauguration. Even in that short time, however, his ineffectiveness had been demonstrated. During the war Garfield fought at Shiloh and later at Chickamauga. In two years he rose from lieutenant colonel to major general. In 1863 he won a seat in Congress, where his oratorical and managerial skills brought him to prominence in the affairs of the Republican party.

Garfield was studious and industrious and had wide-ranging interests. His weakness was indecisiveness—what an admirer described as a "want of certainty." He did not enjoy waving the bloody shirt, but when hard-pressed politically—as when his name was linked with the Crédit Mobilier railroad scandal—he would lash out at the South in an effort to distract the voters.

Although eager to improve the efficiency of the government and resentful of the "intellectual dissipation" resulting from time wasted listening to the countless appeals of office seekers, he often wilted under pressure from the spoilsmen. Only on fiscal policy did he take a firm stand: He opposed categorically all inflationary schemes.

In this 1880 campaign lithograph by Currier & Ives, "Farmer Garfield" uses a scythe made of honesty, ability, and patriotism to cut a swath to the White House through brush infested by snakes like Falsehood and Malice. One snake bears the countenance of Garfield's predecessor, Hayes.

Political patronage proved to be Garfield's undoing. The Republican party in 1880 was split into two factions, the "Stalwarts" and the "Half-Breeds." The Stalwarts, led by New York Senator Roscoe Conkling, believed in the blatant pursuit of the spoils of office. The Half-Breeds did not disagree but behaved more circumspectly, hoping to attract the support of independents. Competition for office was the main reason for their rivalry.

Garfield had been a compromise choice at the 1880 Republican convention. His election precipitated a great battle over patronage, the new president standing in a sort of no-man's land between the factions. He did stand up to the most grasping politicians, resisting in particular the demands of Senator Conkling. By backing the investigation of a post office scandal and by appointing a Half-Breed collector of the Port of New York, he infuriated the Stalwarts. In July 1881 an unbalanced Stalwart lawyer named Charles J. Guiteau shot Garfield in the Washington railroad station. After lingering for weeks, the president died on September 19.

The assassination of Garfield elevated Chester A. Arthur to the presidency. Arthur was a New York lawyer. An abolitionist, he became an early convert to the Republican party and rose rapidly in its local councils. In 1871 Grant gave him the juiciest political plum in the country, the collectorship of the Port of New York, which he held until removed by Hayes in 1878 for refusing to keep his hands out of party politics.

James A. Garfield, mortally wounded. After failing to locate the bullet, surgeons called in Alexander Graham Bell, the famous inventor. Bell conceived of a device, pictured here, that anticipated the mine detector. Bell's machine failed to locate the bullet, however, perhaps because the metal bed springs interfered with its operation. Garfield died, either from the bullet or the surgeon's unsuccessful attempts to extricate it.

The vice presidency was the only elective position that Arthur had ever held. Before Garfield's death, he had paid little attention to questions like the tariff and monetary policy, being content to take in fees ranging upward of $50,000 a year as collector of the port and to oversee the operations of the New York customs office, with its hordes of clerks and laborers. (During Arthur's tenure, the novelist Herman Melville was employed as an "outdoor inspector" by the custom house.) Of course, Arthur was an unblushing defender of the spoils system, though in fairness it must be said that he was personally honest and an excellent administrator.

The tragic circumstances of his elevation to the presidency sobered Arthur considerably. Although he was a genial, convivial man, perhaps overly fond of good food and flashy clothes, he comported himself with great dignity as president. He handled patronage matters with restraint, and he gave at least nominal support to the movement for civil service reform, which had been strengthened by the public's indignation at the assassination of Garfield. In 1883 Congress passed the Pendleton Act, "classifying" about 10 percent of all government jobs and creating the bipartisan Civil Service Commission to administer competitive examinations for these positions. The law made it illegal to force officeholders to make political contributions and empowered the president to expand the list of classified positions at his discretion.

As an administrator Arthur was systematic, thoughtful, businesslike, and at the same time cheerful and considerate. Just the same, he too was a political failure. He made relatively little effort to push his program through Congress. In any case, the Stalwarts would not forgive his "desertion," and the reform element could not forget his past. He did not seek a second term in 1884.

The election of 1884 brought the Democrat Grover Cleveland to the White House. Cleveland grew up in western New York. After studying law, he settled in Buffalo. Although somewhat lacking in the social graces and in intellectual pretensions, he had a basic integrity that everyone recognized; when a group of reformers sought a candidate for mayor in 1881, he was a natural choice. His success in Buffalo led to his election as governor of New York in 1882.

In the governor's chair his no-nonsense attitude toward public administration endeared him to civil service reformers at the same time that his basic conservatism pleased businessmen. When he vetoed a popular bill to force a reduction of the fares charged by the New York City elevated railway on the grounds that it was an unconstitutional violation of the company's franchise, his stock soared. Here was a man who cared more for principle than for the adulation of the multitude, a man of courage—honest, hardworking, and eminently sound. The Democrats nominated him for president in 1884.

The election revolved around personal issues, for the platforms of the parties were almost identical. On the one hand, the Republican candidate, the dynamic James G. Blaine, had an immense following, but his reputation had been soiled by the publication of the "Mulligan letters," which connected him with the corrupt granting of congressional favors to the Little Rock and Fort Smith Railroad. On the other hand, it came out during the campaign that Cleveland, a bachelor, had fathered an illegitimate child. Instead of debating public issues, the Republicans chanted the ditty

> *Ma! Ma! Where's my pa?*
> *Gone to the White House,*
> *Ha! Ha! Ha!*

to which the Democrats countered

> *Blaine, Blaine, James G. Blaine,*
> *The continental liar from the State of Maine.*

The THREAD THAT BINDS THE UNION.

President Grover Cleveland and Frances Folsom in 1888. The couple had married two years earlier; he was 48, and she, 21, the youngest First Lady. Her popularity blunted criticisms that Cleveland, a bachelor, had earlier fathered an illegitimate child. When he lost the 1888 election, his wife predicted that she would return as First Lady. Four years later, she did.

Blaine lost more heavily in the mudslinging than Cleveland, whose quiet courage in saying, "Tell the truth" when his past was brought to light contrasted favorably with Blaine's glib and unconvincing denials. A significant group of eastern Republicans, known as mugwumps, campaigned for the Democrats. However, Blaine ran a strong race against a general pro-Democratic trend; Cleveland won the election by fewer than 25,000 votes. The change of 600 ballots in New York would have given that state, and the presidency, to his opponent.

As a Democrat, Cleveland had no stomach for refighting the Civil War. Civil service reformers overestimated his commitment to their cause, for he believed in rotation in office. He would not summarily dismiss Republicans, but he thought that when they had served four years, they "should as a rule give way to good men of our party." He did, however, insist on honesty and efficiency regardless of party. As a result, he made few poor appointments.

Cleveland had little imagination and too narrow a conception of his powers and duties to be a successful president. His appearance perfectly reflected his character: A squat, burly man weighing well over 200 pounds, he could defend a position against heavy odds, yet he lacked flexibility. He took a fairly broad view of the powers of the federal government, but he thought it unseemly to put pressure on Congress, believing in "the entire independence of the executive and legislative branches."

Toward the end of his term Cleveland bestirred himself and tried to provide constructive leadership on the tariff question. The government was embarrassed by a large revenue surplus, which Cleveland hoped to reduce by cutting the duties on necessities and on raw materials used in manufacturing. He devoted his entire annual message of December 1887 to the tariff, thereby focusing public attention on the subject. When worried Democrats reminded him that an election was coming up and that the tariff might cause a rift in the organization, he replied simply: "What is the use of being elected or re-elected, unless you stand for something?"

In that contest, Cleveland obtained a plurality of the popular vote, but his opponent, Benjamin Harrison, grandson of President William Henry Harrison, carried most of the key northeastern industrial states by narrow margins, thereby obtaining a comfortable majority in the Electoral College, 233 to 168.

Although intelligent and able, Harrison was too reserved to make a good politician. One observer called him a "human iceberg." During the Civil War he fought under Sherman at Atlanta and won a reputation as a stern, effective disciplinarian. In 1876 he ran unsuccessfully for governor of Indiana, but in 1881 was elected to the Senate.

Harrison believed ardently in protective tariffs, stating firmly, if illogically, that he was against "cheaper costs" because cheaper costs seemed "necessarily to involve a cheaper man and woman under the coat." His approach to fiscal policy was conservative, though he was freehanded in the matter of veterans' pensions. He would not use "an apothecary's scale," he said, "to weigh the rewards of men who saved the country." No more flamboyant waver of the bloody shirt existed.

Harrison professed to favor civil service reform, but fashioned an unimpressive record on the question. He appointed the vigorous young reformer Theodore Roosevelt to the Civil Service Commission and then proceeded to undercut him systematically. Before long the frustrated Roosevelt was calling the president a "cold blooded, narrow minded, prejudiced, obstinate, timid old psalm singing Indianapolis politician."

President Benjamin Harrison swapping political office for electioneering support as depicted by a cartoonist, a practice that civil service reformers insisted corrupted national politics. In point of fact, "Little Ben" was among the least given to patronage appointments among post–Civil War presidents.

Harrison accomplished little. The Republicans lost control of Congress in 1890, and two years later Grover Cleveland swept back into power, defeating Harrison by more than 350,000 votes.

CROPS AND COMPLAINTS

The vacuity of American politics may well have stemmed from the complacency of the middle-class majority. The country was growing; no foreign enemy threatened it; the poor were mostly recent immigrants, blacks, and others with little influence, who were easily ignored by those in comfortable circumstances. However, one important group in society suffered increasingly as the years rolled by: the farmers. Out of their travail came the force that finally, in the 1890s, brought American politics face to face with the problems of the age.

Immediately after the Civil War, wheat sold at nearly $1.50 a bushel, and in the early 1870s it was still worth well over a dollar. By the mid-1890s the average price stood in the neighborhood of 60 cents. Cotton, the great southern staple, which sold for more than 30 cents a pound in 1866 and 15 cents in the early 1870s, at times in the 1890s fell below 6 cents.

The tariff on manufactured goods appeared to aggravate the farmers' predicament, and so did the domestic marketing system, which enabled a multitude of middlemen to gobble up a large share of the profits of agriculture. The shortage of credit, particularly in the South, was an additional burden. Furthermore, the improvements in transportation that made it practicable for farmers in Australia, Canada, Russia, and Argentina to sell their produce in western European markets increased the competition faced by Americans seeking to dispose of surplus produce abroad.

Throughout the mid-1880s farmers on the Plains had experienced boom conditions. Adequate rainfall produced bountiful harvests, credit was available, and property values rose rapidly. In the 1880s the population of Kansas increased by 43 percent, that of Nebraska by 134 percent, that of the Dakotas by 278 percent. This agricultural expansion contributed to the destruction of open-range cattle raising and changed the economy of cattle towns like Dodge City, which came to depend more on farmers than on cowboys and ranchers for business.

Speculative booms occurred periodically in every frontier district; like all others, this one collapsed when settlers and investors took a more realistic look at the prospects of the region. In this case special circumstances turned the slump into a catastrophe. A succession of dry years shattered the hopes of the farmers. The downward swing of the business cycle in the early 1890s completed the devastation. Settlers who had paid more for their lands than they were worth and borrowed money at high interest rates to do so found themselves squeezed relentlessly. Thousands lost their farms and returned eastward, penniless and dispirited. The population of Nebraska increased by fewer than 4000 persons in the entire decade of the 1890s.

THE POPULIST MOVEMENT

The agricultural depression triggered a new outburst of farm radicalism, the Alliance movement. Alliances were organizations of farmers' clubs, most of which had sprung up during the bad times of the late 1870s. The first Knights of Reliance group was founded in 1877 in Lampasas County, Texas. As the Farmers Alliance, this organization gradually expanded in northeastern Texas, and after 1885 it spread rapidly throughout the cotton states. Alliance leaders stressed cooperation. Their co-ops bought fertilizer and other supplies in bulk and sold them at fair prices to members. They sought to market their crops cooperatively but could not raise the necessary capital from banks, with the result that some of them began to question the workings of the American financial and monetary system. They became economic and social radicals in the process. In the northern regions a similar though less influential Alliance movement developed.

A gathering of Grangers near Winchester, Illinois, in 1873. Note the bandwagon (literally!) to the left, the women with parasols and bonnets (right), and the American flags (everywhere). This "radical" political movement had the feel of a county fair or religious revival; both had doubtless been held in this same spot.

The alliances adopted somewhat differing policies, but all agreed that agricultural prices were too low, that transportation costs were too high, and that something was radically wrong with the nation's financial system. "There are three great crops raised in Nebraska," an angry rural editor proclaimed in 1890. "One is a crop of corn, one is a crop of freight rates, and one a crop of interest. One is produced by farmers who by sweat and toil farm the land. The other two are produced by men who sit in their offices and behind their bank counters and farm the farmers." All agreed on the need for political action if the lot of the agriculturalist was to be improved.

Although the state alliances of the Dakotas and Kansas joined the Southern Alliance in 1889, for a time local prejudices and conflicting interests prevented the formation of a single national organization. Northern farmers mostly voted Republican, Southerners Democratic, and resentments created during the Civil War lingered in all sections. Cotton-producing Southerners opposed the protective tariff; most Northerners, fearing the competition of foreign grain producers, favored it. Railroad regulation and federal land policy seemed vital questions to Northerners; financial reform loomed most important in southern eyes. Northerners were receptive to the idea of forming a third party, while

Southerners, wedded to the one-party system, preferred working to capture local Democratic machines.

The farm groups entered local politics in the 1890 elections. Convinced of the righteousness of their cause, they campaigned with tremendous fervor. The results were encouraging. In the South, Alliance-sponsored gubernatorial candidates won in Georgia, Tennessee, South Carolina, and Texas; eight southern legislatures fell under Alliance control, and 44 representatives and 3 senators committed to Alliance objectives were sent to Washington. In the West, Alliance candidates swept Kansas and captured a majority in the Nebraska legislature and enough seats in Minnesota and South Dakota to hold the balance of power between the major parties.

Such success, coupled with the reluctance of the Republicans and Democrats to make concessions to their demands, encouraged Alliance leaders to create a new national party. By uniting southern and western farmers, they succeeded in breaking the sectional barrier erected by the Civil War. If they could recruit industrial workers, perhaps a real political revolution could be accomplished. In February 1892, farm leaders, representatives of the Knights of Labor, and various professional reformers, some 800 in all, met at St. Louis. They organized the People's, or Populist, party, and issued a call for a national convention to meet at Omaha in July.

That convention nominated General James B. Weaver of Iowa for president (with a one-legged Confederate veteran as his running mate) and drafted a platform that called for a graduated income tax and national ownership of railroads and the telegraph and telephone systems. To combat deflation, the platform demanded the unlimited coinage of silver and an increase in the money supply "to no less than $50 per capita."

To make the government more responsive to public opinion, the Populists urged the adoption of the initiative and referendum procedures and the election of United States senators by popular vote. To win the support of industrial workers, their platform denounced the use of Pinkerton detectives in labor disputes and backed the eight-hour day and the restriction of "undesirable" immigration.

The Populists saw themselves not as a persecuted minority but as a victimized majority betrayed by what would a century later be called the establishment. They were at most ambivalent about the free enterprise system, and they tended to attribute social and economic injustices not to built-in inequities in the system but to nefarious conspiracies organized by selfish interests in order to subvert the system.

In the one-party South, Populist strategists sought to wean black farmers away from the ruling Democratic organization. Southern black farmers had their own

Mary Elizabeth Lease was a prominent Populist, noted for her rallying cry to "raise less corn and more hell."

Colored Alliance, and even before 1892 their leaders had worked closely with the white alliances. Nearly 100 black delegates had attended the Populist convention at St. Louis. Of course, the blacks would be useless to the party if they could not vote; therefore, white Populist leaders opposed the southern trend toward disfranchising African Americans and called for full civil rights for all.

In the Northwest, the Populists assailed the "bankers' conspiracy" in unbridled terms. Ignatius Donnelly, running for governor of Minnesota, wrote another futuristic political novel, *The Golden Bottle,* and made 150 speeches, vowing to make the campaign "the liveliest ever seen" in the state.

The results proved disappointing, although the Populists did sweep Kansas. They elected numbers of local officials in other western states and cast over a million votes for General Weaver. But the effort to unite white and black farmers in

To this hostile cartoonist, the Populist party was a patchwork coalition of farmers' alliances, urban laborers, prohibitionists, socialists, anarchists, Grangers, and Greenbackers, who were all floating a platform of "lunacy."

the South failed miserably. Conservative Democrats, while continuing with considerable success to attract black voters, played on racial fears cruelly, insisting that the Populists sought to undermine white supremacy. Since most white Populists saw the alliance with blacks as at best a marriage of convenience, this argument had a deadly effect. Elsewhere, even in the old centers of the Granger movement, the party made no significant impression. Urban workers remained aloof.

By standing firmly for conservative financial policies, Cleveland attracted considerable Republican support and won a solid victory over Harrison in the Electoral College, 277 to 145. Weaver's electoral vote was 22.

SHOWDOWN ON SILVER

One conclusion that politicians reached after analyzing the 1892 returns was that the money question, particularly the controversy over the coinage of silver, was of paramount interest to the voters. Despite the wide-ranging appeal of the Populist platform, most of Weaver's strength came from the silver-mining states. By contrast, Cleveland's strong stand for gold proved popular in the Northwest.

In truth, the issue of gold versus silver was superficial; the important question was what, if anything, should be done to check the deflationary spiral. The declining price level benefited bondholders and other people with fixed incomes and injured debtors. Industrial workers profited from deflation except during periods of depression, when unemployment rose—which helps explain why the Populists made little headway among them. Southern farmers, who were prisoners of the crop-lien system, and farmers in the Plains states were hit hard by the downward trend.

By the early 1890s, discussion of federal monetary policy revolved around the coinage of silver. Traditionally, the United States had been on a bimetallic standard. Both gold and silver were coined, the number of grains of each in the dollar being adjusted periodically to reflect the commercial value of the two metals. An act of 1792 established a 15:1 ratio—371.25 grains of silver and 24.75 grains of gold were each worth $1 at the mint. In 1834 the ratio was changed, reducing the value of gold to reflect the new discoveries in California. However, an avalanche of silver from the mines of Nevada and Colorado gradually depressed the price until, around 1874, it again became profitable for miners to coin their bullion. Alas, when they tried to do so, they discovered that the Coinage Act of 1873, taking account of the fact that no silver had been presented to the mint in years, had demonetized the metal.

The silver mines denounced this "Crime of '73," and inflationists, who wanted more money put into circulation regardless of its base, joined them in demanding a return to bimetallism. Conservatives, still fighting the battle against greenback paper money, resisted strongly. The result was a series of compromises.

Silver miners grumbled because their bullion brought in only half what it had in the early 1870s. Debtors noted angrily that because of the general decline in prices, the dollars they used to meet their obligations were worth more than twice as much as in 1865. Advocates of the gold standard feared that unlimited silver coinage would be authorized, "destroying the value of the dollar." When a financial panic brought on by the collapse of the London banking house of Baring Brothers ushered in a severe industrial depression, the confidence of both silverites and "gold bugs" was further eroded.

President Cleveland believed that the controversy over silver had caused the depression by shaking the confidence of the business community and that all would be well if the country returned to a single gold standard. He summoned a special session of Congress, and by exerting immense political pressure he obtained the repeal of the Sherman Silver Purchase Act in October 1893. All that this accomplished was to split the Democratic party, its southern and western wings deserting him almost to a man.

During 1894 and 1895, while the nation floundered in the worst depression it had ever experienced, a series of events further undermined public confidence. In the spring of 1894 several "armies" of the unemployed, the most imposing led by Jacob S. Coxey, an eccentric Ohio businessman, marched on Washington to demand relief. Coxey wanted the government to undertake a program of federal public works and to authorize local communities to exchange non-interest-bearing bonds with the Treasury for $500 million in paper money, the funds to be used to hire unemployed workers to build roads. The scheme, Coxey claimed, would pump money into the economy, provide work for the jobless, and benefit the entire nation by improving transportation facilities.

When Coxey's group of demonstrators, perhaps 500 in all, reached Washington, he and two other leaders were arrested for trespassing on the grounds of the Capitol. Their followers were dispersed by club-wielding policemen. This callous treatment convinced many Americans that the government had little interest in the suffering of the people, an opinion strengthened when Cleveland, in July 1894, used federal troops to crush the Pullman strike.

The next year the Supreme Court handed down several reactionary decisions. In *United States* v. *E. C. Knight Company* it refused to employ the Sherman Antitrust Act to break up the Sugar Trust. In *Pollock* v. *Farmers' Loan and Trust Company* it invalidated a federal income tax law despite the fact that a similar measure levied during the Civil War had been upheld by the Court in *Springer* v. *United States* (1881). Finally, the Court denied a writ of habeas corpus to Eugene

V. Debs of the American Railway Union, who was languishing in prison for disobeying a federal injunction during the Pullman strike.

On top of these indications of official conservatism came a desperate financial crisis. Throughout 1894 the Treasury's supply of gold dwindled as worried citizens exchanged greenbacks (now convertible into gold) for hard money and foreign investors cashed in large amounts of American securities. The government tried to sell bonds for gold to bolster the reserve, but the gold reserve continued to melt away. Early in 1895 it touched a low point of $41 million.

At this juncture a syndicate of bankers headed by J. P. Morgan turned the tide by underwriting a $62 million bond issue, guaranteeing that half the gold would come from Europe. This caused a great public outcry; the spectacle of the nation being saved from bankruptcy by a private banker infuriated millions.

These events, together with the continuing depression, discredited the Cleveland administration. "I haven't got words to say what I think of that old bag of beef," Governor "Pitchfork Ben" Tillman of South Carolina, who had resolutely resisted the Populists in 1892, told a local audience two years later. "If you send me to the Senate, I promise I won't be bulldozed by him."

As the presidential election of 1896 approached, with the Populists demanding unlimited coinage of silver at a ratio of 16:1, the major parties found it impossible to continue straddling the money question. The Populist vote had increased by 42 percent in the 1894 congressional elections. Southern and western Democratic leaders feared that they would lose their following unless Cleveland was repudiated. Western Republicans, led by Senator Henry M. Teller of Colorado, were threatening to bolt to the Populists unless their party came out for silver coinage. After a generation of political equivocation, the major parties had to face an important issue squarely.

The Republicans, meeting to choose a candidate at St. Louis in June 1896, announced for the gold standard. "We are unalterably opposed to every measure calculated to debase our currency or impair the credit of our country," the platform declared. "We are therefore opposed to the free coinage of silver. . . . The existing gold standard must be maintained." The party then nominated Ohio's William McKinley for president. McKinley, best known for his staunch advocacy of the protective tariff yet highly regarded by labor, was expected to run strongly in the Middle West and the East.

The Democratic convention met in July at Chicago. The pro-gold Cleveland element made a hard fight, but the silverites swept them aside. The high point came when a youthful Nebraskan named William Jennings Bryan spoke for silver against gold, for western farmers against the industrial East. Bryan's every sentence provoked ear-shattering applause.

> We have petitioned and our petitions have been scorned; we have entreated, and our entreaties have been disregarded; we have begged, and they have mocked when our calamity came. We beg no longer; we entreat no more; we petition no more. We defy them!

The crowd responded like a great choir to Bryan's oratorical cues. "Burn down your cities and leave our farms," he said, "and your cities will spring up again as if by magic; but destroy our farms and the grass will grow in the streets of every city in the country." He ended with a marvelous figure of speech that set the tone for the coming campaign. "You shall not press down upon the brow of labor this crown of thorns," he warned, bringing his hands down suggestively to his temples. "You shall not crucify mankind upon a cross of gold!" Dramatically, he extended his arms to the side, the very figure of the crucified Christ.

The convention promptly adopted a platform calling for "the free and unlimited coinage of both silver and gold at the present legal ratio of 16 to 1" and went on to nominate Bryan, who was barely 36, for president.

This action put tremendous pressure on the Populists. If they supported the Democrat Bryan, they risked losing their party identity; if they nominated an-

William Jennings Bryan's "Cross of Gold" speech inspired this cartoonist's caricature of it. Bryan's speech in favor of bimetallism was studded with religious references. He described the unlimited coinage of silver and gold as a "holy cause" supported by those who built churches "where they praise their Creator." He concluded with one of the most famous metaphors in American rhetoric: "You shall not press down upon the brow of labor this crown of thorns. You shall not crucify mankind upon a cross of gold."

other candidate, they would ensure McKinley's election. In part because the delegates could not find a person of stature willing to become a candidate against Bryan, the Populist convention nominated him, seeking to preserve the party identity by substituting Watson for the Democratic vice-presidential nominee, Arthur Sewall of Maine.

THE ELECTION OF 1896

Never did a presidential campaign raise such intense emotions. The Republicans from the silver-mining states swung solidly behind Bryan. But many solid-money Democrats, especially in the Northeast, refused to accept the decision of the Chicago convention. Cleveland professed to be "so dazed by the political situation that I am in no condition for speech or thought on the subject." Many others adopted the policy of Governor David B. Hill of New York, who said, "I am a Democrat still—very still." The extreme gold bugs, calling themselves National Democrats, nominated their own candidate, 79-year-old Senator John M. Palmer of Illinois. Palmer ran only to injure Bryan. "Fellow Democrats," he announced, "I will not consider it any great fault if you decide to cast your vote for William McKinley."

At the start the Republicans seemed to have everything in their favor. Bryan's youth and relative lack of political experience—two terms in the House—contrasted unfavorably with McKinley's distinguished war record, his long service in Congress and as governor of Ohio, and his reputation for honesty and good judgment. The severe depression operated in favor of the party out of power, although by repudiating Cleveland the Democrats escaped much of the burden of explaining away his errors. The newspapers came out almost unanimously for the Republicans. Important Democratic papers such as the *New York World,* the *Boston Herald,* the *Baltimore Sun,* the *Chicago Chronicle,* and the *Richmond Times* supported McKinley editorially and even slanted news stories against the Democrats. The *New York Times* accused Bryan of being insane, his affliction being variously classified as "paranoia querulenta," "graphomania," and "oratorical monomania." The Democrats had very little money and few well-known speakers to fight the campaign.

But Bryan proved a formidable opponent. Casting aside tradition, he took to the stump personally, traveling 18,000 miles and making over 600 speeches. He was one of the greatest of orators. A big, handsome man with a voice capable of carrying without strain to the far corners of a great hall yet equally effective before a cluster of auditors at a rural crossroads, he projected an image of absolute sincerity without appearing fanatical or argumentative. At every major stop on his tour, huge crowds assembled. In Minnesota he packed the 10,000-seat St.

Paul Auditorium, while thousands milled in the streets outside. His energy was amazing, and his charm and good humor were unfailing. At one whistle stop, while he was shaving in his compartment, a small group outside the train began clamoring for a glimpse of him. Flinging open the window and beaming through the lather, he shook hands cheerfully with each of the admirers. Everywhere he hammered away at the money question. Yet he did not totally neglect other issues. He was defending, he said, "all the people who suffer from the operations of trusts, syndicates, and combines."

McKinley's campaign was managed by a new type of politician, Marcus Alonzo Hanna, an Ohio businessman. In a sense Hanna was a product of the Pendleton Civil Service Act. When deprived of the contributions of officeholders, the parties turned to business for funds, and Hanna was one of the first leaders with a foot in both camps. Politics fascinated him, and despite his wealth and wide interests, he was willing to labor endlessly at the routine work of political organization.

Hanna aspired to be a kingmaker and early fastened on McKinley, whose charm he found irresistible, as the vehicle for satisfying his ambition. He spent about $100,000 of his own money on the preconvention campaign. His attitude toward the candidate, one mutual friend observed, was "that of a big, bashful boy toward the girl he loves."

Before most Republicans realized how effective Bryan was on the stump, Hanna perceived the danger and sprang into action. Since the late 1880s the character of political organization had been changing. The Civil Service Act was also cutting down on the number of jobs available to reward campaign workers. At the same time, the new mass circulation newspapers and the nationwide press associations were increasing the pressure on candidates to speak openly and often on national issues. This trend put a premium on party organization and consistency—the old political trick of speaking out of one side of the mouth to one audience and out the other to a different audience no longer worked very well. The old military metaphors of political discourse, the terms *campaign* and *spoils* and *standard bearer,* remained, but other more businesslike ones became popular: *boss, machine, lobbyist*. As the federal government became more involved in economic issues, business had more interest in national elections and was more willing to spend money on behalf of candidates whose views they approved. In the campaign of 1888 the Republicans had set up a businessman's "advisory board" to raise money and stir up enthusiasm for Benjamin Harrison.

Hanna understood what was happening to politics. Certain that money was the key to political power, he raised an enormous campaign fund. When businessmen hesitated to contribute, he pried open their purses by a combination of persuasiveness and intimidation. Banks and insurance companies were "assessed" a percentage of their assets, big corporations a share of their receipts, until some $3.5 million had been collected.

Hanna disbursed these funds with efficiency and imagination. He sent 1500 speakers into the doubtful districts and blanketed the land with 250 million pieces of campaign literature, printed in a dozen languages. "He has advertised McKinley as if he were a patent medicine," Theodore Roosevelt, never at a loss for words, exclaimed.

Incapable of competing with Bryan as a swayer of mass audiences, McKinley conducted a "front-porch campaign." Superficially the proceedings were delightfully informal. From every corner of the land, groups representing various regions, occupations, and interests descended on McKinley's unpretentious frame house in Canton, Ohio. Gathering on the lawn—the grass was soon reduced to mud, the fence stripped of pickets by souvenir hunters—the visitors paid their compliments to the candidate and heard him deliver a brief speech, while beside him on the porch his aged mother and adoring invalid wife listened with rapt attention. Then there was a small reception, during which the delegates were given an opportunity to shake their host's hand.

Despite the air of informality, these performances were carefully staged. The delegations arrived on a tightly coordinated schedule worked out by McKinley's staff and the railroads, which operated cut-rate excursion trains to Canton from all over the nation. McKinley was fully briefed on the special interests and attitudes of each group, and the speeches of delegation leaders were submitted in advance. Often his secretary amended these remarks, and on occasion McKinley wrote the visitors' speeches himself. His own talks were carefully prepared, each calculated to make a particular point. All were reported fully in the newspapers. Thus without moving from his doorstep, McKinley met thousands of people from every section of the country.

These tactics worked admirably. On election day McKinley carried the East; the Middle West including even Iowa, Minnesota, and

Beginning with acceptance of the presidential nomination, William McKinley mounted his campaign from his front porch in Canton, Ohio.

North Dakota; and the Pacific coast states of Oregon and California. Bryan won in the South, the Plains states, and the Rocky Mountain region. McKinley collected 271 electoral votes to Bryan's 176, the popular vote being 7,036,000 to 6,468,000.

THE MEANING OF THE ELECTION

The sharp sectional division marked the failure of the Populist effort to unite northern and southern farmers and the triumph of the industrial part of the country over the agricultural. Business and financial interests voted solidly for the Republicans, fearing that Bryan's victory would bring economic chaos. When a Nebraska landowner tried to float a mortgage during the campaign, a loan company official wrote him: "If McKinley is elected, we think we will be in the market, but we do not care to make any investments while there is an uncertainty as to what kind of money a person will be paid back in."

Other social and economic interests were far from being united. Many thousands of farmers voted for McKinley, as his success in states such as North Dakota, Iowa, and Minnesota proved. In the East and in the states bordering the Great Lakes, the agricultural depression was not severe, and farm radicalism was almost nonexistent.

A preponderance of the labor vote also went to the Republicans. In part this resulted from the tremendous pressures that many industrialists applied to their workers. "Men," one manufacturer announced, "vote as you please, but if Bryan is elected . . . the whistle will not blow Wednesday morning." Some companies placed orders for materials subject to cancellation if the Democrats won. Yet coercion was not a major factor, for McKinley was highly regarded in labor circles. While governor of Ohio, he had advocated the arbitration of industrial disputes and backed a law fining employers who refused to permit workers to join unions. During the Pullman strike he had sent his brother to try to persuade George Pullman to deal fairly with the strikers. He had invariably based his advocacy of high tariffs on the argument that American wage levels would be depressed if foreign goods could enter the country untaxed. Mark Hanna too had the reputation of always giving his employees a square deal. The Republicans carried nearly all the large cities, and in closely contested states such as Illinois and Ohio this made the difference between victory and defeat.

During the campaign, some frightened Republicans had laid plans for fleeing the country if Bryan were elected, and belligerent ones, such as Theodore Roosevelt, then police commissioner of New York City, readied themselves to meet the "social revolutionaries" on the battlefield. Victory sent such people into

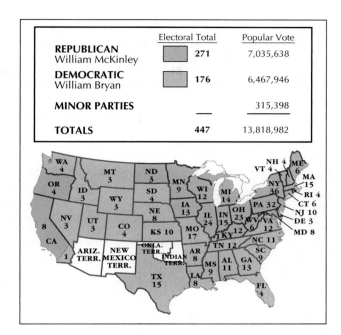

	Electoral Total	Popular Vote
REPUBLICAN William McKinley	271	7,035,638
DEMOCRATIC William Bryan	176	6,467,946
MINOR PARTIES	—	315,398
TOTALS	447	13,818,982

The Election of 1896

transports of joy. Most conservatives concluded that the way of life they so fervently admired had been saved for all time.

However heartfelt, such sentiments were not founded on fact. With workers standing beside capitalists and with the farm vote split, it cannot be said that the election divided the nation class against class or that McKinley's victory saved the country from revolution.

Far from representing a triumph for the status quo, the election marked the coming of age of modern America. The battle between gold and silver, which everyone had considered so vital, had little real significance. The inflationists seemed to have been beaten, but new gold discoveries in Alaska and South Africa and improved methods of extracting gold from low-grade ores soon led to a great expansion of the money supply. In any case, within two decades the system of basing the volume of currency on bullion had been abandoned. Bryan and the "political" Populists who supported him, supposedly the advance agents of revolution, were oriented more toward the past than the future; their ideal was the rural America of Jefferson and Jackson.

McKinley, for all his innate conservatism, was capable of looking ahead toward the new century. His approach was national where Bryan's was basically parochial. Though never daring and seldom imaginative, McKinley was able to deal pragmatically with current problems. Before long, as the United States became increasingly an exporter of manufactures, he would even modify his position on the tariff. And no one better reflected the spirit of the age than Mark Hanna, the outstanding political realist of his generation. Far from preventing change, the outcome of the election of 1896 made possible still greater changes as the United States moved into the twentieth century.

MILESTONES

1873	Congress suspends the coining of silver ("the Crime of '73")
1877	Beginning of Farmers Alliance movement
1878	Bland-Allison Act
1879	Greenback paper money made convertible into gold
1881	Assassination of President Garfield
1883	Pendleton Civil Service Act
1884	Mugwump movement
1887	Interstate Commerce Act
	Cleveland's tariff message
1890	Sherman Silver Purchase Act
1892	Founding of the People's (Populist) party
1893	Panic of 1893
1894	Coxey's Army marches to Washington to demand relief
1895	Supreme Court declares federal income tax unconstitutional (*Pollock v. Farmers' Loan and Trust Company*)
	J. P. Morgan raises $62 million in gold for the Treasury
1896	William Jennings Bryan's "Cross of Gold" speech

22

THE AGE OF REFORM

The period bounded roughly by the end of the nineteenth century and American entry into World War I is usually called the Progressive era. Like all such generalizations about complex subjects, this title involves a great simplification. Whether *progressive* is taken to mean "tending toward change" or "improvement" or is merely used to suggest an attitude of mind, it was neither a unique nor a universal characteristic of the early years of the twentieth century. Progressive elements had existed in earlier periods and did not disappear when the first American soldiers took ship for France. In important ways the progressivism of the time was a continuation of the response to industrialism that began after the Civil War, a response that has not ended. Historians have scoured the sources trying to define and explain the Progressive era, without satisfying everyone. Nevertheless the term *progressive* provides a useful description of this exciting and significant period of American history.

ROOTS OF PROGRESSIVISM

The progressives were never a single group seeking a single objective. The movement sprang from many sources. One was the fight against corruption and inefficiency in government, which began with the Liberal Republicans of the Grant era and was continued by the mugwumps of the 1880s. The struggle for civil service reform was only the first skirmish in this battle; the continuing power of corrupt political machines and the growing influence of large corporations and their lobbyists on municipal and state governments outraged thousands of citizens and led them to seek ways of purifying politics and making the machinery of government at all levels responsive to the majority rather than to special-interest groups.

Progressivism also had roots in the effort to regulate and control big business, which characterized the Granger and Populist agitation of the 1870s and 1890s. The failure of the Interstate Commerce Act to end railroad abuses and of the Sherman Antitrust Act to check the growth of large corporations became increasingly apparent after 1900.

Between 1897 and 1904 the trend toward concentration in industry accelerated. Such new giants as Amalgamated Copper (1899), U.S. Steel (1901), and International Harvester (1902) attracted most of the attention, but even more alarming were the overall statistics. In a single year (1899) more than 1200 firms were absorbed in mergers, the resulting combinations being capitalized at $2.2 billion. By 1904 there were 318 industrial combinations in the country with an aggregate capital of $7.5 billion. People who considered bigness inherently evil demanded that the huge new "trusts" be broken up or at least strictly controlled.

Settlement house workers and other reformers concerned about the welfare of the urban poor made up a third battalion in the progressive army. This was an area in which women made the most important contributions. The working and living conditions of slum dwellers remained abominable, and the child labor problem was particularly acute; in 1900 about 1.7 million children under the age of 16 were working full time—more than the membership of the American Federation of Labor. In addition, laws regulating the hours and working conditions of women in industry were far from adequate, and almost nothing had been done, despite the increased use of dangerous machinery in the factories, to enforce safety rules or to provide compensation or insurance for workers injured on the job. As the number of professionally competent social workers grew, the movement for social welfare legislation gained momentum.

America was becoming more urban, more industrial, more mechanized, more centralized—in short, more complex. This trend put a premium on efficiency and cooperation. It seemed obvious to the progressives that people must become more socially minded, the economy more carefully organized.

By attracting additional thousands of sympathizers to the general cause of reform, the return of prosperity after 1896 fueled the progressive movement. Good times made the average person more tolerant and generous. As long as profits were on the rise, the average employer did not object if labor improved its position too. Middle-class Americans who had been prepared to go to the barricades in the event of a Bryan victory in 1896 became conscience-stricken when they compared their own comfortable circumstances with those of the "huddled masses" of immigrants and native-born poor.

Giant industrial and commercial corporations threatened not so much the economic well-being as the ambitions and sense of importance of the middle class. What owner of a small mill or shop could now hope to rise to the heights attained by Carnegie or merchants like John Wanamaker and Marshall Field? The growth of large labor organizations worried such types. In general, character and moral values seemed less influential; organizations—cold, impersonal, heartless—were coming to control business, politics, and too many other aspects of life.

This development led historian Richard Hofstadter to suggest another explanation of the progressive movement: the status revolution. Numbers of moderately prosperous businessmen, together with members of the professions and other educated people, felt threatened by the increasing power and status of the new tycoons, many of them coarse, domineering, and fond of vulgar display. The antics of machine politicians who made a mockery of the traditions of duty, service, and patriotism associated with statesmanship also troubled them. Comfortably well-off, middle-level businessmen lived in what seemed like genteel poverty compared to a Rockefeller or a Morgan.

Protestant pastors accustomed to the respect and deference of their flocks found their moral leadership challenged by materialistic vestrymen who did not even pay them decent salaries. College professors worried about their institutions falling under the sway of wealthy trustees who had little interest in or respect for learning. Lawyers had been "the aristocracy of the United States," James Bryce recalled in 1905; they were now merely "a part of the great organized system of industrial and financial enterprise."

Such people could support reform measures without feeling that they were being very radical because they were resisting change and because the intellectual currents of the time harmonized with their ideas of social improvement and the welfare state. The new doctrines of the social scientists, the Social Gospel religious leaders, and the philosophers of pragmatism provided a salubrious climate for progressivism. Many of the thinkers who formulated these doctrines in the 1880s and 1890s turned to the task of putting them into practice in the new century. Their number included the economist Richard T. Ely, the philosopher John Dewey, and the Baptist clergyman Walter Rauschenbusch, who in addition to his many books extolling the Social Gospel was active in civic reform movements.

THE MUCKRAKERS

As the diffuse progressive army gradually formed its battalions, a new journalistic fad brought the movement into focus. For many years magazines had been publishing articles discussing current political, social, and economic problems. Henry Demarest Lloyd's first blast at the Standard Oil monopoly appeared in the *Atlantic Monthly* in 1881. Over the years the tempo and forcefulness of this type of literature increased. Then, in the fall of 1902, *McClure's* began two particularly hard-hitting series of articles, one on Standard Oil by Ida Tarbell, the other on big-city political machines by Lincoln Steffens. These articles provoked much comment. When the editor, S. S. McClure, decided to include in the January 1903 issue an attack on labor gangsterism in the coal fields along with installments of the Tarbell and Steffens series, he called attention to the circumstance in a striking editorial.

Something was radically wrong with the "American character," McClure wrote. These articles showed that large numbers of American employers, workers, and politicians were fundamentally immoral. Lawyers were becoming tools

One of McClure's most effective muckrakers, Ida Tarbell, brought to her investigative journalism the well-trained mind of a historian and the indignation of a daughter whose father was done in by big business, specifically the Standard Oil Company.

of big business, judges were permitting evildoers to escape justice, the churches were materialistic, educators seemed incapable of understanding what was happening. "There is no one left; none but all of us," McClure concluded. "We have to pay in the end."

McClure's editorial loosed a chain reaction. The issue sold out quickly. Thousands of readers found their own vague apprehensions brought into focus, some becoming active in progressive movements, more lending passive support.

Other editors jumped to adopt the McClure formula. A small army of professional writers soon flooded the periodical press with denunciations of the insurance business, the drug business, college athletics, prostitution, sweatshop labor, political corruption, and dozens of other subjects. This type of article inspired Theodore Roosevelt, with his gift for vivid language, to compare the journalists to "the Man with the Muck-Rake" in John Bunyan's *Pilgrim's Progress,* whose attention was so fixed on the filth at his feet that he could not notice the "celestial crown" that was offered him in exchange. Roosevelt's characterization grossly misrepresented the literature of exposure, but the label *muckraking* was thereafter affixed to the type. Despite its literal connotations, *muckraker* became a term of honor.

THE PROGRESSIVE MIND

Progressives sought to arouse the conscience of "the people" in order to "purify" American life. They were convinced that human beings were by nature decent, well intentioned, and kind. (After all, the words *human* and *humane* have the same root.) Unlike many earlier reformers, they believed that the source of society's evils lay in the structure of its institutions, not in the weaknesses or sinfulness of individuals. Therefore local, state, and national government must be made more responsive to the will of citizens who stood for the traditional virtues. In the South, many people who considered themselves progressives even argued that poll taxes and other measures designed to disfranchise blacks were reforms because they discouraged a class of people they considered unthinking and shiftless from voting.

When government had been thus reformed, then it must act; whatever its virtues, laissez-faire was obsolete. Businessmen, especially big businessmen, must be compelled to behave fairly, their acquisitive drives curbed in the interests of justice and equal opportunity for all. The weaker elements in society—women, children, the poor, the infirm—must be protected against unscrupulous power.

Despite its fervor and democratic rhetoric, progressivism was paternalistic, moderate, and often softheaded. Typical reformers of the period oversimplified complicated issues and treated their personal values as absolute standards of truth and morality. Thus progressives often acted at cross-purposes; at times some were even at war with themselves. This accounts for the diffuseness of the movement. Cutthroat business practices were criticized by great tycoons seeking to preserve their own positions and by small operators trying to protect themselves against the tycoons. But many tycoons and small operators considered themselves progressives; the former wanted federal regulation of big business and the latter strict enforcement of the antitrust laws, both legitimate "progressive" objectives.

Many progressives who desired to improve the living standards of industrial workers rejected the proposition that workers could help themselves best by organizing powerful national unions. They found it difficult to cooperate with actual working people, who seemed to them unrefined and narrow-minded. Union leaders favored government action to outlaw child labor and restrict immigration but adopted a laissez-faire attitude toward wages-and-hours legislation; they preferred to win these objectives through collective bargaining, thereby justifying their own existence. Many who favored "municipal socialism" (public ownership of streetcar lines, waterworks, and other local utilities) adamantly opposed national ownership of railroads. Progressives stressed individual freedom yet gave strong backing to the drive to deprive the public of its right to drink alcoholic beverages. Few progressives worked more assiduously than Congressman George W. Norris of rural Nebraska for reforms that would increase the power of the ordinary voter, such as the direct primary and popular election of senators, yet Norris characterized the mass of urban voters as "the mob."

The progressives never challenged the fundamental principles of capitalism, nor did they attempt a basic reorganization of society. They would have little to do with the socialist brand of reform. Wisconsin was the most progressive of states, but its leaders never cooperated with the Socialist party of Milwaukee. When socialists threatened to win control of Los Angeles in 1911, California progressives made common cause with reactionary groups in order to defeat them. Many progressives were anti-immigrant, and only a handful had anything to offer blacks, surely the most exploited group in American society.

Some people espoused more radical views. The hard times of the 1890s and the callous reactions of conservatives to the victims of that depression pushed many toward Marxian socialism. In 1900 the labor leader Eugene V. Debs ran for president on the Socialist ticket. He polled fewer than 100,000 votes. When he ran again in 1904 he got more than 400,000, and in later elections still more. Labor leaders hoping to organize unskilled workers in heavy industry were increasingly frustrated by the craft orientation of the American Federation of Labor, and some saw in socialism a way to win rank-and-file backing.

In 1905 Debs; William "Big Bill" Haywood of the Western Federation of Miners; Mary Harris "Mother" Jones, a former organizer for the United Mine Workers; Daniel De Leon of the Socialist Labor party; and a few others organized a new union, the Industrial Workers of the World. The IWW was openly anticapitalist. The preamble to its constitution began: "The working class and the employing class have nothing in common."

But the IWW never attracted many ordinary workers. Haywood, its most prominent leader, was usually a general in search of an army. His forte was attracting attention to spontaneous strikes by unorganized workers, not the patient recruiting of workers and the pursuit of practical goals. Shortly after the founding of the IWW, he was charged with complicity in the murder of an antiunion governor of Idaho after an earlier strike but was acquitted. In 1912 he was closely involved in a bitter and at times bloody strike by textile workers in Lawrence, Massachusetts, which was settled with some benefit to the strikers, and in a strike the following winter and spring by silk workers in Paterson, New Jersey, which was a failure.

Some radicals were concerned chiefly with cultural matters. Most large cities boasted groups of "bohemian" thinkers, by far the most famous being the one centered in New York City's Greenwich Village. The dancer Isadora Duncan, the photographer Alfred Stieglitz, the novelist Floyd Dell, a group of innovative artists, and the playwright Eugene O'Neill rubbed shoulders with Big Bill Haywood of the IWW; the anarchist Emma Goldman; the psychoanalyst A. A. Brill; the militant feminist advocate of birth control, Margaret Sanger; Max Eastman, editor of their organ, *The Masses*; and John Reed, a young Harvard graduate who was soon to become famous for his eyewitness account of the Russian Revolution, *Ten Days That Shook the World*.

Goldman, Haywood, Sanger, and a few others in this group were genuine radicals who sought basic changes in bourgeois society, but most of the Greenwich Village intellectuals were as much concerned with aesthetic as social issues. *The Masses* described itself as "a revolutionary and not a reform magazine . . . a magazine whose final policy is to do as it pleases." Nearly all of them came from middle-class backgrounds. They found the far-different world of the Italian and Jewish immigrants of the Village and its surrounding neighborhoods charming. But they did not become involved in the immigrants' lives the way the settlement house workers did. Their influence on their own times, therefore, was limited. "Do as I say, not as I do" is not an effective way to change minds. They are

The impact of The Silent War, *a 1906 novel by John Ames Mitchell that dealt with the growing class struggle in America, was enhanced by William Balfour-Ker's graphic illustration* From the Depths.

historically important, however, because many of them were genuinely creative people and because many of the ideas and practices they advocated were adopted by later generations.

POLITICAL REFORM: LOCAL AND STATE

To most "ordinary" progressives, political corruption and inefficiency lay at the root of the evils plaguing American society, and nowhere were corruption and inefficiency more obvious than in the nation's cities. Two characteristics of urban life are its anonymity and its complexity. As the cities grew, their antiquated and boss-ridden administrations became more and more disgraceful. For his famous muckraking series for *McClure's,* Lincoln Steffens visited St. Louis, Minneapolis, Pittsburgh, New York, Chicago, and Philadelphia and found them all riddled with corruption.

Beginning in the late 1890s progressives mounted a massive assault on dishonest and inefficient urban governments. In Toledo, Ohio, Samuel M. "Golden

Rule" Jones won election as mayor in 1897 and succeeded in arousing the citizenry against the corrupt officials. Other important progressive mayors were Tom L. Johnson of Cleveland, whose administration Lincoln Steffens called the best in the United States; Seth Low and later John P. Mitchell of New York; and Hazen S. Pingree of Detroit.

City reformers could seldom destroy the machines without changing urban political institutions. A number of middle-sized communities (Galveston, Texas, was the prototype) experimented with a system that integrated executive and legislative powers in the hands of a small elected commission, thereby concentrating responsibility and making it easier to coordinate complex activities. Out of this experiment came the city manager system, under which the commissioners appointed a professional manager to administer city affairs on a nonpartisan basis. Dayton, Ohio, which adopted the plan after the town was devastated by a flood in 1913, offers the best illustration of the city manager system in the Progressive era.

Once the political system had been made responsive to the desires of the people, the progressives hoped to use it to improve society itself. Many cities experimented with "gas and water socialism," taking over public utility companies and operating them as departments of the municipal government. Under "Golden Rule" Jones, Toledo established a minimum wage for city employees, built playgrounds and golf courses, and moderated its harsh penal code. Mayor Seth Low improved New York's public transportation system and obtained passage of the tenement house law of 1901. Mayor Tom Johnson forced a fare cut to 3 cents on the Cleveland street railways.

To carry out this kind of change required the support of state legislatures since all municipal government depends on the authority of a sovereign state. Such approval was often difficult to obtain—local bosses were usually entrenched in powerful state machines, and most legislatures were controlled by rural majorities insensitive to urban needs. Therefore the progressives had to strike at inefficiency and corruption at the state level too.

During the first decade of the new century, Wisconsin, the progressive state par excellence, was transformed by Robert M. La Follette, one of the most remarkable figures of the age. La Follette was born in Primrose, Wisconsin, in 1855. He had served three terms as a Republican congressman (1885–1891) and developed a reputation as an uncompromising foe of corruption before being elected governor in 1900. That the people would always do the right thing if properly informed and inspired was the fundamental article of his political faith. "Machine control is based upon misrepresentation and ignorance," La Follette said. "Democracy is based upon knowledge." His own career seemed to prove his point, for in his repeated clashes with the conservative Wisconsin Republican machine, he won battle after battle by vigorous grassroots campaigning.

Despite the opposition of railroad and lumbering interests, Governor La Follette obtained a direct primary system for nominating candidates, a corrupt practices act, and laws limiting campaign expenditures and lobbying activities. In power he became something of a boss himself. He made ruthless use of patronage, demanded absolute loyalty of his subordinates, and often stretched, or at least oversimplified, the truth when presenting complex issues to the voters.

The success of these policies, which became known as the Wisconsin Idea, led other states to adopt similar programs. Reform administrations swept into office in Iowa and Arkansas (1901); Oregon (1902); Minnesota, Kansas, and Mississippi (1904); New York and Georgia (1906); Nebraska (1909); and New Jersey and Colorado (1910). In some cases the reformers were Republicans, in others Democrats, but in all the example of Wisconsin was influential. By 1910, 15 states had established legislative reference services, most of them staffed by personnel trained in Wisconsin. The direct primary system became almost universal.

Some states went beyond Wisconsin in striving to make their governments responsive to the popular will. In 1902 Oregon began to experiment with the initiative, a system by which a bill could be forced on the attention of the legislature by popular petition, and the referendum, a method for allowing the electorate to approve measures rejected by their representatives and to repeal measures that the legislature had passed. Eleven states, most of them in the West, legalized these devices by 1914.

Progressives also battled for legislation to use state power against business. Women played a particularly important part in these struggles. Sparked by the National Child Labor Committee, organized in 1904, reformers over the next ten years obtained laws in nearly every state banning the employment of young children and limiting the hours of older ones. Many of these laws were poorly enforced, yet when Congress passed a federal child labor law in 1916, the Supreme Court, in *Hammer* v. *Dagenhart* (1918), declared it unconstitutional.

Laws protecting workers against on-the-job accidents were also enacted by many states. Disasters like the 1911 fire in New York City, in which nearly 150 women perished because the Triangle shirtwaist factory had no fire escapes, led to the passage of stricter municipal building codes and factory inspection acts. By 1910 most states had modified the common-law principle that a worker accepted the risk of accident as a condition of employment and was not entitled to compensation if injured unless it could be proved that the employer had been negligent. Gradually the states adopted accident insurance plans, and some began to grant pensions to widows with small children. Most manufacturers favored such

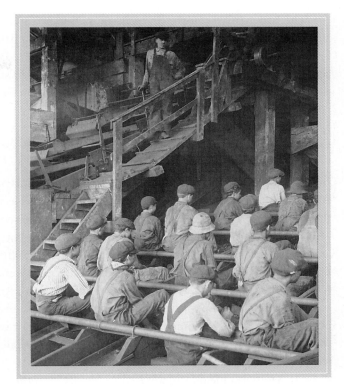

Child labor in the early 1900s was especially evident in the coal mines. Here, in Pittsburgh, Pennsylvania, boys pick through slate in an anthracite mine. Ironically, the seating arrangement of these young workers bears a striking resemblance to students sitting in a schoolhouse.

measures, if for no other reason than that they regularized procedures and avoided costly lawsuits.

The passage of so much state social legislation sent conservatives scurrying to the Supreme Court for redress. Such persons believed that no government had the power to deprive either workers or employers of the right to negotiate any kind of labor contract they wished. When an Oregon law limiting women laundry workers to ten hours a day was challenged in *Muller v. Oregon* (1908), Florence Kelley and Josephine Goldmark of the Consumers' League persuaded Louis D. Brandeis to defend the statute before the Supreme Court.

Progressives also launched a massive if ill-coordinated attack on problems related to monopoly. The variety of regulatory legislation passed by the states between 1900 and 1917 was almost infinite. Wisconsin created a powerful railroad commission staffed with nonpartisan experts; it enacted a graduated income tax and strengthened the state tax commission, which then proceeded to force corporations to bear a larger share of the cost of government; it overhauled the laws regulating insurance companies and set up a small, state-owned life insurance company to serve as a yardstick for evaluating the rates of private companies.

The progressive reform drive also found expression in a variety of congressional initiatives. The Sixteenth Amendment to the Constitution, authorizing federal income taxes, and the Seventeenth, which required the popular election of senators, were both ratified in 1913. Although some 20 states passed presidential primary laws, the cumbersome method of electing presidents was not changed.

POLITICAL REFORM: THE WOMAN SUFFRAGE MOVEMENT

But perhaps the most important federal development was passage of the Nineteenth Amendment in support of woman suffrage. The shock occasioned by the failure of the Fourteenth and Fifteenth Amendments to give women the vote after the Civil War continued to embitter most leaders of the movement. But it resulted in a split among feminists. One group, the American Woman's Suffrage Association, focused on the vote question alone. The more radical National Woman's Suffrage Association (NWSA), led by Elizabeth Cady Stanton and Susan B. Anthony, concerned itself with many issues of importance to women as well as suffrage. The NWSA put the immediate interests of women ahead of everything else. It was deeply involved in efforts to unionize women workers, yet it did not hesitate to urge women to be strikebreakers if they could get better jobs by doing so.

The Victorian idealization of female "purity" and the popular image of women as the revered guardians of home and family confused many reformers. And the trend of nineteenth-century scientific thinking influenced by the Darwinian concept of biological adaptation led to the conclusion that the female personality was different from that of the male and that the differences were inherent, not culturally determined.

These ideas and prejudices enticed feminists into a logical trap. If women were morally superior to men—a tempting conclusion—giving women the vote would improve the character of the electorate. Society would benefit because politics would become less corrupt, war a thing of the past. "City housekeeping has failed," said Jane Addams of

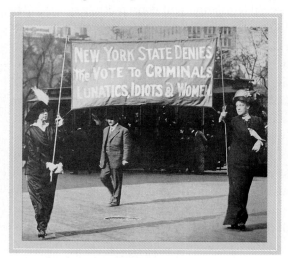

A banner in a 1911 parade carries one of the longest-standing arguments in favor of women getting the vote.

Hull House in arguing for the reform of municipal government, "partly because women, the traditional housekeepers, have not been consulted."

The trouble with this argument (aside from the fact that opponents could easily demonstrate that in states where women did vote, governments were no better or worse than elsewhere) was that it surrendered the principle of equality. In the long run this was to have serious consequences for the women's movement, although the immediate effect of the purity argument was probably to advance the suffragists' cause.

By the early twentieth century there were signs of progress. In 1890 the two major women's groups combined as the National American Woman's Suffrage Association (NAWSA). Stanton and Anthony were the first two presidents of the association, but new leaders were emerging, the most notable being Carrie Chapman Catt, a woman who combined superb organizing abilities and political skills with commitment to broad social reform. The NAWSA made winning the right to vote its main objective and concentrated on a state-by-state approach. Wyoming gave women the vote in 1869, and Utah, Colorado, and Idaho had been won over to women's suffrage by 1896.

The burgeoning of the progressive movement helped as middle-class recruits of both sexes adopted the suffrage cause. California was crucial. In 1896, California voters had rejected the measure. But in 1911, despite determined opposition from saloonkeepers, the proposal barely passed. Within three years, most other western states fell into line. For the first time, large numbers of

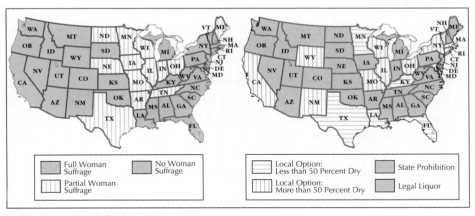

Suffrage and Prohibition, 1917

These maps give a sense of the state-by-state progress of woman suffrage and prohibition by 1917. The Eighteenth Amendment, enforcing national prohibition, passed in 1919; the Nineteenth Amendment, allowing women the right to vote, in 1920. Both amendments were a culmination of reform efforts before and during the Progressive era. The original 1917 version of the temperance map referred to the three "wet" states—New Jersey, Pennsylvania, and Nevada—as "Booze States."

Alva Belmont (left) *and Alice Paul* (right) *served as president and vice president, respectively, of the National Women's party. Here, the two supervise the remodeling work of their political headquarters, a building that, interestingly, stood opposite the U.S. Capitol.*

working-class women began to agitate for the vote. In 1917, bosses at New York City's Tammany Hall, who had engineered the defeat of women's suffrage in that state two years earlier, concluded that passage was inevitable and threw their support to the measure, which passed.

The suffragists then shifted the campaign back to the national level, the lead taken by a new organization, the Congressional Union, headed by Alice Paul and the wealthy reformer Alva Belmont. When President Wilson refused to support the idea of a constitutional amendment granting women the vote, militant women picketed the White House. A number of them, including the daughter of Thomas Bayard, a former senator and secretary of state, were arrested and sentenced to 60 days in the workhouse. This roused a storm of criticism, and Wilson quickly pardoned the picketers. After some hesitation the NAWSA stopped concentrating on the state-by-state approach and began to campaign for a constitutional amendment. Pressure on Congress mounted steadily. The amendment finally won congressional approval in 1918. By 1920 the necessary three-quarters of the states had ratified the Nineteenth Amendment; the long fight was over.

THEODORE ROOSEVELT: COWBOY IN THE WHITE HOUSE

On September 6, 1901, an anarchist named Leon Czolgosz shot President McKinley during a public reception at the Pan-American Exposition at Buffalo, New York. Eight days later McKinley died and Theodore Roosevelt became president of the United States. His ascension to the presidency marked the beginning of a new era in national politics.

Although only 42, by far the youngest president in the nation's history up to that time, Roosevelt brought solid qualifications to the office. Son of a well-to-do New York merchant, he had graduated from Harvard in 1880 and studied law briefly at Columbia, though he did not obtain a degree. In addition to political experience that included three terms in the New York assembly, six years on the United States Civil Service Commission, two years as police commissioner of New York City, another as assistant secretary of the navy, and a term as governor of New York, he had been a rancher in the Dakota Territory and a soldier in the Spanish-American War. He was also a well-known historian: His *Naval War of 1812* (1882), begun during his undergraduate days at Harvard, and his four-volume *Winning of the West* (1889–1896) were valuable works of scholarship, and he had written two popular biographies and other books as well. Politically, he had always been a loyal Republican. He rejected the mugwump heresy in 1884, despite his distaste for Blaine, and during the tempestuous 1890s he vigorously denounced populism, Bryanism, and "labor agitators."

Nevertheless, Roosevelt's elevation to the presidency alarmed many conservatives, and not without reason. He did not fit their conception, based on a composite image of the chief executives from Hayes to McKinley, of what a president should be like. He seemed too undignified, too energetic, too outspoken, too unconventional. It was one thing to have operated a cattle ranch, another to have captured a gang of rustlers at gunpoint; one thing to have run a metropolitan police force, another to have roamed New York slums in the small hours to catch patrolmen fraternizing with thieves and prostitutes; one thing to have commanded a regiment, another to have killed a Spaniard personally.

Theodore Roosevelt in full oratorical flight. No wonder journalists were captivated by him; even when proceeding cautiously, which was most of the time as president, he brought life to national politics.

Roosevelt had been a sickly child, plagued by asthma and poor eyesight, and he seems to have spent much of his adult life compensating for the sense of inadequacy that these troubles bred in him. He repeatedly carried his displays of physical stamina and personal courage and his love of athletics and big-game hunting to preternatural lengths. Henry Adams, who watched Roosevelt's development over the years with a mixture of fear and amusement, said that he was "pure act."

Once, while fox hunting, Roosevelt fell from his horse, cutting his face severely and breaking his left arm. Instead of waiting for help or struggling to some nearby house to summon a doctor, he clambered back on his horse and resumed the chase. "I was in at the death," he wrote next day. "I looked pretty gay, with one arm dangling, and my face and clothes like the walls of a slaughter house." That evening, after his arm had been set and put in splints, he attended a dinner party.

Roosevelt worshiped aggressiveness and was extremely sensitive to any threat to his honor as a gentleman. When another young man showed some slight interest in Roosevelt's fiancée, he sent for a set of French dueling pistols. His teachers found him an interesting student, for he was intelligent and imaginative, if annoyingly argumentative. "Now look here, Roosevelt," one Harvard professor finally said to him, "let me talk. I'm running this course."

Had Roosevelt been the impetuous hothead that conservatives feared, he would have plunged ahead without regard for their feelings and influence. Instead he moved slowly and often got what he wanted by using his executive power rather than by persuading Congress to pass new laws. His domestic program included some measure of control of big corporations, more power for the Interstate Commerce Commission (ICC), and the conservation of natural resources. By consulting congressional leaders and following their advice not to bring up controversial matters like the tariff and currency reform, he obtained a modest budget of new laws.

The Newlands Act (1902) funneled the proceeds from land sales in the West into federal irrigation projects. The Department of Commerce and Labor, which was to include a Bureau of Corporations with authority to investigate industrial combines and issue reports, was established. The Elkins Railroad Act of 1903 strengthened the ICC's hand against the railroads by making the receiving as well as the granting of rebates illegal and by forbidding the roads to deviate in any way from their published rates.

ROOSEVELT AND BIG BUSINESS

Roosevelt soon became known as a trustbuster, and in the sense that he considered the monopoly problem the most pressing issue of the times, this was accurate to an extent. But he did not believe in breaking up big corporations indiscriminately. Regulation seemed the best way to deal with large corporations because, he said, industrial giantism "could not be eliminated unless we were willing to turn back the wheels of modern progress."

With Congress unwilling to pass a stiff regulatory law, Roosevelt resorted to the Sherman Act to get at the problem. Although the Supreme Court decision in the Sugar Trust case seemed to have emasculated that law, in 1902 he ordered the Justice Department to bring suit against the Northern Securities Company.

He chose his target wisely. The Northern Securities Company controlled the Great Northern, the Northern Pacific, and the Chicago, Burlington and Quincy Railroads. It had been created in 1901 after a titanic battle on the New York Stock Exchange between the forces of J. P. Morgan and James J. Hill and those of E. H. Harriman, who was associated with the Rockefeller interests. In their efforts to obtain control of the Northern Pacific, the rivals had forced its stock up to $1000 a share, ruining many speculators and threatening to cause a panic.

Neither side could win a clear-cut victory, so they decided to put the stock of all three railroads in a holding company owned by the two groups. Since Harriman already controlled the Union Pacific and the Southern Pacific, a virtual monopoly of western railroads was effected. The public had been alarmed, for the merger seemed to typify the rapaciousness of the tycoons.

The announcement of the suit caused consternation in the business world. Morgan rushed to the White House. "If we have done anything wrong," he said to the president, "send your man to my man and they can fix it up." Roosevelt was not fundamentally opposed to this sort of agreement, but it was too late to compromise in this instance. Attorney General Philander C. Knox pressed the case vigorously, and in 1904 the Supreme Court ordered the dissolution of the Northern Securities Company.

Roosevelt then ordered suits against the meat packers, the Standard Oil Trust, and the American Tobacco Company. His stock among progressives rose, yet he had not embarrassed the conservatives in Congress by demanding new antitrust legislation.

The president went out of his way to assure cooperative corporation magnates that he was not against size per se. At a White House conference in 1905, Roosevelt and Elbert H. Gary, chairman of the board of U.S. Steel, reached a "gentlemen's agreement" whereby Gary promised "to cooperate with the Government in every possible way." The Bureau of Corporations would conduct an investigation of U.S. Steel, Gary allowing it full access to company records. Roosevelt in turn promised that if the investigation revealed any corporate malpractices, he would allow Gary to set matters right voluntarily, thereby avoiding an antitrust suit.

There were limits to the effectiveness of such arrangements. Standard Oil agreed to a similar détente and then reneged, refusing to turn over vital records to the bureau. The Justice Department brought suit against the company under the Sherman Act, and eventually it was broken up at the order of the Supreme Court. Roosevelt would have preferred a more binding kind of regulation, but when he asked for laws giving the government supervisory authority over big combinations, Congress refused to act.

ROOSEVELT AND THE COAL STRIKE

Roosevelt made remarkable use of his executive power during the anthracite coal strike of 1902. In June the United Mine Workers (UMW), led by John Mitchell, laid down their picks and demanded higher wages, an eight-hour day, and recognition of the union. Most of the anthracite mines were owned by railroads. Two years earlier the miners had won a 10 percent wage increase in a similar strike, chiefly because the owners feared that labor unrest might endanger the election of McKinley. Now the coal companies were dead set against further concessions; when the men walked out, they shut down their properties and prepared to starve the strikers into submission.

The strike dragged on through summer and early fall. The miners conducted themselves with great restraint, avoiding violence and offering to submit their claims to arbitration. As the price of anthracite soared with the approach of winter, sentiment in their behalf mounted.

The owners' spokesman, George F. Baer of the Reading Railroad, proved particularly inept at public relations. Baer stated categorically that God was on the side of management, but when someone suggested asking an important Roman Catholic prelate to arbitrate the dispute, he replied icily: "Anthracite mining is a business and not a religious, sentimental or academic proposition."

Roosevelt shared the public's sympathy for the miners, and the threat of a coal shortage alarmed him. Early in October he summoned both sides to a conference in Washington and urged them as patriotic Americans to sacrifice any "personal consideration" for the "general good." His action enraged the coal operators, for they believed he was trying to force them to recognize the union. They refused even to speak to the UMW representatives at the conference and demanded that Roosevelt end the strike by force and bring suit against the union under the Sherman Act. Mitchell, aware of the immense prestige that Roosevelt had conferred on the union by calling the conference, cooperated fully with the president.

Roosevelt took a bold step: He announced that unless a settlement was reached promptly, he would order federal troops into the anthracite regions, not to break the strike but to seize and operate the mines.

The threat of government intervention brought the owners to terms. In March 1903 a commission appointed by Roosevelt granted the miners a 10 percent wage increase and a nine-hour workday.

"Jack and the Wall Street Giants" show-
ing a diminutive Teddy Roosevelt, armed
solely with the sword of "Public Service,"
taking on the behemoths of Wall Street,
among them railroad barons James J.
Hill and Jay Gould and financier J. P.
Morgan. Roosevelt, in fact, was as likely
to preach to the giants as to slay them.

To the public the incident seemed a perfect illustration of the progressive spirit—in Roosevelt's words, everyone had received a "square deal." Roosevelt, however, was the main winner in the dispute. The public acclaimed him as a fearless, imaginative, public-spirited leader. Without calling on Congress for support, he had expanded his own authority and hence that of the federal government. His action marked a major forward step in the evolution of the modern presidency.

TR's Triumphs

By reviving the Sherman Act, settling the coal strike, and pushing moderate reforms through Congress, Roosevelt ensured that he would be reelected president in 1904. Progressives, if not captivated, were at least pleased by his performance. Conservative Republicans offered no serious objection. Sensing that Roosevelt had won over the liberals, the Democrats nominated a conservative, Judge Alton B. Parker of New York, and bid for the support of eastern industrialists.

This strategy failed, for businessmen continued to eye the party of Bryan with intense suspicion. They preferred, as the *New York Sun* put it, "the impulsive candidate of the party of conservatism to the conservative candidate of the party which the business interests regard as permanently and dangerously impulsive." Despite his resentment at Roosevelt's attack on the Northern Securities Company, J. P. Morgan contributed $150,000 to the Republican campaign. Other tycoons gave with equal generosity. Roosevelt swept the country, carrying even the normally Democratic border states of Maryland and Missouri.

Encouraged by the landslide and the increasing militancy of progressives, Roosevelt pressed for more reform legislation. His most imaginative proposal was a plan to make the District of Columbia a model progressive community. He suggested child labor and factory inspection laws and a slum clearance program, but Congress refused to act. Likewise, his request for a minimum wage for railroad workers was rejected.

He had greater success when he proposed still another increase in the power of the Interstate Commerce Commission. Rebating remained a serious problem. With progressive state governors demanding federal action and farmers and manufacturers, especially in the Midwest, clamoring for relief against discriminatory rates, Roosevelt was ready by 1905 to make railroad legislation his major objective. The ICC should be empowered to fix rates, not merely to challenge unreasonable ones. It should have the right to inspect the private records of the railroads since fair rates could not be determined unless the true financial condition of the roads was known.

Because these proposals struck at rights that businessmen considered sacrosanct, many congressmen balked. But Roosevelt applied presidential pressure, and in June 1906 the Hepburn bill became law. It gave the commission the power to inspect the books of railroad companies, to set maximum rates (once a complaint had been filed by a shipper), and to control sleeping car companies, owners of oil pipelines, and other firms engaged in transportation. In all, the Hepburn Act made the ICC a more powerful and more active body.

Congress also passed meat inspection and pure food and drug legislation. In 1906 Upton Sinclair published *The Jungle,* a devastating exposé of the filthy conditions in the Chicago slaughterhouses. Sinclair was more interested in writing a socialist tract than he was in meat inspection, but his book, a best-seller, raised a storm against the packers. After Roosevelt read *The Jungle* he sent two officials to Chicago to investigate. Their report was so shocking, he said, that its publication would "be well-nigh ruinous to our export trade in meat." He threatened to release the report, however, unless Congress acted. After a hot fight, the meat inspection bill passed. The Pure Food and Drug Act, forbidding the manufacture and sale of adulterated and fraudulently labeled products, rode through Congress on the coattails of this measure.

Roosevelt has probably received more credit than he deserves for these laws. He had never been deeply interested in pure food legislation, and he considered Dr. Harvey W. Wiley, chief chemist of the Department of Agriculture and the leader of the fight for this reform, something of a crank. He compromised with opponents of meat inspection cheerfully, despite his loud denunciations of the evils under attack.

To advanced liberals Roosevelt's achievements seemed limited when placed beside his professed objectives and his smug evaluations of what he had done. How could he be a reformer and a defender of established interests at the same time? Roosevelt

Before the passage of the Pure Food and Drug Act in 1906, manufacturers were free to use any ingredients they chose. Many "tonics" kept their promises of increased vigor by delivering doses of cocaine, alcohol, or other narcotics.

found no difficulty in holding such a position. As one historian has said: "He stood close to the center and bared his teeth at the conservatives of the right and the liberals of the extreme left."

ROOSEVELT TILTS LEFT

As the progressive movement advanced, Roosevelt advanced with it. He never accepted all the ideas of what he called its "lunatic fringe," but he took steadily more liberal positions. He always insisted that he was not hostile to business interests, but when those interests sought to exploit the national domain, they had no more implacable foe. Conservation of natural resources was dear to his heart and probably his most significant achievement as president. He placed some 150 million acres of forest lands in federal reserves, and he strictly enforced the laws governing grazing, mining, and lumbering.

As Roosevelt became more liberal, conservative Republicans began to balk at following his lead. The sudden panic that struck the financial world in October 1907 speeded the trend. Government policies had no direct bearing on the panic, which began with a run on several important New York trust companies and spread to the Stock Exchange when speculators found themselves unable to borrow money to meet their obligations. In the emergency Roosevelt authorized the deposit of large amounts of government cash in New York banks. He informally agreed to the acquisition of the Tennessee Coal and Iron Company by U.S. Steel when the bankers told him that the purchase was necessary to end the panic. In spite of his efforts, conservatives insisted on referring to the financial collapse as "Roosevelt's panic," and they blamed the president for the depression that followed on its heels.

Roosevelt, however, turned left rather than right. In 1908 he came out in favor of federal income and inheritance taxes, stricter regulation of interstate corporations, and reforms designed to help industrial workers. He denounced "the speculative folly and the flagrant dishonesty" of "malefactors of great wealth," further alienating conservative, or Old Guard, Republicans, who resented the attacks on their integrity implicit in Roosevelt's statements. When the president began criticizing the courts, the last bastion of conservatism, he lost all chance of obtaining further reform legislation. As he said himself, during his last months in office "stagnation continued to rage with uninterrupted violence."

WILLIAM HOWARD TAFT: THE LISTLESS PROGRESSIVE, OR MORE IS LESS

But Roosevelt remained popular and politically powerful; before his term ended, he chose William Howard Taft, his secretary of war, to succeed him and easily obtained Taft's nomination. William Jennings Bryan was again the Democratic candidate. Campaigning on Roosevelt's record, Taft carried the country by well over a million votes, defeating Bryan 321 to 162 in the Electoral College.

Taft was intelligent, experienced, and public spirited; he seemed ideally suited to carry out Roosevelt's policies. Born in Cincinnati in 1857, educated at Yale, he had served as an Ohio judge, as solicitor general of the United States under Benjamin Harrison, and then as a federal circuit court judge before accepting McKinley's assignment to head the Philippine Commission in 1900. His success as civil governor of the Philippines led Roosevelt to make him secretary of war in 1904.

Taft supported the Square Deal loyally. This, together with his mentor's ardent endorsement, won him the backing of most progressive Republicans. Yet the Old Guard liked him too; although outgoing, he had none of the Roosevelt impetuosity and aggressiveness. His genial personality and his obvious desire to avoid conflict appealed to moderates.

However, Taft lacked the physical and mental stamina required of a modern chief executive. Although not lazy, he weighed over 300 pounds and needed to rest this vast bulk more than the job allowed. He liked to eat in leisurely fashion, to idle away mornings on the golf course, to take an afternoon nap. Campaigning bored him; speech making seemed a useless chore. The judicial life was his real love; intense partisanship dismayed and confused him. He was too reasonable to control a coalition and not ambitious enough to impose his will on others. He found extremists irritating and persistent people (including his wife) difficult to resist. He supported many progressive measures, but he never absorbed the progressive spirit.

Taft honestly wanted to carry out most of Roosevelt's policies. He enforced the Sherman Act vigorously and continued to expand the national forest reserves. He signed the Mann-Elkins Act of 1910, which empowered the ICC to suspend rate increases without waiting for a shipper to complain and established the Commerce Court to speed the settlement of railroad rate cases. An eight-hour day for all persons engaged in work on government contracts, mine safety legislation, and several other reform measures received his approval. He even summoned Congress into special session specifically to reduce tariff duties—something that Roosevelt had not dared to attempt.

But Taft had been disturbed by Roosevelt's sweeping use of executive power. "We have got to work out our problems on the basis of law," he insisted. Whereas Roosevelt had excelled at maneuvering around congressional opposition and at finding ways to accomplish his objectives without waiting for Congress to act, Taft adamantly refused to use such tactics. His restraint was in many ways admirable, but it reduced his effectiveness.

In case after case, Taft's lack of vigor and his political ineptness led to trouble. In the matter of the tariff, he favored downward revision. When the special session met in 1909, the House promptly passed a bill that was in line with his desires. But Senate protectionists restored the high rates of the act of 1897 on most items. A group of insurgent senators, led by Robert La Follette of Wisconsin, fought these changes, producing masses of statistics to show that the proposed schedules on cotton goods, woolens, and other products were unreasonably high.

They were fighting the president's battle, yet Taft did little to help them. He signed the high Payne-Aldrich measure and called it "the best [tariff] bill that the Republican party ever passed." His attitude dumbfounded the progressives.

In 1910 Taft got into difficulty with the conservationists. Although he believed in husbanding natural resources carefully, he did not like the way Roosevelt had circumvented Congress in adding to the forest reserves. He demanded, and eventually obtained, specific legislation to accomplish this purpose. The issue that aroused the conservationists concerned the integrity of his secretary of the interior, Richard A. Ballinger. A less than ardent conservationist, Ballinger returned to the public domain certain waterpower sites that the Roosevelt administration had withdrawn on the legally questionable ground that they were to become ranger stations. Ballinger's action alarmed Chief Forester Gifford Pinchot, the darling of the conservationists. When Pinchot learned that Ballinger intended to validate the shaky claim of mining interests to a large tract of coal-rich land in Alaska, he launched an intemperate attack on the secretary.

In the Ballinger-Pinchot controversy Taft felt obliged to support his own man. The coal lands dispute was complex, and Pinchot's charges were exaggerated. It was certainly unfair to call Ballinger "the most effective opponent the conservation policies have yet had." When Pinchot, whose own motives were partly political, persisted in criticizing Ballinger, Taft dismissed him. He had no choice under the circumstances, but a more adept politician might have found some way of avoiding a showdown.

BREAKUP OF THE REPUBLICAN PARTY

One ominous aspect of the Ballinger-Pinchot affair was that Pinchot was a close friend of Theodore Roosevelt. After Taft's inauguration, Roosevelt had gone off to hunt big game in Africa, bearing in his baggage an autographed photograph of his protégé and a touching letter of appreciation, in which the new president said: "I can never forget that the power I now exercise was a voluntary transfer from you to me." For months, as he trudged across Africa, guns blazing, Roosevelt was out of touch with affairs in the United States. As soon as he emerged from the wilderness in March 1910, bearing more than 3000 trophies, including 9 lions, 5 elephants, and 13 rhinos, he was caught up in the squabble between the progressive members of his party and its titular head. Pinchot met him in Italy, laden with injured innocence and a packet of angry letters from various progressives. His intimate friend Senator Henry Cabot Lodge, essentially a conservative, barraged him with messages, the gist of which was that Taft was lazy and inept and that Roosevelt should prepare to become the "Moses" who would guide the party "out of the wilderness of doubt and discontent" into which Taft had led it.

Roosevelt hoped to steer a middle course, but Pinchot's complaints impressed him. Taft had decided to strike out on his own, he concluded. "No man must render such a service as that I rendered Taft and expect the individual . . . not in the end to become uncomfortable and resentful," he wrote Lodge sadly. Taft sensed the former president's coolness and was offended. He was egged on by his ambitious wife, who wanted him to stand clear of Roosevelt's shadow and establish his own reputation.

Perhaps the resulting rupture was inevitable. The Republican party was dividing into two factions, the progressives and the Old Guard. Forced to choose between them, Taft threw in his lot with the Old Guard. Roosevelt backed the progressives. Speaking at Osawatomie, Kansas, in August 1910, he came out for a comprehensive program of social legislation, which he called the New Nationalism. Besides attacking "special privilege" and the "unfair money-getting" practices of "lawbreakers of great wealth," he called for a broad expansion of federal power. "The betterment we seek must be accomplished," he said, "mainly through the National Government."

The final break came in October 1911, when the president ordered an antitrust suit against U.S. Steel. Roosevelt, of course, opposed breaking up large corporations. "The effort at prohibiting all combination has substantially failed," Taft said. "The way out lies . . . in completely controlling them." He was prepared to enforce the Sherman Act "or die in the attempt." But what angered Roosevelt was Taft's emphasis in the suit on U.S. Steel's absorption of the Tennessee Coal and Iron Company, which Roosevelt had unofficially authorized during the panic of 1907. The government's antitrust brief made Roosevelt appear to have been either an abettor of monopoly or, far worse, a fool who had been duped by the steel corporation. Early in 1912 he declared himself a candidate for the Republican presidential nomination.

Roosevelt plunged into the preconvention campaign with typical energy. He was almost uniformly victorious in states that held presidential primaries, carrying even Ohio, Taft's home state. However, the president controlled the party machinery and entered the national convention with a small majority of the delegates. Since some Taft delegates had been chosen under questionable circumstances, the Roosevelt forces challenged the right of 254 of them to their seats. The Taft-controlled credentials committee, paying little attention to the evidence, gave all but a few of the disputed seats to the president, who then won the nomination on the first ballot.

Had Roosevelt swallowed his resentment and bided his time, Taft would almost certainly have been defeated in the election, and the 1916 Republican nomination would have been Roosevelt's for the asking. But he was understandably outraged by the ruthless manner in which the Taft "steamroller" had overridden his forces. When his leading supporters urged him to organize a third party, and when two of them, George W. Perkins, formerly a partner of the banker J. P. Morgan, and the publisher Frank Munsey, offered to finance the campaign, Roosevelt agreed to make the race.

In August, amid scenes of hysterical enthusiasm, the first convention of the Progressive party met at Chicago and nominated him for president. Announcing that he felt "as strong as a bull moose," Roosevelt delivered a stirring "confession of faith," calling for strict regulation of corporations, a tariff commission, national presidential primaries, minimum wage and workers' compensation laws, the elimination of child labor, and many other reforms.

THE ELECTION OF 1912

The Democrats made the most of the opportunity offered by the Republican schism. Had they nominated a conservative or allowed Bryan a fourth chance, they would probably have ensured Roosevelt's election. Instead, after battling through 46 ballots at their convention in Baltimore, they nominated Woodrow Wilson, who had achieved a remarkable liberal record as governor of New Jersey. Incidentally, Wilson was one of three southern candidates for the nomination, further evidence that the sectional conflicts of Reconstruction had been forgotten.

Although as a political scientist Wilson had criticized the status quo and taken a pragmatic approach to the idea of government regulation of the economy, he had objected strongly to Bryan's brand of politics. In 1896 he voted for the Gold Democratic party candidate instead of Bryan. But by 1912, influenced partly by ambition and partly by the spirit of the times, he had been converted to progressivism. He called his brand of reform the New Freedom.

The federal government could best advance the cause of social justice, Wilson reasoned, by eradicating the special privileges that enabled the "interests" to flourish. Where Roosevelt had lost faith in competition as a way of protecting the public against monopolies, Wilson insisted that competition could be restored. The government must break up the great trusts, establish fair rules for doing business, and subject violators to stiff punishments. Thereafter, the free enterprise system would protect the public from exploitation without destroying individual initiative and opportunity. "If America is not to have free enterprise,

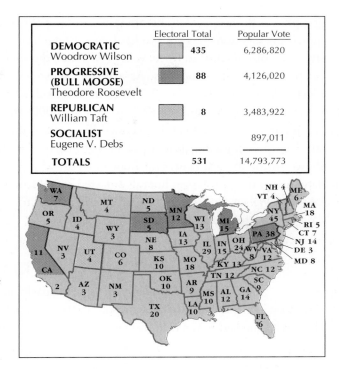

		Electoral Total	Popular Vote
DEMOCRATIC Woodrow Wilson		435	6,286,820
PROGRESSIVE (BULL MOOSE) Theodore Roosevelt		88	4,126,020
REPUBLICAN William Taft		8	3,483,922
SOCIALIST Eugene V. Debs			897,011
TOTALS		531	14,793,773

The Election of 1912

The fourth-largest vote getter in the election of 1912 was Eugene V. Debs of the Socialist party, who gained about 900,000 popular votes (approximately 6 percent of the popular vote) but no electoral votes.

then she can have freedom of no sort whatever," he said. Although rather vague, this argument appealed to thousands of voters who found the growing power of large corporations disturbing, but who hesitated to make the thoroughgoing commitment to government control of business that Roosevelt was advocating.

Roosevelt's reasoning was perhaps theoretically more sound. He called for a New Nationalism. Laissez-faire made less sense than it had in earlier times. The complexities of the modern world seemed to call for a positive approach, a plan, the close application of human intelligence to social and economic problems.

But being more in line with American experience than the New Nationalism, Wilson's New Freedom had much to recommend it. The danger that selfish individuals would use the power of the state for their own ends had certainly not disappeared, despite the efforts of progressives to make government more responsive to popular opinion. Any considerable expansion of national power, as Roosevelt proposed, would increase the danger and probably create new difficulties. Managing so complicated an enterprise as an industrialized nation was sure to be a formidable task for the federal government. Furthermore, individual freedom of opportunity merited the toleration of a certain amount of inefficiency.

To choose between the New Nationalism and the New Freedom, between the dynamic Roosevelt and the idealistic Wilson, was indeed difficult. Thousands grappled with this problem before going to the polls, but partisan politics determined the election. Taft got the hard-core Republican vote but lost the progressive wing of the GOP to Roosevelt. Wilson had the solid support of both conservative and liberal Democrats. As a result, Wilson won an easy victory in the Electoral College, receiving 435 votes to Roosevelt's 88 and Taft's 8. The popular vote was Wilson, 6,286,000; Roosevelt, 4,126,000; and Taft, 3,484,000.

If partisan politics had determined the winner, the election was nonetheless an overwhelming endorsement of progressivism. The temper of the times was shown by the 897,000 votes for Eugene Debs, who was again the Socialist candidate. Altogether, professed liberals amassed over 11 million of the 15 million ballots cast. Wilson was a minority president, but he took office with a clear mandate to press forward with further reforms.

WILSON: THE NEW FREEDOM

No one ever rose more suddenly or spectacularly in American politics than Woodrow Wilson. In the spring of 1910 he was president of Princeton University; he had never held or even run for public office. In the fall of 1912 he

Woodrow Wilson, presiding over the 1906 Princeton commencement, with steel magnate cum educational philanthropist Andrew Carnegie firmly in tow.

was president-elect of the United States. Yet if his rise was meteoric, in a very real sense he had devoted his life to preparing for it. He was born in Staunton, Virginia, in 1856, the son of a Presbyterian minister. As a student he became interested in political theory, dreaming of representing his state in the Senate. He studied law solely because he thought it the best avenue to public office, and when he discovered that he did not like legal work, he took a doctorate at Johns Hopkins in political science.

For years Wilson's political ambitions appeared doomed to frustration. He taught at Bryn Mawr, then at Wesleyan, finally at his alma mater, Princeton. He wrote several influential books, among them *Congressional Government* and *The State,* and achieved an outstanding reputation as a teacher and lecturer. In 1902 he was chosen president of Princeton and soon won a place among the nation's leading educators. He revised the curriculum, introducing many new subjects and insisting that students pursue an organized and integrated course of study. He instituted the preceptorial system, which placed the students in close intellectual and social contact with their teachers. He attracted outstanding young scholars to the Princeton faculty.

In time Wilson's educational ideas and his overbearing manner of applying them got him in trouble with some of Princeton's alumni and trustees. Although his university career was wrecked, the controversies, in which he appeared to be championing democracy and progress in the face of reactionary opponents, brought him at last to the attention of the politicians. Then, in a great rush, came power and fame.

Wilson was an immediate success as president. Since Roosevelt's last year in office Congress had been almost continually at war with the executive branch and with itself. Legislative achievements had been few. Now a small avalanche of important measures received the approval of the lawmakers. In October 1913 the Underwood Tariff brought the first significant reduction of duties since before the Civil War. Food products, wool, iron and steel, shoes, agricultural machinery, and other items that could be produced more cheaply in the United States than abroad were placed on the free list. Rates on most other goods were cut substantially, the object being to equalize foreign and domestic costs. To compensate for the expected loss of revenue, the act provided for a graduated tax on personal incomes.

Two months later the Federal Reserve Act gave the country a central banking system for the first time since Jackson destroyed the Bank of the United States. The measure divided the nation into 12 banking districts, each under the supervision of a Federal Reserve bank, a sort of bank for bankers.

The crown and nerve center of the system was the Federal Reserve Board in Washington, which appointed a majority of the directors of the Federal Reserve banks and had some control over rediscount rates (the commission charged by the reserve banks for performing the rediscounting function). The board provided a modicum of public control over the banks, but the effort to weaken the power of the great New York banks by decentralizing the system proved ineffective. Nevertheless, a true central banking system was created.

When inflation threatened, the reserve banks could raise the rediscount rate, discouraging borrowing and thus reducing the amount of money in circulation. In bad times it could lower the rate, making it easier to borrow and injecting new dollars into the economy. Much remained to be learned about the proper management of the money supply, but the nation finally had a flexible yet safe currency.

In 1914 Congress passed two important laws affecting corporations. One created the Federal Trade Commission (FTC) to replace Roosevelt's Bureau of Corporations. In addition to investigating corporations and publishing reports, this nonpartisan board could issue cease and desist orders against "unfair" trade practices brought to light through its research. The law did not define the term *unfair,* and the commission's rulings could be taken on appeal to the federal courts, but the FTC was nonetheless a powerful instrument for protecting the public against the trusts.

The second measure, the Clayton Antitrust Act, made certain specific business practices illegal, including price discrimination that tended to foster monopolies; "tying" agreements, which forbade retailers from handling the products of a firm's competitors; and the creation of interlocking directorates as a means of controlling competing companies. The act exempted labor unions and agricultural organizations from the antitrust laws and curtailed the use of injunctions in labor disputes. The officers of corporations could be held individually responsible if their companies violated the antitrust laws.

The Democrats controlled both houses of Congress for the first time since 1890 and were eager to make a good record, but Wilson's imaginative and aggressive use of presidential power was decisive. He called the legislators into special session in April 1913 and appeared before them to lay out his program; he was the first president to address Congress in person since John Adams. Then he followed the course of administration bills closely. He had a private telephone line installed between the Capitol and the White House. Administration representatives haunted the cloakrooms and lobbies of both houses. Cooperative congressmen began to receive notes of praise and encouragement, recalcitrant ones stern demands for support, often pecked out on the president's own portable typewriter.

Wilson explained his success by saying, only half humorously, that running the government was child's play for anyone who had managed the faculty of a university. Responsible party government was his objective; he expected individual Democrats to support the decisions of the party majority, and his idealism never prevented him from awarding the spoils of office to city bosses and conservative congressmen, as long as they supported his program. Nor did his career as a political theorist make him rigid and doctrinaire. In practice the differences between his New Freedom and Roosevelt's New Nationalism tended to disappear. The Underwood Tariff and the Clayton Antitrust Act fitted the philosophy Wilson had expounded during the campaign, but the FTC represented a step toward the kind of regulated economy that Roosevelt advocated. So did the Federal Reserve system.

There were limits to Wilson's progressivism, limits imposed partly by his temperament and partly by his philosophy. He objected as strenuously to laws granting special favors to farmers and workers as to those benefiting the tycoons. He considered the provision exempting unions from the antitrust laws unsound. Nor would he push for a federal law prohibiting child labor; such a measure would be unconstitutional, he believed. He also refused to back the constitutional amendment giving the vote to women.

By the end of 1914 the Wilsonian record, on balance, was positive but distinctly limited. The president believed that the major progressive goals had been achieved; he had no plans for further reform. Many other progressives thought that a great deal more remained to be done.

THE PROGRESSIVES AND MINORITY RIGHTS

On one important issue, race relations, Wilson was distinctly reactionary. With a mere handful of exceptions, the progressives exhibited strong prejudices against nonwhite people and against certain categories of whites as well. Many were as unsympathetic to immigrants from Asia and eastern and southern Europe as any of the "conservative" opponents of immigration in the 1880s and 1890s. The Gentlemen's Agreement excluding Japanese immigrants was reached in 1907 at the height of the progressive movement. In the same year, Congress appointed a commission headed by Senator William Dillingham of Vermont to study the immigration question. The Dillingham Commission labored for more than two years and brought forth a 41-volume report that led in 1913 to a bill restricting the number of newcomers to be admitted and reducing especially the influx from eastern and southern Europe. Only the outbreak of war in Europe in 1914, which cut immigration to a trickle, prevented the passage of this measure.

In 1902 Congress passed the Dead Indian Land Act, which made it easier for Indians to sell allotments that they had inherited, and in 1906 another law further relaxed restrictions on land sales. Efforts to improve the education of Indian children continued, but most progressives assumed that only vocational training would help them. Theodore Roosevelt knew from his experiences as a rancher in

Although lynchings were common after the Civil War, by the 1890s they had become public spectacles. Sometimes special "excursion" trains were scheduled, employers released workers, and families would bring picnics to the event. This lynching, viewed by a crowd of 10,000, took place at Paris, Texas, in 1893.

the Dakota Territory that Indians could be as energetic and capable as whites, but he considered these "exceptional." As for the rest, it would be many generations before they could be expected to "move forward" enough to become "ordinary citizens," Roosevelt believed.

To say that African Americans did not fare well at the hands of progressives would be a gross understatement. Populist efforts to unite white and black farmers in the southern states had led to the imposition of further repressive measures. Segregation became more rigid, white opposition to black voting more monolithic. In 1900 the body of a Mississippi black was dug up by order of the state legislature and reburied in a segregated cemetery; in Virginia in 1902 the daughter of Robert E. Lee was arrested for riding in the black section of a railroad car. "Insult is being added to injury continually," a black journalist in Alabama complained. "Have those in power forgotten that there is a God?"

Many progressive women, still smarting from the insult to their sex entailed in the Fourteenth and Fifteenth Amendments and eager to attract southern support for their campaign for the vote, adopted racist arguments. They contrasted the supposed corruption and incompetence of black voters with their own "purity" and intelligence. Southern progressives of both sexes argued that disfranchising blacks would reduce corruption by removing from unscrupulous white politicians the temptation to purchase black votes!

The typical southern attitude toward the education of blacks was summed up in a folk proverb: "When you educate a Negro, you spoil a good field hand." In 1910 only about 8000 black children in the entire South were attending high schools. Despite the almost total suppression of black rights, lynchings continued to occur; between 1900 and 1914 more than 1100 blacks were murdered by mobs, most (but not all) in the southern states. In the rare cases in which local prosecutors brought the lynchers to trial, juries almost without exception brought in verdicts of not guilty.

Booker T. Washington was shaken by this trend, but he could find no way to combat it. The times were passing him by. He appealed to his white southern "friends" for help but got nowhere. Increasingly he talked about the virtues of rural life, the evils of big cities, and the uselessness of higher education for black people. By the turn of the century a number of young, well-educated blacks, most of them Northerners, were breaking away from his accommodationist leadership.

BLACK MILITANCY

William E. B. Du Bois was the most prominent of the militants. Du Bois was born in Great Barrington, Massachusetts, in 1868. His father, a restless wanderer of Negro and French Huguenot stock, abandoned the family, and young William grew up on the edge of poverty. Neither accepted nor openly rejected by the overwhelmingly white community, he devoted himself to his studies, showing such brilliance that his future education was ensured by scholarships: to Fisk University, then to Harvard, then to the University of Berlin. In 1895 Du Bois became the first American black to earn a Ph.D. in history from Harvard; his dissertation, *The Suppression of the African Slave Trade* (1896), remains a standard reference.

Personal success and "acceptance" by whites did not make the proud and sensitive Du Bois complacent. Outraged by white racism and the willingness of many blacks to settle for second-class citizenship, he set out to make American blacks proud of their color—"Beauty is black," he said—and of their African origins and culture.

Like Washington, Du Bois wanted blacks to lift themselves up by their own bootstraps. They must establish their own businesses, run their own newspapers and colleges, write their own literature; they must preserve their identity rather than seek to amalgamate themselves into a society that offered them only crumbs and contempt. At first he cooperated with Washington, but in 1903, in the essay "Of Mr. Booker T. Washington and Others," he subjected Washington's "attitude of adjustment and submission" to polite but searching criticism. Washington had asked blacks to give up political power, civil rights, and the hope of higher education, not realizing that "voting is necessary to modern manhood, that . . . discrimination is barbarism, and that black boys need education as well as white boys." Washington "apologizes for injustice," Du Bois charged. "He belittles the emasculating effects of caste distinctions, and opposes the higher training and ambitions of our brightest minds." Du Bois deemed this totally wrong. "The way for a people to gain their reasonable rights is not by voluntarily throwing them away."

Du Bois was not an uncritical admirer of the ordinary American black. He believed that "immorality, crime, and laziness" were common vices. Quite properly he blamed the weaknesses of blacks on the treatment afforded them by whites, but his approach to the solution of racial problems was frankly elitist. "The Negro race," he wrote, "is going to be saved by its exceptional men," what he called the "talented tenth" of the black population. After describing in vivid detail how white mistreatment had corrupted his people, Du Bois added loftily: "A saving remnant continually survives and persists, continually aspires, continually shows itself in thrift and ability and character." Du Bois, moreover, prided himself on being of mixed races.

Whatever his prejudices, Du Bois exposed both the weaknesses of Washington's strategy and the callousness of white American attitudes. Accommodation was not working. Washington was praised, even lionized by prominent southern whites, yet when Theodore Roosevelt invited him to a meal at the White House they exploded with indignation, and Roosevelt, although not personally prejudiced, meekly backtracked, never repeating his "mistake." He defended his record by saying, "I have stood as valiantly for the rights of the negro as any president since Lincoln." That, sad to relate, was true enough.

A striking likeness of W. E. B. Du Bois drawn by Winold Reiss when Du Bois was in his fifties.

Not mere impatience but despair led Du Bois and a few like-minded blacks to meet at Niagara Falls in July 1905 and to issue a stirring list of demands: the unrestricted right to vote, an end to every kind of segregation, equality of economic opportunity, higher education for the talented, equal justice in the courts, and an end to trade-union discrimination. This Niagara movement did not attract mass support, but it did stir the consciences of some whites, many of them the descendants of abolitionists, who were also becoming disenchanted by the failure of accommodation to provide blacks with real opportunity.

In 1909, the centennial of the birth of Abraham Lincoln, a group of these liberals, including the newspaperman Oswald Garrison Villard (grandson of William Lloyd Garrison), the social worker Jane Addams, the philosopher John Dewey, and the novelist William Dean Howells, founded the National Association for the Advancement of Colored People (NAACP). The organization was dedicated to the eradication of racial discrimination. Its leadership was predominantly white in the early years, but Du Bois became a national officer and the editor of its journal, *The Crisis.*

A turning point had been reached. After 1909 virtually every important leader, white and black alike, rejected the Washington approach. More and more, blacks turned to the study of their past in an effort to stimulate pride in their heritage. In 1915 Carter G. Woodson founded the Association for the Study of Negro Life and History; the following year he began editing the *Journal of Negro History,* which became the major publishing organ for scholarly studies on the subject.

This militancy produced few results in the Progressive era. Theodore Roosevelt behaved no differently than earlier Republican presidents; he courted blacks when he thought it advantageous, turned his back when he did not. When he ran for president on the Progressive ticket in 1912, he pursued a "lily-white" policy, hoping to break the Democrats' monopoly in the South. By trusting in "[white] men of justice and of vision," Roosevelt argued in the face of decades of experience to the contrary, "the colored men of the South will ultimately get justice."

The southern-born Wilson was actively antipathetic to blacks. During the 1912 campaign he appealed to them for support and promised to "assist in advancing the interest of their race" in every possible way. Once elected, he refused even to appoint a privately financed commission to study the race problem. Southerners dominated his administration and Congress; as a result, blacks were further degraded. No fewer than 35 blacks in the Atlanta post office lost their jobs. In Washington employees in many government offices were rigidly segregated, and those who objected were summarily discharged.

Du Bois, who had supported Wilson in 1912, attacked administration policy in *The Crisis.* In November 1914 the militant editor of the *Boston Guardian,* William Monroe Trotter, a classmate of Du Bois at Harvard and a far more caustic critic of the Washington approach, led a delegation to the White House to protest the segregation policy of the government. When Wilson accused him of blackmail, Trotter lost his temper, and an ugly confrontation resulted. The mood of black leaders had changed completely.

By this time the Great War had broken out in Europe. Soon its effects would be felt by every American, by blacks perhaps more than by any other group. In November 1915, a year almost to the day after Trotter's clash with Wilson, Booker T. Washington died. One era had ended; a new one was beginning.

MILESTONES

1890	National American Women's Suffrage Association is founded
1900	Robert La Follette elected governor of Wisconsin
1901	President McKinley is assassinated
1902	National coal strike
	Oregon adopts initiative system for proposing legislation
1904	Northern Securities case revives the Sherman Antitrust Act
	The National Child Labor Committee is established
1905	Industrial Workers of the World (IWW) is founded
1906	Hepburn Act strengthens Interstate Commerce Commission
	Upton Sinclair, *The Jungle*
1907	U.S. Steel absorbs the Tennessee Coal and Iron Company
1908	Theodore Roosevelt convenes National Conservation Conference
	Muller v. *Oregon* upholds law limiting the hours of women
1909	Herbert Croly, *The Promise of American Life*
	NAACP is founded
1910	Ballinger-Pinchot affair
1911	Roosevelt's New Nationalism speech
1912	Roosevelt runs for president on the Progressive party ticket
1913	Sixteenth Amendment authorizes federal income taxes
	Seventeenth Amendment provides for direct election of United States senators
	Underwood Tariff and Federal Reserve Act passed
1914	Federal Trade Commission and Clayton Antitrust Acts passed
1920	Nineteenth Amendment guarantees women the right to vote

23

FROM ISOLATION TO EMPIRE

Americans have always been ambivalent in their attitudes toward other nations, and at no time was this more clearly the case than in the decades following the Civil War. Occupied with exploiting the West and building their great industrial machine, they gave little thought to foreign affairs. Benjamin Harrison reflected a widely held belief when he said during the 1888 presidential campaign that the United States was "an apart nation" and so it should remain. James Bryce made the same point in *The American Commonwealth*. "Happy America," he wrote, stood "apart in a world of her own . . . safe even from menace."

Late-nineteenth-century Americans never ignored world affairs entirely. They had little direct concern for what went on in Europe, but their interest in Latin America was great and growing, in the Far East only somewhat less so. Economic developments, especially shifts in foreign commerce resulting from industrialization, strengthened this interest with every passing year. Whether one sees isolation or expansion as the hallmark of American foreign policy after 1865 depends on what part of the world one looks at.

The disdain of the people of the United States for Europe rested on several historical foundations. Faith in the unique character of American civilization—and the converse of that belief, suspicion of Europe's supposedly aristocratic and decadent society—formed the chief basis of this isolation. Bitter memories of indignities suffered during the Revolution and the Napoleonic Wars and anger at the hostile attitude of the great powers toward the United States during the Civil War strengthened it, as did the dislike of Americans for the pomp and punctilio of European monarchies. Also important was the undeniable truth that the United States was virtually invulnerable to European attack and at the same time incapable of mounting an offensive against any European power. In turning their backs on Europe, Americans were taking no risk and passing up few opportunities—hence their indifference.

ORIGINS OF THE LARGE POLICY: COVETING COLONIES

The nation's interests elsewhere in the world gradually increased. During the Civil War France had established a protectorate over Mexico, installing the Archduke Maximilian of Austria as emperor. In 1866 Secretary of State William H. Seward demanded that the French withdraw, and the United States moved 50,000 soldiers to the Rio Grande. While fear of American intervention was only one of many reasons for their action, the French pulled their troops out of Mexico during the winter of 1866–1867. Nationalist rebels promptly seized and executed Maximilian. In 1867, at the instigation of Seward, the United States purchased Alaska from Russia for $7.2 million, thereby ridding the continent of another foreign power.

In 1867 the aggressive Seward acquired the Midway Islands in the western Pacific, which had been discovered in 1859 by an American naval officer, N. C. Brooks. Seward also made overtures toward annexing the Hawaiian Islands, and he looked longingly at Cuba. In 1870 President Grant submitted to the Senate a treaty annexing the Dominican Republic. He applied tremendous pressure in an effort to obtain ratification, thus forcing a "great debate" on extracontinental expansion. Expansionists stressed the wealth and resources of the country, the markets it would provide, even its "salubrious climate." But the arguments of the opposition proved more persuasive. The distance of the Dominican Republic from the continent and its crowded, dark-skinned population of what one congressman called "semi-civilized, semi-barbarous men who cannot speak our language" made annexation unattractive. The treaty was rejected. Seward had to admit that there was no significant support in the country for his expansionist plans. Prevailing opinion was well summarized by a Philadelphia newspaper: "The true interests of the American people will be better served . . . by thorough and complete development of the immense resources of our existing territory than by any rash attempts to increase it."

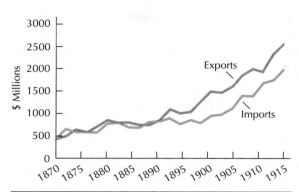

American Foreign Trade, 1870–1914

The internal growth that preoccupied Americans eventually led them to look outward. By the late 1880s the country was exporting a steadily increasing share of its agricultural and industrial output. Exports, only $450 million in 1870, passed the billion-dollar mark early in the 1890s. Imports increased at a rate only slightly less spectacular.

The character of foreign trade was also changing: Manufactures loomed ever more important among exports until in 1898 the country shipped abroad more manufactured goods than it imported. By this time American steelmakers could compete with British producers anywhere in the world. In 1900 one American firm received a large order for steel plates from a Glasgow shipbuilder, and another won contracts for structural steel to be used in constructing bridges for the Uganda Railroad in British East Africa. When a member of Parliament questioned the colonial secretary about the latter deal, the secretary replied: "Tenders [bids] were invited in the United Kingdom . . . [but] one of the American tenders was found to be considerably the lowest in every respect and was therefore accepted." When American industrialists became conscious of their ability to compete with Europeans in far-off markets, they took more interest in world affairs, particularly during periods of depression, when domestic consumption fell.

Shifting intellectual currents further altered the attitudes of Americans. Darwin's theories, applicable by analogy to international relations, gave the concept of manifest destiny a new plausibility. Darwinists like the historian John Fiske argued that the American democratic system of government was so clearly the world's "fittest" that it was destined to spread peacefully over "every land on the earth's surface." In *Our Country* (1885) Josiah Strong found racist and religious justifications for American expansionism, again based on the theory of evolution. The Anglo-Saxon race, centered now in the United States, possessed "an instinct or genius for colonization," Strong claimed. "God, with infinite wisdom and skill is training the Anglo-Saxon race for . . . the final competition of races." Christianity, he added, had developed "aggressive traits calculated to impress its institutions upon mankind." Soon American civilization would "move down upon" Mexico and all Latin America and "out upon the islands of the sea, over upon Africa and beyond." "Can anyone doubt," Strong asked, "that the result of this . . . will be 'the survival of the fittest'?"

The completion of the conquest of the American West encouraged Americans to consider expansion beyond the seas. "For nearly 300 years the dominant fact in American life has been expansion," declared Frederick Jackson Turner, propounder of the frontier thesis. "That these energies of expansion will no longer operate would be a rash prediction." Turner and writers who advanced other expansionist arguments were much influenced by foreign thinking. European liberals had tended to disapprove of colonial ventures, but in the 1870s and 1880s many of them were changing their minds. English liberals in particular began to talk and write about the "superiority" of English culture, to describe the virtues of the "Anglo-Saxon race," to stress a "duty" to spread Christianity among the heathen, and to advance economic arguments for overseas expansion.

Finally, military and strategic arguments were advanced to justify adopting a "large" policy. The powerful Union army had been demobilized rapidly after Appomattox; in the 1880s only about 25,000 men were under arms, their chief occupation fighting Indians in the West. Top army commanders became much concerned with developing and maintaining a professional officer corps.

Half the navy had been scrapped after the war, and the remaining ships were obsolete. While other nations were building steam-powered iron warships, the United States still depended on wooden sailing vessels. In 1867 a British naval publication accurately described the American fleet as "hapless, broken-down, tattered [and] forlorn."

Although no foreign power menaced the country, the decrepit state of the navy vexed many of its officers and led one of them, Captain Alfred Thayer Mahan, to develop a startling theory about the importance of sea power. He explained his theory in two important books, *The Influence of Sea Power Upon History* (1890) and *The Influence of Sea Power Upon the French Revolution and Empire* (1892). According to Mahan, history proved that a nation with a powerful navy and the overseas bases necessary to maintain it would be invulnerable in war and prosperous in time of peace. Applied to the current American situation, this meant that in addition to building a modern fleet, the United States should obtain a string of coaling stations and bases in the Caribbean, annex the Hawaiian Islands,

*A 1904 photograph of Admiral Alfred Thayer
Mahan. Although* The Influence of Sea
Power Upon History *(1890) focused on
seventeenth- and eighteenth-century European
relations, Mahan pointedly cited the inadequacy of the American navy. "Having no foreign
establishments, either colonial or military, the
ships of war of the United States, in war, will be
like land birds, unable to fly far from their own
shores. To provide resting-places for them, where
they can coal and repair, would be one of the
first duties of a government proposing to itself
the development of the power of the Nation
at sea."*

and cut a canal across Central America. A more extensive colonial empire might
follow, but these bases and the canal they would protect were essential first steps
to ensure America's future as a great power.

Writing at a time when the imperialist-minded European nations showed
signs of extending their influence in South America and the Pacific islands, Mahan
attracted many influential disciples. One was Congressman Henry Cabot Lodge
of Massachusetts, a prominent member of the Naval Affairs Committee. Lodge
had married into a navy family and was intimate with the head of the new Naval
War College, Commodore Stephen B. Luce. In 1883 he helped push through
Congress an act authorizing the building of three steel warships, and he consistently advocated expanding and modernizing the fleet. Elevated to the Senate in
1893, Lodge pressed for expansionist policies, basing his arguments on the
strategic concepts of Mahan. "Sea power," he proclaimed, "is essential to the
greatness of every splendid people."

Lodge's friend Theodore Roosevelt was another ardent supporter of the
"large" policy, but he had little influence until McKinley appointed him assistant
secretary of the navy in 1897.

TOWARD AN EMPIRE IN THE PACIFIC

The interest of the United States in the Pacific and the Far East began in the late
eighteenth century, when the first American merchant ship dropped anchor in
Canton harbor. After the Treaty of Wanghia (1844), American merchants in

China enjoyed many privileges and trade expanded rapidly. Christian missionaries began to flock into the country—in the late 1880s, over 500 were living there.

The Hawaiian Islands were an important way station on the route to China, and by 1820 merchants and missionaries were making contacts there. As early as 1854 a movement to annex the islands existed, although it foundered because Hawaii insisted on being admitted to the Union as a state. Commodore Perry's expedition to Japan led to the signing of a commercial treaty (1858) that opened several Japanese ports to American traders.

American influence in Hawaii increased steadily; the descendants of missionary families, most of them engaged in raising sugar, dominated the Hawaiian monarchy. While they made no overt effort to make the islands an American colony, all the expansionist ideas of the era—manifest destiny, Darwinism, Josiah Strong's racist and religious assumptions, and the relentless force of American commercial interests—pointed them in that direction. In 1875 a reciprocity treaty admitted Hawaiian sugar to the United States free of duty in return for a promise to yield no territory to a foreign power. When this treaty was renewed in 1887, the United States obtained the right to establish a naval base at Pearl Harbor. In addition to occupying Midway, America obtained a foothold in the Samoan Islands in the South Pacific.

Sugar planters deposed Hawaii's Queen Liliuokalani, a determined nationalist, in 1893 and requested United States annexation. This 1887 portrait was taken in London during Queen Victoria's jubilee.

During the 1890s American interest in the Pacific area steadily intensified. Conditions in Hawaii had much to do with this. The McKinley Tariff Act of 1890, discontinuing the duty on raw sugar and compensating American producers of cane and beet sugar by granting them a bounty of 2 cents a pound, struck Hawaiian sugar growers hard, for it destroyed the advantage they had gained in the reciprocity treaty.

The following year the death of the complaisant King Kalakaua brought Queen Liliuokalani, a determined nationalist, to the throne. Placing herself at the head of a

"Hawaii for the Hawaiians" movement, she abolished the existing constitution under which the white minority had pretty much controlled the islands and attempted to rule as an absolute monarch. The resident Americans then staged a coup. In January 1893, with the connivance of the United States minister, John L. Stevens, who ordered 150 marines from the cruiser *Boston* into Honolulu, they deposed Queen Liliuokalani and set up a provisional government. Stevens recognized their regime at once, and the new government sent a delegation to Washington to seek a treaty of annexation.

In the closing days of the Harrison administration such a treaty was negotiated and sent to the Senate, but when Cleveland took office in March, he withdrew it. The new president disapproved of the way American troops had been used to overthrow the monarchy. He sent a special commissioner, James H. Blount, to Hawaii to investigate. When Blount reported that the Hawaiians opposed annexation, the president dismissed Stevens and attempted to restore Queen Liliuokalani. Since the provisional government was by that time firmly entrenched, this could not be accomplished peacefully. Because Cleveland was unwilling to use force against the Americans in the islands, however much he objected to their actions, he found himself unable to do anything. The revolutionary government of Hawaii remained in power, independent yet eager to be annexed.

Finally, in July 1898, after the outbreak of the Spanish-American War, Congress annexed the islands by joint resolution, a procedure requiring only a simple majority vote.

TOWARD AN EMPIRE IN LATIN AMERICA

Most of the arguments for extending American influence in the Pacific applied more strongly to Central and South America, where the United States had much larger economic interests and where the strategic importance of the region was clear. Furthermore, the Monroe Doctrine had long conditioned the American people to the idea of acting to protect national interests in the Western Hemisphere.

As early as 1869 President Grant had come out for an American-owned canal across the isthmus of Panama, in spite of the fact that the United States had agreed in the Clayton-Bulwer Treaty with Great Britain (1850) that neither nation would "obtain or maintain for itself any exclusive control" over an interoceanic canal. In 1880, when the French engineer Ferdinand de Lesseps organized a company to build a canal across the isthmus, President Hayes announced that the United States would not permit a European power to control such a waterway.

"The policy of the country is a canal under American control," he announced, another blithe disregard of the Clayton-Bulwer agreement.

When Cleveland returned to power in 1893, the possibility of trouble in Latin America seemed remote, for he had always opposed imperialistic ventures. Yet scarcely two years later the United States was on the verge of war in South America as a result of a crisis in Venezuela, and before this issue was settled Cleveland had made the most powerful claim to American hegemony in the hemisphere ever uttered. The tangled borderland between Venezuela and British Guiana had long been in dispute, Venezuela demanding more of the region than it was entitled to and Great Britain making exaggerated claims and imperiously refusing to submit the question to arbitration.

In July 1895 Cleveland ordered Secretary of State Richard Olney to send a near ultimatum to the British. By occupying the disputed territory, Olney insisted, Great Britain was invading Venezuela and violating the Monroe Doctrine. The note threatened war, but the British ignored it for months. They did not take the United States seriously as a world power, and with reason, for the American navy, although expanding, could not hope to stand up against the British, who had 50 battleships, 25 armored cruisers, and many smaller vessels. When Lord Salisbury, the prime minister and foreign secretary, finally replied, he rejected outright the argument that the Monroe Doctrine had any status under international law and refused to arbitrate what he called the "exaggerated pretentions" of the Venezuelans.

Cleveland was furious. On December 17, 1895, he asked Congress for authority to appoint an American commission to determine the correct line between British Guiana and Venezuela. When that had been done, he added, the United States should "resist by every means in its power" the appropriation by Great Britain of any territory "we have determined of right belongs to Venezuela." Congress responded at once, unanimously appropriating $100,000 for the boundary commission. Popular approval was almost universal.

In Great Britain government and people suddenly awoke to the seriousness of the situation. No one wanted a war with the United States over a remote patch of tropical real estate. In Europe, Britain was concerned about German economic competition and the increased military power of that nation. In addition Canada would be terribly vulnerable to American attack in the event of war. The immense potential strength of the United States could no longer be ignored. Why make an enemy of a nation of 70 million, already the richest industrial power in the world? To fight with the United States, the British colonial secretary realized, "would be an absurdity as well as a crime."

Great Britain agreed to arbitrate the boundary. The war scare subsided. But the incident had the unfortunate effect of adding to the long-held American conviction that the nation could get what it wanted in international affairs by threat and bluster—a dangerous illusion.

THE CUBAN REVOLUTION

On February 10, 1896, scarcely a week after Venezuela and Great Britain had signed the treaty ending their dispute, General Valeriano Weyler arrived in Havana from Spain to take up his duties as governor of Cuba. His assignment to this post was occasioned by the guerrilla warfare that Cuban nationalist rebels had been waging for almost a year. Weyler, a tough and ruthless soldier, set out to administer Cuba with "a salutary rigor." He began herding the rural population into wretched "reconcentration" camps to deprive the rebels of food and recruits. Resistance in Cuba hardened.

The United States had been interested in Cuba since the time of John Quincy Adams and, were it not for northern opposition to adding more slave territory, might well have obtained the island one way or another before 1860. When the Cubans revolted against Spain in 1868, considerable support for intervening on their behalf developed. Hamilton Fish, Grant's secretary of state, resisted this sentiment, and Spain managed to pacify the rebels in 1878 by promising reforms. But change was slow in coming—slavery was not abolished until 1886. The

Instability in Latin America led many to speculate that the United States would play an increasingly dominant role in the region. In Louis Dalrymple's 1895 cartoon, Uncle Sam wins the affection of the damsel Cuba as Spanish misrule and native insurgency lay waste to each other.

worldwide depression of the 1890s hit the Cuban economy hard, and when an American tariff act in 1894 jacked up the rate on Cuban sugar by 40 percent, thus cutting off Cuban growers from the American market, the resulting distress precipitated another revolt.

Public sympathy in the United States went to the Cubans, who seemed to be fighting for liberty and democracy against an autocratic Old World power. Most newspapers supported the rebels; labor unions, veterans' organizations, many Protestant clergymen, a great majority of American blacks, and important politicians in both major parties demanded that the United States give aid. Rapidly increasing American investments in Cuban sugar plantations, now approaching $50 million, were endangered by the fighting and social chaos on the island.

Cuban propagandists in the United States played on American sentiments cleverly. When reports, often exaggerated, of the cruelty of "Butcher" Weyler and the horrors of his reconcentration camps filtered into America, the cry for action intensified. In April 1896 Congress adopted a resolution suggesting that the revolutionaries be granted the rights of belligerents. Since this would have been akin to formal recognition, Cleveland would not go that far, but he did exert diplomatic pressure on Spain to remove the causes of the rebels' complaints, and he offered the services of his government as mediator. The Spanish rejected the suggestion. For a time the issue subsided. The election of 1896 deflected American attention from Cuba, and then McKinley refused to take any action that might disturb Spanish-American relations. Business interests—except those with holdings in Cuba—backed McKinley, for they feared that a crisis would upset the economy, which was just beginning to pick up after the depression. In Cuba General Weyler made some progress toward stifling rebel resistance.

American expansionists, however, continued to demand intervention, and the press, especially Joseph Pulitzer's *New York World* and William Randolph Hearst's *New York Journal,* competing fiercely to increase circulation, kept resentment alive with tales of Spanish atrocities. McKinley remained adamant. Although he warned Spain that Cuba must be pacified, and soon, his tone was friendly and he issued no ultimatum. A new government in Spain relieved the situation by recalling Weyler and promising partial self-government to the Cubans. In a message to Congress in December 1897, McKinley urged that Spain be given "a reasonable chance to realize her expectations" in the island. McKinley was not insensible to Cuba's plight—while far from being a rich man, he made an anonymous contribution of $5000 to the Red Cross Cuban relief fund—but he genuinely desired to avoid intervention.

His hopes were doomed, primarily because Spain failed to "realize her expectations." The fighting in Cuba continued. When riots broke out in Havana in January 1898, McKinley ordered the battleship *Maine* to Havana harbor to protect American citizens.

The explosion of the Maine *in Havana harbor, killing 260 men, caused much speculation in the newspapers and across the nation as to its cause. Many Americans pointed the finger at Spain, a reaction that typified American sentiment toward the Spanish in 1898. What really caused the explosion remains unknown.*

Shortly thereafter Hearst's *New York Journal* printed a letter written to a friend in Cuba by the Spanish minister in Washington, Dupuy de Lôme. The letter had been stolen by a spy. De Lôme, an experienced but arrogant diplomat, failed to appreciate McKinley's efforts to avoid intervening in Cuba. In the letter he characterized the president as a *politicastro*, or "small-time politician," which was a gross error, and a "bidder for the admiration of the crowd," which was equally insulting though somewhat closer to the truth. Americans were outraged, and de Lôme's hasty resignation did little to soothe their feelings.

Then, on February 15, the *Maine* exploded and sank in Havana harbor, 260 of her crew perishing in the disaster. Interventionists in the United States accused Spain of having destroyed the ship and clamored for war. The willingness of Americans to blame Spain indicates the extent of anti-Spanish opinion in the United States by 1898. No one has ever discovered what actually happened. A naval court of inquiry decided that the vessel had been sunk by a submarine mine, but it now seems more likely that an internal explosion destroyed the *Maine*. The Spanish government could hardly have been foolish enough to commit an act that would probably bring American troops into Cuba.

With admirable courage, McKinley refused to panic; but he could not resist the wishes of millions of citizens that something be done to stop the fighting and allow the Cubans to determine their own fate. Spanish pride and Cuban patriotism had taken the issue of peace or war out of the president's hands. Spain could not put down the rebellion, and it would not yield to the nationalists' increasingly extreme demands. To have granted independence to Cuba might have caused the Madrid government to fall, might even have led to the collapse of the monarchy, for the Spanish public was in no mood to surrender. The Cubans, sensing that the continuing bloodshed aided their cause, refused to give the Spanish regime room to maneuver. After the *Maine* disaster, Spain might have agreed to an armistice had the rebels asked for one, and in the resulting negotiations it might well have given up the island. The rebels refused to make the first move. The fighting continued, bringing the United States every day closer to intervention.

The president faced a dilemma. Most of the business interests of the country, to which he was particularly sensitive, opposed intervention. His personal feelings were equally firm. "I have been through one war," he told a friend. "I have seen the dead piled up, and I do not want to see another." Congress, however, seemed determined to act. When he submitted a restrained report on the sinking of the *Maine,* the Democrats in Congress, even most of those who had supported Cleveland's policies, gleefully accused him of timidity. Vice president Garret A. Hobart warned him that the Senate could not be held in check for long; should Congress declare war on its own, the administration would be discredited.

McKinley spent a succession of sleepless nights; sedatives brought him no repose. Finally, early in April, the president drafted a message asking for authority to use the armed forces "to secure a full and final termination of hostilities" in Cuba.

At the last moment the Spanish government seemed to yield; it ordered its troops in Cuba to cease hostilities. McKinley passed this information on to Congress along with his war message, but he gave it no emphasis and did not try to check the march toward war. To seek further delay would have been courageous but not necessarily wiser. Merely to stop fighting was not enough. The Cuban nationalists now insisted on full independence, and the Spanish politicians were unprepared to abandon the last remnant of their once-great American empire. If the United States took Cuba by force, the Spanish leaders might save their political skins; if they meekly surrendered the island, they were done for.

THE "SPLENDID LITTLE" SPANISH–AMERICAN WAR

On April 20, 1898, Congress, by joint resolution, recognized the independence of Cuba and authorized the use of the armed forces to drive out the Spanish. An amendment proposed by Senator Henry M. Teller disclaiming any intention of

*A woman recruiting officer, ac-
companied by a military band,
urging enlistments in New York
City at the outbreak of the
Spanish-American War.
Patriotism, at least, was not
seen as gender-specific.*

adding Cuban territory to the United States passed without opposition. Four days later Spain declared war on the United States.

The Spanish-American War was fought to free Cuba, but the first action took place on the other side of the globe, in the Philippine Islands. Weeks earlier, Theodore Roosevelt, at the time assistant secretary of the navy, had alerted Commodore George Dewey, who was in command of the United States Asiatic Squadron located at Hong Kong, to move against the Spanish base at Manila if war came. Dewey had acted promptly, drilling his gun crews, taking on supplies, giving his gleaming white ships a coat of battle-gray paint, and establishing secret contacts with the Filipino nationalist leader, Emilio Aguinaldo. When word of the declaration of war reached him, Dewey steamed from Hong Kong across the South China Sea with four cruisers and two gunboats. On the night of April 30 he entered Manila Bay, and at daybreak he opened fire on the Spanish fleet at 5000 yards. His squadron made five passes, each time reducing the range; when the smoke had cleared, all ten of Admiral Montojo's ships had been destroyed. Not a single American was killed in the engagement.

Dewey immediately asked for troops to take and hold Manila, for now that war had been declared, he could not return to Hong Kong or put in at any other neutral port. McKinley took the fateful step of dispatching some 11,000 soldiers and additional naval support. On August 13 these forces, assisted by Filipino irregulars under Aguinaldo, captured Manila.

Meanwhile, in the main theater of operations, the United States had won a swift and total victory, though more because of the weakness of the Spanish

Admiral Dewey aboard the Olympia, *directing the attack on the Spanish fleet at Manila Bay, which Dewey suspected of being mined. Dewey's nephew, who commanded a supply ship with the fleet, proposed to lead the way into the bay. "Billy," responded Dewey, "mines or no mines, I am leading the squadron in myself." But Dewey's squadron had arrived before the harbor had been mined and it entered unharmed.*

armed forces than because of the power or efficiency of the American. When the war began, the regular army consisted of about 28,000 men. This tiny force was bolstered by 200,000 hastily enlisted volunteers. In May an expeditionary force gathered at Tampa, Florida. That hamlet was inundated by the masses of men and supplies that descended upon it. Entire regiments sat without uniforms or weapons while hundreds of freight cars jammed with equipment lay forgotten on sidings. Army management was abominable, rivalry between commanders a serious problem. Aggressive units like the regiment of "Rough Riders" raised by Theodore Roosevelt, who had resigned his navy department post to become a lieutenant colonel of volunteers, scrambled for space and supplies, shouldering aside other units to get what they needed. "No words could describe . . . the confusion and lack of system and the general mismanagement of affairs here," the angry Roosevelt complained.

Since a Spanish fleet under Admiral Pascual Cervera was known to be in Caribbean waters, no invading army could safely embark until the fleet could be located. On May 29 American ships found Cervera at Santiago harbor, on the

Spanish-American War: Caribbean Theater

eastern end of Cuba, and established a blockade. In June a 17,000-man expeditionary force commanded by General William Shafter landed at Daiquiri, east of Santiago, and pressed quickly toward the city, handicapped more by its own bad staff work than by the enemy, though the Spanish troops resisted bravely. The Americans sweated through Cuba's torrid summer in heavy wool winter uniforms, ate "embalmed beef" out of cans, and fought mostly with old-fashioned rifles using black powder cartridges that marked the position of each soldier with a puff of smoke whenever he pulled the trigger. On July 1 they broke through undermanned Spanish defenses and stormed San Juan Hill, the intrepid Roosevelt in the van. ("Are you afraid to stand up while I am on horseback?" Roosevelt demanded of one soldier.)

With Santiago harbor in range of American artillery, Admiral Cervera had to run the blockade. On July 3 his black-hulled ships, flags proudly flying, steamed forth from the harbor and fled westward along the coast. Like hounds after rabbits, five American battleships and two cruisers, commanded by Rear Admiral William T. Sampson and Commodore Winfield Scott Schley, ran them down. In four hours the entire Spanish force was destroyed by a hail of 8-inch and 13-inch projectiles (the size of artillery shells refers to their diameter). Damage to the American ships was superficial; only one American seaman lost his life in the engagement.

The end then came abruptly. Santiago surrendered on July 17. A few days later, other United States troops completed the occupation of Puerto Rico. On August 12, one day before the fall of Manila, Spain agreed to get out of Cuba and to cede Puerto Rico and an island in the Marianas (Guam) to the United States. The future of the Philippines was to be settled at a formal peace conference, convening in Paris on October 1.

DEVELOPING A COLONIAL POLICY

Although the Spanish resisted surrendering the Philippines at Paris, they had been so thoroughly defeated that they had no choice. The decision hung rather on the outcome of a conflict over policy within the United States. The war, won at so little cost militarily, produced problems far larger than those it solved. The nation had become a great power in the world's eyes. As a French diplomat wrote a few years later, "[The United States] is seated at the table where the great game is played, and it cannot leave it." European leaders had been impressed by the forcefulness of Cleveland's diplomacy in the Venezuela boundary dispute and by the efficiency displayed by the navy in the war. The annexation of Hawaii and other overseas bases intensified their conviction that the United States was determined to become a major force in international affairs.

But were the American people determined to exercise that force? The debate over taking the Philippine Islands throws much light on their attitudes. The imagination of Americans had been captured by the trappings of empire, not by its essence. It was titillating to think of a world map liberally sprinkled with American flags and of the economic benefits that colonies might bring, but most citizens were not prepared to join in a worldwide struggle for power and influence. They entered blithely on adventures in far-off regions without facing the implications of their decision.

Since the United States (in the Teller Amendment) had abjured any claim to Cuba, even though the island had long been desired by expansionists, logic dictated that a similar policy be applied to the Philippines, a remote land few Americans had ever thought about before 1898. But expansionists were eager to annex the entire archipelago. Even before he had learned to spell the name, Senator Lodge was saying that "the Phillipines [sic] mean a vast future trade and wealth and power," offering the nation a greater opportunity "than anything that has happened . . . since the annexation of Louisiana."

President McKinley adopted a more cautious stance, but he too favored "the general principle of holding on to what we can get." A speaking tour of the Midwest in October 1898, during which he experimented with varying degrees of commitment to expansionism, convinced him that the public wanted the islands. Business opinion had shifted dramatically during the war. Business leaders were now calling the Philippines the gateway to the markets of the Far East.

THE ANTI-IMPERIALISTS

The war had produced a wave of unifying patriotic feeling. It greatly furthered reconciliation between the North and the South; two major generals, for example, were Confederate veterans. But victory raised new divisive questions. An important minority objected strongly to the United States's acquisition of overseas possessions. Persons as different in interest and philosophy as the tycoon Andrew Carnegie and the labor leader Samuel Gompers, as the venerable Republican Senator George Frisbie Hoar of Massachusetts and "Pitchfork Ben" Tillman, the southern Democratic firebrand, together with the writers Mark Twain and William Dean Howells, the reformers Lincoln Steffens and Jane Addams, and the educators Charles W. Eliot of Harvard and David Starr Jordan of Stanford united in opposing the annexation of the Philippines.

The anti-imperialists insisted that since no one would consider statehood for the Philippines, it would be unconstitutional to annex them. It was a violation of the spirit of the Declaration of Independence to govern a foreign territory without the consent of its inhabitants, Senator Hoar argued; by taking over "vassal states" in "barbarous archipelagoes" the United States was "trampling . . . on our own great Charter, which recognizes alike the liberty and the dignity of individual manhood."

McKinley was not insensitive to this appeal to idealism and tradition, which was the fundamental element in the anti-imperialist argument. But he rejected it for several reasons. Many people who opposed Philippine annexation were neither idealists nor constitutional purists. Partisanship led numbers of Democrats to object. Other anti-imperialists were governed by racial and ethnic prejudices, as Senator Hoar's statement indicates. They opposed not expansion as such—Carnegie, for example, was eager to have Canada added to the Union—but expansion that brought under the American flag people whom they believed unfit for American citizenship. Labor leaders particularly feared the competition of "the Chinese, the Negritos, and the Malays" who presumably would flood into the United States if the Philippines were taken.

More compelling to McKinley was the absence of any practical alternative to annexation. Public opinion would not sanction restoring Spanish authority in the Philippines or allowing some other power to have them. That the Filipinos were sufficiently advanced and united socially to form a stable government if granted independence seemed unlikely. Senator Hoar believed that "for years and for generations, and perhaps for centuries, there would have been turbulence, disorder and revolution" in the islands if they were left to their own devices.

Strangely—for he was a kind and gentle man—Hoar faced this possibility with equanimity. McKinley was unable to do so. The president searched the depths of his soul and could find no solution but annexation. Of course the state of public feeling made the decision easier, and he probably found the idea of presiding over an empire appealing. Certainly the commercial possibilities did not escape him. In the end it was with a heavy sense of responsibility that he ordered the American peace commissioners to insist on acquiring the Philippines. To salve the feelings of the Spanish the United States agreed to pay $20 million for the archipelago, but it was a forced sale, accepted by Spain under duress.

The peace treaty faced a hard battle in the United States Senate, where a combination of partisan politics and anticolonialism made it difficult to amass the two-thirds majority necessary for ratification. McKinley had shrewdly appointed three senators, including one Democrat, to the peace commission. This predisposed many members of the upper house to approve the treaty, but the vote was close. William Jennings Bryan, titular head of the Democratic party, could probably have prevented ratification had he urged his supporters to vote nay. Although he was opposed to taking the Philippines, he did not do so. To reject the treaty would leave the United States technically at war with Spain and the fate of the Philippines undetermined; better to accept the islands and then grant them independence. The question should be decided, Bryan said, "not by a minority of the Senate but by a majority of the people" at the next presidential election. Perplexed by Bryan's stand, a number of Democrats allowed themselves to be persuaded by the expansionists' arguments and by McKinley's judicious use of patronage; the treaty was ratified in February 1899 by a vote of 57 to 27.

THE PHILIPPINE INSURRECTION

The national referendum that Bryan had hoped for never materialized. Bryan himself confused the issue in 1900 by making free silver a major plank in his platform, thereby driving conservative anti-imperialists into McKinley's arms. Moreover, early in 1899 the Filipino nationalists under Aguinaldo, furious because the United States would not withdraw, took up arms. A savage guerrilla war resulted, one that cost far more in lives and money than the "splendid little" Spanish-American conflict.

Like all conflicts waged in tangled country chiefly by small, isolated units surrounded by a hostile civilian population, neither side displayed much regard for the "rules" of war. Goaded by sneak attacks and instances of cruelty to captives, American soldiers, most of whom had little respect for Filipinos to begin with, responded in kind. Civilians were rounded up, prisoners tortured, property destroyed. Horrifying tales of rape, arson, and murder by United States troops filtered into the country, providing ammunition for the anti-imperialists. "You

Emilio Aguinaldo, shown here with his young son, commanded Filipino insurgents who worked with Commodore Dewey to help overthrow Spanish rule of the Philippines in 1898. He later took up arms against the United States in a brutal three-year struggle when President McKinley opposed granting independence to the islands.

seem to have about finished your work of civilizing the Filipinos," Andrew Carnegie wrote angrily to one of the American peace commissioners. "About 8000 of them have been completely civilized and sent to Heaven. I hope you like it." In fact, far more than 8000 Filipinos lost their lives during the conflict, which raged for three years. More than 70,000 American soldiers had to be sent to the islands before the resistance was crushed, and about as many of them lost their lives as had perished in the Cuban conflict.

A commission that had been sent to the Philippines by McKinley in 1899 before the fighting started to study the problem attributed the insurrection to the ambitions of the nationalist leaders and recommended that the Philippines be granted independence at an indefinite future date. In 1900 McKinley sent another commission, this one headed by William Howard Taft, a federal judge, to establish a government. Taft, a warmhearted, affable man, took an instant liking to the Filipinos, and his policy of encouraging them to participate in the territorial government attracted many converts. In July 1901 he became the first civilian governor of the Philippines.

Actually, the reelection of McKinley in 1900 settled the Philippine question so far as most Americans were concerned. Anti-imperialists still claimed that it was unconstitutional to take over territories without the consent of the local population. Their reasoning, while certainly not specious, was unhistorical. No American government had seriously considered the wishes of the American Indians, the French and Spanish settlers in Louisiana, the Eskimos of Alaska, or the people of Hawaii when it had seemed in the national interest to annex new lands.

CUBA AND THE UNITED STATES

Nevertheless, grave constitutional questions arose as a result of the acquisitions that followed the Spanish-American War. McKinley acted with remarkable independence in handling the problems involved in expansion. He set up military governments in Cuba, Puerto Rico, and the Philippines without specific congressional authority. But eventually both Congress and the Supreme Court took a hand in shaping colonial policy. In 1900 Congress passed the Foraker Act, establishing a civil government for Puerto Rico. It did not give the Puerto Ricans either American citizenship or full local self-government, and it placed a tariff on Puerto Rican products imported into the United States.

The tariff provision was promptly challenged in the courts on the grounds that Puerto Rico was part of the United States, but in *Downes* v. *Bidwell* (1901) the

Supreme Court upheld the legality of the duties. In this and other "insular cases" the reasoning of the judges was more than ordinarily difficult to follow. ("We suggest, without intending to decide, that there may be a distinction between certain natural rights enforced in the Constitution . . . and what may be termed artificial or remedial rights," the *Downes* opinion held.) The effect, however, was clear: the Constitution did not follow the flag; Congress could act toward the colonies almost as it pleased. A colony, one dissenting justice said, could be kept "like a disembodied shade, in an indeterminate state of ambiguous existence for an indefinite period."

While the most heated arguments raged over Philippine policy, the most difficult colonial problems concerned the relationship between the United States and Cuba, for there idealism and self-interest clashed painfully. Despite the desire of most Americans to get out of Cuba, an independent government could not easily be created. Order and prosperity did not automatically appear when the red and gold ensigns of Spain were hauled down from the flagstaffs of Havana and Santiago.

The insurgent government was feeble, corrupt, and oligarchic, the Cuban economy in a state of collapse, life chaotic. The first Americans entering Havana found the streets littered with garbage and the corpses of horses and dogs. All public services were at a standstill; it seemed essential for the United States, as McKinley said, to give "aid and direction" until "tranquillity" could be restored.

As soon as American troops landed in Cuba trouble broke out between them and the populace. Most American soldiers viewed the ragged, half-starved insurgents as "thieving dagoes" and displayed an unfortunate racial prejudice against their dark-skinned allies. The novelist Stephen Crane, who covered the war for Pulitzer's *New York World,* reported: "Both officers and privates have the most lively contempt for the Cubans. They despise them."

When McKinley established a military government for Cuba late in 1898, it was soon embroiled with local leaders. Then an eager horde of American promoters descended on Cuba in search of profitable franchises and concessions. Congress put a stop to this exploitation by forbidding all such grants as long as the occupation continued.

In the end the United States did withdraw, after doing a great deal to modernize sugar production, improve sanitary conditions, establish schools, and restore orderly administration. In November 1900 a Cuban constitutional convention met at Havana and proceeded without substantial American interference or direction to draft a frame of government. The chief restrictions imposed by this document on Cuba's freedom concerned foreign relations; at the insistence of the United States, it authorized American intervention whenever necessary "for the preservation of Cuban independence" and "the maintenance of a government adequate for the protection of life, property, and individual liberty." Cuba had to promise to make no treaty with a foreign power compromising its independence and to grant naval bases on its soil to the United States.

This arrangement, known as the Platt Amendment, was accepted, after some grumbling, by the Cubans. It had the support of most American opponents of imperialism. The amendment was a true compromise: It safeguarded American interests while granting to the Cubans real self-government on internal matters. In May 1902 the United States turned over the reins of government to the new republic. The next year the two countries signed a reciprocity treaty tightening the economic bonds between them.

True friendship did not result. Although American troops occupied Cuba only once more, in 1906, and then at the specific request of Cuban authorities, the United States repeatedly used the threat of intervention to coerce the Cuban government. American economic penetration proceeded rapidly and without regard for the well-being of the Cuban peasants, many of whom lived in a state of peonage on great sugar plantations. Nor did the Americans' good intentions make up for their tendency to consider themselves innately superior to the Cubans and to overlook the fact that Cubans did not always wish to adopt American customs and culture.

THE UNITED STATES IN THE CARIBBEAN

If the purpose of the Spanish-American War had been to bring peace and order to Cuba, the Platt Amendment was a logical step. The same purpose soon necessitated a further extension of the principle, for once the United States accepted the role of protector and stabilizer in part of the Caribbean, it seemed desirable, for the same economic, strategic, and humanitarian reasons, to supervise the entire region.

The Caribbean countries were economically underdeveloped, socially backward, politically unstable, and desperately poor. Everywhere a few families owned most of the land and dominated social and political life. The mass of the people were uneducated peasants, many of whom were little better off than slaves. Rival cliques of wealthy families struggled for power, force being the usual method of effecting a change in government. Most of the meager income of the average Caribbean state was swallowed up by the military or diverted into the pockets of the current rulers.

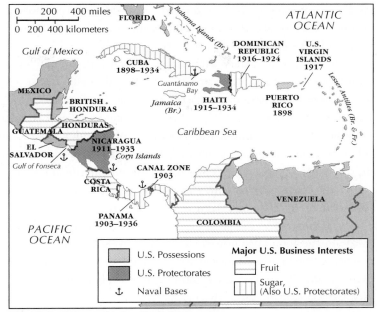

The United States in the Caribbean

Puerto Rico was ceded by Spain to the United States after the Spanish-American War; the Virgin Islands were bought from Denmark; the Canal Zone was leased from Panama. The ranges of dates following Cuba, the Dominican Republic, Haiti, Nicaragua, and Panama cover those years during which the United States either had troops in occupation or in some other way (such as financial) had a protectorate relationship with that country.

Cynicism and fraud poisoned the relations of most of these nations with the great powers. European merchants and bankers systematically cheated their Latin American customers, who in turn frequently refused to honor their obligations. Foreign bankers floated Caribbean bond issues on outrageous terms, while revolutionary Caribbean governments annulled concessions and repudiated debts with equal disdain for honest business dealing.

In 1903 the Dominican Republic defaulted on bonds totaling some $40 million. When European investors urged their governments to intervene, President Theodore Roosevelt announced that under the Monroe Doctrine the United States could not permit foreign nations to intervene in Latin America. But, he added, Latin American nations should not be allowed to escape their obligations. "If we intend to say 'Hands off' . . . sooner or later we must keep order ourselves," he told Secretary of War Elihu Root.

The president did not want to make a colony of the Dominican Republic. "I have about the same desire to annex it as a gorged boa constrictor might have to swallow a porcupine wrong-end-to," he said. He therefore arranged for the United States to take charge of the Dominican customs service—the one reliable source of revenue in that poverty-stricken country. Fifty-five percent of the customs duties would be devoted to debt payment, the remainder turned over to the Dominican government to care for its internal needs. Roosevelt defined his policy, known as the Roosevelt Corollary to the Monroe Doctrine, in a message to Congress in December 1904. "Chronic wrongdoing" in Latin America, he stated with his typical disregard for the subtleties of complex affairs, might require outside intervention. Since, under the Monroe Doctrine, no other nation could step in, the United States must "exercise . . . an international police power."

In the short run this policy worked admirably. Dominican customs were honestly collected for the first time and the country's finances put in order. The presence of American warships in the area provided a needed measure of political stability. In the long run, however, the Roosevelt Corollary caused a great deal of resentment in Latin America, for it added to nationalist fears that the United States wished to exploit the region for its own benefit.

THE OPEN DOOR POLICY

The insular cases, the Platt Amendment, and the Roosevelt Corollary established the framework for American policy both in Latin America and in the Far East. Coincidental with the Cuban rebellion of the 1890s, a far greater upheaval had convulsed the ancient empire of China. In 1894–1895, Japan easily defeated China in a war over Korea. Alarmed by Japan's aggressiveness, the European powers hastened to carve out for themselves new spheres of influence along China's coast. After the annexation of the Philippines, McKinley's secretary of state, John Hay, urged on by business leaders fearful of losing out in the scramble to exploit the Chinese market, tried to prevent the further absorption of China by the great powers.

For the United States to join in the dismemberment of China was politically impossible because of anti-imperialist feeling, so Hay sought to protect American interests by clever diplomacy. In a series of "Open Door" notes (1899) he asked the powers to agree to respect the trading rights of all countries and to impose no discriminatory duties within their spheres of influence. Chinese tariffs should continue to be collected in these areas and by Chinese officials.

The replies to the Open Door notes were at best noncommittal, yet Hay blandly announced in March 1900 that the powers had "accepted" his suggestions! In reality nothing had been accomplished; the imperialist nations did not extend their political control of China only because they feared that by doing so they might precipitate a major war among themselves. Nevertheless, Hay's action marked a revolutionary departure from the traditional American policy of isolation, a bold advance into the complicated and dangerous world of international power politics.

Within a few months of Hay's announcement the Open Door policy was put to the test. Chinese nationalists, angered by the spreading influence of foreign governments, launched the so-called Boxer Rebellion. They swarmed into Peking and drove foreigners within the walls of their legations, which were placed under siege. For weeks, until an international rescue expedition (which included 2500 American soldiers) broke through to free them, the fate of the foreigners was unknown. Fearing that the Europeans would use the rebellion as a pretext for further expropriations, Hay sent off another round of Open Door notes announcing that the United States believed in the preservation of "Chinese territorial and administrative entity" and in "the principle of equal and impartial trade with all parts of the Chinese Empire." This broadened the Open Door policy to include all China, not merely the European spheres of influence.

Hay's diplomacy was superficially successful. Although the United States maintained no important military force in the Far East, American business and commercial interests there were free to develop and to compete with Europeans. But once again European jealousies and fears rather than American cleverness were responsible. When the Japanese, mistrusting Russian intentions in Manchuria, asked Hay how he intended to implement his policy, he replied meekly that the United States was "not prepared . . . to enforce these views on the east by any demonstration which could present a character of hostility to any other power." The United States was being caught up in the power struggle in the Far East without having faced the implications of its actions.

In time the country would pay a heavy price for this unrealistic attitude, largely because of the emergence of Japan as a significant threat to American interests in the Far East.

Relations with Japan worsened in 1906 when the San Francisco school board, responding to local opposition to the influx of cheap labor from Japan, instituted a policy of segregating Asian children in a special school. Japan protested, and President Roosevelt persuaded the San Franciscans to abandon segregation in exchange for his pledge to cut off further Japanese immigration. He accomplished this through a "Gentlemen's Agreement" (1907) in which the Japanese promised not to issue passports to laborers seeking to come to America. Yet Japanese resentment at American racial prejudice was great; many Americans talked fearfully of the "yellow peril."

Theodore Roosevelt was preeminently a realist in foreign relations. "Don't bluster," he once said. "Don't flourish a revolver, and never draw unless you intend to shoot." In the Far East he failed to follow his own advice. He considered the situation in that part of the world fraught with peril. The Philippines, he said, were "our heel of Achilles," indefensible in case of a Japanese attack. He suggested privately that the United States ought to "be prepared for giving the islands independence . . . much sooner than I think advisable from their own standpoint."

Yet while Roosevelt did not appreciably increase American naval and military strength in the Orient, neither did he stop trying to influence the course of events in the area, and he took no step toward withdrawing from the Philippines. He sent the fleet on a world cruise to demonstrate its might to Japan but knew well that this was mere bluff. "The 'Open Door' policy," he advised his successor, "completely disappears as soon as a powerful nation determines to disregard it." Nevertheless he allowed the belief to persist in the United States that the nation could influence the course of Far Eastern history without risk or real involvement.

THE PANAMA CANAL

In the Caribbean region American policy centered on building an interoceanic canal across Central America. Expanding interests in Latin America and the Far East made a canal necessary, a truth pointed up during the war with Spain by the two-month voyage of USS *Oregon* around South America from California waters to participate in the action against Admiral Cervera's fleet at Santiago. The first step was to get rid of the old Clayton-Bulwer Treaty with Great Britain, which barred the United States from building a canal on its own. In 1901 Lord Pauncefote, the British ambassador, and Secretary of State John Hay negotiated an agreement abrogating the Clayton-Bulwer pact and giving America the right to build and, by implication, fortify a transisthmian waterway. The United States agreed in turn to maintain any such canal "free and open to the vessels of commerce and of war of all nations."

One possible canal route lay across the Colombian province of Panama, where the French-controlled New Panama Canal Company had taken over the franchise of the old De Lesseps company. Only 50 miles separated the oceans in Panama. The terrain, however, was rugged and unhealthy. While the French company had sunk much money into the project, it had little to show for its efforts aside from some rough excavations. A second possible route ran across

Nicaragua. This route was about 200 miles long but was relatively easy since much of it traversed Lake Nicaragua and other natural waterways.

President McKinley appointed a commission to study the alternatives. It reported that the Panamanian route was technically superior, but recommended building in Nicaragua because the New Panama Canal Company was asking $109 million for its assets, which the commission valued at only $40 million. Lacking another potential purchaser, the French company lowered its price to $40 million, and after a great deal of clever propagandizing by Philippe Bunau-Varilla, a French engineer with heavy investments in the company, President Roosevelt settled on the Panamanian route.

In January 1903 Secretary of State Hay negotiated a treaty with Tomás Herrán, the Colombian chargé d'affaires in Washington. In return for a 99-year lease on a zone across Panama 6 miles wide, the United States agreed to pay Colombia $10 million and an annual rent of $250,000. The Colombian senate, however, unanimously rejected this treaty, in part because it did not adequately protect Colombian sovereignty over Panama and in part because it hardly seemed fair that the New Panama Canal Company should receive $40 million for its frozen assets and Colombia only $10 million. The government demanded $15 million directly from the United States, plus $10 million of the company's share.

A little more patience might have produced a mutually satisfactory settlement, but Roosevelt looked upon the Colombians as highwaymen who were "mad to get hold of the $40,000,000 of the Frenchmen." ("You could no more make an agreement with the Colombian rulers," Roosevelt later remarked, "than you could nail currant jelly to a wall.") When Panamanians, egged on by the French company, staged a revolution in November 1903, he ordered the cruiser *Nashville* to Panama. Colombian government forces found themselves looking down the barrels of the guns of the *Nashville* and shortly thereafter eight other American warships. The revolution succeeded.

Roosevelt instantly recognized the new Republic of Panama. Secretary Hay and the new Panamanian minister, Bunau-Varilla, then negotiated a treaty granting the United States a zone 10 miles wide in perpetuity, on the same terms as those rejected by Colombia. Within the Canal Zone the United States could act as "the sovereign of the territory . . . to the entire exclusion of . . . the Republic of Panama." The United States guaranteed the independence of the republic. The New Panama Canal Company then received its $40 million.

Historians have condemned Roosevelt for his actions in this shabby affair, and with good reason. It was not that he fomented the revolution, for he did

President Theodore Roosevelt on a steam shovel at the Culebra cut in Panama. The setting caused him to think of the Spanish conquistadors and English explorers who had preceded him in the region. He observed that while nothing remained of their efforts, the Panama Canal was the "greatest engineering feat of the ages" that would last as long as "our civilization."

not. Separated from the government at Bogotá by an impenetrable jungle, the people of Panama province had long wanted to be free of Colombian rule. Since an American-built canal would bring a flood of dollars and jobs to the area, they were prepared to take any necessary steps to avoid having the United States shift to the Nicaraguan route. Nor was it that Roosevelt prevented Colombia from suppressing the revolution. He sinned, rather, in his disregard of Latin American sensibilities. He referred to the Colombians as "dagoes" and insisted smugly that he was defending "the interests of collective civilization" when he overrode their opposition to his plans. "They cut their own throats," he said. "They tried to hold us up; and too late they have discovered their criminal error."

If uncharitable, Roosevelt's analysis was not entirely inaccurate, yet it did not justify his haste in taking Panama under his wing. "Have I defended myself?" Roosevelt asked Secretary of War Root. "You certainly have, Mr. President," Root retorted. "You were accused of seduction and you have conclusively proved that you were guilty of rape." Throughout Latin America, especially as nationalist

The Panama Canal Zone

Following many negotiations, construction on the Panama Canal began in 1904. After many delays and hardships, it was completed in 1914.

sentiments grew stronger, Roosevelt's intolerance and aggressiveness in the canal incident bred resentment and fear.

In 1921 the United States made amends by giving Colombia $25 million. Colombia in turn recognized the independence of the Republic of Panama, but Panama was independent only in name because the United States controlled the canal. Meanwhile, the first vessels passed through the canal in 1914—and American hegemony in the Caribbean expanded.

Roosevelt's successor, William Howard Taft, tried to influence events in this region without intervening militarily. He called this policy "dollar diplomacy," his reasoning being that economic penetration would bring stability to underdeveloped areas and power and profit to the United States without the government's having to commit troops or spend public funds.

Under Taft the State Department won a place for American bankers in an international syndicate engaged in financing railroads in Manchuria. When Nicaragua defaulted on its foreign debt in 1911, the department arranged for American bankers to reorganize Nicaraguan finances and manage the customs service. Although the government truthfully insisted that it did not "covet an inch of territory south of the Rio Grande," dollar diplomacy provoked further apprehension in Latin America. Efforts to establish similar arrangements in Honduras, Costa Rica, and Guatemala all failed. In Nicaragua orderly administration of the finances did not bring internal peace. In 1912, 2500 American marines and sailors had to be landed to put down a revolution.

Economic penetration proceeded briskly. American investments in Cuba reached $500 million by 1920, and smaller but significant investments were made in the Dominican Republic and in Haiti. In Central America the United Fruit Company accumulated large holdings in banana plantations, railroads, and other ventures. Other firms plunged heavily into Mexico's rich mineral resources.

"NONCOLONIAL IMPERIAL EXPANSION"

The United States deserves fair marks for effort in its foreign relations following the Spanish-American War, barely passable marks for performance, and failing marks for results. If one defines imperialism narrowly as a policy of occupying and governing foreign lands, American imperialism lasted for an extremely short time. With trivial exceptions, all the American colonies—Hawaii, the Philippines, Guam, Puerto Rico, the Guantanamo base, and the Canal Zone— were obtained between 1898 and 1903. In retrospect it seems clear that the urge to own colonies was only fleeting; the legitimate questions raised by the anti-imperialists and the headaches connected with the management of overseas possessions soon produced a change of policy.

By the eve of World War I the United States had become a world power and had assumed what it saw as a duty to guide the development of many countries with traditions far different from its own. The American people, however, did not understand what these changes involved. While they stood ready to extend their influence into distant lands, they did so with little awareness of the implications of their behavior for themselves or for other peoples. The national psychology, if such a term has any meaning, remained fundamentally isolationist. Americans understood that their wealth and numbers made their nation strong and that geography made it virtually invulnerable. Thus they proceeded to do what they wanted to do in foreign affairs, limited more by their humanly flexible consciences than by any rational analysis of the probable consequences. This policy seemed safe enough—in 1914.

MILESTONES

1850	Clayton-Bulwer Treaty
1858	Commercial treaty with Japan
1867	Alaska purchased from Russia
1871	Treaty of Washington, settling the *Alabama* claims
1875	Hawaiian reciprocity treaty
1885	Josiah Strong, *Our Country*
1889	First pan-American conference
1890	A. T. Mahan, *The Influence of Sea Power*
1891	*Baltimore* crisis with Chile
1893	Overthrow of Queen Liliuokalani of Hawaii
1895	Venezuela boundary dispute
1898	*Maine* explodes in Havana harbor
	Outbreak of Spanish-American War
	Battle of Manila Bay
	Battle of San Juan Hill
	Annexation of Hawaii
1899	Open Door notes
1900	Platt Amendment to the Cuban constitution
1901	Hay-Pauncefote Treaty
	Supreme Court decides insular cases on control of colonies
1902	Venezuela bond dispute
1904	Roosevelt Corollary to the Monroe Doctrine
1907	"Gentlemen's Agreement" with Japan

24

WOODROW WILSON AND THE GREAT WAR

Woodrow Wilson's approach to foreign relations was well-intentioned and idealistic but somewhat confused. He knew that the United States had no wish to injure any foreign state and assumed that all nations would recognize this fact and cooperate. He wanted to help the republics of Latin America achieve stable democratic governments and improve the living conditions of their people. Imperialism was, in his eyes, immoral. But he felt obliged to sustain and protect American interests abroad. The maintenance of the Open Door in China and the completion of the Panama Canal were as important to him as they were to Theodore Roosevelt.

Wilson's view of nations with traditions different from those of the United States was shortsighted and provincial. His attitude resembled that of nineteenth-century Christian missionaries: He wanted to spread the gospel of American democracy, to lift and enlighten the unfortunate and the ignorant—but in his own way. "I am going to teach the South American republics to elect good men!" he told one British diplomat.

WILSON'S "MORAL" DIPLOMACY

Wilson set out to raise the moral tone of American foreign policy by denouncing dollar diplomacy. Encouraging bankers to lend money to countries like China, he said, implied the possibility of "forcible interference" if the loans were not repaid, and that would be "obnoxious to the principles upon which the government of our people rests." To seek special economic concessions in Latin America was "unfair" and "degrading." The United States would deal with Latin American nations "upon terms of equality and honor."

In certain small matters Wilson succeeded in conducting American diplomacy on this idealistic basis. When the Japanese attempted, in the notorious Twenty-One Demands (1915), to reduce China almost to the status of a Japanese protectorate, he persuaded them to modify their conditions slightly.

Where more important interests were concerned, Wilson sometimes failed to live up to his promises. Because of the strategic importance of the Panama Canal, he was unwilling to tolerate "unrest" anywhere in the Caribbean. Within months of his inauguration he was pursuing the same tactics that circumstances had forced on Roosevelt and Taft. The Bryan-Chamorro Treaty of 1914, which gave the United States an option to build a canal across Nicaragua, made that country virtually an American protectorate and served to maintain in power an unpopular dictator, Adolfo Díaz.

A much more serious example of missionary diplomacy occurred in Mexico. In 1911, a liberal coalition overthrew the dictator Porfirio Díaz, and this government was in turn toppled by Victoriano Huerta, an unabashed reactionary who murdered his predecessor in office. But Huerta was committed to maintaining the stability that foreign investors desired. Most of the European powers promptly recognized his government.

The American ambassador, together with important American financial and business interests in Mexico and in the United States, urged Wilson to do so too, but he refused. "I will not recognize a government of butchers," he said. This was unconventional; nations do not ordinarily consider the means by which a foreign regime has come to power before deciding to establish diplomatic relations.

Wilson brought enormous pressure to bear against Huerta. He dragooned the British into withdrawing recognition. He dickered with other Mexican factions. He demanded that Huerta hold free elections. Huerta would not yield an inch. Indeed, he drew strength from Wilson's effort to oust him, for even his enemies resented American interference in Mexican affairs. Frustration, added to his moral outrage, weakened Wilson's judgment.

The tense situation exploded in April 1914, when a small party of American sailors was arrested in the port of Tampico, Mexico. When the Mexican government refused to supply the apology demanded by the sailors' commander, Wilson fastened on the affair as an excuse for sending troops into Mexico.

The invasion took place at Veracruz. Instead of meekly surrendering the city, the Mexicans resisted tenaciously, suffering 400 casualties before falling back. This bloodshed caused dismay throughout Latin America. Huerta, hard-pressed by Mexican opponents, abdicated. On August 20, 1914, General Venustiano Carranza entered Mexico City in triumph.

Carranza favored representative government, but he proved scarcely better than the tyrant Huerta in controlling the country. One of his own generals, Francisco "Pancho" Villa, rose against him and seized control of Mexico City.

Wilson now made a monumental blunder. Villa professed to be willing to co-operate with the United States, and Wilson, taking him at his word, gave him his support. However, Villa was little more than an ambitious bandit with no other objective than personal power. Carranza, though no radical, was committed to social reform. Fighting back, he drove the Villistas into the northern provinces.

Wilson finally realized the extent of Carranza's influence in Mexico, and in October 1915 he recognized the Carranza government. Still his Mexican troubles were not over. Early in 1916, Villa, seeking to undermine Carranza by forcing the United States to intervene, stopped a train in northern Mexico and killed 16 American passengers. Then he crossed into New Mexico and burned the town of Columbus, killing 19. Having learned his lesson, Wilson would have preferred to bear even this assault in silence, but public opinion forced him to send American troops under General John J. Pershing across the border in pursuit of Villa.

Villa proved impossible to catch. Cleverly he drew Pershing deeper and deeper into Mexico, and this alarmed Carranza, who insisted that the Americans withdraw. Several clashes occurred between Pershing's men and Mexican regulars, and for a brief period in June 1916 war seemed imminent. Wilson now acted bravely and wisely. Early in 1917 he recalled Pershing's force, leaving the Mexicans to work out their own destiny.

EUROPE EXPLODES IN WAR

On June 28, 1914, in the Austro-Hungarian provincial capital of Sarajevo, Gavrilo Princip, a young student, assassinated the Archduke Franz Ferdinand, heir to the imperial throne. Princip was a member of the Black Hand, a Serbian terrorist organization. He was seeking to further the cause of Serbian nationalism. Instead his rash act precipitated a general European war. In little more than a month, following a complex series of diplomatic challenges and responses, two great coalitions, the Central Powers (chiefly Germany and Austria-Hungary) and the Allied Powers (chiefly Great Britain, France, and Russia), were locked in a brutal struggle that brought one era in world history to a close and inaugurated another.

The outbreak of what contemporaries were soon to call the Great War caught Americans psychologically unprepared; few understood the significance of what had happened. The almost unanimous reaction of Americans, aside from dismay, was that the conflict did not concern them. They were wrong, for this was a world war, and Americans were sure to be affected by its outcome.

During World War I, advancing armies unloosed ferocious artillery barrages to destroy deeply entrenched en-emy positions. Before the Third Battle of Ypres, the British fired four and a half million shells at German de-fenses, pulverizing the landscape. But as the British moved forward they became mired in mud; they lost 300,000 men in the action. Few Americans perceived the special horrors of this type of warfare.

There were good reasons, aside from a failure to understand the significance of the struggle, why the United States sought to remain neutral. Over a third of its 92 million inhabitants were either European-born or the children of European immigrants. Sentimental ties bound them to the lands of their ancestors. American involvement would create new internal stresses in a society already strained by the task of assimilating so many diverse groups. War was also an affront to the prevailing progressive spirit, which assumed that human beings were reasonable, high-minded, and capable of settling disputes peaceably. Along with the traditional American fear of entanglement in European affairs, these were ample reasons for remaining aloof.

FREEDOM OF THE SEAS

Under international law, neutrals could trade freely with any belligerent. Americans were prepared to do so, but because the British fleet dominated the North Atlantic, they could not. The situation was similar to the one that had prevailed during the Napoleonic Wars. The British declared nearly all commodities, even foodstuffs, to be contraband of war. They forced neutral merchant ships into Allied ports in order to search them for goods headed for the enemy. Many cargoes were confiscated, often without payment. American firms that traded with the Central Powers were "blacklisted," which meant that no British subject could deal with them. When Americans protested, the British answered that in a battle for survival, they dared not adhere to old-fashioned rules of international law.

Had the United States insisted that Great Britain abandon these "illegal" practices, as the Germans demanded, no doubt it could have had its way. The British foreign secretary, Sir Edward Grey, later admitted: "The ill-will of the United States meant certain defeat. The object of diplomacy, therefore, was to secure the maximum of blockade that could be enforced without a rupture with the United States." It is ironic that an embargo, which failed so ignominiously in Jefferson's day, would have been almost instantly effective if applied at any time after 1914, for American supplies were vital to the Allies.

Wilson faced a dilemma. To allow the British to make the rules meant siding against the Central Powers. Yet to insist on the old rules (which had never been strictly obeyed in wartime) meant siding against the Allies because that would have deprived them of much of the value of their naval superiority. *Nothing* the United States might do would be truly impartial.

In any event, the immense expansion of American trade with the Allies made an embargo unthinkable. While commerce with the Central Powers fell to a trickle, that with the Allies soared from $825 million in 1914 to over $3.2 billion in 1916. An attempt to limit this commerce would have raised a storm; to have eliminated it would have caused a catastrophe. Munitions makers and other businessmen did not want the United States to enter the war. Neutrality suited their purposes admirably.

Britain and France soon exhausted their ready cash, and by early 1917 they had borrowed well over $2 billion. Although these loans violated no principle of international law, they fastened the United States more closely to the Allies' cause.

During the first months of the Great War, the Germans were not especially concerned about neutral trade or American goods because they expected to crush the Allied armies quickly. When their first swift thrust into France was blunted along the Marne River and the war became a bloody stalemate, they began to challenge the Allies' control of the seas. Unwilling to risk their battleships and cruisers against the much larger British fleet, they resorted to a new weapon, the submarine, commonly known as the U-boat (for *Unterseeboot*). German submarines played a role in World War I not unlike that of American privateers in the Revolution and the War of 1812: They ranged the seas stealthily in search of merchant ships. However, submarines could not operate under the ordinary rules of war, which required that a raider stop its prey, examine its papers and cargo, and give the crew and passengers time to get off in lifeboats before sending it to the bottom. When surfaced, U-boats were vulnerable to the deck guns that many merchant ships carried; they could even be sunk by ramming, once they had stopped and put out a boarding party. Therefore, they commonly launched their torpedoes from below the surface without warning, often resulting in a heavy loss of life.

In February 1915 the Germans declared the waters surrounding the British Isles a zone of war and announced that they would sink without warning all enemy merchant ships encountered in the area. Since Allied vessels sometimes flew neu-

"U-Boote Heraus!"("U-boats go get 'em!"). A German poster aimed at encouraging its submarine crews.

tral flags to disguise their identity, neutral ships entering the zone would do so at their own risk. This statement was largely bluff, for the Germans had only a handful of submarines at sea; but they were feverishly building more.

Wilson—perhaps too hurriedly, considering the importance of the question—warned the Germans that he would hold them to "strict accountability" for any loss of American life or property resulting from violations of "acknowledged [neutral] rights on the high seas." He did not distinguish clearly between losses incurred through the destruction of *American* ships and those resulting from the sinking of other vessels. If he meant to hold the Germans responsible for injuries to Americans on *belligerent* vessels, he was changing international law as arbitrarily as the Germans were. Secretary of State Bryan, who opposed Wilson vigorously on this point, stood on sound legal ground when he said: "A ship carrying contraband should not rely upon passengers to protect her from attack—it would be like putting women and children in front of an army."

Correct or not, Wilson's position reflected the attitude of most Americans. It seemed barbaric to them that defenseless civilians should be killed without warning, and they refused to surrender their "rights" as neutrals to cross the North Atlantic on any ship they wished. The depth of their feeling was demonstrated

NOTICE!

TRAVELLERS intending to embark on the Atlantic voyage are reminded that a state of war exists between Germany and her allies and Great Britain and her allies; that the zone of war includes the waters adjacent to the British Isles; that, in accordance with formal notice given by the Imperial German Government, vessels flying the flag of Great Britain, or of any of her allies, are liable to destruction in those waters and that travellers sailing in the war zone on ships of Great Britain or her allies do so at their own risk.

IMPERIAL GERMAN EMBASSY
WASHINGTON, D. C., APRIL 22, 1915.

Three weeks before the Lusitania *was torpedoed, this notice appeared in the classified sections of Washington newspapers.*

when, on May 7, 1915, the submarine *U-20* sank the British liner *Lusitania* off the Irish coast. Nearly 1200 persons, including 128 Americans, lost their lives in this catastrophe.

The torpedoing of the *Lusitania* caused as profound and emotional a reaction in the United States as that following the destruction of the *Maine* in Havana harbor. Wilson, like McKinley in 1898, was shocked, but he kept his head. He demanded that Germany disavow the sinking, indemnify the victims, and promise to stop attacking passenger vessels. When the Germans quibbled about these points, he responded with further diplomatic correspondence rather than with an ultimatum.

In one sense this was sound policy. The Germans pointed out that they had published warnings in American newspapers saying they considered the *Lusitania* subject to attack, that the liner was carrying munitions, and that on past voyages it had flown the American flag as a *ruse de guerre*. It would have been difficult politically for the German government to back down before an American ultima-

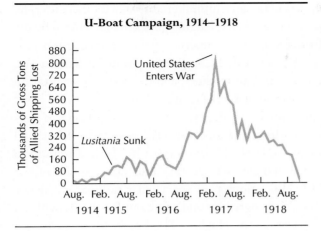

U-Boat Campaign, 1914–1918

Thousands of Gross Tons of Allied Shipping Lost

United States Enters War

Lusitania Sunk

880 800 720 640 560 480 400 320 240 160 80 0

Aug. Feb. Aug. Feb. Aug. Feb. Aug. Feb. Aug.
1914 1915   1916   1917   1918

tum; however, after dragging the controversy out for nearly a year, it apologized and agreed to pay an indemnity. After the torpedoing of the French channel steamer *Sussex* in March 1916 had produced another stiff American protest, the Germans at last promised, in the *Sussex* pledge, to stop sinking merchant ships without warning.

THE ELECTION OF 1916

Part of Wilson's confusion in 1916 resulted from the political difficulties he faced in his fight for reelection. He had won the presidency in 1912 only because the Republican party had split in two. Now Theodore Roosevelt, the chief defector, had become so incensed by Wilson's refusal to commit the United States to the Allied cause that he was ready to support almost any Republican in order to guarantee the president's defeat. At the same time, many progressives were complaining about Wilson's unwillingness to work for further domestic reforms. Unless he could find additional support, he seemed likely to be defeated. He attacked the problem by wooing the progressives. In January 1916 he appointed Louis D. Brandeis to the Supreme Court. In addition to being an advanced progressive, Brandeis was Jewish, the first American of that religion appointed to the Court. Wilson's action won him many friends among people who favored fair treatment for minority groups. In July he bid for the farm vote by signing the Farm Loan

Act to provide low-cost loans based on agricultural credit. Shortly thereafter, he approved the Keating-Owen Child Labor Act, barring goods manufactured by the labor of children under 16 from interstate commerce, and a workers' compensation act for federal employees. He persuaded Congress to pass the Adamson Act, establishing an eight-hour day for railroad workers, and he modified his position on the tariff by approving the creation of a tariff commission.

Each of these actions represented a sharp reversal. In 1913 Wilson had considered Brandeis too radical even for a Cabinet post. The new farm, labor, and tariff laws were all examples of the kind of "class legislation" he had refused to countenance in 1913 and 1914. Wilson was putting into effect much of the Progressive platform of 1912. His actions paid spectacular political dividends when Roosevelt refused to run as a Progressive and came out for the Republican nominee, Associate Justice Charles Evans Hughes. The Progressive convention then endorsed Hughes, who had compiled a fine liberal record as governor of New York, but many of Roosevelt's 1912 supporters felt that he had betrayed them and voted for Wilson.

The key issue in the campaign was American policy toward the warring powers. Wilson intended to stress preparedness, which he was now wholeheartedly supporting. However, during the Democratic convention, the delegates shook the hall with cheers whenever orators referred to the president's success in keeping the country out of the war. One spellbinder, referring to the *Sussex* pledge, announced that the president had "wrung from the most militant spirit that ever brooded above a battlefield an acknowledgement of American rights and an agreement to American demands," and the convention erupted in a demonstration that lasted more than 20 minutes. Thus "He Kept Us Out of War" became the Democratic slogan.

To his credit, Wilson made no promises. "I can't keep the country out of war," he told one member of his Cabinet. "Any little German lieutenant can put us into the war at any time by some calculated outrage." His attitude undoubtedly cost him the votes of extremists on both sides, but it won the backing of thousands of moderates.

The combination of progressivism and the peace issue placed the Democrats on substantially equal terms with the Republicans; thereafter, personal factors probably tipped the balance. Hughes was very stiff (Theodore Roosevelt called him a bearded Woodrow Wilson) and an ineffective speaker; he offended a number of important politicians, especially in crucial California, where he inadvertently snubbed the popular progressive governor, Hiram Johnson; and he equivocated on a number of issues. Nevertheless, on election night he appeared to have won, having carried nearly all the East and Midwest. Late returns gave Wilson

California, however, and with it victory by the narrow margin of 277 to 254 in the Electoral College. He led Hughes in the popular vote, 9.1 million to 8.5 million.

THE ROAD TO WAR

Encouraged by his triumph, appalled by the continuing slaughter on the battle-fields, fearful that the United States would be dragged into the holocaust, Wilson was more genuinely neutral than at any other time during the war, for the Germans had stopped sinking merchant ships without warning and the British had irritated him repeatedly by their arbitrary restrictions on neutral trade. He drafted a note to the belligerents asking them to state the terms on which they would agree to lay down their arms. Unless the fighting ended soon, he warned, neutrals and belligerents alike would be so ruined that peace would be meaning-less.

When neither side responded encouragingly, Wilson, on January 22, 1917, delivered a moving speech aimed, as he admitted, at "the people of the countries now at war" more than at their governments. Any settlement imposed by a victor, he declared, would breed hatred and more wars. There must be "peace without victory," based on the principles that all nations were equal and that every nation-ality group should determine its own form of government. He mentioned, albeit vaguely, disarmament and freedom of the seas, and he suggested the creation of some kind of international organization to preserve world peace. "There must be not a balance of power, but a community of power," he said, and he added, "I am speaking for the silent mass of mankind everywhere."

This noble appeal met a tragic fate. The Germans had already decided to re-nounce the *Sussex* pledge and unleash their submarines against all vessels headed for Allied ports. After February 1, any ship in the war zone would be attacked without warning. Possessed now of more than 100 U-boats, the German military leaders had convinced themselves that they could starve the British people into submission and reduce the Allied armies to impotence by cutting off the flow of American supplies. The United States would probably declare war, but the Germans believed that they could overwhelm the Allies before the Americans could get to the battlefields in force.

Now events moved relentlessly:

February 3: Housatonic *torpedoed. Wilson announces to Congress that he has severed diplomatic relations with Germany. Secretary of State Lansing hands the German ambassador, Count von Bernstorff, his passport.*

February 24: *Walter Hines Page, United States ambassador to Great Britain, transmits to the State Department an intercepted German dispatch (the "Zimmermann telegram") revealing that Germany has proposed a secret alliance with Mexico, Mexico to receive, in the event of war with the United States, "the lost territory in Texas, New Mexico, and Arizona."*

February 25: *Cunard liner* Laconia *torpedoed, two American women perish.*

February 26: *Wilson asks Congress for authority to arm American merchant ships.*

March 1: *Zimmermann telegram released to the press.*

March 4: *President Wilson takes oath of office, beginning his second term.*

March 9: *Wilson, acting under his executive powers, orders the arming of American merchantmen.*

March 12: *Revolutionary provisional government established in Russia.* Algonquin *torpedoed.*

March 15: *Czar Nicholas II of Russia abdicates.*

March 16: City of Memphis, Illinois, Vigilancia *torpedoed.*

March 21: New York World, *a leading Democratic newspaper, calls for declaration of war on Germany. Wilson summons Congress to convene in a special session on April 2.*

March 25: *Wilson calls up the National Guard.*

April 2: *Wilson asks Congress to declare war. Germany is guilty of "throwing to the winds all scruples of humanity," he says. America must fight, not to conquer, but for "peace and justice. . . . The world must be made safe for democracy."*

April 4, 6: *Congress declares war—the vote, 82–6 in the Senate, 373–50 in the House.*

The bare record conceals Wilson's agonizing search for an honorable alternative to war. To admit that Germany posed a threat to the United States meant confessing that interventionists had been right all along. To go to war meant, besides sending innocent Americans to their deaths, allowing "the spirit of ruthless brutality [to] enter into the very fibre of our national life."

The president's Presbyterian conscience tortured him relentlessly. He lost sleep, appeared gray and drawn. When someone asked him which side he hoped would win, he answered petulantly, "Neither." "He was resisting," Secretary of State Lansing recorded, "the irresistible logic of events." In the end Wilson could satisfy himself only by giving intervention an idealistic purpose. The war had become a threat to humanity. Unless the United States threw its weight into the balance, Western civilization itself might be destroyed. Out of the long bloodbath must come a new and better world. The war must be fought to end, for all time, war itself. Thus in the name not of vengeance and victory but of justice and humanity he sent his people into battle.

MOBILIZING THE ECONOMY

America's entry into the Great War determined its outcome. The Allies were running out of money and supplies; their troops, decimated by nearly three years in the trenches, were disheartened and rebellious. In February and March 1917, U-boats sent over a million tons of Allied shipping to the bottom of the Atlantic. The outbreak of the Russian Revolution in March 1917, at first lifting the spirits of the Western democracies, led to the Bolshevik takeover under Lenin. The Russian armies collapsed; by December 1917 Russia was out of the war and the Germans were moving masses of men and equipment from the eastern front to France. Without the aid of the United States, it is likely that the war would have ended in 1918 on terms dictated from Berlin. Instead American men and supplies helped contain the Germans' last drives and then push them back to final defeat.

It was a close thing, for the United States entered the war little better prepared to fight than it had been in 1898. The conversion of American industry to war production had to be organized and carried out without prearrangement. Confusion and waste resulted. The hurriedly designed shipbuilding program was an almost total fiasco. The gigantic Hog Island yard, which employed at its peak over 34,000 workers, completed its first vessel only after the war ended. Airplane, tank, and artillery construction programs, all too large to begin with, developed too slowly to affect the war. The big guns that backed up American soldiers in 1918 were made in France and Great Britain; of the 8.8 million rounds of artillery ammunition fired by American troops, a mere 8000 were manufactured in the United States. Congress authorized the manufacture of 20,000 airplanes, but only a handful, mostly British-designed planes made in America, got to France.

American pilots such as the great "ace" Captain Eddie Rickenbacker flew British Sopwiths and De Havillands or French Spads and Nieuports. Theodore Roosevelt's son Quentin was shot down while flying a Spad over Château Thierry in July 1918.

The problem of mobilization was complicated. It took Congress six weeks of hot debate merely to decide on conscription. Only in September 1917, nearly six months after the declaration of war, did the first draftees reach the training camps, and it is hard to see how Wilson could have speeded this process appreciably.

Wilson was a forceful and inspiring war leader once he grasped what needed to be done. He displayed both determination and unfailing patience in the face of frustration and criticism. Raising an army was only a small part of the job. The Allies had to be supplied with food and munitions, and immense amounts of money had to be collected.

After several false starts, Wilson placed the task in the hands of the War Industries Board (WIB). The board was given almost dictatorial power to allocate scarce materials, standardize production, fix prices, and coordinate American and Allied purchasing. Evaluating the mobilization effort raises interesting historical questions. The antitrust laws were suspended and producers were encouraged, even compelled, to cooperate with one another. Government regulation went far beyond what the New Nationalists had envisaged in 1912.

As for the New Freedom variety of laissez-faire, it had no place in a wartime economy. The nation's railroads, strained by immensely increased traffic, became progressively less efficient. A monumental tie-up in December and January 1917–1918 finally persuaded Wilson to appoint Secretary of the Treasury William G. McAdoo director-general of the railroads, with power to run the roads as a single system. McAdoo's Railroad Administration pooled all railroad equipment, centralized purchasing, standardized accounting practices, and raised wages and passenger rates.

Wilson accepted the kind of government-industry agreement developed under Theodore Roosevelt that he had denounced in 1912. Prices were set by the WIB at levels that allowed large profits—U.S. Steel, for example, despite high taxes, cleared over half a billion dollars in two years. It is at least arguable that producers would have turned out just as much even if compelled to charge lower prices.

Mobilization required close cooperation between business and the military. However, the army, suspicious of civilian institutions, resisted cooperating with them. Wilson finally compelled the War Department to place officers on WIB committees, and when the army discovered that its interests were not injured by the system, the foundation was laid for what was later to be known as the "industrial-military complex," the alliance between business and military leaders that was to cause so much controversy after World War II.

The problem of mobilizing agricultural resources was solved more quickly, and this was fortunate because in April 1917 the British had on hand only a six-week supply of food. As food administrator Wilson appointed Herbert Hoover, a mining engineer who had headed the Belgian Relief Commission earlier in the war. Acting under powers granted by the Lever Act of 1917, Hoover set the price of wheat at $2.20 a bushel in order to encourage production. He established a

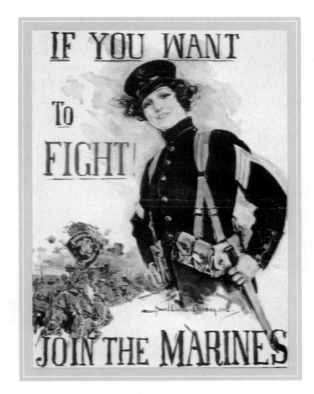

IF YOU WANT To FIGHT! JOIN THE MARINES

A pretty young woman, head cocked with a jaunty smile, teases the viewer. Why, when women could not themselves enlist, did the government artist display this one in uniform and holding a bayonet? The implied answer is that if a woman could show enough spunk to fight, men could—and should—do so, too.

government corporation to purchase the entire American and Cuban sugar crop, which he then doled out to American and British refiners. To avoid rationing he organized a campaign to persuade consumers to conserve food voluntarily. One slogan ran "If U fast U beat U boats"; another, "Serve beans by all means."

"Wheatless Mondays" and "meatless Tuesdays" were the rule, and although no law compelled their observance, the public responded patriotically. Boy Scouts dug up backyards and vacant lots to plant vegetable gardens; chefs devised new recipes to save on scarce items; restaurants added horsemeat, rabbit, and whale steak to their menus and doled out butter and sugar to customers in minuscule amounts. Mothers pressured their children to "Hooverize" their plates. Chicago residents were so successful in making use of leftovers that the volume of raw garbage in the city declined from 12,862 tons to 8,386 tons per month.

Without subjecting its own citizens to serious inconvenience, the United States increased food exports from 12.3 million tons to 18.6 million tons. Farmers, of course, profited greatly: Their real income went up nearly 30 percent between 1915 and 1918.

WORKERS IN WARTIME

With the army siphoning so many men from the labor market and with immigration reduced to a trickle, unemployment disappeared and wages rose. Although the cost of living soared, imposing hardships on people with fixed incomes, the boom produced unprecedented opportunities.

Americans, always a mobile people, pulled up their roots in record numbers. Disadvantaged groups, especially blacks, were particularly attracted by jobs in big-city factories. Early in the conflict, the government began regulating the wages and hours of workers building army camps and manufacturing uniforms. In April 1918 Wilson created the National War Labor Board, headed by former president Taft and Frank P. Walsh, a prominent lawyer, to settle labor disputes. The board considered more than 1200 cases and prevented many strikes. The War Labor Policies Board, chaired by Felix Frankfurter of the Harvard Law School, set wages-and-hours standards for each major war industry. Since these were determined in consultation with employers and representatives of labor, they speeded the unionization of workers by compelling management, even in antiunion industries like steel, to deal with labor leaders. Union membership rose by 2.3 million during the war.

However, the wartime emergency roused the public against strikers; some conservatives even demanded that war workers, like soldiers, be conscripted. While he opposed strikes that impeded the war effort, Wilson set great store in preserving the individual worker's freedom of action. It would be "most unfortunate . . . to relax the laws by which safeguards have been thrown about labor," he said. "We must accomplish the results we desire by organized effort rather than compulsion."

Trends in the steel industry reflect the improvement of the lot of labor in wartime. Wages of unskilled steelworkers more than doubled. Thousands of southern blacks flocked into the steel towns. Union organizers made inroads in many plants, and by the summer of 1918 they were preparing an all-out effort to unionize the industry. If the world was to be made safe for democracy, they argued, there must be "economic democracy [along] with political democracy."

PAYING FOR THE WAR

Wilson managed the task of financing the war effectively. The struggle cost the United States about $33.5 billion, not counting pensions and other postwar expenses. About $7 billion of this was lent to the Allies, but since this money was spent largely in America, it contributed to the national prosperity.

Over two-thirds of the cost of the war was met by borrowing. Five Liberty and Victory Loan drives, spurred by advertising, parades, and other appeals to patriotism, persuaded the people to open their purses. Industrialists, eager to inculcate in their employees a sense of personal involvement in the war effort, conducted campaigns in their plants. Some went so far as to threaten "A Bond or Your Job," but more typical was the appeal of the managers of the Gary, Indiana, plant of U.S. Steel, who published bond advertisements in six languages in order to reach their immigrant workers.

In addition to borrowing, the government collected about $10.5 billion in taxes during the war. A steeply graduated income tax took more than 75 percent of the incomes of the wealthiest citizens. A 65 percent excess-profits tax and a 25 percent inheritance tax were also enacted. Thus although many individuals made fortunes from the war, its cost was distributed far more equitably than that of the Civil War.

PROPAGANDA AND CIVIL LIBERTIES

Wilson was preeminently a teacher and preacher, a specialist in the transmission of ideas and ideals. He excelled at mobilizing public opinion and inspiring Americans to work for the better world he hoped would emerge from the war. In April 1917 he created the Committee on Public Information (CPI), headed by the journalist George Creel. Soon 75,000 speakers were deluging the country with propaganda prepared by hundreds of CPI writers. They pictured the war as a crusade for freedom and democracy, the Germans as a bestial people bent on world domination.

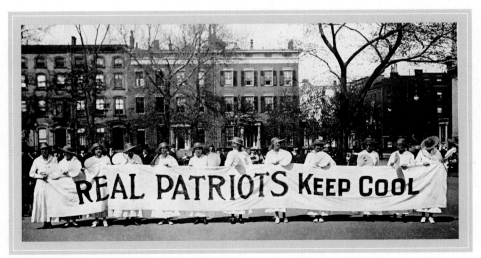

These members of the Woman's Peace party urge Wilson to find a way to stay out of the war in Europe. They are carrying fans to reinforce their message.

A large majority of the nation supported the war enthusiastically. But thousands of persons—German Americans and Irish Americans, for example; people of pacifist leanings such as Jane Addams, the founder of Hull House; and some who thought both sides in the war were wrong—still opposed American involvement. Creel's committee and a number of unofficial "patriotic" groups allowed their enthusiasm for the conversion of the hesitant to become suppression of dissent. People who refused to buy war bonds were often exposed to public ridicule and even assault. Those with German names were persecuted without regard for their views; some school boards outlawed the teaching of the German language; sauerkraut was renamed "liberty cabbage." Opponents of the war of unquestionable patriotism were subjected to coarse abuse. A cartoonist pictured Senator Robert La Follette, who had opposed entering the war, receiving an Iron Cross from the German militarists, and the faculty of his own University of Wisconsin voted to censure him.

Although Wilson spoke in defense of free speech, his actions opposed it. He signed the Espionage Act of 1917, which imposed fines of up to $10,000 and jail sentences ranging to 20 years on persons convicted of aiding the enemy or obstructing recruiting, and he authorized the postmaster general to ban from the mails any material that seemed treasonable or seditious.

In May 1918, again with Wilson's approval, Congress passed the Sedition Act, which made "saying anything" to discourage the purchase of war bonds a crime, with the proviso that investment counselors could still offer "bona fide and not disloyal advice" to clients. The law also made it illegal to "utter, print, write, or publish any disloyal, profane, scurrilous, or abusive language" about the government, the Constitution, or the uniform of the army or navy. Socialist periodicals such as *The Masses* were suppressed, and Eugene V. Debs was sentenced to 10 years in prison for making an antiwar speech. Ricardo Flores Magón, an anarchist, was sentenced to 20 years in jail for publishing a statement criticizing Wilson's Mexican policy, an issue that had nothing to do with the war.

These laws went far beyond what was necessary to protect the national interest. Citizens were jailed for suggesting that the draft law was unconstitutional and for criticizing private organizations like the Red Cross and the YMCA. One woman was sent to prison for writing, "I am for the people, and the government is for the profiteers."

The Supreme Court upheld the constitutionality of the Espionage Act in *Schenck* v. *United States* (1919), a case involving a man who had mailed circulars to draftees urging them to refuse to report for induction into the army. Free speech has limits, Justice Oliver Wendell Holmes, Jr., explained. No one has the right to cry, "Fire!" in a crowded theater. When there is a "clear and present danger" that a statement would threaten the national interest, it can be repressed by law. In peacetime Schenck's circulars would be permissible, but not in time of war.

WARTIME REFORMS

Many progressives believed that the war was creating the sense of common purpose that would stimulate the people to act unselfishly to benefit the poor and to eradicate social evils. Patriotism and public service seemed at last united. Secretary of War Newton D. Baker, a prewar urban reformer, expressed this attitude in supporting a federal child labor law: "We cannot afford, when we are losing boys in France, to lose children in the United States."

Men and women of this sort worked for a dozen causes only remotely related to the war effort. The women's suffrage movement was brought to fruition, as was the campaign against alcohol. Both the Eighteenth Amendment, outlawing alcoholic beverages, and the Nineteenth, giving women the vote, were adopted at least in part because of the war. Reformers began to talk about health insurance. The progressive campaign against prostitution and venereal disease gained strength, winning the enthusiastic support both of persons worried about inexperienced local girls being seduced by the soldiers and of those concerned lest prostitutes lead innocent soldiers astray.

The effort to wipe out prostitution around military installations was a cause of some misunderstanding with the Allies, who provided licensed facilities for their troops as a matter of course. When the premier of France graciously offered to supply prostitutes for American units in his country, Secretary Baker is said to have remarked: "For God's sake . . . don't show this to the President or he'll stop the war." Apparently Baker had a rather peculiar sense of humor. After a tour of the front in France, he assured an American women's group that life in the trenches was "far less uncomfortable" than he had thought and that not a single American doughboy was "living a life which he would not be willing to have [his] mother see him live."

BLACKS IN WARTIME

The wartime "great migration" of southern blacks to northern cities where jobs were available brought them important economic benefits. Actually, the emigration of blacks from the former slave states began with emancipation, but the mass exodus that many people had expected was slow to materialize. Between 1870 and 1890 only about 80,000 blacks moved to northern cities. Compared with the influx from Europe and from northern farms, this number was inconsequential. The black proportion of the population of New York City, for example, fell from over 10 percent in 1800 to under 2 percent in 1900.

Around the turn of the century, as the first postslavery generation reached maturity and as southern repression increased, the northward movement quickened—about 200,000 blacks migrated between 1890 and 1910. Then, after 1914, the war boom drew blacks north in a flood. Agents of northern manufacturers

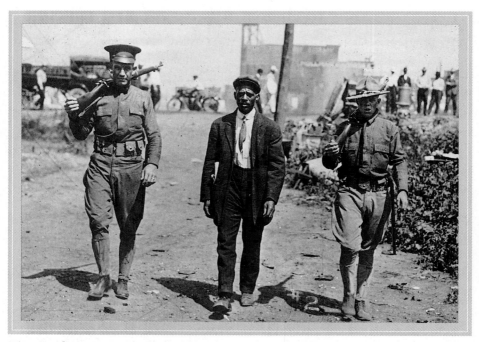

When manufacturers in East Saint Louis, Illinois, sought to weaken labor unions by hiring African American workers from Mississippi and western Tennessee, the white workers went on a rampage. When the dust had cleared, much of East Saint Louis had burned down and several dozen blacks and a few whites were dead. Here several National Guardsmen lead a man to safety.

flocked into the cotton belt to recruit them in wholesale lots. "Leave the benighted land," urged the *Chicago Defender,* a newspaper with a considerable circulation in southern states. "Get out of the South." Half a million made the move between 1914 and 1919. The African American population of New York City rose from 92,000 to 152,000, that of Chicago from 44,000 to 109,000, that of Detroit from 5700 to 41,000.

Life for the newcomers was difficult; many whites resented them; workers feared them as potential strikebreakers yet refused to admit them into their unions. In East St. Louis, Illinois, where employers had brought in large numbers of blacks in an attempt to discourage local unions from striking for higher wages, a bloody riot erupted during the summer of 1917 in which nine whites and an undetermined number of blacks were killed. As in peacetime, the Wilson administration was at worst antagonistic and at best indifferent to blacks' needs and aspirations.

There were two black regiments in the regular army and a number of black national guard units when the war began, and once these outfits were brought up to combat strength, no more volunteers were accepted. Indeed, at first no blacks were conscripted; Southerners in particular found the thought of giving large numbers of guns to blacks and teaching them how to use them most disturbing. However, blacks were soon drafted, and once they were, a larger proportion of them than whites were taken. One Georgia draft board exempted more than 500 of 815 white registrants and only 6 of the 202 blacks in its jurisdiction before its members were relieved of their duties. After a riot in Texas in which black soldiers killed 17 white civilians, black recruits were dispersed among many camps for training to lessen the possibility of trouble.

In the service, all blacks were placed in segregated units. Only a handful were commissioned officers. Despite the valor displayed by black soldiers in the Civil War and the large role played by black combat units in the Spanish-American War, where five blacks had won the Congressional Medal of Honor, most blacks, even those sent overseas, were assigned to labor battalions, working as stevedores and common laborers. But many fought and died for their country. Altogether about 200,000 served overseas. There were black Red Cross nurses in France, and some blacks held relatively high posts in government agencies in Washington, the most important being Emmett J. Scott, who was special assistant for Negro affairs in the War Department.

W. E. B. Du Bois supported the war wholeheartedly. He praised Wilson for making, at last, a strong statement against lynching, which had increased to a

The 369th Infantry Regiment in trenches with French army helmets, gear, and weapons, 1918. The members of the 369th were attached to the French army in order to avoid placing black combat troops under U.S. Army command.

shocking extent during the previous decade. He even went along with the fact that the handful of black officer candidates were trained in a segregated camp. "Let us," he wrote in *The Crisis,* "while the war lasts, forget our special grievances and close ranks shoulder to shoulder with our fellow citizens and the allied nations that are fighting for democracy."

Many blacks condemned Du Bois's accommodationism (which he promptly abandoned when the war ended), but most saw the war as an opportunity to demonstrate their patriotism and prove their worth. For the moment the prevailing mood was one of optimism. "We may expect to see the walls of prejudice gradually crumble"—this was the common attitude of blacks in 1917 and 1918. If winning the war would make the world safe for democracy, surely blacks in the United States would be better off when it was won. Whether or not this turned out to be so was (and still is) a matter of opinion.

AMERICANS:
TO THE TRENCHES AND OVER THE TOP

All activity on the home front had one ultimate objective: defeating the Central Powers on the battlefield. This was accomplished. The navy performed with special distinction. In April 1917, German submarines sank more than 870,000 tons of Allied shipping; after April 1918, monthly losses never reached 300,000 tons. The decision to send merchant ships across the Atlantic in convoys screened by destroyers made the reduction possible. Checking the U-boats was essential because of the need to transport American troops to Europe. Slightly more than 2 million soldiers made the voyage safely. Those who crossed on fast ocean liners were in little danger as long as the vessel maintained high speed and followed a zigzag course, a lesson learned from the *Lusitania,* whose captain had neglected both precautions. Those who traveled on slower troop transports benefited from the protection of destroyers and also from the fact that the Germans concentrated on attacking supply ships. They continued to believe that inexperienced American soldiers would not be a major factor in the war.

The first units of the American Expeditionary Force (AEF), elements of the regular army commanded by General John J. Pershing, reached Paris on Independence Day, 1917. They took up positions on the front near Verdun in October. Not until the spring of 1918, however, did the "doughboys" play a significant role in the fighting, though their mere presence boosted French and British morale.

Pershing, as commander of the AEF, insisted on maintaining his troops as independent units; he would not allow them to be filtered into the Allied armies as

The Western Front, 1918

reinforcements. This was part of a perhaps unfortunate general policy that reflected America's isolationism. (Wilson always referred to the other nations fighting Germany as "associates," not as "allies.")

In March 1918 the Germans launched a great spring offensive, their armies strengthened by thousands of veterans from the Russian front. By late May they had reached a point on the Marne River near the town of Château-Thierry, only 50 miles from Paris. Early in June the AEF fought its first major engagements, driving the Germans back from Château-Thierry and Belleau Wood.

In this fighting only about 27,500 Americans saw action, and they suffered appalling losses. Nevertheless, when the Germans advanced again in the direction of the Marne in mid July, 85,000 Americans were in the lines that withstood their charge. Then, in the major turning point of the war, the Allied armies counterattacked. Some 270,000 Americans participated, helping to flatten the German bulge between Reims and Soissons. By late August the American First Army, 500,000 strong, was poised before the Saint-Mihiel salient, a deep extension of the German lines southeast of Verdun. On September 12 this army, buttressed by French troops, struck and in two days wiped out the salient.

Late in September began the greatest American engagement of the war. No fewer than 1.2 million doughboys drove forward west of Verdun into the Argonne Forest. For over a month of indescribable horror they inched ahead through the tangle of the Argonne and the formidable defenses of the

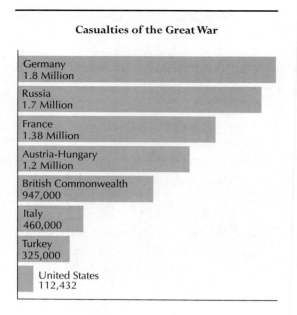

Casualties of the Great War

Germany
1.8 Million

Russia
1.7 Million

France
1.38 Million

Austria-Hungary
1.2 Million

British Commonwealth
947,000

Italy
460,000

Turkey
325,000

United States
112,432

Hindenburg line, while to the west, French and British armies staged similar drives. In this one offensive the AEF suffered 120,000 casualties. Finally, on November 1, they broke the German center and raced toward the vital Sedan-Mézières railroad. On November 11, with Allied armies advancing on all fronts, the Germans signed the armistice, ending the fighting.

PREPARING FOR PEACE

The fighting ended on November 11, 1918, but the shape of the postwar world remained to be determined. European society had been shaken to its foundations. Confusion reigned. People wanted peace yet burned for revenge. Millions faced starvation. Other millions were disillusioned by the seemingly purposeless sacrifices of four years of horrible war. Communism—to some an idealistic promise of human betterment, to others a commitment to rational economic and social planning, to still others a danger to individual freedom, toleration, and democracy—having conquered Russia, threatened to envelop Germany and much of the defunct Austro-Hungarian Empire, perhaps even the victorious Allies. How could stability be restored? How could victory be made worth its enormous cost?

Woodrow Wilson had grasped the significance of the war while most statesmen still thought that triumph on the battlefield would settle everything automatically. As early as January 1917 he had realized that victory would be wasted if the winners permitted themselves the luxury of vengeance. Such a policy would disrupt the balance of power and lead to economic and social chaos. The victors must build a better society, not punish those they believed had destroyed the old.

In a speech to Congress on January 8, 1918, Wilson outlined a plan, known as the Fourteen Points, designed to make the world "fit and safe to live in." The peace treaty should be negotiated in full view of world opinion, not in secret. It should guarantee the freedom of the seas to all nations, in war as in peacetime. It should tear down barriers to international trade, provide for a drastic reduction of armaments, and establish a colonial system that would take proper account of the interests of the native peoples concerned. European boundaries should be redrawn so that no substantial group would have to live under a government not of its own choosing.

More specifically, captured Russian territory should be restored, Belgium evacuated, Alsace-Lorraine returned to France, the heterogeneous nationalities of Austria-Hungary accorded autonomy. Italy's frontiers should be adjusted "along clearly recognizable lines of nationality," the Balkans made free, Turkey divested of its subject peoples, an independent Polish state (with access to the Baltic Sea) created. To oversee the new system, Wilson insisted, "a general association of nations must be formed under specific covenants for the purpose of affording mutual guarantees of political independence and territorial integrity to great and small states alike."

Wilson's Fourteen Points for a fair peace lifted the hopes of people everywhere. After the guns fell silent, however, the vagueness and inconsistencies in his list became apparent. Complete national self-determination was impossible in Europe; there were too many regions of mixed population for every group to be satisfied. Self-determination, like the war itself, also fostered the spirit of nationalism that Wilson's dream of international organization, a league of nations, was designed to deemphasize. Furthermore, the Allies had made territorial commitments to one another in secret treaties that ran counter to the principle of self-determination, and they were not ready to give up all claim to Germany's colonies. Freedom of the seas in wartime posed another problem; the British flatly refused to accept the idea. In every Allied country, millions rejected the idea of a peace without indemnities. They expected to make the enemy pay for the war, hoping, as Sir Eric Geddes, first lord of the Admiralty, said, to squeeze Germany "as a lemon is squeezed—until the pips squeak."

Wilson assumed that the practical benefits of his program would compel opponents to fall in line. He had the immense advantage of seeking nothing for his own country and the additional strength of being leader of the one important nation to emerge from the war richer and more powerful than it had been in 1914.

Yet this combination of altruism, idealism, and power was his undoing; it intensified his tendency to be overbearing and undermined his judgment. He had never found it easy to compromise. Once, when he was president of Princeton, he got into an argument over some abstract question with a professor while shooting a game of pool. To avoid acrimony, the professor finally said: "Well, Doctor Wilson, there are two sides to every question." "Yes," Wilson answered, "a right side and a wrong side." Now, believing that the fate of humanity hung on his actions, he was unyielding. Always a preacher, he became in his own mind a prophet—almost, one fears, a kind of god.

In the last weeks of the war Wilson proved to be a brilliant diplomat, first dangling the Fourteen Points before the German people to encourage them to overthrow Kaiser Wilhelm II and then pressuring Allied leaders to accept the Fourteen Points as the basis for the peace. Under the armistice, Germany had to withdraw behind the Rhine River and surrender its submarines, together with quantities of munitions and other materials. In return it received the assurance of the Allies that the Wilsonian principles would prevail at the Paris Peace Conference.

Wilson then came to a daring decision: He would personally attend the conference as a member of the United States Peace Commission. This was a precedent-shattering step, for no president had ever left American territory while in office. (Taft, who had a summer home on the St. Lawrence River in Canada, never vacationed there during his term, believing it unconstitutional.)

Wilson probably erred in going to Paris, but not because of the novelty or possible illegality of the act. By going, he was turning his back on obvious domestic problems. Western farmers believed that they had been discriminated against during the war, since wheat prices had been controlled while southern cotton had been allowed to rise unchecked from 7 cents a pound in 1914 to 35 cents in 1919. The administration's drastic tax program had angered many businessmen. Labor, despite its gains, was restive in the face of reconversion to peacetime conditions.

Wilson had increased his political difficulties by making a partisan appeal for the election of a Democratic Congress in 1918. Republicans, who had in many instances supported his war program more loyally than the Democrats, considered the action a gross affront. The appeal failed; the Republicans won majorities in both houses. Wilson appeared to have been repudiated at home at the very moment that he set forth to represent the nation abroad. Most important, Wilson intended to break with the isolationist tradition and bring the United States into a league of nations. Such a revolutionary change would require explanation; he should have undertaken a major campaign to convince the American people of the wisdom of this step.

THE PARIS PEACE CONFERENCE AND THE VERSAILLES TREATY

Wilson arrived in Europe a world hero. He toured England, France, and Italy briefly and was greeted ecstatically almost everywhere. The reception tended to increase his sense of mission and to convince him, in the fashion of a typical pro-

The "Big Four" at the Hotel Crillon in Paris. First row, from the left: Orlando of Italy, Lloyd George of Great Britain, Clemenceau of France, and Wilson of the United States.

gressive, that whatever the European politicians might say about it, "the people" were behind his program.

When the conference settled down to its work, control quickly fell into the hands of the so-called Big Four: Wilson, Prime Minister David Lloyd George of Great Britain, Premier Georges Clemenceau of France, and Prime Minister Vittorio Orlando of Italy. Wilson stood out in this group but did not dominate it. His principal advantage in the negotiations was his untiring industry. He alone of the leaders tried to master all the complex details of the task.

The 78-year-old Clemenceau cared only for one thing: French security. He viewed Wilson cynically, saying that since mankind had been unable to keep God's Ten Commandments, it was unlikely to do better with Wilson's Fourteen Points. Lloyd George's approach was pragmatic and almost cavalier. He sympathized with much that Wilson was trying to accomplish but found the president's frequent sermonettes about "right being more important than might, and justice being more eternal than force" incomprehensible. "If you want to succeed in politics," Lloyd George advised a British statesman, "you must keep your conscience well under control." Orlando, clever, cultured, a believer in international cooperation but inflexible where Italian national interests were concerned, was not the equal of his three colleagues in influence. He left the conference in a huff when they failed to meet all his demands.

Europe After World War I

The conference labored from January to May 1919 and finally brought forth the Versailles Treaty. American liberals whose hopes had soared at the thought of a peace based on the Fourteen Points found the document abysmally disappointing.

The peace settlement failed to carry out the principle of self-determination completely. It gave Italy a large section of the Austrian Tyrol, though the area contained 200,000 people who considered themselves Austrians. Other German-speaking groups were incorporated into the new states of Poland and Czechoslovakia. Japan was allowed to take over the Chinese province of Shantung, and the Allies swallowed up all the German colonies in Africa and the Far East.

The victors forced Germany to accept responsibility for having caused the war—an act of senseless vindictiveness as well as a gross oversimplification—and to sign a "blank check," agreeing to pay for all damage to civilian properties and even future pensions and other indirect war costs. This reparations bill, as finally determined, amounted to $33 billion. Instead of attacking imperialism, the treaty attacked German imperialism; instead of seeking a new international social order based on liberty and democracy, it created a great-power entente designed to crush Germany and to exclude Bolshevist Russia from the family of nations. It said nothing about freedom of the seas, the reduction of tariffs, or disarmament. To those who had taken Wilson's "peace without victory" speech and the Fourteen Points literally, the Versailles Treaty seemed an abomination.

The complaints of the critics were individually reasonable, yet their conclusions were not entirely fair. The new map of Europe left fewer people on "foreign" soil than in any earlier period of history. Although the Allies seized the German colonies, they were required, under the mandate system, to render the League of Nations annual accounts of their stewardship and to prepare the inhabitants for eventual independence. Above all, Wilson had persuaded the powers to incorporate the League of Nations in the treaty.

Wilson expected the League of Nations to make up for all the inadequacies of the Versailles Treaty. Once the League had begun to function, problems like freedom of the seas and disarmament would solve themselves, he argued, and the relaxation of trade barriers would surely follow. The League would arbitrate international disputes, act as a central body for registering treaties, and employ military and economic sanctions against aggressor nations. Each member promised (Article 10) to protect the "territorial integrity" and "political independence" of all other members. No nation could be made to go to war against its will, but Wilson emphasized that all were *morally* obligated to carry out League decisions. By any standard, Wilson had achieved a remarkably moderate peace, one full of hope for the future. Except for the war guilt clause and the heavy reparations imposed on Germany, he could be justly proud of his work.

THE SENATE REJECTS THE LEAGUE OF NATIONS

When Wilson returned from France, he finally directed his attention to the task of winning public approval of his handiwork. A large majority of the people probably favored the League of Nations in principle, though few understood all its implications or were entirely happy with every detail. Wilson had persuaded the Allies to accept certain changes in the original draft to mollify American opposition. No nation could be forced to accept a colonial mandate, and "domestic questions" such as tariffs and the control of immigration and the Monroe Doctrine were excluded from League control.

Many senators found these modifications insufficient. Even before the peace conference ended, 37 Republican senators signed a manifesto, devised by Henry Cabot Lodge of Massachusetts, opposing Wilson's League and demanding that the question of an international organization be put off until "the urgent business of negotiating peace terms with Germany" had been completed. Wilson rejected this suggestion icily. Further alterations were out of the question. "Anyone who op-

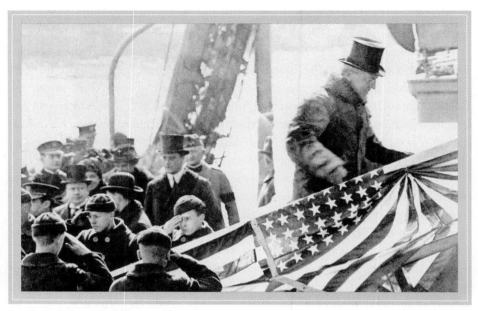

President Woodrow Wilson departing for Europe in December 1918 to negotiate the end of the Great War. A few weeks earlier, Wilson had "begged" voters to elect a Democratic Congress so that he could "continue to be your unembarrassed spokesman in affairs at home and abroad." But the Republicans won three dozen additional seats in Congress, undermining Wilson's claims to speak for the nation.

poses me . . . I'll crush!" he told one Democratic senator. "I shall consent to nothing. The Senate must take its medicine." Thus the stage was set for a monumental test of strength between the president and the Republican majority in the Senate.

Partisanship, principle, and prejudice clashed mightily in this contest. A presidential election loomed. Should the League prove a success, the Republicans wanted to be able to claim a share of the credit, but Wilson had refused to allow them to participate in drafting the document. This predisposed all of them to favor changes. Politics aside, genuine alarm at the possible sacrifice of American sovereignty to an international authority led many Republicans to urge modification of the League covenant, or constitution. Personal dislike of Wilson and his high-handed methods motivated others. Yet the noble purpose of the League made many reluctant to reject it entirely. The intense desire of the people to have an end to the long war made GOP leaders hesitate before voting down the Versailles Treaty, and they could not reject the League without rejecting the treaty.

Wilson could count on the Democratic senators almost to a man, but he had to win over many Republicans to obtain the two-thirds majority necessary for ratification. Republican opinion divided roughly into three segments. At one extreme were some dozen "irreconcilables," led by the shaggy-browed William E.

Massachusetts Republican Senator Henry Cabot Lodge was an ardent opponent of the League of Nations. His staunch opposition delayed ratification of the Versailles Treaty in the Senate for weeks and caused much friction between himself and President Wilson.

Borah of Idaho, an able and kindly person of progressive leanings but an uncompromising isolationist. Borah claimed that he would vote against the League even if Jesus Christ returned to earth to argue in its behalf, and most of his followers were equally inflexible. At the other extreme stood another dozen "mild" reservationists who were in favor of the League but who hoped to alter it in minor ways, chiefly for political purposes. In the middle were the "strong" reservationists, senators willing to go along with the League only if American sovereignty were fully protected and if it were made clear that their party had played a major role in fashioning the final document.

Senator Lodge, the leader of the Republican opposition, was a haughty, rather cynical, intensely partisan individual. He possessed a keen intelligence, a mastery of parliamentary procedure, and, as chairman of the Senate Foreign Relations Committee, a great deal of power. Although not an isolationist, he had little faith in the League. He also had a profound distrust of Democrats, especially Wilson, whom he considered a hypocrite and a coward. The president's pious idealism left him cold. While perfectly ready to see the country participate actively in world affairs, Lodge insisted that its right to determine its own best interests in every situation be preserved. He had been a senator since 1893 and an admirer of senatorial independence since early manhood. When a Democratic president tried to ram the Versailles Treaty down the Senate's throat, he fought him with every weapon he could muster.

Lodge belonged to the strong reservationist faction. His own proposals, known as the Lodge Reservations, 14 in number to match Wilson's Fourteen Points, limited the United States' obligations to the League and stated in unmistakable terms the right of Congress to decide when to honor these obligations. The most important reservation applied to Article 10 of the League covenant, which committed signatories to protect the political independence and territorial integrity of all member nations. Wilson had rightly called Article 10 "the heart of the Covenant." One of Lodge's reservations made it inoperable so far as the United States was concerned "unless in any particular case the Congress . . . shall by act or joint resolution so provide."

Lodge performed brilliantly, if somewhat unscrupulously, in uniting the three Republican factions behind his reservations. He got the irreconcilables to agree to them by conceding their right to vote against the final version in any event, and he held the mild reservationists in line by modifying some of his demands and stressing the importance of party unity. Reservations—as distinct from amendments—would not have to win the formal approval of other League members. In addition, the Lodge proposals dealt forthrightly with the problem of reconciling traditional concepts of national sovereignty with the new idea of world cooperation. Supporters of the League could accept them without sacrifice of principle. Wilson, however, refused to agree. "Accept the Treaty with the Lodge reservations?" the president snorted when a friendly senator warned him that he must accept a compromise. "Never! Never!"

This foolish intransigence seems almost incomprehensible in a man of Wilson's intelligence and political experience. In part his hatred of Lodge accounts for it, in part his faith in his League. His physical condition in 1919 also played a role. At Paris he had suffered a violent attack of indigestion that was probably a symptom of a minor stroke. Thereafter, many observers noted small changes in his personality, particularly increased stubbornness and a loss of good judgment. Instead of making concessions, the president set out early in September on a nationwide speaking crusade to rally support for the League. In three weeks, Wilson traveled some 10,000 miles by train and gave forty speeches, some of them brilliant. But they had little effect on senatorial opinion, and the effort drained his last physical reserves. On September 25, after an address in Pueblo, Colorado, he collapsed. The rest of the trip had to be canceled. A few days later, in Washington, he suffered a severe stroke that partially paralyzed his left side.

For nearly two months the president was almost totally cut off from affairs of state, leaving supporters of the League leaderless while Lodge maneuvered the reservations through the Senate. Gradually, popular attitudes toward the League shifted. Organized groups of Italian, Irish, and German Americans, angered by what they considered unfair treatment of their native lands in the Versailles Treaty, clamored for outright rejection. The arguments of the irreconcilables persuaded many citizens that Wilson had made too sharp a break with America's isolationist past and that the Lodge Reservations were therefore necessary.

A coalition of Democratic and moderate Republican senators could easily have carried the treaty. That no such coalition was organized was Wilson's fault. Lodge obtained the simple majority necessary to add his reservations to the treaty merely by keeping his own party united. When the time came for the final roll call on November 19, Wilson, bitter and emotionally distraught, urged the Democrats to vote for rejection. "Better a thousand times to go down fighting than to dip your colors to dishonorable compromise," he explained to his wife. Thus the amended treaty failed, 35 to 55, the irreconcilables and the Democrats voting against it. Lodge then allowed the original draft without his reservations to come to a vote. Again the result was defeat, 38 to 53. Only one Republican cast a ballot for ratification.

Dismayed but not yet crushed, friends of the League in both parties forced reconsideration of the treaty early in 1920. Neither Lodge nor Wilson would yield an inch. Lodge, who had little confidence in the effectiveness of any league of nations, was under no compulsion to compromise. Wilson, who believed that the League was the world's best hope, did have such a compulsion. Yet he would not compromise either, and this ensured the Treaty's defeat.

Wilson's behavior is further evidence of his physical and mental decline. Probably he was incompetent to perform the duties of his office. Had he died or stepped down, the treaty, with reservations, would almost certainly have been ratified. When the Senate balloted again in March, half the Democrats voted for the treaty with the Lodge Reservations. The others, mostly southern party regulars, joined the irreconcilables. Together they mustered 35 votes, 7 more than the one-third that meant defeat.

THE RED SCARE

The activities of radicals in the labor movement led millions of citizens to associate unionism and strikes with the new threat of communist world revolution. Although there were only a relative handful of communists in the United States, Russia's experience persuaded many people that a tiny minority of ruthless revolutionaries could take over a nation of millions if conditions were right. Communists appointed themselves the champions of workers; labor unrest attracted them magnetically. When strikes broke out, some accompanied by vio-

The *"red scare"* that followed the Great War caused panic and new racial violence throughout the nation. Paranoid delusions of *"dangerous aliens"* and *"foreign subversives"* were prevalent, as this cartoon demonstrates.

lence, many people interpreted them as communist-inspired preludes to revolution. Louis Wiley, an experienced *New York Times* reporter, told a friend at this time that anarchists, socialists, and radical labor leaders were "joining together with the object of overthrowing the American Government through a bloody revolution and establishing a Bolshevist republic."

Organized labor in America had seldom been truly radical. The Industrial Workers of the World (IWW) had made little impression in most industries. But some labor leaders had been attracted to socialism, and many Americans failed to distinguish between the common ends sought by communists and socialists and the entirely different methods by which they proposed to achieve those ends. When a general strike paralyzed Seattle in February 1919, the fact that a procommunist had helped organize it sent shivers down countless conservative spines. When the radical William Z. Foster began a drive to organize the steel industry at about this time, the fears became more intense. In September 1919 a total of 343,000 steelworkers walked off their jobs, and in the same month the Boston police struck. Violence marked the steel strike, and the suspension of police protection in Boston led to looting and fighting that ended only when Governor Calvin Coolidge (who might have prevented the strike had he acted earlier) called out the National Guard.

During the same period a handful of terrorists caused widespread alarm by attempting to murder various prominent persons, including John D. Rockefeller, Justice Oliver Wendell Holmes, Jr., and Attorney General A. Mitchell Palmer. Although the terrorists were anarchists and anarchism had little in common with communism, many citizens lumped all extremists together and associated them with a monstrous assault on society.

What aroused the public even more was the fact that most radicals were not American citizens. Wartime fear of alien saboteurs easily transformed itself into peacetime terror of foreign radicals. In place of Germany, the enemy became the lowly immigrant, usually an Italian or a Jew or a Slav and usually an industrial worker. In this muddled way, radicalism, unionism, and questions of racial and national origins combined to make many Americans believe that their way of life was in imminent danger. That few immigrants were radicals, that most workers had no interest in communism, and that the extremists themselves were faction-ridden and irresolute did not affect conservative thinking. From all over the country came demands that radicals be ruthlessly suppressed. Thus the "red scare" was born.

Attorney General Palmer was the key figure in the resulting purge. He had been a typical progressive, a supporter of the League of Nations and such reforms as women's suffrage and child labor legislation. But pressure from Congress and his growing conviction that the communists really were a menace led him to join the "red hunt." Soon he was saying of the radicals: "Out of the sly and crafty eyes of many of them leap cupidity, cruelty, insanity, and crime; from their lopsided faces, sloping brows, and misshapen features may be recognized the unmistakable criminal type."

In August 1919, Palmer established within the Department of Justice the General Intelligence Division, headed by J. Edgar Hoover, to collect information about clandestine radical activities. In November, Justice Department agents in a dozen cities swooped down on the meeting places of an anarchist organization known as the Union of Russian Workers. More than 650 persons, many of them unconnected with the union, were arrested but in only 43 cases could evidence be found to justify deportation.

Nevertheless, the public reacted so favorably that Palmer, thinking now of winning the 1920 Democratic presidential nomination, planned an immense roundup of communists. He obtained 3000 warrants, and on January 2, 1920, his agents, reinforced by local police and self-appointed vigilantes, struck simultaneously in 33 cities.

About 6000 persons were taken into custody, many of them citizens and therefore not subject to the deportation laws, many others unconnected with any radical cause. Some were held incommunicado for weeks while the authorities searched for evidence against them. In a number of cases, individuals who went to visit prisoners were themselves thrown behind bars on the theory that they too must be communists. Hundreds of suspects were jammed into filthy "bullpens," beaten, and forced to sign "confessions."

The public tolerated these wholesale violations of civil liberties because of the supposed menace of communism. Gradually, however, protests began to be heard, first from lawyers and liberal magazines, then from a wider segment of the population. No revolutionary outbreak had taken place. Of 6000 seized in the Palmer raids, only 556 proved liable to deportation. The widespread ransacking of communists' homes and meeting places produced mountains of inflammatory literature but only three pistols.

Palmer, attempting to maintain the crusade, announced that the radicals planned a gigantic terrorist demonstration for May Day, 1920. In New York and other cities thousands of police were placed on round-the-clock duty; federal troops stood by anxiously. But the day passed without even a rowdy meeting. Suddenly Palmer appeared ridiculous. The red scare swiftly subsided.

THE ELECTION OF 1920

Wilson still hoped for vindication at the polls in the presidential election, which he sought to make a "great and solemn referendum" on the League. He would have liked to run for a third term, but in his enfeebled condition he attracted no support among Democratic leaders. The party nominated James M. Cox of Ohio.

Cox favored joining the League, but the election did not produce the referendum on the new organization that Wilson desired. The Republicans, whose candidate was another Ohioan, Senator Warren G. Harding, equivocated shamelessly on the issue. The election turned on other matters, largely emotional. Disillusioned by the results of the war, many Americans had had their fill of idealism. They wanted, apparently, to end the long period of moral uplift and reform agitation that had begun under Theodore Roosevelt and return to what Harding called "normalcy."

To the extent that the voters were expressing opinions on Wilson's League, their response was overwhelmingly negative. Senator Harding, a strong reservationist, swept the country, winning over 16.1 million votes to Cox's 9.1 million. In July 1921, Congress formally ended the war with the Central Powers by passing a joint resolution.

The defeat of the League was a tragedy both for Wilson, whose crusade for a world order based on peace and justice ended in failure, and for the world, which was condemned to endure another, still more horrible and costly war. Perhaps this dreadful outcome could not have been avoided. Had Wilson compromised and Lodge behaved like a statesman instead of a politician, America would have joined the League, but it might well have failed to respond when called on to meet its obligations. As events soon demonstrated, the League powers acted pusillanimously and even dishonorably when challenged by aggressor nations.

Yet it might have been different had the Senate ratified the Versailles Treaty. What was lost when the treaty failed was not peace but the possibility of peace, a tragic loss indeed.

MILESTONES

1914	United States invades Veracruz, Mexico
	Outbreak of war in Europe
1915	U-boat torpedoes *Lusitania*
	United States recognizes the Carranza government in Mexico
1916	Louis D. Brandeis named to Supreme Court
	Adamson Act gives railroad workers the eight-hour day
	"Pancho" Villa burns Columbus, New Mexico
1917	Wilson's "peace without victory" speech
	Germany resumes unrestricted submarine warfare
	United States declares war on Central Powers
	Herbert Hoover named food administrator
	Bernard Baruch named head of War Industries Board
	Ex-President Taft heads War Labor Board
1918	Sedition Act
	Republicans gain control of both houses of Congress
	Armistice ends the Great War
1919	Steel strike
	Red scare, climaxing in the Palmer raids
	Paris Peace Conference
	Senate rejects Versailles Treaty
1920	Senate again rejects Versailles Treaty

25

POSTWAR SOCIETY
AND CULTURE:
CHANGE AND ADJUSTMENT

T he Great War seemed to many of those who lived through it a turning point in history, the real division separating the nineteenth from the new twentieth century. Actually most of what seemed characteristically new to the people of the 1920s had begun to appear well before 1917, and the changes they noticed were still going on. They were in the midst of adjusting to new social, cultural, and economic forces, forces that were to shape their lives and those of their children and grandchildren.

CLOSING THE GATES TO NEW IMMIGRANTS

The ending of the red scare did not herald the disappearance of xenophobia. It was perhaps inevitable and possibly wise that some limitation be placed on the entry of immigrants into the United States after the war. An immense backlog of prospective migrants had piled up during the conflict, and the desperate postwar economic condition of Europe led hundreds of thousands to seek better circumstances in the United States. Immigration increased from 110,000 in 1919 to 430,000 in 1920 and to 805,000 in 1921, with every prospect of continuing to rise.

In 1921 Congress, reflecting a widespread prejudice against eastern and southern Europeans, passed an emergency act establishing a quota system. Each year 3 percent of the number of foreign-born residents of the United States in

1910 (about 350,000 persons) might enter the country. Each country's quota was based on the number of its nationals in the United States in 1910. This meant that only a relative handful of the total would be from southern and eastern Europe. In 1924 the quota was reduced to 2 percent and the base year shifted to 1890, thereby lowering further the proportion of southern and eastern Europeans admitted.

In 1929 Congress established a system that allowed only 150,000 immigrants a year to enter the country. Each national quota was based on the supposed origins of the entire white population of the United States in 1920, not merely on the foreign-born. Here is an example of how the system worked:

$$\frac{\text{Italian quota}}{150,000} = \frac{\text{Italian-origin population, 1920}}{\text{White population, 1920}}$$

$$\frac{\text{Italian quota}}{150,000} = \frac{3,800,000}{95,500,000}$$

Italian quota = 6000 (approximately)

The system was complicated and unscientific, for no one could determine with accuracy the "origins" of millions of citizens. More seriously, it ignored America's long history of constantly changing ethnic heterogeneity. The motto *E Pluribus Unum,* conceived to represent the unity of the original 13 states, applied even more appropriately to the blending of different cultures into one nationality. The new law sought to freeze the mix, to turn the American melting pot into a kind of gigantic ice cube.

The United States had closed the gates. The National Origins Act caused the foreign-born percentage of the population to fall from about 13 percent in 1920 to 4.7 percent in 1970. Instead of an open, cosmopolitan society eager to accept, in Emma Lazarus's stirring line, the "huddled masses yearning to breathe free," America now became committed to preserving a homogeneous, "Anglo-Saxon" population.

Distaste for the "new" immigrants from eastern Europe, many of whom were Jewish, expanded into a more general anti-Semitism in the 1920s. American Jews, whether foreign-born or native, were subjected to increasing discrimination, not because they were slow in adopting American ways but because (being ambitious and hardworking, as immigrants were supposed to be) many of them were getting ahead in the world somewhat more rapidly than expected. Prestigious colleges like Harvard, Yale, and Columbia that had in the past admitted Jews based on their academic records now imposed unofficial but effective

"Give me your tired, your poor, your huddled masses yearning to breathe free, the wretched refuse of your teeming shore"—these words of Emma Lazarus, inscribed at the base of the Statue of Liberty, tell only part of the story. Most immigrants were young and hopeful, like this family at Ellis Island; many were resolute and ambitious. The restriction of immigration during the 1920s, meant to exclude misfits, also deprived the nation of such as these.

quotas. Medical schools also established quotas, and no matter how talented, most young Jewish lawyers and bankers could find places only in so-called "Jewish" firms.

NEW URBAN SOCIAL PATTERNS

The Census of 1920 revealed that for the first time a majority of Americans (54 million in a population of 106 million) lived in "urban" rather than "rural" places. These figures are somewhat misleading when applied to the study of social attitudes because the Census classified anyone in a community of 2500 or more as urban. Of the 54 million "urban" residents in 1920, over 16 million lived in villages and towns of fewer than 25,000 persons and the evidence suggests strongly that a large majority of them held ideas and values more like those of rural citizens than like those of city dwellers. But the truly urban Americans, the one person in four who lived in a city of 100,000 or more—and particularly the nearly 16.4 million who lived in metropolises of at least half a million—were increasing

steadily in number and influence. More than 19 million persons moved from
farms to cities in the 1920s,
and the population living in
centers of 100,000 or more
increased by about a third.

Being a city dweller
meant far more than changing one's physical surroundings. It affected family
structure, educational opportunities, and dozens of

Among the poor, women and children helped supplement the family income by taking in piecework. This family is sewing garters.

other aspects of human existence. Indeed, since most of the changes in the relations of husbands, wives, and children that had occurred in the nineteenth century were related to the fact that people were leaving farms to work in towns and
cities, these trends continued and were intensified in the early twentieth century
as more and more people settled in urban centers. In addition, couples continued
to marry more because of love and physical attraction than because of social position or economic advantage or because of the wishes of their parents. In each
decade, people married slightly later in life and had fewer children.

Earlier differences between working-class and middle-class family structures
persisted. In 1920 about a quarter of the American women who were working
were married, but less than 10 percent of all married women were working.
Middle-class married women who worked were nearly all either childless or
highly paid professionals who were able to employ servants. Most male skilled
workers now earned enough to support a family in modest comfort so long as
they could work steadily, but an unskilled laborer still could not. Wives in most
such families helped out, usually by taking in laundry or doing piecework sewing
for jobbers.

By the 1920s the idea of intrafamily democracy had emerged. In such families
husbands and wives would deal with each other as equals, which given existing
conditions meant sharing housework and child care, downplaying male authority,
and stressing mutual satisfaction in sexual and other matters. On the one hand,
they should be friends and lovers, not merely housekeepers, earners of money,
and producers of children. Procreation did not have to be the main purpose of
matrimony, but if there were children, they should be left as free as possible to
develop in their own way; rigid discipline was limiting and therefore wrong. On
the other hand, advocates of these companionate relationships believed that there

was nothing particularly sacred about marriage; divorce should be made easier for couples that did not get along, provided they did not have children.

Much attention was given at this time to "scientific" child raising. Child-care experts (a new breed) agreed that routine medical examinations and good nutrition were of central importance, but they were divided about how the socialization and psychological development of the young should be handled. One school stressed rigid training: Children could be "spoiled" by indulgence; toilet training should begin early in infancy; thumb sucking should be suppressed; too much kissing could turn male youngsters into "mama's boys." "Children are made not born," John B. Watson, a former president of the American Psychological Association who was also a vice president of the important J. Walter Thompson advertising agency, explained in *The Psychological Care of Infant and Child* (1928). "Never hug and kiss them, never let them sit in your lap. If you must, kiss them once on the forehead when they say good night."

Another school favored a more permissive approach. Toilet training could wait; parents should pay attention to their children's expressed needs, not impose a generalized set of rules on them. In *The Companionate Marriage* (1927), Benjamin B. Lindsey, a juvenile court judge, suggested a kind of trial marriage, a period during which a young couple could get used to each other before undertaking to raise a family. By practicing contraception such couples could separate without doing serious damage to anyone if they decided to end the relationship. If the relationship remained firm and loving, it would become a traditional marriage and their children would grow up in a loving environment that would help them to become warm, well-adjusted adults.

Lindsey was one among many "experts" who advocated more freedom for young people and open discussion of all questions related to sex. He was most concerned about the welfare of children, whose natural sexuality, he insisted, was being stupidly repressed by Victorian prudes. Others put more emphasis on married women's rights and the injustice of the double standard. Still others were interested in breaking down nineteenth-century sexual taboos for all people, married or single.

The growth of large cities further loosened social constraints on sexuality. Amidst the sea of people that surged down the streets or into the subways, the solitary individual acquired a freedom derived from anonymity. Homosexuals, in particular, developed a set of identifying signals and fashioned a distinctive culture in the parks, cafeterias, nightclubs, and rooming houses of the big cities. Because most others wrongly assumed that male homosexuality was characterized by effeminacy, they were mostly unaware of the extent of the emerging gay culture. But by the late 1920s and early 1930s homosexual parades, dances, and nightclub acts had become public events.

THE YOUNGER GENERATION

The Great War profoundly affected the generation born around the turn of the century. It had raised, and its outcome dashed, their hopes for the future. Now the narrowness and prudery of so many of their elders and the stuffy conservatism of nearly all politicians seemed not merely old-fashioned but ludicrous. The actions of red-baiters and reactionaries led them to exaggerate the importance of their right to express themselves in bizarre ways. Their models and indeed some of their leaders were the prewar Greenwich Village bohemians.

The 1920s has been described as the Jazz Age, the era of "flaming youth," when young people danced to syncopated "African" rhythms, careened about the countryside in automobiles in search of pleasure and forgetfulness, and made gods of movie stars and professional athletes. This view of the period bears a superficial resemblance to reality. "Younger people," one observer noted in 1922, were attempting "to create a way of life free from the bondage of an authority that has lost all meaning." But the resemblance is only superficial; they certainly appreciated having a good time, and like any generation moving from adolescence to maturity, the young people of the 1920s were eager to understand the world and make their way in it. They were more unconventional than their grandparents primarily because they were adjusting to more profound and more rapid changes in their world than their grandparents could have imagined.

By the 1920s paying calls was being replaced by *dating;* the young man called only to "pick up" his "date," the two to go off, free of parental supervision, to whatever diversion they wished. Dating developed many conventions out of keeping with the trend toward freedom in sexual matters of which it was a part. A man asked a woman "for a date" because dating meant going somewhere and spending money, and the man was expected to do the transporting and pay the bill. This made the woman doubly dependent; under the old system, *she* provided the refreshments, and there was no taboo against her doing the inviting.

But there is no question that for the young people of the 1920s, relations between the sexes were becoming more relaxed and uninhibited. Respectable young women smoked cigarettes, something previously done in public only by prostitutes and bohemian types. They cast off their heavy corsets, wore lipstick and "exotic" perfumes, and shortened both their hair and their skirts, the latter rising steadily from instep to ankle to calf to knee and beyond as the decade progressed. For decades female dressmakers and beauty salon proprietors had sold their own beauty products and potions. By 1920, however, new cosmetic corporations, managed primarily by men, appropriated the products and marketing strategies of local women entrepreneurs and catered to national mass markets.

Freudian psychology and the more accessible ideas of the British "sexologist" Havelock Ellis reached steadily deeper into the popular psyche. According to A. A. Brill, the chief American popularizer of Freud's theories, the sex drive was irrepressible. "Love and sex are the same thing," he wrote. "The urge is there, and whether the individual desires it or no, it always manifests itself." Since sex was "the central function of life," Ellis argued, it must be "simple and natural and pure and good." Bombarded by these exciting ideas, to say nothing of their own inclinations, young people found casting off their inhibitions more and more tempting.

Conservatives bemoaned what they described as the breakdown of moral standards, the fragmentation of the family, and the decline of parental authority—all with some reason. Nevertheless, society was not collapsing. Much of the rebelliousness of the young, like their particular style of dress, was faddish in nature, in a sense a kind of youthful conformity. This was particularly true of college students. Every aspect of their extracurricular life (which was consuming a steadily larger share of most students' time and energy to begin with) was governed by elaborate rituals. Fraternity and sorority initiations, "proms," attendance at Saturday afternoon football games, styles of dress, and college slang, seemingly aspects of independence and free choice, were nearly everywhere shaped and controlled by peer pressure.

But young people's new ways of relating to one another, while influenced by the desire to conform, were not mere fads and were not confined to people under 30. This can be seen most clearly in the birth control movement, the drive to legalize the use of contraceptives.

THE "NEW" WOMAN

The young people of the 1920s were more open about sex and perhaps more sexually precocious than the young had been before the war. This does not mean that most of them engaged in sexual intercourse before marriage or that they tended to marry earlier. Single young people might "believe in" birth control, but relatively few (at least by modern standards) had occasion to practice it. Contraception was a concern of married people, and particularly of married women.

The leading American proponent of birth control in the 1920s, actually the person who coined the term, was Margaret Sanger, one of the less self-centered Greenwich Village bohemians. Before the war she was a political radical, a friend of Eugene Debs, "Big Bill" Haywood, and the anarchist Emma Goldman. Gradually, however, her attention focused on the plight of the poor women she encountered while working as a nurse; many of these women were burdened by large numbers of children yet knew nothing about contraception. Sanger began to

This photograph of Margaret Sanger was taken during her trial in January 1917. Having opened the nation's first birth control clinic in Brooklyn, New York, she was convicted of disseminating information on contraception and served 30 days in prison. Friends had advised Sanger to dress conservatively and affect a "Madonna type" persona, much as she appeared here, with her son. Despite her demure clothing, her eyes express her characteristic assertiveness.

write articles and pamphlets designed to enlighten them, but when she did so she ran afoul of the Comstock Act of 1873, an antiobscenity law that banned the distribution of information about contraception from the mails. She was frequently in trouble with the law, but she was persistent to the edge of fanaticism. In 1921 she founded the American Birth Control League and two years later a research center.

The medical profession, though wary of the issue, gave some support to the birth control movement, as did the eugenicists, who claimed that unless the fecundity of "unfit" types (people others might describe simply as poor) was curbed, "race suicide" would result. Sanger accepted support wherever it could be found; by the end of the decade she was no longer on the cutting edge of the movement or even a very radical feminist. But by that time resistance to the use of contraception was crumbling.

Although 10.6 million women were working outside the home by the end of the decade (compared with 8.4 million in 1920), sex-based restrictions continued to affect women. More women worked, but most of the jobs they held were still menial or of a kind that few men wanted: domestic service, elementary school teaching, clerical work, selling behind a counter. One of the worst blows fell in 1923 when in the case of *Adkins* v. *Children's Hospital,* the Supreme Court declared a federal law that limited the hours of work for women in the District of Columbia unconstitutional.

Where they competed for jobs with men, women usually received much lower wages. Women's Bureau studies demonstrated this repeatedly; yet when the head of the bureau, Mary Anderson, tried to get employers to raise women's wages, most of them first claimed that the men had families to support, and when she reminded them that many female employees also had family responsibilities, they told her that there was a "tacit understanding" that women were to make less than men. "If I paid them the same," one employer said, "there would be a revolution." Efforts to get the American Federation of Labor to take up the issue met with failure; few of the unions in the federation admitted women.

The number of women college graduates continued to expand, but the colleges placed more emphasis on subjects like home economics that seemed designed to make them better housewives rather than professional nutritionists or business executives. As one Vassar College administrator (a woman!) said, colleges should provide "education for women along the lines of their chief interests and responsibilities, motherhood and the home."

The 1920s proved disillusioning to feminists, who now paid a price for their single-minded pursuit of the right to vote in the Progressive era. After the ratification of the Nineteenth Amendment, Carrie Chapman Catt was exultant: "We are no longer petitioners," she announced, "but free and equal citizens." Many activists, assuming the battle won, lost interest in agitating for change. They believed that the suffrage amendment had given them the one weapon needed to achieve whatever women still lacked. In fact, it soon became apparent that women did not vote as a bloc. Many married women voted for the candidates their husbands supported.

When radical feminists discovered that voting did not automatically bring true equality, they founded the Women's party and began campaigning for an equal rights amendment. Their leader, Alice Paul, a dynamic if somewhat single-issue person, disdained specific goals such as disarmament, ending child labor, and liberalized birth control. Total equality for women was the one objective. The party considered protective legislation governing the hours and working conditions of women discriminatory. This caused the so-called social feminists, who believed that children and working women needed the protection provided by such laws, to break away.

The battle for the equal rights amendment persisted through the 1930s, but it was lost. By the end of that decade the movement was moribund.

POPULAR CULTURE: MOVIES AND RADIO

The postwar decade saw immense changes in popular culture. Unlike the literary flowering of the era, these changes seemed in tune with the times, not a reaction against them. This was true in part because they were products as much of technology as of human imagination.

The first motion pictures were made around 1900, but the medium only came into its own after the Great War. The early films, such as the eight-minute epic *The Great Train Robbery* (1903), were brief, action-packed, and unpretentious. Professional actors and most educated people viewed them with amused contempt. But their success was instantaneous with recent immigrants and many other slum dwellers. In 1912 there were nearly 13,000 movie houses in the United States, more than 500 in New York City alone. Many of these places were converted stores called nickelodeons because the admission charge was only 5 cents.

In the beginning the mere recording of movement seemed to satisfy the public, but success led to rapid technical and artistic improvements and consequently to more cultivated audiences. David W. Griffith's 12-reel *Birth of a Nation* (1915) was a particularly important breakthrough in both areas, although Griffith's

Artist John Sloan considers the new popular pastime of the movies in Movies, Five Cents *(1907). The girl (center) casts an eager glance back at the viewer. Perhaps she, like the couple on the screen, would like to be smooching.*

sympathetic treatment of the Ku Klux Klan of Reconstruction days angered blacks and white liberals.

By the mid-1920s the industry, centered in Hollywood, California, was the fourth largest in the nation in capital investment. Films moved from the nickelodeons to converted theaters. So large was the audience that movie "palaces" seating several thousand people sprang up in the major cities. *Daily* ticket sales averaged more than $10 million. With the introduction of talking movies, *The Jazz Singer* (1927) being the first of significance, and color films a few years later, the motion picture reached technological maturity. Costs and profits mounted; by the 1930s million-dollar productions were common.

The motion picture made positive contributions to American culture. Beginning with the work of Griffith, filmmakers created an entirely new theatrical art, using close-ups to portray character and heighten tension and broad, panoramic shots to transcend the limits of the stage. They employed, with remarkable results, special lighting effects, the fade-out, and other techniques impossible in the live theater. Movies enabled dozens of established actors to reach wider audiences and developed many first-rate new ones. As the medium matured, it produced many dramatic works of high quality. At its best the motion picture offered a breadth and power of impact superior to anything on the traditional stage.

Even more pervasive than the movies in its effects on the American people was radio. Wireless transmission of sound was developed in the late nineteenth century by many scientists in Europe and the United States. During the war radio was put to important military uses and was strictly controlled, but immediately thereafter the airwaves were thrown open to everybody.

Radio was briefly the domain of hobbyists, thousands of "hams" broadcasting in indiscriminate fashion. Even under these conditions, the manufacture of radio equipment became a big business. In 1920 the first commercial station (KDKA in Pittsburgh) began broadcasting, and by the end of 1922 over 500 stations were in operation. In 1926 the National Broadcasting Company, the first continent-wide network, was created.

It took little time for broadcasters to discover the power of the new medium. When one pioneer interrupted a music program to ask listeners to phone in requests, the station received 3000 calls in an hour. The immediacy of radio explained its tremendous impact. As a means of communicating the latest news, it had no peer; beginning with the broadcast of the 1924 presidential nominating conventions, all major public events were covered live. Advertisers seized on radio too; it proved to be as effective a way to sell soap as to transmit news.

Advertising had mixed effects on broadcasting. The sums paid by businesses for air time made possible elaborate entertainments performed by the finest actors and musicians, all without cost to listeners. However, advertisers hungered

Would women believe the claims of cosmetics advertisements? In a 1927 survey of housewives in Columbus, Ohio, Pond's Company found that two-thirds of the women could not even recall the company's advertisements. Younger women, however, were more impressionable. The J. Walter Thompson advertising agency found that many Vassar students unconsciously used the exact phrases from advertising copy to describe various cosmetics.

for mass markets. They preferred to sponsor programs of little intellectual content, aimed at the lowest tastes and utterly uncontroversial. And good and bad alike, programs were constantly interrupted by irritating pronouncements extolling the supposed virtues of one commercial product or another.

In 1927 Congress limited the number of stations and parceled out wavelengths to prevent interference. Further legislation in 1934 established the Federal Communications Commission (FCC), with power to revoke the licenses of stations that failed to operate in the public interest. But the FCC placed no effective controls on programming or on advertising practices.

THE GOLDEN AGE OF SPORTS

The extraordinary popularity of sports in the postwar period can be explained in a number of ways. People had more money to spend and more free time to fill. Radio was bringing suspenseful, play-by-play accounts of sports contests into millions of homes, thus encouraging tens of thousands to want to see similar events with their own eyes. New means of persuasion developed by advertisers to sell lipstick, breakfast cereal, and refrigerators were applied with equal success to sporting events and to the athletes who participated in them.

Newly built Yankee Stadium, on opening day of the 1923 baseball season. Babe Ruth hit his first home run and soon Yankee Stadium was dubbed "the House that Ruth Built." That year, perhaps his best, Ruth hit 41 home runs, batted .393, and drew 170 walks. He got on base more than half the times he appeared at the plate. Ruth's feats matched the colossal appearance of Yankee Stadium, whose arches evoked the imperial grandeur of ancient Rome.

There had been great athletes before; indeed probably the greatest all-around athlete of the twentieth century was Jim Thorpe, a Sac and Fox Indian who won both the pentathalon and the decathalon at the 1912 Olympic Games, made Walter Camp's All-American football team in 1912 and 1913, then played major league baseball for several years before becoming a pioneer founder and player in the National Football League. But what truly made the 1920s a golden age was a coincidence—the emergence in a few short years of a remarkable collection of what today would be called superstars.

Of them, the greatest by far was "the Sultan of Swat," baseball's Babe Ruth. Ruth not only dominated baseball, he changed it from a game ruled by pitchers and low scores to one in which hitting was more greatly admired. Originally himself a brilliant pitcher, his incredible hitting ability made him more valuable in the outfield, where he could play every day. Before Ruth, John "Home Run" Baker was the most famous slugger; his greatest home run total was 12, achieved shortly before the Great War. Ruth hit 29 in 1919 and 54 in 1920, his first year with the New York Yankees. By 1923 he was so feared that he was given a base on balls more than half the times he appeared at the plate.

The achievements of outstanding athletes had a cumulative effect. New stadiums were built, and they were filled by "the largest crowds that ever witnessed athletic sports since the fall of Rome." Record crowds paying unprecedented sums attended all sorts of events.

Football was the preeminent school sport. At many colleges football afternoons came to resemble religious rites both in their formality, with their cheerleaders and marching bands, and in the fervor of the crowds. A national magazine entitled a 1928 article "The Great God Football," and the editor of a college newspaper denounced "disloyal" students who took seats in the grandstand where they could see what was happening on the field, rather than encouraging the team by doing their bit in the student cheering section in the end zone.

Tens of thousands of men and women took up tennis, golf, swimming, and calisthenics. Social dancing became more energetic. The turkey trot, a popular prewar dance, led in the next decade to the Charleston and what one historian called "an imitative swarm of hops, wriggles, squirms, glides and gallops named after all the animals in the menagerie."

URBAN-RURAL CONFLICTS: FUNDAMENTALISM

These were buoyant times for people in tune with the times—the young, the devil-may-care, factory workers with money in their pockets, many different types. But nearly all of them were city people. However, the tensions and hostilities of the 1920s exaggerated an older rift in American society—the conflict between urban and rural ways of life. To many among the scattered millions who tilled the soil and among the millions who lived in towns and small cities, the new city-oriented culture seemed sinful, overly materialistic, and unhealthy. To them change was something to be resented and resisted.

Yet there was no denying its fascination. Made even more aware of the appeal of the city by radio and the automobile, farmers and townspeople coveted the comfort and excitement of city life at the same time that they condemned its vices. Rural society proclaimed the superiority of its ways at least in part to protect itself from temptation. Change, omnipresent in the postwar world, must be resisted even at the cost of individualism and freedom.

One expression of this resistance was a resurgence of religious fundamentalism. Although it was especially prevalent among Baptists and Methodists, fundamentalism was primarily an attitude of mind, profoundly conservative, rather than a religious idea. Fundamentalists rejected the theory of evolution, indeed all knowledge about the origins of the universe and the human race that had been discovered during the nineteenth century.

In Baptism in Kansas *(1928), John Steuart Curry viewed sympathetically the sincerity and depth of feeling that marked the revival of religious fundamentalism in much of rural America during the 1920s. Curry was a leader of the rural regionalist painters, seeking, he said, to show the "struggle of man against nature."*

Urban sophisticates tended to dismiss fundamentalists as boors and hayseed fanatics, yet the persistence of old-fashioned ideas was understandable. In rural areas where educational standards were low and culture relatively static, old ideas remained unchallenged. The power of reason, so obvious in a technologically advanced society, seemed much less obvious to rural people. Farmers, living in close contact with the capricious, elemental power of nature, tended to have more respect for the force of divine providence than did city people. Beyond this, the majesty and beauty of the King James translation of the Bible, the only book in countless rural homes, made it extraordinarily difficult for many persons to abandon their belief in its literal truth.

What made crusaders of the fundamentalists, however, was their resentment of modern urban culture. Although in some cases they harassed liberal ministers, their religious attitudes had little public significance; their efforts to impose their views on public education were another matter. The teaching of evolution must be prohibited, they insisted. Throughout the 1920s they campaigned vigorously for laws banning discussion of Darwin's theory in textbooks and classrooms. By 1929 five southern states had passed laws prohibiting the teaching of evolution in the public schools.

Their greatest asset in this unfortunate crusade was William Jennings Bryan. Age had not improved the "Peerless Leader." After leaving Wilson's Cabinet in 1915 he devoted much time to religious and moral issues, but without applying himself conscientiously to the study of these difficult questions. He went about the country charging that "they"—meaning the mass of educated Americans—had "taken the Lord away from the schools." He denounced the use of public money to undermine Christian principles, and he offered $100 to anyone who would admit to being descended from an ape. His immense popularity in rural areas assured him a wide audience, and no one came forward to take his money.

The fundamentalists won a minor victory in 1925, when Tennessee passed a law forbidding instructors in the state's schools and colleges to teach "any theory that denies the story of the Divine Creation of man as taught in the Bible." Although the bill passed both houses by big majorities, most legislators voted aye only because they dared not expose themselves to charges that they disbelieved the Bible. Educators in the state, hoping to obtain larger school appropriations from the legislature, hesitated to protest. Governor Austin Peay, an intelligent and liberal-minded man, feared to veto the bill lest he jeopardize other measures he was backing. "Probably the law will never be applied," he predicted when he signed it. Even Bryan, who used his influence to obtain passage of the measure, urged—unsuccessfully—that it include no penalties.

On learning of the passage of this act, the American Civil Liberties Union announced that it would finance a test case challenging its constitutionality if a Tennessee teacher would deliberately violate the statute. Urged on by friends, John T. Scopes, a young biology teacher in Dayton, reluctantly agreed to do so. He was arrested. A battery of nationally known lawyers came forward to defend him, and the state obtained the services of Bryan himself. The "Monkey Trial" became an overnight sensation.

Clarence Darrow, chief counsel for the defendant, stated the issue clearly. "Scopes isn't on trial," he said, "civilization is on trial. The prosecution is opening the doors for a reign of bigotry equal to anything in the Middle Ages. No man's belief will be safe if they win." The comic aspects of the trial obscured this issue. Big-city reporters like H. L. Mencken of the *Baltimore Evening Sun* flocked to Dayton to make sport of the fundamentalists. Scopes's conviction was a foregone conclusion; after the jury rendered its verdict, the judge fined him $100.

Nevertheless the trial exposed both the stupidity and the danger of the fundamentalist position. The high point came when Bryan agreed to testify as an expert witness on the Bible. In a sweltering courtroom, both men in shirt sleeves,

the lanky, rough-hewn Darrow cross-examined the aging champion of fundamentalism, exposing his childlike faith and his scientific ignorance. Bryan admitted to believing that Eve had been created from Adam's rib and that a whale had
swallowed Jonah. "I believe in a God that can make a whale and can make a man
and make both do what He pleases," he explained.

The Monkey Trial ended badly for nearly everyone concerned. Scopes
moved away from Dayton; the judge, John Raulston, was defeated when he
sought reelection; Bryan died in his sleep a few days after the trial. But fundamentalism continued to flourish, not only in the nation's backwaters but in many
cities, brought there by rural people in search of work. In retrospect, even the
heroes of the Scopes trial—science and freedom of thought—seem somewhat
less stainless than they did to liberals at the time. The account of evolution in the
textbook used by Scopes was far from satisfactory, yet it was advanced as unassailable fact. The book also contained statements that to the modern mind seem
at least as bigoted as anything that Bryan said at Dayton. In a section on the "Races
of Man," for example, it described Caucasians as "the highest type of all . . . represented by the civilized white inhabitants of Europe and America."

URBAN-RURAL CONFLICTS: PROHIBITION

The conflict between the countryside and the city was fought on many fronts,
and in one sector the rural forces achieved a quick victory. This was the prohibition of the manufacture, transportation, and sale of alcoholic beverages by the
Eighteenth Amendment, ratified in 1919. Although there were some big-city advocates of prohibition, the Eighteenth Amendment, in the words of the historian
Andrew Sinclair, marked a triumph of the "Corn Belt over the conveyor belt."

The temperance movement had been important since the age of Jackson; it
was a major issue in many states during the Gilded Age, and by the Progressive
era powerful organizations like the Anti-Saloon League and the Women's
Christian Temperance Union were seeking to have drinking outlawed entirely.
Indeed, prohibition was a typical progressive reform, moralistic, backed by the
middle class, and aimed at frustrating "the interests"—in this case the distillers.

World War I aided the prohibitionists by increasing the need for food. The
Lever Act of 1917 outlawed the use of grain in the manufacture of alcoholic beverages, primarily as a conservation measure. The prevailing dislike of foreigners
helped the dry cause still more: Beer drinking was associated with Germans.
State and local laws had made a large part of the country dry by 1917. National
prohibition became official in January 1920.

During Prohibition, rival gangs in many big cities contended for control of the lucrative (and illegal) sale of liquor. On Valentine's Day, 1929, Al Capone's gangsters, in police uniforms, barged into a garage at 2122 North Clark Street, Chicago, lined up the members of the George "Bugs" Moran gang, and shot them.

This "experiment noble in purpose," as Herbert Hoover called it, achieved a number of socially desirable results. It reduced the national consumption of alcohol from 2.6 gallons per capita in the period just before the war to under 1 gallon in the early 1930s. Arrests for drunkenness fell off sharply, as did deaths from alcoholism. Fewer workers squandered their wages on drink. If the drys had been willing to legalize beer and wine, the experiment might have worked. Instead, by insisting on total abstinence, they drove thousands of moderates to violate the law. Strict enforcement became impossible, especially in the cities.

In areas where sentiment favored prohibition strongly, liquor remained difficult to find. Elsewhere, anyone with sufficient money could obtain it easily. Smuggling became a major business, *bootlegger* a household word. Private individuals busied themselves learning how to manufacture "bathtub gin." Many druggists issued prescriptions for alcohol with a free hand. The manufacture of wine for religious ceremonies was legal, and consumption of sacramental wine jumped by 800,000 gallons during the first two years of prohibition. The saloon disappeared, replaced by the speakeasy, a supposedly secret bar or club, operating under the benevolent eye of the local police.

That the law was often violated does not mean that it was ineffective, any more than violations of laws against theft and murder mean that those laws are ineffective. Although gangsters such as Alphonse "Scarface Al" Capone of Chicago were engaged in the liquor traffic, their "organizations" existed before the passage of the Eighteenth Amendment. But prohibition widened already serious rifts in the social fabric of the country. Besides undermining public morality by encouraging hypocrisy, it almost destroyed the Democratic party as a national organization. Democratic immigrants in the cities hated it, but southern Democrats sang its praises, often while continuing to drink (the humorist Will Rogers quipped that Mississippi would vote dry "as long as the voters could stagger to the polls").

The hypocrisy of prohibition had a particularly deleterious effect on politicians, a class seldom famous for candor. Members of Congress catered to the demands of the powerful lobby of the Anti-Saloon League yet failed to grant adequate funds to the Prohibition Bureau. Nearly all the prominent leaders, Democrat and Republican, from Wilson and La Follette to Hoover and Franklin D. Roosevelt, equivocated shamelessly on the liquor question. By the end of the decade almost every competent observer recognized that prohibition at least needed to be overhauled, but the well-organized and powerful dry forces rejected all proposals for modifying it.

THE KU KLUX KLAN

The most horrible manifestation of the social malaise of the 1920s was the revival of the Ku Klux Klan. This new Klan, founded in 1915 by William J. Simmons, a former preacher, admitted only native-born white Protestants. The distrust of foreigners, blacks, Catholics, and Jews implicit in this regulation explains why it flourished in the social climate that spawned religious fundamentalism, immigration restriction, and prohibition. In 1920 two unscrupulous publicity agents, Edward Y. Clarke and Elizabeth Tyler, got control of the movement and organized a massive membership drive, diverting a major share of the initiation fees into their own pockets. In a little over a year they enrolled 100,000 recruits, and by 1923 they claimed the astonishing total of 5 million.

Simmons gave his society trappings and mystery calculated to attract gullible and bigoted people who yearned to express their frustrations and hostilities without personal risk. Klansmen masked themselves in white robes and hoods and enjoyed a childish mumbo jumbo of magnificent-sounding titles and dogmas (kleagle, klaliff, kludd; kloxology, kloran). They burned crosses in the night, organized mass demonstrations to intimidate people they disliked, and put pressure on businessmen to fire black workers from better-paying jobs.

A Ku Klux Klan initiation ceremony photographed in Kansas in the 1920s. During its peak influence at mid-decade, Klan endorsement was essential to political candidates in many areas of the West and Midwest. Campaigning for reelection in 1934, an Indiana congressman testified, "I was told to join the Klan, or else."

The Klan had relatively little appeal in the Northeast or in metropolitan centers in other parts of the country, but it found many members in middle-sized cities and in the small towns and villages of midwestern and western states like Indiana and Oregon. The scapegoats in such regions were immigrants, Jews, and especially Catholics. The rationale was an urge to return to an older, supposedly finer America and to stamp out all varieties of nonconformity. Klansmen "watched everybody," themselves safe from observation behind their masks and robes. They persecuted gamblers, "loose" women, violators of the prohibition laws, and anyone who happened to differ from them on religious questions or who belonged to a "foreign race."

The very success of the Klan led to its undoing. Factionalism sprang up, and rival leaders squabbled over the large sums that had been collected from the membership. The cruel and outrageous behavior of the organization roused both liberals and conservatives in every part of the country. And of course its victims joined forces against their tormentors. When the powerful leader of the Indiana Klan, a middle-aged reprobate named David C. Stephenson, was convicted of assaulting and causing the death of a young woman, the rank and file abandoned the organization in droves. The Klan remained influential for a number of years, contributing to the defeat of the Catholic Alfred E. Smith in the 1928 presidential election, but it ceased to be a dynamic force after 1924. By 1930 it had only some 9000 members.

SACCO AND VANZETTI

The excesses of the fundamentalists, the xenophobes, the Klan, the red-baiters, and the prohibitionists disturbed American intellectuals profoundly. More and more they became alienated, bitter, and contemptuous of those who appeared to control the country. Yet their alienation came at the very time that society was growing more dependent on brains and sophistication. This compounded the confusion and disillusionment characteristic of the period.

Nothing demonstrates this fact so clearly as the Sacco and Vanzetti case. In April 1920 two men in South Braintree, Massachusetts, killed a paymaster and a guard in a daring daylight robbery of a shoe factory. Shortly thereafter Nicola Sacco and Bartolomeo Vanzetti were charged with the crime, and in 1921 they were convicted of murder. Sacco and Vanzetti were anarchists and Italian immigrants. Their trial was a travesty of justice. The presiding judge, Webster Thayer, conducted the proceedings like a prosecuting attorney; privately he referred to the defendants as "those anarchist bastards."

The case became a cause célèbre. Prominent persons throughout the world protested, and for years Sacco and Vanzetti were kept alive by efforts to obtain a new trial. Vanzetti's quiet dignity and courage in the face of death wrung the hearts of millions. "You see me before you, not trembling," he told the court. "I never commit a crime in my life. . . . I am so convinced to be right that if you could execute me two times, and if I could be reborn two other times, I would live again and do what I have done already." When, in August 1927, the two were at last electrocuted, the disillusionment of American intellectuals with prevailing values was profound. Some historians, impressed by modern ballistic studies of Sacco's gun, now suspect that he, at least, may have been guilty. Nevertheless, the truth and the shame remain: Sacco and Vanzetti paid with their lives for being radicals and aliens, not for any crime.

THE "NEW NEGRO"

The postwar reaction brought despair for many blacks. Aside from the barbarities of the Klan, they suffered from the postwar middle-class hostility to labor (and from the persistent reluctance of organized labor to admit black workers into its ranks). The increasing presence of southern blacks in northern cities also caused conflict. Some 393,000 settled in New York, Pennsylvania, and Illinois in the 1920s, most of them in New York City, Philadelphia, and Chicago. The black population of New York City more than doubled between 1920 and 1930.

In earlier periods blacks in northern cities had tended to live together, but in small neighborhoods scattered over large areas. Now the tendency was toward concentration in what came to be called ghettos.

Even in small northern cities where they made up only a tiny proportion of the population, blacks were badly treated. When Robert S. and Helen M. Lynd made their classic sociological analysis of "Middletown" (Muncie, Indiana), they discovered that although black and white children attended the same schools, the churches, the larger movie houses, and other places of public accommodation were segregated. The local YMCA had a gymnasium where high school basketball was played, but the secretary refused to allow any team with a black player to use it. Even the news in Muncie was segregated. Local papers chronicled the affairs of the black community—roughly 5 percent of the population—under the heading "In Colored Circles."

Coming after the hopes inspired by wartime gains, the disappointments of the 1920s produced a new militancy among many blacks. In 1919, W. E. B. Du Bois wrote in *The Crisis*: "We are cowards and jackasses if . . . we do not marshal every ounce of our brain and brawn to fight . . . against the forces of hell in our own land." He increased his commitment to black nationalism, organizing a series of Pan African Conferences in an effort—futile, as it turned out—to create an international black movement.

Du Bois never made up his mind whether to work for integration or black separatism. Such ambivalence never troubled Marcus Garvey, a West Indian whose Universal Negro Improvement Association attracted hundreds of thousands of followers in the early 1920s. Garvey had nothing but contempt for whites, for light-skinned blacks like Du Bois, and for organizations such as the NAACP, which sought to bring whites and blacks together to fight segregation and other forms of prejudice. "Back to Africa" was his slogan; the black man must "work out his salvation in his motherland." (Paradoxically, Garvey's ideas won the enthusiastic support of the Ku Klux Klan and other white racist groups.)

Garvey's message was naive, but it served to build racial pride among the masses of poor and unschooled blacks. He dressed in elaborate braided uniforms, wore a plumed hat, drove about in a limousine. Both God and Christ were black, he insisted. He organized black businesses of many sorts, including a company that manufactured black dolls. He established a corps of Black Cross nurses and a Black Star Line Steamship Company to transport blacks back to Africa.

More sophisticated black leaders like Du Bois detested Garvey, whom they thought something of a charlatan. Garvey's motives are at this distance unclear, and part of his troubles resulted only from his being a terrible businessman. In 1923 his steamship line went into bankruptcy. He was convicted of defrauding the thousands of his supporters who had invested in its stock and was sent to prison. Nevertheless, his message, if not his methods, helped to create the "New Negro," proud of being black and prepared to resist both mistreatment and white ideas. "Up you mighty race, you can accomplish what you will!"

Black separatist Marcus Garvey and his followers were one of many factions of the black movement during the 1920s and 1930s. Other groups, such as the NAACP, worked to bring blacks and whites together, rather than segregating them further.

The ghettos produced compensating advantages for blacks. One effect, not fully utilized until later, was to increase their political power by enabling them to elect representatives to state legislatures and to Congress and to exert considerable influence in closely contested elections. More immediately, city life stimulated self-confidence; despite their horrors, the ghettos offered economic opportunity, political rights, and freedom from the everyday debasements of life in the South. The ghetto was a black world where black men and women could be themselves.

Black writers, musicians, and artists found in the ghettos both an audience and the "spiritual emancipation" that unleashed their capacities. Jazz, the great popular music of the age, was largely the creation of black musicians working in New Orleans before the turn of the century. By the 1920s it had spread throughout the country and to most of the rest of the world. White musicians and white audiences took it up— in a way it became a force for racial tolerance and understanding.

Jazz meant improvisation, and both players and

audiences experienced in it a kind of liberation. Jazz was the music of the 1920s in part because it expressed the desire of so many people to break with tradition and throw off conventional restraints. Surely this helps to explain why it was so important to blacks.

Harlem, the largest black city in the world, became in the 1920s a cultural capital, center of the "Harlem Renaissance." Black newspapers and magazines flourished along with theatrical companies and libraries. Du Bois opened *The Crisis* to young writers and artists, and a dozen "little" magazines sprang up. Langston Hughes, one of the best poets of the era, described the exhilaration of his first arrival in this city within a city, a magnet for every black intellectual and artist. "Harlem! I . . . dropped my bags, took a deep breath, and felt happy again."

ECONOMIC EXPANSION

Despite the turmoil of the times and the dissatisfactions expressed by some of the nation's best minds, the 1920s was an exceptionally prosperous decade. Business boomed, real wages rose, unemployment declined. The United States was as rich as all Europe; perhaps 40 percent of the world's total wealth lay in American hands. Little wonder that business leaders and other conservatives described the period as a "new era."

The prosperity rested on many bases, one of which was the friendly, hands-off attitude of the federal government, which bolstered the confidence of the business community. The Federal Reserve Board kept interest rates low, a further stimulus to economic growth. Pent-up wartime demand helped to power the boom; the construction business in particular profited from a series of extremely busy years. The continuing mechanization and rationalization of industry provided a more fundamental stimulus to the economy. From heavy road-grading equipment and concrete mixers to devices for making cigars and glass tubes, from pneumatic tools to the dial telephone, machinery was replacing human hands at an ever more rapid rate. Industrial output almost doubled between 1921 and 1929 without any substantial increase in the industrial labor force. Greater use of power, especially of electricity, also encouraged expansion—by 1929 the United States was producing more electricity than the rest of the world combined.

Most important, American manufacturing was experiencing a remarkable improvement in efficiency. The method of breaking down the complex processes of production into many simple operations and the use of interchangeable parts were nineteenth-century innovations; in the 1920s they were adopted on an almost universal scale. The moving assembly line, which carried the product to the worker, first devised by Henry Ford in his automobile plant in the decade before

World War I, speeded production and reduced costs. In ten years the hourly out-put of Ford workers quadrupled. The time-and-motion studies of Frederick W. Taylor, developed early in the century, were applied in hundreds of factories after the war. Taylor's method was to make careful analyses of each step and move-ment in the manufacturing process. Then workers would be taught exactly how best to perform each function. Taylor described his system as "enforced standard-ization" made possible by the "enforced cooperation" of workers. "Taylorism" alarmed some union leaders, but no one could deny the effectiveness of "scien-tific shop management" methods.

THE AGE OF THE CONSUMER

The growing ability of manufacturers to produce goods meant that great effort had to be made to create new consumer demands. Advertising and salesmanship were raised almost to the status of fine arts. Bruce Barton, one of the advertising

This 1925 magazine adver-tisement for a Cadillac Coach shows how twentieth-century businesses sought to link nineteenth-century symbols of wealth (horseback riding, the coat-of-arms of nobility, flower gardens) with symbolic expressions of modernity, en-capsulated by the indepen-dence of short-haired, fash-ionably dressed young women.

"geniuses" of the era, wrote a best-selling book, *The Man Nobody Knows* (1925), in which he described Jesus as the "founder of modern business," the man who "picked up twelve men from the bottom ranks . . . and forged them into an organization that conquered the world." In 1930 no less a personage than Eleanor Roosevelt, wife of the governor of New York, gave a testimonial for a leading breakfast cereal, which had, she said, "undoubtedly played its part" in building the "robust physique" of her teenage son, John.

Producers concentrated on making their goods more attractive and on changing models frequently to entice buyers into the market. The practice of selling goods on the installment plan helped bring expensive items within the reach of the masses. Inventions and technological advances created new or improved products: radios, automobiles, electric appliances such as vacuum cleaners and refrigerators, gadgets like cigarette lighters, and new forms of entertainment like motion pictures. These influences interacted much as the textile industry in the early nineteenth century and the railroad industry after the Civil War had been the "multipliers" of their times.

Undoubtedly the automobile had the single most important impact on the nation's economy in the 1920s. Although well over a million cars a year were being regularly produced by 1916, the real expansion of the industry came after 1921. Output reached 3.6 million in 1923 and fell below that figure only twice during the remainder of the decade. By 1929, 23 million private cars clogged the highways, an average of nearly one per family.

The auto industry created industries that manufactured tires and spark plugs and other products. It consumed immense quantities of rubber, paint, glass, nickel, and petroleum products. It triggered a gigantic road-building program: there were 387,000 miles of paved roads in the United States in 1921, 662,000 miles in 1929. Thousands of persons found employment in filling stations, roadside stands, and other businesses catering to the motoring public. The tourist industry profited, and the shift of population from the cities to the suburbs was accelerated.

The automobile made life more mobile yet also more encapsulated. It changed recreational patterns and family life. It created a generation of tinkerers and amateur mechanics and explorers. In addition, it profoundly affected the way Americans thought. It gave them a freedom never before imagined. The owner of the most rickety jalopy could travel further, faster, and far more comfortably than a monarch of old with his blooded steeds and gilded coaches.

These benefits were real and priceless. But cars came to have a symbolic significance that was equally important: They gave their owners a feeling of power and status similar to that which owning a horse gave to a medieval knight.

According to some authorities the typical American cared more about owning an automobile than a house.

In time there were undesirable, even dangerous results of the automotive revolution: roadside scenery disfigured by billboards, gas stations, and other enterprises aimed at satisfying the traveler's needs; horrendous traffic jams; soaring accident rates; air pollution; the neglect of public transportation, which was an important cause of the deterioration of inner cities. All these disadvantages were noticed during the 1920s, but in the springtime of the new industry they were discounted. The automobile seemed an unalloyed blessing—part toy, part tool, part symbol of American freedom, prosperity, and individualism.

HENRY FORD

The person most responsible for the growth of the automobile industry was Henry Ford, a self-taught mechanic from Greenfield, Michigan. Ford was not a great inventor or one of the true automobile pioneers. He was not even the first person to manufacture a good low-priced car (that being the achievement of Ransom E. Olds, producer of the "Merry Oldsmobile"). He had two brilliant insights. The first was, in his words, "get the prices down to the buying power." Through mass production, cars could be made cheaply enough to put them within reach of the ordinary citizen. In 1908 he designed the Model T Ford, a simple, tough box on wheels. In a year he proved his point by selling 11,000 Model T's. Thereafter, relentlessly cutting costs and increasing efficiency by installing the assembly-line system, he expanded production at an unbelievable rate. By 1925 he was turning out more than 9000 cars a day, one approximately every 10 seconds, and the price of the Model T had been reduced to below $300.

Ford grasped the importance of high wages in stimulating output (and selling more automobiles). This was his second insight. The assembly line simplified the laborer's task and increased the pace of work; at the same time it made each worker much more productive. Jobs became boring and fatiguing, absenteeism and labor turnover serious problems. To combat this difficulty, in 1914 Ford established the $5 day, an increase of about $2 over prevailing wages. The rate of turnover in his plant fell 90 percent, and although critics charged that he recaptured his additional labor costs by speeding up the line, his policy had a revolutionary effect on wage rates. Later he raised the minimum to $6 and then to $7 a day.

Ford's profits soared along with sales; since he owned the entire company, he became a billionaire. He also became an authentic folk hero: His homespun style, his dislike of bankers and sophisticated society, and his intense individualism endeared him to millions. He stood as a symbol of the wonders of the American system—he had given the nation a marvelous convenience at a low price, at the same time enriching himself and raising the living standards of his thousands of employees.

Unfortunately, Ford had the defects of his virtues in full measure. He paid high wages but refused to deal with any union and he employed spies to investigate the private lives of his workers, and gangsters and thugs to enforce plant discipline. When he discovered a worker driving any car but a Ford, he had him dismissed. So close was the supervision in the factory that workers devised the "Ford whisper," a means of talking without moving one's lips.

Success made Ford stubborn. The Model T remained essentially unchanged for nearly 20 years. Other companies, notably General Motors, were soon turning out better vehicles for very little more money. Customers, increasingly affluent and style-conscious, began to shift to Chevrolets and Chryslers. Finally, in 1927, Ford shut down all operations for 18 months in order to retool for the Model A. His competitors rushed in during this period to fill the vacuum. Although his company continued to make a great deal of money, Ford never regained the dominant position he had held for so long.

Ford was enormously uninformed, yet—because of his success and the praise the world heaped on him—he did not hesitate to speak out on subjects far outside his area of competence, from the evils of drink and tobacco to medicine and international affairs. He developed political ambitions and published virulent anti-Semitic propaganda. He said he would not give 5 cents for all the art in the world.

While praising his talents as a manufacturer, historians have not dealt kindly with Ford the man, in part no doubt because he once said, "History is more or less the bunk."

THE AIRPLANE

Henry Ford was also an early manufacturer of airplanes, and while the airplane industry was not economically important in the 1920s, its development in that decade laid the basis for changes in lifestyles and attitudes at least as momentous as those produced by the automobile. The invention of the internal combustion gasoline engine, with its extremely high ratio of power to weight, made the airplane possible, which explains why the early experiments with "flying machines" took place at about the same time that the prototypes of the modern automobile were being manufactured. Wilbur and Orville Wright made their famous flight at Kitty Hawk, North Carolina, in 1903, five years before Ford produced his Model T. Another pair of brothers, Malcolm and Haimes Lockheed, built their Model G, one of the earliest commercial planes (commercial in the sense that they used it to take passengers up at $5 a ride) in 1913.

Charles Lindbergh with his famed plane, The Spirit of
St. Louis. *His 1927 flight from New York to Paris
made him an instant American hero.*

World War I speeded the advance of airplane technology, and most of the planes built in the 1920s were intended for military use. Practical commercial air travel was long delayed. Aerial acrobats, parachute jumpers, wing walkers, and other daredevils who put on shows at county fairs and similar places where crowds gathered were the principal civilian aviators of the 1920s. They "barnstormed" from town to town, living the same kind of inbred, encapsulated lives that circus people did, their chief rewards being the sense of independence and pride that the successful performance of their highly skilled but risky trade provided.

The great event of the decade for aviation, still an achievement that must strike awe in the hearts of reflective persons, was Charles A. Lindbergh's nonstop flight from New York to Paris in May 1927. It took more than 33 hours for Lindbergh's single-engine *Spirit of St. Louis* to cross the Atlantic, a formidable physical achievement for the pilot as well as an example of skill and courage. When the public learned that the intrepid "Lucky Lindy" was handsome, modest, uninterested in converting his new fame into cash, and a model of propriety (he neither drank nor smoked), his role as American hero was ensured. It was a role Lindbergh detested—one biographer has described him as "by nature solitary"—but could not avoid.

Lindbergh's flight enormously increased public interest in flying, but it was a landmark in aviation technology as well. The day of routine passenger flights was at last about to dawn. In July 1927, a mere two months after the *Spirit of St. Louis* touched down at Le Bourget Field in France, William E. Boeing of Boeing Air Transport began flying passengers and mail between San Francisco and Chicago, using the M-40, a plane of his own design and manufacture. Early in 1928 he changed the company name to United Aircraft and Transport. Two years later Boeing produced the first all-metal low-wing plane and, in 1933, the twin-engine 247, a prototype for many others.

In retrospect the postwar era seems even more a period of transition than it appeared to most people at the time. Rarely had change come so swiftly, and rarely had old and new existed side by side in such profusion. Creativity and reaction, hope and despair, freedom and repression—the modern world in all its unfathomable complexity was emerging.

MILESTONES

1908   Henry Ford begins production of his Model T automobile

1914   Ford establishes the $5 day for autoworkers

1919   Eighteenth Amendment outlaws alcoholic beverages

             Nineteenth Amendment gives women the vote

1920   Sinclair Lewis, *Main Street*

             F. Scott Fitzgerald, *This Side of Paradise*

             First commercial radio station, KDKA, begins broadcasting

1921   Margaret Sanger founds the American Birth Control League

1923   Supreme Court overturns the law limiting hours of work for women

1925   Scopes trial in Dayton, Tennessee

1926   Gertrude Ederle swims the English Channel

             Ernest Hemingway, *The Sun Also Rises*

1927   Charles A. Lindbergh flies solo from New York to Paris

             Execution of Sacco and Vanzetti

             The Jazz Singer is the first motion picture with sound

             Jack Dempsey loses heavyweight boxing title to Gene Tunney

             Babe Ruth hits 60 home runs

1930   Bobby Jones wins the United States and British amateur and open golf championships

26

❯——✦——❮

THE NEW ERA: 1921–1933

The men who presided over the government of the United States from 1921 to 1933 were Warren G. Harding, Calvin Coolidge, and Herbert Hoover. Harding was a newspaperman by trade, publisher of the *Marion Star,* with previous political experience as a legislator and lieutenant governor in his home state, Ohio, and as a United States senator. No president, before or since, looked more like a statesman; few were less suited for running the country.

Coolidge was a taciturn, extremely conservative New Englander with a long record in Massachusetts politics climaxed by his inept but much admired suppression of the Boston police strike while governor. Harding referred to him as "that little fellow from Massachusetts." Coolidge preferred to follow public opinion and hope for the best. "Mr. Coolidge's genius for inactivity is developed to a very high point," the correspondent Walter Lippmann wrote. "It is a grim, determined, alert inactivity, which keeps Mr. Coolidge occupied constantly." Hoover was best known for his work as food administrator during the Great War and for his many speeches about "progressive individualism" delivered while serving as secretary of commerce under Harding and Coolidge.

HARDING AND "NORMALCY"

Harding won the 1920 Republican nomination because the party convention could not decide between General Leonard Wood, who represented the Theodore Roosevelt progressives, and Frank Lowden, governor of Illinois. His genial nature and lack of strong convictions made him attractive to many of the politicos after eight years of the headstrong Wilson. During the campaign he exasperated sophisticates by his ignorance and imprecision. He coined the famous vulgarism *normalcy* as a substitute for the word *normality*; referred, during a speech before a group of actors, to Shakespeare's play "Charles the Fifth," and committed numerous other blunders. "Why does he not get a private secretary who can clothe . . . his 'ideas' in the language customarily used by educated men?" one Boston gentleman demanded of Senator Lodge, who was strongly supporting Harding. Lodge, ordinarily a stickler for linguistic exactitude, replied acidly that he found Harding a paragon by comparison with Wilson, "a man who wrote English very well without ever saying anything." A large majority of the voters, untroubled by the candidate's lack of erudition, shared Lodge's confidence that Harding would be a vast improvement over Wilson.

Harding has often been characterized as lazy and incompetent. In fact, he was hardworking and politically shrewd; his major weaknesses were indecisiveness and an unwillingness to offend. He turned the most important government departments over to efficient administrators of impeccable reputation: Charles Evans Hughes, in the State Department; Herbert Hoover in the Commerce Department; Andrew Mellon in the Treasury; and Henry C. Wallace in Agriculture. He kept track of what these men did but seldom initiated policy in their areas. However, Harding gave many lesser offices, and a few of major importance, to the unsavory "Ohio Gang" headed by Harry M. Daugherty, whom he made attorney general.

The president was too kindly, too well-intentioned, and too unambitious to be dishonest. He appointed corrupt officials like Daugherty, Secretary of the Interior Albert B. Fall, Director of the Mint "Ed" Scobey, and Charles R. Forbes, head of the new Veterans Bureau, out of a sense of personal obligation or because they were old friends who shared his taste for poker and liquor. Before 1921 he had enjoyed officeholding; he was adept at mouthing platitudes, a loyal party man who seldom questioned the decisions of his superiors. In the lonely eminence of the White House, whence, as President Harry Truman later said, the buck cannot be passed, he found only misery. "The White House is a prison," he complained. "I can't get away from the men who dog my footsteps. I am in jail."

"THE BUSINESS OF THE UNITED STATES IS BUSINESS"

Secretary of the Treasury Mellon, multimillionaire banker and master of the aluminum industry, dominated the administration's domestic policy. Mellon set out to lower the taxes of the rich, reverse the low-tariff policies of the Wilson period, return to the laissez-faire philosophy of McKinley, and reduce the national debt by cutting expenses and administrating the government more efficiently.

In principle his program had considerable merit. Tax rates designed to check consumer spending in time of war and to raise the huge sum needed to defeat the Central Powers were undoubtedly hampering economic expansion in the early 1920s.

Yet Mellon carried his policies to unreasonable extremes. He proposed eliminating inheritance taxes and reducing the tax on high incomes by two-thirds, but he opposed lower rates for taxpayers earning less than $66,000 a year, apparently not realizing that economic expansion required greater mass consumption as well. Freeing the rich from "oppressive" taxation, he argued, would enable them to invest more in potentially productive enterprises, the success of which would create jobs for ordinary people. Little wonder that Mellon's admirers called him the greatest secretary of the treasury since Alexander Hamilton.

Mellon succeeded in balancing the budget and reducing the national debt by an average of over $500 million a year. So committed were the Republican leaders to retrenchment that they even resisted the demands of veterans, organized in the politically potent American Legion, for an "adjusted compensation" bonus.

That the business community heartily approved the policies of Harding and Coolidge is not surprising. Both presidents were uncritical advocates of the business point of view. "We want less government in business and more business in government," Harding pontificated, to which Coolidge added, "The business of the United States is business." Harding and Coolidge used their power of appointment to convert regulatory bodies like the Interstate Commerce Commission (ICC) and the Federal Reserve Board into probusiness agencies that ceased almost entirely to restrict the activities of the industries they were supposed to be controlling. The ICC became almost the reverse of what it had been in the Progressive era. The Federal Trade Commission, in the words of one bemused academic, seemed to be trying to commit hara-kiri.

THE HARDING SCANDALS

At least Mellon was honest. The Ohio gang used its power in the most corrupt way imaginable. The worst scandal involved Secretary of the Interior Albert B. Fall, a former senator. In 1921 Fall arranged with the complaisant Secretary of the Navy Edwin Denby for the transfer to the Interior Department of government oil reserves being held for the future use of the navy. He then leased these properties to private oil companies. Edward L. Doheny's Pan-American Petroleum Company got the Elk Hills reserve in California; the Teapot Dome re-

Warren G. Harding looked presidential, and his voice was suitably deep and resonant. Yet he lacked mental agility and discipline. Republican Senator Frank Brandegee explained Harding's nomination by proclaiming him "the best of the second-raters," and thus the natural compromise between contending factions in the party.

serve in Wyoming was turned over to Harry F. Sinclair's Mammoth Oil Company. When critics protested, Fall explained that it was necessary to develop the Elk Hills and Teapot Dome properties because adjoining private drillers were draining off the navy's oil. Nevertheless, in 1923 the Senate ordered a full-scale investigation, conducted by Senator Thomas J. Walsh of Montana. It soon came out that Doheny had "lent" Fall $100,000 in hard cash, handed over secretly in a "little black bag." Sinclair had given Fall over $300,000 in cash and negotiable securities.

Although the three culprits escaped conviction on the charge of conspiring to defraud the government, Sinclair was sentenced to nine months in jail for contempt of the Senate and for tampering with a jury, and Fall was fined $100,000 and given a year in prison for accepting a bribe. In 1927 the Supreme Court revoked the leases and the two reserves were returned to the government.

The public still knew little of the scandals when, in June 1923, Harding left Washington on a speaking tour that included a visit to Alaska. His health was poor and his spirits low, for he had begun to understand how his "Goddamn friends" had betrayed him. On the return trip from Alaska, he came down with what his physician, an incompetent crony whom he had made surgeon general of the United States, diagnosed as ptomaine poisoning resulting from his having eaten a tainted Japanese crab. In fact the president had suffered a heart attack. He died in San Francisco on August 2.

Few presidents have been more deeply mourned by the people at the moment of their passing. Harding's kindly nature, his very ordinariness, increased his human appeal. Three million people viewed his coffin as it passed across the country. When the scandals came to light, sadness turned to scorn and contempt. The poet e. e. cummings came closer to catching the final judgment of Harding's contemporaries than has any historian:

> the first president to be loved by his
> "bitterest enemies" is dead
> the only man woman or child who wrote
> a simple declarative sentence with seven grammatical
> errors "is dead"
> beautiful Warren Gamaliel Harding
> "is" dead
> he's
> "dead"
> if he wouldn't have eaten them Yapanese Craps
> somebody might hardly never not have been
> unsorry, perhaps

COOLIDGE PROSPERITY

Had he lived, Harding might well have been defeated in 1924 because of the scandals. Vice President Coolidge, unconnected with the troubles and not the type to surround himself with cronies of any kind, seemed the ideal person to clean out the corrupt officials. After he had replaced Attorney General Daugherty with Harlan Fiske Stone, dean of the Columbia University Law School, the scandals ceased to be a serious political handicap for the Republicans.

Coolidge soon became the darling of the conservatives. His admiration for businessmen and his devotion to laissez-faire knew no limit. "The man who builds a factory builds a temple," he said in all seriousness. "The Government can do more to remedy the economic ills of the people by a system of rigid economy in public expenditures than can be accomplished through any other action." Andrew Mellon, whom he kept on as secretary of the treasury, became his mentor in economic affairs.

Coolidge won the 1924 Republican nomination easily. The Democrats, badly split, required 103 ballots to choose a candidate. The southern wing, dry, anti-immigrant, pro-Klan, had fixed on William G. McAdoo, Wilson's secretary of the treasury. The eastern, urban, wet element supported Governor Alfred E. Smith of New York, child of the slums, a Catholic who had compiled a distinguished

Calvin Coolidge's quiet presidential style was a sharp contrast to the outspoken one of Warren Harding. When Coolidge died in 1933, humorist Dorothy Parker remarked, "How could they tell?"

record in social welfare legislation. After days of futile politicking, the party compromised on John W. Davis, a conservative corporation lawyer closely allied with the Morgan banking interests.

Dismayed by the conservatism of Coolidge and Davis, Robert M. La Follette, backed by the farm bloc, the Socialist party, the American Federation of Labor, and numbers of intellectuals, entered the race as the candidate of a new Progressive party. The Progressives adopted a neopopulist platform calling for the nationalization of railroads, the direct election of the president, the protection of labor's right to bargain collectively, and other reforms.

The situation was almost exactly the opposite of 1912, when one conservative had run against two liberals and had been swamped. Coolidge received 15.7 million votes, Davis 8.4 million, La Follette 4.8 million. In the Electoral College La Follette won only his native Wisconsin; Coolidge defeated Davis, 382 to 136. Conservatism was clearly the dominant mood of the country.

While Coolidge reigned, complacency was the order of the day. "The country," the president reported to Congress in 1928, "can regard the present with satisfaction, and anticipate the future with optimism."

PEACE WITHOUT A SWORD

Presidents Harding and Coolidge handled foreign relations in much the same way they managed domestic affairs. Harding deferred to senatorial prejudice against

Here Big Business is depicted as a wanton "flapper," gyrating to the music of Coolidge. Nicknamed "Silent Cal," the president was famously staid.

executive domination in the area and let Secretary of State Charles Evans Hughes make policy. Coolidge adopted a similar course. In directing foreign relations, they faced the obstacle of a resurgent isolationism. The same forces of war-bred hatred, postwar disillusion, and fear of communist subversion that produced the red scare at home led Americans to back away from close involvement in world affairs. The bloodiness and apparent senselessness of the Great War convinced millions that the only way to be sure it would not happen again was to "steer clear" of "entanglements." That these famous words had been used by Washington and Jefferson in vastly different contexts did not deter the isolationists of the 1920s from attributing to them the same authority they gave to Scripture. On the other hand, far-flung American economic interests, the need for both raw materials for industry and foreign markets for America's growing surpluses of agricultural and manufactured goods, made close attention to and involvement in developments all over the world unavoidable.

Isolationist sentiments, therefore, did not deter the government from seeking to advance American interests abroad. The Open Door concept remained predominant; the State Department worked to obtain opportunities in underdeveloped countries for exporters and investors, hoping both to stimulate the American economy and to bring stability to "backward" nations. Although this policy sometimes roused local resentments because of the tendency of the United States to support entrenched elites while the mass of peasants and city workers lived in poverty, it also resulted in a further retreat from active interventionism.

The first important diplomatic event of the period revealed a great deal about American foreign policy after the World War. During the war, Japan had greatly increased its influence in the Far East, especially in Manchuria, the northeastern province of warlord-dominated China. To maintain the Open Door in China, it would be necessary to check Japanese expansion. But there was little hope of restoring the old spheres of influence, which the mass of Chinese people bitterly resented. In addition, Japan, the United States, and Great Britain were engaged in expensive naval building programs, a competition none of them really wanted but from which all dared not withdraw unilaterally.

In November 1921, hoping to reach a general agreement with China, Japan, and the Europeans that would keep China open to the commerce of all and slow the armaments race, Secretary of State Hughes convened a conference in Washington. By the following February the Washington Conference had drafted three major treaties and a number of lesser agreements.

In the Five-Power Treaty, the United States, Great Britain, France, Japan, and Italy agreed to stop building battleships for ten years and to reduce their fleets of capital ships to a fixed ratio, with Great Britain and the United States limited to 525,000 tons, Japan to 315,000 tons, and France and Italy to 175,000 tons. The new ratio was expected to produce a balance of forces in the Pacific.

The Four-Power Treaty, signed by the United States, Great Britain, Japan, and France, committed these nations to respect one another's interests in the islands of the Pacific and to confer in the event that any other country launched an attack in the area.

All the conferees signed the Nine-Power Treaty, agreeing to respect China's independence and to maintain the Open Door. On the surface, this was of monumental importance to the United States since it seemed to mean that Japan had given up its territorial ambitions on the Asian mainland and that both the Japanese and the Europeans had formally endorsed the Open Door concept.

By taking the lead in drafting these agreements, the United States regained some of the moral influence it had lost by not joining the League of Nations. The treaties, however, were uniformly toothless. The signers of the Four-Power pact agreed only to consult in case of aggression in the Pacific; they made no promises to help one another or to restrict their own freedom of action. As President Harding assured the Senate, "there [was] no commitment to armed force, no alliance, no written or moral obligation to join in defense."

The naval disarmament treaty said nothing about the number of other warships that the powers might build, about the far more important question of land and air forces, or about the underlying industrial and financial structures that controlled the ability of the nations to make war. In addition, the 5:5:3 ratio actually enabled the Japanese to dominate the western Pacific. It made the Philippine Islands indefensible and exposed Hawaii to possible attack. In a sense these American bases became hostages of Japan. Yet Congress was so unconcerned about Japanese sensibilities that it refused to grant any immigration quota to Japan under the National Origins Act of 1924, even though the formula applied to other nations would have allowed only 100 Japanese a year to enter the country. The law, Secretary Hughes warned, produced in Japan "a sense of injury and antagonism instead of friendship and cooperation."

Hughes did not think war a likely result, but Japanese resentment of "white imperialism" played into the hands of the military party in that nation. Many Japanese army and navy officers considered war with the United States inevitable.

As for the key Nine-Power Treaty, Japan did not abandon its territorial ambitions in China, and China remained so riven by conflict among the warlords and so resentful of the "imperialists" that the economic advantages of the Open Door turned out to be small indeed.

The United States entered into all these agreements without realizing their full implications and not really prepared to play an active part in Far Eastern affairs. "We have no favorites in the present dog fight in China," the head of the Far Eastern division of the State Department wrote of the civil war going on there in 1924. "They all look alike to us."

THE PEACE MOVEMENT

The Americans of the 1920s wanted peace but would neither surrender their prejudices and dislikes nor build the defenses necessary to make it safe to indulge these passions. "The people have had all the war, all the taxation, and all the military service that they want," President Coolidge announced in 1925.

Peace societies flourished, among them the Carnegie Endowment for International Peace, designed "to hasten the abolition of war, the foulest blot upon our civilization," and the Woodrow Wilson Foundation, aimed at helping "the liberal forces of mankind throughout the world . . . who intend to promote peace by the means of justice."

So great was the opposition to international cooperation that the United States refused to accept membership on the World Court, although this tribunal could settle disputes only when the nations involved agreed.

The culmination of this illusory faith in preventing war by criticizing it came with the signing of the Kellogg-Briand Pact in 1928. The treaty was born in the fertile brain of French Foreign Minister Aristide Briand, who was eager to collect allies against possible attack by a resurgent Germany. In 1927 Briand proposed to

Leaders of the Women's International League for Peace and Freedom assembled at the end of the Great War to argue in favor of United States participation in a worldwide peace organization such as the League of Nations. Jane Addams is in front, fourth from left; at her left is Mrs. Robert La Follette, wife of the Wisconsin senator.

Secretary of State Frank B. Kellogg that their countries agree never to go to war with each other. Kellogg found the idea as repugnant as any conventional alliance, but American isolationists and pacifists found the suggestion fascinating. They plagued Kellogg with demands that he negotiate such a treaty.

To extricate himself from this situation, Kellogg suggested that the pact be broadened to include all nations. Now Briand was angry. Like Kellogg, he saw how meaningless such a treaty would be, especially when Kellogg insisted that it be hedged with a proviso that "every nation is free at all times . . . to defend its territory from attack and it alone is competent to decide when circumstances require war in self-defense." Nevertheless, Briand too found public pressures irresistible. In August 1928, at Paris, diplomats from 15 nations bestowed upon one another an "international kiss," condemning "recourse to war for the solution of international controversies" and renouncing war "as an instrument of national policy." Seldom has so unrealistic a promise been made by so many intelligent people. Yet most Americans considered the Kellogg-Briand Pact a milestone in the history of civilization: The Senate, habitually so suspicious of international commitments, ratified it 85 to 1.

THE GOOD NEIGHBOR POLICY

In the face of continued radicalism and instability in Mexico, which caused Americans with interests in land and oil rights to suffer heavy losses, President Coolidge acted with forbearance. His appointment of Dwight W. Morrow, a patient, sympathetic ambassador, resulted in an improvement in Mexican-American relations. The Mexicans were able to complete their social and economic revolution in the 1920s without significant interference by the United States.

Under Coolidge's successor, Herbert Hoover, the United States began at last to treat Latin American nations as equals. Hoover reversed Wilson's policy of trying to teach them "to elect good men." The Clark Memorandum (1930), written by Undersecretary of State J. Reuben Clark, disassociated the right of intervention in Latin America from the Roosevelt Corollary. The corollary had been an improper extension of the Monroe Doctrine, Clark declared. The right of the United States to intervene depended rather on "the doctrine of self-preservation."

The distinction seemed slight to Latin Americans, but since it seemed unlikely that the existence of the United States could be threatened in the area, it was important. By 1934 the marines who had been occupying Nicaragua, Haiti, and the Dominican Republic had all been withdrawn and the United States had renounced the right to intervene in Cuban affairs, thereby abrogating the Platt Amendment to the Cuban constitution. Unfortunately, the United States did little to try to improve social and economic conditions in the Caribbean region, so the underlying envy and resentment of "rich Uncle Sam" did not disappear.

THE TOTALITARIAN CHALLENGE

The futility and danger of isolationism were exposed in September 1931 when the Japanese, long dominant in Chinese Manchuria, marched in an army and converted the province into a puppet state named Manchukuo. This violated both the Kellogg-Briand and Nine-Power Pacts. China, now controlled by General Chiang Kai-shek, appealed to the League of Nations and to the United States for help. Neither would intervene. When League officials asked about the possibility of American cooperation in some kind of police action, President Hoover refused to consider either economic or military reprisals. The United States was not a world policeman, he said. The Nine-Power and Kellogg-Briand Treaties were "solely moral instruments."

In January 1932 Japan attacked Shanghai, the bloody battle marked by the indiscriminate bombing of residential districts. When the League at last officially condemned their aggressions, the Japanese withdrew from the organization and extended their control of northern China. The lesson of Manchuria was not lost on Adolf Hitler, who became chancellor of Germany on January 30, 1933.

It is easy, in surveying the diplomatic events of 1920–1929, to condemn the United States and the European democracies for their unwillingness to stand up

Japanese troops advancing through the ruins of the Chinese city of Shanghai, in March 1932, a year after Japan had seized Manchuria. Five years later, Japan embarked on the conquest of all China.

for principles, their refusal to resist when Japan and later Germany and Italy embarked on the aggressions that led to World War II. It is also proper to place some of the blame for the troubles of the era on the same powers: They controlled much of the world's resources and were primarily interested in holding on to what they had.

WAR DEBTS AND REPARATIONS

The democracies did not take a strong stand against Japan in part because they were quarreling about other matters. Particularly divisive was the controversy over war debts—those of Germany to the Allies and those of the Allies to the United States. The United States had lent more than $10 billion to its comrades in arms. Since most of this money had been spent on weapons and other supplies in the United States, it might well have been considered part of America's contribution to the war effort. The public, however, demanded full repayment—with interest. "These were loans, not contributions," Secretary of the Treasury Mellon firmly declared. Even when the Foreign Debt Commission scaled down the interest rate from 5 percent to about 2 percent, the total, to be repaid over a period of 62 years, amounted to more than $22 billion.

Repayment of such a sum was virtually impossible. In the first place, the money had not been put to productive use. Dollars lent to build factories or roads might be expected to earn profits for the borrower, but those devoted to the purchase of shells only destroyed wealth.

The Allies tried to load their obligations to the United States, along with the other costs of the war, on the backs of the Germans. They demanded reparations amounting to $33 billion. If this sum were collected, they declared, they could rebuild their economies and obtain the international exchange needed to pay their debts to the United States. But Germany was reluctant even to try to pay such huge reparations, and when Germany defaulted, so did the Allies.

Everyone was bitterly resentful: the Germans because they felt they were being bled white; the Americans, as Senator Hiram Johnson of California would have it, because the wily Europeans were treating the United States as "an international sucker"; the Allies because, as the French said, "*l'oncle Shylock*" (a play on the names Uncle Sam and Shylock, the moneylender in Shakespeare's *Merchant of Venice*) was demanding his pound of flesh with interest. "If nations were only business firms," Clemenceau wrote President Coolidge in 1926, "bank notes would determine the fate of the world. . . . Come see the endless lists of dead in our villages."

Everyone shared the blame: the Germans because they resorted to a runaway inflation that reduced the mark to less than one trillionth of its prewar value, at least in part in hopes of avoiding their international obligations; the Americans because they refused to recognize the connection between the tariff and the debt question; the Allies because they made little effort to pay even a reasonable proportion of their obligations.

In 1924 an international agreement, the Dawes Plan, provided Germany with a $200 million loan designed to stabilize its currency. Germany agreed to pay about $250 million a year in reparations. In 1929 the Young Plan further scaled down the reparations bill. In practice, the Allies paid the United States about what they collected from Germany. Since Germany got the money largely from private American loans, the United States would have served itself and the rest of the world far better had it written off the war debts at the start. In any case, in the late 1920s Americans stopped lending money to Germany, the Great Depression struck, Germany defaulted on its reparations payments, and the Allies then gave up all pretense of meeting their obligations to the United States. The last token payments were made in 1933. All that remained was a heritage of mistrust and hostility.

THE ELECTION OF 1928

Meanwhile, dramatic changes had occurred in the United States. The climax of Coolidge prosperity came in 1928. The president—somewhat cryptically, as was his wont—decided not to run again, and Secretary of Commerce Hoover, whom he detested, easily won the Republican nomination. Hoover was the intellectual leader, almost the philosopher, of the New Era. American capitalists, he believed, had learned

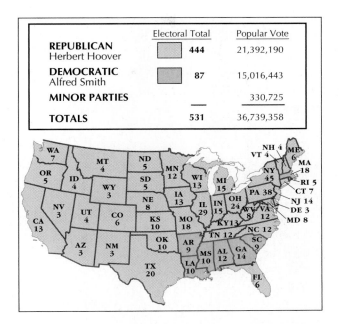

	Electoral Total	Popular Vote
REPUBLICAN Herbert Hoover	444	21,392,190
DEMOCRATIC Alfred Smith	87	15,016,443
MINOR PARTIES	—	330,725
TOTALS	531	36,739,358

The Election of 1928

to curb their selfish instincts. Voluntary trade associations could create "codes of business practice and ethics that would eliminate abuses and make for higher standards."

Although stiff and uncommunicative and entirely without experience in elective office, Hoover made an admirable candidate in 1928. His roots in the Midwest and West (Iowa-born, he was raised in Oregon and educated at Stanford University in California) neatly balanced his outstanding reputation among eastern business tycoons. He took a "modern" approach to both capital and labor; businessmen should cooperate with one another and with their workers too. He opposed both union busting and trustbusting.

The Democrats, having had their fill of factionalism in 1924, could no longer deny the nomination to Governor Al Smith. Superficially, Smith was Hoover's antithesis. Born and raised in New York's Lower East Side slums, affable, witty, determinedly casual of manner, he had been schooled in machine politics by Tammany Hall. He was a Catholic, Hoover a Quaker; he was a wet, while Hoover supported prohibition; he dealt easily with people of every race and nationality, while Hoover had little interest in and less knowledge of blacks and immigrants.

Unwilling to challenge the public's complacent view of Coolidge prosperity, the Democrats adopted a conservative platform. This strategy failed miserably. Nothing Smith could do or say was capable of convincing many businessmen that he was a better choice than Hoover. His Catholicism, his brashness, his criticism of prohibition, his machine connections, and his urban background hurt him in rural areas, especially in the normally Democratic South.

Herbert Hoover relaxing during the 1928 presidential campaign. "That man has been offering me advice for the last five years," President Coolidge said of his secretary of commerce, "all of it bad."

In the election Hoover won a smashing triumph, 444 to 87 in the Electoral College, 21.4 million to 14 million in the popular vote. All the usually Democratic border states and even North Carolina, Florida, and Texas went to the Republicans, along with the entire West and the Northeast save for Massachusetts and Rhode Island.

After this defeat the Democratic party appeared on the verge of extinction. Nothing could have been further from the truth. The religious question and his big-city roots had hurt Smith, but the chief reason he lost was prosperity—and the good times were soon to end. Hoover's overwhelming victory also concealed a political realignment that was taking place. Working-class voters in the cities, largely Catholic and unimpressed by Coolidge prosperity, had swung heavily to the Democrats. In 1924 the 12 largest cities had been solidly Republican; in 1928 all went Democratic. In agricultural states like Iowa, Smith ran far better than Davis had in 1924, for Coolidge's vetoes of bills designed to raise farm prices had caused considerable resentment. A new coalition of urban workers and dissatisfied farmers was in the making.

ECONOMIC PROBLEMS

The American economic system of the 1920s had grave flaws. Certain industries did not share in the good times. The coal business, suffering from the competition of petroleum, entered a period of decline. The production of cotton and woolen cloth also lagged because of the competition of new synthetics, principally rayon. The industry began to be plagued by falling profit margins and chronic unemployment.

The movement toward consolidation in industry, somewhat checked during the latter part of the Progressive era, resumed; by 1929, 200 corporations controlled nearly half the nation's corporate assets. General Motors, Ford, and Chrysler turned out nearly 90 percent of all American cars and trucks. Four tobacco companies produced over 90 percent of the cigarettes. One percent of all financial institutions controlled 46 percent of the nation's banking business. Even retail merchandising, traditionally the domain of the small shopkeeper, reflected the trend. The A & P food chain expanded from 400 stores in 1912 to 17,500 in 1928. The Woolworth chain of five-and-ten-cent stores experienced similar growth.

The trade association movement flourished; producers formed voluntary organizations to exchange information, discuss policies toward government and the public, and "administer" prices in their industry. Usually the largest corporation, such as U.S. Steel in the iron and steel business, became the "price leader," its competitors, some themselves giants, following slavishly.

The success of the trade associations depended in part on the attitude of the federal government, for such organizations might well have been attacked under the antitrust laws. Their defenders argued that the associations made business more efficient and prevented violent gyrations of prices and production. President Harding accepted this line of reasoning. Secretary of Commerce Hoover put the facilities of his department at the disposal of the associations. "We are passing from a period of extremely individualistic action into a period of associational activities," Hoover stated. After Coolidge became president, the Antitrust Division of the Justice Department itself encouraged the trade associations to cooperate in ways that had previously been considered violations of the Sherman Act.

Even more important to the trade associations were the good times. With profits high and markets expanding, the most powerful producers could afford to share the bounty with smaller, less efficient competitors.

The weakest element in the economy was agriculture. Farm prices slumped and farmers' costs mounted. Besides having to purchase expensive machinery in order to compete, farmers were confronted by high foreign tariffs and in some cases quotas on the importation of foodstuffs. As crop yields per acre rose, chiefly because of the increased use of chemical fertilizers, agricultural prices fell further.

Despite the efforts of the farm bloc, the government did little to improve the situation. President Harding opposed direct aid to agriculture as a matter of principle. "Every farmer is a captain of industry," he declared. "The elimination of competition among them would be impossible without sacrificing that fine individualism that still keeps the farm the real reservoir from which the nation draws so many of the finest elements of its citizenship."

Thus, while most economic indicators reflected an unprecedented prosperity, the boom time rested on unstable foundations. The problem was mainly one of maldistribution of resources. Productive capacity raced ahead of buying power. Too large a share of the profits was going into too few pockets. The 27,000 families with the highest annual incomes in 1929 received as much money as the 11 million with annual incomes of under $1500, the minimum sum required at that time to maintain a family decently. High earnings and low taxes permitted huge sums to pile up in the hands of individuals who did not invest the money productively. A good deal of it went into stock market speculation, which led to the "big bull market" and eventually to the Great Depression.

THE STOCK MARKET CRASH OF 1929

In the spring of 1928, prices on the New York Stock Exchange, already at a historic high, began to surge ahead. As the presidential campaign gathered momentum, the market increased its upward pace, stimulated by the candidates' efforts to outdo each other in praising the marvels of the American economic system. "Glamor" stocks skyrocketed—Radio Corporation of America rose from under 100 to 400 between March and November. A few conservative brokers expressed alarm, warning that most stocks were grossly overpriced. The majority scoffed at such talk. "Be a bull on America," they urged. "Never sell the United States short."

During the first half of 1929 stock prices climbed still higher. A mania for speculation swept the country, thousands of small investors putting their savings in common stocks. Then, in September the market wavered. Amid volatile fluctuations stock averages eased downward. Most analysts contended that the stock exchange was "digesting" previous gains. A Harvard economist expressed the prevailing view when he said that stock prices had reached a "permanently high plateau" and would soon resume their advance.

On October 24 a wave of selling sent prices spinning. Nearly 13 million shares changed hands—a record. Bankers and politicians rallied to check the decline, as they had during the Panic of 1907. President Hoover assured the people that "the business of the country . . . is on a sound and prosperous basis." But on October 29, the bottom seemed to drop out. More than 16 million shares were sold, prices plummeting. The boom was over.

HOOVER AND THE DEPRESSION

The collapse of the stock market did not cause the depression; stocks rallied late in the year, and business activity did not begin to decline significantly until the spring of 1930. The Great Depression was a worldwide phenomenon caused chiefly by economic imbalances resulting from the chaos of the Great War. In the United States too much wealth had fallen into too few hands, with the result that consumers were unable to buy all the goods produced. The trouble came to a head mainly because of the easy-credit policies of the Federal Reserve Board and the Mellon tax structure, which favored the rich. Its effects were so profound and prolonged because the politicians (and for that matter the professional economists) did not fully understand what was happening or what to do about it.

The chronic problem of underconsumption operated to speed the downward spiral. Unable to rid themselves of mounting inventories, manufacturers closed plants and laid off workers, thereby causing demand to shrink further. Automobile output fell from 4.5 million units in 1929 to 1.1 million in 1932. When Ford closed his Detroit plants in 1931, some 75,000 workers lost their jobs, and the decline in auto production affected a host of suppliers and middlemen as well.

The financial system cracked under the strain. More than 1300 banks closed their doors in 1930, 3700 more during the next two years. Each failure deprived thousands of persons of funds that might have been used to buy goods; when the Bank of the United States in New York City became insolvent in December 1930, 400,000 depositors found their savings immobilized. And of course the industrial depression worsened the depression in agriculture by further reducing the demand for American foodstuffs. Every economic indicator reflected the collapse. New investments declined from $10 billion in 1929 to $1 billion in 1932, and the national income fell from over $80 billion to under $50 billion in the same brief period. Unemployment, under 1 million at the height of the boom, rose to at least 13 million.

President Hoover was an intelligent man, experienced in business matters and knowledgeable in economics. Secretary of the Treasury Mellon believed that the economy should be allowed to slide unchecked until the cycle had found its bottom. "Let the slump liquidate itself," Mellon urged. "Liquidate labor, liquidate stocks, liquidate the farmers. . . . People will work harder, live a more moral life. Values will be adjusted, and enterprising people will pick up the wrecks from less competent people." Hoover realized that such a policy would cause unbearable hardship for millions. He rejected Mellon's advice to let the depression run its course.

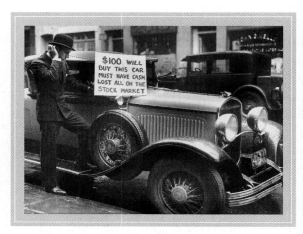

With the collapse of the stock market, Walter Thornton's assets evaporated but his debts remained. To help cover them he sold this snappy roadster for $100, a fraction of its original cost.

Hoover's program for ending the depression evolved gradually. At first he called on businessmen to maintain prices and wages. The government should cut taxes in order to increase consumers' spendable income, institute public works programs to stimulate production and create jobs for the unemployed, lower interest rates to make it easier for businesses to borrow in order to expand, and make loans to banks and industrial corporations threatened with collapse and to home owners unable to meet mortgage payments. He called for an expansion of state and local relief programs and urged all who could afford it to give more to charity. Above all he tried to restore public confidence. The economy was basically healthy; the depression was only a minor downturn; prosperity was "just around the corner."

Although Hoover's plans were theoretically sound, they failed to check the economic slide, in part because of curious limitations in his conception of how they should be implemented. He placed far too much reliance on his powers of persuasion and the willingness of citizens to act in the public interest without legal compulsion. He urged manufacturers to maintain wages and keep their factories in operation, but the manufacturers, under the harsh pressure of economic realities, soon slashed wages and curtailed output sharply. He permitted the Federal Farm Board (created under the Agricultural Marketing Act of 1929) to establish semipublic stabilization corporations with authority to buy up surplus wheat and cotton, but he refused to countenance crop or acreage controls. The stabilization corporations poured out hundreds of millions of dollars without checking falling agricultural prices because farmers increased production faster than the corporations could buy up the excess for disposal abroad.

Hoover resisted proposals to shift responsibility from state and local agencies to the federal government, despite the fact—soon obvious—that they lacked the resources to cope with the emergency. By 1932 the federal government, with Hoover's approval, was spending $500 million a year on public works projects, but because of the decline in state and municipal construction, the total public outlay fell nearly $1 billion below what it had been in 1930. More serious was his refusal, on constitutional grounds, to allow federal funds to be used for the relief of individuals. State and municipal agencies and private charities must take care of the needy.

Unfortunately the depression was drying up the sources of private charities just as the demands on these organizations were expanding. State and municipal agencies were swamped at a time when their capacities to tax and borrow were shrinking. By 1932 more than 40,600 Boston families were on relief (compared with 7400 families in 1929); in Chicago 700,000 persons—40 percent of the workforce—were unemployed. Only the national government possessed the power and the credit to deal adequately with the crisis.

Yet Hoover would not act. He set up a committee to coordinate local relief activities but insisted on preserving what he called "the principles of individual and local responsibility." For the federal government to take over relief would "lead to the super-state where every man becomes the servant of the state and real liberty is lost."

As time passed and the depression worsened, Hoover put more stress on the importance of balancing the federal budget, reasoning that since citizens had to live within their limited means in hard times, the government should set a good example. This policy was counterproductive; by reducing its expenditures the government made the depression worse. By June 1931 the budget was nearly $500 million in the red.

Hoover understood the value of pumping money into a stagnant economy. He might have made a virtue of necessity. The difficulty lay in the fact that nearly all "informed" opinion believed that a balanced budget was essential to recovery. The most prestigious economists insisted on it; so did business leaders, labor leaders, and even most socialists. In 1932, when the House of Representatives refused to vote a tax increase, the Democratic Speaker compelled reconsideration of the bill by asking those "who do not want to balance the budget to rise." Not a single member did so. As late as 1939 a public opinion poll revealed that over 60 percent of the people (even 57.5 percent of the unemployed) favored reducing government expenditures to balance the budget. When Hoover said, "prosperity cannot be restored by raids on the public Treasury," he was mistaken, but it is equally wrong to criticize him for failing to understand what almost no one understood in the 1930s.

Much of the contemporary criticism of Hoover and a good deal of that heaped on him by later historians was unfair. Yet his record as president shows that he was too rigidly wedded to a particular theory of government to cope effectively with the problems of the day. Since these problems were in a sense insoluble—no one possessed enough knowledge and intelligence to understand

Some unemployed men loitered around factories and warehouses, hoping to snatch temporary jobs. Others took to the road to find work elsewhere. Many adult women returned to live with their parents or other relatives. Lest they be mistaken for prostitutes, women generally avoided relief lines such as this one in Chicago.

entirely what was wrong or enough authority to enforce the proper corrective measures—flexibility and a willingness to experiment were essential to any program aimed at restoring prosperity. Hoover lacked these qualities. He was his own worst enemy, being too uncompromising to get on well with the politicians and too aloof to win the confidence and affection of ordinary people. He had too much faith in himself and his plans. When he failed to achieve the results he anticipated, he attracted, despite his devotion to duty and his concern for the welfare of the country, not sympathy but scorn.

THE ECONOMY HITS BOTTOM

During the spring of 1932, as the economy sounded the depths, thousands of Americans faced starvation. In Philadelphia during an 11-day period when no relief funds were available, hundreds of families existed on stale bread, thin soup, and garbage. In the nation as a whole, only about one-quarter of the unemployed were receiving any public aid. In Birmingham, Alabama, landlords in poor districts gave up trying to collect rents, preferring, one Alabama congressman told a Senate committee, "to have somebody living there free of charge rather than to have the house . . . burned up for fuel [by scavengers]." Many people were evicted, and they often gathered in ramshackle communities constructed of packing boxes, rusty sheet metal, and similar refuse on swamps, garbage dumps, and other wasteland. People began to call these places "Hoovervilles."

Thousands of tramps roamed the countryside begging and scavenging for food. At the same time, food prices fell so low that farmers burned corn for fuel. In Iowa and Nebraska farmers organized "farm holiday" movements, refusing to ship their crops to market in protest against the 31-cent-a-bushel corn and 38-cent-a-bushel wheat prices. They blocked roads and rail lines, dumped milk, overturned trucks, and established picket lines to enforce their boycott. The world seemed to have been turned upside down. Professor Felix Frankfurter of the Harvard Law School remarked only half humorously that henceforth the terms B.C. and A.D. would mean "Before Crash" and "After Depression."

The national mood ranged from apathy to resentment. In 1931 federal immigration agents and local groups in the Southwest began rounding up Mexican

Evicted from their homes, many unemployed gravitated to vacant industrial property, where they erected hovels from scraps of lumber, tarpaper, and cardboard. This shantytown is on the outskirts of Seattle.

Americans and deporting them. Only some of those returned to Mexico had entered the United States illegally. Unemployed Mexicans were ejected because they might become public charges, those with jobs because they were presumably taking bread from the mouths of citizens. "Capitalism is dying," the socialist theologian Reinhold Niebuhr remarked in 1932, "and . . . it ought to die."

In June and July 1932, 20,000 World War veterans marched on Washington to demand immediate payment of their "adjusted compensation" bonuses. When Congress rejected their appeal, some 2000 refused to leave, settling in a jerrybuilt camp of shacks and tents at Anacostia Flats, a swamp bordering the Potomac. President Hoover, alarmed, charged incorrectly that the "Bonus Army" was largely composed of criminals and radicals and sent troops into the Flats to disperse it with bayonets, tear gas, and tanks. The task was accomplished amid much confusion; fortunately no one was killed. The protest had been aimless and not entirely justified, yet the spectacle of the United States government chasing unarmed veterans with tanks appalled the nation.

The unprecedented severity of the depression led some persons to favor radical economic and political changes. The disparity between the lots of the rich and the poor, always a challenge to democracy, became more striking and engendered considerable bitterness. "Unless something is done to provide employment," two labor leaders warned Hoover, "disorder . . . is sure to arise. . . . There is a growing demand that the entire business and social structure be changed because of the general dissatisfaction with the present system."

The Communist party gained few converts among farmers and industrial workers, but a considerable number of intellectuals, alienated by the trends of the 1920s, responded positively to the communists' emphasis on economic planning and the total mobilization of the state to achieve social goals. Even the cracker-barrel humorist Will Rogers was impressed by reports of the absence of serious unemployment in Russia. "All roads lead to Moscow," the former muckraker Lincoln Steffens wrote.

THE DEPRESSION AND ITS VICTIMS

Depression is a word used by economists but also by psychologists, and the depression of the 1930s had profound psychological effects on its victims as well as the obvious economic ones. Almost without exception people who lost their jobs first searched energetically for new ones, but when they remained unemployed for more than a few months they sank gradually into apathy. E. Wight Bakke, a Yale sociologist who interviewed hundreds of unemployed men in the United States and England during the depression, described the final stage of decline as "permanent readjustment," by which he meant that the long-term jobless simply

This photograph by Dorothea Lange captures the despair of a typical migrant California family during the depression. Many women had no other choice but to stay in tent cities or makeshift shelters with their children while their husbands searched for work.

gave up. The settlement house worker Lillian Wald came to a similar conclusion. Unemployed people at her famous Henry Street settlement, she noticed, had lost both "ambition and pride."

Simple discouragement alone does not explain why so many of the jobless reacted this way. People who had worked all their adult lives often became ashamed of themselves when they could not find a job. Professor Bakke reported that half the unemployed people in New Haven that he interviewed never applied for public assistance no matter how desperate their circumstances. A purely physiological factor was often involved as well. When money ran low, people had to cut down on relatively expensive foods like fruit, meat, and dairy products. In New York City, for example, milk consumption fell by a million quarts a day. In nutritional terms people consumed more carbohydrates and less food rich in energy-building vitamins and proteins. Listlessness (another word for apathy) often resulted.

The depression affected the families of the jobless in many ways. It caused a dramatic drop in the birthrate, from 27.7 per thousand population in 1920 to 18.4 per thousand in the early 1930s, the lowest in American history. Sometimes it strengthened family ties. Some unemployed men spent more time with their children and helped their wives with cooking and housework. Others, however, became impatient when their children demanded attention, refused to help around the house, sulked, or took to drink.

Two boys, barefoot, at a clinic in Arkansas. In 1914 a Rockefeller Foundation study determined that hookworm, which caused debilitating anemia in the rural South, commonly entered the body through the feet. Although Arkansas legislators denounced the study as a plot to force Arkansans to buy northern shoes for their children, the Rockefeller Foundation persisted in the campaign, which was backed by federal health officials in the 1930s.

The influence of wives in families struck by unemployment tended to increase, and in this respect women suffered less psychologically from the depression. They were usually too busy trying to make ends meet to become apathetic. But the way they used this influence varied. Some wives were sympathetic, others scornful, when the "breadwinner" came home with empty hands. When the wife of an unemployed man managed to find a job, the result could be either gratitude and pride or bitter resentment on the man's part, resentment or a sense of liberation on the woman's.

Children often caused strains in families. Parental authority declined when there was less money available to supply children's needs. Some youngsters became angry when their allowance was cut or when told they could not have something they particularly wanted. Some adolescents found part-time jobs to help out. Others refused to go to school. If there is any generalization about the effects of the depression on family relations it is probably an obvious one—where relationships were close and loving they became stronger, where they were not, the results could be disastrous.

THE ELECTION OF 1932

As the end of his term approached, President Hoover seemed to grow daily more petulant and pessimistic. The depression, coming after 12 years of Republican rule, probably ensured a Democratic victory in any case, but his attitude as the election neared alienated many voters and turned defeat into rout.

Confident of victory, the Democrats chose Governor Franklin Delano Roosevelt of New York as their presidential candidate. Roosevelt owed his nomi-

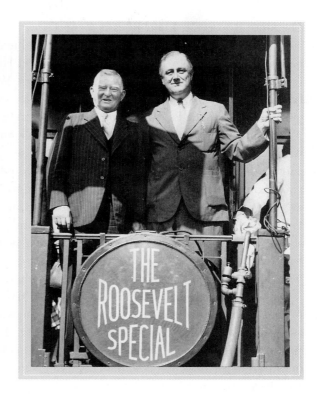

A vigorous-looking Franklin D. Roosevelt campaigning for the presidency in 1932. His vice-presidential running mate, John N. Garner, and the conveniently placed post allowed the handicapped candidate to stand when greeting voters along the way.

nation chiefly to his success as governor. Under his administration, New York had led the nation in providing relief for the needy and had enacted an impressive program of old-age pensions, unemployment insurance, and conservation and public power projects. In 1928, while Hoover was carrying New York against Smith by a wide margin, Roosevelt won election by 25,000 votes. In 1930 he swept the state by a 700,000-vote majority, double the previous record. He also had the advantage of the Roosevelt name (he was a distant cousin of the inimitable T. R.), and his sunny, magnetic personality contrasted favorably with that of the glum and colorless Hoover.

Roosevelt was far from being a radical. He was born to wealth and social status in Dutchess County, New York, in 1882. Pampered in childhood by a doting yet domineering mother, he was educated at the exclusive Groton School and then at Harvard. Ambition as much as the desire to render public service motivated his career in politics; even after an attack of polio in 1921 left him badly crippled in both legs, he refused to abandon his hopes for high office. During the 1920s he was a hardworking member of the liberal wing of his party. He supported Smith for president in 1924 and 1928.

To some observers Roosevelt seemed rather a lightweight intellectually. When he ran for the vice presidency, the *Chicago Tribune* commented: "If he is

Theodore Roosevelt, Elihu Root is Gene Debs, and Bryan is a brewer." Twelve years later many critics judged him too irresolute, too amiable, too eager to please all factions to be a forceful leader. Herbert Hoover thought he was "ignorant but well-meaning," and the political analyst Walter Lippmann, in a now-famous observation, called him "a pleasant man who, without any important qualifications for the job, would very much like to be President."

Despite his physical handicap—he could walk only a few steps, and then only with the aid of steel braces and two canes—Roosevelt was a marvelous campaigner. He traveled back and forth across the country, radiating confidence and good humor even when directing his sharpest barbs at the Republicans. Like every great political leader, he took as much from the people as he gave them, understanding the causes of their confusion and sensing their needs. "I have looked into the faces of thousands of Americans," he told a friend. "They have the frightened look of lost children. . . . They are saying: 'We're caught in something we don't understand; perhaps this fellow can help us out.'"

Roosevelt soaked up information and ideas from a thousand sources—from professors like Raymond Moley and Rexford Tugwell of Columbia, from politicians like the Texan vice-presidential candidate, John N. Garner, from social workers, businessmen, and lawyers. To those seeking specific answers to the questions of the day, he was seldom satisfying. On such vital matters as farm policy, the tariff, and government spending, he equivocated, contradicted himself, or remained silent.

Nevertheless Roosevelt's basic position was unmistakable. There must be a "re-appraisal of values," a "New Deal." Instead of adhering to conventional limits on the extent of federal power, the government should do whatever was necessary to protect the unfortunate and advance the public good. Lacking concrete answers, Roosevelt advocated a point of view rather than a plan: "The country needs bold, persistent experimentation. It is common sense to take a method and try it. If it fails, admit it frankly and try another. But above all, try something."

The popularity of this approach was demonstrated in November. Hoover, who had lost only eight states in 1928, won only six, all in the Northeast, in 1932. Roosevelt amassed 22.8 million votes to Hoover's 15.8 million and carried the Electoral College, 472 to 59.

During the interval between the election and Roosevelt's inauguration in March 1933, the Great Depression reached its nadir. The holdover "lame duck" Congress, last of its kind, proved incapable of effective action. President Hoover, perhaps understandably, hesitated to institute changes without the cooperation of his successor. Roosevelt, for equally plausible reasons, refused to accept responsibility before assuming power officially. The nation, curiously apathetic in the face of so much suffering, drifted aimlessly, like a sailboat in a flat calm.

MILESTONES

1921   Budget and Accounting Act

Washington Disarmament Conference

1922   Fordney-McCumber Tariff protecting "infant industries"

1923   President Harding dies

Teapot Dome and other Harding scandals exposed

1924   Dawes Plan restructures German reparations payments

National Origins Act establishes immigration quotas

1927   McNary-Haugen farm relief bill vetoed by President Coolidge

1928   Kellogg-Briand Treaty "outlaws" war as "an instrument of national policy"

1929   New York Stock Exchange crash ends big bull market

Young Plan further reduces German reparations

1930   Clark Memorandum renounces Roosevelt Corollary to Monroe Doctrine

Hawley-Smoot Tariff raises duties on foreign manufactures

1931   Japanese invasion of Manchuria

Hoover moratorium on war debts

1932   Bonus marchers in Washington dispersed by troops

Reconstruction Finance Corporation created

Franklin D. Roosevelt elected president

27

❯❯———◆———❮❮

THE NEW DEAL: 1933–1941

As the date of Franklin Roosevelt's inauguration approached, the banking system disintegrated—no word less strong portrays the extent of the collapse. Starting in the rural West and spreading to major cities like Detroit and Baltimore, a financial panic swept the land. Depositors lined up before the doors of even the soundest institutions, desperate to withdraw their savings. Hundreds of banks were forced to close. In February, to check the panic, the governor of Michigan declared a "bank holiday," shutting every bank in the state for eight days. Maryland, Kentucky, California, and a number of other states followed suit; by inauguration day four-fifths of the states had suspended all banking operations.

THE HUNDRED DAYS

Something drastic had to be done. The most conservative business leaders were as ready for government intervention as the most advanced radicals. Partisanship, while not disappearing, was for once subordinated to broad national needs. A sign of this change came in February, even before Roosevelt took office, when Congress submitted to the states the Twenty-first Amendment, putting an end to prohibition. Before the end of the year the necessary three-quarters of the states had ratified it, and the prohibition era was over.

But it was unquestionably Franklin D. Roosevelt who provided the spark that reenergized the American people. His inaugural address reassured the country and at the same time stirred it to action. "The only thing we have to fear is fear itself. . . . This Nation asks for action, and action now. . . . I assume unhesitatingly the leadership of this great army of our people. . . ." Many such lines punctuated the brief address, which concluded with a stern pledge: "In the event that Congress shall fail . . . I shall not evade the clear course of duty that will then confront me. I shall ask the Congress for the one remaining instrument to meet the crisis—broad Executive power to wage a war against the emergency."

The inaugural captured the heart of the country; almost half a million letters of congratulation poured into the White House. When Roosevelt summoned Congress into special session on March 9, the legislators outdid one another to enact his proposals into law. "I had as soon start a mutiny in the face of a foreign foe as . . . against the program of the President," one representative declared. In the following "Hundred Days" serious opposition, in the sense of an organized group committed to resisting the administration, simply did not exist.

Roosevelt had the power and the will to act but no comprehensive plan of action. He and his eager congressional collaborators proceeded in a dozen directions at once, sometimes wisely, sometimes not, often at cross-purposes with themselves and one another. One of the first administration measures was the Economy Act, which reduced the salaries of federal employees by 15 percent and cut various veterans' benefits. Such belt-tightening measures could only make the Depression worse. But most New Deal programs were designed to stimulate the economy. All in all, an impressive body of new legislation was placed on the statute books.

On March 5 Roosevelt declared a nationwide bank holiday and placed an embargo on the exportation of gold. To explain the complexities of the banking problem to the public, Roosevelt delivered the first of his "fireside chats" over a national radio network. "I want to talk for a few minutes with the people of the United States about banking," he explained. His warmth and steadiness reassured millions of listeners. A plan for reopening the banks under Treasury Department licenses was devised, and soon most of them were functioning again, public confidence in their solvency restored. This solved the problem, but it also determined that banks would remain private institutions. Reform, not revolutionary change, had been decided upon at the very start of Roosevelt's presidency.

In April, Roosevelt took the country off the gold standard, hoping thereby to cause prices to rise. Before the session ended, Congress established the Federal Deposit Insurance Corporation (FDIC) to guarantee bank deposits. It also forced

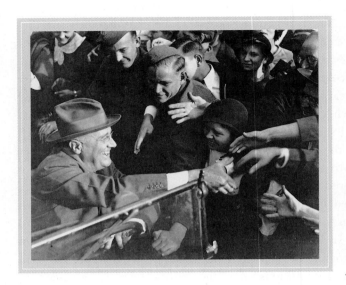

Well-wishers greet the president at Warm Springs, Georgia, in 1933. Franklin's "first-class temperament" compensated for his "second-class intellect," Justice Oliver Wendell Holmes famously observed.

the separation of investment banking and commercial banking concerns while extending the power of the Federal Reserve Board over both types of institutions, and it created the Home Owners Loan Corporation (HOLC) to refinance mortgages and prevent foreclosures. It passed the Federal Securities Act requiring promoters to make public full financial information about new stock issues and giving the Federal Trade Commission the right to regulate such transactions.

THE NATIONAL RECOVERY ADMINISTRATION (NRA)

Problems of unemployment and industrial stagnation had high priority during the Hundred Days. Congress appropriated $500 million for relief of the needy, and it created the Civilian Conservation Corps to provide jobs for men between the ages of 18 and 25 in reforestation and other conservation projects. To stimulate industry, Congress passed one of its most controversial measures, the National Industrial Recovery Act (NIRA). Besides establishing the Public Works Administration with authority to spend $3.3 billion, this law permitted manufacturers to draw up industrywide codes of "fair business practices." Under the law producers could agree to raise prices and limit production without violating the antitrust laws. The law gave workers the protection of minimum wage and maximum hours regulations and guaranteed them the right "to organize and bargain collectively through representatives of their own choosing," an immense stimulus to the union movement.

The NIRA was a variant on the idea of the corporate state. This concept envisaged a system of industrywide organizations of capitalists and workers (supervised by the government) that would resolve conflicts internally, thereby avoiding wasteful economic competition and dangerous social clashes. It was an outgrowth of the trade association idea, although Hoover, who had supported voluntary associations, denounced it because of its compulsory aspects. It was also similar to experiments being carried out by the fascist dictator Benito Mussolini in Italy and by the Nazis in Adolf Hitler's Germany. It did not, of course, turn America into a fascist state, but it did herald an increasing concentration of economic power in the hands of interest groups, both industrialists' organizations and labor unions.

The act created a government agency, the National Recovery Administration (NRA), to supervise the drafting and operation of the business codes. Drafting posed difficult problems, first because each industry insisted on tailoring the agreements to its special needs and second because most manufacturers were unwilling to accept all the provisions of Section 7a of the law dealing with the rights of labor. While thousands of employers agreed to the pledge "We Do Our Part" in order to receive the Blue Eagle symbol of NRA, many were more interested in the monopolistic aspects of the act than in boosting wages and encouraging unionization. In practice, the codes were drawn up by the largest manufacturers in each industry.

The effects of the NIRA were both more and less than the designers of the system had intended. In a sense it tried to accomplish the impossible—to change the very nature of business ethics and control the everyday activities of millions of individual enterprises. At the practical level, it did not end the Depression. There was a brief upturn in the spring of 1933, but the expected revival of industry did not take place; in nearly every case the dominant producers in each industry used their power to raise prices and limit production rather than to hire more workers and increase output.

Beginning with the cotton textile code, however, the agreements succeeded in doing away with the centuries-old problem of child labor in industry. They established the principle of federal regulation of wages and hours and led to the organization of thousands of workers, even in industries where unions had seldom been significant. Within a year John L. Lewis's United Mine Workers expanded from 150,000 members to half a million. About 100,000 automobile workers joined unions, as did a comparable number of steelworkers.

Labor leaders used the NIRA to persuade workers that Roosevelt wanted them to join unions—which was something of an overstatement. In 1935, because the craft-oriented American Federation of Labor (AFL) had displayed little enthusiasm for enrolling unskilled workers on an industrywide basis, John L. Lewis, together with officials of the garment trade unions, formed the Committee for Industrial Organization (CIO) and set out to rally workers in each of these mass-production industries into one union without regard for craft lines. Since a union containing all the workers in a factory was easier to organize and direct than separate craft unions, this was a far more effective way of unionizing factory labor. The AFL expelled these unions, however, and in 1938 the CIO became the Congress of Industrial Organizations. Soon it rivaled the AFL in size and importance.

THE AGRICULTURAL ADJUSTMENT ADMINISTRATION (AAA)

Roosevelt was more concerned about the plight of the farmers than that of any other group because he believed that the nation was becoming overcommitted to industry. The Agricultural Adjustment Act of May 1933 combined compulsory restrictions on production with government subsidies to growers of wheat, cotton, tobacco, pork, and a few other staple crops. The money for these payments was raised by levying processing taxes on middlemen such as flour millers. The object was to lift agricultural prices to "parity" with industrial prices, the ratio in most cases being based on the levels of 1909–1914, when farmers had been reasonably prosperous. In return for withdrawing part of their land from cultivation, farmers received "rental" payments from the Agricultural Adjustment Administration (AAA).

Since the 1933 crops were growing when the law was passed, Secretary of Agriculture Henry A. Wallace, son of Harding's secretary of agriculture and himself an experienced farmer and plant geneticist, decided to pay farmers to destroy the crops in the field. Cotton planters plowed up 10 million acres, receiving $100 million in return. Six million baby pigs and 200,000 pregnant sows were slaughtered. Such ruthlessness appalled observers, particularly when they thought of the millions of hungry Americans who could have eaten all that pork.

Thereafter, limitation of acreage proved sufficient to raise some agricultural prices considerably. Tobacco growers benefited, and so did those who raised corn and hogs. The price of wheat also rose, though more because of bad harvests than because of the AAA program. But dairy farmers and cattlemen were hurt by the law, as were the railroads (which had less freight to haul) and, of course, consumers. Many farmers insisted that the NRA was raising the cost of manufactured goods more than the AAA was raising the prices they received for their crops. "While the farmer is losing his pants to his creditors," one Iowan complained, "NRA is rolling up his shirt. [Soon] we'll have a nudist colony."

A far more serious weakness of the program was its effect on tenant farmers and sharecroppers, many of whom lost their livelihoods when owners took land out of production to obtain AAA payments. In addition many landowners substituted machinery for labor. In the Cotton Belt more than 100,000 tractors were purchased by farmers during the 1930s. Each could do the work of several tenant or sharecropping families. Yet acreage restrictions and mortgage relief helped thousands of others. The law was a remarkable attempt to bring order to the chaotic agricultural economy.

THE TENNESSEE VALLEY AUTHORITY (TVA)

Another achievement of the Hundred Days was the creation of the Tennessee Valley Authority (TVA). During World War I the government had constructed a hydroelectric plant at Muscle Shoals, Alabama, to provide power for factories manufacturing synthetic nitrate explosives. After 1920 farm groups and public power enthusiasts, led by Senator George W. Norris of Nebraska, had blocked administration plans to turn these facilities over to private capitalists, but their efforts to have the site operated by the government had been defeated by presidential vetoes.

The Tennessee Valley Authority

Although the Tennessee Valley Authority (TVA) never fully became the regional planning organization its sponsors had anticipated, the TVA nevertheless was able to expand the hydroelectric plants at Muscle Shoals, Alabama, and build dams, power plants, and transmission lines to service the surrounding area.

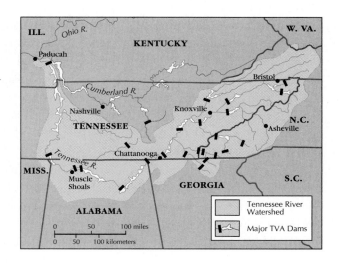

Roosevelt wanted to make the Tennessee Valley area a broad experiment in social planning. Besides expanding the hydroelectric plants at Muscle Shoals and developing nitrate manufacturing in order to produce cheap fertilizers, he envisioned a coordinated program of soil conservation, reforestation, and industrialization.

Over the objections of private power companies, led by Wendell L. Willkie of the Commonwealth and Southern Corporation, Congress passed the TVA Act in May 1933. This law created a board authorized to build dams, power plants, and transmission lines and to sell fertilizers and electricity to individuals and local communities. The board could undertake flood control, soil conservation, and reforestation projects and improve the navigation of the Tennessee River. Although the TVA never became the comprehensive regional planning organization some of its sponsors had anticipated, it improved the standard of living of millions of inhabitants of the valley. In addition to producing electricity and fertilizers and providing a "yardstick" whereby the efficiency—and thus the rates—of private power companies could be tested, it took on other functions ranging from the eradication of malaria to the development of recreational facilities.

THE NEW DEAL SPIRIT

By the end of the Hundred Days the country had made up its mind about Roosevelt's New Deal, and despite the vicissitudes of the next decade, it never changed it. A large majority labeled the New Deal a solid success. Considerable recovery had taken place, but more basic was the fact that Roosevelt, recruiting an army of officials to staff the new government agencies, had infused his administration with a spirit of bustle and optimism.

Dozens of people who lived through those stirring times have left records that reveal the New Deal spirit. "Come at once to Washington," Senator Robert La Follette, Jr., son of "Fighting Bob," telegraphed Donald Richberg, an old Theodore Roosevelt progressive. "Great things are under way." "I have been in a constant spin of activity," another New Dealer wrote a friend. "I feel as if I were alive all over, and that this cockeyed world is taking us somewhere." Justice Harlan Fiske Stone of the Supreme Court recorded: "Never was there such a change in the transfer of government."

Although Roosevelt was not much of an intellectual, his openness to suggestion made him eager to draw on the ideas and energies of experts of all sorts. New Deal agencies soon teemed with college professors and young lawyers without political experience.

Within the administrative maze that Roosevelt created, rival bureaucrats battled to enforce their views. The "spenders," led by Columbia economist Rexford

G. Tugwell, clashed with those favoring strict economy, who gathered around Lewis Douglas, director of the budget. Roosevelt mediated between the factions. Washington became a battleground for dozens of special interest groups: the Farm Bureau Federation, the unions, the trade associations, the silver miners. The NRA aimed frankly at raising the prices paid by consumers of manufactured goods; the AAA processing tax came ultimately from the pocketbooks of ordinary citizens.

THE UNEMPLOYED

At least 9 million persons were still without work in 1934 and hundreds of thousands of them were in real need. Here is the recollection of Malcolm Little, later famous as the radical black leader, Malcolm X:

> By 1934, we really began to suffer. This was about the worst depression year, and no one we knew had enough to eat or live on. . . . There was a bakery where, for a nickel, a couple of us children would buy a tall flour sack of day-old bread and cookies. . . . But there were times when there wasn't even a nickel and we would be so hungry we were dizzy. My mother would boil a big pot of dandelion greens and we would eat that.

Yet the Democrats confounded the political experts, including their own, by increasing their already large majorities in both houses of Congress in the 1934 elections. All the evidence indicates that most of the jobless continued to support

Unemployment and Federal Action, 1929–1941

Unemployment of non-farm workers reached nearly 40 percent by early 1933. The Federal Employment Relief Act (FERA) of May 1933 was followed by the Civil Works Administration (CWA) later that year, and then by the Works Progress Administration (WPA) in April 1935.

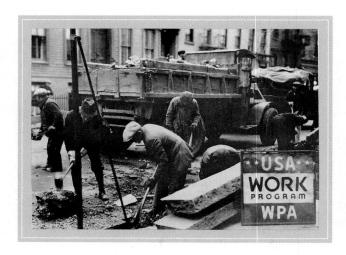

Otherwise unemployed workers removing curbstones in a street-widening project. WPA undertakings extended from carving nature trails in wilderness regions of the Far West to constructing bridges in the heart of New York City.

the administration. Their loyalty can best be explained by Roosevelt's unemployment policies.

In May 1933 Congress had established the Federal Emergency Relief Administration (FERA) and given it $500 million to be dispensed through state relief organizations. Roosevelt appointed Harry L. Hopkins, an eccentric but brilliant and dedicated social worker, to direct the FERA. Hopkins insisted that the unemployed needed jobs, not handouts. In November he persuaded Roosevelt to create the Civil Works Administration (CWA) and swiftly put 4 million people to work building and repairing roads and public buildings, teaching, decorating the walls of post offices with murals, and utilizing their special skills in dozens of other ways.

The cost of this program frightened Roosevelt—Hopkins spent about $1 billion in less than five months—and he soon abolished the CWA. But an extensive public works program was continued throughout 1934 under the FERA. Despite charges that many of the projects were "boondoggles," thousands of roads, bridges, schools, and other structures were built or refurbished.

In May 1935 Roosevelt put Hopkins in charge of the Works Progress Administration (WPA). By the time this agency was disbanded in 1943 it had found employment for 8.5 million people. Besides building public works, the WPA made important cultural contributions. It developed the Federal Theatre Project, which put actors, directors, and stagehands to work; the Federal Writers' Project, which turned out valuable guidebooks, collected local lore, and published about 1000 books and pamphlets; and the Federal Art Project, which employed painters and sculptors. In addition, the National Youth Administration created part-time jobs for more than 2 million high school and college students.

At no time during the New Deal years did unemployment fall below 10 percent of the workforce, and in some places it was much higher. Unemployment in Boston, for instance, ranged between 20 and 30 percent throughout the 1930s. WPA did not go far enough, chiefly because Roosevelt could not escape his fear of drastically unbalancing the budget. Halfway measures did not stimulate the economy. The president also hesitated to undertake projects that might compete with private enterprises. Yet his caution did him no good politically; the business interests he sought to placate were becoming increasingly hostile to the New Deal.

THREE EXTREMISTS: LONG, COUGHLIN, AND TOWNSEND

Roosevelt's moderation roused extremists both on the left and on the right. The most formidable was Louisiana's Senator Huey Long, the "Kingfish." Raised on a farm in northern Louisiana, Long was successively a traveling salesman, a lawyer, state railroad commissioner, governor, and, after 1930, United States senator. By 1933 he ruled Louisiana with the absolutism of an oriental monarch. Long was controversial in his day and so he has remained. He was certainly a demagogue. Yet the plight of all poor people concerned him deeply. More important, he tried to do something about it.

Although U. S. Senator Huey Long of Louisiana supported FDR in 1932, "the Kingfish" had changed his mind two years later, when this picture was taken. He opposed Roosevelt's large government bureaucracies, such as the National Recovery Administration (NRA), and sought more aggressive income redistribution. Also, he wanted to be president.

Long did not question segregation or white supremacy, nor did he suggest that Louisiana blacks should be allowed to vote. He used the word *nigger* with total un–self-consciousness, even when addressing northern black leaders. But he treated black-baiters with scathing contempt. When Hiram W. Evans, imperial wizard of the Ku Klux Klan, announced his intention to campaign against him in Louisiana, Long told reporters: "Quote me as saying that that Imperial bastard will never set foot in Louisiana, and that when I call him a sonofabitch I am not using profanity, but am referring to the circumstances of his birth."

As a reformer, Long stood in the populist tradition; he hated bankers and "the interests." He believed that poor people, regardless of color, should have a chance to earn a decent living and get an education. His arguments were simplistic, patronizing, possibly insincere, but effective. "Don't say I'm working for niggers," he told one northern journalist. "I'm for the poor man—all poor men. Black and white, they all gotta have a chance. . . . 'Every Man a King'—that's my slogan."

Raffish, totally unrestrained, yet shrewd—a fellow southern politician called him "the smartest lunatic I ever saw"—Long had supported the New Deal at the start. But partly because he thought Roosevelt too conservative and partly because of his own ambition, he soon broke with the administration. While Roosevelt was probably more hostile to the big financiers than to any other interest, Long denounced him as "a phoney" and a stooge of Wall Street. "I can take him," he boasted in a typical sally.

By 1935 Long's "Share Our Wealth" movement had a membership of over 4.6 million. His program called for the confiscation of family fortunes of more than $5 million and a tax of 100 percent on incomes over $1 million a year, the money to be used to buy every family a "homestead" (a house, a car, and other necessities) and provide an annual family income of $2000 to $3000, plus old-age pensions, educational benefits, and veterans' pensions. As the 1936 election approached, he planned to organize a third party to split the liberal vote. He assumed that the Republicans would win the election and so botch the job of fighting the Depression that he could sweep the country in 1940.

Less powerful than Long but more widely influential was Father Charles E. Coughlin, the "Radio

Father Charles Coughlin, the "Radio Priest," whose weekly program reached 30 to 45 million listeners nationwide, photographed in Detroit as he promoted his National Union for Social Justice.

Priest." A genial Irishman of Canadian birth, Coughlin in 1926 began broadcasting a weekly religious message over station WJR in Detroit. His mellifluous voice and orotund rhetoric attracted a huge national audience, and the Depression gave him a secular cause. In 1933 he had been an eager New Dealer, but his dislike of New Deal financial policies—he believed that inflating the currency would end the Depression—and his need for ever more sensational ideas to hold his radio audience led him to turn against the New Deal. By 1935 he was calling Roosevelt a "great betrayer and liar."

Although Coughlin's National Union for Social Justice was especially appealing to Catholics, it attracted people of every faith, particularly in the lower-middle-class districts of the big cities. Some of his talks caused more than a million people to send him messages of congratulation; contributions amounting to $500,000 a year flooded his headquarters. Coughlin attacked bankers, New Deal planners, Roosevelt's farm program, and the alleged sympathy of the administration for communists and Jews, both of which Coughlin denounced in his weekly talks. His program resembled fascism more than any leftist philosophy, but he posed a threat, especially in combination with Long, to the continuation of Democratic rule.

Another rapidly growing movement alarmed the Democrats in 1934–1935: Dr. Francis E. Townsend's campaign for "old-age revolving pensions." Townsend, a retired California physician, colorless and low-keyed, had an oversimplified and therefore appealing "solution" to the nation's troubles. The pitiful state of thousands of elderly persons, whose job prospects were even dimmer than those of the mass of the unemployed, he found shocking. He advocated paying every person aged 60 years and over a pension of $200 a month, the only conditions being that the pensioners not hold jobs and that they spend the entire sum within 30 days. Their purchases, he argued, would stimulate production, thereby creating new jobs and revitalizing the economy. A stiff transactions tax, collected whenever any commodity changed hands, would pay for the program.

Economists quickly pointed out that with about 10 million persons eligible for the Townsend pensions, the cost would amount to $24 billion a year—roughly half the national income. But among the elderly the scheme proved extremely popular. Townsend Clubs, their proceedings conducted in the spirit of revivalist camp meetings, flourished everywhere, and the *Townsend National Weekly* reached a circulation of over 200,000. Although most Townsendites were anything but radical politically, their plan, like Long's Share Our Wealth scheme, would have revolutionized the distribution of wealth in the country. The movement marked the emergence of a new force in American society. With medical advances lengthening the average life span, the percentage of old people in the population was rising. The breakdown of close family ties in an increasingly mobile society now caused many of these citizens to be cast adrift to live out their last years poor, sick, idle, and alone.

With the possible exception of Long, the extremists had little understanding of practical affairs. (It could be said that Townsend knew what to do with money but not how to get it, and Coughlin knew how to get money but not what to do with it.) Collectively they represented a threat to Roosevelt; their success helped to make the president see that he must move boldly to restore good times or face serious political trouble in 1936.

Political imperatives had much to do with Roosevelt's decisions, and the influence of Justice Brandeis and his disciples, notably Felix Frankfurter, was great. They urged Roosevelt to abandon his probusiness programs, especially the NRA, and stress restoring competition and taxing corporations more heavily. The fact that most businessmen were turning away from him encouraged the president to accept this advice; so did the Supreme Court's decision in *Schecter* v. *United States* (May 1935), which declared the National Industrial Recovery Act unconstitutional.

THE SECOND NEW DEAL

Existing laws had failed to end the Depression. Extremists were luring away some of Roosevelt's supporters, and conservatives had failed to appreciate his moderation. The voters, heartened by the partial success of early New Deal measures, had responded by further increasing the Democrats' control of Congress in the 1934 elections and were clamoring for further reforms. But the Supreme Court had declared many key New Deal measures unconstitutional. For these many reasons, Roosevelt, in June 1935, launched what historians call the Second New Deal.

There followed the "Second Hundred Days," one of the most productive periods in the history of American legislation. The National Labor Relations Act—commonly known as the Wagner Act—restored the labor guarantees wiped out by the *Schecter* decision. It gave workers the right to bargain collectively and prohibited employers from interfering with union organizational activities in their factories. A National Labor Relations Board (NLRB) was established to supervise plant elections and designate successful unions as official bargaining agents when a majority of the workers approved. It was difficult to force some big corporations to bargain "in good faith," as the law required, but the NLRB could conduct investigations of employer practices and issue cease and desist orders when "unfair" activities came to light.

Civilian Labor Force and Labor Union Membership, 1929–1941

Union membership more than doubled in the years from 1936 to 1941, from less than 5 million to more than 10 million.

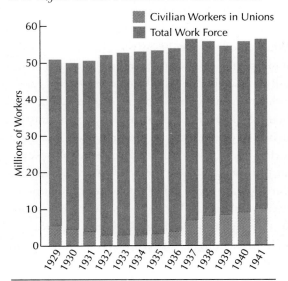

The Social Security Act of August 1935 set up a system of old-age insurance, financed partly by a tax on wages (paid by workers) and partly by a tax on payrolls (paid by employers). It created a state-federal system of unemployment insurance, similarly financed. Liberal critics considered this social security system inadequate because it did not cover agricultural workers, domestics, self-employed persons, and some other groups particularly in need of its benefits. Health insurance was not included, and because the size of pensions depended on the amount earned, the lowest-paid workers could not count on much support after reaching 65. Yet the law was of major significance. Over the years the pension payments were increased and the classes of workers covered expanded.

The Rural Electrification Administration (REA), created by executive order, also began to function during this remarkable period. The REA lent money at low interest rates to utility companies and to farmer cooperatives interested in bringing electricity to rural areas. When the REA went into operation, only one farm in ten had electricity; by 1950 only one in ten did not.

Whether the Second New Deal was more radical than the first depends largely on the vantage point from which it is considered. Measures like the Social Security Act had greater long-range effect on American life than the legislation of the First Hundred Days but were fundamentally less revolutionary than laws like the National Industrial Recovery Act and the Agricultural Adjustment Act, which attempted to establish a planned economy.

Herbert Hoover epitomized the attitude of conservatives when he called the New Deal "the most stupendous invasion of the whole spirit of Liberty that the nation has witnessed." Undoubtedly many opponents of the New Deal sincerely believed that it was undermining the foundations of American freedom. The cost of the New Deal also alarmed them. By 1936 some members of the administration had fallen under the influence of the British economist John Maynard Keynes, who argued that the world Depression could be conquered if governments would deliberately unbalance their budgets by reducing interest rates and taxes and by increasing expenditures to stimulate consumption and investment.

Roosevelt never accepted Keynes's theories; he conferred with the economist in 1934 but could not grasp the "rigmarole of figures" with which Keynes deluged him. Nevertheless the imperatives of the Depression forced him to spend more than the government was collecting in taxes; thus he adopted in part the Keynesian approach. Conservative businessmen considered him financially irresponsible, and the fact that deficit spending seemed to be good politics made them seethe with rage.

THE ELECTION OF 1936

The election of 1936 loomed as a showdown. "America is in peril," the Republican platform declared. The GOP candidate, Governor Alfred M. Landon of Kansas, was a former follower of Theodore Roosevelt, a foe of the Ku Klux Klan in the 1920s, and a believer in government regulation of business. But he was a poor speaker, colorless, and handicapped by the reactionary views of many of his backers. Against the charm and political astuteness of Roosevelt, Landon's arguments—chiefly that he could administer the government more efficiently than the president—made little impression. He won the support of some anti–New Deal Democrats, among them two former presidential candidates, Al Smith and John W. Davis, but this was not enough.

The radical fringe put a third candidate in the field, Congressman William Lemke of North Dakota, who ran on the Union party ticket. Father Coughlin, denouncing Roosevelt as the "dumbest man ever to occupy the White House," rallied his National Union for Social Justice behind Lemke; Dr. Townsend also supported him. However, the extremists were losing ground by 1936. Huey Long had fallen victim to an assassin in September 1935. The Townsendites fell under a cloud because of rumors that some of their leaders had their fingers in the organization's treasury. Father Coughlin's slanderous assaults on Roosevelt caused a backlash. Lemke got only 892,000 votes.

On election day the country gave the president a tremendous vote of confidence. He carried every state but Maine and Vermont. The Republicans elected only 89 members of the House of Representatives and their strength in the Senate fell to 16, an all-time low. In dozens of city and state elections, Democratic candidates also made large gains. Both Roosevelt's personality and his program had captivated the land. He seemed irresistible, the most powerfully entrenched president in the history of the United States.

Roosevelt did not win in 1936 because of the inadequacies of his foes. Having abandoned his efforts to hold the businessmen, whom he now denounced as "economic royalists," he appealed for the votes of workers and the underprivileged. The new labor unions gratefully poured thousands of dollars into the campaign to reelect him. Black voters switched to the Democrats in record numbers. Farmers liked Roosevelt because of his evident concern for their welfare: When the Supreme Court declared the Agricultural Adjustment Act unconstitutional (*United States* v. *Butler,* 1936), he immediately rushed through a new law, the Soil Conservation and Domestic Allotment Act, which accomplished the same objective by paying farmers to divert land from commercial crops to soil-building plants like clover and soybeans. Countless elderly persons backed Roosevelt out of gratitude for the Social Security Act. Home owners were grateful for his program guaranteeing mortgages—eventually about 20 percent of all urban private dwellings were refinanced by the Home Owners Loan Corporation—and for the Federal Housing Administration, which, beginning in 1934, made available low-cost, long-term loans for modernizing old buildings and constructing new ones.

ROOSEVELT TRIES TO UNDERMINE THE SUPREME COURT

On January 20, in his second inaugural address, Roosevelt spoke of the plight of millions of citizens "denied the greater part of what the very lowest standards of today call the necessities of life." A third of the nation, he added without exaggeration, was "ill-housed, ill-clad, ill-nourished." He interpreted his landslide victory as a mandate for further reforms, and with his prestige and his immense congressional majorities, nothing appeared to stand in his way. Nothing, that is, except the Supreme Court.

Throughout Roosevelt's first term the Court had stood almost immovable against increasing the scope of federal authority and broadening the general power of government, state as well as national, to cope with the exigencies of the Depression. Of the nine justices, only Louis Brandeis, Benjamin N. Cardozo, and Harlan Fiske Stone viewed the New Deal sympathetically. Four others—James C. McReynolds, Willis Van Devanter, Pierce Butler, and George Sutherland— were intransigent reactionaries. Chief Justice Charles Evans Hughes and Justice Owen J. Roberts, while more open-minded, tended to side with the reactionaries on many questions.

Much of the early New Deal legislation, pushed through Congress at top speed during the Hundred Days, had been drafted without proper regard for the Constitution. Even the liberal justices considered the National Industrial Recovery Act unconstitutional (the *Schechter* decision was a unanimous one).

The reactionaries on the Court seemed governed by no consistent constitutional philosophy; they tended to limit the police power of the states when wages-and-hours laws came before them and to interpret it broadly when state laws restricting civil liberties were under consideration. In 1937 all the major measures of the Second Hundred Days appeared doomed. The Wagner Act had little chance of winning approval, experts predicted. Lawyers were advising employers to ignore the Social Security Act, so confident were they that the Court would declare it unconstitutional.

Faced with this situation, Roosevelt decided to ask Congress to shift the balance on the Court by increasing the number of justices, thinly disguising the purpose of his plan by making it part of a general reorganization of the judiciary. A member of the Court who reached the age of 70 would have the option of retiring at full pay. Should such a justice choose not to retire, the president was to appoint an additional justice, up to a maximum of six, to ease the burden of work for the aged jurists who remained on the bench.

Roosevelt knew that this measure would run into resistance, but he expected that the huge Democratic majorities in Congress could override any opposition and that the public would back him solidly. No astute politician had erred so badly in estimating the effects of an action since Stephen A. Douglas introduced the Kansas-Nebraska bill in 1854.

Although polls showed the public fairly evenly divided on the "Court-packing" bill, the opposition was vocal and influential. To the expected denunciations of conservatives were added the complaints of liberals fearful that the principle of court packing might in the future be used to subvert civil liberties. What, Senator Norris asked, would have been the reaction if a man like Harding had proposed such a measure? Opposition in Congress was immediate and intense;

This cartoon is unsubtle: A vigorous Roosevelt has lassoed the Supreme Court, which now must gallop in tandem with his (second) New Deal. Roosevelt's image, even among critics, is that of a powerful leader; all but forgotten is the fact that Roosevelt's legs had atrophied from polio.

many who had cheerfully supported every New Deal bill came out against the plan. The press denounced it, and so did most local bar associations. Chief Justice Hughes released a devastating critique; even the liberal Brandeis—the oldest judge on the court—rejected the bill out of hand.

For months Roosevelt stubbornly refused to concede defeat, but in July 1937, he had to yield. Minor administrative reforms of the judiciary were enacted, but the size of the Court remained unchanged.

The struggle did result in saving the legislation of the Second New Deal. Alarmed by the threat to the Court, Justices Hughes and Roberts, never entirely committed to the conservative position, beat a strategic retreat on a series of specific issues. While the debate was raging in Congress, they sided with the liberals in upholding first a minimum wage law of the state of Washington that was little different from a New York act the Court had recently rejected, then the Wagner Act, then the Social Security Act. In May, Justice Van Devanter retired and Roosevelt replaced him with Senator Hugo Black of Alabama, a New Dealer. The conservative justices thereupon gave up the fight, and soon Roosevelt was able to appoint enough new judges to give the Court a large pro–New Deal majority. No further measure of significance was declared unconstitutional during his presidency. The Court fight hurt Roosevelt severely. His prestige never fully re-covered. Conservative Democrats who had feared to oppose him because of his supposedly invulnerable popularity took heart and began to join with the Republicans on key issues. When the president summoned a special session of Congress in November 1937 and submitted a program of "must" legislation, not one of his bills was passed.

THE NEW DEAL WINDS DOWN

The Court fight marked the beginning of the end of the New Deal. Social and eco-nomic developments contributed to its decline, and the final blow originated in the area of foreign affairs. With unemployment high, wages low, and workers relatively powerless against their employers, most Americans had liked New Deal labor legis-lation and sympathized with the industrial unions whose growth it stimulated. The NRA, the Wagner Act, and the CIO's organization of industries like steel and auto-mobiles changed the power structure within the economy. What amounted to a revolution in the lives of wage earners had occurred. Aside from the obvious changes—higher wages, shorter hours, paid vacations, insurance of various kinds—unionization had meant fair methods of settling disputes about work prac-tices and a measure of job security based on seniority for tens of thousands of work-ers. The CIO in particular had done much to increase the influence of labor in pol-itics and to bring blacks and other minorities into the labor movement.

In 1937 a series of "sit-down strikes" broke out, beginning at the General Motors plant in Flint, Michigan. Striking workers barricaded themselves inside the factories; when police and strikebreakers tried to dislodge them, the strikers drove them off with barrages of soda bottles, tools, spare parts, and crockery. The tolerant attitude of the Roosevelt administration ensured the strikers immunity against government intervention. "It is illegal," Roosevelt said of the General Motors strike, "but shooting it out . . . [is not] the answer. . . . Why can't those fel-lows in General Motors meet with the committee of workers?" Fearful that all-out efforts to clear their plants would result in the destruction of expensive ma-chinery, most employers capitulated to the workers' demands. All the automobile manufacturers but Henry Ford quickly came to terms with the United Automobile Workers.

The major steel companies, led by U.S. Steel, recognized the CIO and granted higher wages and a 40-hour week. The auto and steel unions alone boasted more than 725,000 members by late 1937; other CIO units conquered the rubber industry, the electrical industry, the textile industry, and many more.

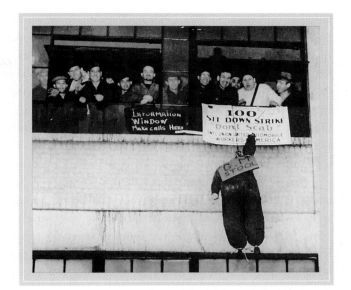

A group of sit-down strikers inside the Chevrolet plant in Flint, Michigan, looking out. They are hanging a "G-M stool [pigeon]" in effigy. The sign directly above the dummy reminds fellow workers: "Don't Scab."

These gains and the aggressive way in which the unions pursued their objectives gave many members of the middle class second thoughts concerning the justice of labor's demands. Sit-down strikes, the disregard of unions for the "rights" of nonunion workers, and the violence that accompanied some strikes seemed to many not merely unreasonable but also a threat to social order. The enthusiasm of such people for all reform cooled rapidly.

While the sit-down strikes and the Court fight were going on, the New Deal suffered another heavy blow. Business conditions had been gradually improving since 1933. Heartened by the trend, Roosevelt, who had never fully grasped the importance of government spending in stimulating recovery, cut back sharply on the relief program in June 1937, with disastrous results. Between August and October the economy slipped downward like sand through a chute. Stock prices plummeted; unemployment rose by 2 million; industrial production slumped. This "Roosevelt recession" further damaged the president's reputation, and for many months he aggravated the situation by adopting an almost Hoover-like attitude. "Everything will work out all right if we just sit tight and keep quiet," he actually said.

While the president hesitated, rival theorists within his administration warred. The Keynesians, led by WPA head Harry Hopkins, Marriner Eccles of the Federal Reserve, and Secretary of the Interior Harold Ickes, clamored for stepped-up government spending. The conservatives, led by Treasury Secretary Henry Morgenthau, Jr., advocated retrenchment. Perhaps confused by the conflict, Roosevelt seemed incapable of decisive action.

In April 1938 Roosevelt finally committed himself to heavy deficit spending. At his urging Congress passed a $3.75 billion public works bill. Two major pieces of legislation were also enacted at about this time. A new AAA program (February 1938) set marketing quotas and acreage limitations for growers of staples like wheat, cotton, and tobacco and authorized the Commodity Credit Corporation to lend money to farmers on their surplus crops.

The second measure, the Fair Labor Standards Act, abolished child labor and established a national minimum wage of 40 cents an hour and a maximum workweek of 40 hours, with time and a half for overtime. Although the law failed to cover many of the poorest-paid types of labor, its passage meant wage increases for 750,000 workers. In later years many more classes of workers were brought within its protection, and the minimum wage was repeatedly increased.

These measures further alienated conservatives without dramatically improving economic conditions. The resistance of many Democratic members of Congress to additional economic and social "experiments" hardened. As the 1938 elections approached, Roosevelt decided to go to the voters in an effort to strengthen party discipline and reenergize the New Deal. He singled out a number of conservative Democratic senators, notably Walter F. George of Georgia, Millard F. Tydings of Maryland, and "Cotton Ed" Smith of South Carolina, and tried to "purge" them by backing other Democrats in the primaries.

The purge failed. Southern voters liked Roosevelt but resented his interference in local politics. Smith dodged the issue of liberalism by stressing the question of white supremacy. Tydings emphasized Roosevelt's "invasion" of Maryland. In Georgia the president's enemies compared his campaign against George to General Sherman's march across the state during the Civil War. All three senators were easily renominated and then reelected in November. In the nation at large the Republicans made important gains for the first time since Roosevelt had taken office. The Democrats maintained nominal control of both houses of Congress, but the conservative coalition, while unable to muster the votes to do away with accomplished reforms, succeeded in blocking additional legislation.

SIGNIFICANCE OF THE NEW DEAL

After World War II broke out in 1939, the Great Depression was swept away on a wave of orders from the beleaguered European democracies. For this prosperity, Roosevelt received much undeserved credit. His New Deal had not returned the

The proliferation of federal agencies during the New Deal inspired cartoonists. In this example, Swift's Gulliver (Uncle Sam) is tied down by the Lilliputian Brain Trusters.

country to full employment. Despite the aid given to the jobless, the generation of workers born between 1900 and 1910 who entered the 1930s as unskilled laborers had their careers permanently stunted by the Depression. Far fewer rose to middle-class status than at any time since the 1830s and 1840s.

Roosevelt's willingness to experiment with different means of combating the Depression made sense because no one really knew what to do; however, his uncertainty about the ultimate objectives of the New Deal was counterproductive. He vacillated between seeking to stimulate the economy by deficit spending and trying to balance the budget; between a narrow "America first" economic nationalism and a broad-gauged international approach; between regulating monopolies and trustbusting; between helping the underprivileged and bolstering those already strong. At times he acted on the assumptions that the United States had a "mature" economy and that the major problem was overproduction. At other

times he appeared to think that the answer to the Depression was more production. He could never make up his mind whether to try to rally liberals to his
cause without regard for party or to run the government as a partisan leader,
conciliating the conservative Democrats.

Roosevelt's fondness for establishing new agencies to deal with specific problems vastly increased the federal bureaucracy, indirectly added to the influence of
lobbyists, and made it more difficult to monitor government activities. His cavalier attitude toward constitutional limitations on executive power, which he justified as being necessary in a national emergency, set in motion trends that so increased the prestige and authority of the presidency that the balance among the
executive, legislative, and judicial branches was threatened.

Yet these are criticisms after the fact; they ignore what one historian has
called the "sense of urgency and haste" that made the New Deal "a mixture of accomplishment, frustration, and misdirected effort." On balance, the New Deal
had a constructive impact. By 1939 the country was committed to the idea that
the federal government should accept responsibility for the national welfare and
act to meet specific problems in every necessary way. What was most significant
was not the proliferation of new agencies or the expansion of federal power.
These were continuations of trends already a century old when the New Deal began. The importance of the "Roosevelt revolution" was that it removed the issue
from politics. "Never again," the Republican presidential candidate was to say in
1952, "shall we allow a depression in the United States."

Because of New Deal decisions, many formerly unregulated areas of
American life became subject to federal authority: the stock exchange, agricultural prices and production, labor relations, old-age pensions, relief of the needy.
If the New Deal failed to end the Depression, it effected changes that have—so
far, at least—prevented later economic declines from becoming catastrophes. By
encouraging the growth of unions, the New Deal probably helped workers obtain
a larger share of the profits of industry. By putting a floor under the income of
many farmers, it checked the decline of agricultural living standards, though not
that of the agricultural population. The social security program, with all its inadequacies, lessened the impact of bad times on an increasingly large proportion of
the population and provided immense psychological benefits to all.

Among other important social changes, the TVA and the New Deal rural
electrification program made farm life literally more civilized. Urban public
housing, while never undertaken on a massive scale, helped rehabilitate some of
the nation's worst slums. Government public power projects, such as the giant
Bonneville and Grand Coulee dams in the Pacific Northwest, were only the most
spectacular part of a comprehensive New Deal program to develop the natural

resources of the country. Exploitation of the natural resources of the West was checked, and a start was made toward the proper national management of the land and water of the region, along with its petroleum, lumber, and other resources. The NIRA and later labor legislation forced employers to reexamine their role in American life and to become more socially conscious. The WPA art and theater programs widened the horizons of millions. All in all, the spirit of the New Deal heightened the people's sense of community, revitalized national energies, and stimulated the imagination and creative instincts of countless citizens.

WOMEN AS NEW DEALERS: THE NETWORK

Largely because of the influence of Eleanor Roosevelt and Molly Dewson, head of the Women's Division of the Democratic National Committee, the Roosevelt administration employed far more women in positions of importance than any earlier one. Secretary of Labor Frances Perkins, the first woman appointed to a Cabinet post, had been active in labor relations for more than 20 years, as secretary of the Consumers' League during the progressive period, as a factory inspector immediately after the war, and as chair of the New York State Industrial Commission. As secretary of labor she helped draft New Deal labor legislation and kept Roosevelt informed on various labor problems outside the government.

Eleanor Roosevelt dispensing soup to the needy. As a wealthy young socialite, she exhibited little interest in public matters. But after Eleanor discovered that Franklin was having an affair with her own social secretary, Lucy Mercer, Eleanor began to change. Her marriage, she confided to a friend, ceased to have any "fundamental love to draw on." Liberated and energized, she threw herself into social and political reform.

In addition to Perkins, there were dozens of other women New Dealers. Dewson and Eleanor Roosevelt headed an informal but effective "network"—women in key posts who were always seeking to place reform-minded women in government jobs.

Through her newspaper column "My Day" and as a speaker on public issues, Eleanor Roosevelt became a major political force. Her influence was large, especially in the area of civil rights, where the administration needed constant prodding.

She was particularly identified with efforts to obtain better treatment for blacks, in and out of government. Her best-known action occurred in 1939 after the Daughters of the American Revolution (DAR) refused to permit the use of their Washington auditorium for a concert by the black contralto Marian Anderson. Eleanor Roosevelt resigned from the DAR in protest, and after the President arranged for Anderson to sing at the Lincoln Memorial, she persuaded a small army of dignitaries to sponsor the concert. An interracial crowd of 75,000 people attended the performance. The *Chicago Defender,* an influential black newspaper, noted that the First Lady "stood like the Rock of Gibraltar against pernicious encroachments on the rights of minorities." (A disgruntled white Southerner made the same point differently: "She goes round telling the Negroes they are as good as anyone else.")

BLACKS DURING THE NEW DEAL

The shift of black voters from the Republican to the Democratic party during the New Deal years was one of the most significant political turnarounds in American history. In 1932 when things were at their worst, fewer blacks defected from the Republican party than the members of any other traditionally Republican group. Four years later, however, blacks voted for Roosevelt in overwhelming numbers.

Blacks supported the New Deal for the same reasons that whites did, but how the New Deal affected blacks in general and racial attitudes specifically are more complicated questions. Claiming that he dared not antagonize southern congressmen, whose votes he needed for his recovery programs, Roosevelt did nothing about civil rights before 1941 and relatively little thereafter. For the same reason, many southern white liberals hesitated to support racial integration for fear that other liberal causes could be injured as a result.

Many of the early New Deal programs treated blacks as second-class citizens. Blacks were often paid at lower rates than whites under NRA codes (and so joked that NRA stood for "Negro Run Around" and "Negroes Ruined Again"). The early farm programs shortchanged black tenants and sharecroppers. Blacks in the

Black sharecroppers evicted from their tenant farms were photographed by Arthur Rothstein along a Missouri road in 1939. Rothstein was one of a group of outstanding photographers who created a unique "sociological and economic survey" of the nation between 1936 and 1942 under the aegis of the Farm Security Administration.

Civilian Conservation Corps were assigned to all-black camps. TVA developments were rigidly segregated, and almost no blacks got jobs in TVA offices. New Deal urban housing projects inadvertently but nonetheless effectively increased the concentration of blacks in particular neighborhoods. Because the Social Security Act excluded agricultural laborers and domestic servants, it did nothing for hundreds of thousands of poor black workers or for Mexican American farmhands in the Southwest. In 1939 unemployment was twice as high among blacks as among whites, and whites' wages were double the level of blacks' wages.

The fact that members of racial minorities got less than they deserved did not keep most of them from becoming New Dealers: Half a loaf was more than any American government had given blacks since the time of U. S. Grant. As one black minister explained, "[Negroes] have never been so crazy as to wait for things to be perfect."

In the labor movement the new CIO unions accepted black members, and this was particularly significant because these unions were organizing industries—steel, automobiles, and mining among others—that employed large numbers of blacks. Thus, while black Americans suffered horribly during the Depression, New Deal efforts to counteract its effects brought them some relief and a measure of hope. And this became increasingly true with the passage of time. During Roosevelt's second term, blacks found far less to criticize than had been the case earlier.

A NEW DEAL FOR INDIANS

New Deal policy toward American Indians built on earlier trends but carried them further. During the Harding and Coolidge administrations more Indian land had passed into the hands of whites, and agents of the Bureau of Indian Affairs had tried to suppress elements of Indian culture that they considered "pagan" or "lascivious." In 1924 Congress finally granted citizenship to all Indians, but it was still generally agreed by whites that Indians should be treated as wards of the state. Assimilation had failed; Indian languages and religious practices, patterns of family life, Indian arts and crafts had all resisted generations of efforts to "civilize" the tribes.

Government policy took a new direction in 1933 when President Roosevelt named John Collier commissioner of Indian affairs. In the 1920s Collier had studied the Indians of the Southwest and been appalled by what he learned. He became executive secretary of the American Indian Defense Association and, in 1925, editor of a reform-oriented magazine, *American Indian Life*. By the time he was appointed commissioner, the Depression had reduced perhaps a third of the 320,000 Indians living on reservations to penury.

Collier tried to revive the spirits of these people. He favored a pluralistic approach, seeking to help the Indians preserve their ancient cultures but also (somewhat contradictorily) to help them earn more money and make use of modern medical advances and modern techniques of soil conservation. He was particularly eager to encourage the revival of tribal governments that could represent the Indians in dealings with the United States government and function as community service centers.

In part because of Collier's urging, Congress passed the Indian Reorganization Act of 1934. This law did away with the Dawes Act allotment system and enabled Indians to establish tribal governments with powers like those of cities, and it encouraged Indians to return individually owned lands to tribal control. About 4 million of the 90 million acres of Indian land lost under the allotment system were returned to the tribes.

New Deal Indian policy was controversial—among Indians as well as among white groups. Some critics charged Collier with trying to turn back the clock.

Others attacked him as a segregationist and claimed that he was trying to restore "pagan" religious practices and convert the Indians to communism.

In truth the problem was more complicated than Collier had imagined. Indians who owned profitable allotments, such as those in Oklahoma who held valuable oil and mineral rights, did not relish turning over their land to tribal control. In New Mexico the Navajos, whose lands had relatively little commercial value, nonetheless voted decisively against going back to the communal system. All told, 77 of 269 tribes voted against communal holdings.

Collier resigned in 1945, and in the 1950s Congress "terminated" most government efforts aimed at preserving Indian cultures. Nevertheless, like so many of its programs, the New Deal's Indian policy was a bold effort to deal constructively with a long-standing national problem.

THE ROLE OF ROOSEVELT

How much of the credit for New Deal policies belongs personally to Franklin D. Roosevelt is debatable. He had little to do with many of the details and some of the broad principles behind the New Deal. His knowledge of economics was skimpy, his understanding of many social problems superficial, his political philosophy distressingly vague. The British leader Anthony Eden described him as "a conjurer, skillfully juggling with balls of dynamite, whose nature he failed to understand."

Nevertheless, every aspect of the New Deal bears the brand of Roosevelt's remarkable personality. Rexford Tugwell has left one of the best-balanced judgments of the president. "Roosevelt was not really very much at home with ideas," Tugwell explained. But he was always open to new facts, and something within him "forbade inaction when there was something to be done." Roosevelt constructed the coalition that made the program possible; his humanitarianism made it a reform movement of major significance. Although considered by many a terrible administrator

When Eleanor Roosevelt learned of Franklin's affair with the widowed Lucy Mercer (above), the president promised never to see Mercer again. But she was with him when he died in April 1945.

because he encouraged rivalry among his subordinates, assigned different agencies overlapping responsibilities, failed to discharge many incompetents, and frequently put off making difficult decisions, he was in fact one of the most effective chief executives in the nation's history. His seemingly haphazard practice of dividing authority among competing administrators unleashed the energies and sparked the imaginations of his aides.

Like Andrew Jackson, Roosevelt maximized his role as leader of all the people. His informal biweekly press conferences kept the public in touch with developments and himself in tune with popular thinking. His "fireside chats" convinced millions that he was personally interested in each citizen's life and welfare, as in a way he was. At a time when the size and complexity of the government made it impossible for any one person to direct the nation's destiny, Roosevelt managed the minor miracle of personifying that government to 130 million people. Under Hoover, a single clerk was able to handle the routine mail that flowed into the office of the president from ordinary citizens. Under Roosevelt, the task required a staff of 50.

While the New Deal was still evolving, contemporaries recognized Roosevelt's right to a place beside Washington, Jefferson, and Lincoln among the great presidents. The years have not altered their judgment. Yet as his second term drew toward its close, some of his most important work still lay in the future.

THE TRIUMPH OF ISOLATIONISM

Franklin Roosevelt was at heart an internationalist, but like most world leaders in the 1930s, he placed revival of his own country's limping economy ahead of general world recovery. In April 1933 he took the United States off the gold standard, hoping that devaluing the dollar would make it easier to sell American goods abroad. The following month the World Economic Conference met in London. Delegates from 64 nations sought ways to increase world trade, perhaps by a general reduction of tariffs and the stabilization of currencies. After flirting with the idea of currency stabilization, Roosevelt threw a bombshell into the conference by announcing that the United States would not return to the gold standard. His decision increased international ill feeling, and the conference collapsed. The German financier Hjalmar Schacht announced smugly that Roosevelt was adopting the maxim of the great *Führer,* Adolf Hitler: "Take your economic fate in your own hands."

Against this background, vital changes in American foreign policy took place. Unable to persuade the country to take positive action against aggressors, internationalists like Secretary of State Stimson had begun in 1931 to work for a discretionary arms embargo law to be applied by the president in time of war against whichever side had broken the peace. By early 1933 Stimson had obtained Hoover's backing for an embargo bill, as well as the support of President-elect Roosevelt. First the munitions manufacturers and then the isolationists pounced on it, and in the resulting debate it was amended to make the embargo apply to *all* belligerents.

Instead of providing an effective if essentially negative tool for influencing international affairs, a blanket embargo would intensify America's ostrichlike isolationism. Stimson's policy would have permitted arms shipments to China but not to Japan, which might have discouraged the Japanese from attacking. As amended, the embargo would have automatically applied to both sides, thus removing the United States as an influence in the conflict. Although Roosevelt accepted the change, the internationalists in Congress did not, and when they withdrew their support the measure died.

The attitude of the munitions makers, who opposed both forms of the embargo, led to a series of studies of the industry. The most important was a Senate investigation (1934–1936) headed by Gerald P. Nye of North Dakota. Nye was convinced that "the interests" had conspired to drag America into World War I; his investigation was more an inquisition than an honest effort to discover what American bankers and munitions makers had been doing between 1914 and 1918. The committee's staff, ferreting into subpoenaed records, uncovered sensational facts about the lobbying activities and profits of various concerns. The Du Pont company's earnings, for example, had soared from $5 million in 1914 to $82 million in 1916. When one senator suggested to Irénée Du Pont that he was displaying a somewhat different attitude toward war than most citizens, Du Pont replied coolly: "Yes; perhaps. You were not in the game, or you might have a different viewpoint."

Munitions makers had profited far more from neutrality than from American participation in the war, but the Nye report convinced millions of citizens that the bankers who had lent the Allies money and the "merchants of death" who had sold them arms had tricked the country into war and that the "mistake" of 1917 must never be repeated.

The danger of another world war mounted steadily as Germany, Italy, and Japan repeatedly resorted to force to achieve their expansionist aims. In March 1935 Hitler instituted universal military training. In May Mussolini massed troops in Italian Somaliland, using a trivial border clash as a pretext for threatening the ancient kingdom of Ethiopia.

Congress responded by passing the Neutrality Act of 1935, which forbade the sale of munitions to all belligerents whenever the president should proclaim that a state of war existed. Americans who took passage on belligerent ships after such a proclamation had been issued would do so at their own risk. Roosevelt would have preferred a discretionary embargo or no new legislation at all, but he dared not rouse the ire of the isolationists by vetoing the bill.

In October 1935 Italy invaded Ethiopia and Roosevelt invoked the new neutrality law. Secretary of State Cordell Hull asked American exporters to support a "moral embargo" on the sale of oil and other products not covered by the act. His plea was ignored; oil shipments to Italy tripled between October and January. Italy quickly overran and annexed Ethiopia. In February 1936 Congress passed a second neutrality act forbidding all loans to belligerents.

Then, in the summer of 1936, civil war broke out in Spain. The rebels, led by the reactionary General Francisco Franco and strongly backed by Italy and Germany, sought to overthrow the somewhat leftist Spanish Republic. Here, clearly, was a clash between democracy and fascism, and the neutrality laws did not apply to civil wars. However, Roosevelt now became more fearful of involvement than some isolationists. The president believed that American interference might cause the conflict in Spain to become a global war, and he was wary of antagonizing the substantial number of American Catholics who were sympathetic to the Franco regime. At his urging Congress passed another neutrality act broadening the arms embargo to cover civil wars.

Isolationism now reached its peak. A public opinion poll revealed in March 1937 that 94 percent of the people thought American policy should be directed

In August 1940 the Committee to Defend America by Keeping Out of the War sponsored an Emergency Peace Mobilization meeting to denounce conscription. The meeting, held at the Chicago Stadium, drew some 15,000 people.

at keeping out of all foreign wars rather than trying to prevent wars from breaking out. In April Congress passed still another neutrality law. It continued the embargo on munitions and loans, forbade Americans to travel on belligerent ships, and gave the president discretionary authority to place the sale of other goods to belligerents on a cash-and-carry basis. In theory this would preserve the nation's profitable foreign trade without the risk of war; in fact it played into the hands of the aggressors. While German planes and cannons were turning the tide in Spain, the United States was denying the hard-pressed Spanish loyalists even a case of cartridges.

"With every surrender the prospects of a European war grow darker," Claude G. Bowers, the American ambassador to Spain, warned. The *New York Herald Tribune* pointed out that the neutrality legislation was literally reactionary—designed to keep the United States out of the war of 1914–1918, not the conflict looming on the horizon. President Roosevelt, in part because of domestic problems such as the Supreme Court packing struggle and the wave of sit-down strikes, and in part because of his own vacillation, seemed to have lost control over the formulation of American foreign policy. The American people, like wild creatures before a forest fire, were rushing in blind panic from the conflagration.

WAR AGAIN IN EUROPE

There were limits beyond which Americans would not go. In July 1937 the Japanese again attacked China, pressing ahead on a broad front. Roosevelt believed that invoking the neutrality law would only help the well-armed Japanese. Taking advantage of the fact that neither side had formally declared war, he allowed the shipment of arms and supplies to both sides.

Then the president went further. Speaking in Chicago in October, he condemned nations—he mentioned none by name—who were "creating a state of international anarchy and instability from which there is no escape through mere isolation or neutrality." The way to deal with "the epidemic of world lawlessness" was to "quarantine" it. Evidently Roosevelt had no specific plan in mind; nevertheless the "quarantine speech" produced a windy burst of isolationist rhetoric that forced him to back down. "It's a terrible thing," he said, "to look over your shoulder when you are trying to lead—and to find no one there."

Roosevelt came gradually to the conclusion that resisting aggression was more important than keeping out of war, but when he did, the need to keep the country united led him at times to be less than candid in his public statements. Hitler's annexation of Austria in March 1938 caused him deep concern. The Nazis' vicious anti-Semitism had caused many of Germany's 500,000 Jewish citizens to seek refuge abroad. Now 190,000 Austrian Jews were under Nazi control. When Roosevelt learned that the Germans were burning synagogues, expelling Jewish children from schools, and otherwise mistreating innocent people, he said that he "could scarcely believe that such things could occur." But public opinion opposed changing the immigration law so that more refugees could be admitted, and the president did nothing.

In September 1938 Hitler demanded that Czechoslovakia cede the German-speaking Sudetenland to the Reich. British Prime Minister Neville Chamberlain and French Premier Edouard Deladier, in a conference with Hitler at Munich, yielded to Hitler's threats and promises and persuaded the Czechs to surrender the region. Roosevelt failed again to speak out. But when the Nazis seized the rest of Czechoslovakia in March 1939, Roosevelt called for "methods short of war" to demonstrate America's determination to check the fascists.

When Hitler threatened Poland in the spring of 1939, demanding the free city of Danzig and the Polish Corridor separating East Prussia from the rest of Germany, and when Mussolini invaded Albania, Roosevelt urged Congress to repeal the 1937 neutrality act so that the United States could sell arms to Britain and France in the event of war. Congress refused. "Captain," Vice-President Garner told Roosevelt after counting noses in the Senate, "you haven't got the votes," and the president, perhaps unwisely, did not press the issue.

Hitler's troops invaded Poland with tremendous force and firepower. The Nazi occupiers rounded up the Jewish residents of the Warsaw ghetto and deported them to slave labor camps that soon became mass extermination camps.

In August 1939 Germany and Russia signed a nonaggression pact, prelude to their joint assault on Poland. On September 1 Hitler's troops invaded Poland, at last provoking Great Britain and France to declare war. Roosevelt immediately asked Congress to repeal the arms embargo. In November, in a vote that followed party lines closely, the Democratic majority pushed through a law permitting the sale of arms and other contraband on a cash-and-carry basis. Short-term loans were authorized, but American vessels were forbidden to carry any products to the belligerents. Since the Allies controlled the seas, cash-and-carry gave them a tremendous advantage.

The German attack on Poland effected a basic change in American thinking. Keeping out of the war remained an almost universal hope, but preventing a Nazi victory became the ultimate, if not always conscious, objective of many citizens. In Roosevelt's case it was perfectly conscious, although he dared not express his feelings candidly because of isolationist strength in Congress and the country. He moved slowly, responding to rather than directing the course of events.

Cash-and-carry did not stop the Nazis. Poland fell in less than a month; then, after a winter lull that cynics called the "phony war," Hitler loosed his armored divisions. Between April 9 and June 22 he taught the world the awful meaning of *Blitzkrieg*—lightning war. Denmark, Norway, the Netherlands, Belgium, and France were successively overwhelmed. The British army, pinned against the sea at Dunkirk, saved itself from annihilation only by fleeing across the English Channel. After the French submitted to his harsh terms on June 22, Hitler controlled nearly all of western Europe.

Roosevelt responded to these disasters in a number of ways. In the fall of 1939, reacting to warnings from Albert Einstein and other scientists that the Germans were trying to develop an atomic bomb, he committed federal funds to a top-secret atomic energy program. Even as the British and French were falling back, he sold them, without legal authority, surplus government arms. When Italy entered the war against France, the president called the invasion a stab in the back. During the first five months of 1940 he asked Congress to appropriate over $4 billion for national defense. To strengthen national unity he named Henry L. Stimson secretary of war and another Republican, Frank Knox, secretary of the navy.

After the fall of France, Hitler attempted to bomb and starve the British into submission. The epic air battles over England during the summer of 1940 ended in a decisive defeat for the Nazis, but the Royal Navy, which had only about 100 destroyers, could not control German submarine attacks on shipping. Far more destroyers were needed. In this desperate hour, Prime Minister Winston Churchill, who had replaced Chamberlain in May 1940, asked Roosevelt for 50 old American destroyers to fill the gap.

The navy had 240 destroyers in commission and more than 50 under construction. But direct loan or sale of the vessels would have violated both international and American laws. Any attempt to obtain new legislation would have roused fears that the United States was going down the path that had led it into World War I. Long delay if not outright defeat would have resulted. Roosevelt therefore arranged to "trade" the destroyers for six British naval bases in the Caribbean. In addition, Great Britain leased bases in Bermuda and Newfoundland to the United States.

The destroyers-for-bases deal was a masterful achievement. It helped save Great Britain, and at the same time it circumvented isolationist prejudices since the president could present it as a shrewd bargain that bolstered America's defenses. A string of island bastions in the Atlantic was more valuable than 50 old destroyers.

Lines were hardening throughout the world. In September 1940, despite last-ditch isolationist resistance, Congress enacted the first peacetime draft in American history. Some 1.2 million draftees were summoned for one year of service, and 800,000 reservists were called to active duty. That same month Japan signed a mutual-assistance pact with Germany and Italy. This Rome-Berlin-Tokyo axis fused the conflicts in Europe and Asia, turning the struggle into a global war.

A THIRD TERM FOR FDR

In the midst of these events the 1940 presidential election took place. Why Roosevelt decided to run for a third term is a much-debated question. Partisanship had something to do with it, for no other Democrat seemed so likely to carry the country. Nor would the president have been human had he not been tempted to hold on to power, especially in such critical times. His conviction that no one else could keep a rein on the isolationists was probably decisive. In any case, he was easily renominated. Vice President Garner, who had become disenchanted with Roosevelt and the New Deal, did not seek a third term; at Roosevelt's dictation, the party chose Secretary of Agriculture Henry A. Wallace to replace him.

By using concern about the European war to justify running for a tradition-breaking third term, Roosevelt brought down on his head the hatred of conservative Republicans and the isolationists of both major parties, just when they thought they would be rid of him. The leading Republican presidential candidates were Senator Robert A. Taft of Ohio, son of the former president, and District Attorney Thomas E. Dewey of New York, who had won fame as a "racket buster" and political reformer. Taft was considered conservative and lacking in political glamor; Dewey, barely 38, seemed too young and inexperienced. Instead the Republicans nominated the darkest of dark horses, Wendell L. Willkie of Indiana, the utility magnate who had led the fight against the TVA in 1933.

Despite his political inexperience and Wall Street connections, Willkie made an appealing candidate. He was an energetic, charming, openhearted man. His rough-hewn, rural manner (one Democrat called him "a simple, barefoot Wall Street lawyer") won him wide support in farm districts. Willkie had difficulty, however, finding issues on which to oppose Roosevelt. Good times were at last returning. The New Deal reforms were too popular and too much in line with his own thinking to invite attack. He believed as strongly as the president that America could no longer ignore the Nazi threat.

In the end Willkie focused his campaign on Roosevelt's conduct of foreign relations. A preponderance of the Democrats favored all-out aid to Britain, while most Republicans still wished to avoid foreign "entanglements." But the crisis was causing many persons to shift sides. Among interventionists, organizations like the Committee to Defend America by Aiding the Allies, headed by Republican William Allen White, and the small but influential Century Group contained members of both parties. So did the isolationist America First Committee, led by Robert E. Wood of Sears Roebuck and the famous aviator Charles A. Lindbergh.

While rejecting the isolationist position, Willkie charged that Roosevelt intended to make the United States a participant in the war. "If you reelect him," he told one audience, "you may expect war in April 1941," to which Roosevelt retorted (disingenuously, since he knew he was not a free agent in the situation), "I have said this before, but I shall say it again and again and again: Your boys are not going to be sent into any foreign wars." In November Roosevelt carried the country handily, though by a smaller majority than in 1932 or 1936. The popular vote was 27 million to 22 million, the electoral count 449 to 82.

THE UNDECLARED WAR

The election encouraged Roosevelt to act more boldly. When Prime Minister Churchill informed him that the cash-and-carry system would no longer suffice because Great Britain was rapidly exhausting its financial resources, he decided at once to provide the British with whatever they needed. Instead of proposing to lend them money, a step certain to rouse memories of the vexatious war debt controversies, he devised the lend-lease program, one of his most ingenious and imaginative creations.

First he delivered a "fireside chat" that stressed the evil intentions of the Nazis and the dangers that a German victory would create for America. Aiding Britain should be looked at simply as a form of self-defense. "As planes and ships and guns and shells are produced," he said, American defense experts would decide "how much shall be sent abroad and how much shall remain at home." When the radio talk provoked a favorable public response, Roosevelt went to Congress in January 1941 with a plan calling for the expenditure of $7 billion for war materials that the president could sell, lend, lease, exchange, or transfer to any country whose defense he deemed vital to that of the United States. After two months of debate, Congress gave him what he had asked for.

Although the wording of the Lend-Lease Act obscured its immediate purpose, the saving of Great Britain, the president was frank in explaining his plan. He coupled his demand for heavy military expenditures with his enunciation of the idealistic "Four Freedoms"—freedom of speech, freedom of religion, freedom from want, and freedom from fear—for which, he said, the war was being fought.

After the enactment of lend-lease, aid short of war was no longer seriously debated. The American navy began to patrol the North Atlantic, shadowing German submarines and radioing their locations to British warships and planes. In April 1941 United States forces occupied Greenland; in May the president declared a state of unlimited national emergency. After Hitler invaded the Soviet Union in June, Roosevelt moved slowly, for anti-Soviet feeling in the United States was intense. But it was obviously to the nation's advantage to help any country that was resisting Hitler's armies. In November, $1 billion in lend-lease aid was put at the disposal of the Russians.

Meanwhile, Iceland was occupied in July 1941, and the draft law was extended in August—by the margin of a single vote in the House of Representatives. In September the German submarine *U-652* fired a torpedo at the destroyer U.S.S. *Greer* in the North Atlantic. The *Greer,* which had provoked the attack by tracking *U-652* and flashing its position to a British plane, avoided the torpedo and dropped 19 depth charges in an effort to sink the submarine.

Roosevelt (nothing he ever did provided more ammunition for his critics) announced that the *Greer* had been innocently "carrying mail to Iceland." He called the U-boats "the rattlesnakes of the Atlantic" and ordered the navy to "shoot on sight" any German craft in the waters south and west of Iceland and to convoy merchant vessels as far as that island. After the sinking of the destroyer U.S.S. *Reuben James* on October 30, Congress voted to allow the arming of American merchant ships and to permit them to carry cargoes to Allied ports. For all practical purposes, though not yet officially, the United States had gone to war.

MILESTONES

1933	Civilian Conservation Corps (CCC)
	Federal Emergency Relief Administration (FERA)
	Agricultural Adjustment Administration (AAA)
	Tennessee Valley Authority (TVA)
	Home Owners Loan Corporation (HOLC)
	National Recovery Administration (NRA)
	Federal Deposit Insurance Corporation (FDIC)
	Public Works Administration (PWA)
	Civil Works Administration (CWA)
1934	Securities and Exchange Commission (SEC)
	Federal Communications Commission (FCC)
	Federal Housing Administration (FHA)
1935	Works Progress Administration (WPA)
	Resettlement Administration (RA)
	Rural Electrification Administration (REA)
	National Youth Administration (NYA)
	National Labor Relations Board (NLRB)
1937	FDR withdraws "court-packing" legislation
1938	FDR supports deficit spending
1939	Secret "nonaggression" pact between Germany and Soviet Union

28

---※◆───────◆※---

WAR AND PEACE

B y December 1941 the United States was in fact at war, but it is hard to see how a formal declaration could have come about had it not been for Japan. Japanese American relations had worsened steadily after Japan resumed its war on China in 1937. In September 1940, Congress prohibited all sales of scrap iron to Japan. Japan immediately signed a treaty of alliance with Germany and Italy, which prompted Roosevelt to extend the embargo to include machine tools and other items. The Japanese pushed ahead relentlessly despite the economic pressures.

THE ROAD TO PEARL HARBOR

Neither the United States nor Japan wanted war. Roosevelt considered Germany by far the more dangerous enemy and was alarmed by the possibility of engaging in a two-front war. In the spring of 1941 Secretary of State Hull conferred in Washington with the Japanese ambassador, Kichisaburo Nomura, in an effort to resolve their differences. Hull showed little appreciation of the political and military situation in the Far East. He demanded that Japan withdraw from China and promise not to attack the Dutch and French colonies in Southeast Asia.

Japan might well have accepted limited annexations in the area in return for the removal of American trade restrictions, but Hull seemed bent on converting the Japanese to pacifism by exhortation. He insisted on total withdrawal, to which even the moderates in Japan would not agree. When Hitler invaded the Soviet Union, thereby removing the threat of Russian intervention in the Far East, Japan decided to occupy Indochina even at the risk of war with the United States. Roosevelt retaliated (July 1941) by freezing Japanese assets in the United States and clamping an embargo on oil. He hoped that the Japanese war machine, deprived of American oil, would grind to a halt.

Now the war party in Japan assumed control. Nomura was instructed to tell Hull that his country would refrain from further expansion if the United States and Great Britain would cut off all aid to China and lift the economic blockade. Japan promised to pull out of Indochina once "a just peace" had been established with China. When the United States rejected these demands, the Japanese prepared to assault the Dutch East Indies, British Malaya, and the Philippines. To immobilize the United States Pacific fleet, they planned a surprise aerial raid on the Hawaiian naval base at Pearl Harbor.

An American cryptanalyst, Colonel William F. Friedman, had cracked the Japanese diplomatic code: the Japanese were making plans to attack in early December. But in the hectic rush of events, both military and civilian authorities failed to make effective use of the information collected. They expected the blow to fall somewhere in Southeast Asia, possibly in the Philippines.

The garrison at Pearl Harbor was alerted against "a surprise aggressive move in any direction." The commanders there, Admiral Husband E. Kimmel and General Walter C. Short, believing an attack impossible, took precautions only against Japanese sabotage. Thus when planes from Japanese aircraft carriers swooped down upon Pearl Harbor on the morning of December 7, they found easy targets. In less than two hours they reduced the Pacific Fleet to a smoking ruin: two battleships destroyed, six others heavily battered, nearly a dozen lesser vessels put out of action. More than 150 planes were wrecked; over 2300 servicemen were killed and 1100 wounded.

Never had American arms suffered a more devastating or shameful defeat. The official blame was placed chiefly on Admiral Kimmel and General Short. They might well have been more alert, but responsibility for the disaster was widespread. Military and civilian officials in Washington had failed to pass on all that they knew to Hawaii or even to one another. On the other hand, the crucial intelligence about the coming attack that the code breakers provided was mixed with masses of other information and was extremely difficult to evaluate.

On December 8 Congress declared war on Japan. Formal war with Germany and Italy was still not inevitable—isolationists were far more ready to resist the "yellow peril" in Asia than to fight in Europe. The Axis powers, however, honored their treaty obligations to Japan and on December 11 declared war on the United States. America was now fully engaged in the great world conflict.

Japan's surprise attack on Pearl Harbor on December 7, 1941, killed more than 2300 American servicemen and launched the United States into World War II. President Roosevelt asked Congress for a declaration of war the next day, calling the attack "a date that will live in infamy."

MOBILIZING THE HOME FRONT

War placed immense strains on the American economy and produced immense results. About 15 million men and women entered the armed services; they, and in part the millions more in Allied uniforms, had to be fed, clothed, housed, and supplied with equipment ranging from typewriters and paper clips to rifles and grenades, tanks and airplanes. Congress granted wide emergency powers to the president. It refrained from excessive meddling in administrative problems and in military strategy. However, while the Democrats retained control of both houses throughout the war, their margins were relatively narrow. A coalition of conservatives in both parties frequently prevented the president from having his way and exercised close control over expenditures.

Roosevelt was an inspiring war leader but not a very good administrator. Any honest account of the war on the home front must reveal glaring examples of confusion, inefficiency, and pointless bickering. The squabbling and waste characteristic of the early New Deal period made relatively little difference—what mattered then was raising the nation's spirits and keeping people occupied; efficiency was less than essential, however desirable. But in wartime, the nation's fate, perhaps that of the entire free world, depended on delivering weapons and supplies to the battlefronts.

Roosevelt's greatest accomplishment was his inspiring of industrialists, workers, and farmers with a sense of national purpose. In this respect his function duplicated his earlier role in fighting the Depression, and he performed it with even greater success.

A sense of the tremendous economic expansion caused by the demands of war can most easily be captured by reference to official statistics of production. In 1939 the United States was still mired in the Great Depression. The gross national product amounted to about $91.3 billion. In 1945, after allowing for changes in the price level, it was $166.6 billion. More specifically, manufacturing output nearly doubled and agricultural output rose 22 percent. In 1939 the United States turned out fewer than 6000 airplanes, in 1944 more than 96,000. Shipyards produced 237,000 tons of vessels in 1939, 10 million tons in 1943.

This growth was especially notable in the South and Southwest. This region got a preponderance of the new army camps built for the war as well as a large share of the new defense plants. Southern productive capacity increased by about 50 percent, and southern per capita output, while still low, crept closer to the national average.

Wartime experience proved that the Keynesian economists were correct in saying that government spending would spark economic growth. About 8 million people were unemployed in June 1940. After Pearl Harbor, unemployment virtually disappeared, and by 1945 the civilian workforce had increased by nearly 7 million. Military mobilization had begun well before December 1941, by which time 1.6 million men were already under arms. Economic mobilization proceeded much more slowly, mainly because the president refused to centralize authority. For months after Pearl Harbor various civilian agencies squabbled with the military over everything from the allocation of scarce raw materials to the technical specifications of weapons. Roosevelt refused to settle these conflicts.

THE WAR ECONOMY

Yet by early 1943 the nation's economic machinery had been converted to a wartime footing and was functioning effectively. Supreme Court Justice James F. Byrnes resigned from the Court to become a sort of "economic czar." His Office of War Mobilization had complete control over priorities and prices. Rents, food prices, and wages were strictly regulated, and items in short supply were rationed to consumers. While wages and prices had soared during 1942, after April 1943 they leveled off. Thereafter the cost of living scarcely changed until controls were lifted after the war.

Expanded industrial production together with conscription caused a labor shortage that increased the bargaining power of workers. At the same time, the national emergency required some limitation on the workers' right to take advantage of this power. After Pearl Harbor, Roosevelt created a National War Labor Board (NWLB) to arbitrate disputes and stabilize wage rates, and he banned all changes in wages without NWLB approval. In the "Little Steel" case (July 1942), the NWLB laid down the rule that wage increases should not normally exceed 15 percent of the rates of January 1941, a figure roughly in line with the increase in the cost of living since that date.

Prosperity and stiffer government controls added significantly to the strength of organized labor; indeed, the war had more to do with institutionalizing industrywide collective bargaining than the New Deal period. As workers recognized the benefits of union membership, they flocked into the organizations. Strikes declined sharply, but some crippling work stoppages did occur.

Wages and prices remained in fair balance. Overtime work fattened paychecks, and labor contracts calling for paid vacations, premium pay for night work, and various forms of employer-subsidized health insurance were added

Men and Women in the Labor Force, 1940–1945
In 1940 about 75 percent of workers in the labor force—82 million—were men, and the other 25 percent—28 million—were women. By the end of World War II, in 1945, nearly 8 million more women had entered the workforce, as compared to 5 million more men. The balance of the labor force had shifted to roughly 70 percent men, 30 percent women.

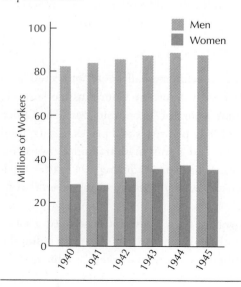

benefits. The war effort had almost no adverse effect on the standard of living of the average citizen, a vivid demonstration of the productivity of the American economy. The manufacture of automobiles ceased and pleasure driving became next to impossible because of gasoline rationing, but most civilian activities went on much as they had before Pearl Harbor. Because of the need to conserve cloth, skirts were shortened, cuffs disappeared from men's trousers, and the vest passed out of style. Plastics replaced metals in toys, containers, and other products. While items such as meat, sugar, and shoes were rationed, they were doled out in amounts adequate for the needs of most persons. Americans had both guns and butter; belt-tightening of the type experienced by the other belligerents was unheard of.

The federal government spent twice as much money between 1941 and 1945 as in its entire previous history. This made heavy borrowing necessary. The national debt, which stood at less than $49 billion in 1941, increased by more than that amount each year between 1942 and 1945 and totaled nearly $260 billion when the war ended. However, more than 40 percent of the total was met by taxation, a far larger proportion than in any earlier war.

The income tax, which had never before touched the mass of white-collar and industrial workers, was extended downward until nearly everyone had to pay it. To collect efficiently the relatively small sums paid by most persons, Congress adopted the payroll-deduction system proposed by Beardsley Ruml, chairman of the Federal Reserve Bank of New York. Employers withheld the taxes owed by workers from their paychecks and turned the money over to the government.

The steeply graduated tax rates, combined with a general increase in the income of workers and farmers, effected a substantial shift in the distribution of wealth in the United States. The poor became richer, while the rich, if not actually poorer, collected a smaller proportion of the national income. The wealthiest 1 percent of the population had received 13.4 percent of the national income in 1935 and 11.5 percent in 1941. In 1944 this group received 6.7 percent.

WAR AND SOCIAL CHANGE

Enormous social effects stemmed from this shift, but World War II altered the patterns of American life in so many ways that it would be wrong to ascribe the transformations to any single source. Never was the population more fluid. The millions who put on uniforms found themselves transported first to training camps in every section of the country and then to battlefields scattered from Europe and Africa to the far reaches of the Pacific. Burgeoning new defense plants, influenced by a government policy of locating them in "uncongested areas," drew other millions to places like Hanford, Washington, and Oak Ridge,

Tennessee, where great atomic energy installations were constructed, and to the aircraft factories of California and other states. As in earlier periods the trend was from east to west and from the rural South to northern cities. The population of California increased by more than 50 percent in the 1940s, that of other far western states almost as much.

During the war the marriage rate rose steeply, from 75 per thousand adult women in 1939 to 118 in 1946. A kind of backlog existed because many people had been forced to put off marrying and having children for financial reasons during the Great Depression. Now wartime prosperity put an end to that problem at the same time that large numbers of young couples were feeling the need to put down roots before the husbands went off to risk death in distant lands. The population of the United States had increased by only 3 million during the Depression decade of the 1930s; during the next *five* years it rose by 6.5 million.

MINORITIES IN TIME OF WAR: BLACKS, HISPANICS, AND INDIANS

The war affected black Americans in many ways. Several factors operated to improve their lot. One was their own growing tendency to demand fair treatment. Another was the reaction of Americans to Hitler's barbaric treatment of millions of Jews, an outgrowth of his doctrine of "Aryan" superiority. These barbarities compelled millions of white citizens to reexamine their views about race. If the nation expected blacks to risk their lives for the common good, how could it continue to treat them as second-class citizens? Black leaders pointed out the inconsistency between fighting for democracy abroad and ignoring it at home. "We want democracy in Alabama," the NAACP announced, and this argument too had some effect on white thinking.

Blacks in the armed forces were treated more fairly than they had been in World War I. They were enlisted for the first time in the air force and the Marines, and they were given more responsible positions in the army and navy. The army commissioned its first black general. Some 600 black pilots won their wings. Altogether about a million served, about half of them overseas. The extensive and honorable performance of these units could not be ignored by the white majority.

However, segregation in the armed services was maintained. Especially in and around army camps in the southern states, rigid segregation proved shocking to many northern white soldiers. In some cases German prisoners of war were seated in front of black American soldiers at camp movies. Such practices led frequently to rioting and even to local mutinies among black recruits.

At the outset of the war, blacks in the army and navy were forced into all-black units, and they were banned entirely from the elite air corps and Marines. Eventually the Army Air Corps accepted some black fliers, many of whom had trained at the Tuskegee Institute. Although the Tuskegee Airmen, such as Leroy Bryant Jr., flew successful missions over North Africa, France, and Germany, they were kept in a segregated unit.

The navy continued to confine black and Hispanic sailors to demeaning, non-combat tasks, and black soldiers were often provided with inferior recreational facilities and otherwise mistreated in and around army camps, especially those in the South. In 1943 William Hastie, a former New Dealer who was serving as an adviser on racial matters to Secretary of War Stimson, resigned in protest because of the "reactionary policies and discriminatory practices of the Army and Air Forces in matters affecting Negroes."

However, economic realities operated significantly to the advantage of black civilians. More of them had been unemployed in proportion to their numbers than any other group; now the labor shortage brought employment for all. More than 5 million blacks moved from rural areas to cities between 1940 and 1945 in search of work. At least a million of them found defense jobs in the North and on the west coast, many of which involved developing valuable skills that had been difficult for blacks to acquire before the war because of the racial policies of trade unions and many employers. The black population of Los Angeles, San Francisco, Denver, Buffalo, Milwaukee, and half a dozen other important cities more than doubled in that brief period. The migrants were mostly forced to live in dreadful urban ghettoes, but their very concentration (and the fact that outside the South blacks could vote freely) made them important politically.

These gains failed to satisfy black leaders. The NAACP, which increased its membership from 50,000 in 1940 to almost 405,000 in 1946, adopted a more militant stance than in World War I. Discrimination in defense plants seemed far less tolerable than it had in 1917–1918. A. Philip Randolph, president of the Brotherhood of Sleeping Car Porters, organized a march of blacks on Washington in 1941 to demand equal opportunity for black workers. Fearing possible violence and the wrath of southern congressmen, Roosevelt tried to persuade Randolph to call off the march. "It would make the country look bad" and "help the Germans," he claimed. But Randolph persisted, and Roosevelt finally agreed to issue an order prohibiting discrimination in plants with defense contracts.

Prejudice and mistreatment did not cease. In areas around defense plants white resentment of the black "invasion" mounted. By 1943, 50,000 new blacks had crowded into Detroit. A wave of strikes disrupted production at U.S. Rubber and several former automobile plants where white workers laid down their tools to protest the hiring of blacks. In June a race riot marked by looting and bloody fighting raged for three days. By the time federal troops restored order, 25 blacks and 9 whites had been killed. Rioting also erupted in New York and many other cities.

In Los Angeles the attacks were upon Hispanic residents. Wartime employment needs resulted in a reversal of the Depression policy of forcing Mexicans out of the Southwest, and many thousands flocked north in search of work. Most had to accept menial jobs. But work was plentiful, and they, as well as resident Spanish-speaking Americans, experienced rising living standards.

A larger proportion of Mexican American men served in the armed forces than the national average, but some young civilian Hispanics in the Los Angeles region adopted a kind of civilian dress known as a zoot suit. These "uniforms" consisted of broad-brimmed fedoras, long coats, and pegged trousers. "Zoot suiters" tended to have money in their pockets, and their behavior (like their costume) was not always as circumspect as many local residents would have preferred. A grand jury undertook an investigation, and the Los Angeles City Council even debated banning the wearing of zoot suits. In 1943 rioting broke out when sailors on shore leave, apparently resenting these prosperous-appearing "foreign" civilians, began roaming the area attacking anyone they could find in a zoot suit.

There were at least understandable reasons why some city dwellers resented the zoot suiters, but these did not justify the way they acted. Still worse, the willingness of white leaders to tolerate attacks on blacks and Hispanics at a time when national unity was so necessary was particularly frustrating. For example, blood plasma from blacks and whites was kept separately even though the two "varieties" were indistinguishable and the process of storing plasma had been devised by a black doctor, Charles Drew.

Blacks became increasingly embittered. Roy Wilkins, head of the NAACP, put it this way in 1942: "No Negro leader with a constituency can face his members today and ask full support for the war in the light of the atmosphere the government has created." Many black newspaper editors were so critical of the administration that conservatives demanded they be indicted for sedition.

Roosevelt would have none of that, but the militants annoyed him; he felt that they should hold their demands in abeyance until the war had been won. Apparently he failed to realize the depth of black anger, and in this he was no different from the majority of whites. A revolution was in the making, yet in 1942 a poll revealed that a solid majority of whites still believed that black Americans were satisfied with their place in society. The riots of 1943 undoubtedly disabused some of them of this illusion.

Concern about national unity did lead to a reaction against the New Deal policy of encouraging Indians to preserve their ancient cultures and develop self-governing communities. There was even talk of going back to the allotment system and trying to assimilate Indians into the larger society. John Collier resigned as commissioner of Indian affairs in disgust in 1945. In fact, the war encouraged

In World War II the U.S. government adopted the Navajo Indian language as a radio code. Navajos (who became known as "Code Talkers") were recruited, trained, and sent to Marine combat units already deployed. As the enemy was unable to break the code, confidential information was able to flow between the various units. Here two Navajos operate a portable radio set in the Bougainville jungle in 1943.

assimilation in several ways. More than 24,000 Indians served in the armed forces, an experience that brought them in contact with new people, new places, and new ideas. Many thousands more left the reservations to work in defense industries in cities all over the country.

THE TREATMENT OF GERMAN AMERICANS AND ITALIAN AMERICANS

Although World War II affected the American people far more drastically than had World War I, it produced much less intolerance and fewer examples of the repression of individual freedom of opinion. People seemed able to distinguish between Italian fascism and Italian Americans and between the government of Nazi Germany and Americans of German descent in a way that had escaped their parents. The fact that few Italian Americans admired Mussolini and that nearly all German Americans were vigorously anti-Nazi helps explain this. So does the fact that both groups were well organized and prepared to use their considerable political power if necessary to protect themselves from abuse.

But the underlying public attitude was more important. Americans went to war in 1941 without illusions and without enthusiasm, determined to win but expecting only to preserve what they had. They therefore found it easier to tolerate dissent, to view the dangers they faced realistically, and to concentrate on the real foreign enemy without venting their feelings on domestic scapegoats. The nation's 100,000 conscientious objectors met with little hostility.

INTERNMENT OF THE JAPANESE

The relatively tolerant treatment accorded most people makes the nation's policies toward American citizens of Japanese extraction all the more difficult to comprehend. Generals on the west coast were understandably unnerved by the Japanese attack on Pearl Harbor and warned that people of Japanese descent might engage in sabotage or espionage for Japan. "The Japanese race is an enemy race," General John L. Dewitt claimed. The 112,000 Americans of Japanese ancestry, the majority of them native-born citizens, were "potential enemies." "The very fact that no sabotage has taken place to date," Dewitt observed, "is a disturbing and confirming indication that such action will be taken." This is like arguing that the driver with a perfect record is for that reason due to have an accident. Secretary of War Stimson proposed the relocation of the west coast people of Japanese extraction, including American citizens, to internment camps in Wyoming,

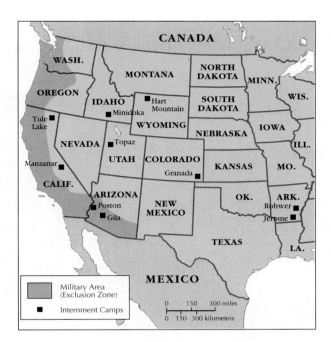

**Japanese American
Internment Camps**

Arizona, and other interior states. President Roosevelt concurred but weakly suggested: "Be as responsible as you can."

The Japanese were properly indignant but also baffled, in some cases hurt more than angry. "We didn't feel Japanese. We felt American," one woman, the mother of three small children, recalled many years later. Some Japanese Americans refused to submit to military authorities. Gordon Hirabayashi, an American citizen and senior at the University of Washington, refused to report for transportation to an internment camp. After being convicted and sentenced to prison, he decided to appeal. Previous Supreme Courts had ruled that the government could deprive Americans of their freedoms during war only when the "military necessity" was compelling. By the time the Supreme Court ruled on his and similar cases, the Japanese military had been thrown back in the Pacific; no invasion was even conceivable. Yet the justices worried that if they declared the internment policy to be unconstitutional, they would appear, Justice Felix Frankfurter put it, "out of step" with the nation. In June 1943, the Court upheld the conviction of Hirabayashi. Finally, in *Ex parte Endo,* it forbade the internment of loyal Japanese American citizens. Unfortunately the latter decision was not handed down until December 1944.

Identification tags hung from the collars of the Mochida children as they posed with their parents for pho-tographer Dorothea Lange. The date was May 8, 1942, and the family was awaiting transportation from their home in Hayward, California, to an internment camp.

WOMEN'S CONTRIBUTION TO THE WAR EFFORT

With economic activity on the rise and millions of men going off to war, a sudden need for more women workers developed. The trends of the 1920s—more women workers and more of them married—soon accelerated. By 1944, 6.5 million additional women had entered the workforce, and at the peak of war production in 1945, more than 19 million women were employed, many of them in well-paying industrial jobs. Additional thousands were serving in the armed forces: 100,000 in the Women's Auxiliary Army Corps, others in navy, marine, and air corps auxiliaries.

At first there was considerable resistance to what was happening. About one husband in three objected in principle to his wife taking a job. Many employers in so-called heavy industry and in other fields traditionally dominated by men doubted that women could handle such tasks.

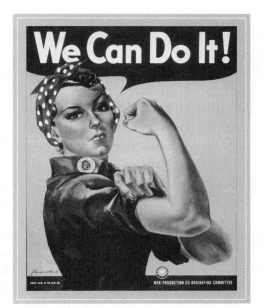

Posters such as this one helped persuade 2 million women to take jobs in defense plants. It suggests that although defense work required determination and strength, women who undertook such jobs would not lose their femininity (note the lipstick and mascara). In fact, most young women were given monotonous work on assembly lines; fewer than 1 in 20 were assigned to skilled jobs.

Unions frequently made the same point, usually without much evidence. A Seattle official of the International Brotherhood of Boilermakers and Iron Ship-builders said of women job applicants: "They don't understand. . . . If one of these girls pressed the trigger on the yard rivet guns, she'd be going one way and the rivet the other." Actually, many women were soon doing "men's work" in the shipyards. The Seattle taxicab union objected to women drivers on the grounds that "drivers are forced to do things and go places that would be embarrassing for a woman to do."

These male attitudes lost force in the face of the escalating demand for labor. That employers usually did not have to pay women as much as men made them attractive, as did the fact that they were not subject to the draft. A breakthrough occurred when the big Detroit automobile manufacturers agreed to employ women on their wartime production lines. Soon women were working not only as riveters and cab drivers but also as welders, as machine tool operators, and in dozens of other occupations formerly the exclusive domain of men.

Few wartime jobs were easy, and for women there were special burdens, not the least of which was the prejudice of many of the men they worked with. For married women there was housework to do after a long day. One War Manpower Commission bureaucrat figured out that Detroit defense plants were losing 100,000 woman-hours a month because of employees taking a day off to do the family laundry. Although the government made some effort to provide day-care facilities, there were never nearly enough; this was one reason why relatively few women with small children entered the labor market during the war.

The war also affected the lives of women who did not take jobs. Families by the tens and hundreds of thousands pulled up stakes and moved to the centers of war production, such as Detroit and southern California. Housing was always in short supply in these areas, and while the men went off to the familiar surroundings of yard and factory, their wives had to cope with cramped quarters, ration books, the absence of friends and relatives, the problems encountered by their children in strange schools and playgrounds, in some situations even with outdoor toilets. With so many people living among strangers and in unstable circumstances it is not surprising that crime, juvenile delinquency, and prostitution increased, as indeed they did in other parts of the country too.

Newly married wives of soldiers and sailors (known generally as "war brides") often followed their husbands to training camps, where life was often as difficult as it was around defense plants. Those who did not faced other problems—adjusting to being married without having had much experience of marriage, loneliness, and worry. Whatever their own behavior, war brides quickly learned that society applied a double standard to infidelity, especially when it involved a man presumably risking his life in some far-off land. There was a general relaxation of sexual inhibitions, part of a decades-long trend but accelerated by the war. So many hasty marriages, followed by long periods of separation, also brought a rise in divorces, from about 170 per thousand marriages in 1941 to 310 per thousand in 1945.

Of course "ordinary" housewives also had to deal with shortages, ration books, and other inconveniences during the war. In addition most took on other duties and bore other burdens, such as tending "victory gardens" and preserving their harvests, using crowded public transportation when there was no gas for the family car, mending and patching old clothes when new ones were unavailable, participating in salvage drives, and doing volunteer work for hospitals, the Red Cross, or various civil defense and servicemen's centers.

ALLIED STRATEGY: EUROPE FIRST

Only days after Pearl Harbor, Prime Minister Churchill and his military chiefs met in Washington with Roosevelt and his advisers. In every quarter of the globe, disaster threatened. The Japanese were gobbling up the Far East. Hitler's armies, checked outside Leningrad and Moscow, were preparing for a massive attack in the direction of Stalingrad, on the Volga River. German divisions under General

Erwin Rommel were beginning a drive across North Africa toward the Suez Canal. U-boats were taking a heavy toll in the North Atlantic. British and American leaders believed that eventually they could muster enough force to smash their enemies, but whether or not the troops already in action could hold out until this force arrived was an open question.

The decision of the strategists was to concentrate first against the Germans. Japan's conquests were in remote and, from the Allied point of view, relatively unimportant regions. If Russia surrendered, Hitler could throw all of German might against Great Britain. If it were defeated, Hitler's position in Europe might prove impregnable.

But how to strike at Hitler? American leaders wanted a second front in France, at least by 1943, and the Russians, with their backs to the wall and bearing the full weight of the German war machine, heartily agreed. Churchill, however, was more concerned with protecting Britain's overseas possessions than with easing the pressure on the Soviet Union. He advocated instead air bombardment of German industry combined with an attempt to drive the Germans out of North Africa, and his argument carried the day.

During the summer of 1942 Allied planes began to bomb German cities. In a crescendo through 1943 and 1944, British and American bombers pulverized the centers of Nazi might. While air attacks did not destroy the German army's capacity to fight, they hampered war production, tangled communications, and brought the war home to the German people in awesome fashion. Humanitarians deplored the heavy loss of life among the civilian population, but the response of the realists was that Hitler had begun indiscriminate bombing, and victory depended on smashing the German war machine.

In November 1942 an Allied army commanded by General Dwight D. Eisenhower struck at French North Africa. After the fall of France, the Nazis had set up a puppet regime in those parts of France not occupied by their troops, with headquarters at Vichy in central France. This collaborationist Vichy government controlled French North Africa. But the North African commandant, Admiral Jean Darlan, promptly switched sides when Eisenhower's forces landed. After a brief show of resistance, the French surrendered.

The Allies were willing to do business with Darlan despite his record as a collaborator. This angered General Charles de Gaulle, who had organized a government in exile immediately after the collapse of France and who considered himself the true representative of the French people. Many Americans agreed with de Gaulle, but the arrangement with Darlan paid large dividends. Eisenhower was able to press forward quickly against the Germans. In February 1943 at Kasserine Pass in the desert south of Tunis, American tanks met Rommel's Afrika Korps.

World War II, European Theater

The battle ended in a standoff, but with British troops closing in from their Egyptian bases to the east, the Germans were soon trapped and crushed. In May, after Rommel had been recalled to Germany, his army surrendered.

In July 1943, while air attacks on Germany continued and the Russians slowly pushed the Germans back from the gates of Stalingrad, the Allies invaded Sicily from Africa. In September they advanced to the Italian mainland. Mussolini had already fallen from power and his successor, Marshal Pietro Badoglio, surrendered. However, the German troops in Italy threw up an almost impregnable defense across the rugged Italian peninsula. The Anglo-American army inched forward, paying heavily for every advance. Monte Cassino, halfway between Naples and Rome, did not fall until May 1944, the capital itself not until June; months of hard fighting remained before the country was cleared of Germans. The Italian campaign was an Allied disappointment even though it weakened the enemy.

GERMANY OVERWHELMED

By the time the Allies had taken Rome, the mighty army needed to invade France had been collected in England under Eisenhower's command. On D-day, June 6, 1944, the assault forces stormed ashore at five points along the coast of Normandy, supported by a great armada and thousands of planes and paratroops. Against fierce but ill-coordinated German resistance, they established a beach-head: Within a few weeks a million troops were on French soil.

Thereafter victory was assured, though nearly a year of hard fighting lay ahead. In August the American Third Army under General George S. Patton, an eccentric but brilliant field commander, erupted southward into Brittany and then veered east toward Paris. Another Allied army invaded France from the Mediterranean in mid-August and advanced rapidly north. Free French troops were given the honor of liberating Paris on August 25. Belgium was cleared by British and Canadian units a few days later. By mid-September the Allies were fighting on the edge of Germany itself.

The front now stretched from the Netherlands along the borders of Belgium, Luxembourg, and France all the way to Switzerland. If the Allies had mounted a

(text continues on page 928)

A second wave of American troops approaching code-named Omaha Beach at Normandy. The first wave had become entangled in obstacles and proved to be easy targets for the Germans, dug into the cliffs ahead. By the end of the day, 2000 of the Americans at Omaha Beach were dead or wounded, but a beachhead had been established.

Saving Private Ryan

Steven Spielberg's *Saving Private Ryan* (1998), starring Tom Hanks, has been widely praised as the most realistic combat movie ever made. This judgment is based chiefly on its re-creation of the June 6, 1944, Allied assault on Omaha Beach during the invasion of Normandy. The camera focuses on Hanks, rain dripping from helmet, huddled in a crowded landing vessel. Explosions rumble in the distance. The ship plows through heavy seas toward a blackened brow of land (see the photograph on page 925) Around him, men vomit. Explosions become louder and sharper. Nearby ships strike mines and blow up; others are obliterated by shell fire. Hanks's landing craft lurches to avoid the mayhem. Like hail against a tin roof, gunfire riddles the landing craft. Some of the men are hit, and the others hunch lower, still vomiting. A deafening din envelops the ship as its bow opens. A curtain of bullets instantly cuts down the men in front. Hanks and several others leap into the sea. They sink: the ship has stopped far short of the beach. As bullets tear into the water, ripping into those still submerged, Hanks struggles to the surface. He swims, weaponless, toward the beach.

He has crossed the threshold of hell, and over the next 15 minutes viewers descend with him the rest of the way.

Saving Private Ryan differs from other combat films not in the graphic horror of the bloodshed, but in its randomness. The audience expects Hanks to survive the opening scenes of the movie in which he stars, and he does. But all other bets are off: a valiant exploit, a kind gesture, a handsome face—none influences the grim lottery of battle. A medic frenziedly works on a severely wounded man, injecting morphine, compressing arteries, and binding wounds. "Why can't you bastards give us a chance!" the medic screams. That is the point: When huge armies converge, hurling high explosives and steel at each other, one's chances of survival are unaffected by ethics or aesthetics.

But having made this point with heart-pounding emphasis, the movie subverts it. Hanks, unnerved and dispirited, for a time hunkers down in the relative safety of the seawall. Then he begins to do his job and others rally around him. They blast a hole through obstacles, crawl toward the concrete fortifications above, penetrate trench defenses, blow up bunkers, and seize the hill. Many perish in the effort; Hanks, an infantry captain, is among the survivors.

Then comes a new mission, which occupies the remainder of the movie. George C. Marshall, U.S. Army Chief of Staff, has learned of a Mrs. Ryan who has been notified on a single day that three of her sons were killed in action. Her fourth son, James, a private in the 101st Airborne, has just been parachuted into Normandy behind German lines. Marshall orders that he be returned to safety. This mission is given to Hanks and the eight surviving members of his platoon. They march inland, encounter snipers, ambushes, and, in the final scenes, a large detachment of German armored vehicles. But they also find Private Ryan (played by Matt Damon).

Along the way, the movie asks many provocative questions, such as whether war improves those who fight. "I think this is all good for me, sir," one earnest soldier confides to Hanks. "Really," Hanks says with a faint smile, "how is that?" The soldier cites Ralph Waldo Emerson: "War educates the senses. Calls into action the will. Perfects the physical constitution." "Emerson had a way of finding the bright side," Hanks deadpans, and the movie endorses his cynicism. Delirious and catatonic soldiers stumble across the battlefield. Others, terrified and jittery, shoot enemy soldiers that have surrendered. A sniper, intoning Old Testament verses, takes aim at unsuspecting enemies. Hanks's hand twitches uncontrollably, a physical manifestation of a disordered soul. War, demonstrably, has not made men better.

Except in one sense, and that may be all that matters: Hanks and his men have repeatedly demonstrated a willingness to give up their lives for others. Indeed, the movie's central dilemma concerns the moral arithmetic of sacrifice. Is it right to risk eight men to save one? To send a thousand men to near certain death in an initial assault to improve the chances of those that fol-

Tom Hanks, Matt Damon, and Edward Burns in Saving Private Ryan.

Three U.S. soldiers on the Normandy beaches.

low? To make one generation endure hell so that another may have freedom? The movie provides no ready answers. But in nearly the final scene it does issue a challenge. Hanks, mortally wounded, is lying amidst the corpses of his platoon, and he beckons to Ryan, who is unhurt. "Earn this," Hanks says, vaguely gesturing to the others.

Saving Private Ryan was part of a wave of nostalgic appreciation during the 1990s for the generation that had won World War II. A spate of books, movies, and TV-documentaries were other expressions of this phenomenon. On accepting the Oscar for his film, Spielberg thanked his father, a World War II vet, "for showing me that there is honor in looking back and respecting the past."

But respect for the past entails getting it right, and the movie makes some significant errors and omissions. For one, it suggests that the men huddled at the base of the seawall blew up the concrete bunkers on their own. This was not possible. In fact, commanders of destroyers took their ships close to the beaches and fired countless heavy shells into the fortifications, allowing the infantry to move up the hills.

The movie also shows the German soldiers as uniformly expert and professional. But the German army had been decimated by losses in Russia. The army manning the Normandy defenses included many units composed mostly of old men, boys, or conscripted soldiers from Poland or Russia. Many surrendered as soon as they encountered American soldiers.

Yet the movie provides a fair rendering of many other elements of the battle: the inaccuracy of aerial bombing, which missed most of the beach fortifications; the confusion caused when hundreds of landing craft failed to reach their destination; the destruction of scores of gliders, which crashed into high hedgerows while attempting to land behind German lines.

Saving Private Ryan captures the effect of war on soldiers. Many men at Omaha Beach, like those depicted in the movie, were shattered by the experience. One private, nearly hit by a shell, recalled that he burst into tears. "My buddies got me behind a burned-out craft, where I cried for what seemed like hours. I cried until tears would no longer come. To this day I've never shed another." Other men confessed that, after the terror of a firefight, they shot Germans who had raised their arms in surrender. "In my opinion any enemy shot during this intense action had waited too long to surrender," one G.I. declared.

Yet through it all, some men, like the captain portrayed by Hanks, drew heroism from some unfathomed depths of the soul. One real soldier at Omaha Beach remembered "a captain and two lieutenants who demonstrated courage beyond belief as they struggled to bring order to the chaos around them."

Saving Private Ryan is not a fully accurate representation of the attack on Omaha Beach, but it depicts—realistically and memorably— how soldiers conferred meaning on the heedless calculus of modern warfare.

massive assault at any one point, as the British Field Marshal Bernard Montgomery urged, the struggle might have been brought to a quick conclusion. Although the two armies were roughly equal in size, the Allies had complete control of the air and 20 times as many tanks as the foe. The pressure of the advancing Russians on the eastern front made it difficult for the Germans to reinforce their troops in the west. But General Eisenhower believed a concentrated attack too risky. He prepared instead for a general advance.

While he was regrouping, the Germans on December 16 launched a counterattack, planned by Hitler himself, against the Allied center in the Ardennes Forest. The Germans hoped to break through to the Belgian port of Antwerp, thereby splitting the Allied armies in two. The plan was foolhardy and therefore unexpected, and it almost succeeded. The Germans drove a salient ("the bulge") about 50 miles into Belgium. But once the element of surprise had been overcome, their chance of breaking through to the sea was lost. Eisenhower concen-

On February 13 and 14, 1945, British and American incendiary bombs razed Dresden, the cultural capital of Germany. Some 35,000 perished. The purpose of the raid was to terrorize and demoralize the German people; the city's few war industries were not even targeted. This picture was taken more than a year after the bombing.

**Nazi Concentration
Camps**

trated first on preventing them from broadening the break in his lines and then on blunting the point of their advance. By late January 1945 the old line had been reestablished.

The Battle of the Bulge cost the United States 77,000 casualties and delayed Eisenhower's offensive, but it exhausted the Germans' last reserves. The Allies then pressed forward to the Rhine, winning a bridgehead on the far bank of the river on March 7. Thereafter, another German city fell almost daily. With the Russians racing westward against crumbling resistance, the end could not be long delayed. In April, American and Russian forces made contact at the Elbe River. A few days later, with Russian shells reducing his capital to rubble, Hitler, by then probably insane, took his own life in his Berlin air raid shelter. On May 8 Germany surrendered.

As the Americans drove swiftly forward in the late stages of the war, they began to overrun Nazi concentration camps where millions of Jews had been murdered. The Americans were horrified by what they discovered, but they should not have been surprised. Word of this holocaust, in which no less than 6 million people were slaughtered, had reached the United States much earlier. At first the news had been dismissed as propaganda, then discounted as grossly exaggerated. Hitler was known to hate Jews and to have persecuted them, but that he could

Once into Germany the Third Army advanced so quickly in the spring of 1945 that it came upon military installations almost without warning. The photograph here is of General Dwight D. Eisenhower inspecting the condition of the concentration camp at Gotha, Germany, where slain inmates had been left unburied by their fleeing captors.

order the murder of millions of innocent people, even children, seemed beyond belief. By 1943, however, the truth could not be denied.

Little could be done about those already in the camps, but there were thousands of refugees in occupied Europe who might have been spirited to safety. President Roosevelt declined to make the effort; he even refused to bomb the Auschwitz death camp in Poland or the rail lines used to bring victims to its gas chambers on the grounds that the destruction of German soldiers and military equipment took precedence over any other objective. Thus, when American journalists entered the camps with the advancing troops, saw the heaps of still-unburied corpses, and talked with the emaciated survivors, their reports caused a storm of protest in America. Why Roosevelt acted as he did has never been satisfactorily explained.

THE NAVAL WAR IN THE PACIFIC

Defeating Germany first had not meant abandoning the Pacific region entirely to the Japanese. While armies were being trained and material accumulated for the

European struggle, much of the available American strength was diverted to maintaining vital communications in the Far East and preventing further Japanese expansion.

The navy's aircraft carriers had escaped destruction at Pearl Harbor, a stroke of immense good fortune because, without most tacticians realizing it, the airplane had revolutionized naval warfare. Commanders discovered that carrier-based planes were far more effective against warships than the heaviest naval artillery because of their greater range and more concentrated firepower. Battleships made excellent gun platforms from which to pound shore installations and support land operations, but aircraft were of prime importance against other vessels.

This truth was demonstrated in May 1942 in the Battle of the Coral Sea. Having captured an empire in a few months without the loss of any warship larger than a destroyer, the Japanese believed the war already won. This led them to overextend themselves.

The Coral Sea lies northeast of Australia and south of New Guinea and the Solomon Islands. Japanese mastery of these waters would cut Australia off from

World War II, Pacific Theater

Hawaii and thus from American aid. Admiral Isoroku Yamamoto had dispatched a large fleet of troopships screened by many warships to attack Port Moresby, on the southern New Guinea coast. On May 7–8 planes from the American carriers *Lexington* and *Yorktown* struck the convoy's screen, sinking a small carrier and damaging a large one. Superficially, the battle seemed a victory for the Japanese, for their planes mortally wounded the *Lexington* and sank two other ships, but the troop transports had been forced to turn back—Port Moresby was saved. Although large numbers of cruisers and destroyers took part in the action, none came within sight or gun range of an enemy ship. All the destruction was wrought by carrier aircraft.

Encouraged by the Coral Sea "victory," Yamamoto decided to force the American fleet into a showdown battle by assaulting the Midway Islands, west of Hawaii. His armada never reached its destination. Between June 4 and 7 control of the central Pacific was decided entirely by air power. American dive bombers sank four large Japanese carriers. About 300 Japanese planes were destroyed. The United States lost only the *Yorktown* and a destroyer. Thereafter the initiative in the Pacific war shifted to the Americans, but victory came slowly and at painful cost.

American land forces were under the command of Douglas MacArthur, a brilliant but egocentric general whose judgment was sometimes distorted by his intense concern for his own reputation. MacArthur was in command of American troops in the Philippine Islands when the Japanese struck in December 1941. After his heroic but hopeless defense of Manila and the Bataan peninsula, President Roosevelt had him evacuated by PT boat to escape capture.

Thereafter MacArthur was obsessed with the idea of personally leading an American army back to the Philippines. Although many strategists believed that the islands should be bypassed in the drive on the Japanese homeland, in the end MacArthur convinced the Joint Chiefs of Staff, to liberate the island. Two separate drives were undertaken, one from New Guinea toward the Philippines under MacArthur, the other through the central Pacific toward Tokyo under Admiral Chester W. Nimitz.

ISLAND HOPPING

Before commencing this two-pronged advance, the Americans had to eject the Japanese from the Solomon Islands in order to protect Australia from a flank attack. Beginning in August 1942, a series of land, sea, and air battles raged around Guadalcanal Island in this archipelago. Once again American airpower was decisive, although the bravery and skill of the ground forces that actually won the island must not be underemphasized. American pilots, better trained and with tougher planes than the Japanese, had a relatively easier task. They inflicted losses five to six times heavier on the enemy than they sustained themselves. Japanese airpower disintegrated progressively during the long battle, and this in turn helped the fleet to take a heavy toll on the Japanese navy. By February 1943 Guadalcanal had been secured.

In the autumn of 1943 the American drives toward Japan and the Philippines got under way at last. In the central Pacific campaign the Guadalcanal action was repeated on a smaller but equally bloody scale from Tarawa in the Gilbert Islands to Kwajelein and Eniwetok in the Marshalls. The Japanese soldiers on these islands fought for every foot of ground. They had to be blasted and burned from tunnels and concrete pillboxes with hand grenades, flamethrowers, and dynamite. They almost never surrendered. But Admiral Nimitz's forces were in every case victorious. By midsummer of 1944 this arm of the American advance had taken Saipan and Guam in the Marianas. Now land-based bombers were within range of Tokyo.

Meanwhile, MacArthur was leapfrogging along the New Guinea coast toward the Philippines. In October 1944 he made good his promise to return to the islands, landing on Leyte, south of Luzon. Two great naval clashes in Philippine waters, the Battle of the Philippine Sea (June 1944) and the Battle for Leyte Gulf (October 1944), completed the destruction of Japan's sea power and reduced its air force to a band of fanatical suicide pilots called *kamikazes,* who tried to crash bomb-laden planes against American warships and airstrips. The *kamikazes* caused much damage but could not turn the tide. In February 1945 MacArthur liberated Manila.

The end was now inevitable. B-29 Superfortress bombers from the Marianas rained high explosives and firebombs on Japan. The islands of Iwo Jima and Okinawa, only a few hundred miles from Tokyo, fell to the Americans in March and June 1945. But such was the tenacity of the Japanese soldiers that it seemed possible that it would take another year of fighting and a million more American casualties to subdue the main Japanese islands.

BUILDING THE ATOM BOMB

At this point came the most controversial decision of the entire war, and it was made by a newcomer on the world scene. In November 1944 Roosevelt had been elected to a fourth term, easily defeating Thomas E. Dewey. Instead of renominating Henry A. Wallace for vice president, whom conservatives considered too radical, the Democratic convention had nominated Senator Harry S Truman of Missouri, a reliable party man well liked by professional politicians. Then, in April 1945, President Roosevelt died of a cerebral hemorrhage. Thus it was Truman, a man painfully conscious of his limitations yet equally aware of the power and responsibility of his office, who had to decide what to do when, in July 1945, American scientists placed in his hands a new and awful weapon, the atomic bomb.

After Roosevelt had responded to Albert Einstein's warning in 1939, government-sponsored atomic research had proceeded rapidly, especially after the establishment of the so-called Manhattan Project in May 1943. The manufacture of the element plutonium at Hanford, Washington, and of uranium 235 at Oak Ridge, Tennessee, continued, along with the design and construction of a transportable atomic bomb at Los Alamos, New Mexico, under the direction of J. Robert Oppenheimer. Almost $2 billion was spent before a successful bomb was exploded at Alamogordo, in the New Mexican desert, on July 16, 1945. As that first mushroom cloud formed over the desert, Oppenheimer recalled the prophetic words of the ancient Hindu text, the *Bhagavad Gita:* "I am become death, the shatterer of worlds."

Should a bomb with the destructive force of 20,000 tons of TNT be employed against Japan? By striking a major city, its dreadful power could be demonstrated convincingly, yet doing so would bring death to tens of thousands of Japanese civilians. Many of the scientists who had made the bomb now argued against its use. Others suggested alerting the Japanese and then staging a demonstration explosion at sea, but that idea was discarded because of concern that the bomb might fail to explode.

Truman was torn between his awareness that the bomb was "the most terrible thing ever discovered" and his hope that using it "would bring the war to an end." The bomb might cause a revolution in Japan, might lead the emperor to intervene, might even persuade the military to give up. Considering the hundreds of thousands of Americans who would surely die in any conventional invasion of Japan and, on a less humane level, influenced by a desire to end the Pacific war before the Soviet Union could intervene effectively and thus claim a role in the peacemaking, the president chose to go ahead.

The moral soundness of Truman's decision has been debated ever since. There is no doubt that hatred of the Japanese had something to do with the decision. What is often forgotten by those who deplore it is the fact that while the immediate result was the death of many thousands of innocent Japanese civilians, far more Japanese would have died—many more than the Americans who would have perished—if Japan had had to be invaded.

Hiroshima's Museum of Science and Industry was reduced to a skeleton in the atomic bomb blast. City officials decided to preserve the wreckage as a memorial.

Truman and all his key military and civilian advisers really had no choice. Imagine the public reaction if the bomb had not been used and if an invasion of Japan had resulted in hundreds of thousands of American casualties. In any case, on August 6 the Superfortress *Enola Gay* dropped an atomic bomb on Hiroshima, killing about 78,000 persons (including 20 American prisoners of war) and injuring nearly 100,000 more out of a population of 344,000. Over 96 percent of the buildings in the city were destroyed or damaged. Three days later, while the stunned Japanese still hesitated, a second atomic bomb, the only other one that had so far been assembled, blasted Nagasaki. This second drop was less defensible morally, but it had the desired result. On August 15 Japan surrendered.

Thus ended the greatest war in history. Its cost was beyond calculation. No accurate count could be made even of the dead; we know only that the total was in the neighborhood of 20 million. As in World War I, American casualties—291,000 battle deaths and 671,000 wounded—were smaller than those of the other major belligerents. About 7.5 million Russians died in battle, 3.5 million Germans, 1.2 million Japanese, and 2.2 million Chinese; Britain and France, despite much smaller populations, suffered losses almost as large as did the United States. And far more than in World War I, American resources, human and material, had made victory possible.

No one could account the war a benefit to humanity, but in the late summer of 1945 the future looked bright. Fascism was dead. The successful wartime diplomatic dealings of Roosevelt, Churchill, and the Soviet dictator, Joseph Stalin, encouraged many to hope that the communists were ready to cooperate in

Nagasaki under atomic bomb attack on August 9, 1945. Two planes of the 20th Air Force participated in the mission—one to carry the bomb, the other to serve as an escort. The new atomic age had begun.

rebuilding Europe. In the United States isolationism had disappeared; the message of Wendell Willkie's best-selling *One World,* written after a globe-circling tour made by the 1940 Republican presidential candidate at the behest of President Roosevelt in 1942, appeared to have been absorbed by the majority of the people.

Out of the death and destruction had come technological developments that seemed to herald a better world as well as a peaceful one. Improvements in surgery and other medical advances gave promise of saving millions of lives, and the development of penicillin and other antibiotics, which had greatly reduced the death rate among troops, would perhaps banish all infectious diseases.

Above all, there was the power of the atom. The force that seared Hiroshima and Nagasaki could be harnessed to serve peaceful needs, the scientists promised, with results that might free humanity forever from poverty and toil. The period of reconstruction would be prolonged, but with all the great powers adhering to the new United Nations charter, drafted at San Francisco in June 1945, international cooperation could be counted on to ease the burdens of the victims of war and help the poor and underdeveloped parts of the world toward economic and political independence. Such at least was the hope of millions in the victorious summer of 1945.

WARTIME DIPLOMACY

That hope was not to be realized, in large part because of a conflict that developed between the Soviet Union and the western Allies. During the course of World War II every instrument of mass persuasion in the country had been directed toward convincing the people that the Russians were fighting America's battle as well as their own. Even before Pearl Harbor, former Ambassador Joseph E. Davies wrote in his best-selling *Mission to Moscow* (1941) that the communist leaders were "a group of able, strong men" with "honest convictions and integrity of purposes" who were "devoted to the cause of peace for both ideological and practical reasons." Communism was based "on the same principle of the 'brotherhood of man' which Jesus preached."

During the war Americans with as different points of view as General Douglas MacArthur and Vice President Henry A. Wallace took strongly pro-Soviet positions, and American newspapers and magazines published many laudatory articles about Russia. *Life* reported that Russians "think like Americans." In 1943 *Time* named Stalin its Man of the Year. The film *Mission to Moscow,* a whitewash of the dreadful Moscow treason trials of the 1930s based on Ambassador Davies's book, portrayed Stalin as a wise, grandfatherly type, puffing comfortably on an old pipe. In *One World* (1943) Wendell Willkie wrote glowingly of the Russian people, their "effective society," and their simple, warmhearted leader. When Willkie suggested jokingly to Stalin that if he continued to make progress in improving the education of his people he might educate himself out of a job, the dictator "threw his head back and laughed and laughed," Willkie recorded.

These views of the character of Joseph Stalin were naive, to say the least, but the identity of interest of the United States and the Soviet Union was very real during the war. The Soviets repeatedly expressed a willingness to cooperate with the Allies in dealing with postwar problems. Russia was one of the 26 signers of the Declaration of the United Nations (January 1942), in which the Allies promised to eschew territorial aggrandizement after the war, to respect the right of all peoples to determine their own form of government, to work for freer trade and international economic cooperation, and to force the disarmament of the aggressor nations.

In May 1943 the Soviet Union dissolved the Comintern, its official agency for the promulgation of world revolution. The following October, during a conference in Moscow with the Allies, Soviet Foreign Minister V. M. Molotov joined in setting up a European Advisory Commission to divide Germany into occupation zones after the war. That December, at a conference held in Teheran, Iran, Roosevelt, Churchill, and Stalin discussed plans for a new league of nations. When Roosevelt described the kind of world organization he envisaged, the Russian dictator offered a number of constructive suggestions.

Between August and October 1944, Allied representatives met at Dumbarton Oaks, outside Washington. The chief Russian delegate, Andrei A. Gromyko, opposed limiting the use of the veto by the great powers on the future United

Churchill, Roosevelt, and Stalin photographed at the week-long Yalta conference in February 1945. By April 1945, Roosevelt was dead.

Nations (UN) Security Council, but he did not take a deliberately obstructionist position. At a conference held at Yalta in the Crimea in February 1945 Stalin joined Roosevelt and Churchill in the call for a meeting in April at San Francisco to draft a charter for the UN. "We argued freely and frankly across the table," Roosevelt reported later. "But at the end, on every point, unanimous agreement was reached. I may say we achieved a unity of thought and a way of getting along together." Privately Roosevelt characterized Stalin as "a very interesting man" whose rough exterior clothed an "old-fashioned elegant European manner." He referred to him almost affectionately as "that old buzzard" and on one occasion called him "Uncle Joe" to his face. At Yalta, Stalin gave Roosevelt a portrait photograph, with a long Cyrillic inscription in his small, tightly written hand.

The UN charter drafted at the 50-nation San Francisco Conference gave each UN member a seat in the General Assembly, a body designed for discussion rather than action. The locus of authority in the new organization resided in the Security Council, "the castle of the great powers." This consisted of five permanent members (the United States, the Soviet Union, Great Britain, France, and China) and six others elected for two-year terms.

The Security Council was charged with responsibility for maintaining world peace, but any great power could block UN action whenever it wished to do so. The United States insisted on this veto power as strongly as the Soviet Union did. In effect the charter paid lip service to the Wilsonian ideal of a powerful international police force, but it incorporated the limitations that Henry Cabot Lodge had proposed in his 1919 reservation to Article X of the League Covenant, which relieved the United States from the obligation of enforcing collective security without the approval of Congress.

ALLIED SUSPICION OF STALIN

Long before the war in Europe ended, however, the Allies had clashed over important policy matters. Most Allied leaders, including Roosevelt, admitted privately during the war that the Soviet Union would annex territory and possess preponderant power in Eastern Europe after the defeat of Germany, but they never said this publicly. They believed that free governments could somehow be created in countries like Poland and Bulgaria that the Soviets would trust enough to leave to their own devices. "The Poles," Winston Churchill said early in 1945, "will have their future in their own hands, with the single limitation that they must honestly follow . . . a policy friendly to Russia. This is surely reasonable."

However reasonable, Churchill's statement was impractical. The Polish question was a terribly difficult one. The war, after all, had been triggered by the German attack on Poland; the British in particular felt a moral obligation to restore that nation to its prewar independence. During the war a Polish government in exile was set up in London, and its leaders were determined—especially after the discovery in 1943 of the murder of some 5000 Polish officers several years earlier at Katyn, in Russia, presumably by the Soviet secret police—to make no concessions to Soviet territorial demands. Public opinion in Poland (and indeed in all the states along Russia's western frontier) was not so much anti-Soviet as anti-Russian. Yet the Soviet Union's legitimate interests (to say nothing of its power in the area) could not be ignored.

YALTA AND POTSDAM

At the Yalta Conference, Roosevelt and Churchill agreed to Soviet annexation of large sections of eastern Poland. In return they demanded that free elections be held in Poland itself. "I want this election to be . . . beyond question," Roosevelt told Stalin. "It should be like Caesar's wife." In a feeble attempt at a joke he added: "I did not know her but they said she was pure." Stalin agreed, almost certainly without intending to keep his promise. The elections were never held; Poland was run by a pro-Soviet puppet regime.

Stalin apparently could not understand why his allies were so concerned about the fate of a small country remote from their strategic spheres. That they professed to be concerned seemed to him an indication that they had some secret, devious purpose. He could see no difference (and "revisionist" American historians agree with him) between the Soviet Union's dominating Poland and maintaining a government there that did not reflect the wishes of a majority of the Polish people and the United States's dominating many Latin American nations and supporting unpopular regimes within them. Roosevelt, however, was worried about the political effects that Soviet control of Poland might have in the United States. Polish Americans would be furious if the United States allowed the Russians to control their homeland.

But had Roosevelt described the difficulties to the Poles and the rest of the American people more frankly, their reaction might have been less angry. In any case, when he realized that Stalin was going to act as he pleased, Roosevelt was furious. "We can't do business with Stalin," he said shortly before his death in April 1945. "He has broken every one of the promises he made at Yalta." In July 1945, following the surrender of Germany, the new president, Harry Truman, met with Stalin and Churchill at Potsdam, outside Berlin. Stalin rejected all arguments that he loosen his hold on Eastern Europe, and Truman (who received news of the successful testing of the atom bomb while at Potsdam) made no concessions. But he was impressed by Stalin. The dictator was "smart as hell," he wrote in his diary. "Stalin was an SOB," the plainspoken president explained to some officers while returning to the United States from Potsdam on the cruiser *Augusta*. Then he added: "Of course he thinks I'm one too."

On both sides suspicions were mounting, positions hardening. Yet all the advantages seemed to be with the United States. Was this not, as Henry Luce, the publisher of *Time* had declared, "the American century," an era when American power and American ideals would shape the course of events the world over? Besides its army, navy, and air force and its immense industrial potential, among the nations the United States alone possessed the atomic bomb.

MILESTONES

1941   Roosevelt creates Fair Employment Practices Committee (FEPC)

Japanese attack on Pearl Harbor

1942   West coast Japanese ordered to relocation camps

Fall of the Philippines

Battle of the Coral Sea

Battle of Midway

American troops invade North Africa

1943   Manhattan Project to make atomic bomb

Race riots in Detroit and Los Angeles

Invasion of Italy

Teheran Conference

1944   Allied invasion of Normandy, France

Liberation of Paris

Battle of the Bulge

1945   Yalta Conference

San Francisco Conference to draft UN Charter

Germany surrenders (V-E Day)

Capture of Okinawa

Atom bomb tested at Alamogordo, New Mexico

Potsdam Conference

Atom bombs dropped on Hiroshima and Nagasaki, Japan

Japan surrenders (V-J Day)

29

THE AMERICAN CENTURY

I n late 1945 most Americans were probably more concerned with what was happening at home than with foreign developments, and no one was more aware of this than Harry Truman. When he received the news of Roosevelt's death, he claimed that he felt as though "the moon, the stars, and all the planets" had suddenly fallen upon him. Although he could not have been quite as surprised as he indicated (Roosevelt was known to have been in extremely poor health), he was acutely conscious of his own limitations.

Truman was born in Missouri in 1884. After his service in a World War I artillery unit, he opened a men's clothing store in Kansas City. The store failed in the postwar depression. Truman then became a minor cog in the political machine of Democratic boss Tom Pendergast. In 1934 he was elected to the United States Senate, where he proved to be a loyal but obscure New Dealer. He first attracted national attention during World War II when his "watchdog" committee on defense spending, working with devotion and efficiency, saved the government immense sums. This led to his nomination and election as vice president.

As president, Truman sought to carry on in the Roosevelt tradition. Curiously, he was at the same time humble and cocky, even brash—both idealistic and cold-bloodedly political. He adopted liberal objectives only to pursue them sometimes by rash, even repressive means. Too often he insulted opponents instead of convincing or appeasing them. Complications tended to confuse him, in which case he either dug in his heels or struck out blindly, usually with unfortunate results. On balance, however, he was a strong and in many ways a successful president.

THE POSTWAR ECONOMY

Nearly all the postwar leaders were worried by the possibility of a serious depression, and nearly all accepted the necessity of employing federal authority to stabilize the economy and speed national development. The Great Depression and the huge government expenditures made necessary by the war had proven the theories of John Maynard Keynes and convinced Democrats and Republicans alike that it was possible to prevent sharp swings in the business cycle and therefore to do away with serious unemployment by monetary and fiscal manipulation.

When World War II ended, nearly everyone wanted to demobilize the armed forces, remove wartime controls, and reduce taxes. Yet everyone also hoped to prevent any sudden economic dislocation, to check inflation, and to make sure that goods in short supply were fairly distributed. Neither the politicians nor the public was able to reconcile these conflicting objectives. Labor wanted price controls retained but wage controls lifted; industrialists wished to raise prices and keep the lid on wages. Farmers wanted subsidies but opposed price controls and the extension of social security benefits to agricultural workers.

In this difficult situation President Truman failed to win either the confidence of the people or the support of Congress. On the one hand, he proposed a comprehensive program of new legislation that included a public housing scheme, aid to education, medical insurance, civil rights guarantees, a higher minimum wage, broader social security coverage, additional conservation and public power projects patterned after the TVA, increased aid to agriculture, and the retention of anti-inflationary controls. On the other hand, he ended rationing and other controls and signed a bill cutting taxes by some $6 billion. Whenever opposition to his plans developed, he vacillated between compromise and inflexibility.

Yet the country weathered the reconversion period with remarkable ease. The pent-up demand for houses, automobiles, clothing, washing machines, and countless other products, backed by the war-enforced savings of millions, kept factories operating at capacity. Economists had feared that the flood of millions of veterans into the job market would cause serious unemployment. But when the veterans returned (more than 60,000 of them accompanied by foreign brides), few went without work for long. Because of the boom, the demand for labor was large and growing. In addition, the government made an unprecedented educational opportunity available to veterans. Instead of a general bonus, which would have stimulated consumption and inflation, in 1944 Congress passed the GI Bill of Rights, which made subsidies available to veterans so they could continue their educations, learn new trades, or start new businesses. Nearly 8 million veterans took advantage of the education and training grants, greatly to their long-term advantage, and thus to the country's.

In June 1947 Congress, now with a Republican majority, passed the Taft-Hartley Act over the veto of President Truman. The measure outlawed the closed shop (a provision written into many labor contracts requiring new workers to join the union before they could be employed) and declared illegal secondary boycotts and strikes called as a result of disputes between unions over the right to represent workers. Most important, it authorized the president to seek court injunctions to prevent strikes that in his opinion endangered the national interest. The injunctions would hold for 80 days—a "cooling-off" period during which a presidential fact-finding board could investigate and make recommendations. If the dispute remained unresolved after 80 days, the president was to recommend "appropriate action" to Congress.

The Taft-Hartley Act made the task of unionizing unorganized industries more difficult, but it did not seriously hamper existing unions. Although it outlawed the closed shop, it permitted union shop contracts, which forced new workers to join the union after accepting employment.

AT HOME AND AT WORK

The trend toward early marriage and a large family, begun during the war, continued and indeed accelerated when the conflict ended. In one year, 1946, more than 10 percent of all the single females over the age of 14 in the country got married. Government policies buttressed the inclinations of the people: to encourage taxpayers to have children, the federal government granted income tax deductions for dependents. The birthrate soared.

The period was marked by a cultural reaffirmation of domesticity. A 1947 survey by the *Woman's Home Companion* found that among possible careers, its readers favored nursing, clerical, retailing, and teaching because these jobs offered the best preparation for women's "prime objective": marriage. Popular magazines like *Woman's Home Companion* and the *Ladies' Home Journal*, full of articles such as "Keep Those Home Fires Burning—With Hobbies" and "See How to Knit a Baby Blanket," showed college-educated women how to make a "career" of home management and child development.

Scholars agreed that women belonged at home. In 1947 psychoanalyst Marynia Farnham explained that the female reproductive organs predisposed women to the protective and nurturing tasks of child rearing; women who pursued careers in the competitive world of business would forever be at odds with their bodies. Dr. Benjamin Spock, whose *Common Sense Guide to Baby and Child Care* first appeared in 1946 and sold 24 million copies during the next quarter century, insisted that a mother's most important job was to shore up her children's sense of self by providing continuous support and affection. Women who worked outside the home necessarily "neglected" their children. The child who was "mildly neglected," Spock added, was apt to grow up "mildly disturbed." Harvard sociologist Talcott Parsons, the leading social scientist of the era, found a yet more compelling justification for female domesticity. The evolution of modern industrial society, he maintained, was linked to the specialization of gender roles. Advanced societies benefited from women performing the "expressive" tasks of family life, and men, the "instrumental" tasks of running economic and political systems. Women who worked outside the home not only endangered the mental well-being of themselves and their children, but also retarded the progress of humanity.

Men were expected to cede management of the domestic sphere to women. Hollywood, its cameras pointed as ever directly at the concerns of audiences, underscored this point. In films such as *Life with Father* (1947), *Mr. Blandings Builds His Dream House* (1948), *Cheaper by the Dozen* (1950) and *Father of the Bride* (1950), irascible or befuddled patriarchs blunder into delicate family matters, only to be gently eased out of harm's way by their understanding and savvy wives. Television picked up on these and similar themes and hammered away at them each week in shows like Robert Young's ironically titled *Father Knows Best* (1954–1962) and Jackie Gleason's equally ironic take on working-class marriage, *The Honeymooners* (1953–1956). Even Lucille Ball and Vivian Vance, the screwball housewives in the popular sitcom *I Love Lucy* (1952–1957), had a better grasp of family dynamics than their stumblebum spouses.

Although men assumed prominent roles in some domestic rituals, such as presiding over the barbecue or carving the holiday turkey, their chief responsibility was to earn enough money to sustain the family. This was considerably easier than in the past. From 1949 through 1975, unemployment never exceeded 7 percent, and during the mid-1960s it fell well below 4 percent. For those who had lived during the Great Depression the dominant social fact of the postwar era was the availability of work. As early as 1948, half the United Auto Workers questioned by Columbia sociologist C. Wright Mills told him that they "hardly ever" worried about losing their jobs.

But the *character* of work was changing in unsettling ways. The Second World War accelerated the growth of giant corporations, whose complex, global operations were built on mountains of paper. Regiments of managers ran the systems, and vast armies of clerical workers processed the expanded flow of information. In 1870, 1 in 160 workers was employed in clerical work; by 1950, that figure was 1 in 8. One-fifth of all manufacturing employees worked in offices.

The shift in work patterns was reflected in the decline of sales as an occupation, and of the salesman as the exemplar of the entrepreneurial individualist. The moment was captured in Arthur Miller's *Death of a Salesman* (1949), a play that provided both the epitaph and explanation for the salesman's demise: Willy Loman (Low-man?) was a prickly loner, ill-equipped to take a place in the bland bureaucracies that were dominating the postwar economic landscape. Salesmen's functions were increasingly taken over by advertising departments. The salesman was replaced by the "organization man." The phrase came from sociologist William H. Whyte's 1956 best-selling book by that title. The organization man went to college, maintained a B average, joined sports teams and clubs, and found work in a large corporation. He subordinated his own interests, even his taste in clothes, to the requirements of the company. His wife was also affected by this pressure. In 1951 *Fortune* magazine cautioned her against drinking at company dinners because "it may go down in a dossier." "Be attractive," it added. "There is a strong correlation between executive success and the wife's appearance."

Blue-collar workers and clerical employees were not as subject to these pressures, but studies reveal that they did not differ in their attitudes toward marriage and child rearing. "The vast changes . . . are pervasive," two demographers concluded. "Social and economic variables . . . such as race, ethnic status, education and residence, do not indicate differences with respect to trends in fertility."

The growth of suburbs gave a geographic dimension to the changing roles of husbands and wives. In the postwar years the federal government encouraged single-family home construction by allowing home owners to deduct mortgage interest from their income taxes and by making low-cost mortgages available through the Federal Housing Administration.

New suburbs appeared almost like mushrooms after a spring rain. With their streets named after flowers or pleasant emotional states (the large postwar suburb of Levittown, near Philadelphia, featured Friendly Lane, Graceful Lane, Good Lane, and Shelter Lane), the suburbs were to function as havens for work-weary men.

This image, powerfully reiterated in television shows and films, sacrificed none of its allure because it was unrealistic. Impressed as a child with the prim family life depicted in *Leave It to Beaver,* the poet Gary Soto, who grew up in the Mexican-American *barrio* in Fresno, California, tried without success to persuade his family to dress for dinner.

In fact, the suburban world was unreal even for many of the women who inhabited it. More women were leaving the home during the day to find work in

A photograph of one of the two Levittown's (this one in New York), taken just three years after builder William Levitt commenced the development. He devised a 27-step system for mass-producing houses. The first was to lay the foundation; the last, to sweep the floors. At the peak of production, 30 houses were completed each day. The houses were cheap—most cost less than $8000—but Levitt nevertheless turned a profit of $1000 on each.

the burgeoning clerical and service sector. In 1940, only one in four civilian employees was female, one-third of them married. Three decades later, four in ten paid employees were women, two-thirds of them married. Perhaps 20 million women—after returning home from work, fixing dinner, putting the children to bed, and doing a load of laundry—collapsed in front of the television set and watched domestic heroines such as Donna Reed vacuuming the house in high heels and pearls, making clothes and cakes from scratch, soothing the fragile psyches of her husband and children, and otherwise living a fantasy that accorded with the views of Farnham, Spock, and Parsons.

THE CONTAINMENT POLICY

Although ordinary people seemed to concentrate almost compulsively on their personal affairs, foreign policy issues vexed the Truman presidency. Repeatedly Stalin made it clear that he had no intention of even consulting with Western leaders about his domination of Eastern Europe, and he seemed intent on extending his power deep into war-devastated central Europe. The Soviet Union also controlled Outer Mongolia, parts of Manchuria, and northern Korea, and it had annexed the Kurile Islands and regained the southern half of Sakhalin Island from Japan. It was fomenting trouble in Iran. By January 1946 Truman had decided to stop "babying" the Russians. "Only one language do they understand," he noted in a memorandum. "How many divisions have you?"

Truman's problem—and it would bedevil American policy makers for years—was that Stalin had far more divisions than anyone else. Truman, a seasoned politician, had swiftly responded to the postwar clamor to "bring the boys home." In the two years following the surrender of Japan, the armed forces of the United States had dwindled from 6 million to 1.5 million. Stalin, who kept domestic foes out of office by having them shot, ignored domestic pressure to demobilize the Red Army, estimated by U.S. intelligence at 5 million strong in 1947.

Stalin and the Red Army evoked the specter of Hitler's troops preparing to pour across the north European plains. Like Hitler, Stalin was a cruel dictator who championed an ideology of world conquest. Averill Harriman, American ambassador to the Soviet Union, warned that communist ideology exerted an "outward thrust" more dangerous than Nazism. George Kennan, a scholarly foreign officer who also had served in Moscow, thought that ideology was more symptom than cause. Marxism, he wrote, merely provided the intellectual "fig-leaf of morality and respectability" for naked Soviet aggression. In an influential article, "The Sources of Soviet Conduct," published anonymously in the July 1947 issue of *Foreign Affairs,* Kennan argued that the instability and illegitimacy of the Soviet regime generated explosive internal pressures. These forces, vented outward, would cause the USSR to expand "constantly, wherever it is permitted to move" until it filled "every nook and cranny available to it in the basin of world power." A policy of "long-term, patient but firm and vigilant containment" was the best means of dealing with the Soviet Union.

THE ATOM BOMB:
A "WINNING" WEAPON?

Although Truman authorized use of the atom bomb to force the surrender of Japan, he had hoped that a demonstration of the weapon's power also would inhibit Stalin and serve as a counterweight to the numerically superior Red Army. Stalin, however, refused to be intimidated. "Atomic bombs are meant to frighten those with weak nerves," he told advisers. His resolve had been stiffened as a result of Soviet espionage. Stalin knew that the American atomic arsenal— slightly more than a dozen bombs in 1947—was insufficient to destroy the Soviet Union's military machine.

The atomic bomb was a doubtful deterrent for another reason. Sobering accounts of the devastation of Hiroshima and Nagasaki and the suffering of the victims of radiation poisoning left many Americans uneasy. J. Robert Oppenheimer, director of the atom bomb design team, informed government officials that most scientists in the Manhattan Project would not continue such work. "I feel we have blood on our hands," he told President Truman. "Never mind," Truman snapped. "It'll all come out in the wash." Yet even Truman came to doubt whether the American people would again "permit" their president to use atomic weapons for aggressive purposes.

In November 1945 the United States suggested that the UN supervise all nuclear energy production, and the General Assembly created an Atomic Energy Commission to study the question. In June 1946 Commissioner Bernard Baruch offered a plan for the eventual outlawing of atomic weapons. Under this proposal UN inspectors operating without restriction anywhere in the world would ensure that no country made bombs clandestinely. When, at an unspecified date, the system was established successfully, the United States would destroy its stockpile of bombs.

Most Americans thought the Baruch plan magnanimous, and some considered it positively foolhardy, but the Soviets rejected it. They would neither permit UN inspectors in the Soviet Union nor surrender the Soviet Union's veto power over Security Council actions dealing with atomic energy. They demanded that the United States destroy its bombs at once. American leaders did not comply; for years to come, they believed, the atom bomb would be, in Baruch's words, their "winning weapon." Exactly how, they could not say.

A TURNING POINT IN GREECE

The strategy of containment began to take shape early in 1947 as a result of a crisis in Greece. Greek communists, waging a guerrilla war against the monarchy, were receiving aid from communist Yugoslavia and Bulgaria. Great Britain had been assisting the monarchists but could no longer afford this drain on its resources. In February 1947 the British informed President Truman that they would cut off aid to Greece.

The British predicament forced American policymakers to confront the fact that their European allies had not been able to rebuild their war-weakened economies. The communist "Iron Curtain" (a phrase coined by Winston Churchill) seemed about to close down on another nation. As Undersecretary of State Dean Acheson put it, the "corruption" of Greece might "infect" the entire Middle East and then spread "through Asia Minor and Egypt" and on to "Italy and France."

Truman therefore asked Congress to approve what became known as the Truman Doctrine. If Greece or Turkey fell to the communists, he said, all of the Middle East might be lost. To prevent this "unspeakable tragedy," he asked for $400 million in military and economic aid to Greece and Turkey. "It must be the policy of the United States to support free peoples who are resisting attempted subjugation by armed minorities or by outside pressures," he said.

By exaggerating the consequences of inaction and by justifying his request on ideological grounds, Truman obtained his objective. The result was the establishment of a right-wing, military-dominated government in Greece. In addition, by not limiting his request to the specific problem posed by the situation in Greece, Truman caused considerable concern in many countries.

The political threat to western Europe certainly loomed large in 1947. With the region, in the words of Winston Churchill (the great phrase maker of the era), "a rubble-heap, a charnel house, a breeding-ground of pestilence and hate," the entire continent seemed in danger of falling into communist hands without the Soviet Union raising a finger.

THE MARSHALL PLAN
AND THE LESSON OF HISTORY

In a 1946 speech entitled "The Lesson of History," George C. Marshall, army chief of staff during World War II, reminded Americans that after World War I, the United States had pursued a "negative course" that made possible Hitler's rise to power. This time, Marshall noted, the people of the United States must be prepared to act. In 1947 Marshall was named secretary of state. He proceeded to outline an extraordinary plan by which the United States would finance the re-

In June 1948 the Soviet Union cut off all water and road traffic into West Berlin. Truman's plan to airlift food and fuel to provision 2.5 million people seemed impossible, but during the 15 months of the Berlin crisis, planes such as this one, landing every four minutes, delivered nearly 2.5 million tons of supplies.

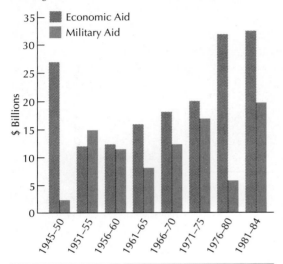

United States Foreign Aid, 1945–1984

In 1945 the dollar was worth over four times its value in 1984, so in uninflated dollars United States foreign aid has lessened over the years, especially during the decade 1971 to 1980. Even so, the total amount of United States foreign assistance from 1945 to 1984 was more than $280 billion.

construction of the European economy. "Hunger, poverty, desperation, and chaos" were the real enemies of freedom and democracy, Marshall said. The need was to restore "the confidence of the European people in the economic future of their own countries." Even the Soviet Union and Soviet-bloc nations would be eligible for American aid.

The European powers eagerly seized upon Marshall's suggestion. They set up a 16-nation Committee for European Economic Cooperation, which soon submitted plans calling for up to $22.4 billion in American assistance.

The Soviet Union and its European satellites were tempted by the offer of aid and sent representatives to the initial planning meetings. But Stalin grew anxious that American capital would draw his satellites into the American orbit. He recalled his delegates and demanded that the Eastern European nations do likewise. Those who hesitated were ordered to report to the Kremlin. "I went to Moscow as the Foreign Minister of an independent sovereign state," Jan Masaryk of Czechoslovakia commented bitterly. "I returned as a lackey of the Soviet government."

In February 1948 a communist coup took over the Czechoslovak government; Masaryk fell (or more likely was pushed) out a window to his death. These

Europe After World War II

Note the "Iron Curtain" separating the two power blocs. West Germany was created out of the merged French, British, and United States Zones in 1947, as was West Berlin. The Russian Zone became East Germany. The Berlin Wall was built later, in 1961, to keep an estimated 700 people a day from fleeing from East to West Germany.

strong-arm tactics brought to mind the Nazi takeover of Czechoslovakia a decade earlier, and helped persuade Congress to appropriate over $13 billion for the Marshall aid program. Results exceeded all expectations. By 1951 Western Europe was booming.

But Europe was now divided in two. In the West, where American-influenced governments were elected, private property was respected if often taxed heavily, and corporations gained influence and power. In the East, where the Soviet Union imposed its will and political system on client states, deep-seated resentment festered among subject peoples.

In March 1948, Great Britain, France, Belgium, the Netherlands, and Luxembourg signed an alliance aimed at social, cultural, and economic collaboration. The Western nations abandoned their understandable but counterproductive policy of crushing Germany economically. They instituted currency reforms in their zones and announced plans for creating a single West German Republic with a large degree of autonomy.

In June 1948 the Soviet Union retaliated by closing off surface access to Berlin from the West. For a time it seemed that the Allies must either fight their way into the city or abandon it to the communists. Unwilling to adopt either alternative, Truman decided to fly supplies to the capital from Frankfurt, Hanover, and Hamburg. American C-47 and C-54 transports shuttled back and forth in fair weather and foul, carrying enough food, fuel, and other goods necessary to maintain more than 2 million West Berliners. The Berlin airlift put the Soviets in an uncomfortable position; if they were determined to keep supplies from West Berlin, they would have to start the fighting. They were not prepared to do so. In May 1949 they lifted the blockade.

DEALING WITH JAPAN AND CHINA

Containment worked well in Europe, at least in the short run; in the Far East, where the United States lacked powerful allies, it was more expensive, less effective, and in most instances less justified. V-J Day found the Far East a shambles. Much of Japan was a smoking ruin. In China chaos reigned: Nationalists under Chiang Kai-shek dominated the south, communists under Mao Zedong controlled the northern countryside, and Japanese troops still held most northern cities. President Truman acted decisively and effectively with regard to Japan, unsurely and with unfortunate results where China was concerned. Even before the Japanese surrendered, he had decided not to allow the Soviet Union any significant role in the occupation of Japan. A four-power Allied Control Council was established, but American troops commanded by General MacArthur governed the country.

MacArthur displayed exactly the proper combination of imperiousness, tact, and intelligence needed to accomplish his purposes. The Japanese, revealing the same remarkable adaptability that had made possible their swift Westernization in the latter half of the nineteenth century, accepted political and social changes that involved universal suffrage and parliamentary government, the encouragement of labor unions, the breakup of some large estates and industrial combines, and the deemphasis on the importance of the emperor. Japan lost its far-flung island empire and all claim to Korea and the Chinese mainland but emerged economically strong, politically stable, and firmly allied with the United States.

The difficulties in China were probably insurmountable. Truman tried to bring Chiang's nationalists and Mao's communists together. He sent General Marshall to China to seek a settlement, but neither Chiang nor Mao would make significant concessions. Mao was convinced—correctly, as time soon proved—that he could win all China by force, while Chiang, presiding over a corrupt and incompetent regime, grossly exaggerated his popularity among the Chinese people. In January 1947 Truman recalled Marshall and named him secretary of state. Soon thereafter civil war erupted in China.

THE ELECTION OF 1948

In the spring of 1948 President Truman's fortunes were at low ebb. Public opinion polls suggested that a majority of the people considered him incompetent or worse. The Republicans seemed so sure to win the 1948 presidential election that many prominent Democrats began to talk of denying Truman the nomination. Governor Dewey, who again won the Republican nomination, ran confidently (even complacently), certain that he would carry the country.

Truman's position seemed hopeless because he had alienated both southern conservatives and northern liberals. The Southerners were particularly distressed because in 1946 the president had established a Committee on Civil Rights, which had recommended antilynching and anti–poll tax legislation and the creation of a permanent Fair Employment Practices Commission. When the Democratic convention adopted a strong civil rights plank, the southern delegates walked out. Southern conservatives then founded the States' Rights ("Dixiecrat") party and nominated J. Strom Thurmond of South Carolina for president.

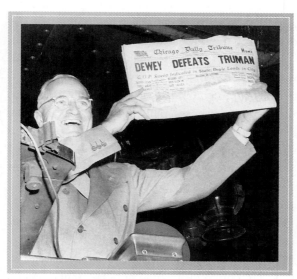

In 1948 the strongly Republican Chicago Daily Tribune guessed its postelection editions before all the returns were in. For Truman, it was the perfect climax to his hard-won victory.

As for the liberals, in 1947 a group that believed Truman's containment policy a threat to world peace organized a new Progressive party and nominated former Vice President Henry A. Wallace. With two minor candidates sure to cut into the Democratic vote, the president's chances seemed minuscule.

Promising to "give 'em hell," Truman launched an aggressive whistle-stop campaign. Traveling by rail, he made several hundred informal but hard-hitting speeches.

He excoriated the "do-nothing" Republican Congress, which had rejected his program and passed the Taft-Hartley Act, and he warned labor, farmers, and consumers that if Dewey won, Republican "gluttons of privilege" would do away with all the gains of the New Deal years.

Millions were moved by Truman's arguments and by his courageous fight against great odds. The success of the Berlin airlift during the presidential campaign helped him considerably, as did disaffection among normally Republican Midwestern farmers. The Progressive party fell increasingly into the hands of communist sympathizers, driving away many liberals who might otherwise have supported Wallace.

Dewey's smug, lackluster speeches failed to attract independents. One party satirized his campaign by boiling it down to four platitudes: "Agriculture is important." "Our rivers are full of fish." "You cannot have freedom without liberty." "The future lies ahead." The president, therefore, was able to reinvigorate the New Deal coalition, and he won an amazing upset victory on election day. He collected 24.1 million votes to Dewey's 21.9 million, the two minor candidates being held to about 2.3 million. In the Electoral College his margin was a thumping 303 to 189.

CONTAINING COMMUNISM ABROAD

During Truman's second term the confrontation between the United States and the Soviet Union dominated the headlines. To strengthen ties with the European democracies, in April 1949 the North Atlantic Treaty was signed in Washington. The United States, Great Britain, France, Italy, Belgium, the Netherlands, Luxembourg, Denmark, Norway, Portugal, Iceland, and Canada agreed "that an armed attack against one or more of them in Europe or North America shall be considered an attack against them all" and that in the event of such an attack each would take "individually and in concert with the other Parties, such action as it deems necessary, including the use of armed force." The pact established the North Atlantic Treaty Organization (NATO).

In September 1949 the Soviet Union detonated an atomic bomb. Truman had expressed doubts that the Soviets could build such sophisticated weapons. But when the explosion was confirmed, he called for rapid expansion of the American nuclear arsenal. He also asked his advisers to determine whether the United States should develop a new weapon thousands of times more destructive than atomic bombs. The "super" or hydrogen bomb would replicate the fusion process on the surface of the sun. The Atomic Energy Commission argued that there was no military use for hydrogen bombs, which would destroy hundreds of

Joseph Stalin, far right, on January 4, 1950, his 70th birthday. Next to him is Nikolai Bulganin, former head of the Soviet military, and Mao Zedong, recently victorious in the Chinese civil war. Mao and Stalin were negotiating a "treaty of friendship."

square miles and precipitate a dangerous arms race with the Soviet Union. The Joint Chiefs of Staff disagreed. Even if the hydrogen bomb could not be used in battle, they argued, its mere existence would intimidate enemies; and, the military men added, the Soviets would themselves build a hydrogen bomb whether or not the United States did so. (Unbeknownst to American leaders, Stalin had in fact already commenced developing a hydrogen bomb.) On January 31, 1950, Truman publicly announced that "though none wants to use it" he had no choice but to proceed with development of a hydrogen bomb.

In Asia the effort to contain communism in China had failed utterly. By the end of 1949 communist armies had administered a crushing defeat to the nationalists. The remnants of Chiang Kai-shek's forces fled to the island of Formosa, now called Taiwan. The "loss" of China to communism strengthened right-wing elements in the Republican party. They charged that Truman had not backed the nationalists strongly enough and that he had stupidly underestimated Mao's dedication to the cause of world revolution.

Despite a superficial plausibility, neither charge made much sense. American opinion would not have supported military intervention, and such intervention unquestionably would have alienated the Chinese people. That *any* American action could have changed the outcome in China is unlikely. The United States probably gave the nationalists too much aid rather than too little.

Containment had relied on American money, materials, and know-how, but not on American soldiers. In early 1950, Truman proposed to pare the budget by further reducing the nation's armed forces. Truman also called for a thorough review of the concept of containment. Dean Acheson, who recently had succeeded George Marshall as secretary of state, supervised the study. In March, it was submitted to the National Security Council, assigned a numerical designation (NSC-68), classified top secret, and sent to the nation's military and diplomatic leaders for review.

The document echoed the ringing rhetoric of George Kennan. The Soviet Union, it declared, was engaged in a worldwide assault on free institutions: "A defeat of free institutions anywhere is a defeat everywhere." NSC-68 differed from previous analyses, however, by calling for a massive expansion of the nation's armed forces. In the absence of "superior aggregate military strength," it concluded, containment was "no more than a policy of bluff." Instead of relying on other nations to stop the spread of communism, the United States itself had to develop military forces sufficient for the task *anywhere in the world.* Military spending therefore had to be increased by a staggering 350 percent to nearly $50 billion. The strategy could not fail: If the Soviet Union neglected to keep up with the American armed forces, it would no longer pose a threat, and if it attempted to match the high levels of American military spending, its less efficient economic system would collapse from the strain.

The document was submitted to Truman on April 7, 1950. His initial reaction was cool. He demanded that it be kept secret. He also persisted in attempts to slice off a billion dollars from the next year's $14 billion military budget. Within a few months, however, events in Korea changed his mind.

HOT WAR IN KOREA

After the Second World War the province of Korea was taken from Japan and divided at 38° north latitude into the Democratic People's Republic in the north, backed by the Soviet Union, and the Republic of Korea in the south, backed by the United States and the UN. Both powers withdrew their troops from the peninsula. The Russians left behind a well-armed local force, but the Republic of Korea's army was small and ill trained.

American strategists, while seeking to "contain" communism in the Far East, had decided that military involvement on the Asiatic mainland was impracticable. America's first line of defense was to be its island bases in Japan and the Philippines. In a speech in January 1950 Acheson deliberately excluded Korea from what he described as the "defensive perimeter" of the United States in Asia. It was up to the South Koreans, backed by the UN, to protect themselves, Acheson said. This encouraged the North Koreans to attack. When their armored

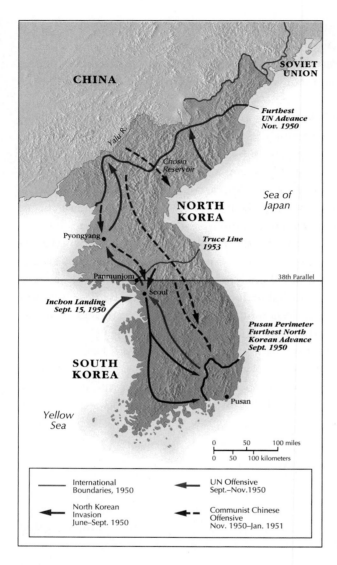

The Korean War, 1950–1953

divisions, led by 150 Soviet-made tanks, struck suddenly across the 38th parallel in June 1950, the South Koreans were unable to stop them.

Truman was at his family home in Independence, Missouri, when Acheson telephoned with the news of the North Korean attack. "Dean," Truman replained, "we've got to stop the sons of bitches no matter what." He hastened to Washington. On the flight, he recalled how the communists in Korea were acting "just as Hitler, Mussolini, and the Japanese had acted ten, fifteen, and twenty years earlier." "If this were allowed to go unchallenged," he concluded, "it would mean a third world war, just as similar incidents had brought on the second world war." With the backing of the UN Security Council (but without asking Congress to declare war), he sent American planes into battle. Ground troops soon followed. Truman also ordered the adoption of NSC-68 "as soon as feasible."

Nominally the Korean War was a struggle between the invaders and the United Nations. General MacArthur, placed in command, flew the blue UN flag over his headquarters, and 16 nations supplied troops for his army. However, more than 90 percent of the forces employed were American. At first the North Koreans pushed them back rapidly, but in September a front was stabilized around the port of Pusan, at the southern tip of Korea. Then MacArthur executed a brilliant amphibious maneuver, striking at the west coast city of Inchon, about 50 miles south of the 38th parallel. Outflanked, the North Koreans retreated in disorder. By October the battlefront had moved north of the 1945 boundary.

General MacArthur now proposed the conquest of North Korea, even if it meant bombing "privileged sanctuaries" on the Chinese side of the Korean border. Less sanguine military officials balked at taking on China but urged occupying North Korea to protect the future security of the south. A few of Truman's civilian advisers, the most important being George Kennan, opposed advancing beyond the 38th parallel, fearing intervention not only by the Red Chinese but also by the Soviets. "When we start walking inland from the tip of Korea, we have about a 10,000 mile walk if we keep going," Kennan pointed out. "We are going to have to stop somewhere."

Truman authorized MacArthur to advance as far as the Yalu River, the boundary between North Korea and China. It was an unfortunate decision, an example of how power, once unleashed, so often gets out of hand. As the advance progressed, ominous rumblings came from north of the Yalu. Foreign Minister Chou En-lai warned that the Chinese would not "supinely" tolerate seeing their neighbors being "savagely invaded by imperialists." Chinese "volunteers" began to turn up among the captives taken by UN units.

Alarmed, Truman flew to Wake Island, in the Pacific, to confer with MacArthur, but the general, who had a low opinion of Asian soldiers, assured him that the Chinese would not dare to intervene. If they did, he added, his army would crush them easily; the war would be over by Christmas.

Seldom has a general miscalculated so badly. Ignoring intelligence reports and dividing his advancing units recklessly, he drove toward the Yalu. Suddenly, on November 26, 33 Chinese divisions, hidden in the interior mountains of Korea, smashed through the center of MacArthur's line. Overnight a triumphant advance became a bloody, disorganized retreat. MacArthur now spoke of the "bottomless well of Chinese manpower" and justified his earlier confidence by claiming that he was fighting "an entirely new war."

The UN army rallied south of the 38th parallel, and MacArthur then urged that he be permitted to bomb Chinese installations north of the Yalu. He also

The Chinese counteroffensive of November 1950 caught the Americans by surprise and cut off many units.
Here, U.S. Marines retreat southward, harassed by communist Chinese soldiers in the hills. American bombers
blast a way through communist defenses to help the Americans escape.

suggested a naval blockade of the coast of China and the use of Chinese Nationalist troops in Korea. When Truman rejected these proposals on the grounds that they would lead to a third world war, MacArthur, who tended to ignore the larger political aspects of the conflict, attempted to rouse Congress and the public against the president by openly criticizing administration policy. Truman ordered him to be silent, and when the general persisted, he removed him from command.

At first the Korean "police action" had been popular in the United States, but as the months passed and the casualties mounted, many citizens became disillusioned and angry. The war was unresolved when Truman left office: By the time it was over, it had produced 157,000 American casualties, including 54,200 dead.

If the Korean War persuaded Truman to adopt NSC-68, it also exposed the failings of the policy. By conceiving of communism as a monolithic force it tended to make it so, driving Red China and the Soviet Union into each other's arms. By committing American military forces to potential trouble spots throughout the world, it increased the likelihood they would prevail in none.

THE COMMUNIST ISSUE AT HOME

The Korean War highlighted the paradox that, at the pinnacle of its power, the influence of the United States in world affairs was declining. Its monopoly on nuclear

A brilliant commander in the Pacific during World War II, General Douglas MacArthur frequently clashed with President Truman over military strategies in Korea. Here, MacArthur confers with South Korea's President Syngman Rhee during ceremonies proclaiming Korea a republic in August 1948.

weapons had been lost. China had passed into the communist orbit. Elsewhere in Asia and throughout Africa, new nations, formerly colonial possessions of the Western powers, were adopting a "neutralist" position in the cold war. Despite the billions poured into armaments and foreign aid, national security seemed far from ensured.

Internal as well as external dangers loomed. Alarming examples of communist espionage in Canada, in Great Britain, and in the United States itself convinced many citizens that clever conspirators were everywhere at work undermining American security. Both the Republicans and conservative Democratic critics of Truman's domestic policies were charging that he was "soft" on communists.

There were never more than 100,000 communists in the United States, and party membership plummeted after the start of the Cold War. However, the possibility that a handful of spies could do enormous damage fueled a kind of panic that could be used for partisan purposes. In 1947, hoping to defuse the communists-in-government issue by being more zealous in pursuit of spies than his critics, Truman established a Loyalty Review Board to check up on government employees. The program made even sympathy for a long list of vaguely defined "totalitarian" or "subversive" organizations grounds for dismissal. During the following 10 years about 2700 government workers were discharged, only a relative handful of them for legitimate reasons. A much larger number resigned.

In 1948 Whittaker Chambers, an editor of *Time* who had formerly been a communist, charged that Alger Hiss, president of the Carnegie Endowment for International Peace and a former State Department official, had been a communist in the 1930s. Hiss denied the charge and sued Chambers for libel. Chambers then produced microfilms purporting to show that Hiss had copied classified documents for dispatch to Moscow. Hiss could not be indicted for espionage because of the statute of limitations; instead he was charged with perjury. His first trial resulted in a hung jury; his second, ending in January 1950, in conviction and a five-year jail term.

If a distinguished official such as Hiss had been disloyal, anything seemed possible. The case fed the fears of those who believed in the existence of a powerful communist underground in the United States. The disclosure in February 1950 that a British scientist, Klaus Fuchs, had betrayed atomic secrets to the Russians heightened these fears, as did the arrest and conviction of his American associate, Harry Gold, and two other Americans, Julius and Ethel Rosenberg, on the same charge.

Although they were not major spies and the information they revealed was not important, the Rosenbergs were executed, to the consternation of many liberals in the United States and elsewhere. However, information gathered by other spies had speeded the Soviet development of nuclear weapons. This fact encouraged some Republicans to press the communists-in-government issue hard.

McCARTHYISM

In February 1950, an obscure senator, Joseph R. McCarthy of Wisconsin, introduced this theme in a speech to the even less well known Ohio County Republican Womens' Club of Wheeling, West Virginia. "The reason we find ourselves in a position of impotency," he stated, "is not because our only powerful potential enemy has sent men to invade our shores, but rather because of the traitorous actions of those who have been treated so well by this nation." The State Department, he added, was "infested" with communists. "I have here in my hand a list of 205—a list of names that were known to the Secretary of State as being members of the communist party and who nevertheless are still working and shaping . . . policy."

Why this speech caused a sensation has never been satisfactorily explained. McCarthy had no shred of evidence to back up these statements, as a Senate committee headed by the conservative Democrat Millard Tydings of Maryland soon demonstrated. He never exposed a single spy or secret American communist. One reporter quipped that McCarthy could not tell Karl Marx from Groucho Marx.

But because of the government loyalty program, the Hiss case, and other recent events, thousands of people were too eager to believe him to listen to rea-

Senator Joe McCarthy's unsubstantiated charges of communist infiltration of the army led finally to his downfall.

son. Within a few weeks he was the most talked of person in Congress. Inhibited neither by scruples nor by logic, he lashed out in every direction.

McCarthy was totally unscrupulous. The "big lie" was his most effective weapon: The enormity of his charges and the status of his targets convinced thousands that there must be some truth in what he was saying. Nevertheless, his crude tactics would have failed if the public had not been so worried about communism. The worries were caused by the reality of Soviet military power, the attack on Korea, the loss of the nuclear monopoly, and the stories about spies, some of them true.

DWIGHT D. EISENHOWER

As the 1952 presidential election approached, Truman's popularity was again at a low ebb. Senator McCarthy attacked him relentlessly for his handling of the Korean conflict and his "mistreatment" of General MacArthur. In choosing their candidate, the Republicans passed over the twice-defeated Dewey and their most prominent leader, Senator Robert A. Taft of Ohio, an outspoken conservative, and nominated General Dwight D. Eisenhower.

Eisenhower's popularity did not grow merely out of his achievements in World War II. Although a West Pointer (class of 1915), he struck most persons as anything but warlike. After the bristly, combative Truman, his genial personality

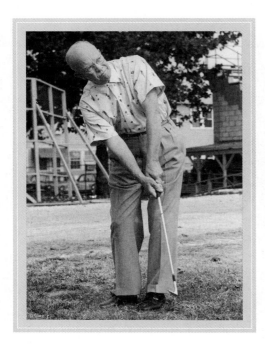

Many critics lampooned Eisenhower for his leisure-time amusements. A popular bumper sticker read: "Ben Hogan [a famous golfer] for President. If We're Going to Have a Golfer for President, Let's Have a Good One." Others have viewed Eisenhower's passion for golf as characteristic of his presidential style: methodical, prudent, and, when in the rough, disarmingly shrewd.

and evident desire to avoid controversy proved widely appealing. In his reluctance to seek political office, Eisenhower reminded the country of George Washington, whereas his seeming ignorance of current political issues was no more a handicap to his campaign than the similar ignorance of Jackson and Grant in their times.

The Democrats nominated Governor Adlai E. Stevenson of Illinois, whose grandfather had been vice president under Grover Cleveland. Stevenson's unpretentiousness was appealing, and his witty, urbane speeches captivated intellectuals. In retrospect, however, it is clear that he had not the remotest chance of defeating the popular Eisenhower. Eisenhower received almost 34 million votes to Stevenson's 27 million, and in the Electoral College his margin was 442 to 89.

Eisenhower was neither a reactionary nor a fool. He was unwilling to do away with existing social and economic legislation or to cut back on military expenditures. Some economists claimed that he reacted too slowly in dealing with business recessions and that he showed insufficient concern for speeding the rate of national economic growth. Yet he adopted an almost Keynesian approach to economic problems; that is, he tried to check downturns in the business cycle by stimulating the economy.

Eisenhower approved the extension of social security to an additional 10 million persons; created a new Department of Health, Education, and Welfare; began the St. Lawrence Seaway project; and in 1955 came out for federal support of education and a highway construction act that eventually produced a 40,000-mile network of superhighways covering every state in the Union. His somewhat doctrinaire belief in decentralization and private enterprise reduced the effectiveness of his social welfare measures, but on balance, he proved to be an excellent politician. He knew how to be flexible without compromising his basic values. His "conservatism" became first "dynamic conservatism" and then "progressive moderation." He summarized his attitude by saying that he was liberal in dealing with individuals but conservative "when talking about . . . the individual's pocketbook." He hoped to strengthen the moderate faction of his party, but despite his extraordinary popularity, he did not succeed in persuading many right-wing Republicans that this was a good idea.

THE EISENHOWER-DULLES FOREIGN POLICY

The American people, troubled and uncertain over the stalemate in Korea, counted on Eisenhower to find a way to employ the nation's immense strength constructively. The new president shared the general feeling that a change of tactics in foreign affairs was needed. He counted on his secretary of state to solve the practical problems.

His choice, John Foster Dulles, was a lawyer with considerable diplomatic experience. He had been an outspoken critic of Truman's foreign policy. In a May 1952 article in *Life* entitled "A Policy of Boldness," he argued that global military containment was both expensive and ineffective: "We cannot build a 20,000 mile Maginot Line or match the Red armies man for man, gun for gun, and tank for tank at any particular time or place their general staff selects." Instead of waiting for the communist powers to make a move and then "containing" them, the United States should put more emphasis on nuclear bombs and less on conventional weapons. Such a "new look" military would be cheaper to maintain than a force of conventional weapons and a large standing army, and it would prevent the United States from being caught up in "local" conflicts like the Korean War. The nation's military forces, spearheaded by its formidable nuclear arsenal, would serve as "a deterrent of war instead of a mere means of waging war after we got into it."

Korea offered the first test of his views. After Eisenhower's postelection trip to Korea failed to bring an end to the war, Dulles signaled his willingness to use tactical nuclear weapons in Korea by showily transferring nuclear warheads from the United States mainland to bomber units stationed in the Far East. He also issued a calculatedly vague warning about tough new measures. Several weeks

Dulles during a 1956 press conference at which he rejected suggestions by Russia and India that the United States suspend further hydrogen bomb tests. His stance and gesture project his "hard-line" approach.

later, in July 1953, the Chinese signed an armistice that ended hostilities but left Korea divided. The administration interpreted the softening of the Chinese position as proof that the nuclear threat had worked. (Dulles was apparently mistaken about the effectiveness of his Korean gambit. In recent years, Chinese officials have said that they were unaware at the time of the American nuclear threats.)

Emboldened by his evident triumph, Dulles again brandished the nuclear threat. Chiang Kai-shek had stationed 90,000 soldiers—one-third of his army—in Quemoy and Matsu, two small islands located a few miles from mainland China. In 1954 the Chinese communists began shelling the islands, presumably in preparation to invade them. Chiang appealed for American protection, warning that loss of the islands would bring about the collapse of Nationalist China. Dulles concurred that the consequences throughout the Far East would be "catastrophic." At a press conference in 1955 Eisenhower announced his willingness to use nuclear weapons to defend the islands, "just exactly as you would use a bullet or anything else." The Chinese communists backed down.

Massive retaliation succeeded, further, in reducing the defense budget. The reliance on a nuclear threat allowed Eisenhower to pare another half million men from the armed forces, saving $4 billion annually. On balance, however, Dulles's strategy was flawed, and many of his schemes were preposterous.

Above all, massive retaliation made little sense when the Soviet Union possessed nuclear weapons as powerful as those of the United States.

McCarthy Self-Destructs

Although the State Department was now controlled by Dulles, a Republican and hard-line anticommunist, Senator McCarthy moderated his attacks on the department not a jot. In 1953 its overseas information program received his special

Senator Joe McCarthy confers with aide Roy Cohn, a tough, young lawyer who had made a reputation prosecuting suspected communists in Manhattan. Cohn intimidated some people by threatening to make public their homosexuality; yet he was himself a homosexual who steadfastly denied it; in 1986 he died of AIDS. His story was symbolized in Tony Kushner's Pulitzer Prize–winning play Angels in America *(1993).*

attention. Despite his attacks, however, its only result was to undermine the morale of Foreign Service officers.

But McCarthy finally overreached himself. Early in 1954 he turned his guns on the army, accusing Pentagon officials of trying to blackmail his committee. The resulting Army-McCarthy hearings, televised before the country, proved the senator's undoing. For weeks his dark scowl, his blind combativeness, and his disregard for every human value stood exposed for millions to see. When the hearings ended in June 1954 after some million words of testimony, his spell had been broken.

The Senate, with President Eisenhower, who despised McCarthy but who considered it beneath his dignity as president to "get into the gutter with that guy," applying pressure behind the scenes, at last moved to censure him in December 1954. This reproof completed the destruction of his influence. Although he continued to issue statements and wild charges, the country no longer listened. In 1957 he died of cirrhosis of the liver.

ASIAN POLICY AFTER KOREA

Shortly after an armistice was finally arranged in Korea in July 1953, new trouble erupted far to the south in the former French colony of Indochina. Nationalist rebels led by the communist Ho Chi Minh had been harassing the French in Vietnam, one of the three puppet kingdoms (the others were Laos and Cambodia) fashioned by France in Indochina after the defeat of the Japanese.

When China recognized the rebels, who were known as the Vietminh, and supplied them with arms, President Truman countered with economic and military assistance to the French, and President Eisenhower continued and expanded this assistance.

Early in 1954 Ho Chi Minh's troops trapped and besieged a French army in the remote stronghold of Dien Bien Phu. Faced with the loss of 20,000 soldiers, France asked the United States to commit its air force to the battle.

By this time the United States was paying about three-quarters of France's expenses in Vietnam, but Eisenhower refused to send in planes. Although the likelihood of communist control of Vietnam worried him, his military judgment warned him against such action. The idea of using American air strikes, he believed, was "just silly." The communists were "secreted all around in the jungle. How are we, in a few air strikes, to defeat them?"

In May the French garrison at Dien Bien Phu surrendered. In July France, Great Britain, the Soviet Union, and China signed an agreement dividing Vietnam along the 17th parallel. France withdrew from the area. The northern sector became the Democratic Republic of Vietnam, controlled by Ho Chi Minh; the southern remained in the hands of the emperor, Bao Dai. An election to settle the future of all Vietnam was scheduled for 1956.

When it seemed likely that the communists would win that election, Ngo Dinh Diem, a conservative anticommunist, overthrew Bao Dai and became president of South Vietnam. The United States supplied his government liberally with aid. The planned election was never held, and Vietnam remained divided.

Dulles responded to the diplomatic setback in Vietnam by establishing the Southeast Asia Treaty Organization (SEATO), but only three Asian nations—the Philippine Republic, Thailand, and Pakistan—joined this alliance.

THE MIDDLE EAST CAULDRON

Within a year the world teetered once again on the brink of war, this time in the Middle East. U.S. policy in that region was influenced by the huge oil resources of Iran, Iraq, Kuwait, and Saudi Arabia—about 60 percent of the world's known reserves—and by the conflict between the new Jewish state of Israel (formerly the British mandate of Palestine) and its Arab neighbors.

Angered by the creation of Israel, the surrounding Arab nations had tried to destroy the country. (The Israeli question had the same impact on Arab emotions that the "bloody shirt" had on Republicans after the Civil War.) But although badly outnumbered, the Israelis were better organized and better armed than the Arabs and drove them off with relative ease. With them departed nearly a million Palestinian Arabs, thereby creating a desperate refugee problem in nearby countries.

President Truman had consistently placed support for Israel before other considerations in the Middle East, partly because of the conviction that survivors of the Nazi holocaust were entitled to a country of their own and partly because of the political importance of the Jewish vote in the United States. Dulles and Eisenhower tried to redress the balance by deemphasizing American support of Israel. In 1952 a revolution in Egypt had overthrown the dissolute King Farouk. Colonel Gamal Abdel Nasser emerged as the strongman of Egypt. The United States was prepared to lend Nasser money to build a huge dam on the Nile at Aswan. The dam was to be the key to an Egyptian irrigation program and a vast source of electric power. However, Eisenhower would not sell Egypt arms. The communists would.

For this reason Nasser drifted toward the communist orbit. When Eisenhower then decided not to finance the Aswan Dam, Nasser responded by nationalizing the Suez Canal. This move galvanized the British and French. Influenced by Dulles's argument that Egypt could be made an ally by cajolery, the British had acceded in 1954 to Nasser's demand that they evacuate their military base at Suez. Now their traditional lifeline to the Far East was at Egypt's mercy. In conjunction with the French, and without consulting the United States, the British decided to take back the canal by force. The Israelis, alarmed by repeated Arab hit-and-run raids along their borders, also attacked Egypt.

Events moved swiftly. Israeli armored columns crushed the Egyptian army in the Sinai Peninsula in a matter of days. France and Britain occupied Port Said, at the northern end of the canal. Nasser blocked the canal by sinking ships in the channel. In the UN the Soviet Union and the United States introduced resolutions calling for a cease-fire. Both were vetoed by Britain and France.

Then Khrushchev threatened to send "volunteers" to Egypt and launch atomic missiles against France and Great Britain if they did not withdraw. Eisenhower also demanded that the invaders pull out of Egypt. In London large crowds demonstrated against their own government. On November 6, only nine days after the first Israeli units invaded Egypt, Prime Minister Anthony Eden, haggard and shaken, announced a cease-fire. Israel withdrew its troops. The crisis subsided as rapidly as it had arisen.

The United States had won a measure of respect in the Arab countries, but at what cost? Its major allies had been humiliated. Their ill-timed attack had enabled the Soviet Union to recover much of the prestige it had lost as a result of its brutal suppression of a Hungarian revolt that had broken out a week before the

Suez fiasco. Eden and French Premier Guy Mollet were claiming with considerable plausibility that Dulles's futile attempt to win Arab friendship without abandoning Israel had placed them in a dilemma.

However, the bad feeling within the Western alliance soon passed. When the Soviet Union seemed likely to profit from its "defense" of Egypt in the crisis, the president announced the Eisenhower Doctrine (January 1957), which stated that the United States was "prepared to use armed force" anywhere in the Middle East against "aggression from any country controlled by international communism." In practice, the Eisenhower Doctrine amounted to little more than a restatement of the containment policy.

EISENHOWER AND KHRUSHCHEV

In 1956 Eisenhower was reelected, defeating Adlai Stevenson even more decisively than he had in 1952. Despite evident satisfaction with their leader, however, the American people were in a sober mood. Hopes of pushing back the Soviet Union with clever strategems and moral fervor were fading. Although the United States detonated the first hydrogen bomb in November 1952, the Soviets followed suit within six months. The cold war between the superpowers had become yet more chilling.

Stalin died in March 1953, and after a period of internal conflict within the Kremlin, Nikita Khrushchev emerged as the new master of Russia. Khrushchev was perhaps the most confusing (and, arguably, confused) figure of the Cold War. Crude and bibulous, prone to violent tantrums and tearful histrionics, he de-

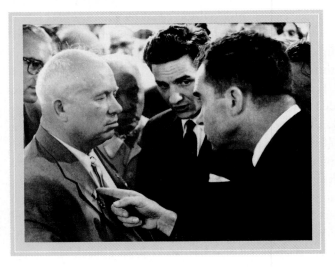

Vice President Richard M. Nixon and Soviet leader Nikita Khrushchev engaged in their "kitchen debate" over the future of capitalism at a Moscow trade fair in 1959. Although this encounter did little to advance United States–Soviet relations, it established Nixon's credentials as a tough negotiator.

lighted in shocking people with words and gestures. In the most famous of these, he pounded his shoe on the table during a debate at the United Nations. Although a product of the Soviet system, Khrushchev recognized its deep failings and resolved to purge it of Stalinism. He released political prisoners from Stalin's gulags, or political prison camps, and told wide-eyed party functionaries that Stalin had committed monstrous crimes.

Eisenhower, a seasoned analyst of military capabilities, understood that Khrushchev's antics were meant to conceal the Soviet Union's many weaknesses: the bitter opposition to Soviet rule among peoples of Eastern Europe; the deficiencies of the overcentralized Soviet economy, especially agriculture; and the bureaucratic ossification of its armed forces. The Soviet Union had kept up a good pace in the nuclear arms race but had not attained nuclear parity. Thousands of American airplanes were based in Europe, northern Africa, and Turkey, placing most Soviet targets within easy range. Heavy Soviet bombers, on the other hand, faced the daunting prospect of lumbering thousands of miles over the Arctic and Pacific Oceans to reach American targets, harried all the while by lightning-fast fighter planes. The United States would win (whatever that meant) any nuclear war.

But this advantage disappeared in the exhaust cloud of a Soviet rocket, launched on October 4, 1957, that carried a 184-pound capsule named Sputnik far above the atmosphere into earth orbit. Soon, American policymakers knew, Soviet missiles capable of reaching American soil would be tipped with nuclear warheads. The nation's far-flung network of bomber defenses had become obsolete, and with it the strategy of massive retaliation.

Several weeks later Khrushchev rubbed hard at the rawest sore in the American psyche: the anguished memory of Pearl Harbor. In an interview with publisher William Randolph Hearst Jr., Khrushchev blustered that the Soviet Union could launch 10 or 20 intercontinental missiles with nuclear warheads "tomorrow." He boasted that the American military was no match for the Soviet military behemoth. This was nonsense and Eisenhower knew it. Yet to point out the weaknesses of the Soviet military—to call Khrushchev's bluff—was potentially to goad the unstable Soviet leader to rash action. While critics at home flayed Eisenhower for allowing a "missile gap" with the Soviet Union, the president testily reassured the American people that they had little to fear, but otherwise remained silent.

In 1957 Dulles underwent surgery for abdominal cancer, and in April 1959 he had to resign. The next month he was dead. Eisenhower never had avoided making decisions in foreign policy, but now he personally took over much of the actual conduct of diplomacy. The key to his approach was restraint; he exercised commendable caution in every crisis. Like U. S. Grant, he was a soldier who hated war. From Korea through the crises over Indochina, Hungary, and Suez, he avoided risky new commitments. His behavior, like his temperament, contrasted sharply with that of the aggressive, oratorically perfervid Dulles.

World opinion was insistent that the great powers stop making and testing nuclear weapons, for every test explosion was contaminating the atmosphere with radioactive debris that threatened the future of all life. Unresolved controversies, especially the argument over divided Germany, might erupt at any moment into a globe-shattering war.

Neither the United States nor the Soviet Union dared ignore these dangers; each therefore adopted a more accommodating attitude. In the summer of 1959 Vice President Richard M. Nixon visited the Soviet Union. Although Nixon's visit was marred by a heated argument with Khrushchev about the virtues of their respective systems, conducted before a gaping crowd in the kitchen of a model American home that had been set up at a Moscow fair, these visits were encouraging.

On May 1, 1960, high over Sverdlovsk, an industrial center deep in the Soviet Union, an American U-2 reconnaissance plane was shot down by antiaircraft fire. The pilot of the plane, Francis Gary Powers, survived the crash, and he confessed to being a spy. His cameras contained aerial photographs of Soviet military installations. When Eisenhower assumed full responsibility for the mission, Khrushchev accused the United States of "piratical" and "cowardly" acts of aggression. In September, Khrushchev told the United Nations that the Soviet Union was turning out nuclear missiles "like sausages from an automatic machine."

LATIN AMERICA AROUSED

Events in Latin America compounded Eisenhower's difficulties. During World War II the United States, needing Latin American raw materials, had supplied its southern neighbors liberally with economic aid. In the period following victory a hemispheric mutual defense pact was signed at Rio de Janeiro in September 1947, and the following year the Organization of American States (OAS) came into being. In the OAS, decisions were reached by a two-thirds vote; the United States had neither a veto nor any special position.

But as the Cold War progressed, the United States neglected Latin American questions. Economic problems plagued the region, and in most nations reactionary governments reigned. Radical Latin Americans accused the United States of supporting cliques of wealthy tyrants, whereas conservatives blamed insufficient American economic aid for the plight of the poor.

Eisenhower, eager to improve relations, stepped up economic assistance. Resistance to communism nonetheless continued to receive first priority. In 1954 the government of Jacobo Arbenz Guzman in Guatemala began to import Soviet weapons. The United States promptly dispatched arms to neighboring Honduras. Within a month an army led by an exiled Guatemalan officer marched into the country from Honduras and overthrew Arbenz. Elsewhere in Latin America, Eisenhower, as Truman had before him, continued to support regimes that were kept in power by the local military.

The depth of Latin American resentment of the United States became clear in the spring of 1958, when Vice President Nixon made what was supposed to be a goodwill tour of South America. Everywhere, he was met with hostility. In Lima, Peru, he was mobbed; in Caracas, Venezuela, students pelted him with eggs and stones. He had to abandon the remainder of his trip. For the first time the American people gained some inkling of Latin American opinion and the social and economic troubles that lay behind it.

That there was no easy solution to Latin American problems was demonstrated by events in Cuba. In 1959 a revolutionary movement headed by Dr. Fidel Castro overthrew Fulgencio Batista, one of the most noxious of the Latin American dictators. Eisenhower recognized the Castro government at once, but the Cuban leader soon began to criticize the United States in highly colored speeches. Castro confiscated American property without providing adequate compensation, suppressed civil liberties, and entered into close relations with the Soviet Union. After he negotiated a trade agreement with the Soviet Union in February 1960, which enabled the Russians to obtain Cuban sugar at bargain rates, the United States retaliated by prohibiting the importation of Cuban sugar into America.

Khrushchev then announced that if the United States intervened in Cuba, he would defend the country with atomic weapons. "The Monroe Doctrine has outlived its time," Khrushchev warned. Shortly before the end of his second term, Eisenhower broke off diplomatic relations with Cuba.

THE CIVIL RIGHTS MOVEMENT

During Eisenhower's presidency a major change occurred in the legal status of American blacks. Eisenhower had relatively little to do with this change, which was part of a broad shift in attitudes toward the rights of minorities in democracies. After 1945 the question of racial equality took on special importance because of the ideological competition with communism. Evidence of color prejudice in the United States damaged the nation's image, particularly in Asia and

Africa, where the United States and the Soviet Union were competing for influence. An awareness of foreign criticism of American racial attitudes, along with resentment that almost a century after the Emancipation Proclamation they were still second-class citizens, produced a growing militancy among American blacks. Eisenhower did complete the integration of the armed forces begun by Truman, but he was temperamentally incapable of a frontal assault on the racial problem. This was done by the Supreme Court, which interjected itself into the civil rights controversy in dramatic fashion in 1954.

Under pressure of litigation sponsored by the NAACP, the Court had been gradually undermining the "separate but equal" principle laid down in *Plessy* v. *Ferguson* in 1896, at least insofar as it applied to higher education. In 1938 it ordered a black student be admitted to the University of Missouri law school because no law school for blacks existed in the state. This decision gradually forced some southern states to admit blacks to advanced programs. "You can't build a cyclotron for one student," the president of the University of Oklahoma confessed when the Court, in 1948, ordered Oklahoma to provide equal facilities. Two years later, when Texas actually attempted to fit out a separate law school for a single black applicant, the Court ruled that truly equal education could not be provided under such circumstances. At lower levels, however, southern discrimination against blacks was extreme. In the 1920s Louisiana had 280 white high schools but only three open to blacks.

In 1953 President Eisenhower appointed California's Governor Earl Warren chief justice of the United States. Convinced that the Court must take the offensive in the cause of civil rights, Warren succeeded in welding his associates into a unit on this question. In 1954 an NAACP-sponsored case, *Brown* v. *Board of Education of Topeka,* came up for decision. The NAACP lawyer, Thurgood Marshall, challenging the "separate but equal" doctrine, submitted a mass of sociological evidence to show that the mere fact of segregation made equal education impossible and did serious psychological damage to both black children and white. Speaking for a unanimous Court, Warren reversed the *Plessy* decision. "In the field of public education, the doctrine of 'separate but equal' has no place," he declared. "Separate educational facilities are inherently unequal." The next year the Court ordered the states to end segregation "with all deliberate speed."

Despite these decisions, few districts in the southern and border states tried to integrate their schools. Many white Southerners who deplored the way blacks were treated in the region nonetheless opposed integrating the schools. As late as September 1956, barely 700 of the South's 10,000 school districts had been de-

Angry jeers from whites rain down on Elizabeth Eckford, one of the first black students to arrive for registration at Little Rock's Central High School in 1957. State troops turned black students away from the school until President Eisenhower overruled the state decision and called in the National Guard to enforce integration.

segregated. The region became more alienated from the rest of the nation than at any time since Reconstruction.

White citizens' councils dedicated to all-out opposition sprang up through-out the South. When the school board of Clinton, Tennessee, integrated the local high school in September 1956, a mob roused by a northern fanatic rioted in protest, shouting "Kill the niggers!" and destroying the property of blacks. The school was kept open with the help of the National Guard until segregationists blew up the building with dynamite. In Virginia the governor announced a plan for "massive resistance" to integration that denied state aid to local school systems that wished to desegregate.

President Eisenhower thought equality for blacks could not be obtained by government edict. He said that the Court's ruling must be obeyed, but he did little to discourage southern resistance to desegregation. "I am convinced that the Supreme Court decision set back progress in the South at least fifteen years," he remarked to one of his advisers. "The fellow who tries to tell me you can do these things by force is just plain nuts."

However, in 1957 events compelled him to act. When the school board of Little Rock, Arkansas, opened Central High School to a handful of black students, the governor of the state, Orval M. Faubus, called out the National Guard to prevent them from attending. Unruly crowds taunted the students and their parents. Eisenhower could not ignore the direct flouting of federal authority. After the mayor of Little Rock sent him a telegram saying, in part, "SITUATION IS OUT OF CONTROL AND POLICE CANNOT DISPERSE THE MOB," Eisenhower dispatched 1000 paratroopers to Little Rock and summoned 10,000

National Guardsmen to federal duty, thus removing them from Faubus's control. The black students then began to attend class. A token force of soldiers was stationed at Central High for the entire school year to protect them.

Resistance strengthened the determination of blacks and many northern whites to make the South comply with the desegregation decision. Besides pressing cases in the federal courts, leaders of the movement organized a voter registration drive among southern blacks. As a result, the administration introduced what became the Civil Rights Act of 1957. It authorized the attorney general to obtain injunctions to stop election officials from interfering with blacks' efforts to register and vote. The law also established a Civil Rights Commission with broad investigatory powers and a Civil Rights Division in the Department of Justice. Enforcing this Civil Rights Act was another matter. A later study of a typical county in Alabama revealed that between 1957 and 1960 more than 700 blacks with high school diplomas were rejected as unqualified by white election officials when they sought to register.

THE ELECTION OF 1960

As the end of his second term approached, Eisenhower somewhat reluctantly endorsed Vice President Richard Nixon as the Republican candidate to succeed him. Nixon had originally skyrocketed to national prominence by exploiting the public fear of communist subversion. "Traitors in the high councils of our government," he charged in 1950, "have made sure that the deck is stacked on the Soviet side of the diplomatic tables." In 1947 he was an obscure young congressman from California; in 1950 he won a seat in the Senate; two years later Eisenhower chose him as his running mate.

Whether Nixon believed what he was saying at this period of his career is not easily discovered; with his "instinct for omnidirectional placation," he seemed wedded to the theory that politicians should slavishly represent their constituents' opinions rather than hold to their own views. He projected an image of almost frantic earnestness, yet he pursued a flexible course more suggestive of calculation than sincerity. Reporters generally had a low opinion of Nixon, and independent voters seldom found him attractive. He was always controversial, distrusted by liberals even when he supported liberal measures.

The Democrats nominated Senator John F. Kennedy of Massachusetts. His chief rival for the nomination, Lyndon B. Johnson of Texas, the Senate majority leader, became his running mate. Kennedy was the son of Joseph P. Kennedy, a wealthy businessman and promoter who had served as ambassador to Great Britain under Franklin Roosevelt. An indifferent student at Harvard, Kennedy in his junior year—1939—traveled with his father to Europe. When Hitler attacked Poland a few months later, Kennedy had the topic for his senior thesis: "Appeasement at Munich," in which he chastised British and American leaders in the 1920s and 1930s for a lack of foresight and resolve. Published in 1940 as *Why England Slept,* the book received favorable reviews and was briefly a best-seller. During World War II, Kennedy served in the Pacific, captaining a torpedo boat. When the boat was sliced in two by a Japanese destroyer, Kennedy showed personal courage in rescuing his men. Besides wealth, intelligence, good looks, and charm, Kennedy had the advantage of his Irish-Catholic ancestry, a particularly valuable asset in heavily Catholic Massachusetts. After three terms in the House, he moved on to the Senate in 1952.

After his landslide reelection in 1958, only Kennedy's religion seemed to limit his political future. No Catholic had ever been elected president, and the defeat of Alfred E. Smith in 1928 had convinced most students of politics (including Smith) that none ever would be elected. Nevertheless, influenced by Kennedy's victories in the Wisconsin and West Virginia primaries—the latter establishing him as an effective campaigner in a predominantly Protestant region—the Democratic convention nominated him.

Kennedy had not been a particularly liberal congressman. He was not involved in the civil rights movement (which was not a major issue in the presidential campaign). He enthusiastically endorsed the Cold War and indicted the Eisenhower administration for falling behind the Soviet Union in the race to build missiles. He admitted frankly that he liked Senator Joseph McCarthy and thought that "he may have something" in his campaign against supposed communists in government. However, as a presidential candidate, he sought to appear more forward-looking. He stressed his youth and "vigor" (a favorite word) and promised to open a "New Frontier" for the country. Nixon ran on the Eisenhower record, which he promised to extend in liberal directions.

A series of television debates between the candidates helped Kennedy by enabling him to demonstrate his maturity and mastery of the issues. Although both candidates laudably avoided it, the religious issue was important. His Catholicism helped Kennedy in eastern urban areas but injured him in many farm districts and throughout the West. Kennedy's victory, 303 to 219 in the electoral college, was paper-thin in the popular vote, 34,227,000 to 34,109,000.

Although Kennedy was rich, white, and a member of the upper crust by any definition, his was a victory of minority groups (Jews, blacks, and blue-collar "ethnics" as well as Catholics gave him overwhelming support) over the traditional white Protestant majority, which went as heavily for Nixon as it had four years earlier for Eisenhower.

MILESTONES

1944	GI Bill of Rights
1945	Franklin Roosevelt dies; Harry Truman becomes president
1946	Benjamin Spock, *Baby and Child Care*
	Baruch plan for control of atomic energy
1947	Taft-Hartley Act
	Truman Doctrine
	"X" (George Kennan), "Sources of Soviet Conduct"
	Marshall Plan proposed
1948–1949	Berlin airlift
1949	North Atlantic Treaty Organization (NATO) established
1950	North Korea invades South Korea
	Alger Hiss convicted of perjury
	Senator McCarthy charges that the State Department is riddled with communists
	UN counterattack in Korea driven back by Red Chinese army
1952	Dwight D. Eisenhower elected president
1953	John Foster Dulles institutes "New Look" foreign policy
	Korean War armistice agreement
1954	Army-McCarthy hearings
	Siege of Dien Bien Phu; French withdraw from Vietnam
	Supreme Court orders school desegregation (*Brown* v. *Board of Education of Topeka*)
1956	Suez crisis
1957	National Guard used to desegregate Central High School in Little Rock, Arkansas
1959	Fidel Castro overthrows Fulgencio Batista, takes power in Cuba
1960	U-2 affair
	United States breaks diplomatic relations with Cuba

30

FROM CAMELOT TO WATERGATE

Having lampooned the Eisenhower administration as stodgy and unimaginative, President Kennedy made a show of his style and wit. He flouted convention by naming his younger brother Robert attorney general. "I can't see that it's wrong to give him a little legal experience before he goes out to practice law," the president quipped. Kennedy also prided himself on being a man of letters, winner of a Pulitzer Prize for *Profiles in Courage*. He quoted Robert Frost and Dante. He played and replayed recordings of Winston Churchill, hoping to imprint the great orator's sonorous cadences on his own flat Bostonian vowels. At the instigation of his elegant wife, Jacqueline, Kennedy surrounded himself with the finest intellects at glittering White House galas to honor Nobel Prize winners and celebrated artists.

Kennedy's campaign slogan—"Let's get this country moving again"—was embodied in his own active life. He played rugged games of touch football with the press corps and romped with his young children in the Oval Office. In an article for *Sports Illustrated* entitled "The Soft American" and published just after the election, Kennedy complained that television, movies, and a comfortable lifestyle had made too many young people flabby. His earliest presidential initiative was a physical fitness campaign in the schools.

Kennedy's image of youthful vigor ("vigah," as he pronounced the word) was enhanced by the beauty and presence of Jacqueline, whose wide-eyed diffidence was commonly misunderstood and universally admired as regal bearing. The im-

979

age was enhanced by Lerner and Loewe's musical *Camelot,* which opened a few weeks before the inauguration. Its evocation of King Arthur, who sought to lead his virile young knights in challenges great and good, suggested the Kennedy White House. (The musical became a favorite of the president; he often listened to cast recordings before going to sleep.) All Washington seemed aglow with excitement and energy. In the words of the administration's chief chronicler, Arthur M. Schlesinger, Jr.: "Never had girls seemed so pretty, tunes so melodious, and evenings so blithe and unconstrained."

Never, too, had the substance of an administration been so closely identified with the style of its president. But the dazzle was misleading. Although quick-witted and intelligent, Kennedy was no intellectual. His favorite reading was the James Bond spy novels of Ian Fleming. He never admitted it publicly, but most of *Profiles in Courage* had been ghostwritten by paid writers.

Nor did the president embody physical fitness. Congenital back problems, aggravated by war injuries, forced Kennedy to use crutches or a cane in private and to take heavy doses of painkillers and amphetamines. The president's permanent "tan" did not result from outdoor exercise, as the public assumed, but from Addison's disease, an often fatal failure of the adrenal glands for which Kennedy gave himself daily injections of cortisone. Though he publicly denied it, Kennedy was chronically ill throughout his presidency.

The president nevertheless engaged in many extramarital sexual affairs. Reporters covering the White House were aware of his often brazen indiscretions, but chose not to intrude on what they regarded as the president's private life.

THE CUBAN CRISIS

"The torch has been passed to a new generation of Americans," Kennedy declared in his inaugural address. Their chief task was to stop the spread of communism. Whereas Eisenhower had relied on the nation's nuclear arsenal to intimidate the Kremlin, Kennedy proposed to challenge communist aggression whenever and wherever it occurred. "We shall pay any price, bear any burden, meet any hardship, support any friend, oppose any foe to assure the survival and the success of liberty," Kennedy intoned. A new breed of cold warrior, Kennedy called on young men and women to serve in the Peace Corps, an organization that he created to mobilize American idealism and technical skills to help developing nations. His was a call for commitment—and action.

Perhaps seduced by his own rhetoric, Kennedy blundered almost immediately. Anti-Castro exiles were eager to organize an invasion of their homeland,

Fidel Castro celebrates in Havana on May 1, 1961, several weeks after the debacle at the Bay of Pigs. Stung by this humiliating defeat, President Kennedy resolved to destroy Castro by other means. "My idea," Robert Kennedy said privately in November, "is to stir things up on the island with espionage, sabotage, general disorder." This CIA program, code-named MONGOOSE, included dozens of schemes to assassinate Castro. Pop-art then imitated life, as weekly television shows such as I Spy *and* Mission: Impossible *featured daffy escapades much like those hatched by MONGOOSE.*

reasoning that the Cuban people would rise up against Castro as soon as "democratic" forces provided the necessary leadership. Under Eisenhower the CIA had begun training some 2000 Cuban exiles in Nicaragua. Kennedy was of two minds about the proposed invasion. Some in his administration opposed it strongly, but his closest advisers, including his brother Robert, urged him to give his approval. In the end he did.

The invaders, 1400 strong, struck in April 1961. They landed at the Bay of Pigs, on Cuba's southern coast. But the Cuban people failed to flock to their lines, and they were soon pinned down by Castro's army and forced to surrender. Because American involvement could not be disguised, the affair exposed the United States to all the criticism that a straightforward assault would have produced, without accomplishing the overthrow of Castro. Worse, it made Kennedy appear impulsive as well as unprincipled. Castro tightened his connections with the Soviet Union.

In June, Kennedy met with Premier Khrushchev in Vienna. Furious over the attempted invasion of Cuba, Khrushchev blustered about grabbing West Berlin. In August, he abruptly closed the border between East and West Berlin and erected a wall of concrete blocks and barbed wire across the city to stop the flow of East Germans into the noncommunist zone. At the same time, the Soviets resumed nuclear testing. Khrushchev ordered the explosion of a series of gigantic hydrogen bombs, including one with a power three thousand times that of the bomb that had devastated Hiroshima.

Khrushchev and Kennedy meet at the summit in Vienna, June 1961. Khrushchev insisted that West Berlin be turned over to communist East Germany; otherwise, he hinted, war might prove inevitable. Kennedy, caught by surprise, failed to mount a powerful defense of why he could do no such thing. "He just beat the hell out of me," Kennedy confided.

Kennedy followed suit: He announced plans to build thousands of nuclear missiles, known as Minutemen, capable of hitting targets on the other side of the world. He expanded the American space program, vowing that an American would land on the moon within ten years. The president called on Congress to pass a large increase in military spending.

In secret, Kennedy resolved to destroy Castro. He ordered military leaders to plan for a full-scale invasion of Cuba. (One of the training maneuvers was code-named ORTSAC—Castro spelled backward.) He also instructed the CIA to undertake "massive activity" against Castro's regime. The CIA devised Operation Mongoose (named for an animal that devours poisonous snakes), a plan to slip spies, saboteurs, and assassins into Cuba. Although never officially endorsed by the president, Mongoose operated under the oversight of Robert Kennedy. Its attempts to assassinate Castro failed.

In 1962 Khrushchev precipitated the most dangerous confrontation of the Cold War. To forestall the anticipated American invasion of Cuba, he moved tanks, heavy bombers, and 42,000 Soviet troops and technicians to the island. But his most fateful step was to sneak guided nuclear missiles into the country and begin constructing launching pads for them. Although the range of these missiles was far less than that of the American Minutemen, if fired from Cuba the Soviet missiles could have delivered nuclear warheads to most of the eastern United States.

On October 22 Kennedy went on television to address the nation. The Soviet buildup was "a deliberately provocative and unjustified change in the status

This photograph, taken by an American U-2 spy plane and released during the Cuban missile crisis, shows the installation of liquid-fueled Soviet missiles. Khrushchev had assumed that the missiles could be kept secret. "Our military specialists informed us that strategic missiles can be reliably concealed in the palm forests of Cuba," one of Khrushchev's advisers recalled. Khrushchev, who assumed that the missiles would be harder to spot if they were in a horizontal position, ordered that the missiles be placed in an upright position only at night. This was a mistake: The U-2's easily detected the missiles in their horizontal position.

quo," he said. He ordered the American navy to stop and search all vessels headed for Cuba and to turn back any containing "offensive" weapons. Kennedy called on Khrushchev to dismantle the missile bases and remove from the island all weapons capable of striking the United States. Any Cuban-based nuclear attack would result, he warned, in "a full retaliatory response upon the Soviet Union."

For days, while the world held its breath, Soviet ships steamed toward Cuba and work on the missile bases continued. Then Khrushchev backed down.

Immediately the president was hailed for his steady nerve and consummate statesmanship; the Cuban missile crisis was widely regarded as his finest hour. Yet in retrospect it appears that he may have overreacted to the missiles in Cuba: a "missile gap" existed but one that favored the United States.

Both Kennedy and Khrushchev were sobered by the missile crisis; afterward neither spoke so glibly about superpower confrontation. They agreed to the installation of a telephone "hot line" between the White House and the Kremlin, so

(text continues on page 986)

Thirteen Days

In October 1962 many people believed that within days they would be dead. The movie *Thirteen Days* (2000), starring Kevin Costner as Kenneth O'Donnell, JFK's appointments secretary, revisits those fears in all their nail-biting vividness. Humanity was saved from nuclear oblivion, the movie contends, only by the steely nerve of President John F. Kennedy, who stared down Soviet aggressors as well as a cabal of trigger-happy U.S. generals.

As the opening credits roll, background scenes mark the crucial events of the Cold War, including the testing of thermonuclear weapons and ICBMs (intercontinental ballistic missiles) capable of delivering nuclear warheads from the United States to the Soviet Union (and vice versa) in less than 30 minutes. As the credits fade, an American U-2 spy plane, flying high over Cuba, takes photos. At this point the movie begins—as did the Cuban missile crisis.

October 15: CIA analysts determine that the Soviet Union has sneaked several dozen medium-range ballistic missiles (MRBMs) into Cuba and is building launching facilities for them. Within a week or two, these missiles will be capable of destroying most American cities. The Soviets, it seems, have sought to alter the strategic balance, perhaps to initiate a sneak attack against the American nuclear arsenal.

October 16: President Kennedy (Bruce Greenwood) hurriedly convenes his top advisers. Former Secretary of State Dean Acheson insists that the president order air strikes against the missiles in Cuba. He predicts that the Soviets will respond by attacking U.S. missiles in Turkey. Obliged to defend Turkey, a member of NATO, the United States will bomb a nuclear facility within the Soviet Union. Perhaps then, he concludes, "cooler heads" will prevail. Kennedy stares at Acheson.

October 17: Secretary of Defense Robert McNamara outlines three options: (1) a surprise bomber attack against Soviet bases in Cuba, followed by an invasion of the island; (2) diplomatic pressure to persuade Soviet Premier Khrushchev to withdraw the missiles; or (3) a naval blockade of Cuba. The Joint Chiefs of Staff unanimously favor bombing and an invasion. "My boys will get those red bastards," declares Curtis LeMay, head of the Strategic Air Command. Kennedy moves toward the blockade option. LeMay seethes.

October 18–21: New reconnaissance photographs show still more Soviet missile sites in Cuba. JFK meets with the Soviet ambassador, Andrei Gromyko, who insists that the Soviet aid to Cuba is purely defensive. "That lying bastard," Kennedy mutters when Gromyko leaves. Preparations for all-out nuclear war intensify.

October 22: Kennedy delivers an "urgent" television address. He informs the nation of the Soviet missiles and announces his decision to impose a blockade of Cuba.

October 23: Some Soviet ships destined for Cuba turn around, but others persist in their course. American warships move to intercept them.

October 25: Prior to an emergency meeting of the United Nations Security Council, Robert Kennedy advises Ambassador Adlai Stevenson to "stick it" to the Soviets. At the subsequent UN session, Stevenson presses the Soviets to say whether they have introduced nuclear missiles into Cuba. "I am prepared to wait for my answer until hell freezes over," Stevenson declares. The Soviet delegate temporizes. Then Stevenson produces photographs of the Soviet missiles.

October 26: The president receives an anguished cable from Khrushchev, calling on him to refrain from igniting a nuclear conflagration. He offers to withdraw the Soviet missiles if the United States will promise not to invade Cuba.

October 27: A second message from Khrushchev, more brusque in tone, includes an additional demand: the United States must withdraw its missiles from Turkey. Kennedy worries that this would harm him politically.

That same day, a Soviet missile in Cuba shoots down a U.S. U-2 plane, killing its pilot. Meanwhile, a Soviet tanker has steamed past the blockade and gives no indication of slowing down. Navy brass inform Secretary of Defense McNamara that the ship will be fired on if it does not stop. "The Navy has been handling

Steven Culp as Robert Kennedy, Bruce Greenwood as President John F. Kennedy, and Kevin Costner as Kenneth O'Donnell, in Thirteen Days.

Photograph of John and Robert Kennedy. O'Donnell is not in the picture—here, nor, as critics of Thirteen Days *insist, in reality.*

blockades since the days of John Paul Jones," an admiral loftily declares. "I don't give a damn about John Paul Jones," McNamara explodes: "There will be no firing on Soviet ships."

October 28: Khrushchev broadcasts his decision to withdraw the Soviet missiles from Cuba. The Soviets "blinked first," American pundits conclude; Kennedy has stared them down.

The movie's account of these and other events is mostly accurate, though sometimes the words are put into someone else's mouth (usually Kevin Costner's). The movie captures John Kennedy's wry elusiveness, Dean Acheson's crisp confidence, Robert Kennedy's youthful impetuousness, and Adlai Stevenson's polished reserve.

But it also contains several significant distortions. The most obvious concerns O'Donnell, who is seen at the center of everything, urging the Kennedys to stand up both to Soviet aggressors and war-hungry American generals. To prevent LeMay from initiating a war on his own, O'Donnell telephones reconnaissance pilots and tells them that if they are fired on they must not inform their commanding officers. Such calls never took place. O'Donnell's role in the crisis was negligible.

Did President Kennedy forestall attempts by the U.S. military to draw the nation into war? The Joint Chiefs of Staff emphatically disapproved of the blockade. And LeMay was certainly intemperate. (During the Vietnam War he advocated bombing Cambodia "into the Stone Age"). But despite the generals' misgivings about Kennedy and his policies, they executed his orders faithfully. For example, after the Soviets shot down the U-2, American warplanes were preparing a retaliatory strike when Kennedy cancelled it. LeMay, though appalled by the order, obeyed it.

Kennedy indisputably exhibited clearheaded judgment and nerve; but two factors, neglected in the movie, were at least as important as his demeanor in resolving the crisis. First, Khrushchev could not go to war because the Soviet Union's military position was weak: indeed, it was the insufficiency of the Soviet nuclear forces that prompted him to send the missiles to Cuba in the first place. If a nuclear war had begun, the Soviet Union would have been annihilated. (Millions of Americans, too, would surely have died.)

Second, Khrushchev was able to satisfy hard-liners within the Soviet military by extracting two concessions from Kennedy: a promise not to invade Cuba, thus ensuring Castro's survival, and a commitment to withdraw U.S. missiles from Turkey. In short, the impasse was resolved by deal-making. This latter provision was kept secret for many years, thus allowing the American people to believe that Kennedy had "stared down" Khrushchev.

that in any future crisis leaders of the two nations could communicate instantly. They also signed a treaty outlawing nuclear testing in the atmosphere. But Khrushchev's bluff had been called—a public humiliation from which he would never recover. Within two years, hard-liners in the Kremlin forced him out of office. His successor, Leonid Brezhnev, was an old-style Stalinist who launched an intensive program of long-range missile development. The nuclear arms race moved to new terrain, uncertain and unimaginably dangerous.

THE VIETNAM WAR

After the French withdrawal from Vietnam in 1954, the Vietnamese people were supposed to determine their own future. But Ngo Dinh Diem, the U.S.-backed leader in the south, feared that he would be defeated by Ho Chi Minh, leader of the nationalist Viet Minh. Diem canceled the election scheduled for 1956. With Eisenhower's help, he attempted to build a new nation: South Vietnam. The United States sent weapons and a handful of American military "advisers" to help Diem equip and train a South Vietnamese army. Ho decided to ignore Diem and consolidate his rule in the north. Those Viet Minh units that remained in the south—they soon came to be known as Vietcong—were instructed to form secret cells and bide their time. During the late 1950s they gained in strength and militancy.

In May 1959 Ho decided that the time had come to overthrow Diem. Vietcong guerrillas infiltrated thousands of villages, ambushed South Vietnamese convoys, and assassinated government officials. Soon the Vietcong controlled large sections of the countryside, some almost within sight of the capital city of Saigon.

By the time Kennedy took office, Diem's government was tottering. As a senator, Kennedy had endorsed Diem and the attempt to build a noncommunist South Vietnam. He called it the "cornerstone of the Free World in Southeast Asia, the keystone in the arch, the finger in the dike." After the Bay of Pigs debacle, furthermore, Kennedy worried that his credibility with Khrushchev had been damaged. "If he thinks I'm inexperienced and have no guts," he told an aide, "we won't get anywhere with him. So we have to act." Vietnam, he added, "looks like the place."

Kennedy sharply increased the American military and economic commitment to South Vietnam. At the end of 1961 there were 3200 American military personnel in the country; within two years, there were more than 16,000, and 120 American soldiers had been killed. Despite the expanded effort, by the summer of 1963 Diem's regime was in ruins. An ardent Catholic, he cracked down on the Buddhists, who, joined by students, protested his repression. Thousands were arrested, and some were shot. In protest, several Buddhist monks became martyrs by setting themselves on fire in public.

Unable to persuade Diem to moderate his policies, Kennedy sent word to dissident Vietnamese generals of his willingness to support them if they ousted Diem. On November 1 several of these generals surrounded the presidential palace with troops and tanks, seized Diem, and killed him. The United States immediately recognized the new junta.

"WE SHALL OVERCOME": THE CIVIL RIGHTS MOVEMENT

Kennedy initially approached the race question with exceeding caution. His razor-thin victory had depended on the votes both of African Americans in northern cities and white Democrats in the Deep South. As president, his visible support for one group would alienate the other. So Kennedy temporized, urging leaders on both sides to show restraint. This proved impossible.

During and after World War II, like a glacier, slowly but with massive force, a demand for change had developed in the South. Its roots lay in southern industrialization; in the shift from small sharecropping holdings to large commercial farms; in the vast wartime expenditures of the federal government on aircraft factories and army bases in the region; in the impact of the GI Bill on southern colleges and universities; and in the gradual development of a southern black middle class.

This change first came to national attention during the Eisenhower administration in the tightly segregated city of Montgomery, Alabama. On Friday, December 1, 1955, Rosa Parks, a seamstress at the Montgomery Fair department store, boarded a bus on her way home from her job. She dutifully took a seat toward the rear as custom and law required. As white workers and shoppers filled the forward section, the driver ordered her to give up her place to a white passenger. Parks, who was also secretary of the Montgomery NAACP chapter, refused. She had decided, she later recalled, that "I would have to know once and for all what rights I had as a human being and a citizen."

She was arrested. Over the weekend, Montgomery's black leaders organized a boycott. "Don't ride the bus . . . Monday," their mimeographed notice ran. "If you work, take a cab, or share a ride, or walk." Monday dawned bitterly cold, but the boycott was a total success.

Most Montgomery blacks could not afford to miss a single day's wages, so the protracted struggle to get to work was difficult to maintain. Black-owned taxis reduced their rates sharply, and when the city declared this illegal, car pools were quickly organized. Few African Americans owned cars. Although nearly everyone who did volunteered, there were never more than 350 cars available to the more than 10,000 people who needed rides to their jobs and back every day. Nevertheless, the boycott went on.

Late in February the Montgomery authorities obtained indictments of 115 leaders of the boycott, but this move backfired because it focused national attention on the situation. A young clergyman, Martin Luther King, Jr., was emerging as the leader of the boycott. A gifted speaker, he became an overnight celebrity. Money poured in from all over the country to support the movement. The boycott lasted for over a year. Finally the Supreme Court declared the local law enforcing racial separation unconstitutional: Montgomery had to desegregate its public transportation system.

This success encouraged blacks elsewhere in the South to band together against segregation. A new organization founded in 1957, the Southern Christian Leadership Conference (SCLC), headed by King, moved to the forefront of the civil rights movement. Other organizations joined the struggle, notably the Congress of Racial Equality (CORE), which had been founded in 1942.

In February 1960 four African American college students in Greensboro, North Carolina, sat down at a lunch counter at a Woolworth's five-and-ten. "We do not serve Negroes," they were told. They returned with more and more demonstrators. By the end of the week over a thousand protesters descended on Woolworth's, led by a phalanx of football players from the nearby black college who cleared the way through a throng of Confederate flag-wavers. "Who do you think you are?" a white demanded. "We the union army," a football player retorted.

In May 1961 black and white foes of segregation organized a "freedom ride" to test the effectiveness of federal regulations prohibiting discrimination in interstate transportation. Boarding two buses in Washington, an integrated group of 13 volunteers took off across the South toward New Orleans. In Alabama they ran into trouble. At Anniston racists set fire to one of the buses, and in Birmingham they were assaulted by a mob. But violence did not stop the freedom riders. Other groups followed, many deliberately seeking arrest to test local segregation ordinances. The resultant court cases repeatedly broke down legal racial barriers throughout the South.

This protracted struggle eventually yielded practical and moral benefits for southern whites as well as blacks. Gradually all but the most unwavering defenders of segregation changed their attitudes. But this took time, and many blacks were unwilling to wait.

Some blacks, contemptuous of white prejudices, were urging their fellows to reject "American" society and all it stood for. In the North, black nationalism became a potent force. Elijah Muhammad, leader of the Black Muslim movement, loathed whites so intensely that he demanded that a part of the United States be set aside exclusively for blacks. He urged his followers to be industrious, thrifty, and abstemious—and to view all whites with suspicion and hatred.

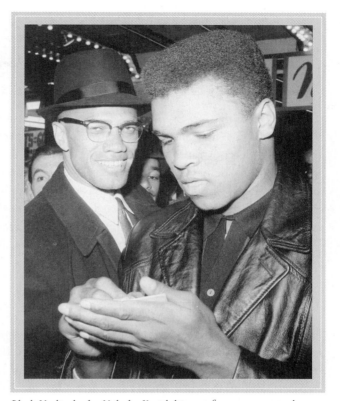

Black Muslim leader Malcolm X with his most famous convert to the Nation of Islam, heavyweight champion Cassius Clay. Clay underscored his conversion by changing his name to Muhammad Ali.

"This white government has ruled us and given us plenty hell, but the time has arrived that you taste a little of your own hell," Muhammad said. "There are many of my poor black ignorant brothers . . . preaching the ignorant and lying stuff that you should love your enemy. What fool can love his enemy?" Another important Black Muslim, Malcolm X, put it this way in a 1960 speech: "For the white man to ask the black man if he hates him is just like the rapist asking the raped, or the wolf asking the sheep, 'Do you hate me?'" "If someone puts a hand on you," he advised blacks on another occasion, "send him to the cemetery."

Ordinary black Southerners became increasingly impatient. In the face of brutal repression by local police, many began to question Martin Luther King's tactic of nonviolent protest. After leading a series of demonstrations in Birmingham, Alabama, in 1963, King was thrown in jail, from which he wrote the following words:

[W]hen you take a cross-country drive and find it necessary to sleep night after night in the uncomfortable corners of your automobile because no motel will accept you; when you are humiliated day in and day out by nagging signs reading "white" and "colored"; when your first name becomes "nigger" and your middle name becomes "boy" ...then you will understand why we find it so difficult to wait.

After Birmingham, President Kennedy finally gave his support to a modest civil rights bill. When this measure ran into stiff opposition in Congress, blacks organized a demonstration in Washington, attended by 200,000 people. At this gathering, King delivered his "I Have a Dream" address, looking forward to a time when racial prejudice no longer existed and people of all religions and colors could join hands and say, "Free at last! Free at last!" Kennedy sympathized with the purpose of the Washington gathering but feared it would make passage of the civil rights bill more difficult rather than easier. As in other areas, he was not a forceful advocate of his own proposals.

Tragedy in Dallas: JFK Assassinated

Through it all, Kennedy retained his hold on public opinion. In the fall of 1963 most observers believed he easily would win a second term. Then, while visiting Dallas, Texas, on November 22, he was shot in the head by an assassin, Lee Harvey Oswald, and died almost instantly. One measure of Kennedy's hold on the public imagination was the outpouring of grief that attended his death. Kennedy had given hope to people who had none. On learning of his death, young black civil rights activist Anne Moody, who later wrote *Coming of Age in*

Jacqueline Kennedy and Robert F. Kennedy returning from the Arlington National Cemetery on November 26, 1963, following the burial of President John F. Kennedy. Not since Lincoln's funeral had there been such an intense display of public grief over the loss of a political leader.

Mississippi, was working as a waitress in a segregated restaurant. "Tears were burning my cheeks," she recalled. Her boss, a Greek immigrant, gently suggested she take the rest of the day off. When she looked up, she saw tears in his eyes too.

Kennedy's assassination precipitated an extraordinary series of events. Oswald had fired on the president with a rifle from an upper story of a warehouse. No one saw him pull the trigger. He was apprehended largely because he panicked and killed a policeman across town later in the day. He denied his guilt, but a mass of evidence connected him with the assassination of the president. Before he could be brought to trial, however, he was himself murdered by Jack Ruby, the owner of a Dallas nightclub. The incident took place in full view of television cameras, while Oswald was being transferred from one place of detention to another.

Each following day brought new revelations. Oswald had defected briefly to the Soviet Union in 1959, then had returned to the United States and formed a pro-Castro organization in New Orleans. Many concluded that some nefarious conspiracy lay at the root of the tragedy. Oswald, the argument ran, was a pawn—either of communists or anticommunists (the conspiracy theories lost none of their appeal for being contradictory)—whose murder was designed to shield from exposure the masterminds who had engineered the assassination. A special commission headed by Chief Justice Earl Warren was convened to analyze the evidence. After a lengthy investigation, they concluded that Oswald had acted alone.

Instead of dampening charges of conspiracy, the Warren Report provoked new doubts. As word leaked out about the earlier CIA assassination attempts against Castro, the failure of the Warren Report even to mention Operation Mongoose made the commission suspect, all the more so since several members, including Allen Dulles, former director of the CIA, had known of the operation. In fact, there is little solid evidence to suggest that Oswald was part of a wider conspiracy. But the decision of Dulles and other commissioners to protect CIA secrets engendered skepticism toward the Warren Commission—and the United States government.

LYNDON BAINES JOHNSON

John F. Kennedy's death made Lyndon B. Johnson president. From 1949 until his election as vice president, Johnson had been a senator and, for most of that time, Senate Democratic leader. He could be heavy-handed or subtle, and also devious, domineering, persistent, and obliging. Many people swore by him; few had the fortitude to swear at him. Above all he knew what to do with political power.

"Some men," he said, "want power so they can strut around to 'Hail to the Chief'. . . . I wanted it to use it."

Johnson, who had consciously modeled his career after that of Franklin D. Roosevelt, considered social welfare legislation his specialty. The contrast with Kennedy could not have been sharper. In his inaugural address, Kennedy had made no mention of domestic issues. Kennedy's plans for federal aid for education, urban renewal, a higher minimum wage, and medical care for the aged were blocked in Congress by Republicans and southern Democrats. The same coalition also defeated his chief economic initiative—a broad tax cut to stimulate the economy. But Kennedy had reacted to these defeats mildly, almost wistfully. He thought the machinery of the federal government was cumbersome and ineffective.

Johnson knew how to make it work. On becoming president, he pushed hard for Kennedy's programs. Early in his career Johnson had voted against a bill making lynching a federal crime, and he also had opposed bills outlawing state poll taxes and establishing the federal Fair Employment Practices Commission. But after he became an important figure in national affairs, he consistently championed racial equality. Now he made it the centerpiece of his domestic policy. "Civil righters are going to have to wear sneakers to keep up with me," he boasted. Bills long buried in committee sailed through Congress. Early in 1964 Kennedy's tax cut was passed. A few months later, an expanded version of another Kennedy proposal became law as the Civil Rights Act of 1964.

THE GREAT SOCIETY

The much-strengthened Civil Rights Act outlawed discrimination by employers against blacks and also against women. It broke down legal barriers to black voting in the southern states and outlawed racial segregation of all sorts in places of public accommodation, such as movie theaters, hotels, and restaurants.

Johnson's success in steering the Civil Rights Act through Congress confirmed his belief that he could be a reformer in the tradition of Franklin Roosevelt. He declared war on poverty and set out to create a "great society" in which poverty no longer would exist.

In 1937 Roosevelt had been accused of exaggeration for claiming that one-third of the nation was "ill-housed, ill-clad, ill-nourished." In fact Roosevelt had underestimated the extent of poverty. Wartime economic growth reduced the percentage of poor people in the country substantially, but in 1960 between 20 and 25 percent of all American families—about 40 million people—were living

LBJ as Texas cowboy, a masculine image he assiduously cultivated. Biographers have suggested that Johnson was torn between the expectations of his father, a crude local politician who flouted polite society, and those of his mother, a refined woman who insisted that her son read poetry and practice the violin. Johnson later told biographer Doris Kearns Goodwin that he persisted in Vietnam because he worried that critics would accuse him of being "an unmanly man. A man without a spine."

below the poverty line, a government standard of minimum subsistence based on income and family size.

The presence of so many poor people in an "affluent" society was deplorable but not difficult to explain. In any community a certain number of people cannot support themselves because of physical, mental, or emotional problems. The United States also included entire regions, the best known being the Appalachian area, that had been bypassed by economic development and no longer provided their inhabitants with adequate economic opportunities.

The primary objective of Johnson's war on poverty was to give poor people the opportunity to improve themselves. The Economic Opportunity Act of 1964 created a mixture of programs, among them a Job Corps similar to the New Deal Civilian Conservation Corps; a community action program to finance local antipoverty efforts; Head Start, an educational program for small children; a work-study program for college students; and a system for training the unskilled unemployed and for lending money to small businesses in poor areas. The programs combined the progressive concept of government aid for those in need with the conservative idea of individual responsibility.

Buttressed by his legislative triumphs, Johnson sought election as president in his own right in 1964. He achieved this ambition in unparalleled fashion. His championing of civil rights won him the almost unanimous support of blacks; his tax policy attracted the well-to-do and the business interests; his war on poverty held the allegiance of labor and other traditionally Democratic groups. His down-home southern antecedents counterbalanced his liberalism on the race question in the eyes of many white Southerners.

The Republicans played into his hands by nominating the conservative Senator Barry M. Goldwater of Arizona, whose objective in Congress had been "not to pass laws but to repeal them." As a presidential candidate he favored such laissez-faire policies as cutting back on the social security system and doing away with the Tennessee Valley Authority. A large majority of voters found Goldwater out-of-date on economic questions and dangerously aggressive on foreign affairs.

In November, Johnson won a sweeping victory, collecting over 61 percent of the popular vote and carrying the whole country except Goldwater's Arizona and five states in the Deep South, where many conservatives were voting more against Johnson's civil rights policies than in favor of Goldwater. While not personally a racist, Goldwater had voted against the Civil Rights Act of 1964 and was opposed to government-mandated school integration.

Quickly Johnson pressed ahead with his Great Society program. In January 1965 he proposed a compulsory hospital insurance system, known as Medicare, for all persons over the age of 65. As amended by Congress, the Medicare Act consisted of Part A, hospital insurance for the retired (funded by increased Social Security taxes), and a voluntary plan, Part B, covering doctors' bills (paid for in part by the government). The law also provided for grants to the states to help pay the medical expenses of poor people, even those below the retirement age of 65. This part of the system was called Medicaid. Before the passage of the Medicare Act, about half of Americans over 65 years old had had no medical insurance.

Next, Congress passed the Elementary and Secondary Education Act in 1965, which supplied federal funds to school districts. Head Start, a program for poor preschoolers, was designed to prepare them for elementary school. It also incidentally improved the children's health by providing medical examinations and nutritious meals.

Still another important reform was the Voting Rights Act of 1965, pressed through Congress by President Johnson after more brutal repression of civil rights demonstrators in the South. This law provided for federal intervention to protect black registration and voting in six southern states. It applied to state and local as well as federal elections.

The Great Society program was one of the most remarkable outpourings of important legislation in American history. The results, however, were mixed. Head Start and a related program to help students in secondary schools prepare for college were unqualified successes. But the 1965 Education Act proved a disappointment. Too many local school districts found ways of using the federal money to cover their ordinary expenses, and the sums actually devoted to programs for the poor failed to improve most students' performances significantly.

Medicare and Medicaid certainly provided good medical treatment for millions of people, but because the patients no longer paid most of the bills, doctors, hospitals, and drug companies were able to raise fees and prices without fear of losing business. Medical costs escalated far more rapidly than the rate of inflation.

The Job Corps, which was designed to help poor people get better-paying jobs by providing them with vocational training, was an almost total failure. The cost of the training was high, relatively few trainees completed the courses, and of those who did, few found jobs in which they could make use of their new skills.

On balance, the achievements of the Great Society were far below what President Johnson had promised and his supporters had envisioned. The same, of course, can be said of most ambitious reform programs—of Reconstruction; of the Progressive movement; certainly of the New Deal, to which Johnson had contributed as a young man. Despite his long political experience, Johnson tried to accomplish too many things too quickly. He relied too heavily on the techniques of political manipulation. Perhaps he was carried away by his good fortune—that he would ever become president must have seemed to a man of his political acumen most unlikely after he failed to win the nomination in 1960. He seized too avidly this unexpected opportunity to make history. Without the crisis atmosphere that had appeared to justify hasty experimentation during the New Deal years, the public judged the results of the Great Society and the president who had shaped it skeptically.

JOHNSON ESCALATES THE WAR

After Diem's assassination, the situation in South Vietnam continued to deteriorate. One military coup followed another, and political instability aggravated military incapacity. President Johnson nevertheless felt that he had no choice but to prop up the South Vietnamese regime. "If I don't go in now," he told an adviser, "they'll be all over me in Congress. They won't be talking about my civil rights bill, or education, or beautification. No sir, they'll push Vietnam up my ass every time."

Johnson decided to punish North Vietnam directly for prosecuting the war in the south. In early 1964 he secretly ordered American warships to escort the South Vietnamese navy on missions far into the Gulf of Tonkin; the South Vietnamese attacked enemy ships and port facilities and landed commandos in North Vietnam. During one spy mission, American destroyers apparently were

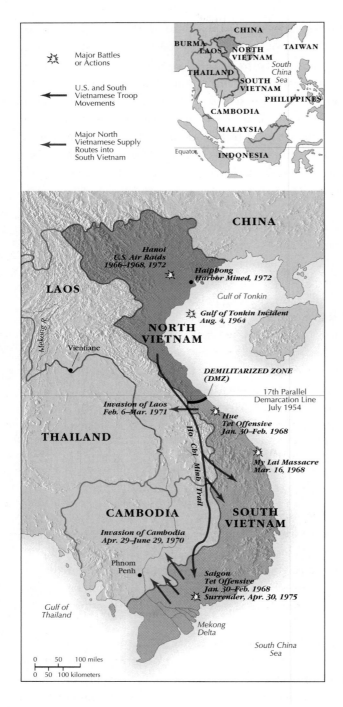

Southeast Asia, 1954–1975

fired on by North Vietnamese gunboats (the action, which occurred on a stormy night, has never been conclusively analyzed). Using this Tonkin "incident" as pretext, Johnson demanded, and in an air of crisis obtained, an authorization from Congress to "repel any armed attack against the forces of the United States and to prevent further aggression." With this blank check, known as the Gulf of Tonkin Resolution, and buttressed by his sweeping defeat of Goldwater in the 1964 presidential election, Johnson authorized air attacks in North Vietnam. By the summer of 1965, American bombers were conducting some 5000 raids each month.

But the hail of bombs on North Vietnam had little effect on the struggle in the south. American intelligence officers concluded that the bombing campaign in the north actually strengthened the people's identification with Ho Chi Minh's government. Worse, the Vietcong expanded the areas under their control in the south. After a fact-finding mission in the war zone, McGeorge Bundy concluded that the prospects were grim for South Vietnam. "The energy and persistence of the Vietcong are astonishing," he reported. "They have accepted extraordinary losses and they come back for more. They show skill in their sneak attacks and ferocity when cornered." If the war was to be won, American soldiers—lots of them—would have to do much of the fighting themselves.

In July 1965 Johnson ordered the first of several huge increases in American ground forces in Vietnam. By the end of 1965, 184,000 Americans were in the field; a year later, 385,000; after another year, 485,000. By the middle of 1968 the number exceeded 538,000. Each increase was met by corresponding increases from the other side. The Soviet Union and China sent no combat troops, but stepped up their aid, and thousands of North Vietnamese regulars filtered across the 17th parallel to join the Vietcong guerrillas.

The new American strategy was not to seize any particular battlefield or terrain as in all previous wars, but to kill as many of the enemy as possible through bloody "search and destroy" operations. As the scope of the action broadened, the number of American casualties rose. The United States was engaged in a full-scale war, one that Congress never declared.

OPPOSITION TO THE WAR

Some Americans claimed that the struggle between the South Vietnamese government and the Vietcong was a civil war in which the United States should not meddle. They stressed the repressive character of the South Vietnamese government as proof that the war was not a contest between democracy and communism. They objected to the massive aerial bombings (more explosives were dropped on Vietnam between 1964 and 1968 than on Germany and Japan combined in World War II), to the use of napalm and other chemical weapons such as the defoliants that were sprayed on forests and crops and that wreaked havoc among noncombatants, and to the killing of civilians by American troops. As chairman of the Foreign Relations Committee, Senator William Fulbright had introduced the Gulf of Tonkin Resolution in 1964. By 1967 he was calling the war "unnecessary and immoral." Above all, opponents of the war deplored the heavy loss of life—over 40,000 American dead by 1970, and hundreds of thousands of Vietnamese.

The cost of the war came to exceed $20 billion a year. But in large part because so many people objected to the war, Johnson refused to ask Congress to raise taxes to pay for it. The resulting deficits forced the government to borrow huge sums, caused interest rates to soar, and pushed prices higher.

Although Johnson's financial policies were shortsighted, if not blatantly irresponsible, and his statements about the war often disingenuous, he and his advisers believed they were defending freedom and democracy. As time passed and the human and financial costs mounted, it became clear that military victory was impossible. Yet American leaders were extraordinarily slow to grasp this fact. Repeatedly they advised the president that just one more escalation (so many more soldiers, so many more air raids) would break the enemy's will to resist. The arrogance bred by America's brief postwar monopoly of nuclear weapons persisted in some quarters long after the monopoly had been lost. This "super-power mentality," the belief that the United States was destined to be a kind of world policeman, was the cause of much future trouble.

THE ELECTION OF 1968

Gradually the opponents of the war gained numbers and strength. They began to include some of the president's advisers. By late 1967 Secretary of Defense Robert F. McNamara, who had methodically tracked kill ratios, troop replacement rates, and nearly every other conceivable statistic, concluded that "the figures didn't add up" and the war could not be won. Deeply despondent, he resigned.

Opposition to the war was especially vehement on college campuses, some students objecting because they thought the United States had no business intervening in the Vietnam conflict, others because they feared being drafted, still others because so many students obtained educational deferments, while young men who were unable to attend college were conscripted.

Then, in November 1967, Eugene McCarthy, a low-keyed, introspective senator from Minnesota, announced his candidacy for the 1968 Democratic presidential nomination. Opposition to the war was his issue.

Stung by the critics, Johnson ordered General William C. Westmoreland, commander of American forces in Vietnam, to reassure the American people on the course of the war. The general obligingly returned to the United States in late 1967 and told the press that he could see "some light at the end of the tunnel."

Suddenly, early in 1968, on the heels of this announcement, North Vietnamese and Vietcong forces launched a general offensive to correspond with their Lunar New Year (called Tet). Striking 39 of the 44 provincial capitals, many other towns and cities, and every American base, they caused chaos throughout South Vietnam. They held Hue, the old capital of the country, for weeks. To root them out of Saigon the Americans had to level large sections of the city. Elsewhere the destruction was total, an irony highlighted by the remark of an American officer after the recapture of the village of Ben Tre: "It became necessary to destroy the town to save it."

The Tet offensive was essentially a series of raids; the communists did not expect to hold the cities indefinitely, and they did not. Their losses were enormous. Nevertheless the psychological impact in South Vietnam and in the United States made Tet a clear victory for the North. American pollsters reported an enormous shift of public opinion against further escalation of the fighting. When Westmoreland described Tet as a communist defeat and yet requested an additional 206,000 troops, McCarthy, who was campaigning in the New Hampshire primary, suddenly became a formidable figure. Thousands of students and other volunteers flocked to the state to ring doorbells on his behalf. On primary election day he polled 42 percent of the Democratic vote.

The political situation was confused. Before the primary, former attorney general Robert F. Kennedy, brother of the slain president, had refused either to seek the Democratic nomination or to support McCarthy, although he disliked Johnson intensely and was opposed to his policy in Vietnam. After McCarthy's success, he announced his candidacy.

Confronting this division in the ranks, President Johnson realized he could no longer hope to be an effective president. In a surprising televised announcement, he withdrew from the race. Vice President Hubert H. Humphrey then announced his candidacy, and Johnson threw the weight of his administration behind him.

Kennedy carried the primaries in Indiana and Nebraska. McCarthy won in Wisconsin and Oregon. In the climactic contest in California, Kennedy won by a small margin. However, immediately after his victory speech in a Los Angeles hotel, he was assassinated by Sirhan Sirhan, an Arab nationalist who had been incensed by Kennedy's support of Israel. In effect, Kennedy's death ensured the nomination of Humphrey.

The contest for the Republican nomination was far less dramatic, although its outcome, the nomination of Richard M. Nixon, would have been hard to predict a few years earlier. After his loss to Kennedy in 1960, Nixon ran unsuccessfully for governor of California in 1962, then moved to New York City and joined a prominent law firm. But he remained active in Republican affairs. In 1964 he had campaigned hard for Goldwater. When no other Republican developed extensive support as the 1968 election approached, Nixon entered the race, swept the primaries, and won an easy first-ballot victory at the Republican convention.

Nixon then astounded the country and dismayed liberals by choosing Governor Spiro T. Agnew of Maryland as his running mate. Agnew was a political unknown. ("Spiro who?" jokesters asked.) Nixon chose him primarily to attract southern votes.

Placating the South seemed necessary because Governor George C. Wallace of Alabama was making a determined bid to win enough electoral votes for his American Independent party to prevent any candidate from obtaining a majority. Wallace was flagrantly antiblack and anti-intellectual. (College professors were among his favorite targets. In attacking them he used such well-worn images as "ivory tower folks with pointed heads" and—more inventive—people without "sense enough to park a bicycle straight.") He seemed sure to attract substantial southern and conservative support. He denounced federal "meddling," the "coddling" of criminals, and the forced desegregation of schools. Nixon's choice of Agnew appeared to be an effort to contend for the groups Wallace was attracting.

This Republican strategy heightened the tension surrounding the Democratic convention, which met in Chicago in late August. Humphrey delegates controlled the convention. The vice president had a solid liberal record on domestic issues, but he had supported Johnson's Vietnam policy with equal solidity. Those who could not stomach the Nixon-Agnew ticket and who opposed the war faced a difficult choice. Several thousand activists, representing a dozen groups and advocating tactics ranging from orderly demonstrations to civil disobedience to indiscriminate violence, descended on Chicago to put pressure on the delegates to repudiate the Johnson Vietnam policy.

In the tense atmosphere that resulted, the party hierarchy overreacted. The mayor of Chicago, Richard J. Daley, whose ability to "influence" election results in a manner favorable to Democrats had often been demonstrated, ringed the convention with policemen to protect it from disruption. This was a reasonable precaution in itself. Inside the building the delegates nominated Humphrey and adopted a war plank satisfactory to Johnson. Outside, however, provoked by the abusive language and violent behavior of radical demonstrators, the police tore into the protesters, in Norman Mailer's graphic phrase, "like a chain saw cutting into wood," while millions watched on television in fascinated horror.

Nixon campaigned at a deliberate, dignified pace. He made relatively few public appearances, relying instead on carefully arranged television interviews and taped commercials. He stressed firm enforcement of the law and his desire

Alarmed by antiwar demonstrators at the 1968 Democratic national convention, Chicago Mayor Richard Daley ordered barbed wire fences erected in an attempt to control access to the convention hall. Protest demonstrations at the convention and Mayor Daley's heavy-handed response persuaded many voters that the fate of the republic would be safer in Republican hands.

"to bring us together." As for Vietnam, he would "end the war and win the peace," by just what means he did not say. Agnew, in his blunt, coarse way, assaulted Humphrey, the Democrats, and left-wing dissident groups. (Critics who remembered Nixon's own political style in the era of Joseph McCarthy called Agnew "Nixon's Nixon.")

The Democratic campaign was badly organized. Humphrey was subjected to merciless heckling from antiwar audiences. He seemed far behind in the early stages. Shortly before election day, however, President Johnson helped him greatly by suspending air attacks on North Vietnam, and in the long run the Republican strategy helped increase his numbers, too. Black voters and the urban poor had no practical choice but to vote Democratic. Gradually Humphrey gained ground, and on election day the popular vote was close: Nixon slightly less than 31.8 million, Humphrey nearly 31.3 million. Nixon's Electoral College margin, however, was substantial—301 to 191. The remaining 46 electoral votes went to Wallace, whose 9.9 million votes came to 13.5 percent of the total. Together, Nixon and Wallace received 57 percent of the popular vote. Nevertheless, the Democrats retained control of both houses of Congress.

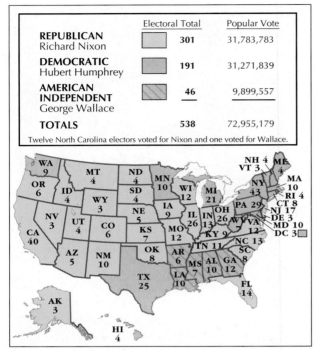

	Electoral Total	Popular Vote
REPUBLICAN Richard Nixon	301	31,783,783
DEMOCRATIC Hubert Humphrey	191	31,271,839
AMERICAN INDEPENDENT George Wallace	46	9,899,557
TOTALS	538	72,955,179

Twelve North Carolina electors voted for Nixon and one voted for Wallace.

The Election of 1968

NIXON AS PRESIDENT: "VIETNAMIZING" THE WAR

When he took office in January 1969, Richard Nixon projected an image of calm and deliberate statesmanship; he introduced no startling changes, proposed no important new legislation. Indeed, he accepted more or less uncritically the New Deal approach to managing the economy. He considered the solution of the Vietnam problem his chief task. When the war in Southeast Asia first had burst on American consciousness in 1954, he had favored military intervention in keeping with the containment policy. As controversy over American policy developed, he had supported most of the actions of Presidents Kennedy and Johnson. During the 1968 campaign he downplayed the Vietnam issue. Although he insisted he would end the war on "honorable" terms if elected, he suggested nothing very different from what Johnson was doing.

In office, Nixon first proposed a phased withdrawal of all non–South Vietnamese troops, to be followed by an internationally supervised election in South Vietnam. The North Vietnamese rejected this scheme and insisted that the United States withdraw its forces unconditionally.

The intransigence of the North Vietnamese left the president in a difficult position. Nixon could not compel the foe to end a war it had begun against the

French nearly a quarter of a century earlier, yet every passing day added to the strength of antiwar sentiment, which, as it expressed itself in ever more emphatic terms, in turn led to deeper divisions in the country. However, large numbers of Americans would not face up to the consequences of ending the war on the communists' terms.

The president responded to the dilemma by trying to build up the South Vietnamese armed forces so that American troops could pull out without South Vietnam being overrun by the communists. He shipped so many planes to the Vietnamese that they came to have the fourth-largest air force in the world. The trouble with this strategy, called Vietnamization, was that for 15 years the United States had been trying without success to make the South Vietnamese capable of defending themselves. Nevertheless, efforts at Vietnamization were stepped up, and in June 1969 Nixon announced that he would soon reduce the number of American soldiers in Vietnam by 25,000. In September he promised that an additional 35,000 troops would be withdrawn.

These steps did not quiet American protesters. On October 15 an antiwar demonstration, Vietnam Moratorium Day, organized by students, produced an unprecedented outpouring of protest all over the country. This massive display produced one of Vice President Agnew's most notorious blasts of adjectival invective: He said that the moratorium was an example of "national masochism" led by "an effete corps of impudent snobs who characterize themselves as intellectuals."

A second Moratorium Day brought a crowd estimated at 250,000 to march past the White House. The president was unmoved. He could not be influenced by protests, he insisted, and passed the time in watching a football game on television.

For a while, events appeared to vindicate Nixon's position. A gradual slowing of military activity in Vietnam had reduced American casualties to what those who did not find the war morally unbearable considered "tolerable" levels. Troop withdrawals continued in an orderly fashion. A new lottery system for drafting men for military duty eliminated some of the inequities in the selective service law.

But the war continued. Early in 1970 reports that in 1968 an American unit had massacred civilians, including dozens of women and children, in a Vietnamese hamlet known as My Lai revived the controversy over the purposes of the war and its corrosive effects on those who were fighting it. The American people, it seemed, were being torn apart by the war.

Nixon's most implacable enemy could have found no reason to think the president wished the war to go on. Its human, economic, and social costs could only vex his days and threaten his future reputation. When he reduced the level of the fighting, the communists merely waited for further reductions. When he

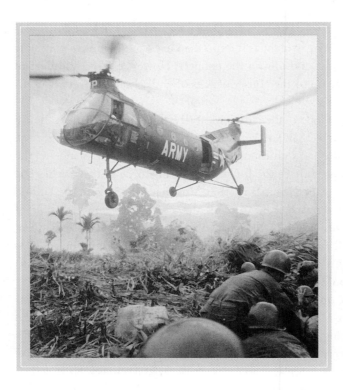

The Vietcong were initially terrified of what they called "angleworms," helicopters that swooped from the sky belching fire and rockets. The Vietcong soon learned to aim two-thirds the distance of the fuselage ahead, so that the helicopter would fly into their bullets. Hundreds of helicopters were shot down by small arms fire.

raised it, many of his own people denounced him. If he pulled out of Vietnam entirely, other Americans would be outraged.

Perhaps Nixon's error lay in his unwillingness to admit his own uncertainty, something the greatest presidents—one thinks immediately of Lincoln and Franklin Roosevelt—were never afraid to do. Facing a dilemma, he tried to convince the world that he was firmly in control of events, with the result that at times he seemed more like a high school valedictorian declaiming sententiously about the meaning of life than the mature statesman he so desperately wished to be. Thus he heightened the tensions he sought to relax—in America, in Vietnam, and elsewhere.

THE CAMBODIAN "INCURSION"

Late in April 1970 Nixon announced that Vietnamization was proceeding more rapidly than he had hoped, that communist power was weakening, and that within a year another 150,000 American soldiers would be extracted from Vietnam. A week later he announced that military intelligence had indicated that the enemy was consolidating its "sanctuaries" in neutral Cambodia and that he was therefore dispatching thousands of American troops to destroy these bases. (American planes had been bombing enemy sites in Cambodia for some time, although this fact was not revealed to the public until 1973.) Nixon even resumed bombing targets in North Vietnam. "You've got to electrify people with bold decisions," he told the Joint Chiefs of Staff. "Let's go blow the hell out of them."

To foes of the war, Nixon's decision seemed so appallingly unwise that some of them began to fear that he had become mentally unbalanced. The contradictions between his confident statements about Vietnamization and his alarmist description of powerful enemy forces poised like a dagger 30-odd miles from Saigon did not seem the product of a reasoning mind. His failure to consult congressional leaders or many of his advisers before drastically altering his policy, the critics claimed, was unconstitutional and irresponsible. His insensitive response to the avalanche of criticism that descended on him further disturbed observers.

Nixon's shocking announcement triggered many campus demonstrations. One college where feeling ran high was Kent State University in Ohio. For several days students there clashed with local police; they broke windows and caused other damage to property. When the governor of Ohio called out the National Guard, angry students showered the soldiers with stones. During a noontime protest on May 4 the guardsmen, who were poorly trained in crowd control, suddenly opened fire. Four students were killed, two of them women who were merely passing by on their way to class.

While the nation reeled from this shock, two black students at Jackson State University were killed by Mississippi state policemen. A wave of student strikes followed, closing down hundreds of colleges, including many that had seen no

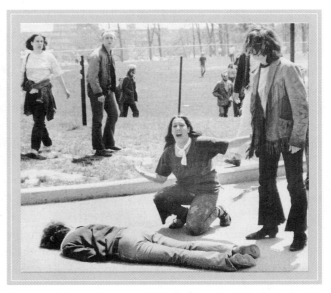

National Guardsmen firing into a crowd of antiwar protesters at Kent State University killed 4 students and injured 11 others. The shootings triggered massive demonstrations and protests across the nation.

previous unrest. Moderate students by the tens of thousands had joined with the radicals.

The almost universal condemnation of the invasion and of the way it had been planned shook Nixon hard. He backtracked, pulling American ground troops out of Cambodia quickly. But he did not change his Vietnam policy, and in fact Cambodia apparently stiffened his determination. As American ground troops were withdrawn, he stepped up air attacks.

The balance of forces remained in uneasy equilibrium through 1971. But late in March 1972 the North Vietnamese again mounted a series of assaults through-out South Vietnam. The president responded with heavier bombing, and he or-dered the approaches to Haiphong and other northern ports sown with mines to cut off the communists' supplies.

Détente with Communism

But in the midst of these aggressive actions, Nixon and his National Security Adviser, Henry Kissinger, devised a bold and ingenious diplomatic offensive, exe-cuted in nearly complete secrecy—from even the State and Defense depart-ments! Nixon and Kissinger made an effective though not always harmonious team. They were both so self-centered that they did not always trust each other. Kissinger, who kept track of his own staff by bugging their phones, accused Nixon's top aides of doing the same to him.

Abandoning a lifetime of treating communism as a single worldwide conspir-acy that had to be contained at all costs, Nixon decided to deal with China and the Soviet Union as separate powers and, as he put it, to "live together and work together" with both. Nixon and Kissinger called the new policy détente, a French term meaning "the relaxation of tensions between governments." But détente was not an expression of friendship so much as an acknowledgment that for decades the policy of containment had driven China and the Soviet Union closer together.

First Nixon sent Kissinger secretly to China and the Soviet Union to prepare the way for summit meetings with the communist leaders. Both the Chinese and the Soviets agreed to the meetings. Then, in February 1972, Nixon and Kissinger, accompanied by a small army of reporters and television crews, flew to Beijing. After much dining, sightseeing, posing for photographers, and consultation with Chinese officials, Nixon agreed to support the admission of China to the United Nations and to develop economic and cultural exchanges with the Chinese. As a result, exports to China increased substantially, reaching $4 billion in 1980. Among other American products, the Chinese were introduced to Coca-Cola, marketed under a name meaning "tasty happiness." Nixon's visit, ending more

President and Mrs. Nixon dining with Chinese communist officials in Beijing in February 1972. Even Nixon's harshest critics conceded that his initiative in reopening United States–China relations was a diplomatic master stroke.

than 20 years of adamantine American refusal to accept the reality of the Chinese revolution, marked a dramatic reversal; as such it was hailed in the United States and elsewhere in the world.

In May 1972, Nixon and Kissinger flew to Moscow. This trip also produced striking results. The mere fact that it took place while war still raged in Vietnam was remarkable. More important, however, the meeting resulted in a Strategic Arms Limitation Treaty (SALT). The two powers agreed to stop making nuclear ballistic missiles and to reduce the number of antiballistic missiles in their arsenals to 200. Nixon also agreed to permit large sales of American grain to the Soviet Union.

By the summer of 1972, with the presidential election looming in the fall, Kissinger redoubled his efforts to negotiate an end to the Vietnam War. By October he and the North Vietnamese had hammered out a settlement calling for a cease-fire, the return of American prisoners of war, and the withdrawal of United States forces from Vietnam. Shortly before the presidential election Kissinger announced that peace was "at hand."

NIXON IN TRIUMPH

A few days later President Nixon was reelected, defeating the Democratic candidate, Senator George McGovern of South Dakota, in a landslide—521 electoral votes to 17. McGovern carried only Massachusetts and the District of Columbia. McGovern's campaign had been hampered by his tendency to advance poorly thought-out proposals, such as his scheme for funneling money directly to the poor, and by his rather bumbling, low-key oratorical style. The campaign marked the historical breakdown of the coalition that Franklin Roosevelt had fashioned and on which he and his Democratic successors, particularly Truman and Johnson, had ridden to power. Of that coalition, only the African Americans voted solidly for McGovern.

Suddenly Nixon loomed as one of the most powerful and successful presidents in American history. His tough-minded but flexible handling of foreign policy questions, even his harsh Vietnamese policy, suggested decisiveness and self-confidence, qualities he had often seemed to lack in his earlier career. His willingness, despite his long history as a militant Cold Warrior, to negotiate with the communist nations indicated a new flexibility and creativity. His landslide victory appeared to demonstrate that a large majority of the people approved of his way of tackling the major problems of the times.

But Kissinger's agreement with the North Vietnamese came apart when Nguyen Van Thieu, the South Vietnamese president, refused to sign it. He claimed that the agreement, by permitting communist troops to remain in the south, would ensure his ultimate defeat. "Why," he asked Kissinger, "are you rushing to get the Nobel Prize?" To Kissinger's chagrin, Nixon sided with Thieu and resumed the bombing of North Vietnam in December 1972, this time sending the mighty B-52s directly over Hanoi and other cities. The destruction they caused was great, but their effectiveness as a means of forcing concessions from the North Vietnamese was at best debatable, and in these strikes for the first time the United States lost large numbers of the big strategic bombers.

In January 1973 a settlement was finally reached. As with the October "agreement," the North Vietnamese retained control of large sections of the south, and they promised to release American prisoners of war within 60 days. Thieu assented this time, largely because Nixon secretly pledged that the United States would "respond with full force" if North Vietnam resumed its offensive. Within several months most prisoners of war were released, and the last American troops were pulled out of Vietnam. More than 57,000 Americans had died in the long war, and over 300,000 more had been wounded. The cost had reached a staggering $150 billion. Nearly a million communist soldiers and 185,000 South Vietnamese soldiers were reported killed.

In 1973, too, Kissinger was named Secretary of State; and he did receive the Nobel Prize for Peace.

THE ECONOMY UNDER NIXON

When Nixon became president in 1969, the major economic problem he faced was inflation. This was caused primarily by the heavy military expenditures and easy-money policies of the Johnson administration. Nixon cut federal spending and balanced the 1969 budget, while the Federal Reserve Board forced up interest rates to slow the expansion of the money supply. When prices continued to rise, there was mounting uneasiness and labor unions demanded large wage increases.

In 1970 Congress passed a law giving the president power to regulate prices and wages. Nixon originally opposed this legislation, but in the summer of 1971 he changed his mind and announced a 90-day price and wage freeze. Then he set up a pay board and a price commission with authority to limit wage and price increases when the freeze ended. These controls did not check inflation completely—and they angered union leaders, who felt that labor was being short-changed—but they did slow the upward spiral.

In handling other domestic issues, the president was less firm. Like President Kennedy, he was primarily interested in foreign affairs. He supported a bold plan for a "minimum income" for poor families, but dropped it when it alarmed his conservative supporters and got nowhere in Congress. But when a groundswell of public support for conserving natural resources and checking pollution led Congress to pass bills creating the Environmental Protection Agency (EPA) and the Clean Air Act of 1970, he signed them cheerfully.

After his triumphant reelection and the withdrawal of the last American troops from Vietnam, Nixon turned to domestic issues, determined, he made clear, to change the direction in which the nation had been moving for decades. He sought, on the one hand, to strengthen the power of the presidency vis-à-vis Congress and, on the other, to decentralize the administration by encouraging state and local management of government programs. He announced that he intended to reduce the interference of the federal government in the affairs of individuals. People should be more self-reliant, he said, and he denounced what he called "permissiveness." Overconcern for the interests of blacks and other minorities must end. Criminals should be punished "without pity." No person or group should be coddled by the state.

These aims brought Nixon into conflict with liberals in both parties, with the leaders of minority groups, and with those alarmed by the increasing power of the executive. The conflict came to a head over the president's anti-inflation policy. After his second inauguration he ended price and wage controls and called for voluntary "restraints." This approach did not work. Prices soared in the most rapid inflation since the Korean War. In an effort to check the rise, Nixon set a rigid limit on federal expenditures. To keep within the limit, he cut back or abolished a large number of social welfare programs and reduced federal grants in support of science and education. He even impounded (refused to spend) funds already appropriated by Congress for purposes of which he disapproved.

The impoundment created a furor on Capitol Hill, but when Congress failed to override his vetoes of bills challenging this policy, it appeared that Nixon was in total command. The White House staff, headed by H. R. Haldeman (called "the Prussian") and John Ehrlichman, dominated the Washington bureaucracy like princes of the blood or oriental viziers and dealt with legislators as though they were lackeys or eunuchs. When asked to account for their actions, they took refuge behind the shield of executive privilege—the doctrine, never before applied so broadly, that discussions and communications within the executive branch were confidential and therefore immune from congressional scrutiny. Critics began to grumble about a new "imperial presidency." No one seemed capable of checking Nixon.

THE WATERGATE BREAK-IN

On March 19, 1973, James McCord, a former agent of the Federal Bureau of Investigation accused of burglary, wrote a letter to the judge presiding at his trial. His act precipitated a series of disclosures that first disrupted and then destroyed the Nixon administration.

McCord had been employed during the 1972 presidential campaign as a security officer of the Committee to Re-elect the President (CREEP). At about 1 A.M. on June 17, 1972, he and four other men had broken into Democratic party headquarters at the Watergate, an apartment house and office building complex in Washington. The burglars were members of an unofficial surveillance group known as "the plumbers." Nixon, who was obsessed by a need to conceal information about his administration, had formed the group after the Pentagon Papers, a confidential report on government policy in Vietnam, had been leaked to the press. The plumbers had been caught rifling files and installing electronic eavesdropping devices.

Two other Republican campaign officials were soon implicated in the affair. Their arrest aroused suspicions that the Republican party was behind the break-in. Nixon denied it. "I can say categorically," he announced on June 22, "that no one on the White House staff, no one in this Administration presently employed, was involved in this very bizarre incident."

Most people evidently took the president at his word despite his well-known deviousness. (He had won the nickname "Tricky Dick" when he first ran for Congress in 1946.) He was far ahead in the polls and seemed so sure to win re-election that it was hard to believe he would stoop to burglary to discover what the Democrats were up to. In any case, the affair did not materially affect the election. When brought to trial early in 1973, most of the Watergate burglars pleaded guilty.

McCord, who did not, was convicted by the jury. Before Judge John J. Sirica imposed sentences on the culprits, however, McCord wrote his letter. High Republican officials had known about the burglary in advance and had paid the defendants "hush money" to keep their connection secret, McCord claimed. Perjury had been committed during the trial.

The truth of McCord's charges swiftly became apparent. The head of CREEP, Jeb Stuart Magruder, and President Nixon's lawyer, John W. Dean III, admitted their involvement. Among the disclosures that emerged over the following months were these:

> That the acting director of the FBI, L. Patrick Gray, had destroyed documents related to the case.
>
> That large sums of money had been paid to the burglars at the instigation of the White House to ensure their silence.
>
> That agents of the Nixon administration had burglarized the office of a psychiatrist, seeking evidence against one of his patients.
>
> That CREEP officials had attempted to disrupt the campaigns of leading Democratic candidates during the 1972 primaries in a number of illegal ways.
>
> That a number of corporations had made large contributions to the Nixon reelection campaign in violation of federal law.
>
> That the Nixon administration had placed wiretaps on the telephones of some of its own officials as well as on those of journalists critical of its policies without first obtaining authorization from the courts.

These revelations led to the dismissal of John Dean and to the resignations of most of Nixon's closest advisers, including Haldeman, Ehrlichman, and Attorney General Richard Kleindienst. They also raised the question of the president's personal connection with the scandals. This he steadfastly denied. He insisted that he would investigate the Watergate affair thoroughly and see that the guilty were punished. He refused, however, to allow investigators to examine White House documents, again on grounds of executive privilege, which he continued to assert in very broad terms.

Garry Trudeau and his politically biting cartoon strip "Doonesbury" enlivened the Vietnam and Watergate years. "Doonesbury" became the first cartoon strip to win a Pulitzer Prize. (Ron Ziegler was President Nixon's press secretary.)

In the teeth of Nixon's denials, John Dean, testifying under oath, stated flatly and in circumstantial detail that the president had been closely involved in the Watergate cover-up. Dean was a persuasive witness, but many people were reluctant to believe that a president could lie so cold-bloodedly to the entire country. Therefore, when it came out during later hearings of the Senate committee investigating the Watergate scandal that the president had systematically made secret tape recordings of White House conversations and telephone calls, the disclosure caused a sensation. It seemed obvious that these tapes would settle the question of Nixon's involvement once and for all. Again Nixon refused to allow access to the evidence.

One result of the scandals and of Nixon's attitude was a precipitous decline in his standing in public opinion polls. Calls for his resignation, even for impeachment, began to be heard. Yielding to pressure, he agreed to the appointment of an "independent" special prosecutor to investigate the Watergate affair, and he promised the appointee, Professor Archibald Cox of Harvard Law School, full cooperation.

Cox swiftly aroused the president's ire by seeking access to White House records, including the tapes. When Nixon refused to turn over the tapes, Cox obtained a subpoena from Judge Sirica ordering him to do so. The administration appealed this decision and lost in the appellate court. Then, while the case was headed for the Supreme Court, Nixon ordered the new attorney general, Elliot Richardson, to dismiss Cox. Both Richardson, who had promised the Senate during his confirmation hearings that the special prosecutor would have a free hand, and his chief assistant, William Ruckelshaus, resigned rather than do as the president directed. The solicitor general, Robert H. Bork, third-ranking officer of the Justice Department, carried out Nixon's order.

These events, which occurred on Saturday, October 20, were promptly dubbed the Saturday Night Massacre. They caused an outburst of public indignation. Congress was bombarded by thousands of letters and telegrams demanding the president's impeachment. The House Judiciary began an investigation to see if enough evidence for impeachment existed.

Once again Nixon backed down. He agreed to turn over the tapes to Judge Sirica with the understanding that relevant materials could be presented to the grand jury investigating the Watergate affair but that nothing would be revealed to the public. He then named a new special prosecutor, Leon Jaworski, and promised him access to whatever White House documents he needed. However, it soon came out that several tapes were missing and that an important section of another had been deliberately erased.

MORE TROUBLES FOR NIXON

The nation had never before experienced such a series of morale-shattering crises. While the seemingly unending complications of Watergate were unfolding during 1973, a number of unrelated disasters struck. First, pushed by a shortage of grain resulting from massive Soviet purchases authorized by détente policy, food prices shot up—wheat from $1.45 a bushel to over $5.00.

Then Vice President Agnew (defender of law and order, foe of permissiveness) was accused of income tax fraud and of having accepted bribes while county executive of Baltimore and governor of Maryland. After vehemently denying all the charges for two months, to escape a jail term Agnew admitted in October that he had been guilty of tax evasion and resigned as vice president. He was fined $10,000 and placed on three years' probation, and the Justice Department published a 40,000-word description of his wrongdoings.

Under the new Twenty-fifth Amendment, President Nixon nominated Gerald R. Ford of Michigan as vice president, and he was confirmed by Congress. Ford had served continuously in Congress since 1949 and as minority leader since 1964. His positions on public issues were close to Nixon's; he was an internationalist in foreign affairs and a conservative and convinced Republican partisan on domestic issues.

THE JUDGMENT ON WATERGATE:
"EXPLETIVE DELETED"

Meanwhile, special prosecutor Jaworski continued his investigation of the Watergate scandals. In March 1974 a grand jury indicted Haldeman; Ehrlichman; former attorney general John Mitchell, who had been head of CREEP at the time of the break-in; and four other White House aides for conspiring to block the Watergate investigation. The jurors also named Nixon an "unindicted co-conspirator," Jaworski having informed them that their power to indict a president was constitutionally questionable. Judge Sirica thereupon turned over the jury's evidence against Nixon to the House Judiciary Committee.

In an effort to check the mounting criticism, late in April Nixon released edited transcripts of the tapes he had turned over to the court the previous November. In addition to much incriminating evidence, the transcripts provided the public with a fascinating and shocking view of how the president conducted himself in private. In conversations he seemed confused, indecisive, and lacking in any concern for the public interest. His repeated use of foul language, so out of keeping with his public image, offended millions. The phrase "expletive deleted," inserted in place of words considered too vulgar for publication in family newspapers, overnight became a catchword.

The publication of the transcripts led even some of Nixon's strongest supporters to demand that he resign. And once the Judiciary Committee obtained the actual tapes, it became clear that the White House transcripts were in crucial respects inaccurate. Much material prejudicial to the president's case had been suppressed. Yet impeaching a president seemed so drastic a step that many people felt more direct proof of Nixon's involvement in the cover-up was necessary. Nixon insisted that all the relevant information was contained in the tapes already surrendered; he adamantly refused to turn over others to the special prosecutor or the Judiciary Committee.

With the defendants in the Watergate case demanding access to tapes that they claimed would prove their innocence, Jaworski was compelled either to obtain them or to risk having the charges dismissed on the grounds that the government was withholding evidence. He therefore subpoenaed 64 additional tapes. Nixon refused to obey the subpoena. Swiftly the case of *United States* v. *Richard M. Nixon* went to the Supreme Court.

In the summer of 1974—after so many months of alarms and crises—the Watergate drama reached its climax. The Judiciary Committee, following months of study of the evidence behind closed doors, decided to conduct its deliberations in open session. While millions watched on television, 38 members of the House of Representatives debated the charges. The discussions revealed both the thoroughness of the investigation and the soul-searching efforts of the representatives to render an impartial judgment. Three articles of impeachment were adopted. They charged the president with obstructing justice, misusing the powers of his office, and failing to obey the committee's subpoenas. Except in the case of the last article, many of the Republicans on the committee joined with the Democrats in voting aye, a clear indication that the full House would vote to impeach.

On the eve of the debates, the Supreme Court had ruled unanimously that the president must turn over the 64 subpoenaed tapes to the special prosecutor. Executive privilege had its place, the Court stated, but no person, not even a president, could "withhold evidence that is demonstrably relevant in a criminal trial." For reasons that soon became obvious, Nixon seriously considered defying the Court. Only when convinced that to do so would make his impeachment and conviction certain did he agree to comply.

He would not, however, resign. Even if the House impeached him, he was counting on his ability to hold the support of at least 34 senators (one-third plus one of the full Senate) to escape conviction. But events were passing beyond his control. The 64 subpoenaed tapes had to be transcribed and analyzed. When they were, Nixon's fate was sealed. Three recorded conversations between the president and H. R. Haldeman on June 23, 1972 (less than a week after the break-in and only one day after Nixon had assured the nation that no one in the White House had been involved in the affair) proved conclusively that Nixon had tried to obstruct justice by engaging the CIA in an effort to persuade the FBI not to follow up leads in the case on the spurious grounds that national security was involved.

The president's defenders had insisted not so much that he was innocent as that solid proof of his guilt had not been demonstrated. Where, in the metaphor of the moment, was the "smoking gun"? That weapon had now been found, and it bore unmistakably the fingerprints of President Richard M. Nixon. The president's chief advisers then pressed him to release the material at once and admit he had erred in holding it back.

This he did on August 5. When they read the new transcripts, all the Republican members of the Judiciary Committee who had voted against the impeachment articles reversed themselves. Understandably, they felt betrayed; they had accepted the president's assurances that all the evidence was in and had gone on record before millions of eyes in his defense. The last remnants of Nixon's congressional support crumbled. Republican leaders told the president categorically that the House would impeach him and that no more than a handful of senators would vote for acquittal.

THE MEANING OF WATERGATE

On August 8 Nixon announced his resignation. "Dear Mr. Secretary," his terse official letter to Secretary of State Kissinger ran, "I hereby resign the Office of President of the United States. Sincerely, Richard Nixon." The resignation took effect at noon on August 9, when Gerald Ford was sworn in as president. "Our long national nightmare is over," he declared.

Within weeks of taking office, Ford pardoned Nixon for whatever crimes he had committed in office, even any, if such existed, that had not yet come to light. Not many Americans wanted to see the ex-president lodged in jail, but pardoning him seemed both illogical and incomprehensible when Nixon had admitted no guilt and had not yet been officially charged with any crime. (Nixon's instant acceptance of the pardon while claiming to have done no wrong was also illogical but not incomprehensible.)

Nixon's own drama is and must remain one of the most fascinating and enigmatic episodes in American history. Despite his fall from the heights because of personal flaws, his was not a tragedy in the Greek sense. When he finally yielded power he seemed without remorse or even awareness of his transgressions. Although he enjoyed the pomp and circumstance attendant on his high office and trumpeted his achievements to all the world, he was devoid of the classic hero's pride. One element in his downfall, preserved for posterity in videotapes of his television appearances, was that even while he was assuring the country of his innocence most vehemently, he did not look like an unsuspecting victim of the machinations of overzealous supporters. Perhaps at some profound level he did not want to be believed.

This explanation of Richard Nixon, however tentative, is at least comforting—it makes him appear less menacing. If it is correct, Americans can deplore the injuries he inflicted on society and still feel a certain compassion for him.

Whether Nixon's disgrace marked the end of one era or the beginning of another is a difficult question. Like most critical moments in human history, it seems in retrospect to have been both. Nixon's détente with the Soviet Union and Red China was surely an early sign of the easing of Cold War tensions characteristic of the decades to follow. Yet the failure of Nixon's interventionist domestic policies, coming just as public disillusionment with the workings of many of the ambitious Great Society programs set in motion under Lyndon Johnson was mounting, put a quietus to the liberal era that had begun with the reforms of the New Deal.

Milestones

1942	Congress of Racial Equality (CORE) founded
1956	Founding of Southern Christian Leadership Conference
1957	Montgomery, Alabama, bus boycott
1960	Founding of Student Nonviolent Coordinating Committee (SNCC)
1961	Bay of Pigs affair
	Freedom riders "invade" South
1962	Cuban Missile Crisis
1963	President Ngo Dihn Diem of South Vietnam assassinated
	Martin Luther King, Jr. writes "Letter from Birmingham Jail"
	President Kennedy assassinated
1964	Gulf of Tonkin Resolution leads to escalation of Vietnam war
	Civil Rights Act
	Economic Opportunity Act
1965	Immigration Act ending national quota system
	Medicare Act
	Elementary and Secondary Education Act
	Clean Air Act
1968	Communist Tet offensive in South Vietnam
	American troop strength in Vietnam reaches 538,000
	Lyndon Johnson withdraws as presidential candidate
	Richard Nixon elected president
1969	Nixon announces "Vietnamization" of the war
1970	Nixon announces "incursion" into Cambodia
	Six students killed at antiwar demonstrations at Kent State and Jackson State Universities
1971	Nixon freezes prices
1972	Break-in at Watergate, Democratic headquarters in Washington, D.C.
	Nixon and Kissinger visit China and the Soviet Union
	Strategic Arms Limitation Treaty (SALT)
1973	House Judiciary Committee begins impeachment hearings
	Vice President Spiro Agnew resigns; Gerald Ford appointed vice president
	Last American troops withdrawn from Vietnam
	Nixon fires special prosecutor Archibald Cox (Saturday Night Massacre)
1974	Supreme Court orders release of Nixon's White House tapes
	Nixon resigns; Gerald R. Ford becomes president

31

SOCIETY IN FLUX

Despite Lyndon Johnson's extravagant style and his landslide defeat of Barry Goldwater in the 1964 presidential election, the tone of his inaugural address in January 1965 was uncharacteristically restrained. The nation was "prosperous, great, and mighty," he said, but "we have no promise from God that our greatness will endure." He was obviously thinking of the enormous changes that were occurring in the country. He spoke of "this fragile existence," and he warned the people that they lived "in a world where change and growth seem to tower beyond the control, and even the judgment of men."

A SOCIETY ON THE MOVE

One reason that American society appeared in flux was that Americans always appeared to be moving. The automobile's influence on transportation was enormous. In the postwar decades the automobile appeared to enter its golden age. During the booming 1920s, when the car became an instrument of mass transportation, about 31 million autos were produced by American factories. During the 1950s, 58 million rolled off the assembly lines; during the 1960s, 77 million.

Gasoline use rose sharply. The more mobile population drove farther in more reliable and more comfortable vehicles over smoother and less congested highways. And the new cars were heavier and more powerful than their predecessors. Gasoline consumption first touched 15 billion gallons in 1931; it soared to

35 billion gallons in 1950 and to 92 billion in 1970. A new business, the motel industry (the word, typically American, was a combination of *motor* and *hotel*) developed to service the millions of tourists and business travelers who burned all this fuel.

The development of the interstate highway system, begun under Eisenhower in 1956, was a major cause of increased mobility. The new roads did far more than facilitate long-distance travel; they accelerated the shift of population to the suburbs and the consequent decline of inner-city districts.

Despite the speeds that cars maintained on them, the new highways were much safer than the old roads. The traffic death rate per mile driven fell steadily, almost entirely because of the interstates. On the other hand, the environmental impact of the system was frequently severe. Elevated roads cut ugly swaths through cities, and the cars they carried released tons of noxious exhaust fumes into urban air. Hillsides were gashed, marshes filled in, forests felled—all in the name of speed and efficiency.

Although commercial air travel had existed in the 1930s and had profited from wartime technical advances in military aircraft, it truly came of age when the first jetliner—the Boeing 707, built in Seattle, Washington—went into service in 1958. Almost immediately jets came to dominate long-distance travel, while railroad passenger service and transatlantic liners declined in importance.

THE ADVENT OF TELEVISION

Another important postwar change was the advent of television as a means of mass communication. By 1961 there were 55 million sets in operation, and by the mid-1960s orbiting government and commercial satellites were relaying pictures from one continent to another instantly.

Television combined the immediacy of radio with the visual impact of films, and it displayed most of the strengths and weaknesses of both in exaggerated form. It swiftly became indispensable to the political system, both for its coverage of public events and as a vehicle for political advertising. Its handling of the events following President Kennedy's assassination and of other news developments made history come alive for tens of millions of viewers.

As for its influence on politics and political campaigning, as early as 1952 the Republicans made effective use of what came to be known as "spots," 20-second tapes of candidate Eisenhower responding to questions about his opinions on issues, important and trivial. In later campaigns candidates for state and local as well as national office spent millions attempting to sell themselves (or attacking

Astronaut Edwin Aldrin on the moon, July 1969. Reflected in his helmet visor are flight commander Neil Armstrong, who took this picture, and part of their spacecraft. Television enabled some 600 million people to see the historic event.

their opponents), often with little regard for the accuracy or relevance of their remarks.

Television also brought sports events before the viewer vividly, attracting enormous audiences and producing so much money in advertising revenue that the economics of professional sports was revolutionized. Team franchises were bought and sold for huge sums, and ordinary players commanded salaries in the hundreds of thousands, stars in the millions.

Some excellent drama was presented, especially on the National Educational Television network, along with many filmed documentaries. However, Newton Minow of the Federal Communications Commission (FCC) called the programming offered by most television stations a "vast wasteland." The lion's share of television time was devoted to uninspired and vulgar serials, routine variety shows, giveaway and quiz programs designed to reveal and revel in the ignorance of the average citizen, and reruns of old movies cut to fit rigid time periods and repeatedly interrupted at climactic points by commercials. Most sets had poor acoustic qualities, which made them inferior instruments for listening to music.

Yet children found television fascinating, remaining transfixed before the screen when—their elders said—they should have been out of doors or curled up with a book.

Still another defect of television was its capacity for influencing the opinions and feelings of viewers. The insistent and strident claims of advertisers punctuated every program with monotonous regularity. Politicians discovered that no other device or method approached television as a means of reaching large numbers of voters with an illusion of intimacy. Because television time was expensive, candidates had to raise huge sums to be able to use the medium—a dangerous state of affairs in a democracy. In time Congress clamped a lid on campaign expenditures, but this action did not necessarily reduce the amounts spent on television, with its capacity to reach so many people.

The importance of the national television networks, NBC, ABC, and CBS, was significantly modified in the 1980s by the rapid growth of cable television companies. Besides bringing the broadcasts of the networks to remote areas, cable made available large numbers of additional channels, thus greatly increasing the variety of materials offered to viewers. The introduction of video cassette recorders (VCRs) further increased the usefulness of television sets, which could be used to copy television programs and to view tapes of old and recent movies in private homes.

THE GROWING MIDDLE CLASS

Another postwar change was the marked broadening of the middle class. In 1947 only 5.7 million American families had what might be considered middle-class incomes—enough to provide something for leisure, entertainment, and cultural activities as well as for life's necessities. By the early 1960s more than 12 million families, about a third of the population, had such incomes.

The percentage of immigrants in the population declined steadily; in 1965 over 95 percent of all Americans were native-born. This trend contributed to social and cultural uniformity. So did the rising incomes of industrial workers and the changing character of their labor. By 1962 about 90 percent of all industrial workers enjoyed such fringe benefits as paid vacations and medical insurance at least partially financed by their employers, and nearly 70 percent participated in pension plans. The merger in 1955 of the two great labor federations, the AFL and the CIO, added to the prestige of all union labor as well as to the power of the new organization.

As blue-collar workers invaded the middle class by the tens of thousands, they moved to suburbs previously reserved for junior executives, shopkeepers, and the like. They shed their work clothes for business suits. They took up golf. In sum, they adopted values and attitudes commensurate with their new status—which helps explain the growing conservatism of labor unions. During the Great Depression, when they were underdogs of sorts, the unions fought for social justice. In the 1960s many union workers seemed more interested in preserving their gains against the ravages of inflation and taxation than they were in social reform.

RELIGION IN CHANGING TIMES

Sociologists and other commentators on contemporary affairs found in the expansion of the middle class another explanation of the tendency of the country to glorify the conformist. They attributed to this expansion the blurring of party lines in politics, the national obsession with moderation and consensus, the complacency of so many Americans, and their tendency, for example, to be more interested in the social aspects of churchgoing than in the moral and philosophical aspects of religion.

Organized religion traditionally deals with eternal values, but it is always influenced by social, cultural, and economic developments. Never had this been more true in America than in the decades after World War II. All the major faiths, despite their differences, were affected. Immediately after the war the prosperity and buoyant optimism of the period led to an expansion of religious activity. The Catholic church alone built over a thousand new schools and more than a hundred hospitals along with countless new churches. By 1950 the Southern Baptists had enrolled nearly 300,000 new members and built some 500 churches for them to worship in.

But while most faiths prospered materially, the faithful tended to accept the world as it was. According to a Gallup poll taken shortly after the war, nearly everyone in America believed in God. However, another poll revealed that many people were woefully ignorant of religious history and doctrine. Large numbers of Christians, for example, were unable to tell pollsters the name of any of the four gospels. Many people tended to belong to a particular religion in order to obtain a particular social position, a sense of being a member of an important institution.

Church and state were by law and the Constitution separate institutions, yet acts of Congress and state legislatures frequently had indirect effects on every aspect of organized religion. New Deal welfare legislation took on a large part of a burden previously borne by church groups. The expansion of higher education resulting from the GI Bill introduced millions of young adults to new ideas and appeared to make people somewhat more tolerant of the beliefs of others, reli-

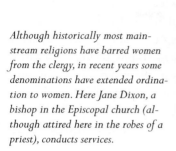

Although historically most mainstream religions have barred women from the clergy, in recent years some denominations have extended ordination to women. Here Jane Dixon, a bishop in the Episcopal church (although attired here in the robes of a priest), conducts services.

gious beliefs included. On the other hand, however, studies showed that better-educated people tended to be less involved in the formal aspects of organized religion, and some became interested in non-Western faiths, such as Zen Buddhism.

Unlike prewar critics who had attacked "rugged individualism," many post–New Deal social critics, alarmed by the conformity of the 1950s, urged people to be more individualistic. One prominent divine complained of "the drive toward a shallow and implicitly compulsory common creed," a "religion-in-general, superficial and syncretistic, destructive of the profounder elements of faith."

The civil rights movement is another illustration of a political and social issue that had important religious implications. So did the war in Vietnam. Many militant blacks (Malcolm X is an early example) were converted to the Muslim faith by its lack of racial bias. Among those in the public eye who became Muslims were the heavyweight champion boxer Cassius Clay, who changed his name to Muhammad Ali, and Lew Alcindor, a basketball star who became Kareem Abdul Jabbar.

Nearly all the denominations played significant roles in the fight for racial justice that erupted after the Supreme Court outlawed segregation. Priests, ministers, and rabbis joined in antiwar demonstrations. Martin Luther King, Jr.'s nonviolent approach was essentially religious, his oratory deeply felt, passionate, but always dignified and controlled.

The enormous outpouring produced by King's March on Washington in 1963 was swelled by many prominent religious leaders, and their example put pressure on both church hierarchies and ordinary members to become civil rights activists. Shocking photographs of police dogs being used to "subdue" demonstrating Catholic nuns in the Deep South converted uncounted thousands to the struggle.

All the social changes of the period had religious ramifications. Feminists objected to male domination of most Christian churches and called for the ordination of female ministers and priests; some religious leaders supported the feminists, but conservatives rejected their ideas out of hand. Every aspect of the sexual revolution, from the practice of couples living together openly outside of marriage to the tolerance of homosexuality and pornography to the legalization of contraception and abortion, caused shock waves in the religious community. The Roman Catholic insistence that the clergy remain celibate resulted in a decline in the number of young Catholics becoming priests and nuns. This dealt a crippling blow to the parochial school system, which depended heavily on the clergy for teachers.

Scientific and technological developments also affected both religious values and the way people worshiped. Darwin's theory of evolution had social effects as well as directly religious ones in the nineteenth and early twentieth centuries, and these were to some extent still unresolved. Many religious groups still believed in the biblical explanation of creation and sought to have "creation theory" taught in the schools.

Radio and television enabled rhetorically skilled preachers to reach millions with emotionally charged messages on religious topics and also on political and social questions. The most successful in the postwar years were the leaders of evangelical protestant sects, and by the 1960s they had mastered television. Whereas most postwar revivalists, the most famous being Billy Graham, stressed interdenominational cooperation, in the 1970s a more militant, fundamentalist type emerged.

These radio preachers often became television preachers. They tended to found churches and educational institutions of their own, and they used the airwaves to raise money to support them. They were extremely conservative both in their religious and in their political, social, and moral views. This brought them into conflict with many other developments of the period. However, in the mid-1980s a number of scandals caused disillusionment and widespread defections among their followers. By 1990 the national television congregation had shrunk drastically.

THE PERILS OF PROGRESS

The many changes of the era help to explain why President Johnson expressed so much uncertainty in his inaugural address. Looking at American society more broadly, two dilemmas seem to have emerged. One was that progress was often self-defeating. Reforms and innovations instituted with the best of motives often made things worse rather than better. Instances of this dilemma, large and small, are so numerous as to defy summary. DDT, a powerful chemical developed to kill insects that were spreading disease and destroying valuable food crops, proved to have lethal effects on birds and fish—and perhaps indirectly on human beings. Goods manufactured to make life fuller and happier (automobiles, detergents, electric power) produced waste products that disfigured the land and polluted air and water. Cities built to bring culture and comfort to millions became pestholes of poverty and depravity.

Change occurred so fast that experience (the recollection of how things had been) tended to become less useful and sometimes even counterproductive as a guide for dealing with current problems. Foreign policies designed to prevent wars, based on knowledge of the causes of past wars, now led to new wars because the circumstances were so different. Parents who sought to transmit to their children the accumulated wisdom of their years found their advice rejected, often with good reason, because that wisdom had little application to the problems their children had to face.

The second dilemma was that modern industrial society placed an enormous premium on social cooperation, at the same time undermining the individual citizen's sense of being essential to the proper functioning of society. The economy was as complicated as a fine watch; a breakdown in any one sector had ramifications that spread swiftly to other sectors. Yet specialization had progressed so far that individual workers had little sense of the importance of their personal contributions and thus felt little responsibility for the smooth functioning of the whole. Effective democratic government required that all voters be knowledgeable and concerned, but few could feel that their individual voices had any effect on elections or public policies. The exhaust fumes of millions of automobiles poisoned the air, but it was difficult to expect the single motorist to inconvenience himself by leaving his car in the garage when his restraint would have no measurable effect on total pollution. "One person just can't feel that she's doing anything," a frustrated teenager wrote. "I can use soap instead of detergent . . . but what good do I feel I'm doing when there are people next door having a party with plastic spoons and paper plates?"

People tried to deal with this dilemma by joining organizations dedicated to achieving particular goals, such as the American Association of Retired People (AARP), the conservationist Sierra Club, and the NAACP. But such groups often became so large that members felt almost as incapable of influencing them as they did of influencing the larger society. The groups were so numerous and had so many conflicting objectives that instead of making citizens more socially minded they often made them more self-centered. The organization—union, club, party, pressure group—was a potent force in society. Yet few organizations were primarily concerned with the common interest, although logic required that the common interest be regarded if individuals or groups were to achieve their special interests.

These dilemmas produced a paradox. The United States was the most powerful nation in the world, its people the best educated, the richest, and probably the most energetic. American society was technologically advanced and dynamic; American traditional values were idealistic, humane, democratic. Yet the nation seemed incapable of mobilizing its resources intelligently to confront the most obvious challenges, its citizens unable to achieve much personal happiness or identification with their fellows, the society helpless in trying to live up to its most universally accepted ideals.

In part the paradox was a product of the strengths of the society and the individuals who made it up. The populace as a whole was more sophisticated. People were more aware of their immediate interests, less willing to suspend judgment and follow leaders or to look on others as better qualified to decide what should be done. They belonged to the "me generation"; they knew that they lived in a society and that their lives were profoundly affected by that society, but they had trouble feeling that they were part of a society.

President Johnson recognized the problem. He hoped to solve it by establishing a "consensus" and building his Great Society. No real consensus emerged; American society remained fragmented, its members divided against themselves and often within themselves. Awareness of the complexities and contradictions of life and human institutions was a mark of increasing maturity but also a source of uncertainty and insecurity.

THE COSTS OF PROSPERITY

The vexing character of modern conditions could be seen in every aspect of life. The gross national product approached and then swiftly passed a trillion dollars, but inflation was becoming increasingly serious. Workers were under constant pressure to demand raises—which only served to drive prices still higher.

Economic expansion resulted in large measure from technological advances, and these too proved to be mixed blessings. As we have seen, World War II needs stimulated the development of plastics like nylon, of synthetic rubber, and of radar, television, and other electronic devices. After the war these products came into their own. Plastics invaded field after field—automobile parts, building materials, adhesives, packaging materials. In the 1950s public utility companies began to manufacture electricity from nuclear fuels because it was cheaper than that produced in coal- or oil-fired plants. But the possibility of catastrophic accidents and the problem of disposing of lethal radioactive waste products soon dampened public enthusiasm for nuclear power. Scientists insisted that the danger from radiation was insignificant, but the possibility of accidents could not be eliminated entirely.

Equally significant was the invention of the electronic computer, which revolutionized the collection and storage of records, solved mathematical problems beyond the scope of the most brilliant human minds, and speeded the work of bank tellers, librarians, billing clerks, statisticians—and income tax collectors. Computers lay at the heart of industrial automation, for they could control the integration and adjustment of the most complex machines. In automobile factories they made it possible to produce entire engine blocks automatically. In steel mills molten metal could be poured into molds, cooled, rolled, and cut into slabs without the intervention of a human hand, the computers locating defects and adjusting the machinery to correct them far more accurately than the most skilled steel worker, and in a matter of seconds. But the computerization of record-keeping and manufacturing raised the problem of how displaced clerks and automobile and steel workers were to find new jobs.

The material benefits of technology commonly had what the microbiologist René Dubos described as "disastrous secondary effects, many of which are probably unpredictable." The consumption of petroleum necessary to produce power began to outstrip supplies, threatening shortages that would disrupt the entire economy. The burning of this fuel released tons of smoke and other polluting gases into the atmosphere, endangering the health of millions. "Life is enriched by one million automobiles," Dubos noted, "but can be made into a nightmare by one hundred million."

The vast outpouring of flimsy plastic products and the increased use of paper, metal foil, and other "disposable" packaging materials seemed about to bury the country beneath mountains of trash. Even an apparently ideal form of scientific advance, the use of commercial fertilizers to boost food output, had unfortunate side effects: Phosphates washed from farmlands into streams sometimes upset the ecological balance and turned the streams into malodorous death traps for aquatic life. Above all, technology increased the capacity of the earth to support people. But as population increased, production and consumption increased, exhausting supplies of raw materials and speeding the pollution of air and water resources. And where would the process end? Viewed from a world perspective, it was obvious that the population explosion must be checked or it would check itself by pestilence, war, starvation, or some combination of these scourges. Yet how to check it?

New Racial Turmoil

President Johnson and most of those who supported his policies expected that the 1964 Civil Rights Act, the Economic Opportunity Act, Medicare and Medicaid, and the other elements in the war on poverty would produce an era of racial peace and genuine social harmony—the Great Society that everyone wanted. The change that occurred in the thinking of the black radical Malcolm X seemed a straw in the wind. In 1964 Malcolm left the Muslims and founded his own Organization of Afro-American Unity. While continuing to stress black self-help and the militant defense of black rights, he now saw the fight for racial equality as part of a larger struggle for all human rights. "What we do . . . helps all people everywhere who are fighting against oppression," he said. Yet as in so many other aspects of modern life, progress itself created new difficulties. Early in 1965 Black Muslim fanatics, furious at his defection, assassinated Malcolm X while he was making a speech in favor of racial harmony.

The assassination was an act of vengeance, not of social protest. More significant was the fact that official white recognition of past injustices was making blacks more insistent that all discrimination be ended. The very process of righting some past wrongs gave them the strength to fight more vigorously. Black militancy, building steadily during the war and the postwar years, had long been ignored by the white majority; in the mid-1960s it burst forth so powerfully that the most smug and obtuse white citizens had to accept its existence.

Even Martin Luther King, Jr., the herald of nonviolent resistance, became more aggressive. "We are not asking, we are demanding the ballot," he said in January 1965. A few weeks after Malcolm's death, King led a march from Selma, Alabama, to Montgomery as part of a campaign to force Alabama authorities to allow blacks to register to vote. King chose Selma because the county in which it was located had a black majority but only 325 registered black voters. He expected the authorities to react brutally, thus attracting public sympathy for the marchers, and he was not disappointed. His marchers were assaulted by state policemen who wielded clubs and tossed canisters of tear gas. Liberal opinion was shocked as never before. Thousands of people descended on Selma to demonstrate their support for the black cause.

The Student Nonviolent Coordinating Committee (SNCC), which had been born out of the struggle for racial integration, had become by the mid-1960s a radical organization openly scornful of integration and interracial cooperation. Many students had been radicalized by the threats and open violence they had experienced while trying to register rural blacks and organize schools for black children in the South and by the foot-dragging of the Kennedy administration in working for racial justice. The slogan of the radicals was "Black Power," an ex-

As a student at Crozier Theological Seminary, Martin Luther King, Jr. excelled at homiletics—the art of preaching. His deep, booming voice and pronounced gestures contributed to his success as a leader in the civil rights movement. "He's damn good," President Kennedy said after seeing King on television.

pression that was given national currency by Stokely Carmichael, chairman of SNCC. Carmichael, a West Indian by birth, had grown up in Harlem. He had worked ceaselessly for black rights in the South, and as a result he had spent considerable time in southern jails, often on such trumped-up charges as pitching a tent on the grounds of a black school. Although willing to work with black moderates such as King, he was adamantly opposed to cooperating with whites of any stripe. "The time for white involvement in the fight for equality has ended," Carmichael announced in 1966. "If we are to proceed toward true liberation, we must set ourselves off from white people." "Integration is a subterfuge for the maintenance of white supremacy," Carmichael said on another occasion. Blacks should have their own schools, their own businesses, their own political parties, their own (African) culture.

Black Power caught on swiftly among militants. This troubled white liberals because people like Carmichael refused "to discriminate between degrees of inequity" among whites. Liberals feared that Black Power would antagonize white conservatives. They argued that since blacks made up only about 11 percent of the population, any attempt to obtain racial justice through the use of naked power was sure to fail.

Meanwhile, black anger erupted in a series of destructive urban riots. The most important occurred in Watts, a ghetto of Los Angeles, in August 1965. A

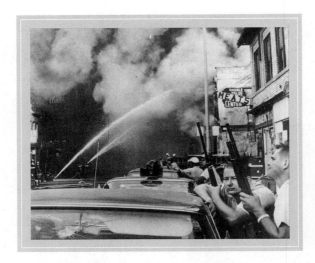

In July 1967 a riot engulfed a 14-square-mile section of Detroit. Police watch for snipers as firefighters attempt to extinguish the flames. Forty-three people were killed, 1300 buildings were reduced to brick and ashes, and thousands were left homeless, most of them African Americans. While surveying the rubble, Mayor Jerome Cavanagh remarked: "It looks like Berlin in 1945."

trivial incident brought thousands into the streets. The neighborhood almost literally exploded: For six days Watts was swept by fire, looting, and bloody fighting between local residents and nearly 15,000 National Guardsmen, called up to assist the police. The following two summers saw similar outbursts in scores of cities.

Then, in April 1968, the revered Martin Luther King, Jr., was murdered in Memphis, Tennessee, by a white man, James Earl Ray. Blacks in more than a hundred cities unleashed their anger in paroxysms of burning and looting. White opinion was shocked and profoundly depressed. The death of King appeared to destroy the hope that his doctrine of pacific appeal to reason and right could solve the racial problem.

Public fear and puzzlement led to many investigations of the causes of the riots, the most important being that of the commission headed by Governor Otto Kerner of Illinois, which President Johnson had appointed after the 1967 riots. The conclusions of most of the studies were complex but fairly clear. Race riots had a long history in the United States, but earlier troubles usually began with attacks by whites that led to black counterattacks. Riots of the Watts type were begun by blacks. Although much white-owned property was destroyed, the fighting was mostly between blacks and law enforcement officers trying to control them.

The rioters were expressing frustration and despair; their resentment was directed more at the social system than at individuals. As the Kerner Commission put it, the basic cause was the "white racism" that deprived blacks of access to good jobs, crowded them into slums, and eroded all hope of escape from such misery. Ghettos bred crime and depravity—as slums always have—and the complacent refusal of whites to invest enough money and energy to help ghetto residents, or even to acknowledge that the black poor deserved help, made the modern slum unbearable. While the ghettos expanded, middle-class whites tended more and more to flee to the suburbs or to call on the police "to maintain law and order," a euphemism for cracking down hard on deviant black behavior no matter how obvious the connection between that behavior and the slum environment.

The victims of racism employed violence not so much to force change as to obtain psychic release; it was a way of getting rid of what they could not stomach, a kind of vomiting. Thus the riots concentrated in the ghettos themselves, smashing, Samson-like, the source of degradation even when this meant self-destruction. When fires broke out in black districts, the firefighters who tried to extinguish them were often showered with bottles and bricks and sometimes shot at, while above the roar of the flames and the hiss of steam rose the apocalyptic chant, "Burn, baby, burn!"

The most frightening aspect of the riots was their tendency to polarize society on racial lines. Advocates of Black Power became more determined to separate themselves from white influence; they exasperated white supporters of school desegregation by demanding schools of their own. Extremists formed the Black Panther party and collected weapons to resist the police. "Shoot, don't loot," the radical H. Rap Brown advised all who would listen. The Panthers demanded public compensation for injustices done to blacks in the past, pointing out that following World War II, West Germany had made payments to Jews to make up for Hitler's persecutions. In 1968 they nominated Eldridge Cleaver for president. Although Cleaver was a convict on parole, he was an articulate and intelligent man whose autobiographical *Soul on Ice* (1967), written in prison, had attracted much praise.

Middle-class city residents often resented what seemed the "favoritism" of the federal government and state and local administrations, which sought through affirmative action to provide blacks with economic opportunities and social benefits. Efforts to desegregate ghetto schools by busing children out of their local neighborhoods were a particularly bitter cause of conflict. These developments caused a powerful white backlash. People already subjected to the pressures caused by inflation, specialization, and rapid change, and worried by rising urban crime rates and welfare costs, found black radicalism infuriating.

NATIVE-BORN ETHNICS

The struggles of blacks for equality went hand in hand with the struggles of those of Mexican descent, principally in the Southwest. After World War I, thousands of immigrants from Mexico flocked into that part of the country, mingling with the far larger native-born Hispanic population. They could do so legally because the restrictive immigration legislation of the 1920s did not apply to Western Hemisphere nations. When the Great Depression struck, Mexican Americans were the first to suffer—about half a million Hispanics who were not citizens were either deported or "persuaded" to return to Mexico. But during World War II and again between 1948 and 1965, federal legislation encouraged the importation of *braceros* (temporary farm workers). Many other Mexicans entered the country illegally. The latter were known as *mojados,* or "wetbacks," because they often slipped over the border by swimming across the Rio Grande.

Many of these Mexicans and other Spanish-speaking people, including the thousands from the territory of Puerto Rico who could immigrate to the mainland legally in unlimited numbers, settled in the big cities, where low-paying but usually steady work was available. They lived in slums called *barrios,* as segregated, crowded, and crime-ridden as the ghettos of the blacks.

Spanish-speaking residents of the Southwest, native- and foreign-born, and to a lesser degree those in the big eastern cities, were for a time largely apolitical; they tended to mind their own business and not "make trouble." But in the 1960s a new spirit of resistance arose. Leaders of the new movement called themselves Chicanos. The Chicanos demanded better schools for their children and easier access to higher education. They urged friends and relatives to take pride in their traditions and culture, to demand their rights, and to organize themselves politically. One Chicano nationalist group tried to secede from New Mexico, an act that brought it into confrontation with the army.

The Chicano leader with the widest influence was César Chávez, who concentrated on what superficially was a more limited goal—organizing migrant farm workers into unions. Chávez grew up in migrant camps in California; he had no schooling beyond the seventh grade. After serving in the navy during World War II, he went to work for the Community Service Organization (CSO), a group seeking to raise the political consciousness of the poor and to develop self-help programs for them. Chávez became general director of the CSO but resigned in 1962 because he felt it was not devoting enough attention to the plight of migrant workers. He then founded the National Farm Workers Association, later known as the United Farm Workers Organizing Committee.

In 1965 the grape pickers in his union in Delano, California, struck for higher wages and union recognition. Chávez, seeing in the strike an opportunity to attack the very structure of the migrant labor system, turned it into a countrywide crusade. Avoiding violence, he enlisted the support of church leaders; he organized sit-ins, a march on the state capital, and then a national consumer boycott of grapes that attracted the support of an estimated 17 million people. He

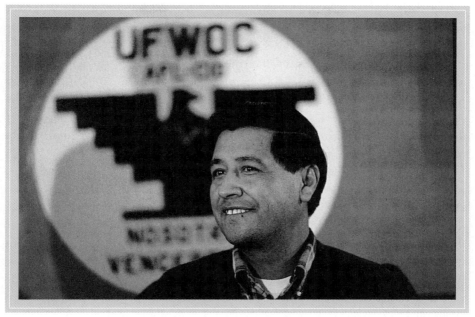

The Mexican American founder of the National Farm Workers Association and later head of the United Farm Workers Organizing Committee, César Chávez successfully organized migrant workers throughout California in the early 1960s and later led a nationwide boycott against California grape producers.

demonstrated convincingly that migrant workers could be unionized and that the demands of minorities for equal treatment did not necessarily lead to separatism and class or racial antagonism.

Nevertheless, racial controversies continued. The struggles of black people for equal treatment in the 1950s and 1960s radicalized many Indians. These militants referred to themselves as Native Americans, not Indians. They used the term *Red Power* as the blacks spoke of Black Power and called their more conservative colleagues "Uncle Tomahawks." The National Indian Youth Council and later the American Indian Movement (AIM) demanded the return of lands taken illegally from their ancestors. They called for self-determination and a concerted effort to revive tribal cultures, even the use of the mind-altering controlled substance peyote in religious ceremonies, and they organized a Pan-Indian movement to advance the cause. Paradoxically, this policy brought them into conflict with traditionalist Indians devoted to local autonomy. (At least 40 Indian languages are still spoken.)

Some AIM leaders sought total separation from the United States; they envisaged setting up states within states, such as the Cherokees had established in

Georgia in Jacksonian days. In 1973 radicals occupied the town of Wounded Knee, South Dakota (site of one of the most disgraceful massacres of Indians in the nineteenth century), and held it at gunpoint for weeks.

While traditionalists resisted the militants, liberal white opinion proved to be generally sympathetic. In 1975 Congress passed the Indian Self-Determination Act, which gave individual tribes much greater control over such matters as education, welfare programs, and law enforcement. The act specifically recognized the government's obligation to ensure "maximum Indian participation" in the management of federal policy in these areas.

Militant ethnic pride characterized the behavior of other racial minorities and of many white Americans too. Blacks donned dashikis and other African garments and wore their hair in natural "Afro" styles. Italian Americans, Polish Americans, and descendants of other "new immigrant" groups eagerly studied their history in order to preserve their culture and where necessary revive dying traditions. The American "melting pot," some historians now argued, had not amalgamated the immigrant strains as completely as had been thought. Ethnic diversity became for some an end to be desired, despite the possibility that differences might as easily inspire conflict as harmonious adjustment.

For all ethnics, the concern for origins was in part nostalgic and romantic. As the number of, say, Greek Americans who had ever seen Greece declined, the appeal of Greek culture and the sense that some Greek Americans had of belonging to a distinct cultural group increased. But for blacks, whose particular origins were obscured by the catastrophe of slavery, awareness of their distinctiveness was more important. Racial pride was a reflection of the new black militancy and the achievements that blacks had made in the postwar period. There was a black on the Supreme Court (Thurgood Marshall, tactician of the fight for school desegregation). President Johnson had named the first black to a Cabinet post (Robert Weaver, secretary of housing and urban development). The first black since Reconstruction (Edward W. Brooke of Massachusetts) was elected to the United States Senate in 1966. A number of large cities elected black mayors.

The color line was broken in major league baseball in 1947, and soon all professional sports were open to black athletes. Whereas the reign of black heavyweight boxing champion Jack Johnson (1908–1915) had inspired an open search for a "white hope" to depose him, and whereas the next black champion, Joe Louis (1937–1949), had been accepted by whites because he "knew his place" and was "well behaved," it was possible for champion Muhammad Ali to be a hero to both white and black boxing fans despite his often bizarre behavior, his militant advocacy of racial equality, and his adoption of the Muslim religion.

Their achievements and advances aside, black Americans had found real self-awareness. The attitude of mind that ran from the lonely Denmark Vesey to Frederick Douglass and to W. E. B. Du Bois had become the black consensus.

RETHINKING PUBLIC EDUCATION

Young people were in the forefront of the fight for the rights of minorities. In a time of uncertainty and discontent, full of conflict and dilemma, youth was affected more strongly than the older generations, and it reacted more forcefully. No institution escaped its criticisms, not even the vaunted educational system, which many students claimed poorly suited their needs. This was still another paradox of modern life, for American public education was probably the best (it was certainly the most comprehensive) in the world.

After World War I, under the impact of Freudian psychology, the emphasis in elementary education shifted from using the schools as instruments of social change, as John Dewey had recommended, to using them to promote the emotional development of the students. "Child-centered" educators played down academic achievement in favor of "adjustment." The change probably stimulated the students' imaginations and may possibly have improved their psychological well-being, but observers soon noted that the system produced poor work habits and fuzzy thinking and fostered plain ignorance. Although "educationists" insisted that they were not abandoning traditional academic subjects, they surely deemphasized them.

The demands of society for rigorous intellectual achievement made this distortion of progressive education increasingly less satisfactory. Following World War II, critics began a concerted assault on the system. The leader of the attack was James B. Conant, former president of Harvard. His book *The American High School Today* (1959) sold nearly half a million copies, and his later studies of teacher education and the special problems of urban schools also attracted wide attention.

Conant flayed the schools for their failure to teach English grammar and composition effectively, for neglecting foreign languages, and for ignoring the needs of both the brightest and the dullest of their students. He insisted that teachers' colleges should place subject matter above educational methodology in their curricula.

The success of the Soviet Union in launching the first Sputnik in 1957 increased the influence of critics like Conant because it dealt a healthy blow to American overconfidence. To match the Soviet achievement, the United States needed thousands of engineers and scientists, and the schools were not turning

High School and College Graduates, 1870–1983

Lyndon Johnson's Elementary and Secondary Education Act, passed in 1965, was a landmark in the century-long expansion of high school education and directly influenced college education in the United States. The most rapid increase in high school graduates occurred between 1920 and 1940, but the number of graduates as a percentage of all people aged 17 was greatest in 1967. The peak period for college graduates, 1945 to 1950, reflects the GI Bill after World War II.

out enough graduates prepared to study science and engineering at the college level. Suddenly the schools were under enormous pressure, for with more and more young people desiring to go to college, the colleges were raising their admission standards. The traditionalists thus gained the initiative, academic subjects a revived prestige. The National Defense Education Act of 1958 supplied a powerful stimulus by allocating funds for upgrading work in the sciences, foreign languages, and other subjects and for expanding guidance services and experimenting with television and other new teaching devices. States encouraged small schools to consolidate into larger units; high schools became larger, as Conant proposed, allowing greater specialization among faculty and more college-level classes. Not until the large high schools were built did administrators perceive that many students, especially from disadvantaged minority groups, felt lost in them.

The post-*Sputnik* stress on academic achievement profoundly affected higher education too. Critics demanded that secondary schools and colleges raise their standards and place more stress on the sciences. Prestige institutions such as Harvard, Yale, Columbia, Stanford, and a dozen other colleges and universities raised their entrance requirements. Then, by the mid-1960s, the children of the baby boom generation were flocking to the nation's high schools and colleges. Population growth and the demands of society for specialized intellectual skills were causing educational institutions to burst at the seams. Enrollments had risen rapidly after World War II, mostly because of the GI Bill; by 1950 there were 2.6 million students in American colleges and universities. Thirty years later there were about 12 million. To bridge the gap between high school and college, two-year community colleges proliferated. Almost unknown before 1920, there were about 1300 two-year colleges by 1980, nearly all of them publicly financed. Enrollment in these institutions rose from 1.3 million in the mid-1960s to 6.4 million in the early 1990s.

The federal and state governments, together with private philanthropic institutions such as the Carnegie Corporation and the Ford Foundation, poured millions of dollars into education at every level—into preschool programs like Head Start, into dormitory and classroom construction, into teacher training, into scholarship funds. At the graduate level the federal government's research and development program provided billions of dollars for laboratories, equipment, professors' salaries, and student fellowships.

STUDENTS IN REVOLT

For a time after World War II, the expansion of higher education took place with remarkable smoothness. The veterans, more mature and eager to make up for lost time, concentrated on their studies, and younger students tended to follow their lead. But in the 1960s the mood changed. The members of this college generation had grown up during the postwar prosperity and had been trained by teachers who were, by and large, New Deal liberals. They had been told that government was supposed to regulate the economy in the general interest, help the weak against the strong, and protect the liberties of all. It seemed to many students not to be performing these functions.

Modern industrial society, with its "soul-less" corporations, its computers, and its almost equally unfeeling human bureaucracies, provided these young people with material comforts and social advantages, but it made them feel insignificant and powerless. Their advantages also made them feel guilty when they thought about the millions of Americans who did not have them. The existence of poverty in a country as rich as the United States seemed intolerable, racial prejudice both stupid and evil. Yet the government seemed incapable of attacking these disgraceful conditions head-on. Still worse in their eyes, the response of their elders to McCarthyism appeared contemptible—craven cowardice of the worst sort—and dangerous. In the age of the atom, rabid anticommunism might end in nuclear war.

All these influences were encapsulated in a manifesto put forth by a small group of students at a meeting of Students for a Democratic Society (SDS), held at Port Huron, Michigan, in 1962. "We are the people of this generation . . . looking uncomfortably to the world we inherit," the Port Huron Statement began. Their main concerns were racial bigotry, the bomb, and the "disturbing paradoxes" associated with these concerns. How could an American reconcile the contradictions between the idea that "all men are created equal" with "the facts of Negro life in the South and the big cities of the North" and between the declared peaceful intentions of the government and its huge "economic and military investments in the Cold War?" Too many people and too many institutions, concentrating on preserving what they own and can command, "have closed their minds to the future."

SDS grew rapidly, powered by rising college enrollments, protest against the escalation of the war in Vietnam, and a seemingly unending list of local campus issues. Radical students generally had little tolerance for injustice, and their dissatisfaction often found expression in public protests. The first great student outburst convulsed the University of California at Berkeley in the fall of 1964. Angry students, many veterans of the 1964 fight for black rights in the South, staged sit-down strikes in university buildings to protest the prohibition of political canvassing on the campus. This Free Speech Movement disrupted the institution over a period of weeks. Hundreds were arrested; the state legislature threatened reprisals; the faculty became involved in the controversy; and the crisis led to the resignation of the president of the University of California, Clark Kerr.

On campus after campus in the late 1960s students organized sit-ins and employed other disruptive tactics. Frequently professors and administrators played into the radicals' hands, being so offended by their methods and manners that they refused to recognize the legitimacy of some of their demands.

At Columbia in 1968, SDS and black students occupied university buildings and refused to leave unless a series of "nonnegotiable" demands (concerning such matters as the university's involvement in secret military research and its relations with minority groups living in the Columbia neighborhood) were met. When, after long delays, President Grayson Kirk called in the police to clear the buildings, a riot broke out in which dozens of students, some of them innocent

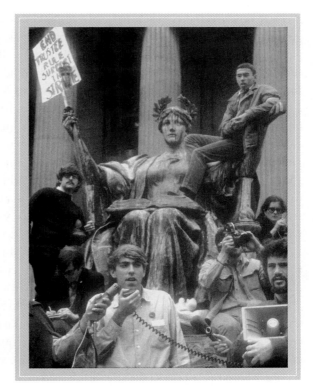

"Alma mater," outside Low Memorial Hall of Columbia University, looks on sedately as SDS leader Mark Rudd denounces the school. Later, Rudd and other radicals climbed these stairs and ordered administrators to vacate the building. The students then occupied the buildings. New York City police subsequently threw the students out.

bystanders, were clubbed and beaten. General student revulsion at the use of the police led to the resignation of Kirk and to the enactment of university reforms.

Equally significant in altering the students' mood was the frustration that so many of them felt with traditional aspects of college life. Regulations that students had formerly merely grumbled about evoked determined, even violent opposition. Dissidents denounced rules that restricted their personal lives, such as prohibitions on the use of alcohol and the banning of members of the opposite sex from dormitories. They complained that required courses inhibited their intellectual development. They demanded a share in the government of their institutions, long the private preserve of administrators and professors.

Beyond their specific complaints, the radicals refused to put up with anything they considered wrong. The knotty social problems that made their elders gravitate toward moderation led these students to become intransigent absolutists. The line between right and wrong became as sharply defined as the edge of a ruler. Racial prejudice was evil: It must be eradicated. War in a nuclear age was insane: Armies must be disbanded. Poverty amid plenty was an abomination: End poverty now. To the counsel that evil can be eliminated only gradually, that misguided persons must be persuaded to mend their ways, that compromise was the path to true progress, they responded with scorn. Extremists among them, observing the weaknesses of American civilization, adopted a nihilistic position—the only way to deal with a "rotten" society was to destroy it.

Critics found the radical students infantile, old-fashioned, and authoritarian: infantile because they refused to tolerate frustration or delay, old-fashioned because their absolutist ideas had been exploded by several generations of philosophers and scientists, authoritarian because they rejected majority rule. As time passed, SDS was plagued by factional disputes. Radical women in the movement, for example, claimed that it was run by male chauvinists; women who sought some say in policy matters, one of them wrote, were met with "indifference, ridicule, and anger."

By the end of the 1960s, SDS had lost much of its influence with the general student body. Nevertheless, it had succeeded in focusing attention on genuine social and political weaknesses both on the campuses and in the larger world.

Black students influenced the academic world in a variety of ways. Almost without exception colleges tried to increase black enrollments through scholarship funds and by lowering academic entrance requirements when necessary to compensate for the poor preparation many black students had received in the schools. This did not mean that the black students were satisfied with college life. Most were not. They tended to keep to themselves and usually had little to do with the somewhat elitist SDS. But they demanded more control over all aspects of their education than did the typical white. They wanted black studies programs taught and administered by blacks. Achievement of these goals was difficult because of the shortage of black teachers and because professors—including most black professors—considered student control of appointments and curricula unwise and in violation of the principles of academic freedom. Nevertheless the general academic response to black demands was accommodating; if confrontations occurred frequently, they were usually resolved by negotiation. Unlike white radical students, blacks tended to confine their demands to matters directly related to local conditions.

THE COUNTERCULTURE

Some young people, known generally as hippies, were so "turned off" by the modern world that they retreated from it, finding refuge in communes, drugs, and mystical religions, often wandering aimlessly from place to place. During the 1960s and 1970s groups of them could be found in every big city in the United

States and Europe. Some hippies, like the poet Allen Ginsberg, one of their elder statesmen, and the novelist Ken Kesey, were genuinely creative people. Ginsberg's dark, desperate masterpiece *Howl,* written apparently while under the influence of drugs in 1955, is perhaps the most widely read poem of the postwar era, certainly a work of major literary significance. *Howl* begins: "I saw the best minds of my generation destroyed by madness, starving hysterical naked," and goes on to describe the wanderings and searchings of these "angelheaded hipsters," a "lost battalion of platonic conversationalists . . . seeking jazz or sex or soup" in Houston, "whoring in Colorado," and "investigating the F.B.I. in beards and shorts" in California, all the while denouncing "the narcotic tobacco haze of Capitalism." *Howl* ends with Ginsberg's indignant, almost frantic assault on that "sphinx of cement and aluminum," the fire god Moloch, the devourer of children.

Others, however, such as the yippies Abbie Hoffman and Jerry Rubin, are best described as professional iconoclasts. (In 1968 yippies went through the motions of nominating a pig named Pigasus for president.) And most hippies were simply unwilling to confront the dilemmas of contemporary existence previously described.

The hippies developed a counterculture so directly opposite to the way of life of their parents' generation as to suggest to critics that they were still dominated by the culture they rejected. They wore old blue jeans and (it seemed) any nondescript garments they happened to find at hand. Male hippies wore their hair long and grew beards. Females avoided makeup, bras, and other devices more conventional women used to make themselves attractive to men. Both sexes rejected the old Protestant ethic; being part of the hippie world meant not caring about money or material goods or power over other people. Love was more important than money or influence, feelings more significant than thought, natural things superior to anything manufactured.

Most hippies resembled the radicals in their political and social opinions. They were disgusted by the dishonesty and sordid antics of so many of the politicians, horrified by the brutality of Vietnam, appalled by racism, contemptuous of the smugness they encountered in the colleges and universities. They believed in conservation, freedom of expression, tolerance, and peace.

But they rejected activism, being almost totally apolitical. Theirs was a world of folk songs and blaring acid rock music, of "be-ins," casual sex, and drugs. Their slogan, "Make love, not war" was more a general pacifist pronouncement than a specific criticism of events in Vietnam, although Vietnam surely had a great deal to do with their underlying pessimism. Indeed, with them passivity was a philosophy, almost a principle. At rock concerts they listened where earlier generations had danced. Hallucinogenic drugs heightened users' "experiences" while they

A sea of faces engulfs Max Yasgur's farm near Woodstock, New York, in 1969, where a half million young people endured mammoth traffic jams to commune with nature and each other. Many smoked pot, romped in the mud, disported in the nude, and otherwise collectively flouted social convention; rock musicians such as Janis Joplin, Jimi Hendrix, and Jefferson Airplane used state-of-the-art amplifiers to repudiate a technocratic world.

were in fact in a stupor; witness "Tune in, turn on, drop out." Another hippie slogan, "Do your own thing," will work in social situations only if no one does anything. Their communes were a far cry from the busy centers of social experimentation of the pre–Civil War Age of Reform.

THE SEXUAL REVOLUTION

Young people made the most striking contribution to the revolution that took place in the late 1960s in public attitudes toward sexual relationships. Here change came with startling swiftness. Almost overnight (it seemed in retrospect) conventional ideas about premarital sex, contraception and abortion, homosexuality, pornography, and a host of related matters were openly challenged. Probably the behavior of the majority of Americans did not alter radically, but the majority's beliefs and practices were no longer automatically acknowledged as the only valid ones. It became possible for individuals to espouse different values and to behave differently with at least relative impunity. Actions that in one decade would have led to social ostracism or even to imprisonment were in the next decade accepted almost as a matter of course.

One of the major changes to occur in the 1970s and 1980s was the willingness of homosexuals to make public their sexual preference in the course of demanding full legal standing and equal rights.

The causes of this revolution were complex and interrelated; one change led to others. More efficient methods of birth control and antibiotics that cured venereal disease removed the two principal practical arguments against sex outside of marriage; with these barriers down, many people found their moral attitudes changing. Alfred C. Kinsey's *Sexual Behavior in the Human Male* (1948), based on thousands of confidential interviews with persons from many walks of life, claimed that half of American men engaged in homosexual activities before adolescence; that 90 percent had masturbated; that between 30 and 45 percent had adulterous sexual relations; that 70 percent had patronized prostitutes; and that 17 percent of farm boys had had sexual relations with animals. Kinsey's data emphasized the diversity of sexual urges, and the foolishness of societal attempts to prescribe narrow standards of morality.

Sexual Behavior in the Human Male shocked many people, and many social scientists pointed out that a large sample was not necessarily representative. When Kinsey published *Sexual Behavior in the Human Female* in 1958, a book that demonstrated that the sexual practices of women were as varied as those of men, he was subjected to a storm of abuse and deprived of the foundation support that had financed his research. (In 1997 historian James H. Jones challenged Kinsey's claims to scientific objectivity. Jones found that Kinsey and some of his researchers organized, participated in, and even filmed all manner of sexual activities involving interview subjects, prostitutes, colleagues, and spouses.)

Nevertheless, Kinsey was during his lifetime called "the Marx of the sexual revolution." Once it became possible to look at sex in primarily physical terms and to accept the idea that one's own urges might not be as uncommon as one had been led to believe, it became much more difficult to object to any sexual activity practiced in private by consenting adults. Homosexuals, for example, began openly to admit their feelings and to demand that the heterosexual society cease to harass and discriminate against them.

That the sexual revolution in its many aspects served useful functions was beyond dispute. Reducing irrational fears and inhibitions was liberating for many persons of both sexes, and it tended to help young people form permanent associations on the basis of deeper feelings than their sexual drives. Women surely profited from the new freedom, just as a greater sharing of family duties by husbands and fathers opened men's lives to many new satisfactions.

But like other changes, the revolution produced new problems, and some of its results were at best ambiguous. For young people, sexual freedom could be very unsettling; sometimes it generated social pressures that propelled them into relationships they were not yet prepared to handle, with grave psychological results. Equally perplexing was the rise in the number of illegitimate births. Easy cures did not eliminate venereal disease; on the contrary, the relaxation of sexual taboos produced what public health officials called a veritable epidemic of gonorrhea, a frightening increase in the incidence of syphilis, and the emergence of a new disease, the acquired immunodeficiency syndrome (AIDS).

Exercising the right to advocate and practice previously forbidden activities involved subjecting people who found those activities offensive—still a large proportion of the population—to embarrassment and even to acute emotional distress. To some people pornography seemed ethically wrong, and to most feminists it seemed degrading to women. Abortion raised difficult legal and moral questions, which exacerbated already serious social conflicts. Clearly, however, the sexual revolution was not about to end, nor the direction of change to be reversed.

WOMEN'S LIBERATION

Sexual freedom also contributed to the revival of the women's rights movement. For one thing, freedom involved a more drastic revolution for women than for men. Effective methods of contraception obviously affected women more directly than men, and the new attitudes heightened women's awareness of the way the old sexual standards and patterns of family living had restricted their entire existence. In fact the two movements interacted with each other in innumerable ways, some clear, others obscure. Concern for better job opportunities and for equal pay for equal work, for example, fed the demand for day-care centers for children.

Still another cause of the new drive for women's rights was concern for improving the treatment of minorities. Participation in and the mere observation of the civil rights movement encouraged American women—as it frequently had in earlier times—to speak out more forcefully for their own rights. Just as white people had callously demeaned and dominated black people until forced to desist by the victims of their prejudice, so, feminists argued, they were being demeaned and dominated by a male-oriented society and must fight back.

One of the leaders of the new women's movement was Betty Friedan. In *The Feminine Mystique* (1963), Friedan argued that advertisers, popular magazines, and other opinion-shaping forces were undermining the capacity of women to use their intelligence and their talents creatively by a pervasive and not very subtle form of brainwashing designed to convince them of the virtues of domesticity. This Friedan deplored. She argued that without understanding why, thousands of women living supposedly happy lives were experiencing vague but persistent feelings of anger and discomfort. "The only way for a woman . . . to know herself as a person is by creative work of her own," she wrote. A "problem that had no name" was stifling women's potential.

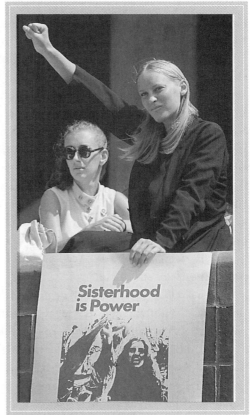

The Feminine Mystique was what later came to be known as "consciousness raising" for thousands of women. Over a million copies were quickly sold. Back in 1922 a committee of physicians and social scientists had queried a thousand middle-class women about their personal lives. To the question: "Is your married life a happy one?" only 116 had answered no. But after her book came out, Friedan was deluged by hundreds of letters from women who had thought that their unease and depression despite their "happy" family life were both unique and unreasonable. Many now determined to expand their horizons by taking jobs or resuming their education.

Friedan had assumed that if able women acted with determination, employers would recognize their abilities and stop discriminating against them. This did not happen. In 1966 she and other femi-

"Sisterhood is Power" proclaimed the radical women's groups as women sought ways to overcome the limitations imposed on them simply because of their gender.

nists founded the National Organization for Women (NOW). Copying the tactics of black activists, NOW called for equal employment opportunities and equal pay as civil rights. "The time has come for a new movement toward true equality for all women in America and toward a fully equal partnership of the sexes," the leaders announced. "The silken curtain of prejudice and discrimination against women" in government, industry, the professions, religion, education, "and every other field of importance" must be drawn back. In 1967 NOW came out for an Equal Rights Amendment to the Constitution, for changes in the divorce laws, and for the legalization of abortion, the right of "control of one's body."

By 1967, however, many younger feminists were arguing that NOW was not radical enough. They deplored its hierarchical structure, its lobbying activities, its stress on attracting celebrities, and its imitation of conventional pressure-group tactics. Equality of the two sexes smacked of "separate but equal" to these women, and indeed, many of them had been first radicalized by the struggle against racial segregation.

Typical was Kate Millett, whose *Sexual Politics* (1970) became a best-seller. Millett called for "a sexual revolution" to do away with "traditional inhibitions and taboos." She denounced male supremacy, which she described as "the institution of patriarchy." She drew a distinction between biological factors, which differentiate men from women and are immutable, and gender, or the learned ways in which men and women relate to one another socially and culturally. These learned ways of behaving are capable of change. For example, Millett said that people must stop thinking of words like *violent* and *efficiency* as male characteristics and *passive* and *tenderness* as female.

The radicals gathered in small consciousness-raising groups to discuss questions as varied as the need for government-provided child-care centers, how best to denounce the annual Miss America contests, and lesbianism. They held conferences and seminars and published magazines, the most widely known being *Ms.*, edited by Gloria Steinem. Academics among them organized women's studies programs at dozens of colleges.

Some radical feminists advocated raising children in communal centers and doing away with marriage as a legal institution. Others described marriage as "legalized rape." Some rejected heterosexuality as a matter of principle.

The militants attacked all aspects of the standard image of the female sex. Avoiding the error of the Progressive era reformers, who had fought for the vote by stressing the supposed purity and high moral character of women, they insisted on total equality. Clichés such as "the fair sex" and "the weaker sex" made them see red. They demanded that men bear as much of the burden of caring for their children, cooking, and housework as women traditionally did. They took courses in self-defense to be able to protect themselves from muggers, rapists,

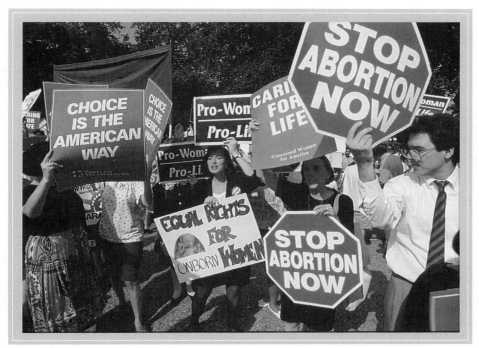

The issue of abortion continues to generate deep feelings among those on both sides of the 1973 Supreme Court Roe v. Wade *decision. In this July 1992 photo, pro-choice adherents, who support the ruling declaring a woman's constitutional right to an abortion, clash with pro-lifers, who seek to overturn the decision, outside the U.S. Supreme Court building.*

and aggressive dates. They denounced the use of masculine words like *chairman* (favoring *chairperson*) and of such terms as *mankind* and *men* to designate people in general. They substituted *Ms.* for both *Miss* and *Mrs.* on the grounds that the language drew no such distinction between unmarried and married men.

Few people escaped being affected by the women's movement. The presence of women in new roles—as television commentators, airline pilots, police officers— did not prove that a large-scale shift in employment patterns had taken place. Yet even the most unregenerate male seemed to recognize that the balance of power and influence between the sexes had been altered. The sexual revolution was not about to end, the direction of change in gender relationships not to be reversed.

Many people in the vanguard of change thought they could catch a glimpse, in the not too distant future, of an egalitarian, tolerant, and fulfilling world. But it is hard to see clearly when one is moving, and American society in the 1960s was in flux. Many soon learned that change begets change, and not always what one expects.

MILESTONES

1948	Norman Mailer, *The Naked and the Dead*
	Alfred C. Kinsey, *Sexual Behavior in the Human Male*
1951	James Jones, *From Here to Eternity*
	J. D. Salinger, *The Catcher in the Rye*
1955	Joseph Heller, *Catch-22*
	Allen Ginsberg, *Howl*
	AFL and CIO merge
1957	Russians launch first *Sputnik*
	Jack Kerouac, *On the Road*
1958	National Defense Education Act
	Alfred C. Kinsey, *Sexual Behavior in the Human Female*
1959	Alaska and Hawaii admitted to the Union
1962	Students for a Democratic Society's Port Huron Statement
1963	Betty Friedan, *The Feminine Mystique*
1964	Free Speech Movement at the University of California
	Malcolm X founds Organization of Afro-American Unity
1965	Malcolm X assassinated
	César Chávez organizes boycott to support grape pickers
1965–1967	Riots in black ghettos
1966	National Organization for Women (NOW) founded
1968	Student strike at Columbia University broken by police
	Martin Luther King, Jr. murdered
1970	Kate Millett, *Sexual Politics*
1975	Indian Self-Determination Act

32

RUNNING ON EMPTY: THE NATION TRANSFORMED

While most Americans watched, transfixed, as the events of Watergate interred the Nixon presidency, few were aware that a battle on the other side of the world was about to transform their lives. On October 6, 1973, the eve of Yom Kippur, the Jewish Day of Atonement, Egypt and Syria attacked the state of Israel. Six years earlier Israel had trounced the Egyptians with humiliating ease, but now Egypt's armored divisions slashed into the Sinai and threatened to slice Israel in half. President Nixon roused himself from a Watergate-induced inertia and airlifted scores of fighter planes and other desperately needed matériel to Israel. In a brilliant counterstroke, the Israelis recrossed the Suez Canal, cut Egyptian supply lines, and forced the invaders to capitulate. But a vengeful Arab world then launched its biggest weapon and aimed it squarely at the United States: It cut off oil shipments to the West.

THE OIL CRISIS

Deprived of access to Middle Eastern oil, the American economy sputtered. The price of oil rose to $12 a barrel, up from $3. This sent prices soaring for nearly everything else. Homes were heated with oil, factories were powered by it, and utility plants used it to generate electricity. Nylon and other synthetic fibers as well as paints, insecticides, fertilizers, and many plastic products were based on petrochemicals. Above all else, oil was refined into gasoline. By the time of the

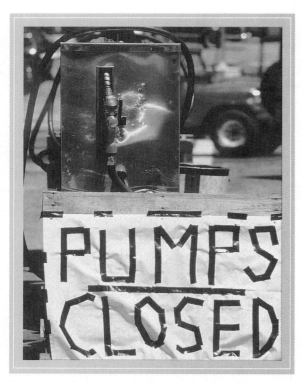

Gas stations all over the country began running out of gas in 1973; the shortage worsened through the winter and into 1974.

Yom Kippur War, American car owners were driving more than a trillion miles a year, the major reason why the United States, formerly a major oil exporter, imported one-third of its oil. The Arab oil embargo pushed up gas prices; service stations intermittently ran out of gasoline and long lines formed at those that remained open.

In the spring of 1974, Henry Kissinger negotiated an agreement that required Israel's withdrawal from some of the territory occupied since the 1967 war; the Arab nations then lifted the oil embargo. But the principal oil exporting nations—Venezuela, Saudi Arabia, Kuwait, Iraq, and Iran—had learned a valuable lesson: if they limited their production of oil, they could drive up its price. After the embargo had ended, their cartel, the Organization of Petroleum Exporting Countries, (OPEC), announced another price increase. Gasoline prices doubled overnight.

American automakers who had scoffed at bulbous Volkswagon "bugs" and tiny Japanese "boxes" now winced as these foreign competitors claimed the new market for small, fuel-efficient, front-wheel-drive cars. American auto companies were unable to respond to this challenge because their contracts with the United Automobile Workers (UAW) linked wages to consumer prices, which had floated upward with the price of oil. As production costs rose, manufacturers needed to sell more of their behemoth models, loaded with expensive options such as air-conditioning, power windows, and stereo systems. They could not profitably sell the small cars the public craved. (In 1982, when Ford belatedly entered the front-wheel-drive market, it lost $40 on each car sold.) By the end of the 1970s, Japanese automakers had captured 30 percent of the entire American automobile market.

FORD AS PRESIDENT

The country greeted the accession of Gerald Ford to the presidency with a collective sigh of relief. Most observers considered Ford unimaginative, certainly not brilliant. But he was hardworking, and—most important under the circumstances—his record was untouched by scandal. Although he was an almost automaton-like Republican partisan, nearly all the Democrats in Congress liked him. He was Nixon's opposite as a person, being gregarious and open, and he stated repeatedly that he took a dim view of Nixon's high-handed way of dealing with Congress. A most ordinary person, earnest but limited, Ford appeared unlikely to venture beyond conventional boundaries or to act rashly. This was what nearly everyone wanted of the president in the wake of Nixon.

But Ford was disinclined to address the great issues of the past generation, social welfare (as established by the New Deal and Great Society programs) and the Cold War, and unprepared to cope with the powerful forces that were already shaking the nation's economic foundation.

Ford identified inflation as the chief economic culprit and asked patriotic citizens to signify their willingness to fight it by wearing WIN (Whip Inflation Now) buttons. Almost immediately the economy entered a precipitous slump. Production fell and the unemployment rate rose to above 9 percent. The president was forced to ask for tax cuts and other measures aimed at stimulating business activity. This made inflation worse and did little to promote employment.

"My fellow Americans, our long national nightmare is over," Gerald Ford announced as he succeeded Richard Nixon in August 1974. Ford's candor and humility reassured a public wearied by the "dirty tricks" and "executive privilege" of the Watergate years.

The economic problems were difficult, and Ford was handicapped by the fact that the Democrats had solid control of Congress, but his performance was at best inept.

THE FALL OF SOUTH VIETNAM

Depressing news about the economy was compounded by events in Vietnam. In January 1975, after two years of a bloody "cease-fire" (Hanoi charged Saigon with 301,000 violations; and Saigon charged its adversary with 35,673), North Vietnam initiated a two-year plan to conquer South Vietnam by striking just south of the 17th parallel. Dispirited and incompetently led, the South Vietnamese fell back, then fled headlong, and finally dissolved with a rapidity that astonished their attackers.

Ford had always supported the Vietnam War. As the military situation deteriorated, he urged Congress to pour more arms into the South to stem the North Vietnamese advance. The legislators flatly refused to do so, and on May 1, 1975 the Viet Cong and North Vietnamese entered Saigon, which they renamed Ho Chi Minh City. The long Vietnam War was finally over.

FORD VERSUS CARTER

Ford's record on the economy and foreign policy did not inspire confidence. After some hesitation he nevertheless decided to seek the Republican presidential nomination in 1976. He fought off a challenge by ex-governor Ronald Reagan of California, a movie actor turned politician who was the darling of the Republican right wing, and won the Republican nomination by a slim majority.

In the meantime the Democrats had chosen James Earl Carter, a former governor of Georgia, as their candidate. Carter's rise from almost total obscurity was even more spectacular than that of George McGovern in the 1972 campaign and was made possible by the same forces: television, the democratization of the delegate-selection process, and the absence of a dominant leader among the Democrats.

Carter had been a naval officer and a substantial peanut farmer and warehouse owner before entering politics. He was elected governor of Georgia in 1970. While governor he won something of a reputation as a southern public official who treated black citizens fairly. (He hung a portrait of Martin Luther King, Jr. in his office.) Carter's political style was informal—he preferred to be called Jimmy. During the campaign for delegates he turned his inexperience in national politics to advantage, emphasizing his lack of connection with the Washington establishment rather than apologizing for it. He repeatedly called attention to his integrity and deep religious faith. "I'll never lie to you," he promised voters, a pledge that no candidate would have bothered to make before Nixon's disgrace. He accumulated delegates steady and won the nomination.

When the final contest began, both candidates were vague with respect to issues, a situation that hurt Carter particularly because he had made so much of honesty and straight talk. Ford stressed the need to control inflation, Carter to attack high unemployment. The election was memorable chiefly for its gaffes: Carter's admission to *Playboy* that he had "lusted after women in my heart" and Ford's declaration in a televised debate, "There is no Soviet domination in Eastern Europe." Voters were left to choose between Carter's seeming ignorance of human frailty and Ford's human frailty of seeming ignorant.

With both candidates stumbling toward the finish line, pundits predicted an extremely close contest, and they were right: Carter won, 297 electoral votes to 241, having carried most of the South, including Texas, and a few large industrial states. A key element in his victory was the fact that he got an overwhelming majority of the black vote (partly on his record in Georgia, partly because Ford had been unsympathetic toward the demands of the urban poor). He also ran well in districts dominated by labor union members. The wish of the public to punish the party of Richard Nixon probably was a further reason for his victory.

THE CARTER PRESIDENCY

Carter shone brightly in comparison with Nixon, and he seemed more forward-looking and imaginative than Ford. He tried to give a tone of democratic simplicity and moral fervor to his administration. After delivering his inaugural address, he walked with his wife Rosalynn and their small daughter Amy in the parade from the Capitol to the White House instead of riding in a limousine. He enrolled Amy, a fourth-grader, in a largely black Washington public school. Soon after taking office he held a "call-in"; for two hours he answered questions phoned in by people from all over the country.

Carter's actual administration of his office did not go nearly so well. He put so many Georgians in important posts that his administration took on a parochial character. The administration developed a reputation for submitting complicated proposals to Congress with great fanfare and then failing to follow up on them. Whatever matter Carter was considering at the moment seemed to absorb him totally—other urgent matters were allowed to drift.

A NATIONAL MALAISE

To Carter, these difficulties were symptomatic of a more fundamental flaw in the nation's soul. In a heralded television speech he complained that "a moral and spiritual crisis" had sapped people's energies and undermined civic pride: "We've learned that piling up material goods cannot fill the emptiness of lives which have no confidence or purpose." Critics responded that the nation needed a president rather than a preacher, and that sermons on the emptiness of consumption rang hollow to those who had lost their jobs or whose paychecks had been shrunk by inflation.

The economic downturn, though triggered by the energy shortage, had more fundamental causes. In the prosperous postwar decades, many companies had become too big and complacent, more attuned to the demands of the corporate bureaucracy than the needs of customers. Workers' boredom lowered productivity. Absenteeism at General Motors and Ford doubled during the 1960s. On an average day in 1970, 5 percent of GM's workforce was missing without explanation, and on Mondays and Fridays one in ten workers failed to show up. That year Lee Iacocca, the president of Ford, was unnerved by employee attitudes during his visit to a plant at Wixcom, Indiana: "I see some young guy who's going full-time to school at Wayne State, his mind is elsewhere, and he doesn't give a shit what he

An abandoned steelmill in Youngstown, Ohio, in 1986. The backbone of American industry throughout the twentieth century, midwestern steel sharply declined in the 1970s and all but collapsed during the 1980s.

builds, he doesn't care and he isn't involved in his job. We can't change a man like that anymore." Incapable of eliminating slipshod work in Ford plants, Iacocca recommended that dealers improve their repair shops.

Two years later simmering discontents among young workers boiled over at the GM assembly division at Lordstown, Ohio. GM had installed robotic welding machines, streamlined the workforce, and accelerated the assembly line: 100 cars passed through the line each hour—40 more than under the previous system. Without authorization from the national UAW, younger workers refused to work at the faster pace, allowing many chassis to pass through untouched and throwing the factory into chaos. "Significant numbers of American workers," the U.S. Department of Health, Education and Welfare concluded, had grown dissatisfied with the "dull, repetitive, seemingly meaningless tasks" of the postwar workplace.

Younger workers were growing impatient, too, with aging union leaders and a system that welded salary increases to seniority. Increasingly the young rejected the postwar accord in which organized labor essentially ceded control of the workplace in return for cost-of-living increases and job security.

Union membership slipped badly from the high point of the mid-1950s, when over one in three nonagricultural workers belonged to unions; by 1978, the proportion had declined to one in four, and by 1990, one in six. During the 1940s and 1950s, most workers voted to join a union, pay dues, and have the organization bargain for them. By 1978, however, union organizers were losing three-fourths of their campaigns to represent workers; and many workers who belonged to unions were opting to get out. Every year, 800 more union shops voted to rescind their affiliation.

STAGFLATION: THE WEIRD ECONOMY

Recessions are part of the natural business cycle: when economies overheat, they eventually cool down. But the economic crisis after 1973 was unsettling because, for the first time in the nation's history, the rising tide of unemployment had failed to extinguish inflation. Millions of workers lost their jobs, yet wages and prices continued to rise. The term "stagflation" (a combination of stagnation and inflation) was coined to describe this anomaly. In 1971 an inflation rate of 5 percent had so alarmed President Nixon that he had imposed a price freeze. By 1975 inflation had soared to 11 percent and by 1979, it peaked at a whopping 13 percent; unemployment ranged from 6 to 10 percent, nearly twice the usual postwar level.

Carter had promised to fight inflation by reducing government spending and balancing the budget and to stimulate the economy by cutting taxes, policies that were very much like those of Nixon and Ford.

Congress raised the minimum wage to help low-paid workers cope with inflation. It pegged Social Security payments to the cost of living index in an effort to protect retirees. Thereafter, when prices rose, Social Security payments went up automatically. The poor and the pensioners got some immediate relief, but the laws made balancing the federal budget more difficult and the increased spending power of the recipients caused further upward pressure on prices. During the decade, social welfare spending more than doubled. The federal deficit soared from $8.7 billion in 1970 to $72.7 billion in 1980. The price spiral seemed unstoppable.

The federal government made matters worse in several ways. Wages and salaries rose in response to inflation, but taxes went up more rapidly because larger dollar incomes put people in higher tax brackets. This "bracket creep" caused resentment and frustration among middle-class families. There were "taxpayer revolts" as many people turned against long-accepted but expensive government programs for aiding the poor. Inflation also increased the government's need for money. Year after year it spent more than it received in taxes. By thus unbalancing the budget it pumped billions of dollars into the economy, and by borrowing to meet the deficits and pushing up interest rates, it increased the costs of all businesses that had to borrow and thereby exacerbated inflation.

Soaring mortgage rates made it more difficult to sell homes. The housing slump meant unemployment for thousands of carpenters, bricklayers, and other construction workers and bankruptcy for many builders. Double-digit interest rates also hurt small businesses seeking to expand. Savings and loan institutions were especially hard-hit because they were saddled with countless mortgages made when rates were as low as 4 and 5 percent. Now they had to pay much more than that to hold deposits and offer even higher rates to attract new money.

"YOU DESERVE A BREAK": FAMILIES UNDER STRAIN

Bad as inflation was in the mid-1970s, it got worse in 1979 when further instability in the Middle East nearly tripled the price of oil, which now reached $34 a barrel. This sent gasoline far over the $1 a gallon price barrier many had thought inconceivable. Within months Ford stock, at 32 in 1978, plummeted to 16; its credit rating with Standard and Poor's fell from AAA to an ignominious BBB. Chrysler, the third largest automaker, tottered near bankruptcy and then fell over the edge, saved in mid-fall only by a $1.2 billion federal loan guarantee. From 1978 to 1982, the jobs of one in three auto workers were eliminated.

When workers—most of them men—lost relatively high-paying jobs in the automobile factories and steel mills, their spouses usually helped to make up for the loss in wages by taking low-paying jobs in restaurants, retail stores, and offices. In 1950, one in four married women had a job outside the home; by 1980, half did.

In 1976 Democratic Senator Lloyd Bentsen, while campaigning for vice president, observed that McDonald's fast-food chain employed more people than U.S. Steel. "There is something very wrong with a nation that is long on hamburgers and short on steel," he declared. In fact, the two phenomena went hand in hand. Overextended families had little time to shop for, prepare, and enjoy leisurely meals around the dinner table. Such families "deserved a break," according to the McDonald's jingle, and often bolted down fast food on the way to or from work or school. "Most people I know have turned their ovens into planters," one harried professional woman said.

For the millions of young women whose gender consciousness had been shaped by Betty Friedan, Kate Millett, and other feminists, the recession struck at the worst possible time. Those who had anticipated a rapid ascent of the corporate ladder discovered that the lower rungs were the first to collapse during the recession. Many abandoned the idea of a career and settled for low-paying, dead-end jobs in the clerical or service sector. Yet some women, especially those who were well-educated, achieved strong gains during the 1970s: female lawyers jumped from 5 to 12 percent of the profession; and accountants, from 25 to 33 percent.

The result was that, just when the feminist movement required a united fight to gain legal parity with men, women increasingly were divided: into an intellectual and professional elite, eager to prove their merits on the job in fair competition with men; and an underpaid and ill-used underclass, vulnerable to the vagaries of a recessionary economy and to the dictates of (mostly male) bosses.

One casualty was the Equal Rights Amendment (ERA), which would make it unconstitutional to deny equal rights "on account of sex." First proposed by the National Woman's party in 1923, the ERA got nowhere. The National Organization for Women (NOW) revived the measure in the 1960s. The House of Representatives approved the ERA in 1971 and the Senate in 1972. By the end of 1972, 22 states had ratified the amendment, only 16 short of the three-fourths needed for the ERA to become part of the constitution.

But in 1973 Phyllis Schlafly, a former vice president of the National Federation of Republican Women and publisher of a conservative newsletter, spearheaded a nationwide campaign against the ERA. She argued that it would subject young women to the military draft, deprive divorced women of alimony and child custody, and make married women legally responsible for providing 50 percent of household income. Although most polls indicated that a majority of voters supported the ERA, Schlafly's words struck a responsive chord among anxious housewives and low-wage-earning women who doubted they could survive the recessionary economy on their own. The ratification campaign lost momentum and stalled, falling just three states short of success.

COLD WAR OR DÉTENTE?

"It is a new world," Carter declared in his first speech on foreign affairs. In contrast to the shadowy dealings and sly gambits of the Nixon-Kissinger years, he based his foreign policy on "constant decency." He announced that he would deal with other nations in a fair and humane way, putting the defense of "basic human rights" before all other concerns. He then cut off aid to Chile and Argentina because of human rights' violations. He also negotiated treaties with Panama that provided for the gradual transfer of the Panama Canal to that nation and guaranteed the canal's neutrality. But he said little about what was going on in a long list of other nations whose citizens' rights were being repressed.

In 1979 another Strategic Arms Limitation Treaty (SALT II) was signed with the Soviet Union, but the following winter the Soviet Union sent troops into Afghanistan to overthrow a government of which it disapproved. Carter denounced the invasion and warned the Russians that he would use force if they invaded any of the countries bordering the Persian Gulf. He withdrew the SALT treaty, which he had sent to the Senate for ratification. He also refused to allow American athletes to compete in the 1980 Olympic games, which were held in Moscow, and he began a new nuclear arms buildup.

Carter's one striking diplomatic achievement was the so-called Camp David Agreement negotiated by Israel and Egypt. Avoiding war in the Middle East was crucial because war in that part of the world was likely to result in the cutting off of oil supplies from the Arab nations. In September 1978 President Anwar Sadat of Egypt and Prime Minister Menachem Begin of Israel came to the United States at Carter's invitation to seek a peace treaty ending the state of war that had existed between their two countries for many years.

For two weeks they conferred at Camp David, the presidential retreat outside the capital, and Carter's mediation had much to do with their successful negotiations. In the treaty Israel promised to withdraw from territory captured from Egypt during the 1967 Israeli-Egypt war. Egypt in turn recognized Israel as a nation, the first Arab country to do so. In 2002, Carter was belatedly awarded the Nobel Peace Prize for his work as intermediary.

THE IRAN CRISIS: ORIGINS

At this point a dramatic shift in the Middle East thrust Carter into the spotlight as never before. On November 4, 1979, about 400 armed Muslim militants broke into the American Embassy compound in Tehran, Iran, and took everyone within the walls captive.

The seizure had roots that ran far back in Iranian history. In the early 1950s liberal and nationalist elements in Iran installed Muhammad Musaddig as premier, and he sought to reduce the power of the Anglo-Iranian Oil Company.

In 1953 the CIA (Operation Ajax), presumably to prevent the nationalization of Iranian petroleum resources and the abolition of the monarchy, organized a coup that resulted in his overthrow.

Iranian militants in Tehran burning the American flag. Such demonstrations attracted millions and helped establish the revolutionary regime's legitimacy among its own people. The alternative means of creating legitimacy, by holding elections, was often rejected on theological (and pragmatic) grounds by Mideast rulers.

The fall of Musaddig enabled the international oil industry to export billions of barrels of cheap oil, but it turned most Iranians against the United States and against his successor: Shah Reza Pahlavi. His unpopularity led the shah to purchase enormous amounts of American arms. Between 1973 and 1978 the shah spent $19 billion on sophisticated F-14 and F-15 fighter planes and other American weapons. Over the years Iran became the most powerful military force in the region.

The shah's unpopularity worsened. Throughout 1977, riots and demonstrations convulsed Iran. When soldiers fired on protesters, the bloodshed caused more unrest, and that unrest, more bloodshed. Over 10,000 civilians were killed, many times that number wounded. In 1978 the whole country seemed to rise against the shah. Finally, in January 1979, he was forced to flee. A revolutionary government headed by a revered religious leader, the Ayatollah Ruhollah Khomeini, assumed power.

Khomeini denounced the United States, the "Great Satan," whose support of the shah, he said, had caused the Iranian people untold suffering. When President Carter allowed the shah to come to the United States for medical treatment for cancer, the seizure of the Tehran embassy resulted.

THE IRAN CRISIS: CARTER'S DILEMMA

The militants announced that the captive Americans would be held hostage until the United States returned the shah to Iran for trial as a traitor. They also demanded that the shah's vast wealth be confiscated and surrendered to the Iranian government. Of course, President Carter rejected these demands. Deporting the shah, who had entered the United States legally, and confiscating his property were not possible under American law. Instead Carter froze Iranian assets in the United States and banned trade with Iran until the hostages were freed.

A stalemate developed. Months passed. Even after the shah, who was terminally ill, left the United States for Panama, the Iranians remained adamant. The crisis produced a remarkable emotional response in the United States. For the first time since the Vietnam War the entire country agreed on something.

Nevertheless the hostages languished in Iran. An intense debate raged within the administration about whether to attempt to rescue them. In April 1980 Carter finally ordered a team of marine commandos flown into Iran in Sea Stallion helicopters in a desperate attempt to free the hostages. The raid was a fiasco. Several helicopters broke down. While the others were gathered at a desert rendezvous south of Tehran, Carter called off the attempt. In the confusion of a

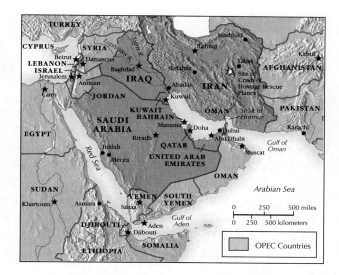

The Middle East

night departure there was a crash and eight commandos were killed. The Iranians made political capital of the incident, gleefully displaying on television the wrecked aircraft and captured American equipment. The stalemate continued. And when the shah died in July 1980, it made no difference to the Iranians.

THE ELECTION OF 1980

Despite the failure of the raid and the persistence of stagflation, Carter had more than enough delegates at the Democratic convention to win nomination on the first ballot. His Republican opponent in the campaign that followed was Ronald Reagan, the former governor of California who had almost defeated Gerald Ford for the nomination in 1976. At 69, Reagan was the oldest person ever nominated for president by a major party. However, his age was not a serious handicap in the campaign; he was physically trim and vigorous and seemed no older than most other prominent politicians.

Reagan had grown up a New Deal Democrat, but during and immediately after World War II he became disillusioned with liberalism. As president of the Screen Actors' Guild he attacked the influence of communists in the movie industry. After his movie career ended (he always insisted that he had not been typed as "the nice guy who didn't get the girl"), Reagan did publicity for General Electric until 1960, then worked for various conservative causes. He campaigned for

Barry Goldwater during the 1964 presidential contest. Reagan won the undying loyalty of supporters of the Vietnam War, as well as the permanent enmity of the left, by proposing that the United States "level North Vietnam, pave it, paint stripes on it, and make a parking lot out of it." In 1966 he was elected governor of California.

The 1980 presidential campaign ranks among the most curious in American history. One of Reagan's opponents at the Republican convention, Congressman John Anderson of Illinois, refused to accept defeat and ran for president as an independent because he thought both Carter and Reagan had little genuine popular support. Indeed, many citizens appeared unable to decide whom they were for; Anderson's problem was that he, too, inspired relatively little enthusiasm.

Both Carter and Reagan spent much time explaining why the other was unsuited to be president. Carter defended his record, though without much conviction. Reagan denounced criminals, drug addicts, and all varieties of immorality and spoke in support of patriotism, religion, family life, and other "old-fashioned" virtues. This won him the enthusiastic backing of fundamentalist religious sects and other conservative groups. He also called for rejection of the SALT II treaty and increased spending on defense, and he promised to transfer some functions of the federal government to the states and to cut taxes. He insisted at the same time that the budget could be balanced and inflation sharply reduced.

Reagan's tendency to depend on popular magazine articles, half-remembered conversations, and other informal sources for his economic "facts" reflected a mental imprecision that alarmed his critics, but his sunny disposition and his easygoing style compared favorably with Carter's personality. The president seemed tight-lipped and tense even when flashing his habitual toothy smile. A television debate between Carter and Reagan pointed up their personal differences, but Reagan's question to the audience: "Are you better off now than you were four years ago?" had more effect on the election than any policy he said he would pursue.

On election day the voting was light, but those who cast ballots gave Reagan over 43 million votes to Carter's 35 million and Anderson's 5.6 million. Dissatisfaction with the Carter administration seems to have determined the result. The Republicans also gained control of the Senate and cut deeply into the Democratic majority in the House of Representatives.

Carter devoted his last weeks in office to the continuing hostage crisis. Perhaps fearing that the new president might take some drastic action, Iran at last agreed to free the hostages in return for the release of its assets in the United States. After 444 days in captivity, the 52 hostages were set free on January 20, the day Reagan was inaugurated.

REAGAN AS PRESIDENT

Despite his amiable, unaggressive style, Reagan acted rapidly once in office. In August 1981 he displayed his determination in convincing fashion when the nation's air traffic controllers went on strike despite the fact that they were forbidden by law to do so. Reagan ordered them to return to work. Most refused; Reagan therefore discharged all 11,400 of them and began a crash program to train replacements. Even after the strike collapsed, the president would not rehire the strikers. The air controllers' union was destroyed.

Reagan hoped to change the direction in which the country was moving. He demanded steep reductions in federal spending and the deficit, to be accomplished by cutting social welfare expenditures, such as welfare, food stamps, and student loans, and by turning many functions of the federal government over to the states. The marketplace, not federal bureaucratic regulations, should govern most economic decisions.

He asked Congress to lower income taxes by 30 percent. When critics objected that this would increase the deficit, the president and his advisers reasoned that the tax cut would leave people with more money, which they would invest in productive ways. The new investment would generate more goods and jobs— and, ultimately, taxes for the federal government. This nostrum became known as Reaganomics.

Helped by the votes of conservative Democrats, Reagan won congressional approval of the Budget Reconciliation Act, which reduced government expenditures on domestic programs by $39 billion. But Congress resisted reducing the

Ronald Reagan rode to the White House in part on promises of reining in the federal government. "It's not my intention to do away with government," Reagan declared in his 1981 inaugural address. "It's rather to make it work— work with us, not over us; to stand by our side, not ride on our back."

politically popular "entitlement" programs, such as Social Security and Medicare, which accounted for about half of the budget.

Congress also enacted most of the tax cuts the president had asked for, lowering individual income taxes by 25 percent over three years. Because the percentage was the same for everyone, high-income taxpayers received a disproportionately large share of the savings. Business taxes were liberalized, and capital gains, gift, and inheritance levies were reduced; workers were given tax breaks to establish their own "individual" retirement accounts (IRAs).

Reagan also eliminated many government regulations affecting businesses. Long and complicated antitrust suits against International Business Machines and American Telephone and Telegraph, two of the largest corporations in the country, were dropped.

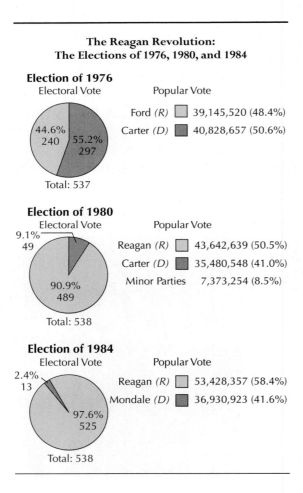

The Reagan Revolution:
The Elections of 1976, 1980, and 1984

Election of 1976

Electoral Vote   Popular Vote

44.6%   55.2%
240   297

Ford *(R)* — 39,145,520 (48.4%)
Carter *(D)* — 40,828,657 (50.6%)

Total: 537

Election of 1980

Electoral Vote   Popular Vote

9.1%
49

90.9%
489

Reagan *(R)* — 43,642,639 (50.5%)
Carter *(D)* — 35,480,548 (41.0%)
Minor Parties — 7,373,254 (8.5%)

Total: 538

Election of 1984

Electoral Vote   Popular Vote

2.4%
13

97.6%
525

Reagan *(R)* — 53,428,357 (58.4%)
Mondale *(D)* — 36,930,923 (41.6%)

Total: 538

Many of Reagan's advisers urged him to reduce the military budget to bring the government's income more nearly in line with its outlays. Instead, reviving the containment policy wholeheartedly, the president insisted that the military buildup was necessary because of the threat posed by the Soviet Union, which he called an "evil empire." In particular, he sought to expand and improve the nation's nuclear arsenal. He made no secret of his wish to create so formidable a nuclear force that the Soviets would have to back down in any confrontation.

In Central America he sought the overthrow of the left-wing government of Nicaragua and the defeat of communist rebels in El Salvador. He even used American troops to overthrow a Cuban-backed regime on the tiny Caribbean island of Grenada.

In 1982 the continuing turmoil in the Middle East plunged the Reagan administration into a new crisis. Israel had invaded Lebanon to destroy Palestine Liberation Organization units that were staging raids on northern Israeli settlements from bases there. Israeli troops easily overran much of the country, but in the process the Lebanese government disintegrated. Reagan agreed to commit American troops to an international peacekeeping force.

Tragedy resulted in October 1983 when a fanatical Muslim crashed a truck loaded with explosives into a building at the Beirut airport housing American marines. The building collapsed, killing 239 marines. Early the next year, prestige or no, Reagan removed the entire American peacekeeping force from Lebanon.

FOUR MORE YEARS

Being a sitting president with an extraordinarily high standing in public opinion polls, Reagan was nominated for a second term at the 1984 Republican convention without opposition. The Democratic nomination went to Walter Mondale of Minnesota, who had been vice president under Carter. Mondale electrified the country by choosing Representative Geraldine Ferraro of New York

Walter Mondale and Geraldine Ferraro held a press conference in Minnesota shortly after the Democratic nominating convention in July 1984.

as his running mate. Being an Italian American and a Catholic, Ferraro was expected to appeal to conservative Democrats who had supported Reagan in 1980 and to win the votes of many Republican women.

Reagan began the campaign with several important advantages. He was especially popular among religious fundamentalists and other social conservatives, and these groups were increasingly vocal. President Nixon had spoken of a "silent majority." By 1980 the kind of people he was referring to were no longer silent. Fundamentalist television preachers were almost all fervent Reaganites and the most successful of them were collecting tens of millions of dollars annually in contributions from viewers. One of these, the Reverend Jerry Falwell, founded Moral Majority and set out to create a new political movement. "Americans are sick and tired of the way the amoral liberals are trying to corrupt our nation," Falwell announced in 1979.

During the first Reagan administration, Moral Majority had become a powerful political force. Falwell was against drugs, the "coddling" of criminals, homosexuality, communism, and abortion, all things that Reagan also disliked. While not openly antiblack, Falwell disapproved of forced busing and a number of other government policies designed to help blacks and other minorities. Of course, Walter Mondale was also against many of the things that Falwell and his followers denounced, but Reagan was against them all. In addition, Reagan was in favor of government aid to private schools run by church groups, something dear to the hearts of Moral Majority despite the constitutional principle of separation of church and state.

But Moral Majority, despite its name, was far from being an actual majority. Reagan's support was much more broadly based. Thousands of working people and an enormous percentage of white southerners, types that had been solidly Democratic during the New Deal and beyond, now voted Republican. The president's personality was another important plus—voters continued to admire his informal yet firm style and his stress on patriotism and other "old-fashioned" virtues.

The tendency of voters to support a sitting president when the economy was on the rise was still another advantage. Unemployment fell to 7 percent, investment finally picked up, and inflation remained low. Interest rates were moving down slowly but steadily.

Mondale, in a daring move, announced that he would *raise* taxes if elected. This promise, most unusual for a person running for office, was an attempt to counter his reputation for political caution.

Most polls showed Reagan far in the lead when the campaign began, and this remained true throughout the contest. Nothing Mondale or Ferraro did or said affected the president's popularity. Bad news, even his own mistakes, had so little effect on his standing that people began to call him "the Teflon president." On election day he got nearly 60 percent of the popular vote and lost only in Minnesota, Mondale's home state, and in the District of Columbia. His Electoral College margin was overwhelming, 525 to 13.

Of all the elements in New Deal coalition, only African Americans, who voted solidly for Mondale, remained loyal. The Democratic strategy of nominating a woman for vice president was a failure; far more women voted for Reagan than for the Mondale-Ferraro ticket.

Reagan's triumph, like the two landslide victories of Dwight Eisenhower in the 1950s, was a personal one. The Republicans made only minor gains in the House of Representatives and actually lost two seats in the Senate.

"THE REAGAN REVOLUTION"

Reagan's agenda for his second term closely resembled that of his first. In foreign affairs, he ran into continuing congressional resistance to his requests for military support for his anticommunist crusade. This was particularly true after Mikhail S. Gorbachev became the Soviet premier in March 1985. Gorbachev seemed far more moderate and flexible than his predecessors. He began to encourage political debate and criticism in the Soviet Union—the policy known as *glasnost*—and he sought to stimulate the stagnant Russian economy by decentralizing administration and rewarding individual enterprise *(perestroika)*.

The arms cuts made at the 1988 Moscow summit showed how Ronald Reagan's ideas about the "evil empire" had changed. Yet Reagan was surprised to find that Mikhail Gorbachev believed "the communist propaganda he's grown up hearing about our country"—above all, that business dominates the government.

Gorbachev also announced that he would continue to honor the unratified SALT II agreement, whereas Reagan, arguing that the Soviet Union had not respected the limits laid down in the pact, seemed bent on pushing ahead with the expansion and modernization of America's nuclear arsenal. Reagan sought funds to develop an elaborate system of missile defenses. He referred to it as the Strategic Defense Initiative (SDI), although it was popularly known as Star Wars. SDI would consist of a network of computer-controlled space stations that would supposedly detect oncoming enemy missiles and destroy them.

When the president realized that the Soviets were eager for an agreement to limit nuclear weapons, he gradually abandoned his talk about Russia being an "evil empire." In October 1986 he met with Gorbachev in Iceland in search of an agreement on arms control. This summit went nowhere. The chief sticking point was SDI, which Gorbachev denounced as "space strike" weaponry that might be used to wipe out Soviet cities. The Iceland setback, however, proved to be temporary, and in 1988 at a second summit, Reagan and Gorbachev signed a treaty eliminating medium-range nuclear missiles.

Reagan nevertheless persisted in pressing for the Star Wars defense-in-space system. Congress, however, boggled at the enormous estimated cost of Star Wars. Costs aside, the idea of relying for national defense on the complex technology involved in controlling machines in outer space suffered a further setback in 1986, when the space shuttle *Challenger* exploded shortly after takeoff, killing its seven-member crew. This disaster put a stop to the program until the cause had been discovered and complex engineering changes made. In 1989 the shuttles began to fly again.

Reagan's basic domestic objectives—to reduce the scope of federal activity, particularly in the social welfare area; to lower income taxes; and to increase the strength of the armed forces—remained constant. Despite the tax cuts already made, congressional leaders of both parties agreed to the Income Tax Act of 1986, which reduced the top levy on personal incomes from 50 percent to 28 percent and the tax on corporate profits from 46 percent to 34 percent.

Liberal members of Congress, remembering how the voters had reacted to Mondale's talk about increasing taxes, found it politically difficult to oppose the measure. But the existing tax system was extremely complicated and full of loopholes benefiting particular interests. The new law did away with most of the tax shelters and special credits that corporations and well-to-do individuals had used to reduce their tax bills. The law also relieved 6 million low-income people from paying any federal income tax at all.

Reagan advanced another of his objectives more gradually. This was his appointment of conservatives to federal judgeships. During his first year in office he appointed Sandra Day O'Connor to the Supreme Court. Justice O'Connor was the first woman ever appointed to the Court, but she was also conservative on most constitutional questions. Reagan made several more appointments in the next few years. By 1988 he had appointed well over half of all the members of the federal bench.

CHANGE AND UNCERTAINTY

But if the "Reagan Revolution" seemed to have triumphed, powerful countering forces were at work that no individual or party could effectively control. For one thing, the makeup of the American people, always in a state of flux, was changing at a rate approaching that of the early 1900s when the "new" immigration had been at its peak. In the 1970s, after the Immigration Act of 1965 had put an end to the national-origins concept, more than 4 million immigrants entered the country, and the vast majority of these newcomers came from Asia and Latin America. This trend continued; of the 643,000 who arrived in 1988, more than 550,000 were from these two regions. More than 111,000 of the immigrants came from East Asian countries, the Philippines, Korea, and Vietnam. In addition, uncounted thousands entered the United States illegally, most crossing the long, sparsely settled border with Mexico. The nation's Hispanic population increased by 53 percent during the 1980s.

Some of the new immigrants were refugees from repressive regimes in Vietnam, Cuba, Haiti, and Central America, and nearly all were poor. Most were hardworking and law abiding and many were well-educated and possessed of valuable skills. But a significant number became public charges and others lawbreakers. Most tended, like their predecessors, to crowd together in ethnic neighborhoods. Spanish could be heard more often than English in large sections of Los Angeles, New York, Miami, and many other cities.

No strong demand for immigration restriction developed, perhaps because so many Americans were themselves the children of immigrants. However, conservatives found it appalling that so many people could enter the country illegally, and even Americans sympathetic to the so-called undocumented aliens agreed that control was desirable. Finally, in 1986, Congress passed a law offering amnesty to illegal immigrants long resident in the country and penalizing employers who hired illegal immigrants in the future. Many persons legalized their status under the new law, but the influx of illegal immigrants continued. Problems developed because some employers refused to hire anyone with a foreign accent on the grounds that they might be "illegals" bearing false papers.

Other trends deeply disturbed thousands of Americans. The postwar population explosion and the following decline in the birthrate assured that great pressure on the Social Security system would be inevitable when the baby boomers born after World War II reached retirement age in the early twenty-first century. More immediately, the traditional family—consisting of a husband and wife and their children, the man a breadwinner, the woman a homemaker and child rearer—seemed in danger of ceasing to be the norm. Year after year more than 1.1 million marriages ended in divorce. The tendency of couples to live together without getting married also continued, helping to explain why the number of illegitimate births rose steadily. So did the number of abortions—from 763,000 in 1974, after abortion was legalized, to an average of 1.3 million a year in the 1980s. However, many young women, married and unmarried, who had chosen careers over motherhood were having second thoughts as they approached the age when having children would no longer be possible.

AIDS

During the 1980s, the nation confronted its most serious health crisis in decades. In the late 1970s, world health officials had spotted the outbreak of yet another viral epidemic in central Africa; but no one noticed that this virus had mutated into a more lethal strain and was spreading to Europe and North America. On June 5, 1981 the Centers for Disease Control (CDC) in Atlanta alerted American health officials to an outbreak of a rare bacterial infection in Los Angeles. What made the outbreak "unusual" was that this particular infection, usually found in infants or older people with fragile immune systems, had struck five healthy young men. All were homosexuals. Within months, all died.

By 1982 the CDC decided to call this new disease acquired immunodeficiency syndrome (AIDS). They learned that AIDS was caused by human immunodeficiency virus (HIV), a lethal virus that destroys the body's defenses against infection, making victims susceptible to many diseases. HIV spread when an infected person's body fluids came in contact with someone else's, most commonly when homosexual men engaged in anal intercourse, or when intravenous drug users shared needles. By the end of the year, the CDC had documented 900 cases of AIDS; the disease was increasing exponentially. Soon HIV contaminated some of the nation's blood banks, and some recipients of transfusions came down with AIDS. In June 1983, when the federal budget approached $1 trillion, Congress finally voted $12 million for AIDS research and treatment.

Not until 1985, when the square-jawed romantic actor Rock Hudson confirmed that he was dying of AIDS, did the subject command widespread public attention. President Reagan, an old friend of Hudson's, publicly acknowledged

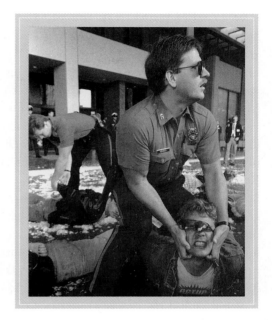

A police officer in Kansas City, Missouri, re-strains an ACT UP! protester, who was demon-strating against doctors at a medical convention in September 1990. ACT UP!, a group of radi-cal AIDS activists, charged the doctors with op-posing new treatments for the disease.

that the disease constituted a grave health crisis. Congress approved Reagan's call for a substantial increase in AIDS funding. But Reagan's appeal was belated and insufficient. By then, nearly 21,000 Americans had died; by 1999, the total number of AIDS-related deaths approached 400,000.

The AIDS epidemic affected public policy and private behavior. A nationwide educational campaign urged "safe" sex, especially the use of condoms, which by 1990 were distributed free in many high schools. Fear of the disease, and of those who suffered from it, exacerbated many people's homophobia. But the AIDS epidemic also forced most people to confront the issue, directly and perhaps for the first time, and thus contributed to a deeper understanding of homosexuality and the complexity of human nature. After Hudson's revelation, for example, the *New York Times* commenced using "gay" and "lesbian," the terms then preferred by the people so identified, instead of "homosexual." Gay and lesbian organizations, the vanguard in the initial war against AIDS, continued to fight for social acceptance and legal rights.

THE NEW MERGER MOVEMENT

The Reagan years witnessed a mad frenzy of corporate mergers. The person most responsible was Michael Milken, a shrewd stockbroker of the firm of Drexel Burnham Lambert. Milken specialized in selling "junk bonds," the debt offerings of companies whose existing debts were already high. He persuaded hundreds of savings and loan associations, insurance companies, pension funds, and other big investors to buy these junk bonds, which, though risky, offered unusually high interest rates. The success of his initial ventures prompted Milken to approach smaller companies, invite them to issue huge numbers of junk bonds, and use the proceeds to acquire larger firms.

In 1985 Ronald Perelman, an aggressive entrepreneur, employed this strategy to perfection. He had recently obtained control of Pantry Pride, a small supermarket chain with a net worth of about $145 million, and wanted to take over Revlon, a $2 billion cosmetics and health care conglomerate. With Milken's help, he sold $1.5 billion in Pantry Pride bonds ("junk," because the debt so greatly exceeded the company's worth) and used that capital to buy Revlon. He then paid off the Pantry Pride bonds by selling off huge chunks of Revlon and amalgamating the remainder of the company into Pantry Pride. The bond purchasers profited handsomely from the high return on the junk bonds, and Perelman made a fortune on the acquisition and reorganization of Revlon. That same year the R. J. Reynolds Tobacco Company purchased the food conglomerate Nabisco for $4.9 billion. Three years later this new giant, RJR Nabisco, was itself taken over by Kohlberg, Kravis, Roberts and Company for $24.9 billion.

During the frenzied decade of the 1980s one-fifth of the Fortune 500 companies were taken over, merged, or forced to go private; in all, some 25,000 mergers and acquisitions were successfully undertaken; their total value was nearly a half-trillion dollars. To make their companies less tempting to cash-hungry raiders, many corporations took on whopping debts or acquired unprofitable companies. By the late 1980s, many American corporations were wallowing in red ink. Debt payments were gobbling up 50 percent of the nation's corporate pretax earnings.

"A Job for Life": Layoffs Hit Home

Most corporations coped with the debt in two ways: they sold assets, such as factories, offices, and warehouses; or they cut costs through layoffs. U.S. Steel, whose rusting mills desperately needed an infusion of capital, instead spent $5 billion to acquire Marathon Oil of Ohio; that decision meant that nearly 100,000 steelworkers lost their jobs. No firm was immune, nor any worker secure. "A job for life" had long been IBM's unofficial but endlessly repeated slogan. As late as 1985, it ran an advertisement to reassure employees: "Jobs may come and go— But people shouldn't." Yet during the next nine years a crippled IBM eliminated 80,000 jobs and more than a third of its workforce. During the 1980s, the total number of employees who worked for the Fortune 500 companies declined by three million; nearly one-third of all positions in middle management were eliminated. Millions of "organization men" (about one-third of whom now were women) were laid off as the organizations themselves "downsized," the corporate euphemism for wholesale firings.

Many of the jobs went abroad, where labor costs were lower and unions nonexistent. In 1980 Xerox of America, realizing that it could no longer compete with its more efficient Japanese subsidiary, transferred contracts to Japan and laid off tens of thousands of American workers. In 1984 Nike closed its American shoe factory and moved sewing operations to Indonesia, where it could hire female workers for a mere 14 cents an hour. In 1986 the chassis for the Mustang, the symbol of American automotive style, was built by Mazda in Hiroshima, Japan.

Towering mountains of private corporate debt nearly were overshadowed by the Everest of public debt held by the federal government itself. Reagan's insistence on a sharp cut in personal taxes and a substantial increase in military expenditures produced huge—and growing—annual federal deficits. When Reagan took office, the total federal debt was 900 million dollars; eight years later, it exceeded two and a half trillion dollars. "No one imagined how bad the outcome would be," explained David Stockman, Reagan's budget director. "It got away from us."

A "BIPOLAR" ECONOMY, A FRACTURED SOCIETY

Although weighed down by debt, the economy did not crash through the floor, as many expected. In 1982 it began to gain strength and by the late 1980s it was growing at a rate unparalleled since the halcyon days of the 1960s. Despite the ominous, persistent increase in corporate layoffs, the stock market soared. Prices were coming down—traditionally evidence of slackening demand—yet the volume of business was growing!

Many economists and pundits warned that the run-up in stock prices was excessive; the bubble would surely burst. These misgivings were seemingly confirmed in 1987, when on a single day, the Dow-Jones industrial average fell 508 points to 1738. But stock prices quickly recovered and embarked on yet another long period of growth.

Although few perceived it at the time, the economy was undergoing a transformation of historic dimensions. Much as the depression after 1893 had strengthened the nation's economy by wiping out thousands of inefficient steel and machinery firms in New England and the Northeast, the seismic economic upheavals of the 20 years after 1973 toppled many of those same industries but

Changing Standards of Living, 1979–1994

thrust up new ones. As weeds grew in the parking lots of the factories of the "Rust Belt" of the Midwest, new companies and new technology industries sprouted in the "Silicon Valley" of California, along Route 128 outside of Boston, and in booming cities such as Seattle, Washington, and Austin, Texas.

By the end of the Reagan era, the economy consisted of two separate and increasingly unequal components: a battered sector of traditional heavy industry, characterized by declining wages and diminishing job opportunities; and an advancing high-tech and service sector dominated by aggressive, innovative, and individualistic entrepreneurs. The older corporations that survived the shakeout of the 1980s were leaner and better equipped to compete in expanding global markets.

Yet American society was becoming as fractured as the bipolar economy from which it drew sustenance. The Reagan tax cuts had disproportionately benefited the wealthy, as had the extraordinary rise of the stock market. Conversely, the economic transformation struck low- or semiskilled wage earners hardest; at the same time, the Reagan administration's shifting of much of the burden of social welfare onto state and local governments reduced benefits to those who lost jobs or could not find work in the strange new economy dominated by information services and bewildering new technologies. At the end of Reagan's second term the standard of living of the poorest fifth of the population (40 million people) was 9 percent lower than it had been in 1979, while that of the wealthiest fifth had risen about 20 percent.

THE IRAN-CONTRA ARMS DEAL

The Reagan administration was generally credited with the nation's successes, and absolved of its failures. The effectiveness of the administration was finally compromised by two self-inflicted wounds involving American policy in Central America and the Middle East.

The Central American problem resulted from a revolution in Nicaragua, where in 1979 leftist rebels had overthrown the dictatorial regime of Anastasio Somoza. Because the victorious Sandinista government was supported by both Cuba and the Soviet Union, President Reagan was determined to force it from power. He backed anti-Sandinista elements in Nicaragua known as the Contras and in 1981 persuaded Congress to provide these "freedom fighters" with arms.

But the Contras made little progress, and many Americans feared that aiding them would lead, as it had in Vietnam, to the use of American troops in the fighting. In October 1984 Congress banned further military aid to the rebels. The president then sought to persuade other countries and private American groups to help the Contras (as he put it) keep "body and soul together."

In the Middle East, the war between Iran and Iraq continued to rage. The chief interest of the United States in the conflict was to make sure that it did not cause the flow of Middle Eastern oil to be cut off. But public opinion in the country was particularly incensed against the Iranians. Memories of the hostage crisis of the Carter years did not fade, and Iran was widely believed to be responsible for the fact that a number of Americans were being held hostage by terrorists in Lebanon. Reagan was famous for opposing bargaining with terrorists. Nevertheless, he was eager to find some way to free the captive Americans. During 1985 he made the fateful decision to allow the indirect shipment of arms to Iran by way of Israel, his hope being that this would result in the hostages being released. When this did not happen, in January 1986 he authorized the secret sale of American weapons directly to the Iranians.

The arms sale was arranged by Marine Colonel Oliver North, an aide of Reagan's national security adviser, Admiral John Poindexter. North, who was already in charge of the administration's effort to supply the Nicaraguan Contras indirectly, used $12 million of the profit from the Iranian sales to provide weapons for the Contras, in plain violation of the Congressional ban on such aid.

News of the sales to Iran and of the use of the profits to supply the Contras came to light in November 1986 and of course caused a sensation. Admiral Poindexter resigned, Colonel North was fired from his job with the Security Council, a special prosecutor was appointed to investigate the affair, and both a presidential committee and a joint congressional committee also began investigations. Reagan insisted that he knew nothing about the aid to the Contras. Critics pointed out that if he was telling the truth it was almost as bad since that meant that he had not been able to control his own administration.

Although he remained personally popular, President Reagan's influence with Congress and his reputation as a political leader plummeted. Comments by reporters ranged from "disengaged" and "gravely uninformed" to "out to lunch." Even earlier Martin Anderson, Reagan's chief economic adviser, had admitted that the president "made decisions like an ancient king or a Turkish pasha, passively letting his subjects serve him."

Reagan was not an able administrator; the Iran-Contra and financial scandals of his administration did not stick to him because he was seldom close enough to the action to get splattered by it. Reagan articulated, simply and persuasively, a handful of concepts—the "evil" character of Soviet communism, the need to get government off people's backs—and in so doing created a political climate conducive to change. Reagan was directly responsible for neither of the great transformations of the late twentieth century—the collapse of the Soviet Union and the restructuring of American corporations. Yet his actions and, indeed, his failures to act indisputably influenced them. His decision to increase military spending and undertake the fantastically expensive SDI ("Star Wars") forced Gorbachev to seek an accommodation with the United States. Reagan's tax cuts precipitated unimaginably large federal deficits, and deregulation unloosed a sordid pack of predators who preyed on the economy. Yet the ensuing Darwinian chaos strengthened those corporations that survived and gave them the muscle to prevail in emerging global markets. "We are the change," Reagan declared in his farewell address. What he had done, exactly, he did not say. Yet the statement, however roseate, vague, and self-congratulatory, was not untrue.

During the preceding 15 years, the American nation, like the automobiles that stretched for blocks in line to buy gasoline during the oil embargo, had been running on empty. The federal government was deeply in debt. Corporations had exhausted their cash reserves. Workers lived in fear of the layoff or bank foreclosure notice. Gone were the fanciful expressions of an earlier era—long and widebodied chassis, roaring V-8 engines, sweeping tail fins, chromium grills like the jaws of a barracuda. Most cars had become simple boxes, trimmed with plastic, whose efficient four-cylinder engines thrummed steadily.

The nation's aspirations, like its cars, had become smaller, more sensible. Politicians muted their rhetoric, rarely issuing grandiose declarations of war against some intractable foe of humanity. Corporate executives spoke of "downsizing" firms rather than building them into empires. And the American people increasingly hunkered down in their own private spaces, which they locked up and wired with alarms.

MILESTONES

1969   American astronauts land on the moon

1973   Proposed Equal Rights Amendment fails to win ratification

Supreme Court guarantees right of abortion in early stages of pregnancy *(Roe* v. *Wade)*

1973–1974   Arab oil embargo

1975   Vietnam War ends

1976   Jimmy Carter elected president

1978   Camp David Agreement between Egypt and Israel

1979   Reverend Jerry Falwell founds Moral Majority

Muslim militants seize U.S. Embassy in Tehran, Iran

United States recognizes People's Republic of China

1980   Soviet troops invade Afghanistan

Ronald Reagan elected president

1981   U.S. hostages in Teheran released

Reagan appoints Sandra Day O'Connor to U.S. Supreme Court

Reagan discharges striking air traffic controllers

1984   Reagan reelected president

1985   Mikhail Gorbachev becomes premier of Soviet Union

1986   Space shuttle *Challenger* explodes, killing seven-member crew

Secret Iran-Contra arms deal exposed

33

MISDEMEANORS
AND HIGH CRIMES

During the final decade of the twentieth century and the opening years of the twenty-first, America was not so much stained by crime as saturated in it. Violent criminals and lesser miscreants held the spotlight partly because the dominant issues of the past were slipping from view. The Soviet Union was collapsing, burying communism in the rubble; and the American economy, after initial hesitation, was gaining momentum and surging forward at breakneck pace. Yet by the turn of the millennium, victory on both fronts seemed hollow. The lifting of the Iron Curtain of Soviet domination allowed smoldering ethnic and religious tensions to flare up in former satellite states. And the superheated "new economy" of the 1990s bubbled with an insubstantial frothiness, as if its gains might evaporate at any moment. Through it all, the American people were so absorbed in their own affairs—gruesome crimes and lurid scandals amidst an exuberant and gaudy materialism—that they failed to perceive the new threat, from abroad and above, that was about to crash into their lives.

THE ELECTION OF 1988

In the absence of the issues of recent decades—the Soviet threat, the energy crisis, stagflation—the presidential election of 1988 might have easily been dominated by a compelling personality. But the candidates were anything but compelling. The selection of George Bush, Reagan's vice president, for the Republican nomination was a foregone conclusion. Bush, the son of a Connecticut senator, had attended an elite private school and Yale College. He served as a pilot during World War II and then settled in Texas, where he worked in the family's oil business. As Republican presidential hopeful, he trumpeted his experience as vice president; but when the Reagan administration was tarnished by the Iran-Contra scandal, Bush claimed that he had been "out of the loop" and thus free of the scandal. When testimony proved otherwise, he dithered. In a cover story, *Newsweek* called him a "wimp."

After winning the nomination, Bush was not helped by his selection of Senator Dan Quayle of Indiana as his running mate. Although Quayle was an ardent supporter of military preparedness, he had avoided the Vietnam draft by enrolling in the Indiana National Guard, and the charge that he had used the influence of his wealthy family to get in the Guard was hard to refute. More seriously, he proved slow-witted in political debate. Gary Trudeau, creator of the political cartoon, "Doonesbury," depicted him as a talking feather.

The Democratic race was far more complicated but scarcely more inspiring. So many lackluster candidates entered the field that wits began to call them "the seven dwarfs." The one candidate who appeared to stand out, Senator Gary Hart of Colorado, wished he hadn't. After newspapers reported allegations of his womanizing, Hart issued a challenge to reporters: "If anybody wants to put a tail on me, go ahead. They'd be very bored." Several did, and were not bored. They found that Hart, who was married, had sailed on a yacht to the Bahamas with an "actress-model." The name of the boat—"Monkey Business"—irreparably suggested what had transpired at sea. Hart withdrew from the race.

Governor Michael Dukakis of Massachusetts, stressing his record as an efficient manager, accumulated delegates steadily. During one debate, however, another Democratic hopeful, Senator Albert Gore of Tennessee, accused Dukakis of handing out "weekend passes for convicted criminals." This referred to a policy, adopted by Massachusetts and many other states, of granting brief furloughs to convicts with satisfactory prison records. Dukakis brushed aside the accusation and went on to win the nomination.

But Lee Atwater, campaign manager for Bush, discovered that during one such furlough Willie Horton, an African American who was serving time in a Massachusetts prison for rape and assault, had stabbed and raped a Maryland woman. "If I can make Willie Horton a household name," Atwater predicted, "we'll win the election." Atwater produced and aired a television advertisement showing prisoners streaming through a revolving door. After describing Horton's record, a voice intoned: "Dukakis wants to do for America what he's done for Massachusetts."

The ad struck a responsive chord among white voters. Dukakis's attempts to shift the focus away from race and crime failed.

The presidential campaign became, in effect, a referendum on violent crime in which Dukakis failed the toughness test. Bush won 54 percent of the vote and carried the Electoral College, 426 to 112.

CRIME AND PUNISHMENT

During the 1980s, the "law and order" movement that had been initiated by Nixon 20 years earlier realized many of its goals. Responding to widespread calls for a crackdown on crime elected officials hired more police, passed tougher laws with mandatory prison sentences, and built additional prisons.

The shift toward capital punishment was symptomatic. During the 1960s only a handful of criminals were executed. When the Supreme Court ruled in 1972 in the *Furman* decision that jury-imposed capital punishment was racially biased and thus unconstitutional, the matter seemed moot: no criminal had been executed since 1967. But many states, responding to a public demand for a crackdown on crime, rewrote capital punishment statutes in light of the *Furman* decision, depriving juries of discretion in sentencing. The Supreme Court upheld

A teenage boy in a Texas jail; most prisons did not allow shoes or belts, which might be fashioned into weapons. During the 1990s, about 19 of 20 prison inmates were male. The great majority had been first arrested during their late teens and early twenties. In 1990, 6 in 10 federal inmates had been convicted of drug charges.

these laws and capital punishment resumed in in 1976. By the 1980s executions were becoming common. During the last quarter of the twentieth century, more than 500 people were executed in the United States.

State legislatures also made it more difficult for prisoners to obtain parole. In 1977, California abolished its parole system and replaced it with mandatory sentencing, which denied convicts the prospect of early release. Ten other states adopted similar restrictions. The proportion of convicts serving long, mandatory sentences increased sharply. In 1993 Hayes Williams, a prisoner at the Louisiana State Penitentiary, commented on the effect of long, fixed sentences on young felons. "When this hits these little crackheads, these little rap-boogity youngsters, that their life been completely taken away from them and they're not going nowhere no more, they gonna go to killing themselves."

Another manifestation of the crackdown on crime was the increase in the nation's prison population. From 1973 to 1980 the number of convicts tripled, and during the 1980s it doubled again. The growth in the nation's prison population during the early 1990s required the construction of a new 1000-bed prison every week. In 1995, California spent twice as much on prisons as on its huge university system. Human Rights Watch reported that the United States incarcerated more people than any country in the world, except perhaps communist China, which did not disclose such information.

"CRACK" AND URBAN GANGS

Several factors intensified the problem of violent crime, especially in the inner cities. One was a shift in drug use. During the 1960s marijuana had become commonly available, especially on college campuses; this was followed by cocaine,

A female Los Angeles police officer hands another officer a piece of rock cocaine found on a teenage member of a gang. Although relatively few women were hired as police officers or firefighters, they fared better in the military. By 1988, the year of this photo, 225,000 women served in the armed forces, over 10 percent of the total.

which was far more powerful and addictive, but so expensive that few could afford it.

During the 1980s growers of coca leaves in Peru and Bolivia greatly expanded production. Drug traffickers in Colombia devised sophisticated systems to transport cocaine to the United States. The price of cocaine dropped from $120 an ounce in 1981 to $50 in 1988.

Still more important was the proliferation of a cocaine-based compound called "crack" because it crackled when smoked. Crack was sold in $10 vials. Many users found that it gave an intense spasm of pleasure that overrode all other desires.

The lucrative crack trade led to bitter turf wars; dealers hired neighborhood youths, armed them with automatic weapons, and told them to drive competitors away. A survey of Los Angeles County in the early 1990s found that more than 150,000 young people belonged to 1000 gangs. Half used drugs; violence had become a fact of life. In 1985, before crack had seized hold of the inner city, there were 147 murders in Washington, D.C.; in 1991, the figure skyrocketed to 482.

Black on black murder had become an important cause of death for African Americans in their twenties. In 1988, Monsta' Kody Scott, who at age 11 pumped shotgun blasts into rival gang members, returned after prison to his Los Angeles neighborhood. He was horrified: gangs no longer merely shot their rivals but "sprayed" them with automatic weapons, 75 rounds to a clip, or blew them away with LAWS rockets. Some ghetto parents, to protect infants from the nightly hail of stray bullets, put them to sleep in bathtubs. In 1995, 30 percent of African American men in their twenties were in prison, or on probation or parole. The recurrent refrain of rap performers—that America was a prison—had become, for many, an everyday reality.

BUSH AS PRESIDENT

In 1989 President Bush, having attacked Dukakis for being soft on crime during the campaign, named a "drug czar" to coordinate various bureaucracies, increased federal funding of local police, and spent $2.5 billion to stop the flow of illegal drugs into the nation. Although the campaign generated plenty of arrests, drugs continued to pour in: as one dealer or trafficker was arrested, another took his place.

Bush also worked to shed the tough image he had cultivated during the campaign. In his inaugural address he said that he hoped to "make kinder the face of the nation and gentler the face of the world." He also displayed a more traditional command of the workings of government and the details of current events than his predecessor, which was reassuring to people put off by Reagan's lack of interest in the details of government. At the same time he pleased right-wing Reagan loyalists by his opposition to abortion and gun control, and by calling for a constitutional amendment prohibiting the burning of the American flag. His standing in the polls soared from high to astronomic.

THE COLLAPSE OF COMMUNISM IN EASTERN EUROPE

One important reason for this was the flood of good news from abroad. The reforms instituted in the Soviet Union by Gorbachev led to demands for similar liberalization by its Eastern European satellites, and Gorbachev responded by announcing that the Soviet Union would not use force to keep communist governments in power in these nations. Swiftly the people of Poland, Hungary, Czechoslovakia, Bulgaria, Romania, and East Germany did away with the repressive regimes that had ruled them throughout the postwar era and moved toward more democratic forms. Except in Romania, where the dictator Nicolae Ceausescu was executed, all these fundamental changes were carried out peacefully.

The End of the Cold War

In October 1989 the hard-line communist leader of East Germany was ousted and his successor opened several gates to allow free passage through the Berlin Wall. West Berliners improved on this conciliatory gesture by tearing the wall down.

Almost overnight the international political climate changed. Soviet-style communism had been discredited. The Warsaw Pact was no longer a significant force. A Soviet attack anywhere was almost unthinkable. The Cold War was over at last. With prodemocratic forces in power in East Germany, demand for reunion with West Germany quickly emerged. In November 1989 the infamous Berlin Wall was torn down, and talks were begun that swiftly led to unification.

President Bush profited from these developments immensely. He expressed moral support for the new governments (and in some cases provided modest financial assistance), but he refrained from embarrassing the Soviets. At a summit meeting in Washington in June 1990 Bush and Gorbachev signed agreements reducing American and Russian stockpiles of long-range nuclear missiles by 30 percent and eliminating chemical weapons. They also announced plans for still further cuts in weaponry, and President Bush agreed to the relaxation of barriers on trade with the Soviet Union, a measure designed to help its limping economy.

In 1989 President Bush sent troops to Panama to overthrow General Manuel Noriega, who had refused to yield power when his figurehead presidential candidate lost a national election. Noriega was under indictment in the United States for drug trafficking, and after temporarily seeking refuge in the Vatican Embassy in Panama, he surrendered to the American forces and was taken to the United States, where he was tried, convicted, and imprisoned.

Bush thus accomplished the objective of the invasion. Latin Americans, however, were alarmed by the way the United States had used force in the region, and the fact that far more Panamanian civilians were killed and wounded in the affair than armed supporters of Noriega.

Meanwhile, in the summer of 1991, civil war broke out in Yugoslavia as Croatia and Slovenia sought independence from the Serbian-dominated central government. This conflict soon became a religious war, pitting Serb and Croatian Christians against Bosnian Muslims. In the Soviet Union, nationalist and anticommunist groups demanded more local control of their affairs. President Gorbachev, who opposed this breakup, sought compromise, backing a draft treaty that would increase local autonomy and further privatize the Soviet economy.

In August, however, before this treaty could be ratified, hard-line communists attempted a coup. They arrested Gorbachev, who was vacationing in the Crimea, and attempted to cow resistance by ordering tanks into Moscow. But Boris Yeltsin, the anticommunist president of the Russian Republic, defied the rebels and roused the people of Moscow. The coup swiftly collapsed. Its leaders were arrested, the Communist party was officially disbanded, and the Soviet Union itself was replaced by a federation of states, of which Russia, led by Yeltsin, was the most important. Gorbachev, who had begun the process of liberation, found himself without a job.

THE WAR IN THE PERSIAN GULF

Early in August 1990, President Saddam Hussein of Iraq suddenly launched an all-out attack on Iraq's tiny neighbor, the oil-rich sheikdom of Kuwait. His pretext was Kuwait's supposed draining off of oil from the Rumalia oil field, much of which lay on the Iraqi side of their border. Saddam hoped to swallow up Kuwait, thus increasing Iraq's already large oil reserves to about 25 percent of the world's total, and then to force up the price of petroleum to replenish his treasury, badly depleted during his war with Iran. His soldiers overran Kuwait swiftly, then systematically carried off everything of value they could back to Iraq. Within a week Saddam annexed Kuwait, and massed troops along the border of neighboring Saudi Arabia.

The Saudis and the Kuwaitis turned to the United States and other nations for help, and it was quickly given. In a matter of days the UN had applied trade

As the routed Iraqi army fled Kuwait, it ignited (literally) an ecological disaster by setting fire to the Kuwaiti oil fields. American soldiers advance past a burning oil well; it took many months before all the wells could be extinguished.

sanctions against Iraq, and at the invitation of Saudi Arabia, the United States (along with Great Britain, France, Italy, Egypt, and Syria) moved troops to Saudi bases.

By November, Bush had increased the American troops in the area from 180,000 to more than 500,000. In late November the UN took the fateful step of authorizing the use of this force if Saddam Hussein did not withdraw from Kuwait by January 15, 1991. Saddam flatly refused to do so.

Congress voted to use force to dislodge Saddam and on January 17, the Americans unleashed an enormous air attack, directed by General Norman Schwartzkopf.

This air assault went on for nearly a month, and it reduced much of Iraq to rubble. The Iraqi forces, aside from firing a number of Scud missiles at Israel and Saudi Arabia and setting fire to hundreds of Kuwaiti oil wells, simply endured the rain of destruction that fell on them daily.

On February 23 Bush issued an ultimatum to Saddam: Pull out of Kuwait or face an invasion. When Saddam ignored the deadline, UN troops, more than 200,000 strong, struck. Between February 24 and February 27 they retook Kuwait, killing tens of thousands of Iraqis in the process and capturing still larger numbers. Some 4000 Iraqi tanks and enormous quantities of other military equipment were destroyed.

Bush then stopped the attack, and Saddam agreed to UN terms that included paying reparations to Kuwait and allowing UN inspectors to determine whether Iraq was developing atomic and biological weapons. Polls indicated that about 90 percent of the American people approved both the president's management of the war and his overall performance as chief executive. These were the highest presidential approval ratings ever recorded.

President Bush and indeed most observers expected Saddam to be driven from power in disgrace by his own people. Indeed, Bush publicly urged the Iraqis to do so. The Kurds in northern Iraq and pro-Iranian Muslims in the south then took up arms, but Saddam used the remnants of his army to crush them. He also refused repeatedly to carry out the terms of the peace agreement, chiefly by hindering the UN inspections for weapons of mass destruction. This led critics to argue that Bush should not have stopped the fighting until Baghdad, the Iraqi capital, had been captured and Saddam's army destroyed.

THE DEFICIT WORSENS

Candidate Bush had promised not to raise taxes, saying in a phrase he would later regret: "Read my lips: No new taxes." As President he recommitted himself to that objective; in fact he even proposed reducing the tax on capital gains. But like his conservative predecessor, Bush could not control the deficit. The "peace dividend" that was to follow the end of the Cold War had to be deferred. The invasion of Panama and the Persian Gulf War were expensive, and Congress obstinately resisted closing local military bases or cutting funding for favored defense contractors. Reducing nonmilitary expenditures, especially popular entitlement programs such as Medicare and social security, also proved nearly impossible.

In 1992, the deficit hit $290 billion. Bush had no choice but to join with Congress in raising the top income tax rate from 28 percent to 31 percent and levying higher taxes on gasoline, liquor, expensive automobiles, and certain other luxuries. This damaged his credibility and angered conservative Republicans. "Read my lips," critics muttered: "No more Bush."

LOOTING THE SAVINGS AND LOANS

An unprecedented drain on the federal treasury was caused by the demise of hundreds of federally-insured savings and loan institutions (S&Ls). S&Ls had traditionally played an important role in nearly every community, and were a secure if sleepy niche in the economy. In the 1980s Congress permitted S&Ls to enter the more lucrative but riskier business of commercial loans and stock investments.

This attracted a swarm of aggressive investors who acquired S&Ls and invested company assets in high-yield but risky junk bonds and real estate deals.

These speculations often failed to generate steady income. Worse, investments in junk bonds, untenanted office buildings, and uninhabited planned communities were often worthless. In October 1987 hundreds of S&Ls were plunged into bankruptcy. In 1988 Michael Milken, the junk bond "guru," was indicted on 98 charges of fraud, stock manipulation, and insider trading. He pleaded guilty, agreed to pay $1.3 billion in compensation, and was sent to jail. Drexel Burnham Lambert, his investment firm, filed for bankruptcy. The junk bond market collapsed.

Hundreds more S&Ls went under. Because their deposits were insured by the federal government, taxpayers were forced to cover the losses. The reserve fund for such purposes—$5 billion—was quickly exhausted. In 1991 Congress allocated $70 billion to close the failing S&Ls, liquidate their assets, and pay off depositors. The Justice Department charged nearly a thousand people for criminal involvement in a mess that, according to most estimates, would eventually cost taxpayers $500 billion. The destruction of the S&Ls was, arguably, the financial crime of the century. That it would spill into the political arena was inevitable.

Michael Milken, who transformed "junk bonds" into fool's gold. Drexel Burnham Lambert Inc., his investment firm, paid him nearly a billion dollars from 1986 through 1987. But in 1986 U.S. Attorney Rudolph Giuliani (later the mayor of New York City) convicted a Milken client of insider trading. Soon Milken himself was under investigation. In 1990 he pleaded guilty to securities charges and was sent to prison. By then, the junk bond market had collapsed, costing investors and the U.S. government many billions of dollars.

WHITEWATER AND THE CLINTONS

William (Bill) Clinton was one of those who got caught up in the maelstrom. He was born William Jefferson Blythe IV, but his father died in a car accident before he was born. Though his stepfather was abusive and an alcoholic, Bill at 15 legally took his stepfather's name. He graduated from Georgetown, won a Rhodes scholarship to study at Oxford University, and graduated from Yale Law school. He returned to Arkansas and was soon elected state attorney general.

In 1977, Clinton and his wife, Hillary Rodham, joined with James McDougal, a banker, to secure a loan to build vacation homes in the Ozarks. But the development, which they named Whitewater, became insolvent. McDougal covered the debts with a loan from a savings and loan company he had acquired.

In 1989 the savings and loan failed, costing the federal government $60 million to reimburse depositors. In 1992 federal investigators claimed that the Clintons had been "potential beneficiaries" of these activities.

By this time Clinton, now governor of Arkansas, was campaigning in the New Hampshire primary for the Democratic nomination for President. Few voters could make much sense of this tangled web of fiduciary finagling, nor did they have much opportunity to do so: another, far more explosive story threatened to sink the Clinton campaign. It came out that Clinton had for many years engaged in an extramarital affair with one Gennifer Flowers; Clinton's standing in the polls tumbled.

Hillary Rodham appeared with her husband on CBS's *60 Minutes* to address the allegations. Bill Clinton indignantly denied Flowers's statements but then issued an earnest if ambiguous appeal for forgiveness. "I have acknowledged causing pain in my marriage," he said. "I think most Americans will know what we're saying; they'll get it." Clinton was right, thus furnishing early evidence of his ability to address the American people directly, but on his own carefully worded terms. He finished second in New Hampshire, captured most of the remaining primaries, and won the Democratic nomination with ease. His choice of running mate—Senator Al Gore of Tennessee, a Vietnam veteran, family man, and environmentalist—helped the ticket considerably.

THE ELECTION OF 1992

While Clinton tiptoed through a minefield of personal scandal, President Bush rested secure in the belief that, after crushing Saddam Hussein's forces in the Gulf War, the 1992 election campaign would be little more than a victory lap. But he encountered unexpectedly stiff opposition within the Republican party.

Young Bill Clinton (left) shakes hands with President John F. Kennedy. "The torch has been passed to a new generation of Americans," Kennedy had declared in his inaugural. "Ask not what your country can do for you—ask what you can do for your country," JFK added. Thirty years later, Clinton's inaugural echoed Kennedy's: "Today, a generation raised in the shadows of the Cold War assumes new responsibilities," Clinton declared. "I challenge a new generation of young Americans to a season of service."

Patrick Buchanan, an outspoken conservative, did well enough to alarm White House strategists. Then Ross Perot, a billionaire Texan, announced his independent candidacy. Perot charged that both major parties were out of touch with "the people." He promised to spend $100 million of his own money on his campaign. Perot's platform had both conservative and liberal planks. He would "take the shackles off of American business," avoid raising taxes, and cut government spending by "getting rid of waste."

Polls quickly revealed that Perot was popular in California, Texas, and other key states that Bush was counting on winning easily. For a time it seemed possible that in a three-way race no one would win a majority of the Electoral College and the election would be thrown into the House of Representatives for the first time since 1824. But when his often-contradictory proposals were attacked in detail, Perot withdrew his candidacy. At the Republican convention in August, Bush was nominated without opposition.

Clinton accused Bush of failing to deal effectively with the lingering economic recession, which had worsened during the summer. He promised to undertake public works projects, to encourage private investment, and to improve the nation's education and health insurance systems. Bush played down the seriousness of the recession, but his jaunty comments offended those who had lost their jobs.

Early polls showed Clinton well ahead, but then Ross Perot reentered the race! On election day, more than 100 million citizens voted, a record. About 44 million voted for Clinton, 38 million for Bush, and 20 million for Perot. Clinton was elected with 370 electoral votes to Bush's 168. Perot did not win any Electoral College votes.

A NEW START: CLINTON

One major reason for Clinton's success was his expressed intention to change health insurance and the welfare system, and to bring the budget deficit under control. His solid knowledge of public issues was impressive, and he created a general impression of mastery and self confidence.

Another reason for Clinton's success was his willingness to reconcile differences. "Cooperation is better than conflict," he said on more than one occasion. But however valuable during a campaign, this reasonableness was sometimes a disadvantage once the power of the presidency was at Clinton's command. He set out to reverse many of the policies of the Reagan-Bush era, but when opposition developed, circumstances often persuaded him to retreat.

This led some critics to argue that Clinton was a poor leader. He had promised to end the ban on gays and lesbians in the armed services, but when the Joint Chiefs and a number of important members of Congress objected, he settled for a policy known as "don't ask, don't tell," meaning that such persons would be allowed to enlist only if they did not openly proclaim their sexual preferences. When relatively minor objections were raised to a number of his important appointments, he tended to back down rather than stand behind his choices.

In July 1993, Clinton used his executive authority to strengthen the Supreme Court majority in favor of upholding the landmark case of *Roe* v. *Wade*. The majority included three conservative justices who had been appointed by Reagan and Bush. Clinton appointed Ruth Bader Ginsberg, a judge known to believe that abortion was constitutional. Clinton also indicated that he would veto any congressional bill limiting abortion rights. He also reversed important Bush policies by signing a revived family leave bill into law and by authorizing the use of fetal tissue for research purposes.

The first major test of the president's will came when he submitted his first budget to Congress. He hoped to reduce the deficit by roughly $500 billion in five years, half by spending cuts, half by new taxes. The proposal for raising new revenue roused a storm of protest.

A number of congressional Democrats refused to go along with Clinton's budget, and since the Republicans in Congress voted solidly against any increase in taxes, the president was forced to accept major changes. Even so the final bill passed by the narrowest of margins. Clinton rightly claimed a victory.

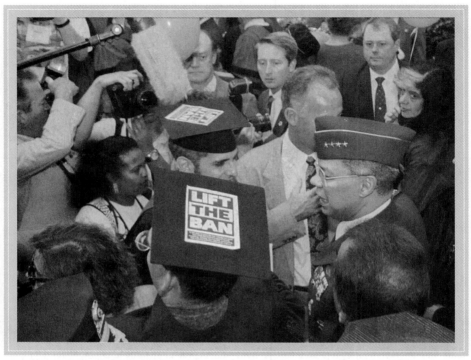

Lifting the military's ban on homosexuals became President Clinton's first order of business following his inauguration. Here, Harvard supporters of the new policy shake hands with Joint Chiefs of Staff Chairman Colin Powell in 1993. Powell, born in the South Bronx of Jamaican immigrants, was named secretary of state in 2001, the first black to hold that post.

He then turned to his long-awaited proposal to reform the nation's ruinously expensive and incomplete health insurance system. A committee headed by his wife had been working for months with no indication that a plan acceptable to the medical profession, the health insurance industry, and ordinary citizens was likely to come from its deliberations. The plan that finally emerged seemed even more complicated and quite possibly more costly than the existing system. It never came to a vote in Congress.

EMERGENCE OF THE REPUBLICAN MAJORITY

The Whitewater scandal, which Clinton had managed to brush aside during the campaign, gnawed at his presidency. Public pressure forced Attorney General

Janet Reno to appoint a special prosecutor, Kenneth W. Starr, a Republican lawyer, to investigate Whitewater and other alleged misdeeds of the Clintons.

More troubles followed. Paula Corbin Jones, a State of Arkansas employee, charged that Clinton, while governor, had invited her to his hotel room and asked her to engage in oral sex. Clinton's attorney denied the accusation and sought to have the case dismissed on the grounds that a president could not be sued while in office. The case commenced a torturous route through the courts.

Eager to take advantage of Clinton's troubles, Republicans looked to the 1994 congressional elections. Led by congressman Newt Gingrich of Georgia, they offered voters an ambitious program to stimulate the economy by reducing both the federal debt and the federal income tax. This would turn many of the functions of the federal government over to the states or to private enterprise. Federally administered welfare programs were to be replaced by block grants to the states. Many measures protecting the environment, such as those making businesses responsible for cleaning up their waste, were to be repealed.

On election day, the Republicans gained control of both houses of Congress. Under the firm direction of Gingrich, now Speaker, the House approved nearly all of the provisions of this "contract with America." This appalled Clinton, who vetoed the 1995 budget drafted by the Republicans. When neither side agreed to a compromise, the government ran out of money and shut down all but essential services.

THE ELECTION OF 1996

The public tended to blame Congress, and particularly Speaker Gingrich, for the shutdown. The president's approval rating rose. But the main issue of the day was the economy, and the upturn during and after 1991 benefited Clinton enormously. By the fall of 1996, unemployment had fallen well below 6 percent, and inflation below 3 percent. The Dow-Jones industrial stock average soared past 6000, more than triple the average in 1987. Clinton was renominated for a second term without opposition.

A number of Republicans competed in their primaries, but after a slow start Bob Dole of Kansas, the Senate majority leader, won the nomination. Dole had been a senator for more than 30 years, but despite his experience he was a poor campaigner, stiff and monotone. His main proposal was a steep reduction of the deficit and a 15 percent income tax cut. Pressed to explain how this could be done without drastic cuts in popular social programs, especially social security and Medicare, he gave a distressingly vague reply. He criticized popular music as "the leading edge of a culture becoming dangerously coarse" and denounced Hollywood for making films that "revel in mindless violence and loveless sex."

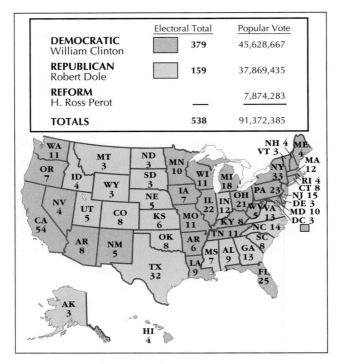

	Electoral Total	Popular Vote
DEMOCRATIC William Clinton	379	45,628,667
REPUBLICAN Robert Dole	159	37,869,435
REFORM H. Ross Perot	—	7,874,283
TOTALS	538	91,372,385

The Election of 1996

When opinion polls showed him falling behind Clinton, he tried to make "trust" the issue, casting himself as the epitome of moral rectitude and Clinton as unprincipled, dishonest, and a libertine. With the polls still against him, he became more and more querulous, accusing "the media," especially the *New York Times,* of being biased in Clinton's favor.

Clinton, a charismatic campaigner, also promised to reduce the deficit, but by a lesser amount, so as to be able to spend more on education, the environment, and social welfare needs. He stressed preparing for the twenty-first century and took, in general, an optimistic view of the economy. Reassured by his pollsters, Clinton ignored Dole's attacks on his character.

On election day Clinton won an impressive victory, sweeping the Northeast, all the Midwest except Indiana, the Upper Mississippi Valley, and the Far West. He divided the South with Dole, who also carried a band of states running north from Texas. Clinton's Electoral College margin was substantial, 379 to 159. The Republicans, however, retained control of both houses of Congress. Many retained, as well, an unquenchable hatred of Clinton.

O. J. SIMPSON AND "THE TRIAL OF THE CENTURY"

The public's attention was often diverted from the political wranglings by a story that seemed scripted for a television melodrama—the murder trial of O. J. Simpson, a former football star for the University of Southern California and the Buffalo Bills. On retiring from football, Simpson, who was black, became an instant celebrity who exploited his good looks and broad, high-wattage smile to make commercials and movies.

On June 12, 1994, his estranged wife, Nicole Brown Simpson, who was white, and another man were found stabbed to death near the entry of her condominium in Brentwood, Los Angeles. Simpson was charged with their murders.

His trial lasted nine riveting months. The victims' blood was found in his car and on his clothing. But defense lawyers discovered that Mark Fuhrman, a detective at the crime scene, had previously made inflammatory remarks about blacks; Simpson's lawyers accused Fuhrman of planting the evidence. After deliberating only four hours, the jury acquitted Simpson. A year later, however, he lost the judgment in civil proceedings on the "wrongful deaths" of the victims and was forced to pay substantial sums to their families.

The media attention to the case—the networks devoted twice as much air time to the Simpson case as to the 1994 political campaign—reflected both its dramatic character and the cultural divide between white and black Americans. To many whites, Simpson was yet another violent black male, while to many African Americans, he was another innocent black abused by a prejudiced criminal justice system. According to polls, 85 percent of blacks agreed with the "not guilty" verdict of the first Simpson trial, while only 34 percent of whites did. For the most part, neither race could understand the other's reasoning.

A RACIAL DIVIDE

Many believed that the cultural chasm between whites and blacks was widening. In 1992 Supreme Court justice Thurgood Marshall observed that educated Americans of each race appeared to have "given up on integration." After the Simpson trial Louis Farrakhan, leader of the black separatist Nation of Islam, called on African American men to express their solidarity by participating in a "Million Man March" on Washington, D.C. Many black leaders, including Jesse Jackson, embraced it. On October 16, 1995 the demonstration attracted perhaps a half million marchers, far more than had participated in Martin Luther King, Jr.'s

"March on Washington" in 1963. But where King welcomed the whites in the audience and declared, "We cannot walk alone," Farrakhan called for "a more perfect union" of the multitude of black men gathered before him.

The persistence of inequality was one reason for the new separatism. In 1972, the incomes of black families were one-third less than those of white families; this was virtually unchanged 20 years later. The leading sectors of the post-1973 economy—technology and information services—placed a premium on education, and here, too, the record in the late 1990s was unsettling. The math and reading scores of 17-year-old African American students rose relative to those of white students in the 1980s. But after 1988 black test scores fell sharply. The extent of the decline—it affected the children of the rich and poor alike, and the students of public and parochial schools—suggests the importance of broader cultural factors.

A significant casualty of the changing tone of race relations was "affirmative action," which gave minorities preference in hiring and college admissions. Initially justified on the grounds that the legacy of slavery and the persistence of racism put blacks at an unfair disadvantage in finding jobs or gaining admission to college, affirmative action programs spread during the 1970s and 1980s. But in July 1995 the Regents of the University of California ordered an end to affirmative action. This decision touched off protests throughout the university system. The protests, however, drew attention to the issue and the following year California voters approved Proposition 209, which abolished racial and gender preferences in all government hiring and education. The U.S. Supreme Court let the law stand. Other states enacted similar laws.

The overt racism of an earlier era, enforced by custom and law, had become socially unacceptable if not explicitly illegal. But as the British writer Godfrey Hodgson observed, Americans in the 1990s appeared to be moving toward "a kind of voluntary apartheid" in which blacks and whites preferred to keep their distance. In 1997, when President Clinton went to Little Rock to celebrate the fortieth anniversary of the desegregation of Central High School, he commented on the deterioration in race relations. The formerly all-white school was now mostly black, as were all public schools in Little Rock. "For the first time since the 1950s, our schools in America are resegregating," he noted.

As ever, race relations defied simple characterization. Opinion polls indicated that attitudes about race were becoming more complicated and ambivalent. By an overwhelming majority whites endorsed the accomplishments of the civil rights movement. Other polls revealed that in 1964 only 1 in 5 whites lived near a black neighbor; by 1994, 3 in 5 whites did so. In 1968 a Gallup poll found that only 17 percent of whites and 48 percent of blacks approved of marriages between blacks and whites; by 1994, the figures had increased to 45 percent of whites and 68 percent of blacks.

But many observed that even when white and black students attended the same schools, learned the same popular songs, and rooted for the same teams, they often attended different classrooms, sat at separate tables in the cafeteria, and occupied voluntarily segregated sections of the bleachers.

VIOLENCE AND POPULAR CULTURE

Popular culture, like athletics, often bridged the racial divide. But some observers took little solace in the broad appeal of youth-focused movies, pop songs, and TV shows. Such entertainment, they contended, romanticized an increasingly bloody culture of crime and violence. They cited as proof increasingly violent movies, pointing out that in *Public Enemy,* reputedly the most violent film of the 1930s, and *Death Wish,* a controversial vigilante fantasy of 1974, the body count reached eight. But three movies released during the late 1980s—*Robocop, Die Hard,* and *Rambo III*—each produced a death tally of 60 or more, nearly one every two minutes. The trend culminated in *Natural Born Killers* (1994), director Oliver Stone's unimaginably violent "spoof" of media violence. Television imitated the movies as the networks crammed violent crime shows into prime time. In 1991 an exhaustive survey found that by the age of eighteen, the average viewer had witnessed some 40,000 murders on TV.

Popular music also acquired a hard, new edge. In 1981 Warner Brothers launched a television channel featuring pop songs set to video. Music TV (MTV) was an instant success; within three years, some 24 million tuned in every day. Michael Jackson's video extravaganza, *Thriller* (1984), transformed the genre. Its surreal images, disjointed editing, and frenzied music set a new standard. Pop music acquired a heavier beat and more explicit lyrics. In 1988 the American Academy of Pediatrics expressed concern that teenagers on the average spent two hours a day watching rock videos. Over half featured violence and three-fourths contained sexually suggestive material.

A new sound called "rap" emerged from the ghetto and spread through radio, cassettes, and CDs. Rap consisted of unpredictably metered lyrics set against an exaggeratedly heavy downbeat. Most early rap performers were African American males. They did not play musical instruments or sing songs so much as convey, in words and gestures, an attitude of defiant, raw rage against whatever challenged their sense of manhood: other young males; women, whom they

Rapper Jay Z, born Shawn Carter, at the Soul Train Awards in Los Angeles in 2001. By then, many rap songs were so filled with obscenities and offensive epithets that the "bleeps" inserted by radio stations became an integral part of the music, an unexpected syncopation that gained power for its illicit suggestiveness.

derided in coarse sexual epithets; and the police. Predictably, raps such as "Cop Killer" and "Illegal Search" contributed to the charge that rap condoned violence and crime.

"I call it crime rhyme," explained rapper Ice-T, "rhyme about actual street events." Some "gangsta" rappers dressed in stylized prison garb—beltless pants and "do-rags."

The appeal of rap quickly spread beyond black audiences. When Dr. Dre (Andrew Young), founder of a gangsta rap group and head of a record firm, discovered that whites bought more rap CDs than blacks, he promoted the career of a young white rapper, Eminem. Born Marshall Bruce Mathers III, Eminem attracted attention with songs such as "Murder, Murder," "Kill You," "Drug Ballad," and "Criminal." He bashed women, gays, his wife, and nearly everyone else. His lyrics were of such surpassing offensiveness that he became an overnight celebrity and instant millionaire. His fans, whom he treated with scorn, were delighted by the universality of his contempt. The list of those suing him included his mother.

The violation of social norms has long been part of adolescence. In the 1830s boys devoured "Davy Crockett" tales that championed sadistic violence and bawdy sexual antics; even during the presumably "conformist" decade of the 1950s young people enjoyed the scatological humor of *Mad Magazine,* the coarse gyrations of Elvis Presley, and the rebellious sexual innuendo of nearly all types of popular music. Anthropologists have suggested that in Western societies adolescence is a transitional stage in which young people delight in "cultural inversions" that turn the social order upside down.

Most consumers of pop violence in the 1990s, like the readers of the Crockett comics or *Mad Magazine,* had little difficulty distinguishing between cultural fantasies and everyday life. But for those who had grown up in ghettoes where gangs ruled the streets and where friends and relatives were commonly swallowed up by the criminal justice system, the culture of violence seemed to legitimate the meanness of everyday life. Moreover, violence and criminality were becoming so much a part of popular culture, and popular culture of adolescent life, that some retreated wholly to imaginative worlds conjured by movies, video games, TV, and pop music. To them, the world of parents and teachers seemed duller and less responsive—less *real*—than the one inside their heads.

A few went so far as to act out destructive fantasies. On October 1, 1997 a 16-year-old boy stabbed his mother, shot and killed two students, and wounded seven others at his high school in Pearl, Mississippi. Over the next 18 months a spate of similar shootings in West Paducah, Kentucky, Jonesboro, Arkansas, and Springfield, Oregon left 5 more students dead and 23 wounded. On April 20, 1999 two teenagers, wearing trenchcoats and armed with automatic weapons, went on a rampage at Columbine High School in Littleton, Colorado. Before shooting themselves to death, they killed 12 students and a teacher and wounded more than 30. Their crime, previewed in a video prepared as a class project, turned out to be a replay of a 1995 movie, "The Basketball Diaries," in which Leonardo Di Caprio, wearing a long, black coat and carrying a shotgun, bursts into school and shoots his classmates and teachers. A month after the Columbine shooting, a 15-year-old shot six students at a high school in Conyers, Georgia.

CLINTON IMPEACHED

Although President Clinton steadfastly denied allegations of womanizing, in January 1998 a judge ruled that Clinton was obliged to testify in the lawsuit Paula Corbin Jones had filed against him. Jones, who sought to strengthen her suit by showing that Clinton had a history of propositioning women, also subpoenaed a former White House intern. Her name was Monica Lewinsky.

Lewinsky and Clinton were separately asked if they had had an affair, and each denied it in turn. When word of their alleged relationship was leaked to the press, Clinton declared in a TV news conference: "I did not have sexual relations with that woman, Miss Lewinsky." Hillary Clinton denounced the allegations as part of a "vast right-wing conspiracy" against her husband.

Unbeknownst to the Clintons, however, Lewinsky had been confiding to Linda Tripp, a former White House employee, and Tripp had secretly tape-recorded some 20 hours of their conversations. She turned these tapes over to special prosecutor Kenneth Starr, whose investigations of the Clintons' roles in the Whitewater scandal had broadened into a more general inquiry. In the Tripp tapes Lewinsky provided intimate details of repeated sexual encounters with the president. Clinton and Lewinsky appeared to have lied under oath. Starr threatened to indict Lewinsky for perjury. In return for immunity from prosecution,

A seemingly anonymous well-wisher from the crowd greets President Bill Clinton. When Clinton was later investigated for having an affair with Monica Lewinsky, a former White House intern, this photograph of the two surfaced. Clinton's lack of discretion struck many as self-destructive.

she repudiated her earlier testimony and admitted that she had engaged in sexual relations with the president and that he and his aides had encouraged her to give misleading testimony in the Jones case.

When called in August to testify on videotape before the Starr grand jury, Clinton conceded that he had engaged in "inappropriate intimate contact" with Lewinsky. But he insisted, "I have not had sex with her as I defined it." When pressed to supply his own definition, he responded with legalistic obfuscation: "My understanding of this definition is it covers contact by the person being deposed with the enumerated areas, if the contact is done with an intent to arouse or gratify." Because Clinton had not intended to arouse or gratify Lewinsky, he had not "had sex" with her. He allowed that this definition was "rather strange."

More legalisms followed. When asked if he had ever been alone with her, he responded, "It depends on how you define alone, but I never really thought we were." When asked if his lawyer had been correct when he had assured the judge in January that "there is absolutely no sex of any kind," Clinton said that the statement was not untrue because "it depends on what the meaning of the word 'is' is."

Clinton's testimony infuriated Starr, who made public Lewinsky's humiliatingly detailed testimony along with the president's deadpanned equivocations. Speaker Newt Gingrich, the driving force behind the conservative Republican resurgence, decided to focus on the Clinton debacle in the November elections. Starr announced that Clinton's deceptive testimony warranted consideration by the House of Representatives for impeachment.

But throughout Clinton's legal battles, opinion polls suggested that two in three Americans approved of his performance as president. Buoyed by the vibrant economy, most Americans blamed the scandal on the intrusive Starr nearly as much as the evasive Clinton. The November election proved disastrous for the Republicans, who nearly lost their majority in the House. Gingrich acknowledged the failure of his strategy and resigned as Speaker, prompting columnist Maureen Dowd to quip: "Who would have thought that the man Lewinsky would bring down would be Newt?"

Clinton's troubles, however, were by no means over. Despite their comeuppance at the polls, Republican leaders in the House initiated impeachment proceedings against him. On the eve of the House impeachment vote, the bizarre episode careened in yet another direction. Clinton ordered a massive air strike on Iraq to punish the Iraqi leader, Saddam Hussein, for failing to provide UN inspectors with full access to sites suspected of producing biological and chemical weapons, as required by the treaty ending the 1991 Persian Gulf War. An intensive bombing campaign lasted three days, forcing a postponement of the impeachment vote.

When deliberations resumed, the House impeached Clinton on the grounds that he had committed perjury and had obstructed justice by inducing Lewinsky and others to give false testimony in the Jones case. The vote closely followed party lines.

The impeachment trial in the Senate began in January 1999. Chief Justice William Rehnquist presided. The Republicans numbered 55, enough to control the proceedings but 12 short of the two-thirds necessary to convict the president and remove him from office. Democrats, while publicly critical of Clinton's behavior, maintained that his indiscretions did not constitute "high crimes and misdemeanors" as specified in the Constitution for removal from office. They prevailed. The article accusing Clinton of perjury was defeated by a vote of 55 to 45; on the article alleging obstruction of justice, the vote was 50 to 50. Clinton remained president.

THE ECONOMIC BOOM AND THE INTERNET

One reason why Clinton survived was the health of the economy. Few wanted to rock the ship of state when it was stuffed with cash.

A significant part of the prosperity came from new technologies such as cellular phones and genetic engineering. But the most important was the development of a revolutionary form of communication: the Internet. Developed in the 1970s by a cluster of U.S. military and academic institutions to coordinate research, the Internet initially proved an awkward means of linking information. Data in one computer did not readily relate to data elsewhere. The Internet was a communication system that lacked a common language.

That was remedied in the early 1990s by Tim Berners-Lee, a British physicist working at a research institute in Switzerland. He devised the software that became the grammar—the "protocols"—of the Internet "language." These included the uniform resource locator (URL), which gave each user a specific address or website; hypertext markup language (HTML), the commands embedded in each website to ensure its compatibility within the system; and the hypertext transfer protocol (HTTP), the routing instructions governing the flow of information through the Internet. With this language, the Internet became the World Wide Web (WWW), a conduit for a stream of electronic impulses flowing among hundreds of millions of computers, electromagnetically organized in silicon chips.

The number of websites increased exponentially, making it difficult to find information on a particular topic. Netscape developed software to enable users to "navigate" or "browse" through the informational sea of the Web. In 1995, software giant Microsoft entered the picture in decisive fashion. It introduced a "point and click" Windows operating system, which made it easy for users of IBM and IBM-compatible computers to issue complex commands. Rather than drown in the coming deluge, Microsoft seized control of it. It competed with Netscape by creating a Web browser—Microsoft Internet Explorer—and embedded its software in the Windows 95 bundle. This provoked howls of protest from Netscape as well as from the largest online service providers: America Online, Compuserve, and Prodigy. Microsoft, they claimed, was threatening to monopolize access to and use of the Internet. (A federal judge concurred, ordering that Microsoft be broken up; but his ruling was overturned on appeal in 2001.)

In the meantime, some visionaries perceived deep veins of real gold in the "virtual reality" of cyberspace. Jeff Bezos, a 1986 summa cum laude graduate of Princeton with a degree in electrical engineering and computer science, took a job in investment banking, quit at age 30, and dreamed of using the Internet to sell books. In 1995 Amazon.com sold its first book. Business took off. Within six years, the company's annual sales approached $3 billion. Bezos had become one of the richest men in the nation.

If Bezos could use the Web for selling books, others imagined they could sell everything from pet food to pornography. (eBay, an Internet auction house, had an online catalogue consisting of three million items.) Many start-up companies (dot-coms, in the argot of the day) consisted of little more than the hubris of the founders. Josh Harris, CEO of a streaming-video company called Pseudo.com, told a reporter: "I'm in a race to take CBS out of business . . . That's why we're going to make the big bucks." Six months later, Pseudo.com failed; CBS did not.

But which ideas were preposterous and which farsighted? Many investors had snickered at Microsoft a decade earlier; they did not want to be left behind again. "Venture capitalists," independent investors seeking to fund emerging "tech" companies, sensed a glittering new economic frontier somewhere down the Internet superhighway, and they poured billions into start-up dot-coms. In 1999 some 200 Internet companies "went public," selling shares in the major stock exchanges. They raised $20 billion easily. Nasdaq, the exchange that specialized in tech companies, saw the value of its stocks skyrocket, its index more than doubling between October 1999 and March 2000.

Analysts watched in amazement as the price of Palm Pilot soared until it nearly surpassed 3ComCorp, which owned nearly all of Palm Pilot! The prices of dot-com stocks kept on climbing though few generated profits; some lacked any revenue whatsoever. In 1999 Amazon, leader among the dot-coms with revenue of several billion dollars, lost $700 million.

By the spring of 2000, with the stock market still surging, dot-coms in the van, a selling wave hit the tech stocks and spilled over to other companies. Stock prices plummeted. Within six months Nasdaq lost nearly half its value. In all, some $2 trillion in stocks and stock funds had disappeared. Some feared that the economy was nearing a recession.

CLINTON'S LEGACY

The Clinton years coincided with the longest economic boom in the nation's history. Clinton deserves considerable credit for the remarkable prosperity of the era. By reducing the federal deficit, interests rates came down, spurring investment and economic growth. By August 1998 unemployment had fallen to 4.5 percent, the lowest level since the 1960s; inflation had eased to a minuscule 1 percent, the lowest level since the 1950s. In 1998 the federal government operated at its first surplus since 1969. Then, as the economy soared during the next two years, so did government income. By the 2000 fiscal year, the surplus hit $237 billion.

Clinton also promoted globalization of the economy. His belief that American corporations and workers could prevail in global markets proved correct. During the last half of the 1990s, the United States led all industrial nations in the rate of growth of its real gross domestic product. But the new global economy harmed many. Some union leaders bitterly asked how their members could compete against convict labor in China or sweatshop workers in Indonesia or

Malaysia. Others complained that the emphasis on worldwide economic growth was generating an environmental calamity. International protests against the World Trade Organization culminated in the disruption of its 2000 meeting in Seattle, when thousands of protesters went on a rampage, setting fires and looting stores.

A decade of prosperity caused the crime wave to subside. Whatever the rewards of crime, it did not pay a steady $13.41 an hour, the average hourly earnings of American workers in 2000. Crime rates also fell because more criminals were in jail, a consequence of aggressive police and stern judges: in 2000, the nation's prison population reached two million.

Clinton's record in foreign affairs was mixed. In 1993 he failed in an effort to assemble an international force to prevent "ethnic cleansing" by Serbian troops against Muslims in Bosnia, formerly part of Yugoslavia. That same year a United States initiative to Somalia, an African nation wracked by civil war and famine, ended in failure when a Somali warlord ambushed and killed 15 American commandos. "Operation Restore Hope," as it was called, did not. In 1999 critics predicted another debacle when Clinton proposed a NATO effort to prevent General Slobodan Milosevic of Yugoslavia from crushing the predominantly Muslim province of Kosovo, which was attempting to secede. But after several months of intense bombing of Serbia, Milosevic withdrew from Kosovo. Within a year, he was forced out of office and into prison, awaiting trial for war crimes before a UN tribunal.

Clinton labored, as had his predecessors in the White House, to broker peace between Israel and the Palestinians; like his predecessors, he failed. In 1993 Yitzhak Rabin, Israeli prime minister, and Yasir Arafat, leader of the Palestinian Liberation Organization, signed an agreement preparing the groundwork for a Palestinian state. But extremists on both sides shattered the fragile accord. In 1994 a heavily armed Israeli burst into a mosque in Hebron and killed 29 Palestinians; the next year Rabin was assassinated by a Jewish zealot. Palestinians, enraged by the construction of Israeli settlements in Palestinian territory, stepped up their campaign of suicide bombings against Israeli soldiers and civilians. Israel retaliated with tank and helicopter attacks on suspected terrorist strongholds. In 2000 Clinton attempted to broker a settlement, whereby Israel would give up lands it had occupied in Palestinian territory, but the talks collapsed and a new wave of violence erupted.

Whatever the successes and shortcomings of his administration, the Clinton presidency will always be linked to his relationship with a White House intern and the impeachment proceedings that ensued. Though by no means the first president to stray from matrimonial propriety, Clinton's behavior, in an era when the media thrived on scandal and crime, was symptomatic of an almost willful self-destructiveness.

THE 2000 ELECTION: BUSH (JR.) WINS BY ONE VOTE

During the 2000 campaign, Vice President Al Gore sought to prove his indispensability to President Clinton, whose administration was credited for the booming economy, as well as his distance from Bill Clinton, whose personal life was discredited by scandal. This was no easy task. Gore showed his loyalty by raising money for the Democratic party, and his independence, by avoiding mention of Clinton. The strategy failed. Gore ran afoul of election laws when he solicited contributions too energetically and in inappropriate places, ranging from a Buddhist temple to the White House itself. And the president, irritated by Gore's

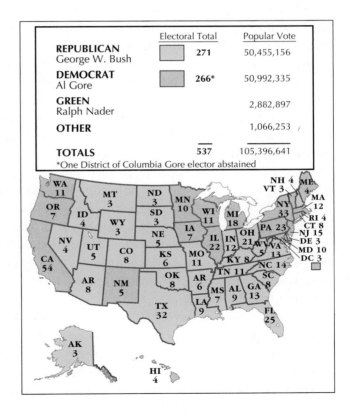

	Electoral Total	Popular Vote
REPUBLICAN George W. Bush	271	50,455,156
DEMOCRAT Al Gore	266*	50,992,335
GREEN Ralph Nader		2,882,897
OTHER		1,066,253
TOTALS	537	105,396,641

*One District of Columbia Gore elector abstained

The Election of 2000

refusal to champion the Clinton record, devoted his energies to his wife's successful campaign to represent New York in the Senate. Gore nevertheless secured the Democratic nomination and chose as running mate Senator Joseph Lieberman of Connecticut, an orthodox Jew.

The leading contender was George W. Bush, son of former President Bush. Like his father, Bush graduated from Yale and worked in the family oil business. He headed a group that bought the Texas Rangers baseball team. Although some doubted Bush's abilities—"What can you say about a partner who traded slugger Sammy Sosa?"—his visible success with the Rangers catapulted him into Texas politics. An effective and personable campaigner, he was elected governor in 1994 and became a front-runner for the presidency six years later.

He was opposed in the Republican primaries by Senator John McCain of Arizona, a Navy pilot who had spent five years in a prisoner-of-war camp in North Vietnam. McCain campaigned to reduce the influence of campaign contributors, a goal as lofty as it was self-serving: he had raised less money than Bush, who prevailed. Bush selected as running mate Richard Cheney, who had served as defense secretary in his father's administration.

Consumer activist and environmentalist Ralph Nader also entered the presidential race, running on the Green Party ticket. This worried Gore, author of *Earth in the Balance;* he had hoped to carry the conservation vote.

The main issue was what to do with the federal surpluses, which by some projections would reach over $1 trillion within five years. Bush called for a substantial tax cut; Gore wanted to increase spending on education and shore up the social security system. But neither issue generated rancor, and the election turned on the character of the candidates.

Gore, though knowledgeable, seemed stiff, and he occasionally indulged in self-serving bombast, as when he claimed to have "invented" the Internet. Bush's principal offense was against the English language. "Rarely is the question asked," he once declaimed, "Is our children learning?" His poetic flights of fancy did not stay aloft long, as when he evoked American aspirations for "wings to take dream" and endorsed economic growth to "make the pie higher." However exaggerated or garbled their messages, the candidates spent a record $1 billion dollars in getting them to the voters.

Having been inundated with advertisements, many on election night breathed a sigh of relief that the election was finally over. They were wrong. By midnight it appeared that Bush had 246 electoral votes, and Gore, 267, with 270 necessary to win; but Florida, with 25 electoral votes, was too close to call. At 2:00 A.M., the major television networks declared Bush the winner. But several hours later, as returns trickled in from late-reporting districts, the television networks reversed themselves and declared Florida—and the election—"too close to call." Bush's lead there was 1784 out of nearly 6 million cast.

After a machine recount, Bush's margin in Florida was reduced to several hundred votes, with Democrats complaining that a punch-card ballot used in some communities was confusing, depriving Gore of thousands of votes; worse, the machines routinely failed to count incompletely punched ballots. His lawyers demanded that the ballots in several predominantly Democratic counties be counted by hand. In some counties hand recounts were initiated, with examiners holding ballots up to the light to determine whether the chad—the "hole" in the punch card—had been sufficiently imprinted to constitute a vote. Republicans countered that Democrats had no right to change voting procedures after the election. They demanded that the hand recounts cease.

Yet when overseas absentee ballots began pouring in, many of them from military personnel, Republicans demanded that technical rules, such as those requiring that ballots be postmarked on or before the election, be waived. Gore objected. The entire election ended up in the courts. On December 12, more than a month after the election, the Supreme Court ruled by a 5–4 vote that the selective hand recounts violated the Constitution's guarantee of equal protection. Bush's margin would stand.

Nationwide, Gore received 51 million votes, Bush, 50.5 million. Nader, who did not win any electoral votes, received 4 million. Pointing to Nader's 98,000 votes in Florida, some Democrats complained that he had elected Bush by siphoning off votes from Gore. But such speculations presume that one can determine the intentions of the voters which, as the vote recount in Florida showed, is sometimes difficult even when staring at their ballots.

TERRORISM INTENSIFIES

After the fall of the Soviet Union, American military might seemed unassailable, and its backing of Israel, unshakeable. Opponents of either now pursued their objectives through terrorism. An early instance of this occurred in October 1985. Four Arabs seized control of the Italian cruise ship *Achille Lauro* in the eastern Mediterranean. After killing an elderly Jewish American tourist and tossing his body into the sea, they surrendered to Egyptian authorities on condition that they be provided with safe passage to Libya on an Egyptian airliner.

The terrorists chose Libya because the president of that nation, Muammar al-Qaddafi, was a bitter enemy of Israel and the United States and an open supporter of terrorist activities. To stop them, President Reagan ordered Navy F-14 jets to intercept the airliner. The jets forced the Egyptian pilot to land in Italy instead of Libya, and the terrorists were taken into custody. Then, after a Libyan-planned bombing of a West German club frequented by American soldiers, Reagan launched an air strike against Libyan bases from airfields in Great Britain.

In December 1988, a bomb tore through the fuselage of a Pan Am 747 jetliner. The plane crashed in Lockerbie, Scotland, killing all 259 on board and 11 on the ground. American and British investigators determined that two Libyans had been responsible for the bombing. The United Nations now joined President Bush in demanding that Libya hand over the two suspects. Qaddafi refused. In 1992 the United Nations retaliated by placing an embargo on air travel and arms sales to Libya. Nearly a decade later, Qaddafi finally relinquished the suspects to an international tribunal.

On February 26, 1993, a tremendous explosion ripped through the parking garage of one of the 110-story twin towers of the World Trade Center in New York City. Smoke and flames engulfed the building. Six people were killed and more than 1000 injured. A serial number from a rented van, which had been packed with explosives, was found among the debris and traced to Islamic fundamentalists.

In February 1995 Ramzi Ahmed Yousef, accused of masterminding the bombing, was captured in Pakistan and returned to New York City for trial. While in custody, Yousef expressed his disappointment that the blast had failed to knock down one of the towers; he had hoped to kill 250,000 people. His action, he had said, had been in retaliation for U.S. aid to Israel. Yousef and three accomplices were convicted and sentenced to life in prison.

On April 19, 1995, another truck exploded just outside the federal building in Oklahoma City and caused it to collapse. Over 850 were injured and 169 killed. Although it was initially assumed that the bombing was the work of Arab terrorists, a former U.S. soldier, Timothy McVeigh, was convicted of the crime and executed.

In November 1995, a car bomb rocked an American military base in Riyadh, Saudi Arabia. Four Islamic militants, enraged that the American bases were supporting air attacks on Iraq, were convicted of the crime in Saudi Arabia and on May 31, 1996 they were publicly beheaded. In retaliation, a truck bomb destroyed another American military complex in Dharan, also in Saudi Arabia. Nineteen servicemen were killed and 500 injured.

In August 1998 truck bombs tore through the American embassies in Nairobi, Kenya, and Dar Es Salaam, Tanzania. Over 200 died, including 12 Americans; 5000 were injured. Those arrested were Islamic extremists. On October 12, 2000, terrorists in a rubber boat laden with explosives rammed a U.S. destroyer, the USS *Cole,* docked in Yemen. The explosion ripped a hole in the ship, killing 17 American sailors and injuring dozens.

A gaping hole in the destroyer USS Cole, *in the port of Aden, Yemen, caused by suicide bombers on October 12, 2000. The attack was linked to Osama bin Laden's Al-Qaeda terrorist network, based in Afghanistan.*

Although more than a dozen terrorist groups operated in the Mideast, suspicion for the spate of terrorist bombings against the United States increasingly focused on Osama bin Laden. The son of a wealthy Saudi businessman, bin Laden ran a terrorist-training organization in Afghanistan.

ATTACK ON THE WORLD TRADE CENTER

At 8:40 on the morning of September 11, 2001, Madeline Amy Sweeney, an attendant on American Airlines Flight 11, placed a cell phone call from the galley of the plane to her supervisor in Boston. In a whisper, she said that four Arab men had slashed the throats of two attendants, forced their way into the cockpit, and taken over the plane. She gave him their seat numbers so that their identities could be determined from the passenger log. The supervisor asked if she knew where the plane was headed. She looked out the window and noted that it was descending rapidly. "I see water and buildings." Then she paused: "Oh my God." The water was the Hudson River, and the buildings were the skyscrapers of lower Manhattan, foremost among them the 110-story twin towers of the World Trade Center.

The hijackers pushed the throttle to full, and the Boeing 767 was traveling at 500 miles per hour at 8:48 when it slammed into the 96th floor of the North

The smoldering twin towers of the World Trade Center after they had been hit by airplanes on September 11, 2001. The jet fuel burned at nearly 2000°F, which caused the steel casing of the towers to expand. The upper floors of the South Tower (left) can be seen pushing outward and twisting. This separated the concrete floors from their steel supports, causing the floors to fall and collapsing the stories below.

tower. A fireball, fed by 16,000 gallons of jet fuel, instantly engulfed eight or nine stories.

Fifteen minutes later a second airliner came into view over Manhattan harbor, banked sharply, and plowed into the 80th floor of the South tower. New York mayor Rudolph Giuliani, who had raced to the scene, asked Fire Chief Peter Ganci, "What should I communicate to people?" "Tell them to get in the stairways," Ganci replied. "I think we can save everyone below the fire." The World Trade Center employed 50,000. As thousands fled the buildings, hundreds of firefighters, Ganci among them, charged up the stairs to rescue those who were trapped.

At 9:30 the White House received word that another hijacked airliner was barreling toward Washington, D.C. Secret Service agents rushed Vice President Richard Cheney to an emergency command bunker far below the White House. At 9:35 the airliner plunged into the Pentagon, which burst into flames. Cheney telephoned President Bush, who was in Sarasota, Florida. The nation was under attack. Bush authorized the Air Force to shoot down any other hijacked airliners. A few minutes later a fourth hijacked airliner crashed into a field in Pennsylvania after passengers had declared their intention—again by cell phone—to retake the plane.

While television viewers absorbed these shocks, they watched as the upper floors of the World Trade Center towers blackened, like charred matches. At 9:59, the South Tower collapsed, followed by the North Tower a half hour later, pulverizing millions of tons of concrete and glass and enveloping lower Manhattan in choking dust. Nearly 3000 lay dead in the mountain of rubble, including Chief Ganci and 350 firemen; several hundred more perished at the Pentagon and in the crash of the airliner in Pennsylvania.

Teams of four or five Arabic-speaking men had hijacked each of the planes. Several of the hijackers were quickly linked to the Al-Qaeda terrorist network run by Osama bin Laden, who had previously been indicted (but not captured) for the 1998 bombing of U.S. embassies in East Africa and the 2000 attack on the USS *Cole*. Bin Laden operated with impunity in Afghanistan, a nation governed by the Taliban, an extremist Islamic group.

That evening President Bush addressed the nation. He spoke simply and with force. "We will find these people," he said of the terrorists. "They will pay." Any government harboring the terrorists—an obvious reference to the Taliban— would be held equally responsible for the attack. Bin Laden, in a video recorded from an undisclosed location, denied involvement in the attack but praised those who carried it out.

Several weeks later, Bush declared that bin Laden would be taken "dead or alive." The president also offered a $25 million reward for his death or capture, an evocation of swift frontier justice that suited the national mood. Within the United States, thousands of Arabs were rounded up and detained; those with visa and immigration violations were imprisoned.

Then more trouble arrived at the Capital, this time in the mail. Several letters addressed to government officials included threatening messages and a white powder consisting of billions of anthrax spores, which could prove fatal if touched or inhaled. Thousands of government employees took antibiotics as a precaution, but some spores had seeped out of the envelopes and killed a half-dozen postal workers and mail recipients.

Bush responded to these multiple threats by creating a Cabinet position, Office of Homeland Security, and naming Pennsylvania governor Tom Ridge to direct it. Several times Ridge issued vague warnings of imminent terrorist attacks. How Americans were to protect themselves, he did not say.

AMERICA FIGHTS BACK

Bush had declared "war on terror," but it was to be a battle unlike any the nation had ever fought. Al-Qaeda had secret terrorist cells in many countries. Bin Laden was ensconced in remote Afghanistan, protected by thousands of Taliban soldiers who had inflicted heavy losses on Soviet invaders in the 1980s. (At the time, the United States had provided bin Laden and the Taliban with money and weapons.) The source of the anthrax letters proved even more problematic, because the spores resembled a strain developed in American military laboratories.

Bush's challenge was all the greater because of his own stated opposition to ill-defined and far-flung military operations. He had chastised the Clinton-Gore administration for "extending our troops all around the world." He underscored his reticence for such ventures by naming Colin Powell secretary of state. Powell, who had been sobered by his experiences in Vietnam, maintained that U.S. troops should only be deployed when their political objective was clear, military advantage overwhelming, and means of disengaging secure. This became known as the Powell doctrine, and Bush had endorsed it during the campaign. But the proposed war against terror adhered to none of its precepts. Now such scruples did not matter; the president had little choice but to fight.

Powell urged many European, Asian, and even Islamic states to crack down on terrorist cells in their countries and to provide assistance in the U.S. military campaign against the Taliban; he also persuaded anti-Taliban factions within Afghanistan to join forces to topple the regime. On September 20 Bush ordered the Taliban to surrender bin Laden and top Al-Qaeda leaders; when the Taliban refused, Bush unloosed missiles and warplanes against Taliban installations and defenses, much like the campaign that had ended Serbian aggression against ethnic Muslims in Kosovo.

For several weeks, Taliban soldiers cowered in bunkers as bombs thudded nearby; but they defended their positions when anti-Taliban forces attacked. Then small teams of elite American soldiers, armed with hand-held computers and satellite-linked navigational devices, joined with anti-Taliban contingents, marking Taliban positions with laser spotters and communicating with high-altitude bombers. These planes, circling at 30,000 feet, dropped electronically guided bombs on Taliban troops with uncanny (but not infallible) accuracy. Now the Taliban soldiers fled; some switched allegiance and joined the anti-Taliban coalition. Within weeks the Taliban were driven from power. Only one American soldier was killed by hostile fire. (A few American soldiers and hundreds of non-combatants were killed by errant bombs.) The United States had won the first battles in the war against terror. But, as Bush repeatedly warned, the campaign against terrorism would occupy the nation for many years. "Let there be no doubt," defense secretary Donald Rumsfeld declared in 2002, "in the years ahead, it is likely we will be surprised again."

THE IMPONDERABLE FUTURE

"Everything's changed"—these words or others like them were heard repeatedly following the attack on the World Trade Center. A generation that had basked in post–Cold War peace and prosperity was now wracked by fear of enemies unknown and unseen. The economic repercussions of the attack were also momentous. Several airlines declared bankruptcy. The travel industry was crippled. The federal surplus was gone in an instant, gobbled up by the unanticipated cost of the war on terrorism. American jurisprudence was transformed overnight by President Bush's threat to try suspected terrorists in secret military tribunals. The political rancor of the Clinton era, rekindled by the disputed vote in the 2000 presidential election, was replaced by bipartisan professions of unity. For such reasons, pundits proclaimed September 11, 2001 "the day that changed America."

But however shocking, the terrorist attack and its aftermath were not without historical precedent. Washington D.C. had been attacked (and burned) during the War of 1812, a profound blow to the nation's pride and security. The campaign against bin Laden and the Taliban also bore some resemblance to U.S. actions against the Barbary Pirates in northern Africa in 1815, and against Francisco "Pancho" Villa in Mexico a century later. Bush's treatment of suspected terrorists was akin to the Alien and Sedition Acts of 1798, Lincoln's suspension of *habeas corpus* during the Civil War, Wilson's suppression of dissent during the First World War, and the internment of alien Japanese and American citizens of Japanese extraction during the Second World War. The renewed sense of national cohesion following the attack (as well as a swift reassertion of politics as usual) has occurred during nearly every American war.

Whether September 11, 2001 will constitute a turning point in American history remains to be seen. Historians are probably better than most other people at explaining how things got to be the way they are at any present moment. This is because events have causes and results, and these are things that historians are trained to study and understand. But historians are no better than anyone else at predicting the future.

In the modern world just about everything that happens is in some way related to everything else that is going on. Far too many things are happening (all producing results of some kind) for anyone to sort out which is going to have what effect on tomorrow's events, let alone those that occur a year from now. "Then" (whether tomorrow or the next year) historians will be able to study those particular events and puzzle out their chief causes—but not "now."

Yet "now" is where we happen to be, and thus this book, so full of events and their causes and results, must end inconclusively. No one knows what will happen next. But not knowing what will happen is one reason why life is so interesting.

MILESTONES

1988 Republican George Bush elected president

1989 Gorbachev allows Eastern European nations to establish independent democratic governments

1990 Iraq invades Kuwait

Germany is reunited

1991 UN forces, led by the United States, drive Iraqi forces from Kuwait

Soviet Union is dissolved; Boris Yeltsin becomes president of Russia

1992 Democrat Bill Clinton elected president

1993 Ruth Bader Ginsberg becomes second woman associate justice of the Supreme Court

Bomb explodes in parking garage of World Trade Center in New York City, killing six and injuring a thousand

1994 Republicans win control of both houses of Congress; Congress defeats Clinton's health care reform plan

Murder trial of O. J. Simpson

1995 Terrorist bomb destroys Alfred P. Murrah Federal Building in Oklahoma City, killing 169

Fiftieth anniversary of founding of United Nations

Microsoft introduces "point and click" Windows operating system for computers

1996 Democrat Bill Clinton reelected president; Republicans retain control of Congress

Measure revamping federal welfare system passed by Congress and signed by President Clinton

1998 Clinton impeached by House of Representatives

U.S. government operates at first surplus since 1969

1999 Clinton aquitted by Senate; remains in office

NATO bombing campaign forces Serbia to halt "ethnic cleansing" in Kosovo

Gun violence in schools escalates; 12 die at Columbine High School in Colorado

2000 Republican George W. Bush elected president when Supreme Court halts Florida recounts

2001 Terrorists fly airplanes into the World Trade Center in New York City and into the Pentagon in Washington, D.C. A fourth plane hijacked by terrorists crashes in Pennsylvania. Over 3000 are killed in these attacks.

United States attacks Taliban in Afghanistan

APPENDIX

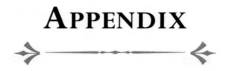

The Declaration of Independence

The Constitution of the United States of America

Amendments to the Constitution

Supplementary Reading

Suggested Websites

Political and Physical Map of the United States

Political Map of the World

The Declaration of Independence

In Congress, July 4, 1776

➤ ———————— ⟵

The Unanimous Declaration
of the Thirteen United States of America,

When, in the course of human events, it becomes necessary for one people to dissolve the political bonds which have connected them with another, and to assume, among the powers of the earth, the separate and equal station to which the laws of nature and of nature's God entitle them, a decent respect to the opinions of mankind requires that they should declare the causes which impel them to the separation.

We hold these truths to be self-evident: That all men are created equal; that they are endowed by their Creator with certain unalienable rights; that among these are life, liberty, and the pursuit of happiness; that, to secure these rights, governments are instituted among men, deriving their just powers from the consent of the governed; that whenever any form of government becomes destructive of these ends, it is the right of the people to alter or to abolish it, and to institute new government, laying its foundation on such principles, and organizing its powers in such form, as to them shall seem most likely to effect their safety and happiness. Prudence, indeed, will dictate that governments long established should not be changed for light and transient causes; and accordingly all experience hath shown that mankind are more disposed to suffer, while evils are sufferable, than to right themselves by abolishing the forms to which they are accustomed. But when a long train of abuses and usurpations, pursuing invariably the same object, evinces a design to reduce them under absolute despotism, it is their right, it is their duty, to throw off such government, and to provide new guards for their future security. Such has been the patient sufferance of these colonies; and such is now the necessity which constrains them to alter their former systems of government. The history of the present King of Great Britain is a history of repeated injuries and usurpations, all having in direct object the establishment of an absolute tyranny over these states. To prove this, let facts be submitted to a candid world.

He has refused his assent to laws, the most wholesome and necessary for the public good.

He has forbidden his governors to pass laws of immediate and pressing importance, unless suspended in their operation till his assent should be obtained; and, when so suspended, he has utterly neglected to attend to them.

He has refused to pass other laws for the accommodation of large districts of people, unless those people would relinquish the right of representation in the legislature, a right inestimable to them, and formidable to tyrants only.

He has called together legislative bodies at places unusual, uncomfortable, and distant from the depository of their public records, for the sole purpose of fatiguing them into compliance with his measures.

He has dissolved representative houses repeatedly, for opposing, with manly firmness, his invasions on the rights of the people.

He has refused for a long time, after such dissolutions, to cause others to be elected; whereby the legislative powers, incapable of annihilation, have returned to the people at large for their exercise; the state remaining, in the mean time, exposed to all the dangers of invasions from without and convulsions within.

He has endeavored to prevent the population of these states; for that purpose obstructing the laws for naturalization of foreigners; refusing to pass others to encourage their migration hither, and raising the conditions of new appropriations of lands.

He has obstructed the administration of justice, by refusing his assent to laws for establishing judiciary powers.

He has made judges dependent on his will alone, for the tenure of their offices, and the amount and payment of their salaries.

He has erected a multitude of new offices, and sent hither swarms of officers to harass our people and eat out their substance.

He has kept among us, in times of peace, standing armies, without the consent of our legislatures.

He has affected to render the military independent of, and superior to, the civil power.

He has combined with others to subject us to a jurisdiction foreign to our constitution, and unacknowledged by our laws, giving his assent to their acts of pretended legislation:

For quartering large bodies of armed troops among us;

For protecting them, by a mock trial, from punishment for any murder which they should commit on the inhabitants of these states;

For cutting off our trade with all parts of the world;

For imposing taxes on us without our consent;

For depriving us, in many cases, of the benefits of trial by jury;

For transporting us beyond seas, to be tried for pretended offenses;

For abolishing the free system of English laws in a neighboring province, establishing therein an arbitrary government, and enlarging its boundaries, so as to render it at once an example and fit instrument for introducing the same absolute rule into these colonies;

For taking away our charters, abolishing our most valuable laws, and altering fundamentally the forms of our governments;

For suspending our own legislatures, and declaring themselves invested with power to legislate for us in all cases whatsoever.

He has abdicated government here, by declaring us out of his protection and waging war against us.

He has plundered our seas, ravaged our coasts, burned our towns, and destroyed the lives of our people.

He is at this time transporting large armies of foreign mercenaries to complete the works of death, desolation, and tyranny already begun with circumstances of cruelty and perfidy scarcely paralleled in the most barbarous ages, and totally unworthy the head of a civilized nation.

He has constrained our fellow-citizens, taken captive on the high seas, to bear arms against their country, to become the executioners of their friends and brethren, or to fall themselves by their hands.

He has excited domestic insurrection among us, and has endeavored to bring on the inhabitants of our frontiers the merciless Indian savages, whose known rule of warfare is an undistinguished destruction of all ages, sexes, and conditions.

In every stage of these oppressions we have petitioned for redress in the most humble terms; our repeated petitions have been answered only by repeated injury. A prince, whose character is thus marked by every act which may define a tyrant, is unfit to be the ruler of a free people.

Nor have we been wanting in our attentions to our British brethren. We have warned them, from time to time, of attempts by their legislature to extend an unwarrantable jurisdiction over us. We have reminded them of the circumstances of our emigration and settlement here. We have appealed to their native justice and magnanimity; and we have conjured them, by the ties of our common kindred, to disavow these usurpations, which would inevitably interrupt our connections and correspondence. They, too, have been deaf to the voice of justice and of consanguinity. We must, therefore, acquiesce in the necessity which denounces our separation, and hold them, as we hold the rest of mankind, enemies in war, in peace friends.

We, therefore, the representatives of the United States of America, in General Congress assembled, appealing to the Supreme Judge of the world for the rectitude of our intentions, do, in the name and by the authority of the good people of these colonies, solemnly publish and declare, that these United Colonies are, and of right ought to be, FREE AND INDEPENDENT STATES; that they are absolved from all allegiance to the British crown, and that all political connection between them and the state of Great Britain is, and ought to be, totally dissolved; and that, as free and independent states, they have full power to levy war, conclude peace, contract alliances, establish commerce, and do all other acts and things which independent states may of right do. And for the support of this declaration, with a firm reliance on the protection of Divine Providence, we mutually pledge to each other our lives, our fortunes, and our sacred honor.

JOHN HANCOCK

Button Gwinnett	Thos. Nelson, Jr	Richd. Stockton
Lyman Hall	Francis Lightfoot Lee	Jno. Witherspoon
Geo. Walton	Carter Braxton	Fras. Hopkinson
Wm. Hooper	Robt. Morris	John Hart
Joseph Hewes	Benjamin Rush	Abra. Clark
John Penn	Benja. Franklin	Josiah Bartlett
Edward Rutledge	John Morton	Wm. Whipple
Thos. Heyward, Junr.	Geo. Clymer	Saml. Adams
Thomas Lynch, Junr.	Jas. Smith	John Adams
Arthur Middleton	Geo. Taylor	Robt. Treat Paine
Samuel Chase	James Wilson	Eldbridge Gerry
Wm. Paca	Geo. Ross	Step. Hopkins
Thos. Stone	Caesar Rodney	William Ellery
Charles Carroll of	Geo. Read	Roger Sherman
Carrollton	Tho. M'Kean	Sam'el Huntington
George Wythe	Wm. Floyd	Wm. Williams
Richard Henry Lee	Phil. Livingston	Oliver Wolcott
Th. Jefferson	Frans. Lewis	Matthew Thornton
Benj. Harrison	Lewis Morris	

The Constitution of the United States of America

PREAMBLE

We the People of the United States, in Order to form a more perfect Union, establish Justice, insure domestic Tranquility, provide for the common defence, promote the general Welfare, and secure the Blessings of Liberty to ourselves and our Posterity, do ordain and establish this Constitution for the United States of America.

ARTICLE 1

Section 1

All legislative Powers herein granted shall be vested in a Congress of the United States, which shall consist of a Senate and House of Representatives.

Section 2

The House of Representatives shall be composed of Members chosen every second Year by the People of the several States, and the Electors in each State shall have the Qualifications requisite for Electors of the most numerous Branch of the State Legislature.

No Person shall be a Representative who shall not have attained to the Age of twenty five Years, and been seven Years a Citizen of the United States, and who shall not, when elected, be an inhabitant of that State in which he shall be chosen.

Representatives and direct Taxes shall be apportioned among the several States which may be included within this Union, according to their respective Numbers, *which shall be determined by adding to the whole Number of free Persons, including those bound to Service for a Term of Years, and excluding Indians not taxed, three fifths of all other Persons.** The actual Enumeration shall be made within three Years after the first Meeting of the Congress of the United States, and within every subsequent Term of ten Years, in such Manner as they shall by Law direct. The Number of Representatives shall not exceed one for every thirty Thousand, but each State shall have at Least one Representative; *and until such enumeration shall be made, the State of New Hampshire shall be entitled to chuse three, Massachusetts eight, Rhode-Island and Providence Plantations one, Connecticut five, New York six, New Jersey four, Pennsylvania eight, Delaware one, Maryland six, Virginia ten, North Carolina five, South Carolina five, and Georgia three.*

When vacancies happen in the Representation from any State, the Executive Authority thereof shall issue Writs of Election to fill such Vacancies.

The House of Representatives shall chuse their Speaker and other Officers; and shall have the sole Power of Impeachment.

Section 3

The Senate of the United States shall be composed of two Senators from each State, *chosen by the Legislature thereof,* for six Years; and each Senator shall have one Vote.

**Passages no longer in effect are printed in italic type.*

Immediately after they shall be assembled in Consequence of the first Election, they shall be divided as equally as may be into three Classes. The Seats of the Senators of the first Class shall be vacated at the Expiration of the second Year, of the second Class at the Expiration of the fourth Year, and of the third Class at the Expiration of the sixth Year so that one third may be chosen every second Year; and if Vacancies happen by Resignation, or otherwise, during the Recess of the Legislature of any state, the Executive thereof may make temporary Appointments until the next Meeting of the Legislature, which shall then fill such Vacancies.

No Person shall be a Senator who shall not have attained to the Age of thirty Years, and been nine Years a Citizen of the United States, and who shall not, when elected, be an Inhabitant of that State for which he shall be chosen.

The Vice President of the United States shall be President of the Senate, but shall have no Vote, unless they be equally divided.

The Senate shall chuse their other Officers, and also a President *pro tempore,* in the Absence of the Vice President, or when he shall exercise the Office of President of the United States.

The Senate shall have the sole Power to try all Impeachments. When sitting for that Purpose, they shall be on Oath or Affirmation. When the President of the United States is tried the Chief Justice shall preside: And no Person shall be convicted without the Concurrence of two thirds of the Members present.

Judgment in Cases of Impeachment shall not extend further than to removal from Office, and disqualification to hold and enjoy any Office of honor, Trust or Profit under the United States: but the Party convicted shall nevertheless be liable and subject to Indictment, Trial, Judgment and Punishment, according to Law.

Section 4

The Times, Places and Manner of holding Elections for Senators and Representatives, shall be prescribed in each State by the Legislature thereof; but the Congress may at any time by Law make or alter such Regulations, except as to the Places of chusing Senators.

The Congress shall assemble at least once in every Year, *and such Meeting shall be on the first Monday in December, unless they shall by Law appoint a different Day.*

Section 5

Each House shall be the Judge of the Elections, Returns and Qualifications of its own Members, and a Majority of each shall constitute a Quorum to do Business; but a smaller Number may adjourn from day to day, and may be authorized to compel the Attendance of absent Members, in such Manner, and under such Penalties as each House may provide.

Each House may determine the Rules of its Proceedings, punish its Members for disorderly Behaviour, and, with the Concurrence of two thirds, expel a Member.

Each House shall keep a Journal of its Proceedings, and from time to time publish the same, excepting such Parts as may in their Judgment require Secrecy; and the Yeas and Nays of the Members of either House on any question shall, at the Desire of one fifth of those Present, be entered on the Journal.

Neither House, during the Session of Congress, shall, without the Consent of the other, adjourn for more than three days, nor to any other Place than that in which the two Houses shall be sitting.

Section 6

The Senators and Representatives shall receive a Compensation for their Services, to be ascertained by Law, and paid out of the Treasury of the United States. They shall in all Cases, except

Treason, Felony and Breach of the Peace, be privileged from Arrest during their Attendance at the Session of their respective Houses, and in going to and returning from the same; and for any Speech or Debate in either House, they shall not be questioned in any other Place.

No Senator or Representative shall, during the Time for which he was elected, be appointed to any civil Office under the Authority of the United States, which shall have been created, or the Emoluments whereof shall have been encreased during such time, and no Person holding any Office under the United States, shall be a Member of either House during his Continuance in Office.

Section 7

All Bills for raising Revenue shall originate in the House of Representatives; but the Senate may propose or concur with Amendments as on other Bills.

Every Bill which shall have passed the House of Representatives and the Senate, shall, before it become a Law, be presented to the President of the United States; If he approve he shall sign it, but if not he shall return it, with his Objections to the House in which it shall have originated, who shall enter the Objections at large on their Journal, and proceed to reconsider it. If after such Reconsideration two thirds of that House shall agree to pass the Bill, it shall be sent, together with the Objections, to the other House, by which it shall likewise be reconsidered, and if approved by two thirds of that House, it shall become a Law. But in all such Cases the Votes of both Houses shall be determined by Yeas and Nays, and the Names of the Persons voting for and against the Bill shall be entered on the Journal of each House respectively. If any Bill shall not be returned by the President within ten Days (Sundays excepted) after it shall have been presented to him, the Same shall be a Law, in like Manner as if he had signed it, unless the Congress by their Adjournment prevent its Return, in which Case it shall not be a Law.

Every Order, Resolution, or Vote to which the Concurrence of the Senate and House of Representatives may be necessary (except on a question of Adjournment) shall be presented to the President of the United States; and before the Same shall take Effect, shall be approved by him, or being disapproved by him, shall be repassed by two thirds of the Senate and House of Representatives, according to the Rules and Limitations prescribed in the Case of a Bill.

Section 8

The Congress shall have Power To lay and collect Taxes, Duties, Imposts and Excises, to pay the Debts and provide for the common Defence and general Welfare of the United States; but all Duties, Imposts and Excises shall be uniform throughout the United States;

To borrow Money on the credit of the United States;

To regulate Commerce with foreign Nations, and among the several States, and with the Indian Tribes;

To establish an uniform Rule of Naturalization, and uniform Laws on the subject of Bankruptcies throughout the United States;

To coin Money, regulate the Value thereof, and of foreign Coin, and fix the Standard of Weights and Measures;

To provide for the Punishment of counterfeiting the Securities and current Coin of the United States;

To establish Post Offices and post Roads;

To promote the Progress of Science and useful Arts, by securing for limited Times to Authors and Inventors the exclusive Right to their respective Writings and Discoveries;

To constitute Tribunals inferior to the supreme Court;

To define and punish Piracies and Felonies committed on the high Seas, and Offences against the Law of Nations;

To declare War, grant Letters of Marque and Reprisal, and make Rules concerning Captures on Land and Water;

To raise and support Armies, but no Appropriation of Money to that Use shall be for a longer Term than two Years;

To provide and maintain a Navy;

To make Rules for the Government and Regulation of the land and naval Forces;

To provide for calling forth the Militia to execute the Laws of the Union, suppress Insurrections and repel Invasions;

To provide for organizing, arming, and disciplining, the Militia, and for governing such Part of them as may be employed in the Service of the United States, reserving to the States respectively, the Appointment of the Officers, and the Authority of training the Militia according to the discipline prescribed by Congress;

To exercise exclusive Legislation in all Cases whatsoever, over such District (not exceeding ten Miles square) as may, by Cession of particular States, and the Acceptance of Congress, become the Seat of the Government of the United States, and to exercise like Authority over all Places purchased by the Consent of the Legislature of the State in which the Same shall be, for the Erection of Forts, Magazines, Arsenals, dock-Yards, and other needful Buildings;—And

To make all Laws which shall be necessary and proper for carrying into Execution the foregoing Powers, and all other Powers vested by this Constitution in the Government of the United States, or in any Department or Officer thereof.

Section 9

The Migration or Importation of such Persons as any of the States now existing shall think proper to admit, shall not be prohibited by the Congress prior to the Year one thousand eight hundred and eight, but a Tax or duty may be imposed on such Importation, not exceeding ten dollars for each Person.

The Privilege of the Writ of Habeas Corpus shall not be suspended, unless when in Cases of Rebellion or Invasion the public Safety may require it.

No Bill of Attainder or ex post facto Law shall be passed.

No Capitation, or other direct, Tax shall be laid, unless in Proportion to the Census or Enumeration herein before directed to be taken.

No Tax or Duty shall be laid on Articles exported from any State.

No Preference shall be given by any Regulation of Commerce or Revenue to the Ports of one State over those of another: nor shall Vessels bound to, or from, one State, be obliged to enter, clear, or pay Duties in another.

No Money shall be drawn from the Treasury, but in Consequence of Appropriations made by Law; and a regular Statement and Account of the Receipts and Expenditures of all public Money shall be published from time to time.

No Title of Nobility shall be granted by the United States: And no Person holding any Office of Profit or Trust under them, shall, without the Consent of the Congress, accept of any present, Emolument, Office, or Title, of any kind whatever, from any King, Prince, or foreign State.

Section 10

No State shall enter into any Treaty, Alliance, or Confederation; grant Letters of Marque and Reprisal; coin Money; emit Bills of Credit; make any Thing but gold and silver Coin a Tender in Payment of Debts; pass any Bill of Attainder, ex post facto Law, or Law impairing the obligation of Contracts, or grant any Title of Nobility.

No State shall, without the Consent of the Congress, lay any Imposts or Duties on Imports or Exports, except what may be absolutely necessary for executing its inspection Laws: and the net Produce of all Duties and Imposts, laid by any State on Imports or Exports, shall be for the Use of the Treasury of the United States; and all such Laws shall be subject to the Revision and Controul of the Congress.

No State shall, without the Consent of Congress, lay any Duty of Tonnage, keep Troops, or Ships of War in time of Peace, enter into any Agreement or Compact with another State, or with a foreign Power, or engage in War, unless actually invaded, or in such imminent Danger as will not admit of delay.

ARTICLE II

Section 1

The executive Power shall be vested in a President of the United States of America. He shall hold his Office during the Term of four Years, and, together with the Vice President, chosen for the same Term, be elected, as follows:

Each State shall appoint, in such Manner as the Legislature thereof may direct, a Number of Electors, equal to the whole Number of Senators and Representatives to which the State may be entitled in the Congress: but no Senator or Representative, or Person holding an Office of Trust or Profit under the United States, shall be appointed an Elector.

The Electors shall meet in their respective States, and vote by Ballot for two Persons, of whom one at least shall not be an Inhabitant of the same State with themselves. And they shall make a List of all the Persons voted for, and of the Number of Votes for each; which List they shall sign and certify, and transmit sealed to the Seat of the Government of the United States, directed to the President of the Senate. The President of the Senate shall, in the Presence of the Senate and House of Representatives, open all the Certificates, and the Votes shall then be counted. The Person having the greatest Number of Votes shall be the President, if such Number be a Majority of the whole number of Electors appointed; and if there be more than one who have such Majority, and have an equal Number of Votes, then the House of Representatives shall immediately chuse by Ballot one of them for President; and if no Person have a Majority, then from the five highest on the List the said House shall in like Manner chuse the President. But in chusing the President, the Votes shall be taken by States, the Representation from each State having one Vote; A quorum for this Purpose shall consist of a Member or Members from two thirds of the States, and a Majority of all the States shall be necessary to a Choice. In every Case, after the Choice of the President, the Person having the greatest Number of Votes of the Electors shall be the Vice President. But if there should remain two or more who have equal Votes, the Senate shall chuse from them by Ballot the Vice President.

The Congress may determine the time of chusing the Electors, and the Day on which they shall give their Votes; which Day shall be the same throughout the United States.

No person except a natural born Citizen, *or a Citizen of the United States, at the time of the Adoption of this Constitution,* shall be eligible to the Office of President; neither shall any Person be eligible to that Office who shall not have attained to the Age of thirty five Years, and been fourteen Years a Resident within the United States.

In Case of the Removal of the President from Office, or of his Death, Resignation, or Inability to discharge the Powers and Duties of the said Office, the Same shall devolve on the Vice President, and the Congress may by Law provide for the Case of Removal, Death, Resignation or Inability, both of the President and Vice President, declaring what Officer shall then act as President, and such Officer shall act accordingly, until the Disability be removed, or a President shall be elected.

The President shall, at stated Times, receive for his Services, a Compensation, which shall neither be encreased nor diminished during the Period for which he shall have been elected, and he shall not receive within that period any other Emolument from the United States, or any of them.

Before he enter on the Execution of his Office, he shall take the following Oath or Affirmation:—"I do solemnly swear (or affirm) that I will faithfully execute the Office of President of the United States, and will to the best of my Ability, preserve, protect and defend the Constitution of the United States."

Section 2

The President shall be Commander in Chief of the Army and Navy of the United States, and of the Militia of the several States, when called into the actual Service of the United States; he may require the Opinion, in writing, of the principal Officer in each of the executive Departments, upon any Subject relating to the Duties of their respective Offices, and he shall have Power to grant Reprieves and Pardons for Offences against the United States, except in Cases of Impeachment.

He shall have Power, by and with the Advice and Consent of the Senate, to make Treaties, provided two thirds of the Senators present concur; and he shall nominate, and by and with the Advice and Consent of the Senate, shall appoint Ambassadors, other public Ministers and Consuls, Judges of the supreme Court, and all other Officers of the United States, whose Appointments are not herein otherwise provided for, and which shall be established by Law: but the Congress may by Law vest the Appointment of such inferior Officers, as they think proper in the President alone, in the Courts of Law, or in the Heads of Departments.

The President shall have Power to fill up all Vacancies that may happen during the Recess of the Senate, by granting Commissions which shall expire at the End of their next Session.

Section 3

He shall from time to time give to the Congress Information of the State of the Union, and recommend to their Consideration such Measures as he shall judge necessary and expedient; he may, on extraordinary Occasions, convene both Houses, or either of them, and in Case of disagreement between them, with Respect to the Time of Adjournment, he may adjourn them to such Time as he shall think proper; he shall receive Ambassadors and other public Ministers; he shall take Care that the Laws be faithfully executed, and shall Commission all the officers of the United States.

Section 4

The President, Vice President and all civil Officers of the United States, shall be removed from Office on Impeachment for, and Conviction of, Treason, Bribery or other high Crimes and Misdemeanors.

ARTICLE III

Section 1

The judicial Power of the United States, shall be vested in one supreme Court, and in such inferior Courts as the Congress may from time to time ordain and establish. The Judges, both of the supreme and inferior Courts, shall hold their offices during good Behaviour, and shall, at stated Times, receive for their Services, a Compensation, which shall not be diminished during their Continuance in Office.

Section 2

The judicial Power shall extend to all Cases, in Law and Equity, arising under this Constitution, the Laws of the United States, and Treaties made, or which shall be made, under their Authority;—to all Cases affecting Ambassadors, other public Ministers and Consuls;—to all Cases of admiralty and maritime Jurisdiction;—to Controversies to which the United States shall be a Party;—to Controversies between two or more States;—*between a State and Citizens of another State;*—between Citizens of different States;—between Citizens of the same State claiming Lands under Grants of different States, and between a State, or the Citizens thereof, and foreign States, Citizens or Subjects.

In all Cases affecting Ambassadors, other public Ministers and Consuls, and those in which a State shall be Party, the supreme Court shall have original Jurisdiction. In all the other Cases before mentioned, the supreme Court shall have appellate Jurisdiction, both as to Law and Fact, with such Exceptions, and under such Regulations as the Congress shall make.

The Trial of all Crimes, except in Cases of Impeachment, shall be by Jury; and such Trial shall be held in the State where the said Crimes shall have been committed, but when not committed within any State, the Trial shall be at such Place or Places as the Congress may by Law have directed.

Section 3

Treason against the United States, shall consist only in levying War against them, or in adhering to their Enemies, giving them Aid and Comfort. No person shall be convicted of Treason unless on the Testimony of two Witnesses to the same overt Act, or on Confession in open Court.

The Congress shall have Power to declare the Punishment of Treason, but no Attainder of Treason shall work Corruption of Blood, or Forfeiture except during the Life of the Person attainted.

ARTICLE IV

Section 1

Full Faith and Credit shall be given in each State to the public Acts, Records, and judicial Proceedings of every other State. And the Congress may by general Laws prescribe the Manner in which such Acts, Records and Proceedings shall be proved, and the Effect thereof.

Section 2

The Citizens of each State shall be entitled to all Privileges and Immunities of Citizens in the several States.

A Person charged in any State with Treason, Felony, or other Crime, who shall flee from Justice, and be found in another State, shall on Demand of the executive Authority of the State from which he fled, be delivered up, to be removed to the State having Jurisdiction of the Crime.

No Person held to Service or Labour in one State, under the Laws thereof, escaping into another, shall, in Consequence of any Law or Regulation therein, be discharged from such Service or Labour, but shall be delivered up on Claim of the Party to whom such Service or Labour may be due.

Section 3

New States may be admitted by the Congress into this Union; but no new State shall be formed or erected within the Jurisdiction of any other State; nor any State be formed by the Junction of two or more States, or Parts of States, without the Consent of the Legislatures of the States concerned as well as of the Congress.

The Congress shall have Power to dispose of and make all needful Rules and Regulations respecting the Territory or other Property belonging to the United States; and nothing in this Constitution shall be so construed as to Prejudice any Claims of the United States, or of any particular States.

Section 4

The United States shall guarantee to every State in this Union a Republican Form of Government, and shall protect each of them against Invasion; and on Application of the Legislature, or of the Executive (when the Legislature cannot be convened) against domestic violence.

ARTICLE V

The Congress, whenever two thirds of both Houses shall deem it necessary, shall propose Amendments to this Constitution, or, on the Application of the Legislatures of two thirds of the several States, shall call a Convention for proposing Amendments, which, in either Case, shall be valid to all Intents and Purposes, as Part of this Constitution, when ratified by the Legislatures of three fourths of the several States, or by Conventions in three fourths thereof, as the one or the other Mode of Ratification may be proposed by the Congress; Provided *that no Amendment which may be made prior to the Year One thousand eight hundred and eight shall in any Manner affect the first and fourth Clauses in the Ninth Section of the first Article;* and that no State, without its Consent, shall be deprived of its equal Suffrage in the Senate.

ARTICLE VI

All Debts contracted and Engagements entered into, before the Adoption of this Constitution, shall be as valid against the United States under this Constitution, as under the Confederation.

This Constitution, and Laws of the United States which shall be made in Pursuance thereof; and all Treaties made, or which shall be made, under the Authority of the United States, shall be the supreme Law of the Land; and the Judges in every State shall be bound thereby, any Thing in the Constitution or Laws of any State to the Contrary notwithstanding.

The Senators and Representatives before mentioned, and the Members of the several State Legislatures, and all executive and Judicial Officers, both of the United States and of the several States, shall be bound by Oath or Affirmation, to support this Constitution; but no religious Test shall ever be required as a Qualification to any Office of public Trust under the United States.

ARTICLE VII

The Ratification of the Conventions of nine States, shall be sufficient for the Establishment of this Constitution between the States so ratifying the Same.

Done in Convention by the Unanimous Consent of the States present the Seventeenth Day of September in the Year of our Lord one thousand seven hundred and Eighty seven and of the Independence of the United States of America the Twelfth.* IN WITNESS whereof We have hereunto subscribed our Names,

GEORGE WASHINGTON
President and Deputy from Virginia

Delaware
GEORGE READ
GUNNING BEDFORD, JR.
JOHN DICKINSON
RICHARD BASSETT
JACOB BROOM

Maryland
JAMES MCHENRY
DANIEL OF ST. THOMAS JENIFER
DANIEL CARROLL

Virginia
JOHN BLAIR
JAMES MADISON, JR.

North Carolina
WILLIAM BLOUNT
RICHARD DOBBS SPRAIGHT
HUGH WILLIAMSON

South Carolina
JOHN RUTLEDGE
CHARLES COTESWORTH PINCKNEY
CHARLES PINCKNEY
PIERCE BUTLER

Georgia
WILLIAM FEW
ABRAHAM BALDWIN

New Hampshire
JOHN LANGDON
NICHOLAS GILMAN

Massachusetts
NATHANIEL GORHAM
RUFUS KING

Connecticut
WILLIAM SAMUEL JOHNSON
ROGER SHERMAN

New York
ALEXANDER HAMILTON

New Jersey
WILLIAM LIVINGSTON
DAVID BREARLEY
WILLIAM PATERSON
JONATHAN DAYTON

Pennsylvania
BENJAMIN FRANKLIN
THOMAS MIFFLIN
ROBERT MORRIS
GEORGE CLYMER
THOMAS FITZSIMONS
JARED INGERSOLL
JAMES WILSON
GOUVERNEUR MORRIS

The Constitution was submitted on September 17, 1787, by the Constitutional Convention, was ratified by the Convention of several states at various dates up to May 29, 1790, and became effective on March 4, 1789.

Amendments to the Constitution

AMENDMENT I

Congress shall make no law respecting an establishment of religion, or prohibiting the free exercise thereof; or abridging the freedom of speech, or of the press; or the right of the people peaceably to assemble, and to petition the Government for a redress of grievances.

AMENDMENT II

A well regulated Militia being necessary to the security of a free State, the right of the people to keep and bear Arms, shall not be infringed.

AMENDMENT III

No Soldier shall, in time of peace be quartered in any house, without the consent of the Owner, nor in time of war, but in a manner to be prescribed by law.

AMENDMENT IV

The right of the people to be secure in their persons, houses, papers, and effects, against unreasonable searches and seizures, shall not be violated, and no Warrants shall issue, but upon probable cause, supported by Oath or affirmation, and particularly describing the place to be searched, and the persons or things to be seized.

AMENDMENT V

No person shall be held to answer for a capital, or otherwise infamous crime, unless on a presentment or indictment of a Grand Jury, except in cases arising in the land or naval forces, or in the Militia, when in actual service in time of War or public danger; nor shall any person be subject for the same offense to be twice put in jeopardy of life or limb; nor shall be compelled in any criminal case to be a witness against himself, nor be deprived of life, liberty, or property, without due process of law; nor shall private property be taken for public use, without just compensation.

AMENDMENT VI

In all criminal prosecutions, the accused shall enjoy the right to a speedy and public trial, by an impartial jury of the State and district wherein the crime shall have been committed, which district shall have been previously ascertained by law, and to be informed of the nature and cause of the accusation; to be confronted with the witnesses against him; to have compulsory process for obtaining witnesses in his favor, and to have the Assistance of Counsel for his defence.

AMENDMENT VII

In Suits at common law, where the value in controversy shall exceed twenty dollars, the right of trial by jury shall be preserved, and no fact tried by a jury, shall be otherwise re-examined in any Court of the United States, than according to the rules of the common law.

Amendment VIII

Excessive bail shall not be required, nor excessive fines imposed, nor cruel and unusual punishments inflicted.

Amendment IX

The enumeration in the Constitution, of certain rights, shall not be construed to deny or disparage others retained by the people.

Amendment X[*]

The powers not delegated to the United States by the Constitution, nor prohibited by it to the States, are reserved to the States respectively, or to the people.

Amendment XI
[Adopted 1798]

The Judicial power of the United States shall not be construed to extend to any suit in law or equity, commenced or prosecuted against one of the United States by Citizens of another State, or by Citizens or Subjects of any Foreign State.

Amendment XII
[Adopted 1804]

The Electors shall meet in their respective states, and vote by ballot for President and Vice President, one of whom, at least, shall not be an inhabitant of the same state with themselves; they shall name in their ballots the person voted for as President, and in distinct ballots the person voted for as Vice President, and they shall make distinct lists of all persons voted for as President, and of all persons voted for as Vice President, and of the number of votes for each, which lists they shall sign and certify, and transmit sealed to the seat of the government of the United States, directed to the President of the Senate;—The President of the Senate shall, in the presence of the Senate and House of Representatives, open all the certificates and the votes shall then be counted;—The person having the greatest number of votes for President, shall be the President, if such number be a majority of the whole number of Electors appointed; and if no person have such majority, then from the persons having the highest numbers not exceeding three on the list of those voted for as President, the House of Representatives shall choose immediately, by ballot, the President. But in choosing the President, the votes shall be taken by states, the representation from each state having one vote; a quorum for this purpose shall consist of a member or members from two-thirds of the states, and a majority of all the states shall be necessary to a choice. And if the House of Representatives shall not choose a President whenever the right of choice shall devolve upon them, before *the fourth day of March* next following, then the Vice President shall act as President, as in the case of the death or other constitutional disability of the President.—The person having the greatest number of votes as Vice President, shall be the Vice President, if such number be a majority of the whole number of Electors appointed, and if no person have a majority, then from the two highest numbers on the list, the Senate shall choose the Vice President; a quorum for the purpose shall consist of two-thirds of the whole number of Senators, and a majority of the whole number shall be necessary to a choice. But no person con-

---

[*]*The first ten amendments (the Bill of Rights) were ratified, and their adoption was certified, on December 15, 1791.*

stitutionally ineligible to the office of President shall be eligible to that of Vice President of the United States.

AMENDMENT XIII
[ADOPTED 1865]

Section 1

Neither slavery nor involuntary servitude, except as a punishment for crime whereof the party shall have been duly convicted, shall exist within the United States, or any place subject to their jurisdiction.

Section 2

Congress shall have power to enforce this article by appropriate legislation.

AMENDMENT XIV
[ADOPTED 1868]

Section 1

All persons born or naturalized in the United States, and subject to the jurisdiction thereof, are citizens of the United States and of the State wherein they reside. No State shall make or enforce any law which shall abridge the privileges or immunities of citizens of the United States; nor shall any State deprive any person of life, liberty, or property, without due process of law; nor deny to any person within its jurisdiction the equal protection of the laws.

Section 2

Representatives shall be apportioned among the several States according to their respective numbers, counting the whole number of persons in each State, excluding Indians not taxed. But when the right to vote at any election for the choice of electors for President and Vice President of the United States, Representatives in Congress, the Executive and Judicial officers of a State, or the members of the Legislature thereof, is denied to any of the male inhabitants of such State, being twenty-one years of age, and citizens of the United States, or in any way abridged, except for participation in rebellion, or other crime, the basis of representation therein shall be reduced in the proportion which the number of such male citizens shall bear to the whole number of male citizens twenty-one years of age in such State.

Section 3

No person shall be a Senator or Representative in Congress, or elector of President and Vice President, or hold any office, civil or military, under the United States, or under any State, who, having previously taken an oath, as a member of Congress, or as an officer of the United States, or as a member of any State legislature, or as an executive or judicial officer of any State, to support the Constitution of the United States, shall have engaged in insurrection or rebellion against the same, or given aid or comfort to the enemies thereof. But Congress may by a vote of two-thirds of each House, remove such disability.

Section 4

The validity of the public debt of the United States, authorized by law, including debts incurred for payment of pensions and bounties for services in suppressing insurrection or rebellion, shall not be questioned. But neither the United States nor any State shall assume or pay any debt or obligation incurred in aid of insurrection or rebellion against the United States, or any claim for the loss or emancipation of any slave; but all such debts, obligations and claims shall be held illegal and void.

Section 5

The Congress shall have power to enforce, by appropriate legislation, the provisions of this article.

AMENDMENT XV
[ADOPTED 1870]

Section 1

The right of citizens of the United States to vote shall not be denied or abridged by the United States or by any State on account of race, color, or previous condition of servitude.

Section 2

The Congress shall have power to enforce this article by appropriate legislation.

AMENDMENT XVI
[ADOPTED 1913]

The Congress shall have power to lay and collect taxes on incomes, from whatever source derived, without apportionment among the several States, and without regard to any census or enumeration.

AMENDMENT XVII
[ADOPTED 1913]

The Senate of the United States shall be composed of two Senators from each State, elected by the people thereof, for six years; and each Senator shall have one vote. The electors in each State shall have the qualifications requisite for electors of the most numerous branch of the State legislatures.

When vacancies happen in the representation of any State in the Senate, the executive authority of such State shall issue writs of election to fill such vacancies: *Provided,* That the legislature of any State may empower the executive thereof to make temporary appointments until the people fill the vacancies by election as the legislature may direct.

This amendment shall not be so construed as to affect the election or term of any Senator chosen before it becomes valid as part of the Constitution.

AMENDMENT XVIII
[ADOPTED 1919, REPEALED 1933]

Section 1

After one year from the ratification of this article the manufacture, sale, or transportation of intoxicating liqours within, the importation thereof into, or the exportation thereof from the United States and all territory subject to the jurisdiction thereof for beverage purposes is hereby prohibited.

Section 2

The Congress and the several States shall have concurrent power to enforce this article by appropriate legislation.

Section 3

This article shall be inoperative unless it shall have been ratified as an amendment to the Constitution by the legislatures of the several States, as provided in the Constitution, within seven years from the date of the submission hereof to the States by the Congress.

AMENDMENT XIX
[ADOPTED 1920]

The right of citizens of the United States to vote shall not be denied or abridged by the United States or by any State on account of sex.

Congress shall have power to enforce this article by appropriate legislation.

AMENDMENT XX
[ADOPTED 1933]

Section 1

The terms of the President and Vice President shall end at noon on the 20th day of January, and the terms of Senators and Representatives at noon on the 3d day of January, of the years in which such terms would have ended if this article had not been ratified and the terms of their successors shall then begin.

Section 2

The Congress shall assemble at least once in every year, and such meeting shall begin at noon on the 3d day of January, unless they shall by law appoint a different day.

Section 3

If, at the time fixed for the beginning of the term of the President, the President elect shall have died, the Vice President elect shall become President. If a President shall not have been chosen before the time fixed for the beginning of his term, or if the President elect shall have failed to qualify, then the Vice President elect shall act as President until a President shall have qualified; and the Congress may by law provide for the case wherein neither a President elect nor a Vice President elect shall have qualified, declaring who shall then act as President, or the manner in which one who is to act shall be selected, and such person shall act accordingly until a President or Vice President shall have qualified.

Section 4

The Congress may by law provide for the case of the death of any of the persons from whom the House of Representatives may choose a President whenever the right of choice shall have devolved upon them, and for the case of the death of any of the persons from whom the Senate may choose a Vice President whenever the right of choice shall have devolved upon them.

Section 5

Sections 1 and 2 shall take effect on the 15th day of October following the ratification of this article.

Section 6

This article shall be inoperative unless it shall have been ratified as an amendment to the Constitution by the legislatures of three fourths of the several States within seven years from the date of its submission.

Amendment XXI
[Adopted 1933]

Section 1

The eighteenth article of amendment to the Constitution of the United States is hereby repealed.

Section 2

The transportation or importation into any State, Territory, or possession of the United States for delivery or use therein of intoxicating liquors in violation of the laws thereof, is hereby prohibited.

Section 3

This article shall be inoperative unless it shall have been ratified as an amendment to the Constitution by conventions in the several States, as provided in the Constitution, within seven years from the date of the submission hereof to the States by the Congress.

Amendment XXII
[Adopted 1951]

Section 1

No person shall be elected to the office of the President more than twice, and no person who has held the office of President, or acted as President, for more than two years of a term to which some other person was elected President shall be elected to the office of the President more than once. But this Article shall not apply to any person holding the office of President when this Article was proposed by the Congress, and shall not prevent any person who may be holding the office of President, or acting as President, during the term within which this Article becomes operative from holding the office of President or acting as President during the remainder of such term.

Section 2

This article shall be inoperative unless it shall have been ratified as an amendment to the Constitution by the legislatures of three-fourths of the several States within seven years from the date of its submission to the States by the Congress.

Amendment XXIII
[Adopted 1961]

Section 1

The District constituting the seat of Government of the United States shall appoint in such manner as the Congress shall direct:

A number of electors of President and Vice President equal to the whole number of Senators and Representatives in Congress to which the District would be entitled if it were a State, but in no event more than the least populous State; they shall be in addition to those appointed by the States, but they shall be considered, for the purposes of the election of President and Vice President, to be electors appointed by a State; and they shall meet in the District and perform such duties as provided by the twelfth article of amendment.

Section 2

The Congress shall have power to enforce this article by appropriate legislation.

AMENDMENT XXIV
[ADOPTED 1964]

Section 1

The right of citizens of the United States to vote in any primary or other election for President or Vice President, for electors for President or Vice President, or for Senator or Representative in Congress, shall not be denied or abridged by the United States or any state by reason of failure to pay any poll tax or other tax.

Section 2

The Congress shall have the power to enforce this article by appropriate legislation.

AMENDMENT XXV
[ADOPTED 1967]

Section 1

In case of the removal of the President from office or his death or resignation, the Vice President shall become President.

Section 2

Whenever there is a vacancy in the office of the Vice President, the President shall nominate a Vice President who shall take the office upon confirmation by a majority vote of both houses of Congress.

Section 3

Whenever the President transmits to the President pro tempore of the Senate and the Speaker of the House of Representatives his written declaration that he is unable to discharge the powers and duties of his office, and until he transmits to them a written declaration to the contrary, such powers and duties shall be discharged by the Vice President as Acting President.

Section 4

Whenever the Vice President and a majority of either the principal officers of the executive departments or of such other body as Congress may by law provide, transmit to the President pro tempore of the Senate and the Speaker of the House of Representatives their written declaration that the President is unable to discharge the powers and duties of his office, the Vice President shall immediately assume the powers and duties of the office as Acting President.

Thereafter, when the President transmits to the President pro tempore of the Senate and the Speaker of the House of Representatives his written declaration that no inability exists, he shall resume the powers and duties of his office unless the Vice President and a majority of either the principal officers of the executive department or of such other body as Congress may by law provide, transmit within four days to the President pro tempore of the Senate and the Speaker of the House of Representatives their written declaration that the President is unable to discharge the powers and duties of his office. Thereupon Congress shall decide the issue, assembling within 48 hours for that purpose if not in session. If the Congress, within 21 days after receipt of the latter written declaration, or, if Congress is not in session, within 21 days after Congress is required to assemble, determines by two-thirds vote of both houses that the President is unable to discharge the powers and duties of his office, the Vice President shall continue to discharge the same as Acting President; otherwise, the President shall resume the powers and duties of his office.

AMENDMENT XXVI
[ADOPTED 1971]

Section 1

The right of citizens of the United States, who are 18 years of age or older, to vote shall not be denied or abridged by the United States or any state on account of age.

Section 2

The Congress shall have the power to enforce this article by appropriate legislation.

AMENDMENT XXVII
[ADOPTED 1992]

No law, varying the compensation for the services of the Senators and Representatives shall take effect, until an election of Representatives shall have intervened.

Supplementary Reading

Prologue | Beginnings

During the 1990s the prehistoric era in North America witnessed an explosion of interest, especially among archaeologists. A global perspective, focusing on geography as a causal force, is outlined in Jared Diamond, *Guns, Germs, and Steel* (1997). David Hurst Thomas, *Exploring Native North America* (2000), provides detailed analyses of representative archaeological sites.

A good survey of the first peoples of North America is David J. Meltzer, *Search for the First Americans* (1993). The "overkill hypothesis" is developed in Paul Martin and Richard Klein, eds., *Quaternary Extinctions* (1984). The best survey on the Southwestern peoples is Linda S. Cordell, *Preshistory of the Southwest* (1997). See also J. J. Brody, *The Anasazi* (1990), David Roberts, *In Search of the Old Ones: Exploring the Anasazi World of the Southwest* (1995), R. Gwinn Vivian, *The Chacoan Prehistory of the San Juan Basin* (1990), John P. Andrews and Todd W. Bostwick, *Desert Farmers at the River's Edge: The Hohokam and Pueblo Grande* (1997), and, on early agriculture, R. G. Matson, *The Origins of Southwestern Agriculture* (1991). For a study of Hopewell peoples, see Bruce D. Smith, *Rivers of Change* (1992).

On the Mississipian societies, see Thomas E. Emerson, *Cahokia and the Archaeology of Power* (1997), Thomas E. Emerson and R. Barry Lewis, eds., *Cahokia and the Hinterlands: Middle Mississippian Cultures of the Midwest* (1991), Biloine W. Young and Robert Fowler, *Cahokia, The Great Native American Metropolis* (2000), Timothy Pauketat, *The Ascent of Chiefs: Cahokia and Mississippian Politics in Native North America* (1994), and Robert A. Birmingham and Leslie Eisenberg, *Indian Mounds of Wisconsin* (2000). For early peoples elsewhere, see Vance T. Holliday, *Paleoindian Geoarchaeology of the Southern High Plains* (1997), and Ruth Kirk and Richard D. Daugherty, *Hunters of the Whale* (1974), for the Makah of the Northwest.

For an overview of political structures, see Robert D. Drennan, *Chiefdoms in the Americas* (1987). That warfare was a product of gender tensions is explored in Bruce G. Trigger, *Natives and Newcomers* (1985). The contention that the early peoples of North America lived in perfect harmony with nature is rebutted in Shepard Krech, *The Ecological Indian* (1999). Another common assumption, based on Native American folklore, of the essentially peaceful character of Southwestern peoples has been challenged by recent studies such as Glen E. Rice and Steven A. Leblanc, eds., *Deadly Landscapes: Case Studies in Prehistoric Southwestern Warfare* (2001), and Tim D. White, *Prehistoric Cannibalism at Mancos* (1992).

Chapter 1 | Alien Encounters: Europe in the Americas

On the explorers and the world they opened up, see Samuel E. Morison, *The European Discovery of America* (1971–1974). Morison's biography of Columbus, *Admiral of the Ocean Sea* (1942), is a classic; for a recent study see Miles Davidson, *Columbus Then and Now* (1997). David Stannard, *American Holocaust* (1992), and Kirkpatrick Sale, *The Conquest of Paradise* (1990) are highly critical of Columbus. See also Donald W. Meinig, *The Shaping of America: Atlantic America, 1492–1800* (1986). The history of Spanish colonization in the Southwest is treated in David J. Weber, *The Spanish Frontier in North America* (1992), and, in the Southeast, in Paul E. Hoffman, *A New Andalucia and a Way to the Orient* (1991). The classic study is Charles Gibson, *Spain in America* (1966). For an imaginative attempt to reconstruct the Native American response, see Ramon Guittierrez, *When Jesus Came, The Corn Mothers Went Away* (1991).

Accounts of the English background of colonization can be found in Nicholas Canny, ed., *The Oxford History of the British Empire: The Origins of Empire* (1998). On French colonization, see William J. Eccles, *The French in North America, 1500–1765* (1998), Carl J. Ekberg, *French Roots in the Illinois Country* (1998), and Carole Blackburn, *Harvest of Souls* (2000), which focuses on the Jesuit Missionaries. John H. Elliott, *The Old World and the New* (1970), analyzes the impact of the discovery of America on Europe.

Contemporary scholarship on Indian-colonist relations focuses on their interactions. Important studies in that vein include Richard White, *Indians, Empires and Republics in the Great Lakes Region, 1650–1815* (1991), James Merrell, *Into the American Woods: Negotiators on the Pennsylvania Frontier* (1999), and Karen Kupperman, *Indians and English: Facing Off in Early America* (2000). See also Jean O'Brien, *Dispossession by Degrees: Indians, Land and Identity in Natick, Massachusetts, 1650–1790* (1997). On the role of infectious diseases, see Alfred W. Crosby, *Ecological Imperialism: The Biological Expansion of Europe, 900–1900* (1993) and, though it deals with a later period, Robert Boyd, *The Coming of the Spirit of Pestilence: Introduced Infectious Diseases and Population Decline among Northwest Coast Indians* (1999).

For a general study of American slave trade, see David Eltis, *The Rise of African Slavery in the Americas* (2000). General surveys of slavery include Ira Berlin, *Many Thousands Gone* (1998), and Peter Kolchin, *American Slavery, 1619–1877* (1993). On the background of black slaves, see Basil Davison and F. K. Buah, *History of West Africa to the Nineteenth Century* (1967).

On Virginia, see David H. Fischer and James C. Kelly, *Bound Away: Virginia and the Westward Movement* (2000), and Edmund S. Morgan, *American Slavery, American Freedom* (1975). Jack P. Greene, *Pursuits of Happiness* (1988), argues for the centrality of the Chesapeake in the formation of American identity. On Roanoke, see Ivor Noel Hume, *The Virginia Adventure* (1994); for Maryland, consult Gloria T. Main, *Tobacco Colony* (1982), and Aubrey C. Land, *Colonial Maryland* (1981); for Carolina, see Roger Ekirch, *Poor Carolina* (1981).

For the middle colonies, see Michael Kammen, *Colonial New York* (1975) and Donna Merwick, *Possessing Albany, 1630–1710: The Dutch and English Experiences* (1990).

Among the important biographies, Edmund Morgan's *The Puritan Dilemma: The Story of John Winthrop* (1981) remains unsurpassed; on Anne Hutchinson, see Selma R. Williams, *Divine Rebel* (1981); for Pennsylvania, see Mary Geiter, *William Penn* (2000); for Virginia, Everett Emerson, *Captain John Smith* (1993); and for Rhode Island, Edwin S. Gaustad, *Liberty of Conscience: Roger Williams in America* (1991).

No student should miss at least dipping into the works of Francis Parkman on the French in America. His *Pioneers of France in the New World* (1855) covers the early period. William Bradford's classic, *Of Plymouth Plantation*, is also well worth sampling.

CHAPTER 2 | AMERICAN SOCIETY IN THE MAKING

Among general interpretations, Daniel J. Boorstin's *The Americans: The Colonial Experience* (1958), emphasizes the modern aspects of colonial society, an idea that is extended far beyond white males in Jon Butler's *Becoming America: The Revolution before 1776* (2000).

On economic conditions, see John J. McCusker and Russell R. Menard, eds., *The Economy of British America, 1607–1789* (1991). For the economic growth of colonial New England, see Margaret Ellen Newell, *From Dependency to Independence* (1998). On the chronologically and geographically uneven development of slavery in America, consult Ira Berlin, *Many Thousands Gone* (1998) and Philip D. Morgan, *Slave Counterpoint* (1998). Also see P. D. Curtin, *The Rise and Fall of the Plantation Complex* (1990). For the institution of slavery generally, see Herbert Klein, *The Middle Passage* (1978), D. B. Davis, *The Problem of Slavery in Western Culture* (1966), and W. D. Jordan, *White Over Black: American Attitudes Toward the Negro* (1968). On indentured servitude see W. D. Galenson, *White Servitude in Colonial America* (1981).

On life in the colonial South, see Thad W. Tate and David Ammerman, eds., *The Chesapeake in the Seventeenth Century* (1979), Allan Kulikoff, *Tobacco and Slaves* (1986), Darrett B. and Anita H. Rutman, *A Place in Time* (1984), and Timothy H. Breen and Stephen Innes, *"Myne Owne Ground": Race and Freedom on Virginia's Eastern Shore* (1980).

Family and community life are surveyed in David F. Hawke, *Everyday Life in Early America* (1988), and Edmund S. Morgan, *The Puritan Family* (1966). See also John Demos, *A Little Commonwealth* (1970), Richard L. Bushman, *From Puritan to Yankee* (1967), Kenneth A. Lockridge, *A New England Town* (1970), and Philip Greven, *Four Generations* (1970). The places of women and children are effectively presented in Laurel T. Ulrich, *Good Wives: Image and Reality in the Lives of Women in Northern New England* (1982), and Philip Greven, *The Protestant Temperament: Patterns of Child-Rearing, Religious Experience, and the Self in Early America* (1980).

The works of Perry Miller remain the starting point for any serious study of the cultural life of colonial New England. Among them, *Errand into the Wilderness* (1956) provides a good introduction. More recent studies, most of which modify Miller's judgments, include David D. Hall, *Worlds of Wonder, Days of Judgment* (1989), and Patricia U. Bonomi, *Under the Cope of Heaven: Religion, Society, and Politics in Colonial America* (1986). Some recent scholarship contends that Puritan practices complemented economic development: for example, John Frederick Martin, *Profits in the Wilderness* (1991), Stephen Innes, *Creating the Commonwealth* (1995), and Mark A. Peterson, *The Price of Redemption* (1997).

The disturbances in Salem Village are discussed in Paul Boyer and Stephen Nissenbaum, *Salem Possessed* (1974), while the subject is considered generally in John Demos, *Entertaining Satan: Witchcraft and the Culture of Early New England* (1982). For a chronicle of the episode in Salem, see Larry D. Gragg, *The Salem Witch Crisis* (1992). On women and witchcraft, see Elizabeth Reis, *Damned Women* (1997), Elaine G. Breslaw, *Tituba, Reluctant Witch of Salem* (1996), and Carol F. Karlsen, *The Devil in the Shape of a Woman* (1987).

For an engaging overview of the ideology of gender authority in the seventeenth century, see Mary Beth Norton, *Founding Mothers and Fathers* (1996). On women and religion in New England, see also Susan Juster, *Disorderly Women* (1994). Karin Wolf, *Not All Wives* (2000), describes the range of women's activities in Philadelphia. For the role of women in Virginia, see Kathleen M. Brown, *Good Wives, Nasty Wenches and Anxious Patriarchs* (1996).

Educational and intellectual developments are treated in Bernard Bailyn, *Education in the Forming of American Society* (1960), and Lawrence A. Cremin, *American Education: The Colonial Experience* (1970).

On the Middle Colonies, for New Jersey see Ned Landsman, *Scotland and Its First American Colony* (1985); for New York, Robert C. Ritchie, *The Duke's Province* (1977), Patricia U. Bonomi, *A Factious People: Politics and Society in Colonial New York* (1971); for Maryland, Lois Green Carr et al., *Robert Cole's World* (1991); and for Pennsylvania, Gary B. Nash, *Quakers and Politics* (1968).

For the interrelationship between settlers and Indians, consult Richard White, *The Middle Ground* (1991), John Demos, *The Unredeemed Captive* (1994), Daniel K. Richter, *Ordeal of the Longhouse* (1992), and Daniel H. Usner, *Indians, Settlers, and Slaves in a Frontier Exchange Economy* (1992).

CHAPTER 3 | AMERICA IN THE BRITISH EMPIRE

The fullest analysis of the British imperial system can be found in the early volumes of Lawrence H. Gipson's *British Empire Before the American Revolution* (1936–1968). See also James A. Henretta, *The Evolution of American Society* (1973), and Michael Kammen, *Empire and Interest* (1974). Jack P. Greene, *Peripheries and Center* (1989), describes how the colonists extended their control of political affairs.

On colonial trade and the mercantilist system, see John J. McCusker and Russell R. Menard, *The Economy of British America* (1985), and Peter J. Marshall, ed., *The Oxford History of the British Empire: The Eighteenth Century* (1998).

Useful interpretive surveys include Greene's *Pursuits of Happiness* (1988) and Jon Butler, *Becoming America: The Revolution Before 1776* (2000). Butler argues for a broad definition of religion, to include magic and popular practices in *Awash in a Sea of Faith* (1990).

On the Great Awakening, Richard Bushman, *From Puritan to Yankee* (1967) emphasizes psycho-social factors while Frank Lambert, *Inventing the 'Great Awakening'* (1999) focuses on the intersection of religion and economics. Catherine A. Brekus, *Strangers and Pilgrims: Female Preaching in America* (1998) addresses a long-neglected subject. See also Patricia U. Bonomi, *Under the Cope of Heaven: Religion, Society, and Politics in Colonial America* (1986). For the Enlightenment, see Henry F. May, *The Enlightenment in America* (1976). Fred Anderson, *The Crucible of War* (2000), is a readable and thorough narrative of the great war for the empire; see also his *A People's Army: Massachusetts Soldiers and Society in the Seven Years' War* (1984).

On the causes of the Revolution, see Pauline Maier, *From Resistance to Revolution* (1972), Edmund S. Morgan, *The Birth of the Republic* (1977), and Edward Countryman, *The American Revolution* (1985). Valuable local studies include Timothy H. Breen, *Tobacco Culture* (1985), on Virginia; Countryman's *A People in Revolution* (1989), on New York; and Thomas M. Doerflinger, *A Vigorous Spirit of Enterprise* (1986), on Philadelphia. Specific issues during the period are treated in Edmund S. and Helen M. Morgan, *The Stamp Act Crisis* (1953), John Shy, *Toward Lexington* (1965), and Alfred F. Young, *The Shoemaker and the Tea Party* (1999).

Bernard Bailyn's *The Ideological Origins of the American Revolution* (1967) and *The Origins of American Politics* (1968) are brilliant analyses of the political thinking and political structure of eighteenth-century America. Other seminal works include Gordon S. Wood, *The Radicalism of the American Revolution* (1992) and Edmund S. Morgan, *Inventing the People: The Rise of Popular Sovereignty in England and America* (1988). See also Pauline Maier, *The Old Revolutionaries* (1980).

The full story of Eunice Williams/Gannenstenhawi is brilliantly told in John Demos, *The Unredeemed Captive* (1994).

CHAPTER 4 | THE AMERICAN REVOLUTION

Good brief surveys of the Revolutionary years are Edward Countryman, *The American Revolution* (1985) and Edmund S. Morgan, *The Birth of the Republic* (1977). The best one-volume account of the war is Piers Mackesey, *The War for America, 1775–1783* (1964). See also Jack Greene, *Understanding the American Revolution* (1995). David Hackett Fischer's account of the Battle of Lexington and Concord in *Paul Revere's Ride* (1994) shows why the colonists won the war. See also John W. Shy, *A People Numerous and Armed* (1990).

Recent accounts of Washington, Jefferson, and John Adams include John E. Ferling, *Setting the World Ablaze* (2000), which provides a good overview of the roles of Washington, Jefferson, and John Adams. See also Joseph Ellis, *Founding Brothers: The Revolutionary Generation* (2000), and David McCullough's *John Adams* (2001).

On the broader context of the Revolution, see Lester Langley, *The Americas in the Age of Revolution, 1750–1850* (1996); Eliga Gould emphasizes the continuity in America of British political culture, *The Persistence of Empire* (2000).

On the Continental Congress and the Articles of Confederation, see Jackson T. Main, *The Sovereign States* (1973) and Jack N. Rakove, *The Beginnings of National Politics* (1979). Peter S. Onuf, *Statehood and Union* (1987), deals with the Northwest Ordinance. Eric Foner, *Tom Paine and Revolutionary America* (1976), is an excellent brief biography. James K. Martin makes a case for his subject in *Benedict Arnold, Revolutionary Hero* (1997).

The classic study of the Declaration of Independence is Carl L. Becker, *The Declaration of Independence* (1922); for a contemporary analysis see Pauline Maier, *American Scripture* (1997) and Jay Fliegelman, *Declaring Independence* (1993).

The early history of the state governments is covered in Willi P. Adams, *The First American Constitutions* (1980). Edward Countryman, *A People in Revolution* (1982), deals with conditions in New York; for Maryland, see Jean B. Lee, *The Price of Nationhood* (1994). The development of political and social ideas, before, during, and after the Revolution, is admirably described and analyzed in Gordon S. Wood, *The Creation of the American Republic* (1969) and *The Radicalism of the American Revolution* (1992).

The classic account of the social and economic effects of the Revolution is J. Franklin Jameson, *The American Revolution Considered as a Social Movement* (1926). Jackson T. Main, *The Social Structure of Revolutionary America* (1965), provides a general picture against which to evaluate the views of Jameson and his critics. See also Carla Pestana and Sharon V. Salinger, eds., *Inequality in Early America* (1999).

The effects of the Revolution on slavery are treated in Winthrop D. Jordan, *White over Black* (1968), and on the Indians, in Colin G. Calloway, *The American Revolution in Indian Country* (1995). For an account of Indians, debtors, and slaves in Virginia, see Woody Holton, *Forced Founders* (1999). Linda K. Kerber, *Women of the Republic* (1980), Mary B. Norton, *Liberty's Daughters* (1980), and Joy Day Buel and Richard Buel, *The Way of Duty* (1984) discuss the effects of the Revolution on women and the family.

On the diplomacy of the Revolution, see Jonathon R. Dull, *A Diplomatic History of the American Revolution* (1985). On the peace negotiations see Andrew Stockley, *Britain and France at the Birth of America* (2001).

CHAPTER 5 | THE FEDERALIST ERA: NATIONALISM TRIUMPHANT

For a good brief survey, see Reginald Horsman, *The New Republic* (2000). On the "critical period," the drafting of the Constitution, see Richard B. Morris, *The Forging of the Union* (1987), and Jackson T. Main, *Political Parties Before the Constitution* (1973). On economic development, see E. J. Ferguson, *The Power of the Purse* (1968) and Curtis P. Nettels, *The Emergence of a National Economy* (1962), which puts this subject in the broader perspective of the period 1775–1815. On the radical western movements, see David P. Szatmary, *Shays' Rebellion* (1980) and Thomas P. Slaughter, *The Whiskey Rebellion* (1986).

The political thinking of the period is discussed lucidly in Jack N. Rakove, *Original Meanings* (1996), Gordon S. Wood, *The Creation of the American Republic* (1969), and Richard Buel, Jr., *Securing the Revolution* (1972). A good general account of the convention is Clinton Rossiter,

1787: The Grand Convention (1966). For Madison's role, see Lance Banning, *The Sacred Fire of Liberty* (1995), Drew R. McCoy, *The Last of the Fathers* (1989), and Gary Rosen, *American Compact* (1999). On Hamilton see Karl-Friedrich Walling, *Republican Empire: Alexander Hamilton on War and Free Government* (1999); Richard Brookhiser's brief biography, *Alexander Hamilton, American* (1999), is sympathetic.

C. A. Beard, *An Economic Interpretation of the Constitution* (1913), caused a veritable revolution in the thinking of historians about the motives of the Founding Fathers, but later works have caused a major reaction away from the Beardian interpretation; see especially Forrest McDonald, *We the People* (1958). Robert A. Rutland, *The Ordeal of the Constitution* (1966), and Jackson T. Main, *The Antifederalists* (1961), are helpful in understanding the opposition to the Constitution, while the *Federalist Papers* of Hamilton, Madison, and Jay, available in many editions, are essential for the arguments of the supporters of the new government. For the Bill of Rights, consult Bernard Schwartz, *The Great Rights of Mankind* (1977).

On the organization of the federal government and the history of the Washington administration, see Carl Prince, *The Federalists and the Origins of the U.S. Civil Service* (1977), an administrative history, and Stanley Elkins and Eric McKitrick, *The Age of Federalism* (1993) and James Roger Sharp, *American Politics in the Early Republic* (1993), more detailed histories of the period. Washington's presidency is treated in detail in the later volumes of Douglas S. Freeman, *George Washington* (1948–1957); for a biography in a single volume, see Richard North Smith's *Patriarch* (1993).

On frontier life, see Laurel Thacher Ulrich, *A Midwife's Tale* (1990) and Alan Taylor, *William Cooper's Town* (1995).

For foreign affairs during the Washington Administration, see Alexander De Conde, *Entangling Alliance: Politics and Diplomacy Under George Washington* (1958), Harry Ammon, *The Genet Mission* (1973), two volumes by Samuel F. Bemis, *Jay's Treaty* (1923) and *Pinckney's Treaty* (1926), Alexander De Conde, *The Quasi-War* (1966), and William Stinchcombe, *The XYZ Affair* (1980).

On the Adams Administration, consult Stephen G. Kurtz, *The Presidency of John Adams* (1957); see also David McCullough, *John Adams* (2001). Paul Nagel's collective biography, *The Adams Women* (1987), provides a superb account of a remarkable family. For the Alien and Sedition Acts, see James M. Smith, *Freedom's Fetters* (1956) and Leonard W. Levy, *Freedom of the Press from Zenger to Jefferson* (1996).

For the political conflict between the coastal sections and the frontiersmen, see Jackson Turner Main, *The Antifederalists* (1961); for another view, see Saul Cornell, *The Other Founders* (1999).

Chapter 6 | Jeffersonian Democracy

No student interested in Jefferson's political and social philosophy should miss sampling his writings. A useful compilation is Merrill D. Peterson, ed., *Thomas Jefferson* (1984). Lance Banning, *The Jeffersonian Persuasion* (1978), is valuable, as are Joyce Appleby, *Capitalism and a New Social Order* (1984) and M. D. Peterson, *Thomas Jefferson and the New Nation* (1970). On the elusive character of Jefferson himself, see Joseph J. Ellis, *American Sphinx* (1997) and Annette Gordon-Reed, *Thomas Jefferson and Sally Hemings* (1997).

For the election of 1800, see Bernard A. Weisberger, *America Afire* (2000). Arnold Rogow, *Fatal Friendship* (1998), describes the relationship of Hamilton and Burr; Roger G. Kennedy, *Burr, Hamilton and Jefferson* (2000) considers the three central figures of the period.

For a general treatment of the Jeffersonian era, consult Marshall Smelser, *The Democratic Republic* (1968). On the parties of the era, see James Roger Sharp, *American Politics in the Early Republic* (1993) and Noble E. Cunningham, Jr., *The Jeffersonian Republicans in Power* (1963); an important monograph is Anthony F. C. Wallace, *Jefferson and the Indians* (1999); on the structure of Jefferson's administration, see Leonard D. White, *The Jeffersonians* (1951); and on Jefferson's management of the administration and of Congress, James S. Young, *The Washington Community* (1966).

Jefferson's battle with the judges can be followed in Richard E. Ellis, *The Jeffersonian Crisis* (1971). For *Marbury v. Madison,* see John A. Garraty, ed., *Quarrels That Have Shaped the Constitution* (1964), and Donald O. Dewey's more detailed *Marshall Versus Jefferson* (1970), as well as R. Kent Newmeyer, *John Marshall and the Heroic Age of the Supreme Court* (2001).

On the Louisiana Purchase, see Alexander De Conde, *The Affair of Louisiana* (1976), Harry Ammon, *James Monroe* (1971), and George Dangerfield, *Chancellor Robert R. Livingston* (1960).

An excellent general treatment of western exploration is contained in Robert A. Billington, *Westward Expansion* (1967). On Lewis and Clark, see Stephen E. Ambrose, *Undaunted Courage* (1996).

The best account of the neutral rights question is Bradford Perkins, *Prologue to War* (1961).

CHAPTER 7 | NATIONAL GROWING PAINS

On Madison, see Lance Banning, *Sacred Fire of Liberty* (1995) and Jack N. Rakove, *James Madison and the Creation of the American Republic* (2002). The best modern account of the causes and course of the War of 1812 is John C. A. Stagg, *Mr. Madison's War* (1983). Irving Brant, *James Madison: Commander-in-Chief* (1961), vigorously defends Madison's handling of the war. Jackson's part in the conflict is described in Robert V. Remini, *Andrew Jackson and the Course of American Empire* (1977). Richard Barbuto, *Niagara 1814: America Invades Canada* (2000) and David Curtis Skaggs and Larry L. Nelson, *The Sixty Years' War for the Great Lakes* (2001), provide accounts of the war in the North.

On the Treaty of Ghent, see Fred L. Engelman, *The Peace of Christmas Eve* (1962) and Bradford Perkins, *Castlereagh and Adams* (1964). For the decline of the Federalist party and the Hartford Convention, consult David H. Fischer, *The Revolution of American Conservatism* (1965), and James M. Banner, *To the Hartford Convention* (1981).

For the postwar diplomatic settlements and the Era of Good Feelings, see James Lewis, *The American Union and the Problem of Neighborhood: The United States and the Collapse of the Spanish Empire, 1783–1829* (1998), George Dangerfield, *The Era of Good Feelings* (1971), and on his famous doctrine, Ernest May, *The Making of the Monroe Doctrine* (1976).

On the economic issues of this period, see George R. Taylor, *The Transportation Revolution* (1958), Bray Hammond, *Banks and Politics in America from the Revolution to the Civil War* (1957), and Roy M. Robbins, *Our Landed Heritage* (1942).

Merrill D. Peterson, *The Great Triumvirate* (1987), is an interesting study of Clay, Calhoun, and Webster. Other biographies of statesmen of the period include Paul C. Nagel, *John Quincy Adams* (1997), Robert Remini, *Daniel Webster* (1997), Irving Bartlett, *John C. Calhoun* (1993), Maurice Baxter, *Henry Clay and the American System* (1995), and Chase C. Mooney, *William H. Crawford* (1974). On the Missouri Compromise, see Glover Moore, *The Missouri Controversy* (1953). See also Paul C. Nagel, *One Nation Indivisible* (1965).

Good studies of Native Americans include John Sugden, *Tecumseh* (1998), R. David Edmonds, *The Potawatomis* (1978), and Michael N. McConnell, *A Country Between: The Upper Ohio Valley and Its Peoples* (1992).

CHAPTER 8 | TOWARD A NATIONAL ECONOMY

On the consumer revolution, see especially Richard Bushman, *The Refinement of America* (1992). The most influential work on the market revolution is Charles Sellers's 1991 book by that title. See also Melvyn Stokes and Stephen Conway, eds., *The Market Revolution in America* (1996). Excellent accounts of the economic transformation at the regional or local level are found in Christopher Clark, *The Roots of Rural Capitalism: Western Massachusetts, 1780–1860* (1991) and John Mack Faragher, *Sugar Creek: Life on the Illinois Prairie* (1986).

On the industrial revolution in America, see Alfred D. Chandler, Jr., *The Visible Hand: The Managerial Revolution in American Business* (1977). On the role of inventors, see Carroll Pursell, *The Machine in America* (1995) and Barbara M. Tucker, *Samuel Slater and the Origins of the American Textile Industry* (1984).

The growth of cities in the Jacksonian era can be traced in Richard C. Wade, *The Urban Frontier* (1957), and Howard Chudacoff, *The Evolution of American Urban Society* (1981). Allen F. Davis and Mark Halle, eds., *The Peoples of Philadelphia* (1973), Sam Bass Warner, Jr., *The Private City: Philadelphia in Three Periods of Its Growth* (1968), Oscar Handlin, *Boston's Immigrants* (1968 ed.), and Peter R. Knights, *The Plain People of Boston* (1971), deal with individual cities.

On immigration and ethnicity, see Dale T. Knoble, *Paddy and the Republic* (1986), Jay P. Dolan, *Immigrant Church: New York's Irish and German Catholics* (1982), and, generally, Philip Taylor, *The Distant Mirror: European Migration to the United States* (1971), and Stephan Thernstrom, ed., *Harvard Encyclopedia of American Ethnic Groups* (1980).

On changes in the nature of work, consult Paul Johnson, *A Shopkeeper's Millennium* (1978), Sean Wilentz, *Chants Democratic* (1984), Bruce Laurie, *Artisans into Workers* (1989), Norman Ware, *The Industrial Worker* (1990), and Anthony F. C. Wallace, *Rockdale* (1978); on women in the early factories, see Mary Blewett, *Men, Women, and Work* (1988) and Thomas Dublin, *Women at Work* (1979). On the lengthening commute to work, see Sam Bass Warner, *The Private City: Philadelphia in Three Periods of Its Growth* (1968).

George Rodger Taylor's *Transportation Revolution* (1951) is the best introduction to the changes in transportation. Evan Cornog describes the origins and impact of the Erie Canal in *The Birth of Empire* (1988). On canal building, consult Ronald E. Shaw, *Canals for a Nation* (1990). Two works by Carter Goodrich, *Government Promotion of American Canals and Railroads* (1960) and *Canals and American Economic Development* (1961), describe the role of government aid in canal construction authoritatively.

On John Marshall, see G. Edward White, *The Marshall Court and Cultural Change* (1991), as well as the sources cited in previous chapters. The most important decisions of the Marshall court in this period are discussed in John A. Garraty, ed., *Quarrels That Have Shaped the Constitution* (1987), and R. Kent Newmyer, *The Supreme Court under Marshall and Taney* (1968).

CHAPTER 9 | JACKSONIAN DEMOCRACY

The nature of Jacksonian democracy was analyzed brilliantly by Alexis de Tocqueville, *Democracy in America* (1835–1840). A. M. Schlesinger, Jr., *The Age of Jackson* (1945), stresses the democratic character of Jacksonianism, a position that has been reworked and revived in Harry L. Watson, *Liberty and Power* (1990). On Jackson's presidency, see Robert V. Remini, *Andrew Jackson and the Course of American Freedom* (1981), and *Andrew Jackson and the Course of American Democracy* (1984). D. T. Miller, *Jacksonian Aristocracy* (1967), and two works by Edward Pessen, *Riches, Class and Power Before the Civil War* (1973) and *Jacksonian America* (1969), describe the growth and extent of economic and class distinctions. Lee Benson, *The Concept of Jacksonian Democracy* (1964), emphasizes the role of ethnic and religious differences in the political disputes of the era. Louis Masur's *1831, Year of Eclipse* (2001), provides an interesting perspective.

A number of contemporary commentaries by foreigners throw much light on Jacksonian democracy. See especially, in addition to Tocqueville, Frances Trollope, *Domestic Manners of the Americans* (1832), Michel Chevalier, *Society, Manners and Politics in the United States* (1961), Harriet Martineau, *Retrospect of Western Travel* (1838) and *Society in America* (1837), and Francis J. Grund, *Aristocracy in America* (1959).

On Jackson's administration of the government and the development of the spoils system, see Leonard D. White, *The Jacksonians* (1954), and Sidney H. Aronson, *Status and Kinship in the Higher Civil Service* (1964); on the development of parties, see Richard P. McCormick, *The Second American Party System* (1966). For an exhaustive analysis of the Whigs, attentive to local variations, see Michael Holt, *The Rise and Fall of the American Whig Party* (1999). A critical account of Jackson's Indian policy appears in Jill Norgren, *The Cherokee Cases* (1996); Robert Remini is more supportive in *Andrew Jackson and His Indian Wars* (2001).

The struggle with the Bank is discussed in Bray Hammond, *Banks and Politics in America from the Revolution to the Civil War* (1957), and John M. McFaul, *The Politics of Jacksonian Finance* (1972). Peter Temin, *The Jacksonian Economy* (1969), minimizes the effects of Jackson's policies on economic conditions. Temin also provides an interesting analysis of economic trends throughout the period.

On the nullification controversy, see Richard E. Ellis, *The Union at Risk* (1987), and William W. Freehling, *The Road to Disunion* (1990), which stresses the close relationship between the nullifiers and the slavery issue.

For the Van Buren administration, see John Niven, *Martin Van Buren* (1983), and Major L. Wilson, *The Presidency of Martin Van Buren* (1984). The election of 1840 is treated in Robert G. Gunderson, *The Log-Cabin Campaign* (1957), and the biographies of Clay and Webster.

CHAPTER 10 | THE MAKING OF MIDDLE-CLASS AMERICA

On Tocqueville and his views of America, see Alexis de Tocqueville, *Democracy in America,* Jacob P. Mayer, ed. (1966 edition); also Andre Jardin, *Alexis de Tocqueville* (1988). For an analysis of the middle class, see Stuart M. Blumin, *The Emergence of the Middle Class* (1989).

On the changing place of the family and the changes within it, see Mary P. Ryan, *Cradle of the Middle Class: The Family in Oneida, New York* (1981), Catherine E. Kelly, *In the New England Fashion: Reshaping Women's Lives in the Nineteenth Century* (1999), Nancy Cott, *The Bonds of Womanhood* (1977), and Carl Degler, *At Odds: Women and Family in America from the Revolution to the Present* (1980).

Fertility and the frontier is examined in Yasukichi Yasuba, *Birth Rates of the White Population in the U.S., 1800–1860* (1962), and John Modell, "Family and Fertility on the Indiana Frontier, 1820," in *American Quarterly* (1971). See also Mary Ryan's work, mentioned above.

The Second Great Awakening has been examined both as a religious and as a social phenomenon. Still useful is Whitney Cross, *The Burned-Over District* (1950), but see also Paul E. Johnson, *A Shopkeeper's Millennium* (1978). Kathryn Teresa Long, *The Revival of 1857–58* (1998) is useful for the later period.

For the origins of feminism, see Nancy Cott, *The Grounding of Modern Feminism* (1987), Ellen C. DuBois, *Feminism and Suffrage: The Emergence of an Independent Women's Movement in America, 1848–1869* (1978), and Linda K. Kerber, *No Constitutional Right to Be Ladies* (1998).

Scholars have recently been interested in the proliferation of unconventional popular ideas during these years. See David S. Reynolds, *Beneath the American Renaissance* (1988) and *Walt Whitman's America* (1995), and John M. Brooke, *The Refiner's Fire* (1994).

On utopianism generally, see Ronald G. Walters, *American Reformers, 1815–1860* (1978), and David B. Davis, ed., *Ante-Bellum Reform* (1967). Enormously influential is the work of a French philosopher, Michel Foucault, who argued in *Madness and Civilization* (1961) and other works that middle-class reforms are best understood as attempts to discipline and control workers and outcasts who might otherwise challenge middle-class hegemony. In this vein see David J. Rothman, *Age of the Asylum: Social Order and Disorder in the New Republic* (1971).

For the Shakers, see Stephen J. Stein, *The Shaker Experience in America* (1992). Richard Bushman, *Joseph Smith and the Beginnings of Mormonism* (1984), provides a good introduction to the subject. For a broader study see Leonard J. Arrington, *The Mormon Experience* (1992).

Accounts of the temperance movement include Barbara L. Epstein, *The Politics of Domesticity* (1981), and William J. Rorabaugh, *The Alcoholic Republic* (1979).

For a general study of the context of abolitionism, see David Grimsted, *American Mobbing, 1828–1861* (1998). For sharply contrasting views of the abolitionist movement, see Stanley Elkins, *Slavery* (1975), and Lewis Perry and Michael Fellman, eds., *Anti-Slavery Reconsidered* (1979). Women's role in the movement is discussed in Julie Roy Jeffrey, *The Great Silent Army of Abolitionism* (1998). The persistence of slavery in the North, a topic that is often overlooked, is examined in Joanne P. Melish, *Disowning Slavery* (1998). Biographical accounts include John L. Thomas, *The Liberator: William Lloyd Garrison* (1963), Gerda Lerner, *The Grimké Sisters from South Carolina* (1967), and Nathan Huggins, *Slave and Citizen: The Life of Frederick Douglass* (1980). On antiabolitionists, see Leonard L. Richards, *Gentlemen of Property and Standing* (1970).

Carolyn L. Karcher, *The First Woman in the Republic: A Cultural Biography of Lydia Maria Child* (1994), Charles Capper, *Margaret Fuller* (1992), Elizabeth Griffith, *In Her Own Rights: The Life of Elizabeth Cady Stanton* (1984), and Kathryn K. Sklar, *Catharine Beecher* (1973), are solid biographies of important women in the era.

CHAPTER 11 | A DEMOCRATIC CULTURE

Useful surveys of cultural and intellectual currents in this period are Daniel Boorstin, *The Americans: The National Experience* (1967), and Rush Welter, *The Mind of America, 1820–1860* (1975). See also Richard Hofstadter, *Anti-intellectualism in American Life* (1963), and Stow Persons, *The Decline of American Gentility* (1975), for a more critical assessment. Francis O. Mattheissen, *American Renaissance* (1941), remains valuable. David S. Reynolds, *Beneath the American Renaissance* (1988), concludes that the major literary figures were merely the most visible aspect of a widespread "subversive" imagination in the antebellum era. In *Carnival on the Page: Popular Print Media in Antebellum America* (2000), Isabelle Lehuu argues that a rowdy and "subversive" popular press was another manifestation of this subversive culture.

On transcendentalism, see Perry Miller, ed., *The American Transcendentalists* (1957). For Emerson, see Robert D. Richardson, *Emerson: The Mind on Fire* (1995). For a critical appraisal, see Quentin Anderson, *The Imperial Self* (1971).

On American literature, Van Wyck Brooks, *The Flowering of New England* (1936), remains a readable survey. Alfred Kazin, *On Native Grounds* (1942), is more critically disposed.

On the cultural life of the South, see Clement Eaton, *The Mind of the Old South* (1964), and Drew Faust, *A Sacred Circle* (1977). On education, see Lawrence A. Cremin, *American Education:*

The National Experience (1980), and C. F. Kaestle, *Pillars of the Republic* (1983). Michael B. Katz, *The Irony of Early School Reform* (1968), questions the motives of the reformers, while Diane Ravitch, *The Revisionists Revised* (1978), questions Katz. Carl F. Kaestle and Maris Vinovskis, *Education and Social Change* (1980), is excellent.

Popular culture is discussed in Carl Bode, *The American Lyceum* (1956) and *The Anatomy of Popular Culture* (1959), and Russell Lynes, *The Tastemakers* (1954). Ann Douglas, *The Feminization of American Culture* (1977), is excellent on the pervasiveness and impact of sentimental literature. Neil Harris, *The Artist in American Society* (1966), puts art in its social setting. See also Barbara Novak, *Nature and Culture: American Landscape Painting* (1980).

The standard sources for the history of American colleges remain Richard Hofstadter, *Academic Freedom in the Age of the College* (1955), and Fred Rudolph, *The American College and University* (1961). But see also David Allmendinger, *Paupers and Scholars* (1975), Ronald Story, *The Forging of an Aristocracy* (1980), and Colin Burke, *American Collegiate Populations* (1982).

Scientific activities are examined in George H. Daniels, *American Science in the Age of Jackson* (1968), William H. Goetzmann, *Exploration and Empire* (1967), William Stanton, *The Great United States Exploring Expedition* (1975), and A. Hunter Dupree, *Science in the Federal Government* (1957).

On Sojourner Truth, see Nell Irvin Painter, *Sojourner Truth* (1996) and, for her time with Mathias, Paul E. Johnson and Sean Wilentz, *Kingdom of Mathias* (1994).

CHAPTER 12 | EXPANSION AND SLAVERY

For the Tyler administration, see Robert J. Morgan, *A Whig Embattled: The Presidency under John Tyler* (1954); on the Whigs more generally, see Michael F. Holt, *The Rise and Fall of the American Whig Party* (1999), and Daniel Walker Howe, *The Political Culture of the American Whigs* (1979).

On diplomatic affairs, see P. A. Varg, *United States Foreign Relations: 1820–1860* (1979), and D. M. Pletcher, *The Diplomacy of Annexation: Texas, Oregon, and the Mexican War* (1973).

The new expansionism is discussed in Frederick Merk, *Manifest Destiny and Mission in American History* (1963) and *The Monroe Doctrine and American Expansionism* (1966). H. N. Smith, *Virgin Land* (1950), is also important for an understanding of this subject. The course of western development is treated in Ray Allen Billington and Martin Ridge, *The Far Western Frontier* (1982). Important recent studies of the California gold rush include Malcolm J. Rohrbough, *Days of Gold* (1997), and Susan Lee Johnson, *Roaring Camp: The Social World of the California Gold Rush* (2000). On the frontier see John D. Unruh, *The Plains Across* (1979), and Francis Parkman's classic account, *The Oregon Trail* (1849). On women and the frontier see John M. Farragher, *Women and Men on the Overland Trail* (1979) and Julie Roy Jeffrey, *Frontier Women* (1979).

For the election of 1844, see James C. N. Paul, *Rift in the Democracy* (1961). The standard biography of Polk is Charles G. Sellers's *James K. Polk* (1957–1966), but see also Paul H. Bergeron, *The Presidency of James K. Polk* (1987). N. A. Graebner, *Empire on the Pacific* (1955), is the fullest analysis of the factors influencing the Oregon boundary compromise.

On the Mexican War, see Robert W. Johannsen, *To the Halls of the Montezumas* (1987), and K. Jack Bauer, *The Mexican War* (1974). John H. Schroeder, *Mr. Polk's War* (1973), discusses American opposition to the conflict. See also Marshall De Bruhl, *Sword of San Jacinto* (1993), a biography of Sam Houston. On the treatment of Mexicans and blacks, see Robert F. Heize and Alan J. Almquist, *The Other Californians* (1971), and Rudolph M. Lapp, *Blacks in Gold Rush California* (1977).

For the Compromise of 1850, see David M. Potter, *The Impending Crisis, 1848–1861* (1976), and Holman Hamilton, *Prologue to Conflict* (1964). See also the biographies of Clay, Calhoun, and

Webster cited in earlier chapters, Robert W. Johannsen, *Stephen A. Douglas* (1973), Holman Hamilton, *Zachary Taylor* (1951), Avery O. Craven, *The Growth of Southern Nationalism* (1953), and Michael A. Morrison, *Slavery and the American West* (1997).

CHAPTER 13 | THE SECTIONS GO THEIR WAY

On slavery, see Kenneth M. Stampp, *The Peculiar Institution* (1956), Eugene D. Genovese, *Roll, Jordan, Roll* (1975), Herbert G. Gutman, *Black Family in Slavery and Freedom* (1976), Brenda Stevenson, *Life in Black and White* (1996), and Walter Johnson, *Soul by Soul: Life Inside the Antebellum Slave Market* (1999), which focuses on New Orleans.

Stanley Elkins's *Slavery* (1959) maintained that the institution infantilized slaves, an argument that provoked great controversy. Recent evidence of slave resistance is documented in John Hope Franklin and Loren Schweninger, *Runaway Slaves* (1999), David Robertson, *Denmark Vesey* (1999), and Douglas R. Egerton, *Gabriel's Rebellion* (1993). An earlier study is Eugene D. Genovese, *From Rebellion to Revolution* (1979).

Excellent regional studies include Peter Coclanis, *The Shadow of a Dream* (1989), for South Carolina, as well as Charles E. Joyner, *Down by the Riverside: A South Carolina Slave Community* (1984), and Ann Patton Malone, *Sweet Chariot: Slave Family and Household Structure in Nineteenth-Century Louisiana* (1992).

Among specialized volumes, Bertram Wyatt-Brown, *Southern Honor* (1982), and Ira Berlin, *Slaves Without Masters* (1975), are important. Richard C. Wade, *Slavery in the Cities* (1964), contends that urban life eroded slavery, while Robert Starobin, *Industrial Slavery in the Old South* (1970) found that the institution could be adapted to industrial purposes. Most local studies take an intermediate position; see, for example, Midori Takagi, *"Rearing Wolves to Our Own Destruction": Slavery in Richmond, Virginia, 1782–1865* (1999).

On the *Amistad* mutiny, see Howard Jones, *Mutiny on The* Amistad (1987).

Irish emigration is the subject of Tim Pat Coogan's expansive *Wherever Green Is Worn* (2000), and Edward Laxton, *The Famine Ships* (1997), as well as the scholarly collection edited by Arthur Gribben, *The Great Famine and the Irish Diaspora in America* (1999). J. Matthew Gallman, *Receiving Erin's Children* (2000) examines the arrival of Irish famine emigrants in Philadelphia. Although fewer sources on German emigration are available in English, see Marianne Wokeck, *Trade in Strangers* (1999).

On industrial developments, see H. J. Habbakuk, *American and British Technology in the Nineteenth Century* (1962), and Nathan Rosenberg, *Technology and American Economic Growth* (1972). George R. Taylor's *The Transportation Revolution* (1951) is outstanding on developments in commerce and communication. John F. Stover, *American Railroads* (1997), is a good survey. Among the specialized studies of railroad development see Sarah Gordon, *Passage to Union* (1997), which considers the political implications of railroad development.

On labor history, many of the books cited in the three previous chapters apply to this one as well. See also Raymond A. Mohl, *Poverty in New York* (1971), and Barbara M. Wertheimer, *We Were There* (1977). For workingmen's political activities, Edward Pessen's *Most Uncommon Jacksonians* (1967) remains valuable.

CHAPTER 14 | THE COMING OF THE CIVIL WAR

The events leading to the Civil War have been analyzed by dozens of historians. Allan Nevins provides the fullest and most magisterial treatment in his *The Ordeal of the Union* (1947) and *The Emergence of Lincoln* (1950). An excellent briefer summary is David M. Potter, *The Impending Crisis*

(1976). For recent perspectives, see Michael Holt's later chapters in *The Rise and Fall of the American Whig Party* (1999), Don E. Fehrenbacher, *Sectional Crisis and Southern Constitutionalism* (1995), Gabor S. Borritt, ed., *Why the Civil War Came* (1996), and Marshall De Rosa, *The Politics of Dissolution* (1998).

On slave resistance, see especially John Hope Franklin and Loren Schweninger, *Runaway Slaves* (1999), William Dusinberre, *Them Dark Days: Slavery in the American Rice Swamps* (1996), and Steven Weisenburger, *Modern Medea: A Family Story of Slavery and Child-Murder from the Old South* (1998).

On the enforcement of the Fugitive Slave Act, see Stanley W. Campbell, *The Slave Catchers* (1970), and Thomas D. Morris, *Free Men All: The Personal Liberty Laws* (1974). Everyone should read Harriet Beecher Stowe's *Uncle Tom's Cabin*. E. L. McKitrick, ed., *Slavery Defended* (1963), contains a typical southern review of *Uncle Tom's Cabin*. Joan Hedrick's *Harriet Beecher Stowe* (1994) is excellent.

For the foreign policy of the 1850s, see C. H. Brown, *Agents of Manifest Destiny* (1980), R. E. May, *The Southern Dream of a Caribbean Empire* (1974), and P. B. Wiley and Korogi Ichiro, *Yankees in the Land of the Gods* (1990). D. S. Spencer, *Louis Kossuth and Young America* (1977) is also worth reading.

On Stephen A. Douglas, see Robert W. Johannsen, *Stephen A. Douglas* (1973).

Sumner's role in the deepening crisis is brilliantly discussed in David H. Donald, *Charles Sumner and the Coming of the Civil War* (1960). Philip S. Klein, *President James Buchanan* (1962), is careful and judicious. See also Donald E. Fehrenbacher, *The Dred Scott Case* (1981).

For Lincoln's own good words, see Abraham Lincoln, *Selections* (2 vols., 1989). The best modern biographies of Lincoln are David H. Donald, *Lincoln* (1995), and Mark Neely, *The Last Best Hope on Earth* (1993). Lincoln's early struggles are thoughtfully examined in Douglas L. Wilson, *Honor's Voice: The Transformation of Abraham Lincoln* (1998). William E. Gienapp, *The Origins of the Republic Party* (1987), and Eric Foner, *Free Soil, Free Labor, Free Men* (1970), are excellent analyses of Republican ideas and policies.

Stephen B. Oates, *To Purge This Land with Blood* (1970), is a readable biography of John Brown.

CHAPTER 15 | THE WAR TO SAVE THE UNION

The best survey of the Civil War period is James M. McPherson, *Battle Cry of Freedom* (1988), but see also Russell F. Weigley, *A Great Civil War* (2000).

On the precipitating events of the war, see Maury Klein, *Days of Defiance: Sumter, Secession and the Coming of the Civil War* (1997), and Wallace Hettle, *The Peculiar Democracy: Southern Democrats in Peace and Civil War* (2001).

For Lincoln, in addition to books mentioned in previous chapters, see Philip Paludan, *The Presidency of Abraham Lincoln* (1994). Lincoln's dealings with the Radicals have been extensively investigated. Hans L. Trefousse, *The Radical Republicans: Lincoln's Vanguard for Racial Justice* (1969), which praises Lincoln's management of the Radicals and minimizes his differences with them, is a good summary, but see also Richard Franklin Bensel, *Yankee Leviathan: The Origins of Central State Authority in America* (1990), and Joel H. Silbey, *A Respectable Minority: The Democratic Party in the Civil War Era* (1977). Mark E. Neely, *The Fate of Liberty* (1991) examines Lincoln's position on civil liberties. Frank Klement, *The Limits of Dissent* (1998) focuses on Clement Vallandigham.

On economic issues, see Heather Cox Richardson, *The Greatest Nation on Earth: Republican Economy Policies during the Civil War* (1997), and Bray Hammond, *Sovereignty and an Empty Purse: Banks and Politics in the Civil War* (1970).

For the movement to make abolition a war aim and the reaction to it, see Michael Vorenberg, *Final Freedom* (2001), and James M. McPherson, *The Struggle for Equality* (1964).

On African Americans in the Union army, see Joseph T. Glatthaar, *Forged in Battle: The Civil War Alliance of Black Soldiers and White Officers* (1990); Peter Burchard, *One Gallant Rush* (1965), recounts the story of Robert Gould Shaw and the Massachusetts 54th. Ervin Jordan, *Black Confederates and Afro-Yankees in Civil War Virginia* (1995) considers a yet more complicated situation. See also Noralee Frankel, *Freedom's Women: Black Women and Families in Civil War Era Mississippi* (1999). See also Iver Bernstein, *The New York City Draft Riots* (1990).

For aspects of economic and social history, see Philip S. Paludan, *"A People's Contest": The Union at War* (1988), Paul W. Gates, *Agriculture and the Civil War* (1965), Anne C. Rose, *Victorian America and the Civil War* (1992), and Robert P. Sharkey, *Money, Class, and Party* (1959). For women and the war, see Drew Gilpin Faust, *Mothers of Invention* (1997), Judith Ann Giesberg, *Civil War Sisterhood: The U.S. Sanitary Commission and Women's Politics in Transition* (2000), and Laura Edwards, *Scarlett Doesn't Live Here Anymore* (2000). Elizabeth Young considers the literary heritage of women and the war in *Disarming the Nation: Women's Writing and the American Civil War* (1999).

For the Confederacy, see Gary W. Gallagher, *The Confederate War* (1997). See also his edited collection, *Lee the Soldier* (1996). Important biographies include William Cooper, *Jefferson Davis, American* (2000). See also Mark Grimsley and Brooks D. Simpson, eds., *Collapse of the Confederacy* (2001), and Steven V. Ash, *When the Yankees Came: Conflict and Chaos in the Occupied South* (1995).

Gerald F. Linderman, *Embattled Courage* (1988) argues that the soldiers on both sides grew disillusioned with the fighting; the persistence of the initial ideals is a theme in James McPherson, *What They Fought For, 1861–1865* (1994), and Reid Mitchell, *The Vacant Chair* (1993).

Among the biographies of Civil War generals, northern and southern, the following are especially noteworthy: Brooks D. Simpson, *Ulysses S. Grant: Triumph over Adversity, 1822–1865* (2000), Jean E. Smith, *Grant* (2001), William S. McFeely, *Grant* (1981), James I. Robertson, *Stonewall Jackson* (1997), Stephen W. Sears, *George B. McClellan* (1988), Stanley P. Hirshson, *The White Tecumseh: A Biography of William T. Sherman* (1997), James L. McDonough, *War so Terrible: Sherman and Atlanta* (1987), Douglass S. Freeman, *R. E. Lee* (1934–1935), and Chester G. Hearn, *Admiral David Glasgow Farragut* (1998).

The diplomacy of the Civil War period is covered in two works by Howard Jones, *Union in Peril* (1992), on British intervention, and *Abraham Lincoln and a New Birth of Freedom* (1999), on issues of slavery. See also John Taylor, *William Henry Seward* (1991).

John C. Waugh, *Reelecting Lincoln* (1997) considers the election of 1864. The assassination of Lincoln and its aftermath is the subject of Jay Winik, *April 1865: The Month That Saved America* (2001).

The legacy of the Civil War is thoughtfully examined in David W. Blight, *Race and Reunion: The Civil War in American Memory* (2001), and Tony Horwitz, *Confederates in the Attic: Dispatches from the Unfinished Civil War* (1998).

CHAPTER 16 | RECONSTRUCTION AND THE SOUTH

The finest of many excellent overviews of the Reconstruction era is Eric Foner's *Reconstruction: America's Unfinished Revolution* (1988). Joel Williamson, *The Crucible of Race* (1984), emphasizes the positive aspects of Reconstruction. For recent general studies, see Don E. Fehrenbacher, *The Slaveholding Republic* (2001), and Pamela Brandwein, *Reconstructing Reconstruction* (1999).

Lincoln's ideas about Reconstruction are analyzed in William C. Harris, *With Charity for All* (1997) and in many of the Lincoln volumes mentioned in earlier chapters. Hans Trefousse, *Andrew*

Johnson: A Biography (1989) is a balanced account. See also Brooks D. Simpson, *The Reconstruction Presidents* (2001).

Conditions in the South during Reconstruction are discussed in Edward Ayers, *The Promise of the New South* (1992). The Freedmen's Bureau is examined in Paul Cimbala, *Under the Guardianship of the Nation* (1997). See also Richard H. Abbott, *The Republican Party and the South* (1986), Michael Perman, *Reunion Without Compromise* (1973), H. N. Rabinowitz, *Race Relations in the Urban South* (1978), James L. Roark, *Masters Without Slaves* (1977), and Leon Litwack, *Been in the Storm Too Long* (1979). Daniel Stowell's *Rebuilding Zion* (1998) explores the religious dimensions of Reconstruction.

On the economic and social effects of Reconstruction, see G. D. Jaynes, *Branches Without Roots: Genesis of the Black Working Class* (1986), Roger L. Ransom and Richard Sutch, *One Kind of Freedom: The Economic Consequences of Emancipation* (1977), and Robert Higgs, *Competition and Coercion* (1977). The ambiguities of dependence and independence as they relate to racial and gender issues are explored in Laura F. Edwards, *Gendered Strife and Confusion* (1997), and Amy Dru Stanley, *From Bondage to Contract* (1998).

On Grant's presidency, see Jean Edwards Smith, *Grant* (2001), Geoffrey Perret, *Ulysses S. Grant* (1997), and W. S. McFeely, *Grant* (1981). On the Republican reform movement, see John G. Sproat, *"The Best Men": Liberal Reformers in the Gilded Age* (1968). For the disputed election of 1876 and the compromise following it, consult C. Vann Woodward, *Reunion and Reaction* (1951), and William Gillette, *Retreat from Reconstruction* (1980).

CHAPTER 17 | IN THE WAKE OF WAR

Recent historians of the West do not regard it as a frontier to be settled, but as a region where white settlers and Native American peoples converged, to the destruction of the latter's way of life. For the older view, see Frederick Jackson Turner's *The Frontier in American History* (1920), which has been updated in Raymond A. Billington and Martin Ridge, *Westward Expansion* (1982). For a summary of the newer interpretation, see Gregory H. Nobles, *American Frontiers* (1997). See also Patricia Nelson Limerick, *The Legacy of Conquest* (1987), and Richard White, *"It's Your Misfortune and None of My Own"* (1991).

On government policy and white attitudes toward Indians, see Robert F. Berkhofer, Jr., *The White Man's Indian* (1978), Robert Wooster, *The Military and U. S. Indian Policy* (1988), and Andrew C. Isenberg, *The Destruction of the Bison* (2000). See also John Sugden, *Tecumseh* (1998), Robert M. Utley, *The Lance and the Shield: The Life and Times of Sitting Bull* (1993), Margaret Coel, *Chief Left Hand* (1981), and Angie Debo, *Geronimo* (1976).

On race relations in the South, see Leon Litwack, *Trouble in Mind* (1998), Glenda E. Gilmore, *Gender and Jim Crow* (1996), Joel Williamson, *The Crucible of Race* (1984), C. Vann Woodward, *The Strange Career of Jim Crow* (1966), and Samuel Spencer, *Booker T. Washington* (1967). For a thoughtful study of the persistence of the black elite in Washington, D.C., see Jacqueline M. Moore, *Leading the Race* (1999). On immigration, see Ronald Takaki, *Strangers from a Different Shore: A History of Asian Americans* (1989), and John Higham, *Strangers in the Land* (1955).

Two superb recent studies have transformed our understanding of the California gold rush: Susan Lee Johnson, *Roaring Camp: The Social World of the California Gold Rush* (2000), and Malcolm J. Rohrbough, *Days of Gold: The California Gold Rush and the American Nation* (1997). Valuable books on the frontier include Elliott West, *Contested Plains: Indians, Goldseekers, and the Rush to Colorado* (1998), and Duane A. Smith, *Rocky Mountain Mining Camps* (1967).

For a compelling account of the development of transcontinental railroads see David Haward Bain, *Empire Express: Building the First Transcontinental Railroad* (1999). See also David

Lavender, *The Great Persuader* (1970), Albro Martin, *James J. Hill* (1976), and Robert G. Athearn, *Union Pacific Country* (1971).

CHAPTER 18 | AN INDUSTRIAL GIANT

Matthew Josephson's classic, *The Robber Barons* (1934), is highly critical but provocative. For a different perspective see John A. Garraty, *The New Commonwealth* (1968). Alfred D. Chandler, Jr., *The Visible Hand* (1977), emphasizes the role of managers in rationalizing the economy; his *Strategy and Structure* (1962) describes the expansion of the size and scope of industrial enterprises. Thomas C. Cochran, whose views are best summarized in *Frontiers of Change* (1981), shows how social and cultural factors impinged on economic rationalization. Recent scholars have developed this point further. John N. Ingham, for example, outlines the persistence of small, specialized firms in *Making Iron and Steel* (1991); Oliver Zunz emphasizes the importance of middle-level managers in *Making America Corporate* (1990). See also Chandler's *Railroads: The Nation's First Big Business* (1965), and Cochran's *Railroad Leaders* (1953). On the ways that technology transformed the way people understood daily life, see David E. Nye, *Electrifying America* (1990).

The nation's expansive economy in the 1990s sparked interest in the leading businessmen and inventors a century earlier: For a detailed study of the key investment figure, see Jean Strouse, *Morgan: American Financier* (1999). Other examples include Harold C. Livesay, *Andrew Carnegie and the Rise of Big Business* (2000); Michael P. Malone, *James J. Hill* (1996); Ron Chernow *Titan* (1998), on John D. Rockefeller and the oil industry; James A. Mackey, *Alexander Graham Bell: A Life* (1997); and Paul Israel, *Edison: A Life of Invention* (1998).

For the radical critics, see John L. Thomas, *Alternative Americas: Henry George, Edward Bellamy, Henry Demarest Lloyd* (1983).

On the growth of unions see David Montgomery, *Beyond Equality* (1967), Leon Fink, *Workingmen's Democracy: The Knights of Labor and American Politics* (1983), and Nick Salvatore, *Eugene V. Debs* (1982). Jo Ann Argersinger, *Making the Amalgamated* (1999) describes the relation of gender and ethnicity in the rise of the clothing workers' union in Baltimore. Robert E. Weird, *Knights Unhorsed* (2000) blames internal dissension for the Knights' rapid decline. Lawrence Blickman, *A Living Wage* (1997) insists that labor radicalism persisted even after unionized workers won steady wages. The important strikes and labor violence of the period are covered in David O. Stowell, *Streets, Railroads, and the Great Strike of 1877* (1999), Robert V. Bruce, *1877: Year of Violence* (1959), Paul Arvich, *The Haymarket Tragedy* (1984), Carl S. Smith, *Urban Disorder and the Shape of Belief* (1995), and Richard Schneirov, ed., *The Pullman Strike and the Crisis of the 1890s* (1999).

CHAPTER 19 | AMERICAN SOCIETY IN THE INDUSTRIAL AGE

Henry Adams, *The Education of Henry Adams* (1918), is a fascinating if highly personal view of the period, and James Bryce, *The American Commonwealth* (1888), while primarily a political analysis, contains a great deal of information about social conditions.

An enormous number of books deal with the social history of late nineteenth-century America. John A. Garraty, *The New Commonwealth* (1968), treats most of the subjects covered in this chapter; Arthur M. Schlesinger's classic study, *The Rise of the City* (1933), provides a wealth of information about social trends. Robert Wiebe's *The Search for Order* (1967) shows how corporate and administrative bureaucracies overspread the nation, while Alan Trachtenberg, *The Incorporation of America* (1982), considers the cultural implications of Wiebe's insight. See also Gunther Barth, *City People* (1980).

On middle-class life and culture, see John Kasson, *Rudeness and Civility* (1990), Karen Halttunen, *Confidence Men and Painted Women* (1982), Burton Bledstein, *The Culture of Professionalism* (1976), and Mark C. Carnes, *Secret Ritual and Manhood in Victorian America* (1989). Karen Lystra, *Searching the Heart* (1989), emphasizes the close character of marriage, and Peter Gay, *The Bourgeois Experience* (1984–1997), argues that the middle classes throughout the Western world were not prudes; the repressive hypothesis is outlined in Ronald Walter, *Primers for Prudery* (1974). On contraception see Janet F. Brodie, *Contraception and Abortion in Nineteenth-Century America* (1994). On the family generally, see Colleen McDannell, *The Christian Home in Victorian America* (1986), and Carl Degler, *At Odds* (1980). On issues of consumption see Daniel Horowitz, *The Morality of Spending* (1985), William Leach, *Land of Desire: Merchants, Power, and the Rise of a New American Culture* (1993), and Elaine S. Abelson, *When Ladies' Go A-Thieving* (1989).

On working-class culture, Keith Peiss, *Cheap Amusements: Working Women and Leisure in Turn-of-the-Century New York* (1983), and Roy Rosenzweig, *Eight Hours for What We Will* (1983) are excellent. Roy Rosenzweig and Elizabeth Blackmar provide an interesting account of cultural tensions between middle and working classes in *The Park and the People: A History of Central Park* (1992).

In *The Uprooted* (1951), a study that influenced a generation of scholars, Oscar Handlin argued that the alien culture of the American city shattered the immigrant's values and sense of self. For more recent studies along these lines, see Francis G. Couvares, *The Remaking of Pittsburgh: Class and Culture in an Industrializing City* (1984), Oliver Zunz, *The Changing Face of Inequality* (1982), and Alan Dawley, *Class and Community* (1976). Humbert S. Nelli, *Italians in Chicago* (1970), and Virginia Yans-McLaughlin, *Family and Community: Italian Immigrants in Buffalo* (1977), and especially John Bodnar, *The Transplanted* (1985), emphasize the resilience and persistence of immigrant values.

A brief interpretive history of urban development is Charles N. Glaab and A. Theodore Brown, *A History of Urban America* (1967). Kenneth T. Jackson, *Crabgrass Frontier* (1985), is a pioneering history of suburban development, and Jon C. Teaford, *The Unheralded Triumph* (1984), gives weight to the accomplishments of the cities as well as to their inadequacies. For the growing pains of American cities, consult Robert H. Bremmer, *From the Depths* (1956), Jacob Riis, *How the Other Half Lives* (1890), and Roy Lubove, *The Progressives and the Slums* (1962).

On the early development of intercollegiate sports, see Ronald A. Smith, *Sports and Freedom: The Rise of Big-Time College Athletics* (1988); on sports and modernization, see Melvin L. Adelman, *A Sporting Time* (1986), and Allen Guttmann, *From Ritual to Record* (1978). The response of religion to industrialism is discussed in Henry F. May, *Protestant Churches and Industrial America* (1949). For the settlement house movement, see Allen F. Davis, *Spearheads for Reform* (1967), Davis's *American Heroine* (1973), a life of Jane Addams, and two classic personal accounts, Jane Addams, *Twenty Years at Hull House* (1910), and Lillian Wald, *The House on Henry Street* (1915).

CHAPTER 20 | INTELLECTUAL AND CULTURAL TRENDS

All the surveys of American intellectual history deal extensively with this period. The modern classics include Louis Hartz, *The Liberal Tradition in America* (1955), Clinton Rossiter, *Conservatism in America* (1962), and Henry S. Commager, *The American Mind* (1950). John Patrick Diggins, *The Promise of Pragmatism* (1994), Jackson Lears, *No Place for Grace: Antimodernism and the Transformation of American Culture, 1880–1920* (1981), and Gail Bederman, *Manliness and Civilization* (1995) are also stimulating.

A recent interpretation of the Chautauqua movement is John E. Tapia, *Circuit Chautauqua* (1997). On journalism, see especially David Nasaw, *The Chief: The Life of William Randolph Hearst* (2000), and George Juergens, *Joseph Pulitzer and the* New York World (1966).

On higher education, see George Marsden, *The Soul of the American University* (1994), and Laurence R. Veysey, *The Emergence of the American University* (1965). Kim Townsend, *Manhood at Harvard* (1996), and William McNeill, *Hutchins' University* (1992), on the University of Chicago, are especially stimulating. Thorstein Veblen, *The Higher Learning in America* (1918), is full of provocative opinions.

Good introductions to law and the social sciences during this period include, respectively, Morton Horwitz, *The Transformation of American Law, 1870–1960* (1992), and Dorothy Ross, *The Origins of American Social Science* (1991). Richard Hofstadter, *Social Darwinism in American Thought* (1944), generated a host of books on the subject. See also Linda Simon, *Genuine Reality: A Life of William James* (1998). The Turner frontier thesis is examined in Wilbur R. Jacobs, *On Turner's Trail* (1994). For trends in educational theory, see Lawrence A. Cremin, *American Education: The Metropolitan Experience* (1988).

On women, see Rosalind Rosenberg, *Beyond Separate Spheres: Intellectual Roots of Modern Feminism* (1982), and Regina Morantz-Sanchez, *Sympathy and Science: Women Physicians in American Medicine* (1985).

On Twain, see Everett Emerson, *Mark Twain: A Literary Life* (1999); on Henry Adams during this period, Edward Chalfant, *Better in Darkness* (1994); on Henry James, Leon Edel, *Henry James* (1953–1962). Interesting studies of art and society include Kathleen Pyne, *Art and the Higher Life: Painting and Evolutionary Thought in Late Nineteenth-Century America* (1996) and Barbara Novak, *Nature and Culture* (1995).

CHAPTER 21 | POLITICS: NATIONAL, STATE, AND LOCAL

The political history of this period is covered in lively and controversial fashion in Matthew Josephson, *The Politicos* (1938), and more solidly and sympathetically in H. Wayne Morgan, *From Hayes to McKinley* (1969). Harold U. Faulkner, *Politics, Reform, and Expansion* (1959), treats the politics of the 1890s in some detail, while Samuel McSeveney, *The Politics of Depression: Political Behavior in the Northeast* (1972), and C. Vann Woodward, *Origins of the New South* (1951), are important regional studies. John A. Garraty, *The New Commonwealth* (1968), attempts to trace the changing character of the political system after 1877.

There are several superb analyses of the political system of the period written by men who studied it firsthand: James Bryce, *The American Commonwealth* (1888), and Woodrow Wilson, *Congressional Government* (1886). On the evolution of political parties, see Paul Kleppner, *The Third Electoral System, 1853–1892* (1979), and Michael E. McGerr, *The Decline of Popular Politics* (1986).

Jon C. Teaford, *The Unheralded Triumph: City Government* (1984), Ballard C. Campbell, *Representative Democracy* (1980), Richard J. Jensen, *The Winning of the Midwest* (1971), and Paul Kleppner, *The Cross of Culture* (1977), are important studies of the character of state and local politics.

The issues of postreconstruction politics are discussed in Gretchen Ritter, *Goldbugs and Greenbacks* (1977), Ross Evans Paulson, *Liberty, Equality and Justice: Civil Rights, Women's Rights and the Regulation of Business, 1865–1932* (1997), Irwin Unger, *The Greenback Era* (1964), Walter T. K. Nugent, *Money and American Society* (1968), Geoffrey Blodgett, *The Gentle Reformers* (1966), and Ari Hoogenboom, *Outlawing the Spoils* (1961).

Among biographies of political leaders, the following are especially worth consulting: Ari Hoogenboom, *Rutherford B. Hayes* (1995), Allan Peskin, *Garfield* (1999), Thomas C. Reeves, *Gentleman Boss: Chester A. Arthur* (1975), and H. Paul Jeffers, *An Honest President* (2000), on Cleveland; see also Allan Nevins, *Grover Cleveland* (1932), Homer E. Socolovsky and Allan B. Spetter, *The*

Presidency of Benjamin Harrison (1987), H. Wayne Morgan, *William McKinley and His America* (1963), and Stephen D. Kantrowitz, *Ben Tillman and the Reconstruction of White Supremacy* (2000).

Populism has been the subject of intensive study. Richard Hofstadter, *The Age of Reform* (1955), takes a dim view of populism as a reform movement; Lawrence Goodwyn, *Democratic Promise: The Populist Movement in America* (1976), calls it "a people's movement of mass democratic aspiration." Elizabeth Sanders, *Roots of Reform* (1999), champions the farmers' political efforts, a position amplified by Gene Clanton, *Congressional Populism and the Crisis of the 1890s* (1998). Peter Argersinger, *The Limits of Agrarian Radicalism: Western Populism and American Politics* (1995), Sheldon Hackney, *Populism to Progressivism in Alabama* (1969), and Steven Hahn, *The Roots of Southern Populism* (1983), are more than local studies. Michael Kazin, *The Populist Persuasion* (1994), insists on the enduring legacy of the movement.

On the depression of the 1890s, consult Charles Hoffman, *The Depression of the Nineties* (1970), Carlos Schwantes, *Coxey's Army* (1985), Stanley Buder, *Pullman* (1967), and Nick Salvatore, *Eugene V. Debs* (1982). On Bryan and the election of 1896, see Paul E. Glad, *The Trumpet Soundeth* (1960), Robert W. Cherny, *A Righteous Cause: William Jennings Bryan* (1985), Stanley L. Jones, *The Presidential Election of 1896* (1964), and Robert F. Durden, *The Climax of Populism* (1965).

CHAPTER 22 | THE AGE OF REFORM

The Progressive era is surveyed in Arthur S. Link, *Woodrow Wilson and the Progressive Era* (1954), Steven J. Diner, *A Very Different Age* (1997), and Daniel T. Rodgers, *Atlantic Crossings: Social Politics in a Progressive Age* (1998). Important interpretations of progressivism include Richard Hofstadter, *The Age of Reform* (1955), Gabriel Kolko, *The Triumph of Conservatism* (1963), and John M. Cooper, Jr., *The Warrior and the Priest: Theodore Roosevelt and Woodrow Wilson* (1983).

The role of muckraking journalism is considered in David M. Chalmers, *The Social and Political Ideas of the Muckrakers* (1964), and Peter Lyon, *Success Story: The Life and Times of S. S. McClure* (1963).

On workers and the radical intellectuals, see Leon Fink, *Progressive Intellectuals and the Dilemmas of Democratic Commitment* (1997), Leslie Fishbein, *Rebels in Bohemia* (1982), Thomas Bender, *New York Intellectuals* (1987), Henry F. May, *The End of American Innocence* (1964), and Nathan G. Hale, *Freud and the Americans* (1971).

Studies of the South include Dewey W. Grantham, *The South in Modern America* (1994), and George B. Tindall, *The Emergence of the New South* (1967). For particular states, consult, for Wisconsin, Nancy Unger, *Fighting Bob La Follette* (2000), and Bernard A. Weisberger, *The La Follettes of Wisconsin* (1994); also Hoyt L. Warner, *Progressivism in Ohio* (1964), Sheldon Hackney, *Populism to Progressivism in Alabama* (1969), and Zane L. Miller, *Boss Cox's Cincinnati* (1968). See also John D. Buenker, *Urban Liberalism and Progressive Reform* (1973). Kenneth Finegold, *Experts and Politicians* (1995), compares the struggles between urban machines and reformers in New York, Cleveland, and Chicago. James J. Connolly, *The Triumph of Ethnic Progressivism* (1998), examines the political dynamics in Boston. J. Anthony Lukas, *Big Trouble* (1997), provides a detailed account of labor strife in Idaho and Colorado.

On the woman suffrage campaign, see Ellen Carol DuBois, *Harriot Stanton Blanch and the Winning of Woman Suffrage* (1997), and Gayle Gullett, *Becoming Citizens: The Emergence and Development of the California Women's Movement, 1880–1911* (2000). Other useful works include Lynn D. Gordon, *Gender and Higher Education in the Progressive Era* (1990), Robyn Muncy, *Creating a*

Female Dominion in American Reform, 1890–1935 (1991), and Paula Baker, *The Moral Frameworks of Public Life: Gender, Politics and the State in Rural New York, 1870–1930* (1991).

Books treating special aspects of progressivism include Edward A. Purcell, *Brandeis and the Progressive Constitution* (2000), and Samuel Haber, *Efficiency and Uplift* (1964). On the regulation of business, see Tony Freyer, *Regulating Big Business: Antitrust in Great Britain and America, 1880–1990* (1992), James Weinstein, *The Corporate Ideal and the Liberal State* (1981), Albro Martin, *Enterprise Denied: Origins of the Decline of American Railroads* (1971), and Naomi Lamoreaux, *The Great Merger Movement in American Business, 1895–1940* (1985).

On blacks, see David Levering Lewis, *W. E. B. DuBois: Biography of a Race, 1868–1919* (1993), and W. E. B. DuBois, *The Fight for Equality* (1919–1963), Charles F. Kellogg, *NAACP: A History of the National Association for the Advancement of Colored People* (1970), and Jack T. Kirby, *Darkness at the Dawning: Race and Reform in the Progressive South* (1972). On the treatment of Indians, consult Frederick E. Hoxie, *A Final Promise: The Campaign to Assimilate the Indians* (1984).

H. W. Brands, *TR* (1997), and William H. Harbaugh, *Power and Responsibility* (1961) provide sound, scholarly treatments of Roosevelt's career. Edmund Morris's *Theodore Rex* (2001) is a more engaging account.

On Taft, see Donald F. Anderson, *William Howard Taft: A Conservative's Conception of the Presidency* (1973), and Paolo E. Coletta, *The Presidency of William Howard Taft* (1973). The Republican party breakup and the history of the Progressive party are discussed in John A. Garraty, *Right-hand Man: The Life of George W. Perkins* (1960).

The standard biography of Wilson is Arthur S. Link, *Wilson* (1947–1965). See also August Heckscher, *Woodrow Wilson* (1991), and John A. Garraty, *Woodrow Wilson* (1956).

CHAPTER 23 | FROM ISOLATION TO EMPIRE

Contemporary attitudes are reflected in Josiah Strong, *Our Country* (1885), and Alfred T. Mahan, *The Influence of Sea Power Upon History* (1890), which provides the clearest presentation of Mahan's thesis.

For post–Civil War diplomatic history, see Milton Plesur, *America's Outward Thrust* (1971), and John A. S. Grenville and George B. Young, *Politics, Strategy, and American Diplomacy: Studies in Foreign Policy* (1966). Walter LaFeber, *The New Empire* (1963), presents a forceful but somewhat overstated argument on the extent of expansionist sentiment, especially on the part of American businessmen. Emily S. Rosenberg, *Financial Missionaries to the World: The Politics and Culture of Dollar Diplomacy, 1900–1930* (1999), shows how cultural and economic forces intersected to promote expansionism.

On Hawaiian annexation, see Merze Tate, *The United States and the Hawaiian Kingdom* (1965). On the Spanish-American War, see John L. Offner, *An Unwanted War: The Diplomacy of the United States and Spain over Cuba, 1895–1898* (1992).

On imperialism, see Thomas D. Schoonover, *The United States in Central America* (1991), David Healy, *U.S. Expansionism: The Imperialist Urge in the 1890's* (1970), and William A. Williams, *The Tragedy of American Diplomacy* (1962). Robert L. Beisner, *Twelve Against Empire: The Anti-imperialists* (1968), contains lively and thoughtful sketches of leading foes of expansion. See also E. Berkeley Tompkins, *Anti-imperialism in the United States* (1970). For colonial problems in the Philippines, see Stuart Creighton Miller, *"Benevolent Assimilation": The American Conquest of the Philippines, 1899–1903* (1982), and H. W. Brands, *Bound to Empire: The United States and the Philippines* (1992). On the Caribbean, see Thomas O'Brien, *The Revolutionary Mission: American Enterprise in Latin*

America, 1900–1945 (1996). David McCullough, *The Path Between the Seas* (1977), is excellent on the history of the Panama Canal.

CHAPTER 24 | WOODROW WILSON AND THE GREAT WAR

For American entry into the Great War, see Ernest R. May, *The World War and American Isolation* (1959), and Edward H. Buehrig, *Woodrow Wilson and the Balance of Power* (1955).

The war on the home front is covered in David M. Kennedy, *Over Here: The First World War and American Society* (1980). Paul A. C. Koistinen, *Mobilizing for Modern War* (1997), examines the emergence of business and military ties during the war. Other useful volumes include Robert D. Cuff, *The War Industries Board* (1973); Stephen L. Vaughn, *Holding Fast the Inner Lines* (1980), which deals with the Committee on Public Information; Donald Johnson, *The Challenge to American Freedoms* (1963); and David Brody, *Steelworkers in America* (1960).

On American military participation, Laurence Stallings, *The Doughboys* (1963), is a good popular account of the American army in France. See also Frank E. Vandiver, *Black Jack: The Life and Times of John J. Pershing* (1977). On blacks in the army, see Arthur E. Barbeau and Florette Henri, *The Unknown Soldiers* (1974). Women's role with the AEF is examined in Susan Zeiger, *In Uncle Sam's Service* (1999).

On the peace settlement, in addition to the biographies of Wilson, consult Thomas J. Knock, *The War to End All Wars: Woodrow Wilson and the Quest for a New World Order* (1992); Arno J. Mayer, *Politics and Diplomacy of Peacemaking* (1967); John M. Cooper, *Breaking the Heart of the World* (2001), focusing on Wilson; John A. Garraty, *Henry Cabot Lodge* (1953); and Ralph Stone, *The Irreconcilables* (1970).

On labor, see David Montgomery, *The Fall of the House of Labor: The Workplace, the State, and American Labor Activism, 1865–1921* (1987). For a detailed study of organized labor in the South, see Bryant Simon, *A Fabric of Defeat* (1998). Kathleen Kennedy, *Disloyal Mothers and Scurrilous Citizens* (1999), examines the intersection of war, gender, and free speech. On radicalism and the red scare, see Robert K. Murray, *The Red Scare* (1955), Stanley Cohen, *A. Mitchell Palmer* (1963), David Brody, *The Steel Strike of 1919* (1965), and E. Anthony Lukas, *Big Trouble* (1997), on labor disturbances in the Far West. On the election of 1920, see Wesley Bagby, *The Road to Normalcy* (1962), Burl Noggle, *Into the Twenties* (1974), and Robert K. Murray, *The Harding Era* (1969). Gina Kolata, a science writer, provides a gripping account of the struggle against disease in *Flu: The Story of the Great Influenza Pandemic of 1918 and the Search for the Virus That Caused It* (1999).

Wilson's handling of foreign relations is discussed in several volumes by Arthur S. Link: *Woodrow Wilson and the Progressive Era* (1954), and *Wilson the Diplomatist* (1957). See also N. Gordon Levin, Jr., *Woodrow Wilson and World Politics* (1968), Lloyd Ambrosius, *Woodrow Wilson and the American Diplomatic Tradition* (1987), and Manfred Jonas, *The United States and Germany* (1984). Latin American affairs under Wilson are treated in Dana G. Munro, *Intervention and Dollar Diplomacy in the Caribbean* (1964).

CHAPTER 25 | POSTWAR SOCIETY AND CULTURE: CHANGE AND ADJUSTMENT

Frederick Lewis Allen, *Only Yesterday* (1931), a classic, disapproved of the gaudy materialism of the 1920s and concluded that its frenetic amusements were symptomatic of a belief that "life was futile and nothing much mattered." William E. Leuchtenburg, *The Perils of Prosperity* (1958) argued that there was much more to the decade than "raccoon coats and bathtub gin," and that important questions were addressed though not resolved. Ann Douglas, *Terrible Honesty: Mongrel Manhattan in the 1920s* (1995), emphasizes the positive aspects of urban life, and Stanley Coben, *Rebellion Against Victorianism* (1991), emphasizes its elements of change. David Goldberg's survey, *Discontented America* (1999), focuses on divisions of race, ethnicity, and class. See also the volumes mentioned in previous chapters.

Leftist scholars have indicted the developments in advertising and consumerism as part of a "cultural hegemony" that sustained corporate profits; see Roland Marchand, *Advertising the American Dream* (1985), T. J. Jackson Lears, *Fables of Abundance: A Cultural History of Advertising* (1994), and Stewart Ewen, *Captains of Consciousness* (1976). That consumption could enrich the human experience is the theme of Warren I. Susman, *Culture as History: The Transformation of American Society in the Twentieth Century* (1984). Ted Ownby, *American Dreams in Mississippi* (1999), considers the positive elements of such beliefs on the South. On the rise of consumer credit, see Lendol Calder, *Financing the American Dream* (1999).

Nativism and immigration restriction are covered in Desmond King, *Making Americans* (2000), and John Higham, *Strangers in the Land* (1955). On changes in the family, see Steven Mintz and Susan Kellogg, *Domestic Revolutions* (1988); on other social trends, John D'Emilio and Estelle Freedman, *Intimate Matters* (1988), George Chauncey, *Gay New York* (1994), and Paula Fass, *The Damned and the Beautiful* (1977).

The "new" woman is discussed in Nancy F. Cott, *The Grounding of Modern Feminism* (1987); William Chafe, *The American Woman* (1972); Ellen Chesler, *Woman of Valor* (1992), on Margaret Sanger and the birth control movement; Dorothy M. Brown, *Setting a Course: American Women in the 1920s* (1987); and Nancy Woloch, *Women and the American Experience* (1971). Women workers are dealt with in Winifred D. Wandersee, *Women's Work and Family Values* (1981).

On popular culture, see Steven J. Ross, *Working-Class Hollywood: Silent Film and the Shaping of Class in America* (1998), Robert Sklar, *Movie-Made America* (1976), Susan J. Douglas, *Inventing American Broadcasting* (1987), and Philip T. Rosen, *The Modern Stentors: Radio Broadcasting and the Federal Government* (1980).

Fundamentalism is treated in Joel A. Carpenter, *Revive Us Again: The Reawakening of American Fundamentalism* (1997); the Scopes trial in Edward J. Larson, *Summer for the Gods: The Scopes Trial and America's Continuing Debate over Science and Religion* (1997), and Paul Conkin, *When All the Gods Trembled* (1998). On prohibition see Andrew Sinclair, *Prohibition: The Era of Excess* (1962), and Stanley Walker, *The Night Club Era* (1999), which focuses on New York. On the Klan, consult Nancy MacLean, *Behind the Mask of Chivalry: The Making of the Second Ku Klux Klan* (1994), Jim Ruiz, *The Black Hood of the Ku Klux Klan* (1998), Kathleen Blee, *Women of the Klan* (1991), and Richard K. Tucker, *The Dragon and the Cross: The Rise and Fall of the Ku Klux Klan in Middle America* (1991).

Francis Russell, *Tragedy in Dedham* (1962), casts doubt on the innocence of Sacco and Vanzetti; see also Paul Avrich, *Sacco and Vanzetti: The Anarchist Background* (1991).

On blacks in Harlem, see Gilbert Osofsky, *Harlem: The Making of a Ghetto* (1965). The Harlem Renaissance is the subject of Steven Watson, *The Harlem Renaissance* (1995), and J. Martin Favor, *Authentic Blackness* (1999).

The literature of the period is analyzed in Alfred Kazin, *On Native Grounds* (1942), Malcolm Cowley, *Exiles Return* (1934), and Edmund Wilson, *The Twenties* (1975). See Jeffrey Meyers, *Scott Fitzgerald: A Biography* (1994) and also his *Hemingway: A Biography* (1999); also Carlos H. Baker,

Hemingway (1956); on Mencken, William R. Manchester, *Disturber of the Peace* (1951); on Lewis, Mark Schorer, *Sinclair Lewis* (1961); on Wharton, R. W. B. Lewis, *Edith Wharton* (1975), and Shari Benstock, *No Gifts from Chance* (1994). On the popularization of literature, see Joan Shelley Rubin, *The Making of Middlebrow Culture* (1992).

On Henry Ford, see Allan Nevins and Frank E. Hill, *Ford* (1954–1957). Clarence Hooker, *Life in the Shadows of the Crystal Palace 1910–1927* (1997), illuminates the role of labor at Ford. John Bell Rae, *The American Automobile Industry* (1984), and James J. Flink, *The Car Culture* (1975), contain interesting material. On women and cars, see Virginia Scharff, *Taking the Wheel* (1991). Beth Bailey, *From Front Porch to Back Seat* (1988), considers the ramifications of the automobile on courtship.

Chapter 26 | The New Era, 1921–1933

The political history of the 1920s is surveyed in Robert K. Murray, *The Politics of Normalcy* (1973), Ellis W. Hawley, *The Great War and the Search for a Modern Order* (1979), Michael Parrish, *Anxious Decades: America in Prosperity and Depression, 1920–1941* (1992), and Geoffrey Parret, *America in the Twenties* (1982).

On the labor history of the postwar decade, see Robert H. Zieger, *Republicans and Labor* (1969). The best brief biography of Harding is Andrew Sinclair, *The Available Man* (1965). Robert Ferrell, *The Presidency of Calvin Coolidge* (1998), is the best study of Coolidge in the White House. On Hoover, see Martin L. Fausold, *The Presidency of Herbert Hoover* (1985), and a narrower monograph, Kendrick A. Clements, *Hoover, Conservatives and Consumerism* (2000).

David Burner, *The Politics of Provincialism* (1968), deals with the Democratic party in the 1920s. On the trade association movement, see Robert F. Himmelberg, *The Origins of the National Recovery Act* (1976).

Diplomatic developments are summarized in Selig Adler, *The Uncertain Giant* (1965); Akira Iriye, *After Imperialism* (1965) and *Across the Pacific* (1967); Stephen Kneeshaw, *The Pursuit of Peace* (1991), on the Kellogg-Briand Pact; Thomas H. Buckley, *The United States and the Washington Conference* (1970); Charles De Benedetti, *Origins of the Modern Peace Movement* (1978); and John H. Wilson, *American Business and Foreign Policy* (1971).

On farm problems, see John D. Hicks, *Twentieth-Century Populism* (1951), and Gilbert C. Fite, *George N. Peek and the Fight for Farm Parity* (1954).

On the election of 1928, see Oscar Handlin, *Al Smith and His America* (1958).

On isolationism, see Robert A. Divine, *The Reluctant Belligerent* (1965) and *The Illusion of Neutrality* (1962). On Latin American relations, see Irwin F. Gellman, *Good Neighbor Diplomacy* (1979).

For the stock market crash, see Robert Sobel, *The Great Bull Market* (1968), and John Kenneth Galbraith, *The Great Crash* (1961). Lester V. Chandler, *America's Greatest Depression* (1970), is a good introduction to the economic problems of the period, but see also Michael A. Bernstein, *The Great Depression* (1987), and John A. Garraty, *The Great Depression* (1986), which puts American developments in world perspective.

Chapter 27 | The New Deal, 1933–1941

The best recent survey of the era is David M. Kennedy, *Freedom From Fear: The American People in Depression and War* (1999). A brief but balanced portrayal of the New Deal is William E. Leuchtenburg, *Franklin D. Roosevelt and the New Deal* (1963). Arthur M. Schlesinger, Jr., *The Age of*

Roosevelt (1957–1960) is a lively and sympathetic narrative. Analytical studies include Maxwell Bloomfield, *Peaceful Revolution* (2000), Ronald Edsforth, *The New Deal* (2000), Alan Brinkley, *Liberalism and Its Discontents* (1998), and Mark Leff, *The Limits of Symbolic Reform* (1984).

Of the many biographies of Roosevelt, see especially Frank Freidel, *Franklin D. Roosevelt* (1952–1973), and James M. Burns, *Roosevelt: The Lion and the Fox* (1956). On Eleanor Roosevelt, see Blanche W. Cook, *Eleanor Roosevelt* (1992–1999), and Lois Scharf, *Eleanor Roosevelt: First Lady of American Liberalism* (1987).

On the Brains Trust, see Elliot A. Rosen, *Hoover, Roosevelt, and the Brains Trust* (1977).

For regional studies, see Bruce Shulman, *From Cotton Belt to Sunbelt* (1991), Charles H. Trout, *Boston, the Great Depression, and the New Deal* (1977), and Richard Lowitt, *The New Deal in the West* (1984).

On the New Deal and agriculture, see *From New Day to New Deal: American Farm Policy from Hoover to Roosevelt, 1928–1933* (1991); on the problems of the Dust Bowl, see James N. Gregory, *American Exodus: The Dust Bowl Migration and Okie Culture in California* (1989).

On the New Deal and business, see Ellis W. Hawley, *The New Deal and the Problem of Monopoly* (1966), Morton Keller, *Regulating the New Economy: Public Policy and Economic Change in America* (1990), and *Regulating a New Society: Public Policy and Social Change in America, 1900–1933* (1994).

On workers and the New Deal, see Edwin Amenta, *Bold Relief: Institutional Politics and the Origins of Modern Social Policy* (1998), Gery Gerstle, *Working-Class Americanism: The Politics of Labor in a Textile City, 1914–1960* (1989), Vicki Ruiz, *Cannery Women, Cannery Lives: Mexican Women, Unionization, and the California Food Processing Industry, 1930–1950* (1987), Lizabeth Cohen, *Making a New Deal: Industrial Workers in Chicago, 1919–1939* (1990), and Melvyn Dubofsky, *The State and Labor in Modern America* (1994).

On constitutional questions, see William E. Leuchtenburg, *The Supreme Court Reborn: The Constitutional Revolution in the Age of Roosevelt* (1995), and Paul L. Murphy, *The Constitution in Crisis Times* (1972).

For the activities of the radical fringe, consult Michael Denning, *The Cultural Front: The Laboring of American Culture in the Twentieth Century* (1996), Donald R. McCoy, *Angry Voices: Left-of-Center Politics in the New Deal Era* (1958), and David H. Bennett, *Demagogues in the Depression* (1969).

On women and gender, apart from the works cited above, see Suzanne Mettler, *Dividing Citizens* (1998), Landon Storrs, *Civilizing Capitalism* (2000), Susan Ware, *Beyond Suffrage: Women in the New Deal* (1981), and *Partner and I* (1987), a life of Molly Dewson. Also Linda Gordon, *Pitied But Not Entitled: Single Mothers and the History of Welfare* (1994), and Susan Ware, *Holding Their Own: American Women in the 1930s* (1982). On New Deal Indian policy, see Kenneth R. Philip, *John Collier's Crusade for Indian Reform* (1977). A chronologically broader but perceptive study is Kenneth R. Philip, *Termination Revisited: American Indians on the Trail to Self-Determination, 1933–1953* (1999).

A provocative analysis of modern art and the New Deal appears in Michael Szalay, *New Deal Modernism* (2000).

On isolationism and the events leading to Pearl Harbor, see Robert A. Divine, *The Reluctant Belligerent* (1965), brief but comprehensive, and *The Illusion of Neutrality* (1962), T. R. Fehrenbach, *F. D. R.'s Undeclared War* (1967), Wayne S. Cole, *Roosevelt and the Isolationists* (1983), and Warren F. Kimball, *The Most Unsordid Act* (1969), on lend-lease.

CHAPTER 28 | WAR AND PEACE

On prewar American–Japanese relations, see Akira Iriye, *After Imperialism* (1965). The best history of the worldwide events leading to the Japanese attack on Pearl Harbor is Waldo Heinrichs, *Threshold of War* (1988), but for more detail see Gordon W. Prange, *At Dawn We Slept* (1981), and Michael S. Stackman, *Target: Pearl Harbor* (1990). Useful overviews include David M. Kennedy, *Freedom from Fear: The American People in Depression and War* (1999), Murray Williamson and Allan R. Millett, *A War to Be Won* (2000), and Warren F. Kimball, *Forged in War: Roosevelt, Churchill and the Second World War* (1997). Mark A. Stoler, *Allies and Adversaries* (2000) focuses on the Joint Chiefs of Staff. Thomas S. Fleming, *The New Dealers' War* (2001), is critical of Roosevelt. See also Michael S. Sherry, *The Rise of American Airpower* (1987).

A recent, sober assessment of Pearl Harbor is Akira Iriye, *Pearl Harbor and the Coming of the Pacific War* (1999). On aerial warfare, see Williamson Murray, *War in the Air, 1914–1945* (1999), and Geoffrey Peret, *Winged Victory* (1993). Paul Fussell, *Wartime: Understanding and Behavior in the Second World War* (1989), provides a realistic rendering of the carnage and chaos of modern warfare. The term *the greatest generation* is from Tom Brokaw's 1998 book by that title.

For a general, brief overview of the home front, see Lewis A. Erenberg and Susan E. Hirsch, *The War in American Culture: Society and Consciousness During World War II* (1996), John Morton Blum, *V Was for Victory* (1976), Doris Kearns Goodwin, *No Ordinary Time* (1995), and Steven Mintz and Susan Kellogg, *Domestic Revolutions* (1988). The effects of the war on women are described in D'Ann Campbell, *Women at War with America* (1984), Karen Anderson, *Wartime Women* (1981), and Susan M. Hartmann, *The Home Front and Beyond* (1982). William M. Tuttle, Jr., *"Daddy's Gone To War": The Second World War in the Lives of America's Children* (1993) offers an interesting perspective. The impact of the war on radical politics is examined in Bill V. Mullen, *Popular Fronts: Chicago and African-American Cultural Politics, 1935–46* (1999).

African American participation is the subject of Nat Brandt, *Harlem at War* (1996), Neil A. Wynn, *The Afro-American and the Second World War* (1993), Dominic J. Capeci, Jr., *Race Relations in Wartime Detroit* (1984), and A. Russell Buchanan, *Black Americans in World War II* (1977). On the relocation of the Japanese, see Roger Daniels, *Concentration Camps USA: Japanese Americans and World War II* (1971), and Peter Irons, *Justice at War* (1984).

Major biographies include Geoffrey Perret, *Eisenhower* (1999), Stephen Ambrose, *Eisenhower* (1983), and Ed Cray, *General of the Army: George C. Marshall* (1990).

Richard Rhodes, *The Making of the Atom Bomb* (1986), is superb. On the decision to use the atomic bomb, see J. Samuel Walker, *Prompt and Utter Destruction* (1997), Gar Alperovitz, *Atomic Diplomacy* (1965), and Martin Sherwin, *A World Destroyed* (1975). Other important books include David S. Wyman, *The Abandonment of the Jews* (1984).

CHAPTER 29 | THE AMERICAN CENTURY

Scholarship on the Cold War is being rapidly transformed as archives and sources in the Soviet Union and the former Soviet-bloc states are becoming available to scholars. For a summary of the implications of these materials, see John L. Gaddis, *We Now Know: Rethinking Cold War History* (1997). His *Strategies of Containment: A Critical Appraisal of Postwar American National Security Policy* (1982) emphasizes a continuity in the postwar goals and a pronounced discontinuity in strategies for attaining them. See also his *The United States and the End of the Cold War* (1992). Thomas G. Paterson, *On Every Front: The Making of the Cold War* (1979) argues that American policymakers were not fettered by public opinion and might have avoided the Cold War. Paterson's *Meeting the Communist Threat* (1988) summarizes the revisionists' criticisms of American policy. Other recent works include Michael Hogan, *A Cross of Iron: Harry S Truman and the Origins of the National Security State* (1998), and Steve Neal, *Harry and Ike* (2001). Earlier criticisms of American policy include Walter La Feber, *America, Russia and the Cold War* (1968), and Daniel Yergin, *Shattered Peace* (1977).

General surveys include William Chafe, *The Unfinished Journey* (1986), James T. Patterson, *Grand Expectations: Postwar America, 1945–1974* (1996), David Halberstam, *The Fifties* (1993), H. W. Brands, *The Devil We Knew: Americans and the Cold War* (1993), John Patrick Diggins, *The Proud Decades, 1941–1960* (1989), and Michael S. Sherry, *In the Shadow of War* (1995).

The evolution of American policy toward nuclear weapons is debated in Gar Alperovitz, *Atomic Diplomacy: Hiroshima and Potsdam* (1985), Gregg Herken, *The Winning Weapon: The Atomic Bomb in the Cold War* (1982), and Melvyn P. Leffler, *A Preponderance of Power: National Security, the Truman Administration, and the Cold War* (1992). An accessible overview is Richard Rhodes, *Dark Sun: The Making of the Hydrogen Bomb* (1995).

The 1948 election is described in Gary Donaldson, *Truman Defeats Dewey* (1999). Postwar domestic politics are also treated in William L. O'Neill, *Riding High* (1986), and Alonzo L. Hamby, *The Imperial Years* (1976). Interpretive works useful for understanding the period include Arthur M. Schlesinger Jr., *The Vital Center* (1949), Richard E. Neustadt, *Presidential Power* (1960), and James M. Burns, *The Deadlock of Democracy* (1964). On the cultural effects of the Cold War, see Elaine Tyler May, *Homeward Bound: American Families in the Cold War* (1988), and Paul Boyer, *By the Bomb's Early Light* (1986).

In addition to works cited in the previous chapter, see also Donald R. McCoy, *The Presidency of Harry S. Truman* (1984). David McCullough's, *Truman* (1992), is accessible and sympathetic; Alonzo L. Hamby's *Man of the People: A Life of Harry S Truman* (1995), is scholarly and analytical.

On Truman's foreign policy, see the biographies, Paul G. Pierpaoli, Jr., *Truman and Korea* (1999), and Michael J. Hogan, *The Marshall Plan* (1987). Roger C. Miller, *To Save a City: The Berlin Airlift* (2000) is a succinct account.

The origins of the Korean War are now becoming clearer. See Bruce Cumings, *The Origins of the Korean War* (1981–1990). Cumings's broader study, *Korea's Place in the Sun* (1997), includes material that has been made available recently. On the war itself, see Stanley Sandler, *The Korean War* (1999). On MacArthur, see Geoffrey Perret, *Old Soldiers Never Die* (1996).

On McCarthyism, Ellen Schrecker, *Many Are the Crimes: McCarthyism in America* (1998), argues that the phenomenon was broader than McCarthy and became institutionalized in the FBI under J. Edgar Hoover. David Caute, *The Great Fear* (1978), is sharply critical. For different views of McCarthy himself, see Thomas C. Reeves, *Life and Times of Joe McCarthy* (1997), and Arthur Herman, *Joseph McCarthy* (2000). On the Hiss case see Allen Weinstein, *Perjury: The Hiss-Chambers Case* (1978), and Sam Tanenhaus, *Whittaker Chambers* (1997).

On the evolution of the suburbs, see Kenneth T. Jackson, *Crabgrass Frontier* (1985). The issue of neighborhood racial segregation is the subject of Thomas J. Sugrue, *The Origins of the Urban Crisis: Race and Inequality in Postwar Detroit* (1996), and Stephen G. Meyer, *As Long as They Don't Move Next Door* (2000).

Eisenhower's own view of his presidency can be found in Dwight D. Eisenhower, *Mandate for Change* (1963) and *Waging Peace* (1965). Recent (and increasingly positive) assessments include Robert Bowie and Richard Immerman, *Waging Peace: How Eisenhower Shaped an Enduring Cold War Strategy* (1998); Ray Takeyh, *The Origins of the Eisenhower Doctrine,* on Suez (2000); and Craig Campbell, *Destroying the Village: Eisenhower and Thermonuclear War* (1998).

Biographies on the central figures, in addition to those cited in the previous chapter, include James Chace, *Acheson* (1998), and Richard H. Immerman, *John Foster Dulles* (1999).

CHAPTER 30 | FROM CAMELOT TO WATERGATE

On Kennedy, consult Richard Reeves, *President Kennedy* (1992), Herbert S. Parmet, *JFK: The Presidency of John F. Kennedy* (1983), and James Giglio, *The Presidency of John F. Kennedy* (1991). Arthur M. Schlesinger, Jr., *A Thousand Days* (1965), and Theodore Sorensen, *Kennedy* (1965), are rich in eyewitness detail but extremely pro-Kennedy. The Kennedy style can be "heard" in Ernest R. May and Philip D. Zelikow, eds., *The Kennedy Tapes: Inside the White House During the Cuban Missile Crisis* (1997). Other works include David E. Kaser, *American Tragedy: Kennedy, Johnson and the Origins of the Vietnam War* (2000), and Lawrence Freedman, *Kennedy's Wars: Berlin, Cuba, Laos, and Vietnam* (2000). See also Mark J. White, *The Cuban Missile Crisis* (1996). Gerald Posner, *Case Closed: Lee Harvey Oswald and the Assassination of JFK* (1994) debunks the assassination theorists.

Robert Caro, *The Years of Lyndon B. Johnson: The Path to Power* (1982) and *Means of Ascent* (1990), are extremely critical; Robert Dallek, *Lone Star Rising: Lyndon Johnson and His Times, 1908–1960* (1991), and *Flawed Giant: Lyndon B. Johnson, 1960–1973* (1998) are more balanced. Recent works include Irwin Unger, *LBJ: A Life* (1999), and H. W. Brands, *The Wages of Globalism: Lyndon Johnson and the Limits of American Power* (1995). See also Doris Kearns Goodwin, *Lyndon Johnson and the American Dream* (1976). On Goldwater, see Robert A. Goldberg, *Barry Goldwater* (1995). Michael Beschloss, ed., *Taking Charge: The Johnson White House Tapes, 1963–1969* (1997), provides a verbatim, previously secret, account.

For civil rights developments, consult Mark Tushnet, *Making Civil Rights Law* (1994), Richard Kluger, *Simple Justice* (1976), and Harvard Sitkoff, *The Struggle for Black Equality* (1993). Karl Evanzz, *The Messenger: The Rise and Fall of Elijah Muhammed* (1999), provides a detailed account of the founder of the Black Muslims; Michael E. Dyson's *Making Malcolm* (1995), is also solid. See also the writings of King and Malcolm X: Martin L. King, Jr., *Stride Toward Freedom* (1958), and Malcolm X, *Autobiography* (1966). Taylor Branch's multivolume biography of Martin Luther King, Jr., is powerful; *Parting the Waters* (1988), covers 1959 through 1963; and *Pillar of Fire* (1988), the following two years. Nicholas Lemann, *The Promised Land: The Great Black Migration and How It Changed America* (1991), is also indispensable.

On the election of 1968, Theodore H. White's *The Making of the President, 1968* (1969), is lively and entertaining. The best biography of Nixon is Stephen Ambrose, *Nixon* (1987–1991), but see also Joan Hoff, *Nixon Reconsidered* (1994), and Herbert S. Parmet, *Richard Nixon and His America* (1990).

The literature on the war in Vietnam is enormous. Recent interpretations include David E. Kaiser, *American Tragedy: Kennedy, Johnson and the Origins of the Vietnam War* (2000), Lawrence Freedman, *Kennedy's Wars: Berlin, Cuba, Laos, and Vietnam* (2000), A. J. Langguth, *Our Vietnam: The War: 1954–1975* (2000), and Robert D. Schulzinger, *A Time for War* (1997). Stanley Karnow, *Vietnam: A History* (1983), is a straightforward narrative account. David Halberstam, *The Best and the Brightest* (1972), contains a mass of detail on the evolution of American policy, based on extensive interviews. Neil Sheehan, *A Bright and Shining Lie* (1988), an account of the war from one American adviser's perspective, provides the best explanation of why the war could not be won. See also Lloyd C. Gardner, *Pay Any Price: Lyndon Johnson and the Wars for Vietnam* (1995).

For the antiwar movement, see Robert Buzzanco, *Masters of War: Military Dissent and Politics in the Vietnam Era* (1996), Rhodri Jeffreys-Jones, *Peace Now!* (1999), and Mary Hershberger, *Traveling* to *Vietnam: American Peace Activists and the War* (1998) on the ending of the war; and John Hagan, *Northern Passage* (2001), for an account of Americans who fled to Canada. See also Randall B. Woods's biography of J. William Fulbright (1998).

On Nixon, in addition to works cited previously, see Richard Reeves, *Richard Nixon: Alone in the White House* (2001). Robert S. Litwak, *Détente and the Nixon Doctrine* (1984), is a useful study of U.S.–Soviet relations in the Nixon era, and Henry Kissinger's memoirs, *White House Years* (1979) and *Years of Upheaval* (1982), are important though, like most such works, self-serving. Walter Isaacson's *Kissinger* (1992) is more balanced. Larry Berman, *No Peace, No Honor* (2001), is sharply critical; also see Christopher Hitchens, *The Trial of Henry Kissinger* (2001). Allen J. Matusow, *Nixon's Economy* (1998), is excellent.

The best analysis of the Watergate affair is Stanley I. Kutler, *The Wars of Watergate* (1990) and *Abuse of Power* (1997), but see also Carl Bernstein and Robert Woodward, *All the President's Men* (1974) and *Final Days* (1976), John W. Dean, *Blind Ambition* (1976), and Leon Jaworski, *The Right and the Power* (1976). On Ford's elevation to the presidency, see James Cannon, *Time and Chance* (2001).

CHAPTER 31 | SOCIETY IN FLUX

Allen J. Matusow, *The Unraveling of America* (1984), William M. O'Neill, *Coming Apart: An Informal History of the 1960s* (1971), and Godfrey Hodgson, *America in Our Time* (1976), are social histories of the period. See also Roger Kimball, *The Long March: How the Cultural Revolution of the 1960s Changed America* (2000), Dominick Cavallo, *A Faction of the Past: The Sixties in American History* (1999), and Thomas Frank, *The Conquest of Cool: Business Culture, Counterculture and the Rise of Hip Consumerism* (1997). Modern art is discussed in Barbara Rose, *American Art Since 1900* (1967), and Diana Crane, *The Transformation of the Avant-Garde* (1987).

On geographic mobility, see the final chapters of Stephan Thernstrom, *The Other Bostonians* (1973). On the automobile, see Jane H. Kay's history/manifesto, *Asphalt Nation* (1997), and Virginia Scharff's *Taking the Wheel: Women and the Coming of the Motor Age* (1992).

For television, see Mary Ann Watson, *The Expanding Vista: American Television in the Kennedy Years* (1994), James L. Baughman, *The Republic of Mass Culture: Journalism, Filmmaking, and Broadcasting in America Since 1941* (1991), and Karal Ann Marling, *As Seen on TV: The Visual Culture of Everyday Life in the 1950s* (1994).

For the causes and character of the poverty and urban problems that led Johnson to devise his Great Society program, see Michael Harrington, *The Other America* (1962), and Oscar Lewis, *La Vida: A Puerto Rican Family in the Culture of Poverty* (1966).

On the black radicals, see, in addition to works cited in the previous chapter, Malcolm X, *Autobiography* (1966), Stokely Carmichael and C. V. Hamilton, *Black Power* (1967), and Eldridge Cleaver, *Soul on Ice* (1967). Other important books on race relations include Taylor Branch's multivolume biography of Martin Luther King, Jr.: *Parting the Waters: 1954–1963* (1988), and *Pillar of Fire: America in the King Years, 1963–1965* (1998). On SNCC, see John Lewis's memoir, *Walking with the Wind* (1998), as well as Clayborne Carson, *In Struggle: SNCC and the Black Awakening of the 1960s* (1981). The neglected role of women in the movement is being addressed by works such as Chana Kai Lee, *For Freedom's Sake: The Life of Fannie Lou Hamer* (1999), and Carolyn Wedin, *Inheritors of the Spirit: Mary White Ovington and the Founding of NAACP* (1998).

Ronald Takaki, *A Different Mirror: A History of Multicultural History* (1993), provides an overview of the contemporary immigrant experience. Rodolfo Acuna, *Occupied America: A History of Chicanos* (2000), Manuel Gonzales, *Mexicanos: A History of Mexicans in the United States* (1999), and Ernesto Vigil, *The Crusade for Justice* (1999), provide surveys of broad trends of Chicano history in the United States. Biographies of César Chávez include Richard Griswold del Castillo and Richard A. Garcia, *A Triumph of the Spirit* (1998), and Joan London and Henry Anderson, *So Shall Ye Reap: The Story of César Chávez and the Farm Workers Movement* (1970). James S. Olson and Raymond Wilson, *Native Americans in the Twentieth Century* (1984), is a good survey.

On education reform, see Diane Ravitch's, *Left Back: A Century of Failed School Reforms* (2000) and *Troubled Crusade: American Education, 1945–1980* (1983).

On militancy among college students, see Roger Rosenblatt, *Coming Apart* (1997), on Harvard; and Todd Gitlin, *The Sixties: Years of Hope, Days of Rage* (1987). David Farber, *Chicago '68* (1988), is more critical of the radicals. See also W. J. Rorabaugh, *Berkeley at War* (1989), and Kenneth Kenniston, *Young Radicals* (1968).

The literature on the women's movement is voluminous. Betty Friedan, *The Feminine Mystique* (1963), is essential, though her account must be modified in light of Daniel Horowitz, *Betty Friedan and the Making of The Feminine Mystique* (1998). Rosalind Rosenberg, *Divided Lives: American Women in the Twentieth Century* (1992), is a good introduction to women's history. See also Jo Freeman, *The Politics of Women's Liberation* (1975), and Susan M. Hartmann, *From Margin to Mainstream: Women and American Politics Since 1960* (1989). Narrower monographs include Dennis A. Deslippe, *"Rights, Not Roses": Unions and the Rise of Working-Class Feminism* (2000).

James H. Jones, *Alfred C. Kinsey: A Public / Private Life* (1997), finds that the researcher's own odd behavior discredits his findings; Jonathan Gathorne-Hardy, *Alfred C. Kinsey: Sex the Measure of All Things* (1998), is less critical. On sexual trends more generally, see Beth Bailey, *Sex in the Heartland* (1999), on Kansas in the 1960s and 1970s.

The early history of the AIDS crisis is movingly told in Randy Shilts, *And the Band Played On* (1987). See also Elizabeth Fee and Daniel M. Fox, eds., *AIDS: The Making of a Chronic Disease* (1992).

CHAPTER 32 | RUNNING ON EMPTY: THE NATION TRANSFORMED

For an overview, see Bruce J. Schulman, *The Great Shift in American Culture, Society, and Politics* (2001). On Gerald Ford, see James M. Cannon, *Time and Chance: Gerald Ford's Appointment with History* (1994), and John R. Greene, *The Presidency of Gerald R. Ford* (1995).

Peter G. Bourne, *Jimmy Carter* (1997), relates his subject's life and policies. Donald Spencer, *The Carter Implosion: Jimmy Carter and the Amateur Style of Diplomacy* (1988), contains its thesis in the title; Robert A. Strong, *Working the World: Jimmy Carter and the Making of American Foreign Policy* (2000), defends Carter's record.

For recent biographies of Reagan, largely informed by interviews, see Deborah H. Strober, *Reagan* (1998), and William Pemberton, *Exit with Honor* (1997). Although Edmund Morris's *Dutch: A Memoir* (1999), which includes fictional characters and footnotes, is not what it purports to be, it nevertheless offers interesting observations. David A. Stockman, *The Triumph of Politics* (1986), contains a frank discussion of administration fiscal policies. Reagan's foreign policy remains controversial. Peter Schweizer, *Victory: The Reagan Administration's Secret Strategy That Hastened the Collapse of the Soviet Union* (1994), summarizes its achievements; Frances FitzGerald, *Way Out There in the Blue: Reagan, Star Wars and the End of the Cold War* (2000), is sharply critical. See also Jay Winik, *On the Brink* (1996). Lisa McGirr, *Suburban Warriors: The Origins of the New American Right* (2001), examines the social dynamics of political change during these years.

On the end of the Cold War, see two volumes by John L. Gaddis, *The Long Peace* (1987) and *The United States and the End of the Cold War* (1992), and Marvin P. Leffler, *A Preponderance of Power* (1992).

The early history of the AIDS crisis is movingly told in Randy Shilts, *And the Band Played On* (1987); see also Elizabeth Fee and Daniel M. Fox, eds., *AIDS: The Making of a Chronic Disease* (1992). John-Manual Andriote examines its impact on gays themselves in *Victory Deferred: How AIDS Changed Gay Life in America* (1999).

On the transformation of the economy, see Daniel Yergin, *The Prize: The Epic Quest for Oil, Money and Power* (1991), and Barry Bluestone and Bennett Harrison, *The Deindustrializing of America* (1982). On Michael Milken and junk bonds, see Harlan Platt, *The Predators Ball* (1988); also James B. Stewart, *Den of Thieves* (1991). On the United States and the global economy, see Robert Kuttner, *The End of Laissez Faire: National Purpose and the Global Economy After the Cold War* (1991), and Henry R. Nau, *The Myth of America's Decline: Leading the World Economy in the 1990s* (1990). On young Bill Gates, see James Wallace, *Hard Drive* (1992). David Bank offers a critical assessment of Gates's later period in *Breaking Windows* (2002).

Chapter 33 | Misdemeanors and High Crimes

Haynes Johnson, *Divided We Fall: Gambling with History in the Nineties* (1994), discusses the first few years of the 1990s; for the end of the Cold War, see Michael R. Beschloss and Strobe Talbot, *At the Highest Levels: The Inside Story of the End of the Cold War*, and John Lewis Gaddis, *The United States and the End of the Cold War* (1992).

Many scholars have attempted to fit the political developments of the era into a traditional framework: see Mary Jo Bane and David Ellwood, *Welfare Realities: From Rhetoric to Reform* (1994), Theodore J. Lowi, *The End of the Republican Era* (1995), and Robert S. McElvaine, *The End of the Conservative Era: Liberalism After Reagan* (1987).

For accounts of the George Bush administration, see Herbert Parmet, *George Bush: The Life of a Lone Star Yankee* (1997), John R. Greene, *The Presidency of George Bush* (2000), and Michael Duffy, *Marching in Place: The Status Quo Presidency of George Bush* (1992). Gary R. Hess provides a thoughtful comparison on war-making processes in *Presidential Decisions for War: Korea, Vietnam and the Persian Gulf* (2001). The Panama invasion is discussed in David Harris, *Shooting the Moon* (2001).

On Clinton prior to his move to the White House, see David Maranniss, *First in His Class: A Biography of Bill Clinton* (1995). The *Starr Report* (1998), though hastily released and published, constituted the evidentiary base and set the tone for the subsequent impeachment debate. See also Richard A. Posner, *An Affair of State: The Investigation, Impeachment, and Trial of President Clinton* (1999). On Clinton's foreign policy, see David Halberstam, *War in a Time of Peace: Bush, Clinton and the Generals* (2001).

On the advance of conservatism, see Godfrey Hodgson, *The World Turned Rightside Up: A History of the Conservative Ascendancy in America* (1996). On the defeat of the ERA, see Mary Francis Berry, *Why ERA Failed* (1986), and Donald G. Mathews and Jane Sherron De Hart, *Sex, Gender, and the Politics of E.R.A.* (1990).

David Courtwright, *Violent Land: Single Men and Social Disorder from the Frontier to the Inner City* (1996) argues that much of the nation's crime has come from single males; for a cultural analysis of the infatuation with aggression, see Richard Slotkin, *Gunfighter Nation: The Myth of the Frontier in Twentieth-Century America* (1992). Bruce Jacobs, *Dealing Crack* (1999), provides a case study of the drug problem.

On race and ethnicity, see David A. Hollinger, *Postethnic America: Beyond Multiculturalism* (1995), Andrew Hacker, *Two Nations: Black and White, Separate, Hostile, Unequal* (1992), and Stephen Thernstrom and Abigail Thernstrom, *America in Black and White: One Nation, Indivisible* (1997).

John Cassidy, *Dot.con* (2002) surveys the Internet economy. For a history of the Internet, see Janet Abbate, *Inventing the Internet* (1999).

On the 2000 election, see David A. Kaplan, *The Accidental President* (2001), Roger Simon, *Divided We Stand: How Al Gore Beat George Bush and Lost the Presidency* (2001), Jeffrey Toobin, *Too Close to Call* (2001), and Richard Posner, *Breaking the Deadlock* (2001).

The literature on terrorism is expanding rapidly. Peter Bergen, *Holy War, Inc.: Inside the Secret World of Osama bin Laden* (2001), offers a preliminary view of that shadowy figure. Thomas L. Friedman, *From Beirut to Jerusalem* (1989), provides a thoughtful assessment of the complex problems of the Middle East.

Suggested Websites

PROLOGUE | BEGINNINGS

Precontact and Colonial Maps
http://www.lib.utexas.edu/maps/americas/
This University of Texas site contains numerous maps from the precontact and colonial periods.

Ancient Mesoamerican Civilization
http://www.angelfire.com/ca/humanorigins/index.html
Kevin L. Callahan of the University of Minnesota Department of Anthropology maintains this page that supplies information regarding Mesoamerican civilizations with well-organized essays and photos.

National Museum of the American Indian
http://www.si.edu/nmai
The Smithsonian Institution museum is dedicated to the Native American experience.

Cahokia Mounds
http://medicine.wush.edu/~mckinney/cahokia/cahokia.html
The Cahokia Mounds State Historical site gives information about this fascinating pre-Columbian North American culture.

Mexico Pre-Colombian History
http://www.mexonline.com/precolum.htm
This site provides information on the Aztecs, Maya, Mexica, Olmec, Toltec, Zapotecs, and other pre-European cultures, as well as information on museums, archaeology, language, and education.

CHAPTER 1 | ALIEN ENCOUNTERS: EUROPE IN THE AMERICAS

Vikings in the New World
http://www.anthro.mankato.msus.edu/prehistory/vikings/vikhome.html
This site explores the history of some of the earliest European visitors to the Americas.

The Columbus Doors
http://xroads.virginia.edu/~cap/columbus/col1.html
On this University of Virginia website, historians discuss the Columbus myth and how it has changed over time.

1492: An Ongoing Voyage
http://www.metalab.unc.edu/expo/1492.exhibit/Intro.html
An exhibit of the Library of Congress, Washington D.C., that includes brief essays and images about early civilizations and contact in the Americas.

The Computerized Information Retrieval System on Columbus and the Age of Discovery
http://www.millersv.edu/~columbus/
The History Department and Academic Computing Services of Millersville University, Pennsylvania, provide this text retrieval system containing more than 1000 articles from various magazines, journals, newspapers, speeches, official calendars, and other sources relating to various encounter themes.

Interacting with Native Americans in New Hampshire
http://seacoastnh.com/history/contact/index.html
This brief history of contact era New Hampshire has interesting links and gives a good picture of the earliest contacts.

The Discoverers' Web
http://www.win.tue.nl/cs/fm/engels/discovery/
Andre Engels offers information on the various exploration efforts.

The Plymouth Colony Archives Project at the University of Virginia
http://www.people.virginia.edu/~jfd3a/
This site contains extensive information about late seventeenth-century Plymouth colony.

Jamestown Rediscovery
http://www.apva.org/
This site, mounted by the Association for the Preservation of Virginia Antiquity, has excellent material on archaeological excavations at Jamestown.

Jamestown
http://www.nps.gov/colo/
This National Park Service site has information on Jamestown and other important colonial historical sites.

Williamsburg
http://www.history.org/
This commercial site explores colonial Williamsburg, Virginia.

William Penn, Visionary Proprietor
http://xroads.virginia.edu/~CAP/PENN/pnhome.html
William Penn had an interesting life, and this University site is a good introduction to the man and some of his achievements.

CHAPTER 2 | AMERICAN SOCIETY IN THE MAKING

LVA Colonial Records Project—Index of Digital Facsimiles of Documents on Early Virginia
http://eagle.vsla.edu/colonial/
Although difficult to negotiate, this site contains reproductions of numerous documents.

Anglicans, Puritans, and Quakers in Colonial America
http://www.mun.ca/rels/ang/texts/
This site provides information on the major religious movements in colonial America.

DSL Archives: Slave Movement During the 18th and 19th Centuries
http://dpls.dacc.wisc.edu/slavedata/index.html
This site explores the slave ships and the slave trade that carried thousands of Africans to the New World.

Witchcraft in Salem Village
http://etext.virginia.edu/salem/witchcraft/
This University of Virginia site offers an extensive archive of the 1692 trials as well as life in late seventeenth-century Massachusetts.

Salem Witchcraft Trials (1692)
http://www.law.umkc.edu/faculty/projects/ftrials/salem/salem.htm
Images, chronology, court and official documents by Dr. Doug Linder of the University of Missouri–Kansas City Law School.

Benjamin Franklin
http://sln.fi.edu/franklin/rotten.html
This Benjamin Franklin Institute site contains information and sources on one of early America's most well-known figures.

Religion and the Founding of the American Republic
http://lcweb.loc.gov/exhibits/religion/religion.html
This Library of Congress site is an online exhibit about religion and the formation of the United States.

DoHistory, Harvard University Film Center
http://www.dohistory.org/
Focusing on the life of Martha Ballard, a late eighteenth-century New England woman, this site employs selections from her diary, excerpts from a book and film about her life, and other primary documents that enable students to conduct their own historical investigation.

CHAPTER 3 | AMERICA IN THE BRITISH EMPIRE

Colonial Era Timeline
http://www.seanet.com/users/pamur/colo.html
This site provides both an outstanding timeline and links to other sites that treat colonial-era issues.

Colonial Documents
http://www.yale.edu/lawweb/avalon/18th.htm
The key documents are reproduced on this Yale University site, as are some important documents from other periods of U.S. history.

Jonathan Edwards
http://www.jonathanedwards.com/
This site includes the text of speeches delivered by Preacher Jonathan Edwards.

The French and Indian War
http://web.syr.edu/~laroux/
This site, treating the French and Indian War, includes chronologies and documents, as well as materials dealing with the French soldiers who fought in the conflict.

The Early America Review
http://earlyamerica.com/
This site explores the colonies through the colonial media.

White Oak Fur Post
http://www.whiteoak.org/
This site documents an eighteenth-century fur trading post among the Indians in the region that would become Minnesota.

CHAPTER 4 | THE AMERICAN REVOLUTION

Revolutionary War Songs
http://www.mcneilmusic.com/rev.html
This site contains colonial and revolutionary era songs.

Maryland Loyalists and the American Revolution
http://users.erols.com/candidus/index.htm
This examination of Maryland's Loyalists promotes the author's book on that subject. Nonetheless, the site has good information about an underappreciated phenomenon, including Loyalist songs and poems.

Canada History
http://www.civilization.ca
Canada and the United States shared a colonial past, but developed along different lines. This site is part of the virtual museum of the Canadian Museum of Civilization Corporation.

Georgia's Rare Map Collection
http://scarlett.libs.uga.edu/darchive/hargrett/maps/colamer.html
http://scarlett.libs.uga.edu/darchive/hargrett/maps/revamer.html
These two University of Georgia sites contain maps of colonial and revolutionary America.

The American Revolution
http://revolution.h-net.msu.edu/
This site accompanies the PBS series *Revolution* with essays and resource links.

Timeline of the American Revolution
http://www.seanet.com/users/pamur/revo.html
This site has both an outstanding timeline of significant events of the War for Independence and related links.

CHAPTER 5 | THE FEDERALIST ERA: NATIONALISM TRIUMPHANT

George Washington at Home
http://www.mountvernon.org/
Pictures and documents from Mount Vernon, the home of the first president, George Washington.

George Washington
http://memory.loc.gov/ammem/gwhtml/gwhome.html
This Library of Congress site contains information on Washington and his papers.

Biographies of the Founding Fathers
http://www.colonialhall.com/
This site provides interesting information about the men who signed the Declaration of Independence and includes a trivia section.

The Federalist Papers
http://www.law.emory.edu/FEDERAL/federalist/
This Emory University site is a collection of the most important Federalist Papers, a series of documents designed to convince people to support the new Constitution and the Federalist party.

The Continental Congress and the Constitutional Convention, 1774–1798
http://memory.loc.gov/ammem/bdsds/bdsdhome.html
The Continental Congress Broadside Collection (253 titles) and the Constitutional Convention Broadside Collection (21 titles) contain 274 documents relating to the work of Congress and the drafting and ratification of the Constitution.

The Constitution and the Amendments
http://www.law.emory.edu/FEDERAL/usconst.html
A searchable Constitution site, especially useful for its information on the Bill of Rights and other constitutional amendments.

The George Washington Papers
http://www.virginia.edu/gwpapers/
This site provides information on the University of Virginia publishing project, with selected documents, essays, and an index to the published volumes.

Archiving Early America
http://earlyamerica.com
Old newspapers provide a window into issues of the past. This site includes the Keigwin and Matthews collection of historical newspapers.

Alexander Hamilton
http://odur.let.rug.nl/~usa/B/hamilton/hamilxx.htm
This site from A Hypertext of American History examines Hamilton's life and influence in the United States during the early national period.

The XYZ Affair
http://gi.grolier.com/presidents/aae/side/xyzaffr.html
This site examines the XYZ affair, the first major crisis of U.S. foreign policy.

CHAPTER 6 | JEFFERSONIAN DEMOCRACY

Thomas Jefferson
http://www.pbs.org/jefferson/
This site, the companion to the PBS series on Jefferson, includes material on how people understand Jefferson today.

Thomas Jefferson Resources Online
http://etext.virginia.edu/jefferson/
"Mr. Jefferson's University," The University of Virginia, provides resources about Jefferson and his times.

The Jefferson Home
http://www.monticello.org/
This site explores Jefferson's gifted mind through an examination of Monticello, Jefferson's unique home.

The Lewis and Clark Expedition
http://www.cp.duluth.mn.us/~tmcs/lewsclrk1.htm
This site offers assorted materials treating the expedition that explored the Louisiana Territory.

Lewis and Clark—The PBS Website
http://www.pbs.org/lewisandclark
This is a companion site to Ken Burns's film, containing a timeline of the expedition, a collection of related links, a bibliography, and more than 800 minutes of unedited, full-length Real Player interviews with seven experts featured in the film.

CHAPTER 7 | NATIONAL GROWING PAINS

Documents from the War of 1812
http://www.yale.edu/lawweb/avalon/diplomacy/br1814m.htm
This site includes the important documents from the War of 1812.

The War of 1812
http://members.tripod.com/~war1812/index.html
This site provides in-depth information about the War of 1812.

The Monroe Doctrine
http://www.yale.edu/lawweb/avalon/monroe.htm
Read the Monroe Doctrine, an important early articulation of U.S. foreign policy, online.

The Seminole Indians of Florida
http://www.seminoletribe.com/
Before becoming president, Andrew Jackson began a war against the Seminole Indians.

CHAPTER 8 | TOWARD A NATIONAL ECONOMY

The Era of the Mountain Men
http://www.xmission.com/~drudy/amm.html
Private letters help students learn about the concerns and environment of the writers and recipients. This site has correspondence from early settlers west of the Mississippi River.

The Marshall Cases
http://odur.let.rug.nl/~usa/D/1801-1825/marshallcases/marxx.htm
John Marshall, and the cases he heard, shaped the form and function of the judicial system in the United States.

Whole Cloth: Discovering Science and Technology Through American Textile History

http://www.si.edu/lemelson/centerpieces/whole_cloth/

The Jerome and Dorothy Lemelson Center for the Study of Invention and Innovation/Society for the History of Technology put together this site, which includes activities and sources about early American manufacturing and industry.

Erie Canal On-Line

http://www.syracuse.com/features/eriecanal

This site, built around the diary of a 14-year-old girl who traveled from Amsterdam to Syracuse, New York, in the early nineteenth century, explores the construction and importance of the Erie Canal.

Midwest History to 1850

http://www.connerprairie.org/historyonline

This site includes a collection of documents and articles relating to Midwest history, with special attention to Indian affairs.

The National Road

http://www.connerprairie.org/historyonline/ntlroad.html

The National Road was a hot political topic in the early republic and was part of the beginning of the developments of America's infrastructure.

CHAPTER 9 | JACKSONIAN DEMOCRACY

Indian Affairs: Laws and Treaties, Compiled and Edited by Charles J. Kappler (1904)

http://www.library.okstate.edu/kappler/

This digitized text at Oklahoma State University includes preremoval treaties with the Five Civilized Tribes and other tribes.

Andrew Jackson and Indian Removal

http://www.iwchildren.org/genocide/shame9.htm

This site offers a critical appraisal of Jackson's Indian removal policy.

The Second Bank of the United States, 1816–1836

http://odur.let.rug.nl/~usa/E/usbank/bank04.htm

The political fighting surrounding the Second Bank of the United States occupied the United States during the Jackson era and led to the rise of the Whig party.

Daniel Webster

http://www.dartmouth.edu/~dwebster

Background information and selected writings from one of the nineteenth-century's most noted orators.

The American Whig Party, 1834–1856

http://odur.let.rug.nl/~usa/E/uswhig/whigsxx.htm

This site treats the rise and fall of an important nineteenth-century political movement.

National Museum of the American Indian
http://www.si.edu/nmai

The Smithsonian Institution maintains this site, providing information about the museum that is dedicated to everything about Native Americans.

CHAPTER 10 | THE MAKING OF MIDDLE-CLASS AMERICA

The Alexis de Tocqueville Tour: Exploring Democracy in America
http://www.tocqueville.org/

Text, images, and teaching suggestions are all part of this companion site to C-SPAN's recent program on de Tocqueville.

Votes for Women: Selections from the National Woman Suffrage Association Collection, 1848–1921
http://memory.loc.gov/ammem/naw/nawshome.html

This Library of Congress site contains books, pamphlets, and other artifacts that document the suffrage campaign.

By Popular Demand: "Votes for Women" Suffrage Pictures, 1850–1922
http://memory.loc.gov/ammem/vfwhtml/vfwhome.html

Portraits, suffrage parades, picketing suffragists, an antisuffrage display, and cartoons commenting on the movement are all part of this Library of Congress site.

Important Black Abolitionists
http://www.loc.gov/exhibits/african/influ.html

An exhibit from the Library of Congress, with pictures and text, that discuss some of the key African American abolitionists and their efforts to end slavery.

1830s Clothing
http://www.connerprairie.org/historyonline/clothing.html

See how clothing worn in the early republic was quite different from what people wear today.

Commerce on the Prairie
http://www.ukans.edu/carrie/kancoll/books/gregg/contents.htm

This University of Kansas site looks at life and commerce on the frontier between the United States and Mexico.

Pioneering the Upper Midwest: Books from Michigan, Minnesota, and Wisconsin, ca. 1820–1910
http://memory.loc.gov/ammem/umhtml/umhome.html

This Library of Congress site looks at first-person accounts, biographies, promotional literature, ethnographic and antiquarian texts, colonial archival documents, and other works from the seventeenth to early twentieth century. It covers many topics and issues that affected Americans in the settlement and development of the upper Midwest.

History of the Suffrage Movement
http://www.rochester.edu/SBA

This site includes a chronology, important texts relating to woman's suffrage, and bibliographical information about Susan B. Anthony and Elizabeth Cady Stanton.

CHAPTER 11 | A DEMOCRATIC CULTURE

America's First Look into the Camera: Daguerreotype Portraits and Views, 1839–1862

http://memory.loc.gov/ammem/daghtml/daghome.html

The Library of Congress's daguerreotype collection consists of more than 650 photographs from the 1839–1864 period. Portraits, architectural views, and some street scenes make up most of the collection.

The Era of the Mountain Men

http://www.xmission.com/~drudy/amm.html

Private letters help students of the past learn about the concerns and environment of the writers and recipients. This site has correspondence from early settlers in the area west of the Mississippi River.

Edgar Allan Poe

http://www.eapoe.org/index.html

The Edgar Allan Poe Society of Baltimore provides the original works, history, criticism, images, and more about the writer.

Eastern State Penitentiary Official Homepage

http://www.easternstate.com/index.html

This is the official website for America's most historical prison; the model for 300 prisons world-wide. Eastern State Penitentiary is now open to the public as a historical site.

CHAPTER 12 | EXPANSION AND SLAVERY

From Slave to Master

http://moa.umdl.umich.edu/cgi/sgml/moa-idx?notisid=ABT6752

This site contains an autobiography of a slave who became a master, with strong comments on the place of blacks in pre–Civil War America.

Sam Houston and the Texas Revolution, 1825–1836

http://www.lnstar.com/mall/texasinfo/shouston.htm

This site provides information on the revolution, including the dynamic Sam Houston.

The Mexican-American War Memorial

http://sunsite.dcaa.unam.mx/revistas/1847

Images and text explain the causes, course, and outcome of the Mexican-American War.

On the Trail in Kansas

http://www.ukans.edu/carrie/kancoll/galtrl.htm

This Kansas Collection site provides good primary sources and images relating to the Oregon Trail and America's early movement westward.

"Been Here So Long": Selections from the WPA American Slave Narratives

http://newdeal.feri.org/asn/index.htm

Slave narratives are some of the most interesting primary sources about slavery.

The African American Odyssey
http://digital.nypl.org/schomburg/images_aa19/
This Library of Congress site includes information on slavery, free blacks, and abolition.

Slave Narratives
http://docsouth.unc.edu/neh/texts.html
This site presents narratives of several slaves housed at the Documents of the American South collection and the University of North Carolina.

The Settlement of African Americans in Liberia
http://www.loc.gov/exhibits/african/perstor.html
This site contains images and text relating to the colonization movement to return African Americans to Africa.

Images of African Americans from the Nineteenth Century
http://digital.nypl.org/schomburg/images_aa19/
The New York Public Library–Schomburg Center for Research in Black Culture site contains numerous visuals of nineteenth-century African Americans.

The Compromise of 1850 and the Fugitive Slave Act
http://www.pbs.org/wgbh/aia/part4
From the series, *Africans in America*, an analysis of the Compromise of 1850 and the effect of the Fugitive Slave Act on black Americans.

The 1850s: An Increasingly Divided Union
http://nac.gmu/mmts/50proto.html
A tutorial skill development site Multi-Media Thinking Skills project that focuses on events in the 1850s leading to the Civil War.

Words and Deeds in American History
http://lcweb2.loc.gov/ammem/mcchtml/corhome.html
A Library of Congress site containing links to Frederick Douglass; the Compromise of 1850; speeches by John C. Calhoun, Daniel Webster, and Henry Clay; and other topics from the Civil War era.

CHAPTER 13 | THE SECTIONS GO THEIR WAYS

"Been Here So Long": Selections from the WPA American Slave Narratives
http://newdeal.feri.org/asn/index.htm
Slave narratives are some of the most interesting primary sources about slavery.

The African American Odyssey
http://digital.nypl.org/schomburg/images_aa19/
This Library of Congress site includes information on slavery, free blacks, and abolition.

The Settlement of African Americans in Liberia
http://www.loc.gov/exhibits/african/perstor.html
This site contains images and text relating to the colonization movement to return African Americans to Africa.

Images of African Americans from the Nineteenth Century
http://digital.nypl.org/schomburg/images_aa19/
The New York Public Library Schomburg Center for Research in Black Culture site contains numerous visuals of nineteenth-century African Americans.

Exploring Amistad
http://amistad.mysticseaport.org/main/welcome.html
The Mystic Seaport Museum, Mystic, Connecticut, maintains this site that includes extensive collections of historical resources relating to the slave revolt aboard the *Amistad*, as well as the subsequent trial.

Amistad Trials (1839–1840)
http://www.law.umkc.edu/faculty/projects/ftrials/amistad/AMISTD.HTM
Dr. Doug Linder at University of Missouri–Kansas City Law School has collected images, chronology, court and official documents for this site.

CHAPTER 14 | THE COMING OF THE CIVIL WAR

Secession Era Editorial Project
http://history.furman.edu/~benson/docs/
Furman University is digitizing editorials about the secession crisis and already includes scores of them on this site.

John Brown Trial Links
http://www.law.umkc/edu/faculty/projects/ftrials/Brown.html
For information about the John Brown trial, this site provides a list of excellent links.

Harriett Beecher Stowe and Uncle Tom's Cabin
http://xroads.virginia.edu/~HYPER/STOWE/stowe.html
This site provides both text and description of Stowe's important books, as well as information about the author's life.

Abraham Lincoln
http://showcase.netins.net/web/creative/lincoln.html
This site both contains useful information about President Lincoln and links to other Web destinations.

Abraham Lincoln Association
http://www.alincolnassoc.com/
This site allows searches of digital versions of Lincoln's papers.

Heroes and Villains in Kansas
http://history.cc.ukans.edu/carrie/kancoll/galhero.htm
The Kansas Collection Gallery profiles the famous and little-known people who made up the history of the state.

Chapter 15 | The War to Save the Union

The American Civil War Homepage
http://sunsite.utk.edu/civil-war/warweb.html
This site has a great collection of hypertext links to the most useful identified electronic files about the American Civil War.

The Valley of the Shadow: Living the Civil War in Pennsylvania and Virginia
http://jefferson.village.virginia.edu/vshadow/vshadow.html
This project tells the histories of two communities on either side of the Mason-Dixon line during the Civil War. It includes narratives and an electronic archive of sources.

Abraham Lincoln
http://showcase.netins.net/web/creative/lincoln.html
This site both contains useful information about President Lincoln and links to other Web destinations.

Abraham Lincoln Association
http://www.alincolnassoc.com/
This site allows digital searches of Lincoln's papers.

Assassination of President Abraham Lincoln
http://memory.loc.gov/ammem/alhtml/alrintr.html
Part of the American Memory series with introduction, timeline, and gallery.

U.S. Civil War Center
http://www.cwc.lsu.edu/
The mission of this site is to "locate, index and/or make available all appropriate private and public data regarding the Civil War and to promote the study of the Civil War from the perspective of all professions, occupations, and academic disciplines."

Selected Civil War Photographs
http://memory.loc.gov/ammem/cwphtml/cwphome.html
This Library of Congress site has more than one thousand photographs, many from Matthew Brady.

A Timeline of the Civil War
http://www.historyplace.com/civilwar/index.html
This site offers a comprehensive Civil War timeline that includes photographs.

National Civil War Association
http://www.ncwa.org/
This site documents one of the many Civil War reenactment organizations in the United States.

Chapter 16 | Reconstruction and the South

The Impeachment of Andrew Johnson
http://www.impeach-andrewjohnson.com/
This HarpWeek site about the impeachment includes images and text from the Reconstruction period.

Diary and Letters of Rutherford B. Hayes
http://www.ohiohistory.org/onlinedoc/hayes/index.cfm
The Rutherford B. Hayes Presidential Center in Fremont, Ohio, maintains this searchable database of Hayes's writings.

Rutherford B. Hayes
http://www.ipl.org/ref/POTUS/rbhayes.html
This site contains information relating to Hayes and his presidency.

Images of African Americans from the Nineteenth Century
http://digital.nypl.org/schomburg/images_aa19/
The New York Public Library Schomburg Center for Research in Black Culture site contains numerous visuals.

Freedman and Southern Society Project
http://www.inform.umd.edu/ARHU/Depts/History/Freedman/home.html
This site contains a chronology and sample documents from several collections or primary sources about emancipation and freedom in the 1860s.

CHAPTER 17 | IN THE WAKE OF WAR

Indian Affairs: Laws and Treaties, Compiled and Edited by Charles J. Kappler (1904)
http://www.library.okstate.edu/kappler
This digitized text at Oklahoma State University includes preremoval treaties with the Five Civilized Tribes and other tribes.

Geronimo
http://odur.let.rug.nl/~usa/B/geronimo/geronixx.htm
This site contains biographical and autobiographical information about the famous Native American who resisted European American domination.

National Museum of the American Indian
http://www.si.edu/nmai
The Smithsonian Institution maintains this site, providing information about the museum. The museum is dedicated to everything about Native Americans.

The Northern Great Plains, 1880–1920: Photographs from the Fred Hulstrand and F. A. Pazandak Photograph Collections
http://memory.loc.gov/ammem/award97/ndfahtml/ngphome.html
This American Memory site from the Library of Congress contains "two collections from the Institute for Regional Studies at North Dakota State University" with "900 photographs of rural and small-town life at the turn of the century." Included are "images of sod homes and the people who built them; images of farms and the machinery that made them prosper; and images of one-room schools and the children who were educated in them."

"California as I Saw It": First-Person Narratives of California's Early Years, 1849–1900

http://memory.loc.gov/ammem/cbhtml/cbhome/html

This site is part of the American Memory series and contains "full texts and illustrations of 190 works documenting the formative era of California's history through eyewitness accounts." It covers the gold rush, the interaction of various groups, and the settling of the region.

CHAPTER 18 | AN INDUSTRIAL GIANT

Alexander Graham Bell Family Papers at the Library of Congress

http://memory.loc.gov/ammem/bellhtml/bellhome.html

This site contains papers from 1862 to 1939, as well as a chronology, images, selected documents, and interpretive essays about Bell.

Alexander Graham Bell Telephone Sketch

http://lcweb2.loc.gov/ammem/bellhtml/bellhome.html

This Library of Congress site has the sketch Bell made of his invention, the telephone.

Anarchist Archives at Pitzer University

http://dwardmac.pitzer.edu/Anarchist_Archives/archivehome.html

This archive includes classic anarchist texts, especially information about and graphics of the Haymarket Riot.

John D. Rockefeller and the Standard Oil Company

http://www.micheloud.com/FXM/SO/

This study with accompanying images by François Micheloud tells of the rise of Rockefeller and his mammoth company.

National Refinery Company

http://www.enarco.com/

This positive history of the company reflects industrial changes of late-nineteenth-century America.

A Short History of American Labor

http://www.unionweb.org/history.htm

This brief essay is adapted from the AFL-CIO *American Federationist,* March 1981.

American Labor History

http://www.geocities.com/CollegePark/Quad/6460/AmLabHist/index.html

This site takes a general look at the history of labor in America.

Labor-Management Conflict in American History

http://www.history.ohio-state.edu/projects/laborconflict/

This Ohio State University site includes primary accounts of some of the major events in the history of the labor-management conflict in the late nineteenth and early twentieth centuries.

Samuel Gompers Papers at the University of Maryland

http://www.inform.umd.edu/HIST/Gompers/web1.html

This site includes information about the papers project. It also has a photo gallery, selected documents, and a brief history of the first president of the American Federation of Labor.

CHAPTER 19 | AMERICAN SOCIETY IN THE INDUSTRIAL AGE

Coal Mining During the Gilded Age and Progressive Era
http://www.history.ohio-state.edu/projects/Lessons_US/Gilded_Age/
Coal_Mining/default.htm
This Ohio State University site examines the development of the coal industry, including the sometimes violent labor-management conflicts.

Touring Turn-of-the-Century America: Photographs from the Detroit Publishing Company, 1880–1920
http://memory.loc.gov/ammem/detroit/dethome.html
This Library of Congress collection has thousands of photographs from turn-of-the-century America.

American Labor History
http://www.geocities.com/CollegePark/Quad/6460/AmLabHist/index.html
This site takes a general look at the history of labor in America.

Inside an American Factory: The Westinghouse Works, 1904
http://lcweb2.loc.gov/ammem/papr/west/westhome.html
Part of the American Memory Project at the Library of Congress, this site provides a glimpse inside a turn-of-the-century factory.

Thorsten Veblen's The Theory of the Leisure Class
http://xroads.virginia.edu/~HYPER/VEBLEN/veb_toc.html
This University of Virginia site includes a picture of Veblen as well as the text of his influential book.

CHAPTER 20 | INTELLECTUAL AND CULTURAL TRENDS

Touring Turn-of-the-Century America: Photographs from the Detroit Publishing Company, 1880–1920
http://memory.loc.gov/ammem/detroit/dethome.html
This Library of Congress collection has thousands of photographs from turn-of-the-century America.

American Authors
http://xroads.virginia.edu/~HYPER/hypertex.html
This University of Virginia site contains hypertexts of the works of many prominent American authors, including Mark Twain, Stephen Crane, and Theodore Dreiser.

Mary Baker Eddy
http://www.tfccs.com/
This site looks at the founding of Christian Science.

I Hear America Singing
http://www.thirteen.org/cgi-bin/ihas.cgi
American music came into its own at the turn of the century, as this fascinating site demonstrates.

African American Women Writers of the Nineteenth Century
http://digital.nypl.org/schomburg/writers_aa19/
The New York Public Library's Schomburg Center for Research in Black Culture maintains this site, which contains a large number of digital texts by African American women of the nineteenth century.

National Arts and Crafts Archives
http://arts-crafts.com/archive/archive.shtml
This site serves as a guide to materials on the arts and crafts movement, which lasted roughly from 1890 to 1929.

National Geographic and the Titanic
http://www.nationalgeographic.com/society/ngo/explorer/titanic/movie.html
This National Geographic site offers historical perspective and balanced coverage of the *Titanic* tragedy.

CHAPTER 21 | POLITICS: NATIONAL, STATE, AND LOCAL

James Garfield
http://www.ipl.org/ref/POTUS/jagarfield.html
This site contains basic data about Garfield's election and presidency, speeches, and an online bibliography.

Benjamin Harrison
http://www.ipl.org/ref/POTUS/bharrison.html
This site contains basic data about Harrison's election and presidency, speeches, and an online bibliography.

Chester Arthur
http://www.ipl.org/ref/POTUS/caarthur.html
This site contains basic data about Arthur's election and presidency, speeches, and an online bibliography.

William Jennings Bryan
http://gi.grolier.com/presidents/aae/side/bryan.html
This site treats the career and ideas of the three-time presidential candidate.

William McKinley
http://www.ipl.org/ref/POTUS/wmckinley.html
This site contains basic data about McKinley's election and presidency, speeches, and an online bibliography.

The Era of William McKinley
http://www.cohums.ohio-state.edu/history/projects/mckinley
This site contains numerous images from various stages of William McKinley's career along with a brief bibliographical essay. This Ohio State University site also has a section with an excellent collection of McKinley-era cartoons.

CHAPTER 22 | THE AGE OF REFORM

History of the Suffrage Movement
http://www.rochester.edu/SBA

This site includes a chronology, important texts relating to woman suffrage, and bibliographical information about Susan B. Anthony and Elizabeth Cady Stanton.

The Conservation Movement, 1850–1920
http://memory.loc.gov/ammem/amrvhtml/conshome.html

This American Memory site brings together scores of primary sources and photographs about "the historical formation and cultural foundations of the movement to conserve and protect America's natural heritage."

African American Perspectives: Pamphlets from the Daniel A. P. Murry Collections, 1818–1907
http://memory.loc.gov/ammem/aap/aaphome.html

This collection includes writings of famous African Americans, including Frederick Douglass, Booker T. Washington, Ida B. Wells-Barnett, Benjamin W. Arnett, Alexander Crummel, and Emanuel Love.

Coal Mining During the Gilded Age and Progressive Era
http://www.history.ohio-state.edu/projects/Lessons_US/Gilded_Age/
Coal_Mining/default.htm

This Ohio State University site examines the development of the coal industry, including the sometimes violent labor–management conflict.

Theodore Roosevelt Association
http://www.theodoreroosevelt.org/

This site contains much bibliographical and research information about Theodore Roosevelt.

NAACP On-line
http://www.naacp.org/past_future/index.html

The National Association for the Advancement of Colored People's official website explains its mission and includes a primary document explaining the start of the NAACP.

The Triangle Shirtwaist Factory Fire, March 25, 1911
http://www.ilr.cornell.edu/trianglefire/

The Kheel Center for Labor–Management Documentation and Cornell University Archives put together this excellent site of oral histories, images, and essays.

Labor–Management Conflict in American History
http://www.history.ohio-state.edu/projects/laborconflict/

This Ohio State University site includes primary accounts of some of the major events in the history of the labor–management conflict.

Bill Haywood Trial (1907)
http://www.law.umkc.edu/faculty/projects/ftrials/haywood/haywood.htm

This site contains images, chronology, court and official documents maintained by Dr. Doug Linder at the University of Missouri–Kansas City Law School.

Theodore Roosevelt
http://www.ipl.org/ref/POTUS/troosevelt.html
This site contains basic data about Roosevelt's election and presidency, speeches, and an online bibliography.

The 1906 San Francisco Earthquake
http://www-socal.wr.usgs.gov/wald/1906/1906.html
This site contains scholarly articles dealing with the earthquake, its source and history.

Federal Reserve Act of 1913
http://odur.let.rug.nl/~usa/E/usbank/bank13.htm
The federal government's role in U.S. banking was finally resolved in 1913.

William Howard Taft
http://www.ipl.org/ref/POTUS/whtaft.html
This site contains basic data about Taft's election and presidency, speeches, and an online bibliography.

CHAPTER 23 | FROM ISOLATION TO EMPIRE

William McKinley
http://www.ipl.org/ref/POTUS/wmckinley.html
This site contains basic data about McKinley's election and presidency, speeches, and an online bibliography.

The Era of William McKinley
http://www.history.ohio-state.edu/projects/mckinley/default.htm
This site contains numerous images from various stages of William McKinley's career along with a brief bibliographical essay. This Ohio State University site also has a section with an excellent collection of McKinley-era cartoons.

William McKinley and the Spanish-American War
http://www.history.ohio-state.edu/projects.mckinley/SpanAmWar.html
Part of the Ohio State University site about William McKinley. This section highlights the Spanish-American War with an essay and photographs.

Sentenaryo/Centennial: The Philippine Revolution and the Philippine-American War
http://www.boondocksnet.com/centennial/index.html
Jim Zwick organizes primary documents, images, and essays focusing on U.S. involvement in the Philippines.

Selected Naval Documents; The Spanish-American War
http://www.history.navy.mil/wars/spanam/sn98-1.htm
The primary documents speak volumes to the activity of the U.S. Navy during the conflict with Spain.

The Spanish-American War
http://lcweb.loc.gov/rr/hispanic/1898/trask.html
This article by historian David Trask includes links to other related sites. The article is provided by the Library of Congress.

The First Open Door Note
http://odur.let.rug.nl/~usa/D/1876-1900/foreignpolicy/opendr.htm
The Open Door note played an important ideological role in U.S. foreign policy at the end of the nineteenth century. Read the text of that document on this site.

Imperialism Web Page
http://www.smplanet.com/imperialism/toc.html
Focusing on the period around 1900, this site puts much information about American imperialism in one place.

Theodore Roosevelt Association
http://www.theodoreroosevelt.org/
This site contains much bibliographical and research information about Theodore Roosevelt.

CHAPTER 24 | WOODROW WILSON AND THE GREAT WAR

Woodrow Wilson
http://www.ipl.org/ref/POTUS/wwilson.html
This site contains basic data about Wilson's election and presidency, speeches, and an online bibliography.

World War I Document Archives
http://www.lib.byu.edu/~rdh/wwi/
This archive contains sources about World War I in general, not just America's involvement.

World War I: Trenches on the Web
http://www.worldwar1.com/index.html
This site provides a mass of data concerning the prosecution of the world's first global war.

American Leaders Speak: Recordings from World War I and the 1920 Election
http://memory.loc.gov/ammem/nfhtml/
This Library of Congress site contains 59 recordings from American leaders at the turn of the century.

The Great Migration in Chicago
http://lcweb.loc.gov/exhibits/african/afam011.html
This site looks at the black experience in the great migration at one prominent destination.

The Flu Epidemic of 1918
http://www.pbs.org/wgbh/amex/influenza/
Today, the flu is an annoyance for most people. Yet in 1918, a major flu epidemic swept the United States, killing 600,000 people.

CHAPTER 25 | POSTWAR SOCIETY AND CULTURE: CHANGE AND ADJUSTMENT

Shadow Ball: The Negro Baseball Leagues
http://www.negro-league.columbus.oh.us/jimcrow1.htm
This Harlan William article examines the African American baseball leagues.

Margaret Sanger Papers Projects
http://www.nyu.edu/projects/sanger/
This site at New York University contains information about Margaret Sanger and digital versions of several of her works.

Harlem: The Mecca of the New Negro
http://etext.lib.virginia.edu/harlem/
This site is the online text of the March 1925 *Survey Graphic* Harlem Number; the journal was the premier social work journal of the decade.

Automotive History at the Michigan Electronic Library
http://mel.org/business/autos-history.html
This page has several links to good sites about automotive history in America.

Harlem 1900–1940: An African American Community
http://www.si.umich.edu/CHICO/Harlem/
The New York Public Library's Schomburg Center for Research in Black Culture hosts this site that includes a database, a timeline, and an exhibit.

William P. Gottlieb Photographs of the Golden Age of Jazz
http://memory.loc.gov/ammem/wghtml/wghome.html
The Music Division of the Library of Congress has numerous images, audio, and scanned articles from the 1940s.

The Scopes Trial
http://xroads.virginia.edu/~UG97/inherit/1925home.html
This site gives general descriptions of the trial and the issues surrounding the landmark case.

Temperance and Prohibition
http://prohibition.history.ohio-state.edu/
This site looks at the temperance movement over time and contains many informative links.

National Arts and Crafts Archives
http://arts-crafts.com/index.html
This site serves as a guide to materials on the arts and crafts movement, which lasted roughly from 1890 to 1929.

The Flappers
http://www.geocities.com/flapper_culture/
This site contains links to information about 1920s popular culture, with special attention to the flapper.

CHAPTER 26 | THE NEW ERA, 1921–1933

The Calvin Coolidge Experience
http://www.geocities.com/CapitolHill/4921/
This site is an unusual look at one of America's less colorful presidents.

The Crash of 1929
http://www.btinternet.com/~dreklind/thecrash.htm
This site includes articles about the stock market crash as well as audio clips.

America from the Great Depression to World War II: Photographs from the FSA and OWI, c. 1935–1945

http://memory.loc.gov/ammem/fsowhome.html

These images in the Farm Security Administration–Office of War Information Collection show Americans from all over the nation experiencing everything from despair to triumph in the 1930s and 1940s.

CHAPTER 27 | THE NEW DEAL, 1933–1941

Voices from the Dust Bowl: The Charles L. Todd and Robert Sonkin Migrant Worker Collection, 1940–1941

http://memory.loc.gov/ammem/afctshtml/tshome.html

Farm Security Administration (FSA) studies of migrant work camps in central California in 1940 and 1941 are the bulk of this site. The collections include audio recordings, photographs, manuscript material, and publications.

The New Deal Network

http://newdeal.feri.org

This database includes photographs, political cartoons, and texts—including speeches, letters, and other historical documents—from the New Deal period.

Franklin Delano Roosevelt

http://www.ipl.org/ref/POTUS/fdroosevelt.html

This site provides information about Roosevelt, the only president to serve more than two terms.

A New Deal for the Arts

http://www.nara.gov/exhall/newdeal/newdeal.html

Artwork, documents, and photographs recount the federal government's efforts to fund artists in the 1930s in this National Archives site.

Eleanor Roosevelt

http://gi.grolier.com/presidents/ea/first/32pw.html

This site provides both information about the first lady and links to other relevant sites.

America from the Great Depression to World War II: Photographs from the FSA and OWI, c. 1935–1945

http://memory.loc.gov/ammem/fsowhome.html

These images in the Farm Security Administration–Office of War Information Collection show Americans from all over the nation experiencing everything from despair to triumph in the 1930s and 1940s.

American Life Histories: Manuscripts from the Federal Writers Project, 1936–1940

http://memory.loc.gov/ammem/wpaintro/wpahome.html

The staff of the Folklore Project of the Federal Writers Project wrote these histories. Typically between 2,000 and 15,000 words, the manuscripts provide a wonderful glimpse into American life.

CHAPTER 28 | WAR AND PEACE

Franklin Delano Roosevelt
http://www.ipl.org/ref/POTUS/fdroosevelt.html
This site provides information about Roosevelt, the only president to serve more than two terms.

America from the Great Depression to World War II: Photographs from the FSA and OWI, c. 1935–1945
http://memory.loc.gov/ammem/fsowhome.html
These images in the Farm Security Administration–Office of War Information Collection show Americans from all over the nation experiencing everything from despair to triumph in the 1930s and 1940s.

A People at War
http://www.nara.gov/exhall/people/people.html
This National Archives exhibit takes a close look at the contributions millions of Americans made to the war effort.

Powers of Persuasion—Poster Art of World War II
http://www.nara.gov/education/teaching/posters/poster.html
These powerful posters at the National Archives were part of the battle for the hearts and minds of the American people.

A-Bomb WWW Museum
http://www.csi.ad.jp/ABOMB/
This site offers information about the impact of the first atomic bomb as well as the background and context of weapons of total destruction.

The United States Holocaust Memorial Museum
http://www.ushmm.org/index.html
This is the official website of the Holocaust Museum in Washington, D.C.

The Seabees During World War II
http://www.seabeecook.com/history/
The Seabees are a U.S. Navy support unit best known for their construction projects. This site provides articles, pictures, and reminiscences of Seabees during the war. This site looks at the war behind the lines.

Tuskegee Airmen
http://www.wpafb.af.mil/museum/history/prewwii/ta.htm
The Air Force Museum at Wright-Patterson Air Force Base maintains this site about the African American pilots of World War II.

Abraham Lincoln Brigade Archives
http://www.alba-valb.org
This Brandeis University site has posters and photographs from the Spanish Civil War and the unit of American volunteers who fought in it.

George C. Marshall
http://www.marshallfoundation.org/
This site, maintained by the George C. Marshall Foundation at the Virginia Military Institute, Lexington, Virginia, provides information on the values and career of U.S. Army Chief of Staff George C. Marshall.

CHAPTER 29 | THE AMERICAN CENTURY

Harry S Truman
http://www.ipl.org/ref/POTUS/hstruman.html
This site contains basic data about Truman's election, presidency, and speeches.

Cold War
http://cnn.com/SPECIALS/cold.war/
This is the companion site to the CNN Perspectives series on the Cold War. It contains information including interactive timelines and a quiz.

The Marshall Plan
http://www.nara.gov/exhall/featured-document/marshall/marshall.html
This National Archives site contains useful information on the Marshall Plan.

Beyond the Playing Field: Jackie Robinson, Civil Rights Advocate
http://www.nara.gov/education/teaching/robinson/robmain.html
This National Archives and Records Administration teaching materials site contains images, essays, and documentation about Robinson and civil rights.

Negro League Baseball On-Line Archives
http://www.negroleaguebaseball.com/
This site includes essays about desegregation, baseball, and Jim Crow as well as images of teams and players.

Korean War Project
http://www.koreanwar.org/
This site has information about the Korean War and is a guide to resources on that conflict.

NATO at 50
http://www.cnn.com/SPECIALS/1999/nato/
This CNN site has an excellent timeline and images that tell the history of the North Atlantic Treaty Organization.

Senator Joe McCarthy—A Multimedia Celebration
http://webcorp.com/mccarthy/
This Webcorp site includes audio and visual excerpts of McCarthy's speeches.

Harry S Truman Library and Museum
http://www.trumanlibrary.org
This presidential library site has numerous photos and important documents relating to Truman.

Dwight David Eisenhower
http://www.ipl.org/ref/POTUS/ddeisenhower.html
This site contains an online bibliography covering Eisenhower's election, presidency, and speeches.

Fifties Website Home Page
http://www.fiftiesweb.com
This entertaining site tells about and samples music and television from the 1950s. It also includes a related links page.

1950s America
http://dept.english.upenn.edu/~afilreis/50s/home.html
This site by University of Pennsylvania Professor Al Filreis contains a large array of 1950s literature and images in an alphabetical index.

Levittown: Documents of an Ideal American Suburb
http://www.uic.edu/~pbhales/Levittown/
The postwar boom in housing made suburban living the cultural norm in America and shaped a generation. The story of the classic suburb, Levittown, is told in pictures and text.

Hollywood and the Movies During the 1950s
http://lib.berkeley.edu/MRC/50sbib.html
This site proves information on cinema and film during the 1950s.

The Dwight D. Eisenhower Library and Museum
http://www.eisenhower.utexas.edu/
This site contains mainly photographs of the president.

Rock and Roll
http://www.rockhall.com/home/
By the late 1950s, rock and roll had become the music of the new generation.

Alaskan Statehood
http://www.nara.gov/education/historyday/alaska/statehd.html
This site contains information on both Alaska's move toward statehood and designing a new U.S. flag.

CHAPTER 30 | FROM CAMELOT TO WATERGATE

John Fitzgerald Kennedy
http://www.ipl.org/ref/POTUS/jfkennedy.html
This online bibliography contains basic data about Kennedy's election, presidency, and speeches.

Lyndon B. Johnson
http://www.ipl.org/ref/POTUS/lbjohnson.html
This site contains basic facts about Johnson's election, presidency, and speeches.

Lyndon B. Johnson Library and Museum
http://www.lbjlib.utexas.edu/
The presidential library site has images and online exhibits.

Vietnam: A Soldier's Perspective
http://www.macomb.k12.mi.us/wq/gb2fr.htm
This site offers assorted resources relating to America's involvement in the Vietnam war.

Vietnam On-Line
http://www.pbs.org/wgbh/pages/amex/vietnam/
From PBS and *The American Experience,* this site contains a detailed, interactive timeline of the war, interpretive essays, and autobiographical reflections.

Civil Rights Oral History Bibliography
http://www-dept.usm.edu/~mcrohb/
This University of Southern Mississippi site includes complete transcripts of selected oral resources.

My Lai Court Martial (1970)
http://www.law.umkc.edu/faculty/projects/ftrials/mylai/mylai.htm
This site contains images, chronology, court and official documents maintained by Dr. Doug Linder at University of Missouri–Kansas City Law School.

United States *v.* Cecil Price et al. *(The "Mississippi Burning" Trial), 1967*
http://www.law.umkc.edu/faculty/projects/ftrials/price&bowers.html
This site contains images, chronology, and court and official documents maintained by Dr. Doug Linder at the University of Missouri–Kansas City Law School.

Richard Milhous Nixon
http://www.ipl.org/ref/POTUS/rmnixon.html
This site contains basic data about Nixon's elections and presidency, speeches, as well as an on-line bibliography.

Watergate
http://www.journale.com/watergate.html
This site contains primary and secondary sources relating to the event that forced Nixon's resignation.

Gerald Rudolph Ford
http://www.ipl.org/ref/POTUS/grford/html
This online bibliography covers Ford's elections, presidency, and speeches.

CHAPTER 31 | SOCIETY IN FLUX

1950s America
http://dept.english.upenn.edu/~afilreis/50s/home.html
This site by University of Pennsylvania Professor Al Filreis contains a large array of 1950s literature and images in an alphabetical index.

Hollywood and the Movies During the 1950s
http://lib.berkeley.edu/MRC/50sbib.html
This site proves information on cinema and film during the 1950s.

Rock and Roll
http://www.rockhall.com/
By the late 1950s, rock and roll had become the music of the new generation.

Martin Luther King, Jr.
http://www.seattletimes.com/mlk/
This *Seattle Times* site has several articles about King and the civil rights movement.

Martin Luther King, Jr. Papers Project
http://www.stanford.edu/group.King/
This Stanford University site has links and selected documents by and concerning Martin Luther King, Jr.

National Civil Rights Museum
http://www.civilrightsmuseum.org
This site allows a virtual tour of the museum with its interpretive exhibits.

The Diggers Archives
http://www.diggers.org/
This site provides information about the San Francisco Diggers, one of the legendary groups in the Haight-Ashbury area from 1966 to 1968.

Gay Rights Movement
http://www.columbia.edu/cu/libraries/events/sw25/case1.html
This site includes articles from the New York City press as well as first-hand accounts of the June 1969 Greenwich Village riots that are today commemorated throughout the country during Gay Pride celebrations.

The Sixties Project
http://lists.village.virginia.edu/sixties/
This University of Virginia site has extensive exhibits, documents, and personal narratives from the 1960s.

Civil Rights Oral History Bibliography
http://www-dept.usm.edu/~mcrohb/
This University of Southern Mississippi site includes complete transcripts of selected oral resources.

1969 Woodstock Festival and Concert
http://www.woodstock69.com/index.html
This site provides pictures and lists of songs from the famous rock festival.

United States *v.* Cecil Price et al. (The "Mississippi Burning" Trial), 1967
http://www.law.umkc.edu/faculty/projects/ftrials/price&bowers.html
This site contains images, chronology, and court and official documents maintained by Dr. Doug Linder at the University of Missouri–Kansas City Law School.

Virtual Museum of Computing
http://vmoc.museophile.sbu.ac.uk
This site relates the history of computing through a series of online exhibits.

The Computer Museum History Center
http://www.computerhistory.org

This site for the Computer Museum History Center features online archives and exhibits tracing decades of computer history.

CHAPTER 32 | RUNNING ON EMPTY: THE NATION TRANSFORMED

Gerald Rudolph Ford
http://www.ipl.org/ref/POTUS/grford/html

This site contains basic data about Ford's presidency, speeches, and an online bibliography.

James Earl Carter, Jr.
http://www.ipl.org/ref/POTUS/jecarter/html

This site contains basic data about Carter's election and presidency, speeches, and an online bibliography.

The 80s Server
http://www.80s.com

Although the best parts of this site are restricted to members, it nonetheless has some great information about the 1980s.

Ronald Wilson Reagan
http://www.ipl.org/ref/POTUS.rwreagan.html

This site contains basic data about Reagan's elections and presidency, speeches, and an online biography.

The 1980s Farm Crisis
http://www.pioneerplanet.com/archive/cent/dox/cent10.htm

In rural America, the 1980s marked a period of great economic turmoil. Many farmers lost their land as prices fell and interest rates rose; in the Midwest the reaction to these circumstances ranged from frustration to violence.

Virtual Museum of Computing
http://vmoc.museophile.sbu.ac.uk

This site relates the history of computing through a series of online exhibits.

The Computer Museum History Center
http://www.computerhistory.org

This site for the Computer Museum History Center features online archives and exhibits tracing decades of computer history.

CHAPTER 33 | MISDEMEANORS AND HIGH CRIMES

Desert Storm
http://www.desert-storm.com/

This site treats U.S. involvement in the 1991 Persian Gulf conflict.

George Herbert Walker Bush
www.ipl.org/ref/POTUS/ghwbush.html
This site contains basic data about Bush's election and presidency, speeches, and an online biography.

The Christian Coalition
http://www.pfaw.org/issues/liberty/
This article about Robert Reed's resignation from the organization elaborates the Christian Coalition agenda.

American Identities
http://xroads.virginia.edu/~YP/ethnic.html
This site suggests resources for studying America's multiple ethnic identities.

William Jefferson Clinton
http://www.ipl.org/ref/POTUS/wjclinton.html
This site contains factual data about Clinton's elections and presidency, speeches, and an online biography.

Investigating the President: The Trial
http://www.cnn.com/ALLPOLITICS/resources/1998/lewinsky/
This CNN site provides information and documents about the scandals surrounding President Clinton and his impeachment.

The O. J. Simpson Trial
http://www.cnn.com/US/OJ/index.html
This site provides basic facts and interpretive essays, plus additional links about the O. J. Simpson trial: the players, the evidence, and the jury.

Kosovo
http://www.cnn.com/SPECIALS/1998/10/kosovo/
This in-depth CNN Interactive site looks at the development and current resolution of the turmoil in Kosovo.

Oklahoma City Bombing
http://www.cnn.com/US/9703/okc.trial/
This CNN Interactive site has information about this recent terrorist act.

The Promise Keepers
http://www.promisekeepers.org
This official site gives information about the men's religious organization.

Why Do Campaign Polls Zigzag So Much?
http://www.psych.purdue.edu/%7Ecodelab/Invalid.Polls.html
This site treats polling and its impact on the 1996 election.

Political and Physical Map of the United States

A-85

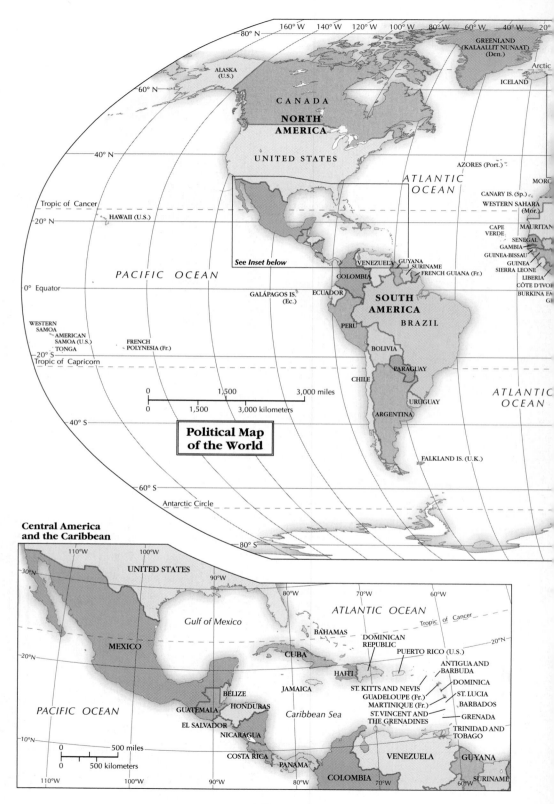

Political Map
of the World

**Central America
and the Caribbean**

A-86

20° E 40° E 60° E 80° E 100° E 120° E 140° E 160° E

ARCTIC OCEAN

See Inset below

RUSSIA

EUROPE

KAZAKHSTAN

MONGOLIA

PACIFIC OCEAN

GEORGIA
ARMENIA
TURKEY
MALTA
TUNISIA CYPRUS

UZBEKISTAN
KYRGYZSTAN
TURKMENISTAN TAJIKISTAN
AZERBAIJAN
AFGHANISTAN

CHINA

N. KOREA
S. KOREA JAPAN

ASIA

ERIA LIBYA
EGYPT

PAKISTAN
NEPAL BHUTAN

TAIWAN

AFRICA

BANGLADESH

NIGER CHAD
SUDAN
ERITREA YEMEN
DJIBOUTI

INDIA
MYANMAR
(BURMA)
THAILAND
CAMBODIA
VIETNAM
LAOS

PHILIPPINES

NORTHERN
MARIANA
IS. (U.S.)
GUAM (U.S.)

MARSHALL
IS.

See Inset below

NIGERIA
BENIN
TOGO
CAMEROON
EQ.
NEA
GABON
TOME
INCIPE
ABINDA
(Ang.)

CENTRAL
AFRICAN REP
ETHIOPIA

SOMALIA

MALDIVES

SRI
LANKA

BRUNEI

MALAYSIA

SINGAPORE

INDONESIA

FEDERATED STATES
OF MICRONESIA

KIRIBATI

RWANDA
DEM. REP OF
THE CONGO
BURUNDI TANZANIA

UGANDA
KENYA

COMOROS
MAYOTTE (Fr.)

SEYCHELLES

INDIAN
OCEAN

PAPUA
NEW
GUINEA

SOLOMON
IS.

TUVALU

ANGOLA
ZAMBIA
MALAWI

VANUATU FIJI

NAMIBIA
BOTSWANA
ZIMBABWE
MOZAMBIQUE

MADAGASCAR
RÉUNION
(Fr.)

MAURITIUS

AUSTRALIA

NEW
CALEDONIA
(Fr.)

SOUTH
AFRICA
SWAZILAND
LESOTHO

NEW
ZEALAND

ANTARCTICA

Southwest Asia

30°E 40°E 50°E TURKM.
TURKEY
CYPRUS LEB.
SYRIA
WEST
ISRAEL BANK
JORDAN
IRAQ
AFGHAN.
IRAN

0   500 miles
0   500 kilometers

KUWAIT
EGYPT
BAHRAIN
QATAR
OMAN
Persian Gulf
SAUDI
ARABIA
UNITED ARAB
EMIRATES
OMAN
Tropic of Cancer
Red Sea
30°N
20°N
Arabian
Sea
SUDAN
ERITREA
YEMEN
40°E 50°E 60°E

Europe

70°N
0° 10°E
Arctic Circle
10°W
60°N
FINLAND
NORWAY
RUSSIA
SWEDEN ESTONIA
LATVIA
North
Sea
DENMARK
LITHUANIA
RUS.
IRELAND UNITED
KINGDOM
50°N
NETH.
GERMANY
POLAND
BELARUS
ATLANTIC
OCEAN
BELG.
LUX.
CZ. REP
SLVK.
AUS. HUNG.
UKRAINE
MOLDOVA
PORTUGAL
FRANCE
SWITZ.
SLOV.
CRO.
BOSNIA-
HERZ.
ROMANIA
SERB.
BULGARIA
Black Sea
SPAIN
ITALY
MAC.
ALB.
GREECE
TURKEY
Mediterranean Sea
20°E
30°E
CYPRUS
MOROCCO ALGERIA TUNISIA

0   500 miles
0   500 kilometers

A-87

CREDITS

CHAPTER 16

537 Library of Congress **539** Library of Congress **542** Library Company of Philadelphia **548** The Granger Collection, New York **550** Library of Congress **551** Library of Congress **554** Culver Pictures, Inc. **556** Alabama Department of Archives and History, Montgomery, Alabama

CHAPTER 17

567 The Granger Collection, New York **575** Brown Brothers, Inc. **579** Sterling Memorial Library, Manuscripts & Archives/Yale University **582** National Archives **583** DeGolyer Library, Southern Methodist University, Dallas, Texas **584** Library of Congress **587** © Bettmann/CORBIS **588** Henry Ford Museum and Greenfield Village **589** Bancroft Library, University of California **590** The Kansas State Historical Society, Topeka **597** Solomon D. Butcher Collection, Nebraska State Historical Society

CHAPTER 18

603 © Tony Arruza/CORBIS **606** Courtesy of Bethlehem Steel Corporation **607** Brown Brothers, Inc. **611** Theobald Chartran, "Andrew Carnegie," (detail), 1895. Carnegie Museum of Art, Gift of Henry Clay Frick, 1896, (96.5) **612** © Bettmann/CORBIS **614** © Collection of The New-York Historical Society **615** The Granger Collection, New York **619** © Bettmann/CORBIS **624** © Bettman/CORBIS **629** North Wind Picture Archives

CHAPTER 19

633 © Bettmann/CORBIS **637** © Bettmann/CORBIS **641** The Granger Collection, New York **644** Culver Pictures, Inc. **646** Library of Congress **648** Culver Pictures, Inc. **651** © Bettmann/CORBIS **652** Thomas Eakins, "Baseball Players Practicing," (detail), 1875. Watercolor; 10 7/8" × 12 7/8". Museum of Art, Rhode Island School of Design Jesse Metcalf and Walter H. Kimball Funds **656** Alice Kellogg Tyler, "Portrait of Jane Addams," 1893. Chicago Historical Society, (P&S-1971.0140)

CHAPTER 20

661 Private Collection, Courtesy of Emily Rauh Pulitzer, Pulitzer Collection. **663** © Bettmann/CORBIS **666** Smith College Archives, Smith College Northampton, MA **670** Jefferson Medical College, Thomas Jefferson University, Philadelphia, (detail) **671** Nebraska State Historical Society, Solomon D. Butcher Collection **673** Left: © Bettmann/CORBIS **673** Right: The Granger Collection, New York **677** © Bettmann/CORBIS **681** Left: Photofest **681** Right: Brown Brothers, Inc

CHAPTER 21

685 Culver Pictures, Inc. **688** Left: Brown Brothers, Inc. **689** Right: The Granger Collection, New York **690** Culver Pictures, Inc. **692** National Museum of American History, Smithsonian Institution **694** © Bettmann/CORBIS **696** © Bettmann/CORBIS **698** Kansas State Historical Society **698** The Granger Collection, New York **702** Culver Pictures, Inc. **705** The Granger Collection, New York

CHAPTER 22

712 Left: © Bettmann/CORBIS **712** Right: Culver Pictures, Inc **716** The New York, Public Library, Astor, Lenox and Tilden Foundations **719** Keystone-Mast Collection, UCR/California Museum of Photography, University of California, Riverside **720** Culver Pictures, Inc **722** © Bettmann/CORBIS **723** Brown Brothers, Inc. **727** Library of Congress **729** The Granger Collection, New York **736** Brown Brothers, Inc. **740** Library of Congress **742** National Portrait Gallery, Smithsonian Institution/Art Resource, NY, (detail)

CHAPTER 23

749 © Bettmann/CORBIS **750** Hawaii State Archives/Historical Records Branch **753** The Granger Collection, New York **755** Chicago Historical Society, (ICHi-08428) **757** © Bettmann/CORBIS **758** Vermont State House **763** © Bettmann/CORBIS **772** Library of Congress

CHAPTER 24

779 Imperial War Museum, London **781** Left: The Granger Collection, New York **782** Right: Brown Brothers, Inc **789** National Archives **791** Photoworld/FPG International/Getty Images **794** © Bettmann/CORBIS **795** National Archives **801** The Granger Collection, New York **804** AP/Wide World Photos **805** Culver Pictures, Inc **808** Chicago Historical Society

CHAPTER 25

814 Culver Pictures, Inc. **815** Courtesy of George Eastman House **819** © Bettmann/CORBIS **821** Courtesy of Mr. and Mrs. Herbert Goldstone, NY **823** Culver Pictures, Inc. **824** © Bettmann/CORBIS **826** Whitney Museum of American Art, (detail) **829** © Bettmann/CORBIS **831** Kansas State Historical Society **834** Hulton Archive/Getty Images **836** Culver Pictures, Inc. **840** Library of Congress

CHAPTER 26

845 Culver Pictures, Inc **847** Culver Pictures, Inc. **848** Culver Pictures, Inc. **851** Library of Congress **853** AP/Wide World Photos **856** © Bettmann/CORBIS **860** © Bettmann/CORBIS **862** © CORBIS **863** University of Washington Libraries, Special Collections Division **865** Library of Congress **866** Franklin D. Roosevelt Library **867** © Bettmann/CORBIS

CHAPTER 27

872 © Bettmann/CORBIS **878** © Bettmann/CORBIS **879** AP/Wide World Photos **880** © Bettman/CORBIS **887** The Granger Collection, New York **889** AP/Wide World Photos **891** © William Gropper/Vanity Fair, Condé Nast Publications, Inc. **893** © Bettmann/CORBIS **895** Library of Congress **897** © CORBIS **900** AP/Wide World Photos **902** © Roger-Viollet/Getty Images

CHAPTER 28

910 SuperStock, New York **915** National Archives **917** Hulton| Archive/Getty Images **920** National Archives **921** National Archives **925** © Bettmann/CORBIS **927** Left: Photofest **927** Right: National Archives **928** Top: © Bettmann/CORBIS **930** Bottom: Culver Pictures, Inc. **935** © Bettmann/Corbis **936** Courtesy of the U.S. Air Force **938** The Granger Collection, New York

CHAPTER 29

947 © Bettmann/CORBIS **950** AP/Wide World Photos **954** © Bettmann/CORBIS **956** © Bettmann/CORBIS **960** National Archives **961** © Bettmann/CORBIS **963** © Bettmann/CORBIS **964** © Bettmann/CORBIS **966** © Bettmann/CORBIS **967** © Bettmann/CORBIS **970** © Elliot Erwitt/Magnum Photos, Inc., (detail) **975** © Bettmann/CORBIS **981** Hulton| Archive/Getty Images

CHAPTER 30

982 © Bettmann/CORBIS **983** © Bettmann/CORBIS **985** Left: The Everett Collection **985** Right: © CORBIS **989** AP/Wide World Photos **990** © Eliott Erwin/Magnum Photos, Inc., (detail) **993** © Bettmann/CORBIS **1001** © Bettmann/CORBIS **1004** © Larry Burrows/TimePix **1005** © John Filo **1007** Magnum Photos, Inc., (detail) **1012** ©1997 G.P. Trudeau. Reprinted with permission of Universal Press Syndicate. All rights reserved.

CHAPTER 31

1020 Courtesy of NASA **1023** © Joe McNally **1029** ©Julian Wasser/TimePix **1030** AP/Wide World Photos **1033** © Robert D./Black Star **1039** Getty Images News Services **1042** © H. Diltz/CORBIS SYGMA **1043** © J.L. Atlan/CORBIS SYGMA **1045** © Owen Franken/Stock Boston, Inc. **1047** © Diana Walker/TimePix

CHAPTER 32

1050 © S. Seitz/Woodfin Camp & Associates **1051** ©Bettman/CORBIS **1054** Liaison/Getty Images **1059** © Sipa Press **1063** © J. L. Atlan/CORBIS SYGMA **1065** © Allan Tannenbaum **1067** © Larry Downing/Woodfin Camp & Associates **1071** AP/Wide World Photos

CHAPTER 33

1080 © Bob Daemmrich/The Image Works **1081** AP/Wide World Photos **1084** AP/Wide World Photos **1086** AP/Wide World Photos **1089** Liasion /Getty Images **1090** Arnie Sachs/Consolidated News Pictures/Liaison/Getty Images **1092** AP/Wide World Photos **1098** AP/Wide World Photos **1100** Getty Images **1109** Getty Images **1110** AP/Wide World Photos

INDEX

Note: Italicized letters *f* and *m* following page numbers indicate figures (photos, illustrations, and graphs) and maps, respectively.